D0688394

WORLD OF CULTURE

PAINTING

Through the Eighteenth Century

by Terisio Pignatti

Newsweek Books, New York

NEWSWEEK BOOKS

Joseph L. Gardner, Editor

Janet Czarnetzki, Art Director
Edwin D. Bayrd, Jr., Associate Editor
Ellen Kavier, Researcher-Writer
Elaine Andrews, Copy Editor

S. Arthur Dembner, President

ARNOLDO MONDADORI EDITORE

Giuliana Nannicini, Editor

Mariella De Battisti, Picture Researcher
Marisa Melis, Editorial Secretary
Enrico Segré, Designer
Giovanni Adamoli, Production Coordinator

Terisio Pignatti's text has been translated from the Italian by Helen Barolini

*Grateful acknowledgment is made for the use of excerpted material on pages
154-179 from the following works:*
Recollections of Rubens by Jacob Burckhardt. Copyright © 1950 by Phaidon
Publishers. Reprinted by permission of Phaidon Publishers, London.
Rembrandt by Jacob Rosenberg. Copyright © 1948 by Phaidon Press. Reprinted by
permission of Phaidon Press and Praeger Publishers.
Stories of the Italian Artists from Vasari. Arranged and translated by E. L. Seeley.
Reprinted by permission of Chatto & Windus and E P. Dutton & Co.
The Writings of Albrecht Dürer. Translated and edited by William M. Conway.
Copyright © 1958 by Peter Owen Ltd. Reprinted by permission of Peter Owen Ltd.
and Sanford J. Greenburger Associates, Inc.

Contents

1

Mankind's First Language

When grass grew on the Sahara, a stone age artist painted these two male dancers on a rock face at Tassili, Algeria. The ornamented figures are rendered in what is known as the late round-headed style and show Egyptian influence in their postures. The white dots probably indicate scarification patterns, while the ochre coloring of the bodies was obtained, as were all ochres, from the iron oxide in sand and clay. To show the human form symbolized an epochal change, for Paleolithic hunter-painters had largely confined themselves to images of the animals in whose domains they lived.

THIRTY THOUSAND YEARS AGO, in a grotto at Pech-Merle in southwest France, an unknown artist-sorcerer placed his hand upon a smooth wall of rock and blew ochre dust from a hollow reed all around it. When he removed his hand, the outline appeared in negative, white on red. The image thus created may fairly be called history's first painting. For thousands of years thereafter, painting served as an indispensable cultural expression. Ancient civilizations as diverse as those of Greece and Egypt, India and China, produced painters of genius, while more modern cultures spawned such great artists as Leonardo, Michelangelo, Rubens, Rembrandt, Monet, and Picasso.

In practice, a painter is that person who traces images upon a surface and presents them to view. The Latin verb *pingere*, to paint, suggests the concept of making images by its analogy with the similar verb *fingere*, whose meaning is to fake in the sense of imitate. That does not mean, however, that the specific task of the painter is the transposition of images from reality alone. True, painters can, and often do, attempt to recreate literally the physical world. However, they also transform that world in a variety of ways: they distort to various degrees; they diminish what is represented until it is rendered abstract; they even arrive at a version that is detached, at least in intention, from any known external reference.

Technically, the painter avails himself of differing means of expression. These include graphic ones such as sketching, etching, and engraving, which rely upon the linear mark, or chromatic ones such as encaustic or fresco colors, watercolors, tempera or oils, glazes, mosaics, enamel, and inlay. The choice of technique and materials is almost never accidental; on the contrary, it is very closely related to the stylistic situation that confronts the painter.

From this viewpoint, painting is defined by the "mark" the artist imparts upon it, that unique and unmistakable effect, determined by his own character, that is called the painter's style. And while style is determined, above all, by imponderable elements of the artist's own temperament, it is to an extent also influenced by the culture in which the artist matures and the social and economic milieu in which he creates his works.

The meaning and value attributed to the term "painting" has changed radically through the centuries, varying greatly from country to country. Nor is it accurate to claim that painting proceeds according to a certain evolutionary pattern, starting from a minimum of faithful representation and arriving at a maximum of abstract perfection. Thirty thousand years ago, the men who painted the wild animals in the Lascaux cave in France or the Altamira cave in Spain had already reached an extraordinary level of proficiency. Therefore, it is not correct to think of a technical evolution toward an ideal point of perfection as a characteristic of painting.

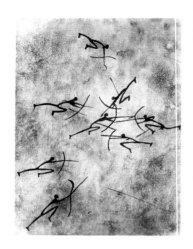

In a sense, however, the painter does have greater freedom than artists who work in other media. From the first creative moment the painter is master of his imagination because he is not limited—as, for example, the sculptor is—by the materials of his medium. Nor does the painter have to obey the physical laws of space, as the architect must. On the contrary, the painter if he chooses can create in his own work some of the effects achieved through these other media. He can stamp upon his work a "plastic" nature that is perceived as sculptural effects, or he can choose forms completely detached from their physicalness, whether these be the weightless figures of the Byzantine mosaics of Hagia Sophia or French Impressionist landscapes that seem to be composed only of light. He can, with equal ease, be a painter who shares some of the concerns of the architect, as was the Italian Renaissance painter Masaccio; his frescoes in the church of Santa Maria del Carmine in Florence reflect, among other things, his interest in the science of perspective, an interest that he shared with his contemporary the architect Brunelleschi. Among recent voices that have been raised to claim the superiority of painting is that of the great Italian sculptor Arturo Martini, who defined sculpture as a "dead tongue" because of the necessity of completing it with the medium of light—that is, with an element that is peculiarly painterly.

This brief survey of painting attempts to account for the various pictorial experiences that have taken place in different times and places. It begins with the most ancient pictorial expressions and ends on the threshold of the contemporary era, the final decade of the eighteenth century. That decisive historic moment not only concludes the time of aristocratic dominion and ushers in the beginning of modern awareness but also marks the abandonment of some of the traditional values and ideals to which painting had, until then, been anchored.

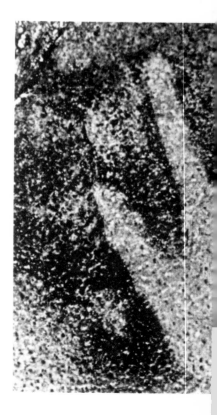

Contemporary man has substituted for a sense of collective values his own individuality. At the same time, art has broken through national confines—becoming first European, then worldwide—and in the process annulled the particular values of the old schools and traditions. It could be affirmed, and only partially paradoxically, that the French Revolution and the Neoclassical movement returned painting to its beginnings, almost canceling its history, in order to restore to the artist his total liberty.

Painting was born in the era of mankind's origin, long before it can be historically determined. The very first traces left by *Homo sapiens*, traces left at the time of the great glacial ages in Europe—from 10,000 to 40,000 years ago—are in fact paintings. And it is these paintings that establish for the first time unequivocal signs of man's civilization:

domestic and wild animals, hunters with lances and arrows, dance rituals and magic—a long series of images that extend along the rock walls of caves rediscovered in France, Spain, northern Africa, and Asia.

The men of the earliest stone age have left the outline of their culture on the walls of these caves. Through these earliest paintings, tribes of hunters expressed their heroic myths and the tribulations and joys of their lives. It is also clear that Paleolithic man attributed magical significance to the painted forms themselves. Anthropologists have in fact established, through observation of the most primitive tribes surviving in our own modern era, that early man thought these painted figures could propitiate the gods of hunting and fishing, activities basic to human survival itself. Even today certain Australian tribes believe that by "imprisoning" a representative animal in paint, others of its breed can be captured. From this comes the necessity of representing animals with maximum fidelity, even to the point of indicating the places a hunter should hit them in order to slay them easily. The painting of the Paleolithic period was thus naturally imitative, and it was closely bound up with ethical, social, and religious values. It became, in short, an intimate part of existence—and perhaps because of this it takes on a character surprisingly persuasive, passionate, and direct.

The oldest image on these pages is that of the stenciled hand below, found in a cave at Pech-Merle, France. It was made by Paleolithic hunters during the early Magdalenian period. The naturalistic bison above, from a cave at Altamira, Spain, dates from middle Magdalenian times, while the schematic archers in combat (above, left) are typical of later, Mesolithic group scenes.

Overleaf: A bull, one of the early Magdalenian paintings in the caves at Lascaux, France, is more than five yards in length.

The prehistoric painter expressed himself through simple techniques, using sharpened flint, for example, to better delineate outlines. The color of his work tended almost always to the red, since the pigment most used was ochre, but shadings from yellow to brown were also possible. Black was obtained with manganese oxide or charcoal. The colors were fixed with oily mediums or with binding ones like blood or egg white. Instead of actual brushes, the stone age artist used his fingers or tufts of feathers held in his hand. Because of these technical characteristics, the vitality of cave painting is extraordinary, constituting perhaps its most striking attribute. Standing out from the pale background of the rock, which was often purposely whitened, those forms take on an unleashed tension, a velocity and rhythm that is wholly their own.

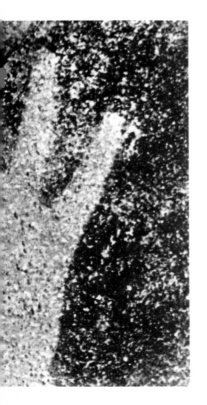

The area where major cave paintings have been found is in Western Europe, straddling the Pyrenees. These caves were first discovered toward the end of the nineteenth century. The Altamira cave near Santander, Spain, was the first to be found. Its discovery by a little girl came about by pure chance in 1869. The paintings themselves are in a room not very distant from the entrance, on a vaulting less than seven feet from the ground—easily observable by a child. On these walls are life-size paintings of twenty bison, along with a few other animals and occasional figures of men in the act of hunting. The color effect is stupifying, with modulations in red and brown ochre between outlines marked in coal black. Some of the gigantic animals are depicted in the act of charging with lowered horns; some are shown resting. The outlines of the bodies seem to vibrate—in the motion of a tail that flails the air, or in that of a mane that darkens a mighty chest. The technique used by the painter of the bison of Altamira is the most advanced of all those known in cave painting, which suggests that he probably worked toward the end of the Paleolithic period, or some 15,000 years ago.

The Lascaux grotto near Montignac in France, which is the other major location of cave painting, contains works that seem at least 10,-000 years more ancient than those of Altamira. Lascaux, unlike the other caves, has a kind of architectural layout, with the large main area that contains the major paintings coming along a long entrance hall. Here the paintings begin on the walls and end overhead, imparting an unusually monumental effect. Two somewhat narrower side wings lead off from the main room, and these are also decorated with paintings and primitive graffiti.

The principal subject of Lascaux is bulls: three gigantic forms, each measuring a good sixteen feet, extend along the walls of the main room, where other animals are also depicted. The dash and vitality of the forms is accentuated by their linear design, which throws them in relief against the light background of rock. Technically, the Lascaux painters favored the outline over the uniformly colored ground. But sometimes, especially in the smaller figures, they used color with a supreme artistry, availing themselves of the "blowing" technique—that is, spraying pulverized pigment from a reed or hollowed bone over the scratched surfaces. Thus herds of horses and deer in ochre red and black file along the borders as if stampeded by the onrush of the immense bulls. In the side wings, scenes unfold with unusual realism, particularly the one showing five deer swimming across a river, only their antlered heads emerging from the water. In a more hidden tunnel, a wounded bison lies on the ground in front of a dying hunter—the first "story" in the history of painting. Even though the paintings of Lascaux are earlier than those at Altamira and such other famous caves as Les Combarelles, Niaux, Trois-Frères, and Font-de-Gaume, they are no less skillful and certainly no less powerful.

In the later stone age, or Neolithic Period, the area where traces of cave painting are found shifts mainly to northern Africa and the Sahara Desert, athwart the Atlas Mountains. Here too are paintings attributed to tribes of hunters and fishermen, paintings imbued with ritual and magic meanings. The artistic interest of these works, however, is of a lower level, and even the best examples, such as those at Wadi Giorat, cannot be compared to the French and Spanish finds.

The Paleolithic deer at lower left date from about 15,000 B.C. and appear in Lascaux's Frieze of the Swimming Deer. The omnipresence of animals is also felt in the ivory engraving above, done by an Eskimo artisan of our own epoch. The masked figure at right, below, was produced by a Mixtec painter of Mexico's Oaxaca highlands around A.D. 1000.

COLLECTION CHARLES RATTON, PARIS

At least a mention should be made of "primitive" civilizations, those in which, as in prehistoric civilizations, the members are still engaged in the most elementary struggle for survival before the forces of nature. The term "primitive civilization" actually refers to two diverse groups: peoples in today's world who have remained at a lower level of achievement; and those distant in time whose development was arrested, so to speak, at an incomplete stage of civilization.

In observing the artistic production of primitive peoples, one is tempted to make comparisons with the art of the prehistoric world. For one thing, primitive art is frequently characterized by those same qualities of ingenuous freshness and creative simplicity that are typical of prehistoric art. For another, simply worked furnishings, decorative or sacredly symbolic sculpture, masks and shields, arms and ritual objects, recall the productions of the stone age and other remote ages in the most diverse places. Unfortunately, exemplars in the field of painting are all too rare, either because paintings were difficult to preserve or because of a tendency to use plastic forms of expression.

The ideal places to document the artistic productions of primitive civilizations are America, Africa, and Oceania. Eskimo painting, for example, is sketched in simple marks on wood or ivory and suggests the simplicity of prehistoric art. By the same token, the art of the Indians of the American Northwest reveals certain animal figurations that have the same ingenuousness and vitality as those at Altamira. As for earlier primitive cultures, the civilizations that arose in Mexico in the first centuries A.D. and were extant right up to the threshold of the contemporary era have left an exceptional legacy. From the culture of Teotihuacán, which thrived in an area located near Mexico City, there remains in addition to the imposing architecture of its temples a few fragmented frescoes. Monstrous divinities with animal heads, bloody battle scenes, and markedly expressive colors all testify to a violent and forceful civilization. The remains of the earlier Maya culture, which thrived in Mesoamerica from 1000 B.C. to the eleventh century A.D., also yield a few pictures. Of these, the eighth-century frescoes of the Temple of Painting at Bonampak in southeast Mexico stand out in particular. Reunions, dances, religious ceremonies, and battles are the subject matter; fiery, dense, and contained within a brutally realistic linear design, this art is once again expressive of both a strong and a volatile primitive civilization.

13

2

The Classical Heritage

THREE THOUSAND YEARS before the birth of Christ, two new and imposing civilizations were to establish themselves—the Sumerian in Mesopotamia and the Egyptian in Africa. It was no mere chance that both civilizations stretched alongside great riverways—the first between the Tigris and the Euphrates rivers, the second beside the Nile—for these rivers were a source of considerable material well-being for the people who lived on their banks. The Sumerians were an Indo-European people who emigrated into verdant Mesopotamia around 3000 B.C. They brought with them traditions and artistic abilities that were already well evolved, and they were thus able to demonstrate immediate and impressive achievements in the fields of architecture and sculpture.

One of Sumeria's most ancient pictorial expressions is the so-called Ur Mosaic, dating from about 2500 B.C. It depicts a march of triumphant kings, warriors, and their captives that unfolds on various levels against an amethyst-colored background. Equally spectacular are the dazzling glazed ceramics that adorn the walls and gates of Babylon and Darius' palace at Susa—all of which date from the seventh to the fifth centuries B.C. But these are not forms of painting in the true sense of the word, and in fact whatever paintings the Sumerians may have done have been destroyed by time and man. One surviving rarity, the fresco fragments from the royal palace of the Amorites, built around 1700 B.C., demonstrates that ancient Mesopotamians were capable of expressing themselves with the same techniques and sensitivity available to other artists of the same epoch. However, Mesopotamian civilization expressed itself first and foremost in its architecture and sculpture, as surviving masterpieces, among them the stupendous reliefs of Nineveh and Persepolis, emphatically indicate.

In the beginning the Egyptians also expressed themselves through plastic and architectural forms, a tendency that was very much in keeping with their singular social and religious concepts. For one thing, from early times until the Christian era the Egyptian sovereign, or pharaoh, was held to be divine. For another, Egypt's complex religion was based upon belief in an afterlife, which was envisoned as an eternity through which man was transported in order to be successively reborn. Egyptian art naturally reflected these social institutions and beliefs: gigantic figures of the pharaohs populated the temples and palaces; mammoth architectural constructions, among them the pyramids,

After smearing the walls of the Amorite palace at Mari on the Euphrates with gesso, a mixture of chalk and glue, Semitic painters outlined this temple servant in black and then colored him and his processional companions with plaster and shades of ochre. Painted almost twenty centuries ago, this citified man is leading a bull to slaughter.

15

served as their burial places; and these were embellished with such monuments of magical significance as the Sphinx.

Only later did painting become a widely used art form. Its diffusion was connected with the development of writing, which for the Egyptians consisted of setting down hieroglyphs, or pictorial symbols, on papyrus sheets. Another factor that spurred the technical development of painting was the need to cover certain older bas-reliefs, which had been executed in soft and undurable stone, with more resistant marble-like and colored surfaces. As a result, the most ancient Egyptian "paintings," which date from about 2700 B.C., are actually painted statues.

In the same epoch we find the first authentic paintings, decorative wall friezes inside tombs. Done in two dimensions, they seem to suggest the idea of a sculptured relief, but the color—for example, that of the well-known Frieze of the Geese from the tomb of Itet–takes on a life of its own. The paintings seem removed from reality, almost "abstract," perhaps because of the presence of the symmetry that remains the primary characteristic of art.

By the period of the New Kingdom (1567-1329 B.C.), painting began to reflect nature more closely. Among noteworthy examples are the numerous frescoes decorating the temple of Queen Hatshepsut at Deir el-Bahri near Thebes and the fresco in the tomb of Thutmose III that depicts the pharaoh and the thousand things necessary for his afterlife. But it is useless to seek even in these paintings lifelike realism. On the contrary, the Egyptian artist seemed insistently to aspire to a form of abstraction, whether by displaying his figures in profile as though they were cut off from a natural atmosphere or by presenting them on a uniform ivory-colored background that annulled any sense of space.

The only exception to this rule is what is certainly the most evocative of ancient Egyptian paintings, the History of Nebamon, which decorated Nebamon's fifteenth-century tomb. Nebamon is shown first as a young prince hunting among the reeds and mysterious flowers of a swamp. Surrounding him are his handmaidens and many birds, animals, and fish. Farther along a banquet is being prepared. Ladies of the court smilingly sniff perfumed bouquets as, to the sound of a double flute played by a long-haired girl, two almost nude ballerinas perform a rhythmic dance. The colors probably have a good part of tempera mixed in with them, which accounts for the most delicate shades of

The three geese below are part of a panel painted in Egypt during the twenty-seventh century B.C. for the tomb of Itet. The artist, who worked with tempera on the stucco wall of the tomb, used the imprint of his paintbrush—clamped reeds bound together—to give a look of realism to the feathers. At right, a nobleman and his wife observe a funeral banquet. This painting was done during the late Eighteenth Dynasty (1580-1300 B.C.), one of the great periods of ancient Egyptian painting.

16

blue, ochre, pale green, and faint azure. The most singular quality, however, is the design: both fluid and precise, it achieves the typical abstract and transcendental effect of Egyptian art but at the same time suggests a warm sense of life.

The numerous other later frescoes found in the Valley of the Kings —such as those in the tomb of Ramses VI depicting Nut, the goddess of night—do not add much to the development of painting. While perfect in technique, their colors and forms are purely decorative. As with the History of Nebamon, their strength lies in their design.

While the Sumerian and Egyptian civilizations were flourishing along their great rivers, civilizations of seafaring mercantile peoples were to arise: the Hittites and the Phoenicians in the eastern Mediterranean and the Cretans and the Mycenaeans in the Aegean. The cradle of their activities was mainly the area around the eastern Mediterranean. The adventurous Phoenicians, however, expanded along the entire coast of northern Africa, founding cities and colonies there. Although

numerous remains of Hittite and Phoenician art have come down to us, they are exclusively in the fields of sculpture and ceramic decoration; nothing remains of their painting.

Artistic production of greater importance emerged from the Cyclades Islands in the Aegean Sea, which by the second millennium B.C. had fallen under the influence of Mycenaean culture. From the most ancient remains of Cycladic art, traces of painting have come down to us, especially painted vases. These are mainly clay vessels with simple decorations of flowers and animal life, but there are also occasional human figures that suggest the linear and expressive realism of much prehistoric painting.

Around 2500 B.C. the center of Mediterranean civilization shifted west to the island of Crete, where it flourished for almost a thousand years. Phaistos, Gournia, Hagia Triada—but mainly Knossos—became centers of extraordinary artistic achievement. It is in Crete that painting finally triumphed as an art form, and it is not incidental that the island is warm and sunny, limpid under almost perennially blue skies. In this unrivaled natural setting was born that religious and heroic tradition that has reached us through the epic poems of Homer.

Excavations undertaken at the beginning of this century, especially at Phaistos and Knossos, have brought to light numerous monuments of Cretan civilization. In the remains of these ancient cities' great palaces, traces of original decoration are surprisingly well preserved. There, in rooms opening onto hidden gardens or onto loggias overlooking stu-

The wasp-waisted Prince of Lilies (right) was executed in low relief on a stucco wall of the Cretan palace at Knossos around 1500 B.C. Egyptian influence is evident in the combination of a frontal torso and the head in profile. The six-foot-tall prince has been recently reconstructed; only the rougher areas are original. With daggers perhaps less handsomely decorated than the iron blade seen above—which depicts a lion hunt in damascened gold—Mycenaean warriors subdued much of Crete in the first millennium B.C.

pendous vistas, fresco painting is triumphant. There are two main styles: decorative, in which great filled-in areas of vivacious colors, geometrically adorned with historic scenes in a "floral" style, create a supreme but abstract elegance; and naturalistic. Surviving fragments of this latter style, dating from the seventeenth century B.C., have a well-merited fame. The Crocus Gatherer, for example, is shown bending over in the shade of a garden filled with fabulous, light-struck bluebells; The Prince of Lilies advances majestically and nimbly among the tall flowers, as if wafted by a fresh spring breeze; and, in The Bull Baiting, slim Mycenaean athletes catapult over the bull's back. In the background, a sky as blue and as transparent as glass evokes the limpidness of the Aegean.

Even as Knossos and the other Cretan cities were adorning them-

Red-figure pottery, the apogee of the Grecian potter's art, reflected such events as that of the goddess Eos, or Dawn, (above, right) laying the stiffened body of her son Memnon to rest. More mundane scenes were also represented, as the portrait above of an Athenian horseman indicates. The outlines of all three figures were sketched on semidry clay and outlined with dark glaze.

selves with amazing monuments, a rough warrior population was moving west from the steppes of Central Asia to occupy various parts of Greece. The Achaeans, as the conquerors called themselves, concentrated around Mycenae, which toward the second half of the second millennium B.C. became the center of a new civilization. Through the works of the poet Homer we can retrace the tangled history of the long wars that culminated in the Achaeans' destruction of Troy. Ultimately even Crete was subjugated by these warriors, and beginning around 1500 B.C. its political and cultural dominion ceased.

The origin of the Hellenic people–who gave the world the prestigious Greek civilization, cradle of Western culture–is sunk in legend. It is said that Hellen, who came from the mountainous zones between Thessaly and Macedonia, descended to the sea with his sons Doris,

Xuthus, and Aeolus. Each of the latter settled with his following in a different region—the Dorians in Greece and Sicily, the Ionians and Aeolians in the Aegean Islands and in Asia Minor. Because of this common tie, the various Greek nations, even though geographically isolated, had a substantial unity of spirit. Both their religion and their form of government fostered an idealism in the Greek people, for the well-ordered system of Olympic divinities governed over by Zeus suggested a universal ideal of harmony and a concept of beauty that bore obvious fruits in the arts.

Politically, communes began to take the place of those authoritarian and brutal governments modeled upon Mycenae. Unlike the Egyptians and Cretans, who submitted themselves to forms of divine monarchy, the Greeks chose their rulers from among themselves, electing them on their merits—thus founding the first democracy. Along with a feeling for beauty and harmony, then, there developed a new moral concept of order and justice. These sensibilities had certain significant effects on the Greek artist: they allowed him a unique freedom of representation, they accounted for his concern with the real world, and, under their influence, his goal became first and foremost the depiction of man as he related to universal ideals.

Everyone knows what Greece means in the world of art; from that civilization came all the manifestations that we now designate as "classical." For centuries afterward, in fact, the canons of architecture and of sculpture derived from the Greek vision. In only four hundred years—which is nothing in comparison to the preceding civilizations that had evolved over millennia—the Greeks executed some of the most marvelous artistic creations in the history of mankind.

The Greeks quickly discovered the grandiosity and monumentality of the architectural form. They built temples that featured colonnades and pediments adorned with huge sculptures, the most splendid of which is the magnificent Parthenon on the Athenian Acropolis. Constructed between 447 and 438 B.C., during Pericles' reign, it was adorned with the work of Phidias, the greatest of all Greek sculptors. In the fourth century B.C., under the Macedonian dominion of Alexander the Great, Greek art reached its apogee. Seeking once more to capture the supreme beauty of the human body, the Alexandrian age bequeathed us the Venus of Milos, its unsurpassed masterpiece.

Painting inevitably played a great role in this wondrous artistic flowering. We know of the works of many great masters of the era through descriptions in literature. There are, for instance, abundant references to Polygnotus, who at the beginning of the fifth century B.C. decorated the portico of the stoa in Athens and the Temple of Castor and Pollux with frescoes and depicted the adventures of Ulysses and the fall of Troy in the sanctuary of Cnidus at Delphi. What is recalled of Polygnotus is his extraordinary ability to convey realism and, in particular, his bravura in portraiture. There are of course references to other fifth-century painters—among them Apollodorus, Parrhasius, and Zeuxis—whose capacity for realism is highly praised. During the rule of Alexander the Great (336-323 B.C.) the painter Apelles achieved preeminence, and there is no lack of mention of him either. We know, for instance,

The warrior-maiden Athena decorates the amphora above, made at the height of the red-figure period (500-475 B.C.). Earlier pottery painters had characteristically created black or red figures upon a light background, as can be seen in the detail of the renowned François Vase at right. The latter painting shows Mesopotamian alignment in both the overlapping arrangement of horses and the developing perspective of the figures.

Overleaf: A white-robed female dancer and her ochre-smeared male partner—figures executed in fresco on the walls of the Tomb of the Lionesses in Tarquinia—reveal the impact of Greek art but show the stability of the sinuous Etruscan line.

that he was admired above all for the vitality of his masterpiece, the Anadiomene Venus, which showed the goddess emerging from the waters of the sea. But of all the works of these great painters, nothing, absolutely nothing, has been recovered. Everything has been destroyed over the centuries, and consequently modern criticism has had to rely upon comparisons with a related art of the same period—vase painting.

The art of painting ceramic vases is as old as the history of Greece. In the beginning the vase painters preferred geometric decorative forms, taking inspiration in part from traditional Egyptian forms, which emphasized symmetry and two-dimensionality. By the seventh and sixth centuries B.C., both in Greece and in her Italian colonies, a new technique for painting vases had evolved. Figures were henceforth incised upon the clay in thin outline, then colored in red or in black, which detached them from the lighter background. This silhouetting technique is characteristic of the sixth century B.C. Among surviving masterpieces from this period is the famous François Vase, named after its discoverer, which shows the marriage of Thetis and Peleus. The vase is signed by the artist Ergotimos.

Around the beginning of the fifth century, vase painters began to reverse their shadings so that lighter figures appeared upon a darker ground. This was achieved by leaving uncovered the reddish ground of earthenware, then surrounding the outlined figures with a uniform

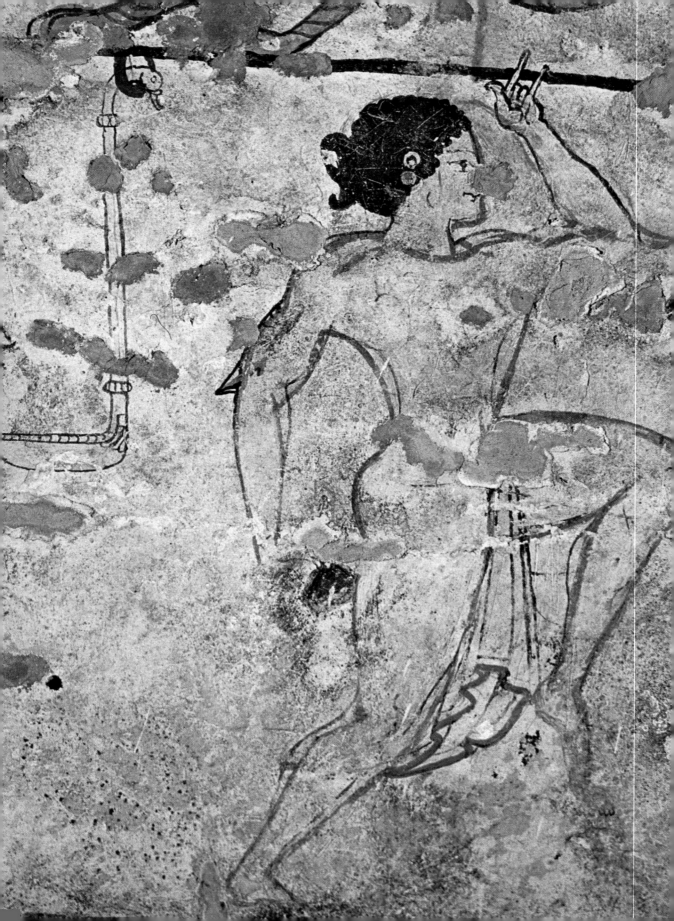

black background. One particular phase in vase painting was the so-called Free Style, established at the beginning of the fifth century; one example is the Achilles Amphora, which is characterized by an airy lightness of the outlined figures, light upon dark. Another work from the time of Polygnotus and Zeuxis, the realistic Orvieto Bowl, shows us the qualities most admired by painters of the classical age.

In the Hellenistic epoch (the fourth and third centuries B.C.), the vase painter completely discarded the contrast between the red and black grounds and designed thin figures, full of shadings, on a white ground. *Lekythi*, slim amphorae with elongated necks, are typical of this period in which delicate figures in attenuated colors appear against white cylindrical forms.

Between the sixth and the fourth centuries B.C. another civilization evolved on the Italian peninsula—the Etruscan. Nothing precisely is recorded of the origin of the Etruscans, and little is known of their social life and their religious beliefs. Arriving perhaps from the north, the Etruscans became a mercantile and seafaring people and established many contacts with the ancient civilizations of the Mediterranean area. Their oldest artistic productions, especially in the field of sculpture and gold working, exhibit a decorative stylization common to the art of the Asiatic populations and the Mesopotamian and Egyptian civilizations. The Etruscans gave major artistic attention to their tombs, which, like those of the Egyptians, were underground and were decorated on the inside with extended frescoes. Through the splendor of these colorful walls, the world of death was cheered by representations of life in endless scenes of dancing, gaming, hunting, and diversion. Most of these tomb frescoes have been discovered at the sites of the great centers founded by the Etruscans; the richest area is near the city of Tarquinia in central Italy. In the earliest of these finds, burial sites dating from the sixth century B.C., the styles are derivative. The appearance of symmetrical forms suggests the influence of Egyptian painting; the spare delineation of the images, however, seems to derive more from the painted ceramics of Greece's Italian colonies.

But by the beginning of the fifth century, the characteristics now considered typical of Etruscan painting had emerged fullblown. These included a marked narrative liveliness, an earthiness, a rougher, more energetic sense of reality than that of the Greeks, an intensity unleashed from the vigorous linear profiles. Etruscan masterpieces include the dancers from the Tomb of the Triclinio, the musicians from the Tomb of the Leopards, and the intensely melancholy women in portraits from the Tomb of the Orco. While the coloring of the earlier Tarquinia frescoes is extremely vivid, with a predominance of reds and whites on light backgrounds, these paintings never seem to impart the feelings of joy or cheerful festivity suggested by those works.

The Romans were the heirs of the Etruscans, and it was they who brought to maturity the technical innovations of Etruscan architecture and sculpture. Even Roman painting is closely associated with the Etruscan, perhaps because Rome's first artists are said to have been Etruscans. Roman art soon acquired a characteristic that distinguished it both from Greek idealism and Etruscan realism, however, and that

From the fifth-century Tomb of the Leopards in Tarquinia comes the double-flute player at right, who strides through life-giving laurel to evoke for the nearby dead memories of happier times. In the mosaic below, which depicts the battle of Issus in 333 B.C., Darius of Persia flees the victorious Alexander (in profile at extreme left). This second-century work was probably based on an earlier painting.

Overleaf: *On the vermilion-painted walls of a Pompeiian villa, a Campanian painter produced this panorama of the Dionysian mysteries.*

was the tendency to represent human actions within the Romans' own historical framework. From this there flowed an eminently concrete concept of life in all its forms—political, religious, and mundane. This characteristic became evident in paintings, whether small portrait tablets in tempera, still lifes, frescoes adorning homes and public buildings, or the mosaic work of villas, baths, and palaces.

The problem of Roman painting is very complex. First of all, the only examples that have been preserved are from a rather brief period concentrated between the dawn of the Augustan Age and the eruption of Vesuvius in A.D. 79, which buried the cities of Pompeii, Herculaneum, and Stabia–and thus preserved their monuments. Moreover, it is quite obvious that the painters active around Rome and in Campania were inspired mainly by extant Greek models from the golden period, which they were able to copy. But since those Greek originals are lost to us today, we have no way of knowing to what extent such inspiration restricted the Roman artist, or whether he was, instead, able to transmute Greek ideas through his own imagination.

For these reasons, it is not accurate to speak of "Roman painting" as if it actually corresponded to a precise cultural unity. Rather, in the works of the Augustan painters in Rome and Pompeii, two principal

and often divergent directions can be discerned: a Greek tendency, termed Neo-Attic, and an indigenous tendency that we can call Roman (or Campanian, after the region around Naples that was the source of its major manifestation). The latter, the most typically Roman painting, has been given the name Summary in order to indicate the rapidity of its execution and the vitality of its images.

The Greek tendency is evident in the few remaining frescoes in Rome, from those of the House of Livia on the Palatine to the Tiber Villa near the Farnesina. There is a fascinating similarity between the Maiden Pouring Perfume and the figurines inscribed on the Attic *lekythi* of the third century B.C. In the former, the maiden's arms are extended, her long, slender legs are gathered under an elegant stool with the tips of her light sandals just barely touching the ground; the happiness and innocence of youth are conveyed through the subtle stroke of a brush that barely outlines the form.

Examples of the other tendency, the one we have called Campanian, are found not in the imperial palaces and aristocratic villas of Rome but at Pompeii and Herculaneum, which were inhabited by merchants, a rich middle class, and working classes—a population not so given to glorification and mythmaking. Here, in the atria and triclinia or on the porticoes of homes, we find architectural patterns painted with the Summary technique; still lifes, sometimes done on wood panels inserted into the wall furniture; scenes of gardens and of animal life whose perspectives suggest far-off views; and, finally, scenes of popular life, often done with overtones of caricature and meant to amuse guests or to denote the practical activities of the owner of the house.

Portraits, too, are abundant in Roman homes. Most often they appear as part of frescoes, or on thin tablets in the manner of those popular in Egypt. The portrait is indubitably an art form congenial to Roman artists, and many painted portraits are unforgettable for their beauty and psychological fascination. Examples include The Baker with His Wife, and The Young Girl Intent upon Writing; the latter is caught in a moment of total concentration, her eyes wide open, her stylus upon her lips.

The greater part of the Pompeiian frescoes illustrates mythological or heroic themes taken from Greek or Latin literature and from religious tradition. In frescoes such as those in the House of Castor and Pollux and the Villa di Boscoreale, the brush work of the Campanian painters gives a new vividness to classical themes. The masterpiece of Roman painting, in the Villa of Mysteries in Pompeii, consists of a long frieze that runs all around the room and depicts the rites of initiation into the cult of Dionysius and Ariadne. Large solemn figures, robed or nude, appear one after another as the story unfolds against a background of the red that is typical of Pompeiian walls done in encaustic. The majestic figures are full-formed but softened by the coloring. Absorbed by the religious tension of the rite, they advance slowly within a space measured by an unerring perspective, their gazes intensely fixed, their steps agile. The main figures are unforgettable: the mistress of the house, the bacchante, the initiate, the flagellant, the beautiful Ariadne in the arms of a rather crude and ecstatic Bacchus.

The fresco portrait of the young girl above was found in a Roman home. She wears golden earrings and green and lavender clothing. The circus charioteer opposite also wears green—to show he represents the green faction of Rome's four horse-racing groups.

Stylization and creative vitality merge in this masterpiece.

Very little has come down to us from the centuries after A.D. 79, and what does remain is mostly in the field of mosaic. The age called Late Roman was important primarily for the diffusion of Roman art outside of Italy. This diffusion was accomplished between the second and fourth centuries A.D., when Rome became mistress of Europe and part of Asia. Late Roman art takes on an essentially naturalistic character in which reality is represented in a particularly vivid manner.

During this period, mosaics became highly developed, especially in the pavements of homes and baths. They drew their subjects mainly from heroic and mythological themes, but some, such as the gladiators in the Baths of Caracalla, utilized scenes from contemporary life. The masterpiece of Late Roman mosaic is that in the mansion called the Imperial Villa near Piazza Armerina in Sicily. Dating from the fourth century A.D., it was only recently discovered. The work consists of a series of more than forty large mosaic pavements, with scenes of hunters, banquets, and sporting activities. Although the painter's origin is shrouded in mystery, he appears to be the last great painter in the Roman tradition. For at the very time that he was working, the new Christian civilization, having been granted freedom of worship by the Emperor Constantine in A.D. 313, was introducing its own subject matter and moral themes, thus inaugurating a new era in Western art.

3

Byzantine Strength,
Roman Elegance

The lifelike and life-promising face of Christ adorns the south gallery of Hagia Sophia, Constantinople's magnificent church, mosque, and museum. The mosaic face was set into a golden background during the thirteenth century. Clay cones were first used as mosaic pieces in Babylon, where they were set into the pavements, and the idea was later taken over by both the Greeks and the Romans. It was Christian artists, however, who elevated mosaic to the walls.

CHRISTIAN ART actually began underground—with the frescoes decorating the Roman catacombs, those subterranean vaults that served both as Christian burial places and centers of refuge and worship. In style these Christian frescoes are similar to contemporary Roman works, all of which derive inspiration from the splendid models at Pompeii, Herculaneum, and Stabia. The Summary art technique almost always characterizes the former, for the very simplicity of that technique is well suited to the innocent freshness of the early Christians' religious sentiment. True early Christian art emerged only after the new cult had been authorized by imperial Rome—that is, in the period between the edicts of Constantine (A.D. 313) and Theodosius (A.D. 383). By then the Church had become strong enough to step into the political vacuum created by the decline of the Roman Empire. And by then the empire had split into two major divisions, with Rome the capital of the West and Byzantium the capital of the East.

Along with these political changes, an important philosophical transformation was taking place: the new Christian belief gave impetus to a view of life that was increasingly individualized, autonomous, and otherworldly. One consequence of this transformation was that artistic expression began to grow in two directions. On the one hand, artists exhibited a tendency to portray political or religious themes in an expressionistic and abstract style, as the Byzantines did; on the other, artists indicated continually growing concern with moral, natural, and human values. These two tendencies became especially apparent during the fourth century, which witnessed the multiplying of monuments to the new faith in architecture and in sculpture, both in Rome and in the outlying provinces.

Painting and mosaics were to develop in the same bifurcated manner in the fourth and fifth centuries. The first approach, a kind of abstract symbolism, is particularly well represented in the mosaics of the first Roman churches. At Santa Prudenziana, erected in Rome in A.D. 402-417, Christ is at the center of an architectural semicircle set along a portico; apostles and allegorical figures of the Church are placed around him in a symmetrical fashion. What is most unusual here is the use of color: brilliant, dense tones that negate a naturalistic view. And yet almost in the same period we can find in Rome manifestations of the other tendency, keyed to reality and employing the Summary technique. Here one thinks of the luxuriant vaulting of vine shoots, the vivid harvest scenes, and the views of birds in flight that decorate the church of Santa Costanza in Rome, one of the first masterpieces of Christian art. An example of the most vivid narrative realism can be found in the early fifth-century mosaics of the nave of Santa Maria Maggiore in Rome, where a series of panels illustrating biblical stories shows white-robed Christians moving against a background of lush green vegetation, azure sky, and clear river waters. The whole suggests the ingenuousness and candidness of the primitive faith.

It is in part from these Roman sources that the fifth- and sixth-century mosaics found in Milan and Ravenna drew their inspiration. But in Ravenna other influences were at work, for that city was an important port, one that served as a surrogate capital following the fall of the Western Empire in A.D. 476 and actually became the capital during the reign of the Goths. After 540, it was also the seat of the Byzantine governor in Italy, playing a key role in the introduction of Byzantine culture to the West. Indeed, it was in Ravenna, during the political and idealogical expansion of Byzantium under the Emperor Justinian in the early 500's, that a legitimately "Byzantine" style developed in Italy.

Visitors to Ravenna today can easily trace in its famed mosaics the coexistence of two cultural worlds. The fifth-century mausoleum of Galla Placidia, for example, offers—in a completely original manner, and for the first time—one of the fundamental innovations of Byzantine art—the fusion of architecture and painting. The mosaic work in the little mausoleum covers all of the vaulting and a good part of the walls, creating an image of unified space, and the tessellated surface seems to rid the walls of their weight and plastic nature.

Among the first Byzantine masterpieces created in Italy are the mosaics of the San Vitale chancel, which were executed in 547 and which depict in two panels the courts of Justinian and Theodora. The two rulers are encircled by dignitaries and handmaidens, all frontally portrayed; third-dimensional perspective, one of the foundations of naturalistic Roman art, is largely ignored. The pavement is colored an incongruous green, and the background is gold. The unknown painter who prepared the outlines of this mosaic incorporated some of the principal elements of Byzantine style, among them an almost symbolic representation of a political or religious theme, a unified relationship between architectural space and abstract decorative touches, a flatness that seemed to put the subjects outside of time or space, and highlights of brilliant color.

Yet the mosaics of Justinian and Theodora in some of their nuances reach insistently back to the Roman tradition. The large, expressively fixed eyes of Theodora, the bishop's marked features, the incisive will of Justinian—all remind us of the portraiture that appeared in sculptures or frescoes of the imperial period. In Ravenna the Roman tradition also appears clearly in the panels of the nave of Sant'Appollinare Nuovo; these scenes from the life of Jesus evidently were inspired by the naturalism of the mosaics in the nave of Santa Maria Maggiore.

Outside Ravenna, Byzantine art of the medieval period developed both in the East and in Europe. In Byzantium itself the greatest trove of

The trustful eyes of the richly dressed matron above, whose portrait was found on the wall of a mid-fourth-century catacomb in Rome, reflect her hope of resurrection. The mosaic lunette of Christ as the Good Shepherd (opposite), from the entry wall of the Galla Placidia mausoleum in Ravenna, is over-arched by designs in white, gold, and brilliant blue.

Overleaf: *Virgins walk in procession along a wall of Sant' Appollinare Nuovo in Ravenna, intent upon presenting their crowns to the Virgin and Child in the church's eastern apse.*

Byzantine painting was the church of Hagia Sophia, built in Justinian's time but decorated at a later period. The ninth-century mosaics in its vestibule are highly stylized rather than realistic, and the vibrantly colored portraits of the Comnenus emperors, dating from the eleventh to the thirteenth centuries, achieve even greater detail through the use of small bits of tile. These portraits feature the characteristic that was to become the hallmark of the school inspired by Byzantine art—a glimmering gold background that encompasses all of the principal figures in an abstract space. The most brilliant Eastern example of this technique is the fourteenth-century mosaic in the vestibule of the church of the Chora monastery in modern Istanbul.

Of equal importance in the history of Byzantine painting is the fresco work done in the south of Yugoslavia. These frescoes, which generally derive from the monastic tradition, differ from those in Constantinople in that they exhibit a three-dimensional tendency in which expressive characters are much more vivid and dynamic—an aspect of

Yugoslav painting that presages the figurative developments of the Romanesque period. The best Balkan mosaics can be found at Nerezi, where the violently expressive *Stories from the Life of Christ* (1164) depict both human piety and divine sufferance. The same tendency can be found in the series of paintings in the thirteenth-century church of Mileseva, which are more toned down in coloring but profoundly vigorous in human expressiveness. These strong dramatic currents also characterize the frescoes that decorate the rock churches of Cappadocia.

Another rich field for the study of Byzantine art is manuscript illumination. In numerous Eastern monasteries—particularly those of the Benedictines—monks spent long hours copying and illustrating religious texts. Their efforts produced what are surely among the most beautiful examples of Byzantine painting, miniatures that embody the elegant style, the symbolism, and the bright colors typical of Byzantine art. These works range from the vivid, incisive representation of the Gospels in the sixth-century Purple Codex of Rossano to the refined chromatic elegance of the ninth-century Gregory Nazianzus Codex. Miniature art evolved throughout the Middle Ages, but it met with particular success in Ireland and in Central Europe during the Carolingian and Ottonian eras. In the great masterpieces from those areas, the Byzantine experience was modified according to local traditions and culture, producing such masterworks as The Book of Kells, The Utrecht Psalter, and The Gospels of Otto III.

In the late Middle Ages, papal Rome also enjoyed a pictorial flowering, and examples of both mosaic and fresco survive from that period. The first of these paintings are indisputably Byzantine in inspiration, although the adaptations are not always successful. In one eighth-century mosaic in the Vatican grottos, for instance, Pope John VII is reduced to tenuous, evanescent profile on a ground of gold that seems to absorb his figure.

Notable in late Roman painting is the prevalence of outlining, which takes on a decorative rhythm of its own. This marked linearity is apparent, for instance, in the eighth-century frescoes of Santa Maria Antiqua in the Roman Forum. These frescoes include a ritualistic image of Saint Giuletta and a spectral Crucifixion, the latter touched by streaks of light that accentuate the dramatic character of the vision without suggesting a naturalistic reality. The linear tension apparent in these paintings becomes still stronger in the ninth century, in frescoes such as *The Ascension* and *The Descent of Christ in Limbo* at San Clemente. In these and other works, the line is no longer simply decorative but is the source of tension and drama.

In the southern provinces of Italy, and especially in Campania, painting combined Byzantine motifs with typically provincial variants. The best examples of this style are the frescoes in the eleventh-century church of Sant'Angelo in Formis, near Capua. Under the guidance of the abbot Desiderio, who was Greek by birth, a Byzantine artist painted a portrait of Saint Michael in the atrium that, with its frontal fixity and limpid, jewel-like coloring, seems to have sprung from an Eastern icon. Yet the stories from the life of Christ that have been painted in the naves retain all the dramatic immediacy of the Germanic

The miniature adorning the tenth-century Egbert Psalter (above) shows the monk Rudoprecht holding a volume of his work. The decorative initial opposite opens the Gospel of St. Matthew in The Book of Kells, named for the Irish monastery where it was kept.

miniatures from which they possibly originate. This amalgamation—which fuses, in a vigorously independent manner, Byzantine motifs and indigenous genres—is called the Benedictine Style because it was originally practiced in the far-flung monasteries of Saint Benedict's order. Interestingly enough, the development of this new expressive form paralleled that of the "vulgar idiom"—that is, those national tongues that were then forming upon the classical roots of Latin and would become the Romance languages.

In fact, both Romance languages and the art that would be called Romanesque had their roots in the successive invasions of barbaric peoples who spilled into the civilized territories of the ancient empire during the early centuries of the Christian era. In Central Europe in particular, the culture of the barbarians—as the Romans designated any people whose language differed from their own—gradually began to superimpose itself upon the Roman culture. Except for miniatures, early examples of paintings from this phase are rare. Perhaps the greatest surviving example is in the little church of Castelseprio near Varese, Italy. Here, in the solitude of the moors that once sheltered important Longobard castles, an unknown fresco painter executed the life of Christ with extreme sensitivity, reviving motifs of "illusionistic" late Roman painting. Yet these motifs are expressed in a turmoil of colors –blazing reds, ochre, greens and yellows, all veiled by an unreal luminosity—and all broken up by a play of lines that recalls Byzantine models. Because of the diversity of influences—late Roman, Byzantine, and Germanic–it is difficult to date the Castelseprio frescoes; the work could have been done at any time between A.D. 600 and 900.

The spread of the Romanesque: detail (upper right) from a fresco of the archangel Michael in the church of San Vincenzo in Galliano, Lombardy, early eleventh century; a vivid detail (below) from a mural showing the martyrdom of Saints Savin and Cyrian in a French church near Poitiers, end of the eleventh century; a detail (center right) from a twelfth-century crypt fresco thought to show David fighting a lion, from the church of Tavent, near Tours; and an unknown saint in a detail (lower right) from a twelfth-century church in Berzé-la-Ville.

Romanesque culture was an intensely national culture, rising from a base of late Roman tradition and synthesizing, over a period of centuries, the most diverse influences. Actually, the term "Romanesque" takes on different meanings in different countries. Despite the work of wandering monks and artists who helped spread certain ideas about technique and subject matter, there was no true and proper "European" style in the Romanesque period. On the contrary, the style of the Romanesque artist was invariably influenced by local circumstances. Thus the term is used simply to refer to the art that developed upon the maturity of the national tongues after the beginning of the eleventh century.

Auguries had suggested that the year 1000 might well bring the end of the world, and consequently the millennium was awaited with terror by the ingenuous populace of Western Europe. To their immense relief, 1000 proved to be a year of rebirth, marked by the flowering of new artistic forms. The establishment of feudalism, with its social hierarchies and agriculturally based manorial system, brought political and economic stability, while the growing power of the Church put a secure base under the artists and artisans of the period, especially as great cathedrals rose along pilgrims' routes.

The earliest examples of Romanesque painting are those found in the Po plain, where, in the years following 1000, important religious edifices were erected. Frescoes in the San Vincenzo church at Galliano, Lombardy, feature figures of archangels, prophets, and Christ in the apse. The impact of these paintings is enormous, both because of the extraordinary dynamic force of the design and because of the choice of colors, which have a limpid, luminous quality. The figures, with their large, almost inhumanly fixed eyes—emphasized by a double circling of the eyelids—recall the mannerism of Byzantine painting in the Balkans.

Romanesque painting had no real importance in Italy until the thirteenth century, when it began to flourish in such areas as Sicily, the Veneto, and Tuscany. The eleventh and twelfth centuries, however, were a time of cultural greatness in other areas. Mural painting, for instance, flourished in France and in Spain. The most striking example of French Romanesque style is to be found at Saint-Savin-sur-Gartempe, near Poitiers. The abbey church in that village was once entirely frescoed, and much of the work has been preserved. What distinguishes the frescoes of Saint-Savin is their elegance of design, which prevails over their coloring. The figures—Moses crossing the Red Sea in a chariot pulled by charging steeds; the monsters of the Apocalypse; the three angels in adoration—convey, as do the most refined late medieval miniatures, a sense of measured proportions as well as symbolically expressed feelings. Any reference to reality has been avoided, and even that linear dynamism that was noted in Italy seems here to have given place to a more rhythmic movement.

Another series of very characteristic French Romanesque paintings is located in the twelfth-century church of Tavant near Tours. These frescoes interpret the life of Jesus through allegorical figures representing the Vices and the Virtues. Typical of the style of the master of Tavant is the decorative fluidity of the lines, which wind around in undulating spires, a perfect accompaniment to the vaults and corbels of the crypt and choir. The figure representing Luxuriousness, for instance, is shown being speared by a lance that is the only straight element in a form made up entirely of curved lines. The figure is one of the most unusual in the fresco and typifies, in the expressiveness of its quivering movement, the symbolic quality that Romanesque painters wanted their images to take on. The paintings of Saint-Savin and Tavant are utterly independent products of the French Romanesque school, but the equally striking frescoes of Berzé-la-Ville, near Cluny, are not. The latter clearly evidence the influence of Carolingian-Ottonian miniatures in their accentuation of classical linear rhythms and in the stylization of their architectural backgrounds.

In this same period—roughly from A.D. 1000 through the thirteenth century—painting in Spain took on a markedly national character. The best surviving examples come from Catalonia and are characterized by the strength of their color, which is always very deep. Catalan design favors a frontal stylization that betrays its far-off Byzantine inspirations; in fact, because of its location along the Mediterranean routes, Spain was much more accessible to Byzantine influence than to that of Carolingian France.

The major period of Sicilian painting paralleled Romanesque developments in Spain, a country with which Sicily had considerable contact because of the island's Mediterranean location. Governed by Moslems between the ninth and eleventh centuries, Sicily was even more receptive to Islamic influences than Iberia. This is amply evidenced in Sicilian architecture, where a proliferation of columns produces a sense of fragmentation of internal space, and a flowering of decorative elements replaces pictorial figurations. At the same time, however, Byzantine tradition was to remain an abiding element of Sicilian painting. The Sicilian painters who decorated the Martorana in Palermo, for example, were obviously inspired by the linear elements and intense colors of the Greek mosaics at Daphne. And Palermo's Palatine Chapel, a twelfth-century masterwork built under the Norman ruler Roger II, contains mosaics that recall the decorative values of the Byzantine tradition. The first of them, *The Entrance into Jerusalem*, assumes a shaded and musical character. The mosaics of the Creation, on the other hand, reflect the influences of Romanesque sculpture in surfaces that are filled with more marked three-dimensional values.

Something similar also took place in Venice, the lagoon republic that became, after 1200, the mistress of the Adriatic and the chief commercial tie between the East and Europe. In the beginning, Venice too revealed her dependence upon Byzantine tradition, or at least upon that of Ravenna and the Dalmatian coast. While many of the frescoes that originally adorned the numerous churches of this city have been lost, the mosaics of the cathedral of Torcello remain to document early Venetian painting. And the oldest of these, which goes back to the sixth century, shows the influence of Ravenna and through Ravenna, Byzantium. But later, in such twelfth-century works as the grandiose *Last Judgment*, as local handiwork began to prevail, the coloring became deeper and more intense, the contours became more dynamic, and modeling was done on more supple surfaces.

A Catalan painter presented Christ, Lord of the Earth, with impressive Spanish features in this twelfth-century fresco from St. Clement's church in Tahull.

We can follow a similar development in the basilica of St. Mark's, perhaps the most important treasury of thirteenth-century painting in all of Europe. The church's older mosaics, such as *The History of Saint Mark*, which dates from the twelfth century, are still Byzantine in many aspects. The *Prayer in the Garden*, finished at the beginning of the thirteenth century, is unified by an exquisite Byzantine decorativeness, at least in its extremely refined, minute mosaic work and the shaded modulation of its colors. However, the mid-thirteenth-century panels of the Arch of the Passion in the center of the basilica, while initiating from Byzantine designs, exhibit a linear tension and a dramatic vigor that identify them as fully Romanesque. These panels were comparable in style to the contemporary sculpture being created in new churches from Modena to Milan, from Parma to Ferrara.

The frescoes ornamenting the atrium of St. Mark's, created during the thirteenth century, sum up the different motifs that underlined Venetian culture. Those done first are semi-Byzantine; later panels, among them the superb series of the Flood, exhibit unadulterated Romanesque characteristics; the final works, done in the late thirteenth century, marked a return to the Byzantine—but with a sense of nature and a characterization of personages anticipating the Gothic manner.

In fact, Neo-Byzantine was the style that prevailed at the end of the thirteenth century, inspiring such outstanding mosaics as those of the cathedral in Monreale near Palermo to the frescoes in the crypt of the basilica in Aquileia near Trieste to the great ornamental fresco in the baptistry in Parma. In general, this last Byzantine wave was received in Europe, as it was in the Balkans, as a return to classicism. The human figure regained the solemnity of the old form and became a center of moral as well as figurative interest, and nature reappeared in backgrounds that included architecture, mountains, and vegetation. But the gold ground so favored by Byzantine mosaicists, a background that had signified the negation of spatial values and of perspective, almost entirely disappeared.

Neo-Byzantine has often been called "the Greek manner," but its meaning can be better understood in the context of the civilizing process that had engulfed all of Europe at this time. The Continent was by then approaching a period of artistic renewal of its French and Germanic origins, a period that would be called Gothic. And it was in this intellectual climate that the Neo-Byzantine style prepared the way for the great artistic flowering that would find its center in the Florence of Dante and Giotto. Two transitional painters of this period were the Florentine Cimabue and the Sienese Duccio. While remaining within the Byzantine tradition, these two artists introduced a greater realism and freedom in their works, thereby presaging the works of the great Florentine painters of the fourteenth century. Cimabue incorporated what had been bequeathed both by the Greek manner and by the strongest Romanesque currents. As a result his *Madonna* in the Uffizi gallery in Florence is at the same time solemn and most human—a Neo-Byzantine symbol in the subtle ornamentation of her dress, but a live person in her intense features and maternal gesture. The frescoed *Crucifixion* in the church of St. Francis at Assisi, for its part, is the most

Suffering is made manifest in Cimabue's thirteenth-century head of Christ (below) from a detail of The Crucifix *in the church of San Domenico, Arezzo. The realism of maternity begins to emerge from the stylized Byzantine tradition in Cimabue's* Madonna and Child in Majesty *(opposite, left); it is even more pronounced in the* Madonna and Child *of Cimabue's student Duccio (opposite, right). Both Madonnas are tempera on wood, and both date from the 1280's.*

realistically dramatic interpretation of the suffering of Christ that had ever been attempted. And the *Crucifix* at Santa Croce—tragically ruined by the 1966 flooding of Florence–represents a harmonious fusion of soft color tones and veiled moral and figurative tension.

In the same years, Duccio seemed to point, above all, to approaching Gothic refinements. He retained the undulant line of the Byzantine tradition as well as the crystalline purity of its gemlike colors. His *Rucellai Madonna*, in the Uffizi, is the tenderest masterpiece of the late thirteenth century, with a rhythmic play of angels around the Virgin's throne that suggests the most delicate of musical pauses and evokes the fineness of a Byzantine ivory. Duccio's masterpiece is a large altar in the Siena cathedral museum that depicts the Virgin and saints in the foreground and the life of Christ in panels in the back. The balanced and harmonious manner of composition, the goldsmith's incisive touch with linear profiles, and the mineral limpidness of colors made this superb work an unsurpassed model for the whole Sienese school that arose in Duccio's wake.

Cimabue and Duccio experimented with ideas that were ultimately to result in dramatically new artistic insights. Working at the very end of the medieval Romanesque period, they anticipated the achievements of Cimabue's pupil Giotto, that great Florentine painter of the fourteenth century who revolutionized Western art.

در حکمت کوکب

4

The East: A Tradition Apart

IN THE PERIOD BETWEEN the high Middle Ages and the fifteenth century, while political, social, and intellectual developments were changing Christian Europe, another great civilization, Islam, arose to the south—and in the extent of its dominion and the importance of the historical events with which it was associated, Islam must be compared with early Roman civilization. Founded by Mohammed in A.D. 622 as a monotheistic religious movement, Islam became, in the span of a century, an invincible military and political power. The nation of Islam was divided into numerous states, or caliphates, that included not only Arabia and Asia Minor but Mediterranean Africa, Spain, and Turkestan. Islam thus entered into contact with the most ancient Asiatic civilizations, those of India and of China, and consequently it became the link between these Far Eastern cultures and Europe.

The origins of Islamic art are as complex as its history, involving as they do Arabic, Turkish, and Persian elements. From the Arabs, Islam took the linear ornamentation—"arabesque"—and the geometric and rhythmic sense that still can be observed today, not only in Islamic painting but also in poetry and music. From the Persians, on the other hand, came a delicately pictorial aspect as well as the evocation of a world of extraordinary figurative fantasy. Especially in the beginning, Islamic art was also influenced by the dominant styles of the countries Islam conquered. Over and above these different influences, the new religion itself acted as a unifying agent. The Koran's emphasis on other-worldly contemplation led artists away from realism and toward that abstract, rhythmic repetition that characterizes Islamic art, making it in large measure ornamental. Typical examples of abstract ornamentation can be seen in the decor of mosques, where grandiose architectural forms are reduced to inconsequentiality by being covered with glazed and vibrantly colored ceramic tiles that repeat the same elegant calligraphic motifs into infinity.

This fifteenth-century miniature, illustrating the adventures of Khwaiu Kermani, typifies the city of Herat's school of Persian illumination. In the garden of the emperor of China, Princess Humayan first meets Prince Humay (lower right).

In religious places, the representation of the human figure is completely avoided, although such representation was not definitely proscribed by the religion. Islam does forcefully oppose idolatry, however, and it was for that reason that Mohammed condemned art that represented divinity with a human likeness. But secular narrative themes and the representation of nature were not at all forbidden; on the contrary, they constituted a notable part of Islamic painting outside of mosques, from book illustration to painted ceramics to the frescoes that decorated the palaces of the ruling class.

The most ancient Islamic paintings are to be found in the remains of the fabulous palaces of Samarra, the destroyed capital of the Abbasids, located in the Iraqi desert north of Baghdad. In the remains of the splendid palace of Jausak a fragment of mid-ninth-century fresco, *Two Dancers*, combines semi-Byzantine linear motifs with a certain density and sensual heaviness that suggests Indian influence. In general, Islamic painting was given over to miniatures that illustrated religious books and poems. The oldest example is the *Poem of Gulsah and Warkah*, which dates from the thirteenth century. The illuminator was of course familiar with Byzantine enameling and miniatures, but certain representations, such as the scenes of knights in combat, are given a magically abstract feeling by the choice of colors (the horses in this case are executed in tones of amethyst and ruby).

Many paintings remain from the period following the thirteenth-century Mongol invasion of the eastern part of the Islamic empire, including Iraq, Syria, and Persia. They are mainly illuminated pages of poems, heroic tales, and histories of the kings. The creators of these miniatures were for the most part Persians, resident in the local courts. In their pictorial styles, which reflect a variety of influences, glimpses and echoes of the Far East are frequently in evidence. For example, on one page of the oldest illuminated manuscript from the Mongol epoch, *The Usefulness of Animals*, the depiction of reedy marshes and flowers is Chinese in manner. Clearly more autonomous is the style of the unknown painter, certainly the most expert illustrator of this period, who was responsible for the fourteenth-century *Book of Kings*. The page that shows Bahram Gur killing a wolf has an extraordinarily realistic force, one that never loses the ceremonial and decorative sense that is typical of Persian illumination.

After Tamerlane's invasion and the establishment of the Timurid dynasty, Persia became the center of Islamic painting, producing true masterpieces. In the capital cities of Tabriz, Shiraz, and above all Herat, fifteenth- and sixteenth-century Persian illuminators experimented with a new concept of space in their efforts to show nature realistically. The greater part of the illuminated page was filled with a close-up view scaled in a heightened perspective; the far area—sky, horizon, and mountains—was depicted only on the topmost part of the page. The most typical example of this style may well be *The Anthology of the Adventures of Khwaiu Kermani*. Here landscape is of transcendant importance, painted with fine brush-strokes and given innumerable shadings. The use of gold for the heavens and of silver for the waters is also characteristic of such fifteenth-century miniatures.

Under the Safavid dynasty, which ruled Persia from the sixteenth to the eighteenth centuries and gave the nation its greatest splendor, Persian painting retained its fundamental character, a combination of vivid imagination and subtle abstraction. The painter Riza-i-Abbasi of Isfahan, in his *Pair of Lovers*, achieved a stylized refinement that, without renouncing pure fantasy, suggests feelings and psychological values that are human and modern. Similar paintings done in fresco are found

Mongol artists of the thirteenth century introduced Syrian, Iraqi, and Persian contemporaries to Chinese landscape painting and the depiction of animals—as can be seen in the mid-fourteenth-century Syrian miniature at right. One of the best portraits of a Mogul emperor is Abdul Masan's study of Prince Jahangir (above), who gazes upon a portrait of his father Akbar.

Overleaf: *Two Persian miniatures, the earlier of which (right) dates from the sixteenth century. The 1632 portrait of Jahangir at left depicts the prince riding with his favorite son, who holds a parasol above his father.*

in a pavillion that served as the entrance to the shah's palace in the magnificent city of Isfahan.

The last interesting evolution in Persian painting came in the middle of the sixteenth century with the movement of artists and expressive traditions into India. Famous artists like Abdel-Samad and Mir Say-yid Ali traveled from Tabriz to the Indian capital of Kabul to demonstrate the "Iranian calligraphic style." Others followed them, and large writing studios were set up where Indian books were illuminated in a style that at first was strongly Persian but gradually changed into what became known as the Mogul style. The principal characteristic of the latter was the marked narrative tendency that hinged mainly on popular traditions and stories or on the mythical adventures of the emperors. The masterpiece of this particular style is the series of miniatures illustrating the history of the house of Timur, which gives us a fully realistic representation of court life among gilded pavilions and green gardens.

Portraiture was the last development of Islamic painting, and it was not by chance that it occurred during the Indian period, for India was in contact with Chinese sources that had already produced masterpieces of portraiture. Among many Persian examples are the early-seventeenth-century portrait of Prince Jahangir, the work of Abdul Masan, that is the most exquisite result of a long pictorial tradition.

Islamic painting came into contact with India in the modern era, but Indian artisitc culture had its own autonomous and far-off origins. At

least two thousand years before Christ, in the fertile plain between the Hindu and Ganges, a rich civilization arose—only to be destroyed by the disastrous Aryan invasions of 1500 B.C. Later dynasties found themselves confronted with other invaders, among them the Persians in the sixth century B.C. and Alexander the Great in the fourth century. Meanwhile, a certain religious unity had been established through the Veda, the sacred writings of Hinduism, which embodied ideas introduced by the Aryans. The sixth century was to witness the rise of another great religion, Buddhism, which was destined to further unify the Indian population by exercising great influence over the arts, which incorporated Buddhist symbolism and acted as a vehicle for representing divine ideals on earth. Innumerable images of a superhuman Buddha, the Enlightened One; of the bodhisattvas, his terrestrial incar-

nations; and of the minor deities comprise the single theme of Indian figurative art throughout the centuries.

Indian artists considered both sculpture and architecture better suited to the exaltation of the divine form than painting. As a result, fresco painting took on a distinctly secular quality between the fourth and seventh centuries A.D., representing not only divine beings but also human. Among the greatest masterpieces of Indian painting are the frescoes in the sanctuaries of Ajanta. They show, in addition to religious episodes, the life of the court with its ceremonies and feasts, the private lives of the princes, the hunt, and the luxury of the palaces. These frescoes are especially noteworthy for their spatial concept, which relies upon circular rhythms rather than geometric or pictorial perspective. This confers upon them a unique musical fluidity that corresponds to the Buddhist concept of life as centered around a divinity or the prince who represents him. The treatment of the female figure in

A miniature of the Indian school of Kishangarh (left) portrays Muni Shri Sukdevji urging Raja Parikshit to renounce his throne. Chinese painting influenced other national art schools but remained uninfluenced at home. On a tile fragment from a tympanum of the first century A.D. (above), men watch animal fights at Shang-lin, the royal zoological park of the Han dynasty. At right, a T'ang nobleman and his servant on horseback.

Overleaf: *Detail from a larger work, probably copied by the Sung dynasty ruler Hui-Tsung (1082-1135) from an original eighth-century T'ang painting called* Ladies Preparing Newly Woven Silk. *In this panel, the silk is being ironed.*

these paintings is unforgettable, especially in the frescoes dating from the fifth and sixth centuries A.D. In the dance episodes in particular, women are imbued with a heavy sensuality.

The Chinese figurative tradition also has ancient origins, going back as it does to the dynasties of the second millennium B.C. What typifies this particular tradition is a singular coherence and unity of forms, one that stems from the close ties that art had with philosophy and religion in ancient China. Many rules that are fundamental in the West are either ignored or contradicted by Chinese art; it is not easy, therefore, for modern man, educated along Western lines, to grasp the meaning of Chinese art in general and Chinese painting in particular.

First of all it should be remembered that China was totally isolated from the rest of the world during the millennia that preceded the

founding of Taoism and Confucianism. The Great Wall of China was more than a defensive barrier; it also stood as silent testament to China's desire for total cultural isolation from the rest of the world. Chinese art thus seems somehow "outside of time," and this helps to explain its incredible continuity through the centuries. Moreover, in the Chinese social hierarchy, closely centered as it was upon the person of the prince and his representatives, the artist was considered an aristocrat, a notion that encouraged art's detachment from life's reality. That artists themselves were part of the cultural elite, just as scholars, philosophers, and poets were, also helps to explain the modern difficulty of interpretation, for paintings were addressed to a learned public, and the artist assumed a basic knowledge on the part of that public that the modern observer frequently lacks. Only at a relatively late stage did Chinese art free itself from submission to the philosophical and religious world.

Chinese painting began with the ornamentation of tombs, for it was the custom to inter a funeral dowry along with each corpse. A few such paintings remain from the third century A.D. They are painted in tempera on bricks and show bands of animals, horses, riders, philosophers, and divinities. Some of the characteristics now thought to be typical of Chinese painting are already evident: light brush-work barely outlines the figures, highlighting forms on a light background and only slightly veiling the figures with faint colors that retain all the freshness of the herb juices from which they were made.

The T'ang period, which lasted from the seventh through the tenth centuries A.D., first introduced the landscape as a foremost element of composition. From then on, silk or thin but resilient paper was to be used as backing for scroll paintings, which could be unrolled vertically to hang from walls or horizontally to be scanned in the privacy of a library. In the following period, the great Sung dynasty, Chinese painters demonstrated an extraordinary ability to depict nature and the human figure. Panoramic views of valleys and mountains, whirling rivers, and dense forests; minute figures of monks and travelers; villages swathed in the soft mist of dawn's first light; white cherry branches or warm, orange-colored flowers and immense green leaves—these are the subjects of numerous scrolls by such painters as the landscape artist Fan Kuan, author of numerous rolls that describe his travels.

The remarkable depiction of landscape in Sung painting corresponded to a particular religious and philosophical belief, one that saw nature as an aspect of the Universal Soul. To communicate this new view of nature the artist turned to new techniques, one of which was a form of ink painting augmented by the most knowledgeable use of wash. In this way Chinese painting, while availing itself of only a single color, was able to attain the most varied atmospheric and tonal effects. When artists did use different pigments, they were always of an extremely light material, watered and shaded and spread with transparent brush-strokes.

Among the major artists who worked to extraordinary effect in ink alone during the late Sung period were members of the Ma family. In melancholy, twilit scenes such as *Awaiting Friends by Lantern Light,* Ma Lin in particular reached the limits of personal lyrical expression.

The curvilinear breakers featured in The Waves and the Moon *(above) are the work of a thirteenth-century Chinese painter. His influence can be clearly seen in the Japanese colored ink drawing opposite. The work of a late-fifteenth-century painter,* The Burning of the Sanjo Palace *depicts a night assault upon a Taira clan stronghold in Kyoto in 1160.*

The well-known Mu Ch'i also devoted himself to landscape painting between A.D. 1250 and 1270, and in works such as *Evening Light on a Fishing Village* he portrayed wide valleys, calm lakes, and mountains sleeping in the evening mists.

At the beginning of the thirteenth century the Mongols under Genghis Khan invaded China, and by the end of the century the Sung dynasty had been destroyed. In its place the great khan's grandson, Kublai Khan, established the Yüan dynasty. Among the Yüan artists who were active in the fourteenth century special attention must be given to Ni Tsan and Wu Chen, the latter of whom was famous for his studies of bamboo.

China was freed from the Mongols by the Ming, who took power in 1368 and reigned for almost three centuries. In the new capital of Peking, the court's painting academies produced artists of great merit whose work remained rooted in Chinese tradition. This typically Chinese imitation of past ways allowed the Ming school to perpetuate itself almost until the modern era, perfecting a style of supreme dignity without ever reaching the lofty heights of the great Sung and Yüan painters of previous epochs.

Along the islands off the eastern coast of Asia, the Japanese civilization was also developing, although in many aspects it remained for a

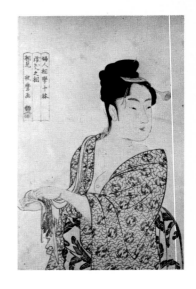

long while a subsidiary of the greater and more ancient Chinese culture. There are few indications of an independent tradition before the establishment of the city of Kyoto in A.D. 794. During this period Buddhism had become diffused in Japan, and divine images became one of the favorite subjects of indigenous painters, who showed no inclination to detach themselves from the tradition established in China.

In the fourteenth-century view of Kyoto seen opposite, the principal figures are executed in the Japanese style, but a Chinese landscape is reflected in parts of the scroll. The development of Japanese naturalism can be seen in the 1791 woodcut (left, above) by Kitagawa Utamaro; it is one of a series of studies of Edo period females. Katsushika Hokusai's Thirty-Six Views of Mount Fuji *(above), another Edo period woodcut, realistically depicts fatigued travelers stopping to rest.*

Only in the twelfth century did a native style assert itself, often in the form of such portraits as that of Minamoto Yoritomo in Kyoto's Jingo-ji Temple. This preference for realistic detail is also expressed in the great narrative scrolls of the period, among them *The Biography of the Priest Ippen.*

In the fourteenth century, under the influence of Zen philosophy, Japanese artists began to move away from religious painting and toward natural themes. The Momoyama and Edo periods that followed furthered this trend, using the traditional landscape theme for elegant gilded folding screens that became a principal element in the furnishing of Japanese houses. The works of the great Japanese painters of the nineteenth century were inspired by that same elegant mannerism. These artists often used the colored woodblock print, rather than the traditional brush, to express themselves.

5

Gothic Dreamworld

Divorced from divinity, a real woman of Tuscany sits spinning outside the door of Saint Anne's apartment—while inside the heretofore barren saint hears she will give birth to the Virgin Mary. Giotto's realistic detail is only a small touch in a larger panel, The Annunciation—*itself only one among many frescoes on the life of Mary and Jesus in Padua's Scrovegni Chapel—but it highlights Giotto's technique.*

BY THE FOURTEENTH CENTURY, Italian artists and art schools so dominated the European scene that it could be said with only slight exaggeration that all the Continent's major painters were Italian. Their grand achievements in fresco and oil corresponded with equally impressive achievements in the other arts—and thus while Giotto and Simone Martini were producing paintings of unsurpassed beauty, poets like Dante, Petrarch, and Boccaccio were making comparable linguistic breakthroughs. These artists were all part of a vast social, economic, and political movement that was revolutionizing life for the peoples of Western Europe. Strong local governments were being established, and the Church was achieving cultural supremacy through the great monastic orders of the Franciscans and Benedictines. The effect of all this was to bring about significant changes in artistic conception.

The painting that came out of fourteenth-century Italy was unquestionably superior to the works of artists in France, Spain, and England. Italian writers of the late Renaissance designated this period as the "Gothic," a term denoting the art of the Goths, and it is clear that the term was meant to be a disparaging one for art works created beyond the Alps. In truth, of course, masterpieces of European art did emerge from these supposedly barbarian trans-Alpine countries—not in the field of painting but in the fields of architecture and sculpture.

The Gothic style owed much to the spiritual ideals of the time. The vertical thrust of Gothic, accentuated by acute arches and elongated windows, increased internal luminosity, and this in turn gave such structures a certain mystical quality. The light of the nave of the Gothic cathedral was said to lead the souls of the faithful toward the light of God. Architects who thought in such terms were not particularly concerned with leaving wall space for paintings, and as a result it was the stained-glass window that became the favored mode of pictorial expression in thirteenth-century France.

In Italy the Gothic style received a different architectural interpretation. More harmonious and more spacious than its northern counterpart, Italian Gothic cleaved to tradition—both the Byzantine tradition, which was still quite alive in the thirteenth century, and the older classical tradition. In fact, a form of classicism was revived in Tuscany and Rome after the middle of the thirteenth century by such sculptors as Nicola and Giovanni Pisano and Arnolfo di Cambio. In their works the

solemnity of the ancient plastic concept takes on a more realistically human quality, strongly psychological and, at times, highly dramatic.

It is evident today that the Gothic period, wrongly defamed during the Renaissance, was actually a major epoch in European culture. During this period a new philosophy of man began to develop, one that was to evolve, in the space of a single century, into the philosophy of Humanism, the underlying inspiration of the Renaissance. For this reason it is wrong to think of the strong-willed Giotto as an anomaly, unconnected with his time. Nothing could be more false, for Giotto took full advantage of the innovations of both his predecessors and his contemporaries. From Nicola Pisano and Arnolfo di Cambio he appropriated classical plasticity and solemnity of architectural composition —and from Giovanni Pisano he took a deeply human and dramatic sense expressed in linear values.

Giotto's masterpieces are the frescoes that adorn the vast, luminous interiors of Italian Gothic cathedrals: Assisi, the Scrovegni Chapel in Padua, Santa Croce in Florence. The artist's use of color and his ability to create a sense of space contribute to the dramatic intensity of these works. In his depiction of the life of St. Francis at Assisi, for instance, Giotto's motifs range from a representation of nature to the portrayal of intense human feelings. In this relatively early work, the color and the monumentality of the forms suggest a kind of mystic abstraction that is typically medieval. Not so the frescoes that Giotto created for the Scrovegni Chapel in 1304 and 1305. Here his coloring is even more

Giotto's first major work included a number of the frescoes in Assisi depicting the life of Saint Francis. A lingering Byzantine stylization can be detected at right in The Miracle of the Chariot. *Rather abstracted mountains (above) persist behind the quite humanized figures of the Holy Family in* The Flight Into Egypt, *another fresco from the Scrovegni Chapel.*

intense—rose, green, turquoise, and purple tones blare against a lapis lazuli sky, and figures appear almost without shadowing, immersed in an astral light. Giotto's color sense was extraordinary, and it often served to underline the dramatic surroundings. For example, the great turquoise cape of the Madonna in *Flight Into Egypt* suggests a ship miraculously guided through a grayish natural setting. And in Giotto's *Annunciation* Saint Anne is garbed in a golden cloak and sits in a tranquil room with green wall-hangings. Lemon yellow, sharp green, and pale violet are used to depict the women mourning Christ in the *Lamentation*. Each is powerful in its unity, further evidence that Giotto's art ranks alongside Dante's in terms of impact upon the fourteenth-century world.

Two of Giotto's contemporaries, the Sienese painters Simone Martini and Ambrogio Lorenzetti, while never approaching Giotto's greatness, also developed new techniques and means of expression. Inspired by his Sienese contemporary Duccio, Martini emerged as the representative of the "new style," an aristocratic synthesis of French refinement and the last Hellenistic echoes. In *Majesty*, painted for the public palace

in 1315, angels and saints surround the Madonna like a flowering garden. The figures are arranged upon the turquoise ground in a harmonious whole, to which the suffused golden light gives a musical unity, and it is almost as if the painter was searching above all for a delicate rhythmic effect, depending for this effect on the flow of a line that creates the forms. Martini's work reflected the cultural climate of fourteenth-century Italy, which was becoming ever more cosmopolitan, the artistic epicenter of Western Europe.

Martini's most famous work, which is one of the matchless masterpieces of the Renaissance, is his *Annunciation*. In the center of this 1333 work, on a ground of gold, an angel and the Virgin are inscribed like two enormous illuminated capital letters in a flow of linear rhythms that follows the three-pointed framework. Such sublime detachment from reality creates the highest degree of lyric suggestiveness, comparable to one of the delicate verses of Martini's poet friend Petrarch.

The work of Ambrogio Lorenzetti is completely different, bound to reality by its subject matter as well as its form. His frescoes, *Good and Bad Government*, in Siena's public palace offer a narrative view not

Two of Siena's painters represent simultaneous trends: Ambrogio Lorenzetti, with his naturalistic mural of the city and surrounding countryside, Good and Bad Government (right), advanced realism; while Simone Martini, with the more delicately decorative style shown in his 1333 tempera Annunciation (above), carried Sienese goldwork to new heights.

Overleaf: *This late-fourteenth-century anonymous work, popularly known as* The Wilton Diptych, *was probably painted to support Richard II's claim to the English throne.*

only of city life but of the surrounding countryside as well. With beautifully warm, golden colors Lorenzetti creates an unforgettable portrait of a large communal city, the social unit that so favored the rebirth of culture and art in Italy.

Toward the close of the fourteenth century, both England and France witnessed the diffusion of a form of "polite" art that reached its maximum development in the following century. One great representative work, *The Wylton Dyptich,* was painted by an anonymous artist around 1395. On one panel King Richard II appears surrounded by his patron saints—Edward the Confessor, Saint Edmund, and Saint John the Baptist. On another panel the Madonna is surrounded by eleven winged angels, all dressed, as is the Madonna herself, in tunics of lapis lazuli blue. The sky, the child's gown, and the hair of the celestial messengers are gold.

Of the same subtly refined character is the art developed in the Bohemian court beginning with the reign of Charles IV, a sovereign of markedly French education. Under Charles' patronage, the *Cycle of Vissi Brod* was completed around 1350. Its nine panels depicting the

International Gothic style in fifteenth-century Europe: from France (left), the "April" illumination for the Limburg brothers' Les très riches heures du duc de Berry; *from Italy (top), Pisanello's mystical tempera,* The Virgin and Child with Saint George and the Abbot Anthony; *from Germany (above), Stefan Lochner's softly modeled* Madonna in the Rose Bower.

life of Christ are among the most singular European paintings of the century, both in the exceptional fineness of their delicately linear design and in their soft naturalism.

Painting in mid-fourteenth-century Venice wavered between recurring Byzantine themes and the more mature forms of Gothic decoration. The era's chief personality, Maestro Paolo Veneziano, reflected that ambivalence; his work could be semi-Byzantine—*The Death of the Virgin* is an excellent example—or softly tender, as is the glowing *Incoronation*. The same uncertainties are apparent in a series of fourteenth-century mosaics in St. Mark's, among them *Salome's Dance* in the great church's famed baptistry.

With the end of the fourteenth century and the beginning of the fifteenth there came to maturity in Europe the pictorial style known as International Gothic, an elegant style that was essentially a cultural product of European courts. This movement probably had its beginning in Paris, and only later spread to Brussels and Ghent, Dijon and Poitiers, Prague, Milan, Verona, and Venice. The movement was encouraged by traveling artists who took their works—Burgundian tapestries, illuminated religious codices, and knightly romances—with them. As a result, themes as well as style became uniform: the undertakings of noble knights; the heroic lives of saints; the days, months, and seasons in the ubiquitous Book of Hours; the luxuriousness of court life. International Gothic was therefore a conventionalized language. It was also a language of almost unparalleled refinement, and it did offer a wide margin for individual creativity.

The justly celebrated Limburg brothers excelled over all other fifteenth-century illuminators. Their *Les Très Riches Heures du duc de Berry* contains illustrations depicting life on the farm alongside the castle, the chores of peasant life, and the visits of lords and ladies in brilliant garb. Giovannino de' Grassi, another master of illumination, worked at the court of the Visconti in Milan, where he illustrated books of hours and calendars of great graphic elegance, among them the justly celebrated *Bergamo Notebook*.

During this same period two Italians, Gentile da Fabriano and Antonio Pisano, called Pisanello, achieved public recognition for their large-size canvases. Gentile, who lived from 1380 to 1427, painted his masterpiece, *The Adoration of the Magi* four years before his death. The "magic lyricism" of his style became, in the younger Pisanello, a fabulous and almost obsessive recreation of knighthood. His frescoes in the church of Sant'Anastasia in Verona and in the ducal palace in Mantua illustrated chivalric myths that were popular at that time. Pisanello recreated a world that was both violent and refined, religious and cruel.

In addition to Italy, where it found favor in the numerous courts that had sprung up, the polite Gothic style was well received in Germany. The figurations of the so-called celestial gardens, done by anonymous artists in the large Rhenish cities, are typical. One master, Stefan Lochner, stands out for his gentle, refined, poetic manner, which is clearly court-inspired. His minute and rounded Madonnas lean against flowering bushes in fantastic gardens, preserving the ingenuous aura of an art refined by a long, aristocratic tradition.

6

Classicism Reborn

IN THE FIRST YEARS of the fifteenth century, while the rest of Europe dozed in the delicate dream world of International Gothic painting, a single city brought to fruition a culture that was completely new and independent, one destined to show an extraordinary poetic force capable of transforming the civilized world. The city was Florence, and the new culture was the Renaissance.

Renaissance is a term that looks simultaneously to the past and to the future. It was coined by Italian art historians of the sixteenth century to contrast the period in which they lived with the grim penumbra of the Dark Ages from which they had so recently emerged. In short, they wanted to underline that this new philosophy of art proposed the "rebirth" of a classical style, inspired by the study of Roman and Greek antiquity that was then preoccupying men of culture.

We now recognize that the medieval period did have high artistic moments, so that what was reborn at the beginning of the fifteenth century in Florence was the classical evaluation of the world rather than art itself. Here the rational awareness of the Humanist philosophers combined with a resurgent interest in nature and the study of physical phenomena, bringing to the arts an entirely new aesthetic outlook. The first result was a science of perspective that allowed a vastly better apprehension of reality.

Florence was favored by an enlightened government, and it also had the good fortune to be the birthplace of artists of exceptional intellect, men who were able to put Renaissance theories into practice. Among the first who were able to synthesize man's capacities to know and to create were the architect Brunelleschi, the sculptor Donatello, and the painter Masaccio. The latter was one of the universal geniuses of painting. His pictorial world conveyed a titanic moral energy and revealed forms of three-dimensional monumentality that had up to then been foreseen only by Giotto. Masaccio's masterpieces were the frescoes done in the last two years of his very brief life, among them *The Trinity*, painted three years before his death in 1428 for the church of Santa Maria Novella. The scene is dominated by the cross, upon which Christ is supported by the Eternal Father. What is striking in this work is Masaccio's use of perspective. The central figures are set in a niche composed of a fronting with pilasters and architraves, columns and arches, and topped with a paneled vaulting of clearly classical inspira-

Obsessed by perspective, Paolo Uccello side-stepped the attempts of his fellow painters in Florence to bring to life the man-centered heroic art of the ancients and stayed within the metaphysics of the Gothic spirit. But he rendered his subject matter in deep perspective, as can be seen in this detail from his Battle of San Romano.

The realism of Giotto was further developed by Masaccio; in the detail of *Adam and Eve* at left, from the Brancacci Chapel frescoes in Florence, it is well-observed human anguish that registers on the faces of the banished pair. Above, the more static grace and the semidivine subjects of Fra Angelico's muted wet-plaster Annunciation bespeak its function as a meditative prop for monks in the monastery of St. Mark, Florence.

tion. (It has been suggested that Brunelleschi himself designed the niche, for the great architect is known to have been a friend of Masaccio's.) Certainly the schemes of all Masaccio's paintings are governed by his consciousness of the laws of space as well as his feeling for order.

Masaccio's supreme work is his *Life of Christ* in the church of the Carmine. In these frescoes the artist reveals the most extraordinary power of pictorial realization that had yet been seen. In the panel entitled *The Tribute Money*, for example, Christ is seen surrounded by the Apostles and is preparing to pay a tribute to the tax collector. At the right, a foreshortened house reinforces the feeling of perspective that has already been emphasized by the circle of Apostles ranged around Christ. The figures are massive and majestic, with a notable sculpted quality that is emphasized by lighting. It is almost as if Masaccio were deliberately neglecting the values of color in order to render volume more conspicuous through the interplay of lights. Masaccio also makes impressive use of light in the panel *The Expulsion of Adam and Eve*. Here the despair and sorrow of mankind is concentrated in the simplified forms of the bodies, mercilessly run through by light.

Meanwhile, there sprang up around Masaccio a generation of painters who made Florence the cradle of the Renaissance. Their number included the serene Fra Filippo Lippi, the dreamy Domenico Veneziano, Paolo Uccello, and Andrea del Castagno. Brother Giovanni da

74

Space can be organized by light and color as well as strict linear perspective. This was the choice of Piero della Francesca in The Baptism of Christ, *shown at left, and in the medallionlike portrait above of his one-eyed patron Federico da Montefeltro. Sandro Botticelli, to please his patron, Lorenzo de' Medici, accented tendrils and draperies with metallic gold in his tempera on canvas* The Birth of Venus *(right).*

Overleaf: *Botticelli's tempera vision of spring,* Primavera.

Fiesole, known as Fra Angelico, is the most interesting of all, however, for this artist, who spent most of his life painting in St. Mark's monastery in Florence, apparently ignored the dramatic revolution initiated by Masaccio. Instead he created slender angels with golden wings announcing glad tidings to timid Madonnas, magical villages under limpid skies populated by cherubs, saints, angelic choirs, and celestial music. This world, suffused as it is with the most delicate Gothic refinement, nevertheless reveals an abiding faith in Christian ideals. If Masaccio represented rational consciousness—an attitude that today would be considered secular—Fra Angelico expressed spiritual consciousness, founded on faith and on the primacy of Christian theology.

Angelico also showed a greater interest in color than Masaccio. But for a supreme display of critical intelligence and chromatic feeling, we must turn to Piero della Francesca. It was he who first effected a synthesis between reality and transcendence by placing men and objects within a familiar framework while using color and light values that were completely imaginary, symbols of an idealized perfection. In *The Baptism of Christ,* for instance, the alabasterlike figure of Jesus

seems bathed in an unreal light, while at the same time the landscape that serves as background for the figures is portrayed naturalistically.

Piero della Francesca's masterpieces are his frescoes for the story of the Cross, begun in 1452. Here the colors, rendered very clear and smoothed by light, create an almost kaleidescopic effect, with a tendency to abstraction that confers a magic quality on the subject. In fact, Piero's use of color, combined as it was with his concern for perspective and lighting, was to influence many of his contemporaries.

In the second half of the fifteenth century, Sandro Botticelli was far and away the most important Tuscan painter. Botticelli had a greatly refined sensibility and a natural inclination toward elegance. From the very beginning his paintings were founded upon an exaltation of linear

rhythms, and he selected as subject matter the triumph of the graceful, happy life of Florence under the leadership of the Medici. Noble ladies are thus depicted in the guise of *The Magnificat* or *The Madonna of the Pomegranate.* Nubile girls move rhythmically through flowering gardens in the *Primavera,* a masterpiece notable for its color, its balance, and its success in capturing the neo-Platonic ideals of love and beauty. Like other Renaissance painters, Botticelli also sought to capture the beauty of the nude figure, his most noteworthy achievement in this area being *The Birth of Venus.* His was a world of aristocratic detachment, expressed through the lyrical rhythm of line and through the use of brilliant color.

With so many great painters in Florence, it is not surprising that new ideals and techniques spread rapidly to other parts of Italy and then to the rest of Europe. (Piero della Francesca, for instance, exercised an important influence on such central Italian artists as Signorelli and Perugino.) But the artistic inheritance from Florence seemed to find the most congenial atmosphere in northern Italy, particularly in the Veneto region. By the 1430's the city of Padua, seat of an ancient university, had already begun to attract Tuscan painters like Filippo Lippi, and Venice had lured others, among them Uccello in 1425 and Andrea del Castagno in 1442. But the artist who more than any other carried the Tuscan Renaissance to the Veneto was the sculptor Donatello, who arrived in Padua in 1443 and stayed there ten years, enthralling the young artists of the region with his designs for the high altar of the church of St. Anthony and the equestrian statue of Gattamelata.

It was through the double exploration of both perspective and realism that painters moved from the stylized late-Byzantine Christs to Andrea Mantegna's extraordinary perspective view (below) of The Dead Christ. *The route often led to sadistic depictions of the sufferings of the saints as well as Christ. In Giovanni Bellini's monochrome* Pietà *at right, however, the fully modeled figures are infused with serenity, as is Leonardo Loredan in Bellini's portrait above.*

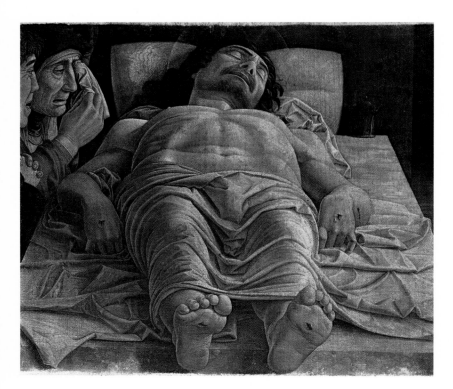

Interestingly enough, the new figurative idiom expounded by the great sculptor attracted painters as well as sculptors, including Andrea Mantegna, Cosmè Tura, and Giovanni Bellini.

Mantegna was one of those whom Donatello inspired. A master draftsman and a student of perspective, Mantegna created figures that seemed at times to be sculptural imitations, intense and dramatic. Mantegna's works also reflect his fascination with antiquity; often he chooses classical subjects, using architectural motifs inspired by the ruins of ancient Rome. His principal works are frescoes, among them an early masterpiece in the church of the Eremitani at Padua—where, between 1448 and 1455, he painted the histories of Saints James and

Christopher in his most classical style. After entering the service of the Duke of Mantua, he painted luminous frescoes on the walls of the Camera degli Sposi that depicted people and events associated with the duke's family, the Gonzagas. The world he created was a realistically faithful one, but it also incorporated the intellectual attitudes of which Mantegna was master.

The happiest consequences of the Paduan experience are to be seen in the school of painting founded in Venice by Jacopo Bellini and perpetuated by his sons, Gentile and Giovanni. And when Mantegna married Jacopo Bellini's daughter, the brothers joined the most advanced current of the early Renaissance. At first Giovanni was faithful to Mantegna's style, drawing with great care and seeking to capture the effects he had noted in the works of his brother-in-law and the great Donatello. He soon began to disengage himself from their influence and strike out on his own, however, and his interest then shifted from draftsmanship to pure color. Bellini's subject matter was quite varied, from the youthful *Pietà* of 1460 to the Madonnas through which he conveyed variations on the theme of maternal love. These works are characterized by a certain aura of melancholy, a delicate sorrow. In his mature period, Bellini

At left, one of Antonello da Messina's versions of the Crucifixion inaccurately emphasizes the tortured positions of the executed. Below, Saint Ursula sleeps in a fifteenth-century room into which an angel walks, in Saint Ursula's Dream from Carpaccio's Saint Ursula Cycle.

was to be influenced in architectural rendering by Piero della Francesca, probably during a trip to central Italy. This added technical skill enabled Bellini to create grandiose altarpieces such as that of Saint Job. In this work one is struck, above all, by atmospheric nuances; every element of color is in perfect harmony with the spiritually sweet and balanced expression of the figures.

Bellini's long career lasted into the sixteenth century, and thus he came into contact with numerous artists of the younger generation. Carpaccio, Giorgione, Titian, all were at one time or another his followers. In turn, the old artist accepted suggestions from them, thereby offering the most extraordinary demonstration of his own capacity to grow. Two painters who came into contact with Bellini in Venice at the close of the fifteenth century were the Sicilian Antonello da Messina and the Venetian Vittore Carpaccio. Antonello was a product of

fifteenth-century Sicilian culture, which was closely bound to medieval Catalan art. In Naples, where he received his artistic education, Antonello became acquainted with the Flemish and French cultures of the early 1400's, absorbing from them an extraordinary sense of reality. As a result he became an excellent portrait painter, capable of conveying faithfully both physiognomy and psychological insights.

In 1475 Antonello went to Venice to execute the altarpiece of San Cassiano. His colors—applied with oils, which he had reintroduced—were already as limped and strong as those of the Flemish masters and became crystalline when combined with light effects inspired by Piero della Francesca. In Venice, Antonello found a compatible cultural atmosphere, and there he created his masterpieces: two versions of the Crucifixion and a striking full-length study of Saint Sebastian. In the latter, the etiolated figure of the young martyr seems to exceed human limitations in its almost geometric beauty, but the setting itself is realistic—city streets, shady porticos, and sunny terraces where elegant personages move naturally in spaces defined by perspective.

Antonello's achievements strongly impressed Carpaccio, who was one of the most extraordinary personalities in all of painting history. Molded in the school of the Bellinis, Carpaccio had the makings of a

Mutilation underlies Carpaccio's Saint George Fighting the Dragon; the dragon's victims sprawl on the ground in various stages of decomposition before the gates of Cairo.

great spinner of tales, his thematic matter coming from simple legends. And yet in paintings based on these stories Carpaccio moved back and forth between realism and an almost magical transfiguration, letting imagination soar freely, mixing truth and dream, setting his images within a perspective of geometric spaces that is almost surrealistic. In the celebrated *Saint Ursula Cycle*, detailed drawings of the colorful, splendid costumes of Venetian gentlemen are interrupted by shimmering stretches of water or sky whose pictorial values take on an abstract and symbolical significance. In *Saint Ursula's Dream*, for example, the saint's room is depicted in all its minute particulars, a perfect "period room" of late-fifteenth-century Venice—but the lone angel who enters silently through the door glides over a shadowy, magical triangle drawn on the pavement.

Carpaccio's second masterpiece, a series of panels in the Scuola degli Schiavoni, tells the stories of Saint Jerome and Saint George. Here color becomes the protagonist, objects in such an atmosphere taking on an absolute, symbolic life, almost passing the bounds of reality. And there can be no doubt that the painters of the next generation—from Giorgione to Titian himself—were inspired by Carpaccio's extremely modern concept of color.

7

Legacy of the Low Countries

The return of man as a heroic creature marked the paintings of the Renaissance artists of Florence and Siena, while the great Flemish artists of the period favored domestic realism—as in Jan van Eyck's Marriage of Giovanni Arnolfini to Giovanna Cenami. *The dog is said to symbolize fidelity and the candle conjugal love. Two witnesses attend the ceremony, their figures visible in the mirror at center rear. One of these guests is thought to be Van Eyck himself.*

WHILE THE FLORENTINE RENAISSANCE was putting an end to the medieval view of life in Italy, another movement, similar in many aspects, was gathering force in northern Europe, first in Flanders and Holland and later in France and Germany as well. After a final, splendid outburst, the motifs of International Gothic, an art form that had achieved stylistic perfection, were fast disappearing. Especially in the Low Countries, the refined life of the aristocracy was coming into contact with the activities of middle-class merchants and craftsmen. A new economic well-being, a faith in the future, and the satisfaction derived from material pleasures induced society to turn wholeheartedly to a much more mundane world-view.

The Flemish artists of the first part of the fifteenth century clearly reflected these new attitudes. Although still dependent upon aristocratic patrons, they began for the first time to choose subjects from contemporary life, observing with new eyes evocative green landscapes broken by cathedral spires and city walls, or uncovering through portraiture the most intimate aspects of daily life. The great Flemish painters of the early fifteenth century thus were essentially realists. In this they differed from Tuscan painters whose "rebirth," influenced by both the noble formality of the ancients and a modern philosophical and geometrical rationality, was essentially idealistic. Indeed, it can be maintained that a true Renaissance spirit was lacking in the north—if by Renaissance we mean the conscious evolution of the spirit and style expressed by the Florentine painters from Masaccio to Piero della Francesca. Yet painters like Jan van Eyck, Rogier van der Weyden, Gheerardt David, Jean Fouquet, and Konrad Witz, who turned to such different cultural and spiritual sources of inspiration, made a substantial leap beyond the polite art of their predecessors, illuminators like the Limburgs or the delicate Stefan Lochner. The fact remains that whatever the movement in the north is called, an extraordinary pictorial culture flourished in the early 1400's in the great Low Country metropolises of Bruges, Ghent, and Louvain.

In 1419 Philip the Good, Duke of Burgundy and protector and patron of artists, transferred his ducal seat to Bruges—and in a short time his court became the center of Flemish artistic civilization. The painter Jan van Eyck, who can be considered the initiator of the new school, was one of the first to join Philip's retinue. A true transitional artist, and gifted with extraordinary creative force, Van Eyck began his career as an illustrator in the manner of the Limburg illuminators. However, Van Eyck soon confronted the reality of nature, executing his masterpiece, the multipaneled painting of *The Mystical Lamb* for the cathedral of Ghent in 1432. Painted on both sides of the panels, this grandiose work covers a wide range of styles and themes, from realistic portraits of the donors, Jos Vijd and his wife, to impressionistic nude figures of Adam and Eve, to various animated episodes in the life of Christ, to an idyllic vision of paradise. The latter is depicted as a green valley strewn with rose bushes and populated by legions of angels and saints. On the horizon splendid cities with palaces and high-spired cathedrals are silhouetted in the flamboyant Gothic style.

Where Van Eyck's art especially arouses our admiring wonder is in interior scenes and in portraits. A superb example is the 1434 wedding

A consistent inconsistency bound the scenes depicted in northern painting: real, almost palpable figures are seen in the detail at left from Van Eyck's Ghent Altarpiece. Patriarchs, poets, philosophers, and prophets sing their adoration of the mystic lamb, who bleeds into a chalice. In the portrait of Chancellor Rolin (right), the two elements of real and unreal are separate yet joined. The old chancellor kneels before the holy figures in a room that is separated from a very real city that is visible through the windows.

portrait of Giovanni Arnolfini and his bride; here Van Eyck's brush work is as delicate as that of an illuminator. The couple stands in a small room, on one side of which a lead-paned window is open, letting a soft light filter in. In the center of the room a rich, bronze candelabrum hangs from the ceiling; it has only one lit candle–a symbol, perhaps, of conjugal love. From the wooden floor a little Maltese dog, a symbol of fidelity, gazes out at us. On a wall in the background a mirror reflects the couple from behind and also reveals the figures of two visitors who are entering the room. Every object is minutely depicted, and this attention to detail creates Van Eyck's special brand of realism.

At times, Van Eyck's passion for detail produced almost supernatural effects. In his 1436 portrait of Chancellor Rolin, the subject kneels before the Virgin and in front of a window, beyond which lies an endless landscape. These hills and vales are seen as through a binocular, treated in microscopic detail. Walled cities and cathedral spires, hills and castles, a river port and loaded boats, a green island, blue mountains that fade into the horizon—all are depicted with an acute clarity that goes far beyond a "natural" landscape.

Van Eyck set the pattern for a Flemish figurative culture that would flourish throughout the fifteenth century. Following his lead Flemish painters abandoned the traditional egg-base tempera for oil colors, a more fluid medium that facilitated the execution of their painstaking paintings, which were done with demanding exactness. Consequently, Flemish color was very different from that of contemporary Tuscan painting; it found a parallel only in certain aspects of Venetian painting at the end of the fourteenth century. Such colors highlight the works of Rogier van der Weyden, who was born in the year 1400. In contrast to Van Eyck, Van der Weyden was inspired not so much by medieval illumination as by the work of painters well grounded in reality—men like the mature Van Eyck himself, or even Robert Campin, the creator of figures of such amazing verity as Saint Barbara. Van der Weyden imposed on his colors a mineral tone, an almost crystalline

Van Eyck's colors did not fade, muddy, or darken but were held by secret formulae in their initial brilliance, causing other painters to interest themselves in the differences between egg-bound, matte-finish tempera on wood and light-reflecting oil on canvas. Although he worked in tempera, Rogier van der Weyden managed to produce remarkably glowing colors without the gold of the decorative painters—for instance, in his Deposition *above. And in his portrait of a veiled woman at right, light suffuses the film of the veil and rounds the soft curves of the face.*

limpidness, and he introduced sudden, sometimes violent contrasts. In *The Deposition* and *The Crucifixion*, he appears at his most dramatic. The latter, one of the most expressive paintings of the period, achieves its effects through the dramatic interplay of violet, azure, and silver-grey colors against a blood-red background.

In 1450 Van der Weyden made a trip to Italy, stopping in Ferrara on his way to Rome. There he became acquainted with the painting of Piero della Francesca, whose influence Van der Weyden was to carry back to Flanders. Traces of this contact with the Italian Renaissance are especially apparent in the artist's late portraits. Indeed, the malleability of his portrait of Francesco d'Este and the crystal purity of *The Veiled Lady* reveal a new tendency to idealize the subject, freeing it from the characteristic burden of Flemish psychological realism in order to give it an aspect of formal beauty.

Flemish painters active in the second half of the fifteenth century were influenced by one of the two great masters who initiated Flemish painting. One of Van Eyck's stylistic descendants was Petrus Christus, creator of *Double Portrait* and *Portrait of a Girl*. (In the latter, Christus turns his fascinated attention to the human figure, which he details as if it were a precious, unfathomable object.) Van der Weyden influenced

In Petrus Christus' Saint Eligius as a Goldsmith, left, the otherworldly quality rests in the saint himself and the worldly reality in the young couple and in the detailed contents of the goldsmith's shop. In Hugo van der Goes' Portinari Altarpiece (a section of which is shown at right), three shepherds gaze in wonder at the glowing babe, who illuminates the delicate face and heavy peasant hands of his virgin mother. Fifteen angels, representing the fifteen joys of the Virgin, have come to rest at various locations.

Overleaf: A section from Joys of the Senses, *the central panel of Hieronymus Bosch's oil-on-panel triptych* The Garden of Earthly Delights, *reveals the Flemish artist's bizarre vision.*

another great master, Dirk Bouts, an artist of Dutch origin who lived in Flanders. His masterpieces can be admired in the cathedral of Louvain, in the panels of the altarpiece of the Sacraments for Saint Peter, created from 1464 through 1467. By means of singularly heightened perspective, Bouts seems to draw the observer into that work, making him a participant in the events and in the protagonist's feelings. Contributing to this particular sensation is the allusive presence of so many other figures, among them two men who are looking from the little window in the background and a mysterious personage in the red cap—the artist perhaps?—who silently lays his hand on the bureau at right.

Another noteworthy artist of the period was Hugo van der Goes, whose Portinari Altarpiece (1476-78) is one of the most extraordinary creations of Flemish art. This huge panel was commissioned by the Tuscan merchant Tommaso Portinari, an agent of the Medici family who resided in Bruges. Members of the Portinari family, including Tommaso, his wife, and three children, therefore appear at the sides of

the Holy Family as they are adored by shepherds and angels. A sense of wonder and amazement is generated by this manger scene, and apposed groups of angels create harmonious relationships of color—pale turquoise, sea blue, gold, and velvety green. In a Delft vase and glass in the center are symbolic lilies and irises together with elegant indigo-blue columbines. Yet the beauty and harmony of these scenes contrast sharply with the figures of roughly dressed shepherds. Reality and fantasy, truth and dream, are thus fused in the art of Van der Goes.

The most faithful interpreter of Flemish society in the late fifteenth century was the painter Hans Memling, who also lived in Bruges. His portraits, whether sacred or secular, share a sense of quiet melancholy that has been expressed in paintings that consistently adhere to reality. In his masterpieces—*The Mystical Matrimony of Saint Catherine*, *The Vision of Saint John at Patmos*, and *The Martyrdom of Saint John the Baptist*—his representation of historical fact is completely believable.

Memling was really the last of the great artists in the fifteenth-century Flemish tradition, for his contemporary Hieronymus Bosch truly stands by himself. Bosch lived in isolation in the little city of 's Herto-genbosch at the southern extremity of Flanders. Unlike his predecessors, who were in full rapport with Flemish society and depicted its most felicitous aspects, Bosch saw a world of intellectual crises and religious doubts. He belonged to an active evangelical fraternity, yet he was driven to the very edge of heresy, skirting areas of the occult with an emphasis that often causes one to doubt his sanity. In such religious works as the *Epiphany*, for instance, the rapt spirituality of the divine personages is in disconcerting contrast to the almost bestial caricatures of earthly beings who are present at the miracle.

In characteristic allegorical paintings like *The Garden of Earthly Delights*, painted around 1500, diabolical jokes and grotesque marvels reveal Bosch's own anguish, which is that of a lost soul who no longer believes in the values of the spirit, who confounds good and evil, who has no moral focus. This large triptych shows the globe, which opens onto a vision of the garden of happiness flanked by earthly hell and paradise. Absurd human figures, horrendous demons, strange birds, and monstrous fish and animals populate that fantastic and terrifying world. Bosch's palette perfectly expresses hallucination, passing from the airiest brilliance of the heavens to hazy reddish shadows flashing with hellish flames. Absolutely singular in its character, Bosch's work concluded the exceptional period of fifteenth-century Flemish painting.

French painting in the fifteenth century was of a lesser order than Flemish. During the first half of the century the former fell under the domination of the latest manifestation of polite Gothic, which had had notable influence upon tapestry weaving, a medium in which the role of the painter was limited to the preparation of the "cartoon" upon which the weaving was then carried out. Early in the century a marvelous series of tapestries was created in Arras, Tours, and Lyon. Later the center of tapestry production moved to Tournai and thence to Brussels, and by 1500 tapestry had become a Flemish specialty.

Fifteenth-century French painting can be said to have reached its highest level in the works of Jean Fouquet. Like so many other artists,

After the fantasies of Bosch, the chaste piety of an adolescent angel appearing to a childlike Virgin in Hans Memling's Annunciation *(left). That same piety veils a luminous face in Memling's portrait of Benedetto Portinari (above), a young member of the Italian family that was stationed in Bruges as agents of the Medici family.*

Fouquet traveled to Italy, and while he was there in about 1445 he
became acquainted with the works of the great Tuscans, from Fra
Angelico to Piero della Francesca. Angelico especially made a lasting
impression upon the Frenchman, and among the few works of Fouquet's that have survived is a diptych comprised of the *Madonna with
Child* and the *Portrait of Etienne Chevalier*. The delicate Madonna—a
likeness of Agnès Sorel, Charles VII's mistress and Fouquet's patron—

seems made of alabaster; the light gently skims over the cold tones and the smoothness of her flesh. But this delicacy and spirituality are but one aspect of Fouquet's paintings, which are also characterized by a realistic portrayal of the contemporary world. In addition to his portraits, Fouquet was renowned for illuminations, many of which survive.

In Germany, despite the flowering of numerous schools in such great Rhenish cities as Cologne and Basel, painting remained at a modest level of achievement throughout the 1400's. The only painter of note was Konrad Witz, whose realism, expressed particularly in the 1435 *Saint Peter* panels, laid the groundwork for that concrete, earthly vision that would become the basis of Germanic painting toward the end of the century. Witz was naturally aware of the achievements of the great Flemish painters, but he also placed his figures in a measured and molded space in a way that suggests he had become familiar—considerably in advance of his compatriots—with the Italian Renaissance. Indeed, this solitary, morose artist was at work just as the countries of northern Europe were about to be touched by that Renaissance, a contact that was to prove highly stimulating—and also extremely hazardous for the autonomy of the national schools.

Jean Fouquet's Madonna (left), believed to have been modeled on a king's mistress, displays the high forehead of infancy—the fashionable hairstyle of the time, produced by shaving the temples. The growing importance of perspective in French painting was eventually felt in tapestry design as well, as the detail at right from The Lady and the Unicorn, *clearly indicates.*

8

Art's Apotheosis

THE FIFTEENTH CENTURY saw the diffusion, in Italy and subsequently in all of Europe, of the first principles of the Renaissance—and the sixteenth century witnessed their triumphal affirmation. In part the Renaissance triumphed because social and economic conditions were increasingly favorable to such developments. In Italy, for example, both the Church and the indigenous feudatories grew more powerful, and as they did, religious and secular rulers became patrons of artists. The ruling houses of other European states soon followed the example of the Italian courts, and the physical and cultural renovation of their residences became commonplace. It is therefore altogether logical that major artistic schools were located near the centers of political and economic power. The Florence of Giuliano de' Medici offered hospitality to Leonardo; the Rome of Popes Julius II and Leo X summoned Raphael and Michelangelo; the Emilian dukedoms nourished a mannerist school that would migrate to the court of King Francis I of France; and the Holy Roman Empire of Maximilian succored Dürer and other great German painters. And in Venice, the splendid palaces of the lagoon city's fabulously wealthy merchants displayed the works of Europe's greatest pictorial school.

The history of High Renaissance painting, like that of the early Renaissance, begins in Florence. Here, in the last quarter of the fifteenth century, Leonardo da Vinci was to establish himself, joining the workshop of the painter and sculptor Andrea Verrocchio. During his apprenticeship Leonardo helped Verrocchio with the famous *Baptism of Christ*, painting one of the two angels kneeling alongside the Baptist. Under the young artist's brush the spiritual elegance associated with Botticelli—who was also apprenticed to Verrocchio—was transformed into a subtle, realistic probing of the human soul.

From the outset Leonardo appeared as a major new historical figure, the artist-scientist. In addition to investigating the laws of physics, mechanics, and botany, he studied anatomy, examined the pictorial values of nature, and explored perspective and color variation in the different strata of the atmosphere. He exhibited a virtuosity never before evidenced in the use of light and shadow, a skill that enabled him to achieve his famous mellow gradation of tones. His works, founded as they were on poetic as well as scientific premises, were not unflawed, however. Indeed, as a result of a multitude of technical and

In this charcoal sketch by Leonardo da Vinci—a cartoon, or preliminary study for a fresco—the very air seems to have been made visible. The four figures include Saint Mary, who rests upon Saint Anne's knee to display the infant Jesus, and Saint John, who watches all three.

Why is it Leonardo's Mona Lisa del Giocondo, the legendary Mona Lisa (top), who is world famous, rather than his Ginevra de' Benci, shown immediately below her? The answer seems to have little to do with the comparative beauty of the two women, but rather with the compositional qualities of the two paintings. Leonardo painted his Virgin of the Rocks (opposite) when he was in his twenties, only to return to the subject several decades later, when his color values were far more cool.

conceptual difficulties, they often remained unfinished, marred by the use of colors still not sufficiently tested. *The Adoration of the Kings*, for example, was an attempt that only partly succeeded. In many areas, especially those treating distant vistas, the drawing is slurred by rapid, dark brush-strokes and furnishes little more than an outline. And yet this unfinished work represented a major breakthrough, pointing toward painting's new vision—one in which the figures were flexible in space, one in which light and shade were used to achieve striking dramatic effects. Leonardo experimented with a kind of clarity of purpose that at once had the force of philosophy and the fascination of poetry.

The masterpiece of Leonardo's naturalistic period is *The Virgin of the Rocks*, begun in 1483 after Leonardo moved from Florence to Milan. Here too the central figure of the Madonna seems to stand out from the background, an effect achieved through the use of chiaroscuro, or light and shade. Under the muted color of Leonardo's palette, the relationship between nature and the figures of the Madonna and the child, Saint John, and the angel became an almost musical harmony.

In the refectory of Santa Maria delle Grazie in Milan, Leonardo labored over his most celebrated work, *The Last Supper*, from 1495 through 1497. Christ and the Apostles are seen at the front of a large room that opens onto a landscape. The figures of the Apostles are arranged in balanced groups, and light-bathed color contributes to the unity of design. *The Last Supper* illustrates the degree to which painting had changed since the time of Masaccio, for whom color took on a plastic meaning, isolating figures in space. For Leonardo and those who followed him, space itself took on color in the thousand nuances of nature, with chiaroscuro and a system of multiple perspective replacing Masaccio's blocks of color.

In this period are Leonardo's two later masterworks, *Mona Lisa* and *The Virgin and Child with Saint Anne*. The former, a portrait of Mona Lisa del Giocondo, was begun in 1503. The enigmatic expression on the face of La Gioconda, as the portrait is sometimes called, has enchanted generations, but the source of her special quality remains elusive. Perhaps it emanates from the barely delineated smile, which suggests thoughts and words only dreamed of. Or perhaps it stems from another source—mountains, lakes, and rivers that encircle the subject and then gradually fade in the vaguely misty atmosphere; or perhaps from Leonardo's idealization of mature beauty, symbolized by the light, velvety touch of the hands—certainly among the most amazing hands ever conceived by an artist. The painting suggests an ancient Greek sculpture, but even more it is a Renaissance philosophical meditation upon the beauty of nature and upon the mystery of the human intellect. La Gioconda, in short, is the ultimate statement of High Renaissance painting, of which Leonardo was the great initiator.

Raphael, born Raffaello Sanzio in Urbino in 1483, also created an idealistic image of the world through painting. Brought up in the cultured, refined atmosphere of Urbino's ducal court, where he was a disciple of the pleasant, mild-mannered Perugino, Raphael set forth a perfectly balanced world-view in his first paintings. In *The Marriage of the Virgin*, to take but one example, space is in flawless perspective,

the frescoes that adorn the ceiling of the Sistine Chapel. Raphael himself used the fresco style in two rooms, the Stanza della Segnatura and the Stanza di Eliodoro, both of which were completed by 1514. One of the frescoes in the first of these rooms, a work called *The School of Athens*, is a representation of ancient Athens' greatest philosophers engaged in discussion. (Interestingly enough, Raphael has given these great personages of antiquity the faces of men of his own time: Archimedes has the face of the architect Bramante, who was then building St. Peter's, and one of Plato's followers bears a remarkable resemblance to Raphael himself.) In the monumental suppleness of these figures, which are draped in the classical manner, there is clear reference to Michelangelo's figures on the Sistine ceiling.

The second of the two rooms presents a surprisingly sudden chromatic change. Here Raphael has chosen a palette that is thicker and softer, one that recalls, in its brilliance, Florentine paintings. The artist may well have had some contact with Venetian painting—which by the beginning of the fifteenth century had become the mistress of coloring —through the Venetian artists Sebastiano del Piombo and Lorenzo Lotto, who were in Rome working in the pope's service. In *The Mass of Bolsena* and *The Freeing of Saint Peter from Prison*, Raphael searched out particular light effects in order to render more brilliant and sumptuous the chromatic texture. And in the many portraits in these frescoes a new interest in color tonality is apparent, as well as a joy in painting that is surprising in such a composed and intellectual artist.

In time Raphael was to be caught up in the frantic artistic activity of the papal court, his prestigious brush enlisted by the new sovereign, Pope Leo X. Raphael's portrait of Leo depicts the pope seated at his work table examining an illuminated missal. The hands of this great prince of the Church, under whose patronage so many splendid works were created, are thin and well cared for; Raphael seems to have transfused them with all the sensitivity, the love of beauty, and the vitality that marked sixteenth-century Italy.

Like Raphael, Michelangelo Buonarroti also had a feeling for classic grandeur. It was he who created the figurative language that is frequently called the perfect synthesis of the High Renaissance ideal. But Michelangelo lived a long life, and it was his fate to assist at the undoing of the very ideals that he had contributed so much to establishing. Michelangelo's personality was strongly marked by his original vocation as a sculptor, even though he successively became an architect and a painter. As a sculptor his first goal was to rediscover the majestic beauty of the classical age, and in fact he first attracted attention with a statue of a sleeping cupid that Cardinal di San Giorgio purchased at Rome as an excavated piece, believing it to be a Roman or Greek work. Shortly thereafter, Michelangelo let it be known—through his transcendant *Pietà* in St. Peter's—that his supposed submissiveness to antiquity involved interpreting the nobility and majesty of classical composition, not renouncing the expressiveness of his own soul. The figure of Mary, bowed over the smooth body of her son, her beautiful face revealing a most human grief, presages all Michelangelo's future efforts, expressing as it does the sublime nature of the spirit.

Portraiture developed to the point where a conviction of substantiality emanates from such panels as Raphael's Portrait of a Cardinal *(above). There is little emphasis on backgrounds in the paintings of Michelangelo, who concentrated, like the sculptor that he was, upon the human body. At right, above, is his too-seldom-admired* Doni Tondo, *which presents the Holy Family as a three-generational grouping; at right below, a detail from the Sistine Chapel frescoes shows a mother and two children climbing to higher ground to escape the oncoming Flood.*

Overleaf: Two ignudi, heavy-muscled youths, observe aspects of the history of man from the ceiling of the Sistine Chapel.

Like his sculpture, Michelangelo's paintings seem to recreate the classical age while remaining contemporary in substance and mood. A representative early example is the *Doni Tondo*, painted during the first decade of the sixteenth century. Only formed figures took on value for Michelangelo, and in this work the atmospheric sense of landscape discovered by Leonardo and employed by Raphael is annulled completely. Even the colors of this early Michelangelo express the artist's disdain for any imitative form of reality. What "realness" there is emanates from the statuesque forms themselves.

In 1505 Pope Julius II summoned Michelangelo to Rome to execute the pontiff's own funeral monument, a project that was to be interrupted by quarrels and court intrigues. Michelangelo's distress and anger over this imbroglio were so great that later writers have referred to the events connected with the project as a tragedy in his life. A year after his arrival, the angry artist left Rome. Julius was able to lure him back at a later date—not to finish the tomb, however, but to fresco the ceiling of the Sistine Chapel in the Vatican. Luckily, the pope insisted upon the completion of this work despite the thousand hesitancies and anguishes that accompanied its execution.

The Sistine Chapel gives us the full measure of Michelangelo's genius. The ceiling is divided into sectors, within which are contained almost three hundred grandiose figures illustrating the story of mankind from the Creation to the Flood, from the travails of the Hebrews to the lives of the Prophets. Michelangelo wanted to represent the anguished, heroic struggle of man against all the physical adversities that oppose his full freedom of spirit—and it was this theme

that gave free rein to the artist's dramatic temperament and to his aspiration for a world where spirit and matter could meet and man could thus achieve a supreme freedom. This epic struggle underlies *The Eternal Father Giving Life to Adam*, moody and full of foreboding, and the despairing tension of the mothers who, during the Flood, try to bring their offspring to safety. Whatever the artist's intentions, the results of his heroic efforts in the Sistine Chapel provide the history of painting with one of its greatest treasures.

In 1541 Michelangelo completed *The Last Judgment* on a wall of the Sistine Chapel. This was a work of the artist's later years, which were increasingly circumscribed by a feeling of isolation and an obsession with obtaining unattainable artistic heights. The fact that many of the artist's later works remained unfinished suggests that by then life appeared to be without any precise rational or moral outline. In *The Last Judgment*, for instance, the figures themselves, in the absence of natural elements to help delineate perspective, reflect Michelangelo's own anguished soul. The subjects of this monumental work, a tangle of nude bodies in the hollow of an unnatural space, move under the gesture of a Christ who is more revenger than brother. Under the weight of doubt, the ideal equilibrium of Raphael's classicism has been undone, replaced by that negative phase of the Renaissance that in so many aspects began with Michelangelo and is called Mannerism.

In general, the term Mannerism derived from the word "manner," which meant the tendency of artists to draw inspiration from the works of the great artists who had preceded them, rather than from nature. Born as a reaction to the style of the early Renaissance, Mannerism expressed itself in "anticlassical" forms that at times tended toward melodrama or a kind of watered-down, intellectualized refinement. The source of this reaction was a growing lack of faith in the ideals and norms of the early Renaissance, and even in Catholicism itself, about which strong doubts had been raised beginning in 1517 with the advent of the Lutheran reform.

Mannerism traces its origins to early sixteenth-century Tuscany, and particularly to the work of Jacopo Pontormo. This singular artist emerged from the Florentine tradition of Leonardo and Raphael, but in contrast to his teacher Andrea del Sarto, whose works were typical expressions of the Renaissance school, Pontormo was to deny the ideals of order and balance, the Florentine feel for nature, and the atmospheric values of color. Instead Pontormo's works were to reveal the extent of the pictorial revolution brought about by the Mannerists. In his version of *The Supper at Emmaus*, Portormo has chosen colors for Christ and the Apostles that are so far from natural that they approach surrealistic expression. Pontormo's masterwork in the Mannerist mode is his *Deposition of Christ* in the church of Santa Felicità in Florence; here green or blue-robed angels are arranged on various levels around a Madonna who seems to be equally exempt from the laws of gravity.

Leonardo's chiaroscuro technique greatly influenced Antonio Allegri da Correggio, founder of an Emilian school of art that was strongly influenced also by Tuscan and Roman Mannerism. A whole group of youthful works, including *The Madonna and Saint John* and *The Holy*

Family, reveal Correggio's gradual absorption of fifteenth-century design into a harmonious atmosphere of fluid color, one shot through by a subtle luminosity that lights up the features of the protagonists. The best examples of Correggio's early works are the frescoes of the abbess's room in the convent of St. Paul in Parma. The freshness of the decorative vegetation, the airy elegance of the youthful figures, the zest for mythology, the homage to Hellenistic motifs—all give these frescoes an especially festive character. A few years later, in the cupolas of St. John the Evangelist and the dome of the cathedral in Parma, Correggio was to attempt grand decorativeness, using dazzling whirls of light.

Certain paintings of the artist's last period are characterized by techniques that would influence the great ambiance painters of the Baroque period. In *The Virgin with Saint Jerome* and the *Danaë*, for instance, sinuous elegance, flowing design, and subtly allusive sensuality are the predominant qualities, while soft colors suggest a spaciousness in depicting natural environment. At times surpassing even the examples of the great innovators, Correggio became the model for the late Baroque era, the favorite artist of painters from Watteau to Tiepolo.

The antitraditional seeds planted by Correggio bore fruit in the works of his follower Parmigianino, a leader of the Mannerist school in northern Italy. After studying the works of Michelangelo in Rome, Parmigianino abandoned Correggio's sensitive softness in favor

Jacopo Pontormo had the Capponi Chapel walled up during the years he painted his dreamlike, poignant Deposition of Christ *(left, above) so that he could work in absolute solitude. His own face is the rapt one staring from the righthand background. Gradually the heroic Renaissance sense of spirit, intellect, and personality was subjected to a more fluid and agitated line—and, in Correggio, whose* Danaë *appears at right, to the sensuality of flesh itself. So long as there is wealth and paint there will be portraits: at left below, a Medici princess sits for Agnolo Bronzino.*

of images of the most aristocratic and intellectual elegance, executed with cold, mineral colors. In *The Madonna with the Long Neck*, pliant design and abstract color are organized according to a series of complex interrelationships: an angel's leg corresponds to a white column, and a bulging, elongated amphora to the sensual torso of the Madonna.

An important phase in the history of Mannerism was to occur in France at the court of Francis I. Around 1540 Francis summoned the greatest of Italy's artists to his château at Fontainebleau, which soon became a center for the diffusion of Italian art in northern Europe. Primaticcio from Bologna joined the Roman Niccolò dell'Abate in creating frescoes for the ballroom, the duchess's chamber, and the so-called Ulysses Gallery. (The mark of Italian Mannerism also extended to the decorative furnishings, from tapestries to sculptures.) The work of the Italian Mannerists served as models for contemporary French artists, among them Jean Cousin, his son Jean, Antoine Caron, and François Clouet. However, the Fontainebleau school did not include Jean Clouet, the greatest French artist of the mid-sixteenth-century and creator of the supreme portrait of Francis I. Rather, Clouet's incisive style recalled the Flemish tradition.

The Veneto school of High Renaissance painting also evolved at the beginning of the sixteenth century. While Leonardo and Raphael, Michelangelo and Correggio were laying the foundations for the richest period in the history of Italian art, the art of the Veneto region remained independent. The school itself included a number of truly exceptional figures, the best known of whom are Giorgione, Titian, and Lorenzo Lotto. Later Veneto painters such as Bassano, Tintoretto, and Paolo Veronese approached Mannerism but never really moved away from their own tradition, which was strongly bound to the pictorial current represented by Giovanni Bellini at the beginning of the sixteenth century. Its characteristic was a kind of "constant picturesqueness" that resolved sixteenth-century naturalism in a triumphal preeminence of color. (This style, in which forms are defined by color, is known as painterly. It differs from linear painting, in which forms are defined by line.) In their use of color, the Venetian painters increasingly disassociated themselves from the rules of design as they were understood in Florence and Rome, and arguments over the relative merits of the linear and painterly styles arose among the leading art critics and historians of the age.

The birth of sixteenth-century Veneto painting is linked to the prestigious name of Giorgio da Castelfranco, called Il Giorgione, who declined to create religious or ceremonial works for court patrons, painting instead for an elite group of philosophers, musicians, literary men, and art lovers. Giorgione's most significant technical innovation was his use of painterly style. His most significant thematic innovation was his lyrical use of landscape, and this was to have a profound effect on the painters who followed him. Giorgione did not simply attempt to portray nature realistically; for him, landscape expressed mood, and it was this attitude that opened new horizons for painters.

Although Giorgione chose both secular and sacred subjects for his canvases, he made the setting secular in all cases. His particular interest

Life is one but art is many. It was Francis I—depicted in the realistic Flemish style in Jean Clouet's portrait at top—who tried to import the Italian Renaissance to France, specifically to Fontainebleau. But what developed at the château was a mannered, often stilted style, visible above in the anonymous portrait bust of Sabina Poppea. Meanwhile, in Venice, the landscape was again being incorporated into allegorical works such as Giorgione's luminous Sleeping Venus *(opposite).*

in nature, whose charms he depicted with the lyrical and pastoral accents in vogue at that time, is the hallmark of Giorgione's style. Thus in Giorgione's only altarpiece, *The Madonna di Castelfranco*, more emphasis is given to the sentimental landscape of green Veneto hills than to the holy personages in the center of the painting. Landscape also predominates in *The Philosophers*. Three figures—who probably represent Aristotle, Averroës, and the Modern Philosopher—are central to this work, but it is the vision of mountains and valleys, plants, trees, and flowers taken directly from nature, which Giorgione has drawn with loving attention.

Giorgione is, then, a realist in the sense that details of nature are drawn as precisely as in Florentine painting, providing a solid ground for his lyricism. Yet the type of realism upon which Giorgione's poetics are founded is not merely imitative, nor does it limit his imagination, which tends naturally toward the lyricism of pastoral literature. Even Giorgione's expressive medium—an extraordinarily warm palette that enriches itself in shadowy or shining tones according to light variations —seems to adapt itself to his poetic concept, which uses physical things to elicit man's most intimate feelings. This poetic quality is evident in Giorgione's masterpiece, *Sleeping Venus*, in which the nude goddess,

reclining before a silent landscape, evokes deepening melancholy.

After Giorgione's premature death from the plague, his *Venus* was retouched by another artist destined to take Giorgione's place in the admiration of the Venetians—Tiziano Vecellio, known as Titian. Titian is supposed to have added the figure of Cupid to the landscape—although today that figure has disappeared—and the younger artist may have contributed to other paintings by Giorgione as well. Titian's work, while clearly influenced by Giorgione, was distinguished by a robust and vigorously sensual style expressed through marked coloration and strong lighting effects. One painting of doubtful attribution, the famous *Country Concert*, seems to show strong evidence of Titian's hand rather than Giorgione's. The musicians and the nudes are a great deal more corporeal and earthly than the Philosophers or the Venus, and they are animated by a sensuality that is violently expressive—and thoroughly typical of Titian.

Titian's artistic reputation grew rapidly during the early decades of the sixteenth century. He was summoned to adorn the altars of churches, creating such complex symphonies of color as the Pesaro Altarpiece in the church of I Frari. He was also attracted by secular themes, intended for the most illustrious representatives of a cynical and sensual aristocracy. Thus he painted the *Bacchanalia* and *Allegories* for the dukes of Ferrara, and *Venus* for Duke Guidobaldo of Urbino. Superficially, the latter was a copy of Giorgione's *Venus*, but Titian's rosy Venus was no melancholy goddess; she was a magnificent courtesan, lying on a huge bed in a sumptuous room.

Gifted with great force of character, Titian emerged as a painter of the highest caliber, and his portraits comprise the richest gallery of the period. Titian managed to combine a formal idealization of his subject with psychological characterization. Thus *The Man with the Glove* becomes the personification of virile melancholy, and *Riminaldi* betrays a sick and insecure personality. In much the same way the dukes of Urbino, magnificently garbed, seem to exult over their exalted status, and King Francis I, swelling with pride, suggests unbridled political power. Even more penetrating, perhaps, are the portraits of Titian's advanced age—those of the leonine Holy Roman Emperor, Charles V, or Pope Paul III with his nephews in Naples.

Titian, who journeyed to Rome in 1545, was unquestionably familiar with the works of Leonardo, Raphael, and Michelangelo, but to speak of any true adherence to Mannerism on his part would be inexact —even though it is evident that Titian's style underwent a dramatic change after midcentury. The architectonic solidity of his early compositions, bound as they were to classic perspective, was replaced by different points of view, expressed in such works as *The Martyrdom of Saint Lawrence* and *The Rape of Europa*. Even color underwent a transformation in these works, becoming dramatically mixed with light.

In his last years Titian's luminosity became ever more evident. The figures in *The Crowning with Thorns* are phantoms lit by torches, and tortuous bands of light play over their robes with magical effects. The *Pietà*, uncompleted at the time of the painter's death, gives testimony to the inexhaustible tragic bent of Titian through the cry of Mary Magda-

To capture Holy Roman Emperor Charles V's powerful gaze, Titian relied upon a close observation of the tenets of the Flemish school—a realism Titian may have been striving for to please the imperial patron who had summoned him to Augsburg to paint this portrait.

lene and the resigned despair of the Madonna. And yet, in the expressive forcefulness of these late works Titian remains firm in his faith in man, whether represented in joy or in suffering.

So powerful was Titian's star that it all but obscured other contemporary painters. As a result, early art historians tended to ignore Lorenzo Lotto, a talented artist who repeatedly offered himself as an alternative to Titian. Lotto also reached maturity in the first decade of the sixteenth century—influenced by Bellini, who was his teacher, and by Dürer, whose overwhelmingly innovative realism he admired. His forte was portraiture, and at the beginning of his career Lotto painted several great portraits. His study of Bishop De Rossi, executed by the twenty-five-year-old painter in 1505, focuses on the subject's ivory features and scarlet cape. Lotto's early altarpieces were less assured, however. They reveal an artist hesitant to choose between the Venetian ideas of the late fifteenth century and a figurative clarity recalling the Flemish painters.

After a period of intense interest in Dürer, Lotto turned up in Rome, where he collaborated with Raphael on the latter's Vatican rooms. The experience transformed him completely, and his great Saint Bartholomew Altarpiece in Bergamo reveals a Lotto inspired by the realistic Lombardy vein. His color has become more subtle and gentle, the forms elegantly balanced. Another of the masterpieces of Lotto's Bergamasco period, the frescoes of Saint Lucia in Villa Suardi at Trescorre, reveal that he was probably the greatest colorist of the sixteenth-century Veneto; the frescoes feature grasses of an unforgettable green, the golden yellow of the ripe harvest, and saints dressed in milky white mantles. All this was portrayed with a narrative joy that constitutes, in his advanced works, Lotto's typical imprint.

And yet Lotto did not meet with fortune in a Venice dominated by Titian; perhaps he was too sensitive, or too given to Mannerist intellectualisms—or even too humble for exuberant Venice. At any rate he was finally forced to emigrate to the Marche region, where he left masterpieces that seem to anticipate Goya.

As youthful painters embarking upon long careers, Titian and Lotto could not help but be aware of Albrecht Dürer, who was without doubt the greatest protagonist of the restless German Renaissance. Born in Nuremberg, and associated from his earliest youth with publishers and Humanists who already had brought to the north the message of Italian classicism, Dürer moved with boundless energy. In 1494 he went to Italy to spend a year in Venice, returning again from 1505 to 1507.

Dürer's most striking quality was his representation of reality. In contrast to his compatriots he proposed an objective approach to nature, and his philosophical soul drew him close to the geniuses of the Italian Renaissance. The majority of the works from his youthful period are drawings or etchings on metal or wood. Evidently Dürer was impelled toward the graphic medium not only by Nuremberg tradition but also by his own need to search out, through the subtlest, softest, most expressive means, the manifold aspects of reality. Certain watercolors, done during his trip to Italy, give precise testimony to his extraordinarily attentive and inquisitive nature and to his marvelous ability to create a natural reality that, in its very exactness and incisive-

Albrecht Dürer, the preeminent figure of the German Renaissance, visited Venice for the first time in the early 1490's. In the course of a subsequent visit, he was to introduce his hard-edged technique—exemplified by the masterful Self Portrait in a Fur Coat—*opposite—to an entire generation of Venetian painters. Dürer's impact is evident in the taut line and austere palette of Lorenzo Lotto's* Portrait of a Young Man, *above.*

ness, goes well beyond simple reproduction. Thus in *The Rabbit*, drawn by pen and then watercolored, flowers, trees, and animals become surprising microcosms, rich with an unfathomable force that discloses a truth more penetrating and profound than nature's reality.

Even in painting a great part of Dürer's ability to fascinate derives from his amazing technical perfection, which seems to surpass even that of the Flemish masters who were his models. The relationship between technical accomplishment and the extraordinary moral energy that emanates from portraits like that of Oswald Krell is obvious. The Venetians themselves must have been amazed at the drawings, prints, and paintings that Dürer showed them during his second stay in their city, a sojourn that began in 1505. In 1506 he began the Altarpiece of Saint

Bartholomew. This *Madonna of the Rosary* made a clean break with the melodic, dreamlike tradition of Bellini's painting. Here instead was an overwhelming series of aggressively lively portraits, of sacred images set like petrified idols within a flowering green landscape, of woods and distant mountains distinct against a limpid sky. Giorgione, Lotto, and Titian were all fascinated by Dürer's art, and his influence is apparent in their works, in an enrichment of motifs and themes that they never could have discovered in the Venetian tradition alone.

The Venetian period was undoubtedly a happy one for Dürer too, for he almost certainly found in the lagoon city the ideal climate for this artistic development. Upon his return home, however, the Humanist glow slowly disappeared from his works in the face of his preoccupation with philosophical and scientific meditations. Even his coloring, while it retained the gloss of a supreme technical brilliance, seemed to cool off. His later works became more complex, reflecting the divergent influences that shaped the artist—Renaissance Italy, with its Humanism, classicism, and realism; and Reformation Germany, with its stern Christianity and sterner attitude toward life. Thus in the Altarpiece of All Saints, completed in 1511, the crowd of the chosen, suspended like a medieval puppet theater against an abstract turquoise sky, is in sharp contrast to the realistic landscape below, with its waters and its mountains that simply vanish into the distance. Nor is it easy to grasp the beauty of such late paintings as *The Four Apostles*, which while powerful and forceful are chilled by chromatic technique.

This renunciation of color value, born of Dürer's desire to stress a new moral attitude, indicates the degree to which the spiritual development of the Lutheran reform in Germany weighed upon the artist in his last years. Other important German artists were inspired by that same moralistic rigor, as well as by a medieval interest in the fantastic. Albrecht Altdorfer, for his part, attempted to create a fantastic world of stupefying lights—a forest lit with beams of gold, an aurora borealis appearing over a battlefield. Matthias Grünewald, on the other hand, reached peaks of hallucination and horror in visions full of expressionistic violence, among them a Crucifixion. In comparison with these masters, the works of Luther's friend Lucas Cranach are slickly elegant. The slim women in *Springtime*, just emerged from their bath and intent upon ministering to the bee sting of a crying Cupid, show what happened to a German art too receptive to Italian influence.

In the second half of the sixteenth century the center of painting in the north shifted from Germany to the Low Countries—where, unhappily, it failed to reach the high level of achievement of the preceding century. The prime motifs were Italian Renaissance forms imported by itinerant painters like Lucas van Leyden and Mabuse, both of whom were deeply struck by Michelangelo and Raphael. Quentin Massys, perhaps the most delicate colorist in all of Flanders, looked to Leonardo da Vinci, and so did landscape painter Joachim Patinir. It is clear, however, that the influences of the Italian Renaissance and of Mannerism were not positive ones for northern painters, who sacrificed their originality in the search for an idealized form that was not congenial.

The only northern painter who truly preserved his own personality

intact was the Flemish artist Pieter Bruegel. Instead of turning to the idealized themes of the Italian Renaissance, Bruegel found sources of artistic inspiration in everyday Flemish life and in the landscape around him. Scenes from *Carnival* and *Lent*, *Children's Games*, and *Parables and Proverbs* recall the work of the great Hieronymous Bosch, although they are more openly laughable and grotesque. Bruegel's range is impressive, and his subjects include religious parables and allegories, landscapes, phantasmagorias, and happy scenes of peasant life. One of his masterpieces is *The Seasons*, from which the unforgettable vision of *Winter* stands out in particular: hunters return to their village under a sky that mirrors the whiteness of the snow and ice. The frozen village itself takes on a surrealistic aspect—the nude branches of trees stark against a leaden sky, highlighted by the snow that rests on them; and hungry birds and skating children fill the air with sharp cries. Bruegel's nature is composed of authentic human feeling, observed with an eye that is serenely understanding.

Color continued to reign triumphant in Venice in the latter half of the 1500's, just as it had in the first part of the century under Giorgione and Titian. In the 1540's, Mannerism had been introduced to Venice by Tuscan and Roman painters, but Veneto artists remained strongly committed to the "creative color" tradition, expressed in the most sumptuous of decorative forms. Venice demanded above all that its painters help beautify the city. The doges redecorated their palace—enlarging the rooms, constructing new ceremonial halls, replacing frescoes damaged by time with great canvases of resounding decorative effect. Paintings also decorated devout church schools like St. Rocco, new churches like St. Sebastian, and private palaces and country villas erected by Sansovino and Palladio, the two greatest architects of the lagoon city's golden age.

Jacopo Tintoretto, an extraordinarily talented decorative painter, created a series of huge canvases for the schools of St. Mark and St. Rocco and for the ducal palace as well. A dynamic chiaroscuro idiom gives these canvases a particular mark, creating chromatic effects from which the molded tension of form reemerges. In fact, even though Tintoretto is Venetian he seems to derive the grandiose monumentality of his figures from Michelangelo. Yet despite the influence of Michelangelo and of Mannerism, Tintoretto also developed an independent style. The burning light of *The Miracle of Saint Mark* and the theatrical violence of the night sky in *The Crucifixion* in St. Rocco are examples of the so-called luminism that characterized a great part of Venetian painting in the late sixteenth century.

Tintoretto's last works reflect an ingenuous but profound faith, undoubtedly unique in the cynical and pragmatic Venice of the "golden century." The angelic choirs of his immense *Paradise*—perhaps the hugest canvas ever painted—or the Apostles and faithful in *The Last Supper* in the church of San Giorgio Maggiore seem to be waiting for an other-worldly life in a real world where matter is humbly reduced to almost monochromatic tones.

Tintoretto's traveling companion and rival in Venice, Paolo Veronese, was of a completely different temperament. Aristocratic and

As the High Renaissance moved northward, it inspired German artists to new heights. At left, above, Dürer's superbly colored portrait of the merchant Oswald Krell. At left, below, the slim subjects of Lucas Cranach's Venus and Cupid as a Honey Thief. *Directly above, a central detail from Grünewald's* Christ.

Overleaf: *Another northerner to survive the southern influence was Pieter Bruegel. In his* Winter, *or* Hunters in the Snow, *the north's full power is felt.*

117

The end of linear perspective, so germane to the Renaissance, came with such works as El Greco's Burial of the Count Orgaz, *a detail of which is shown opposite, and his* View of Toledo, *shown at right. Vertically elongated shapes and extraordinary colors typify the works of El Greco, as does the absence of extremely precise drawing underlying the final painting.*

painter can be traced back to the last flowering of Venetian painting, for Kyriakos Theotokopoulos, called El Greco, was born in Crete and spent his first ten years of artistic activity in Venice. Very little can be attributed to him in that period, which came to a close around 1570 with his polyptych of the Annunciation, a tiny masterpiece that combines Byzantine religious vision with the refined Mannerist mode.

Shortly thereafter El Greco moved to Toledo, Spain, where he found an environment most suited to his mystical temperament, which seems to have been made to order to give form to the artistic ideals of the Counter Reformation. His *Christ Stripped of His Garments* and *The Burial of the Count Orgaz,* both in Toledo, sum up the intensity of El Greco's feelings while reflecting the stylistic influences of his Venetian experience. The colors, however, are very personal, the lightning blues, acid yellows, and eerie greens expressing the hallucinatory world of the artist. Even in landscapes, El Greco tended to bend natural reality. In his fascinating *View of Toledo,* for instance, the Alcazar and the cathedral are illuminated by lightning against a stormy sky highlighted by sinister, unreal colors. In El Greco's works, perspective as it had been conceived by the Italian Renaissance was negated by a simultaneous vision of both foreground and background that opened the doors to the figurative freedom of the Baroque period.

9

Baroque's Long Shadow

THE CLOSE OF THE SIXTEENTH CENTURY marked the end of Europe's golden century of art, for by then all the Renaissance ideals—from faith in a balance between spirit and form to the search for perfect knowledge—had been irrevocably swept away. Seventeenth-century Europe seemed tragically upset by decade-long wars, by pestilence, by natural and economic cataclysms—and man, clearly bewildered, turned to a bigoted and miracle-working faith or sought evasion in the pleasures of a life lived day by day.

On the aesthetic level, art presented a most varied panorama, reflecting the seventeenth century's deep social, economic, and moral contradictions. On the one hand there were the stylized, conventional court paintings that adorned marvelous palaces, embellished grandiose churches, or enriched the collections of princes, from papal Rome to the kingdoms of Spain and of France. On the other, there were the works of such innovative geniuses as Caravaggio, Rembrandt, Vermeer, and La Tour.

This was the century of Descartes and also of the Inquisition, of Galileo and of the Counter Reformation. It is no surprise, therefore, that the artistic culture of the age developed in a tumultuous manner, one classified as Baroque, meaning that it had degenerated into intellectualized and decorative straining for gratuitous effects. Modern criticism has diminished the negative sense of the term Baroque, however, recognizing in it instead an authentic inventiveness and imagination.

Painting in seventeenth-century Europe drew its inspiration from Rome, a city that was thriving under papal patronage. By the turn of the century Michelangelo da Caravaggio had begun to paint in a style that was totally antithetical to the Mannerism of the preceding generation of academic painters. Caravaggio's paintings were like a declaration of war, aimed at a generation of dull academicians. Fortunately, the young painter found patrons among the Roman prelates, particularly Cardinal del Monte, who commissioned *The Story of Saint Matthew* for the church of San Luigi dei Francesi in 1592. One panel, *The Call of Matthew*, reflects the artist's dramatic use of chiaroscuro: a bare tavern room is illuminated by a blazing light that underlines the gesture of the one called by Christ. After painting some other canvases for the church of Santa Maria del Popolo, Caravaggio created *The Deposition of Christ*, a work that expresses tragic feeling with titanic moral power. Violent

Through the stem of a wine glass we see the thumb and draped sleeve of Michelangelo da Caravaggio's Bacchus. *It was through a glass of a different sort that the artist studied his own features for this work, a reputed self-portrait.*

125

light illuminates the figures, which are executed with rare realism.

Unfortunately, the tempestuous Caravaggio's life was brief; he died shortly after he was forced to flee Rome because he had seriously wounded a rival in a brawl. His remarkable work helped determine the course of Italian and European painting, however. In place of the empty rules of Renaissance order and the sterility of Mannerism, Caravaggio proposed man's tormented earthly adventure as the theme of painting.

In the beginning, Caravaggio's protest remained essentially isolated, especially in the Roman art world. The papal city demanded less disturbing art, art that responded to the renewed ideals of science and culture but did not raise questions about the value of a moral order that conformed to the interests of the dominant classes. As a result, the kind of painting that dominated Rome in the first decades of the seventeenth century and that found favor with the economic and political powers responsible for the city's embellishment was much softer than Caravaggio's. Although Caravaggio's work was shunted aside by Rome, it met with quite a different reception in those regions that were more socially and temperamentally congenial to it. In Italy such places included the Lombard region, which was oriented toward rigorous Catholicism, and Naples, where Caravaggio lived and left works. But the most enduring impact of Caravaggio's works was felt in Holland, where Protestantism favored the birth of thoughtful, dramatic painting.

Caravaggio's influence was carried to the north of Europe by itinerant painters, among whom Hendrick Terbrugghen stands out. Terbrugghen left Rome in 1614 after a long sojourn there and promptly resettled in Utrecht, where he became a central figure of a school of

realism that quickly extended itself to the other cities of Holland, among them Haarlem. There the great Frans Hals also came under the influence of the Caravaggio idiom. The result was a remarkably faithful portrait of contemporary society: oil portraits of well-to-do bourgeois couples, soldiers, common people, and the members of guilds, all enlivened by a palette of intense, sanguine tones.

The greatest artist of the Dutch school was Rembrandt van Rijn. His first works, executed in loud colors that owed much to Hals, reveal an Italian point of reference. The rigorously moral climate of Protestantism soon began to have singular effects upon Rembrandt's palette, however, and it grew denser and more given to chiaroscuro. His images became immersed in an almost surreal atmosphere where light seemed to lift the weight of material substance from men and things.

One of Rembrandt's favorite subjects was the self-portrait. Painted over a period of many years, these portraits documented the development of the man as well as of the artist. Rembrandt painted many other portraits as well, of course, both of individuals and of groups. Famous among the latter are *The Anatomy Lesson of Doctor Tulp*, with its cold, accusatory lights, and the so-called *Night Watch* (which actually portrays Captain Banning Cocq's company of arquebusiers in full daylight), a dramatic work of brusque shadings and blinding flashes.

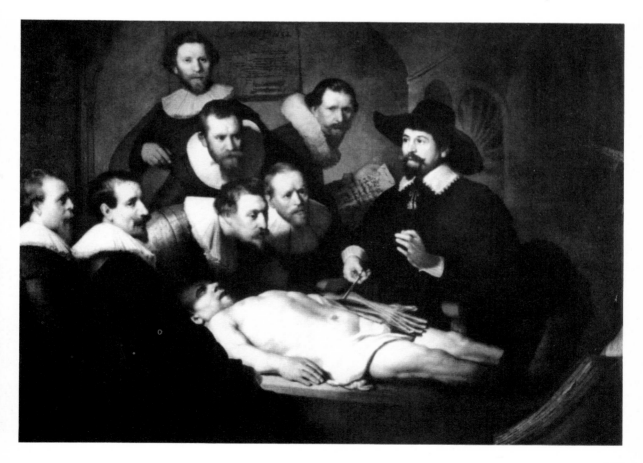

Rembrandt's last years found him sorely burdened by loneliness and financial cares, but his works from this period preserve intact a powerful poetic force founded on a desperate fidelity to truth. For instance, the figures in *Christ at Emmaus*, illuminated against the bare plaster of a wretched room, seem to project an interior light, transcending human nature through the suffering that consumes them. Like Titian in his old age, Rembrandt too left a number of his works "unfinished"; forms detach themselves from smoky backgrounds, animated by brush strokes that reveal the despair that presages death.

In the world of late-seventeenth-century Dutch genre painting where Rembrandt's tragic genius stood out, Jan Vermeer of Delft held an absolutely unique and independent position. Although he painted mainly interiors, the reality of everyday things became dreamlike and almost abstract in Vermeer's hands. From his *Young Girl Asleep* to *The Letter Reader*, from *The Milk Woman* to *The Lady at the Spinet*, the subject it always immobile, almost as if it lacked any real rapport with life. Yet the overall impression is one of serenity. Exquisitely colored and brilliantly executed, those figures seem symbols of the quiet, simple philosophy of life of the Dutch middle class—of whom Vermeer is the authentic narrative poet.

An echo of Caravaggio's realism was apparent in contemporary France as well. French realism subordinated sentimentality to the calculated pictorial effect, however. Louis Le Nain, the first representative of the realistic trend in France, took his usual themes from the life of the peasants, observed in their simplest surroundings. These sympathetic paintings were characterized by artificial illumination from fires and torches, and by punctiliousness of line.

Artificial illumination—which again suggests the influence of Caravaggio—is also characteristic of the works of Georges de La Tour. His Magdalene is depicted in a darkened room by the light of a single oil lamp; the flame diffuses cold, silvery reverberations over the body of the saint, who is shown in the clothing of a simple peasant woman. La Tour's poetry was founded on a deep sentiment for the ideal, which stripped from the figures every specific naturalistic value. At the same time, the artist seemed to be seeking a fundamental simplification of forms, as if he were reducing the living theme to a symbolic image.

This tendency to interpret nature intellectually—rather than cap-

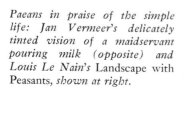

Paeans in praise of the simple life: Jan Vermeer's delicately tinted vision of a maidservant pouring milk (opposite) and Louis Le Nain's Landscape with Peasants, *shown at right.*

ture its transitory aspects impressionistically—remained a characteristic of French art even outside the Caravaggian tradition. We find it, for example, in the work of Nicolas Poussin, the great French classicist who moved permanently to Italy in 1624. In Rome Poussin drew inspiration from ancient sculpture, from the colors of Titian and of Veronese, and from the more academic and measured style of the Carracci family. Venetian echoes are apparent in his youthful canvas *Narcissus and Echo*, painted in 1630, with its brilliant, light-steeped color and generous opulence of human forms. In this work Poussin is already depicting the natural setting according to a rational pattern, with a rigorously calculated perspective.

The influence of Raphael and of classical sculpture only partially extinguished the color of Poussin's later canvases. In works such as *The Epiphany*, colors are sharp but they are also limited to local hues, without taking on any atmospheric values. *The Epiphany* also reveals Poussin's growing philosophical interests; even the gestures lose naturalness, becoming instead expressions of the soul's innermost feelings.

From the lyricism of his first years, Poussin passed on to erudite subjects drawn from Roman history or to didactic ones like the famous series of the Sacraments, in which he explored the symbolic meaning of Church rites. Yet Poussin never lost that delicacy of line and richness of color that characterized his youthful work, and in his final landscapes he tried out colors and light effects with a loving attention to reality. Thus in *Orpheus and Eurydice* myth and reality finally meet in a perfect synthesis of rational form and brilliant color.

The naturalistic art of Claude Lorrain, another expatriate Frenchman living in Rome during Poussin's lifetime, was simpler and more direct, though no less evocative. Lorrain's subject was the Roman landscape, with its lush trees, wide valleys, and mirroring lakes and rivers, scenes populated by figures from mythology or from biblical or Roman history. Lorrain's canvases are symphonies of color, denser and richer than any previously seen but at the same time direct, persuasive, and

In Georges de La Tour's Mary Magdalene with Oil Lamp, *seen opposite, illumination comes from a source within the picture itself. The flame that burns in the oil-filled glass casts its gentle light upon the saint, who seems mesmerized by the flickering glow. For* Narcissus' Death *(left above), Nicolas Poussin chose a more conventional source of light—the sun itself.*

natural—a flaming sunset, a clear morning. Lorrain's contemplative spirit, linked to the rationality of Poussin, who was his master, found expression in pastoral poems of limpid perfection. But he also pointed the way to the great landscape artists who followed him, from Hubert Robert and Fragonard to Turner and Corot.

Thus while Protestant, middle-class Holland fostered the deeply interior art of Rembrandt and Vermeer, Catholic and aristocratic Flanders nourished the decorative magnificence of Roman Baroque. Grandiloquent portraits and grandiose natural scenes were in constant demand to adorn the great residences of Antwerp and Brussels, and the art of Peter Paul Rubens perfectly satisfied such requirements.

Between 1600 and 1608 Rubens lived in various Italian cities, including Venice, Mantua, Genoa, Florence, and Rome. He became familiar with all kinds of Italian art, ranging from Renaissance masterpieces to the paintings of the first Baroque period. Caravaggio made the strongest impression on the young Rubens, especially the master's extraordinary capacity to compose with light and shadow while employing color to its full advantage. One of Rubens' first works upon his return home was *The Descent from the Cross*. An extremely bold composition on the diagonal, it recalls an analagous painting by Caravaggio.

Rubens did not linger long upon tragic themes, naturally inclined as he was to great, decorative painting and to resounding, clear color. The twenty-one large canvases narrating the arrival in France of Queen Marie de Médicis and painted in the years from 1621 through 1625 for the Luxembourg Palace in Paris are glorious proof of this: a whirl of monumental figures, opulent nudes, magnificent wardrobes, from all of which bursts forth an unrestrainable vital energy. Rubens had numerous collaborators, but he himself always added the final touch that gave the mark of genius even to his less inspired works. He became the great decorator of a princely society, providing it with myths of privilege and triumph. Yet despite the nature of his commissions, Rubens was not insensitive to more subtle human qualities, as shown in the numerous portraits of his second wife. In *Hélène Fourment with the Children*, for instance, the most delicate brushwork covers the faint outline and heightens the colored shadows.

Rubens' style was taken up in the eighteenth century by French painters like Watteau and by the great English portraitists. Closer to home, Rubens' influence was apparent in the works of Jacob Jordaens, who celebrated the master's sensual richness in an interpretation at times rustically realistic, at other times almost surrealistic in its glassy, hallucinatory effects.

Anthony Van Dyck was bound even closer to Rubens than Jordaens, but his interests took him in two divergent directions. He was attracted to portrait painting, and often achieved extraordinary results. There are few figures in seventeenth-century Europe, for instance, who give such an impression of nobility and confidence as *The Marchioness Grimaldi*, painted in Genoa in 1622. On the other hand, Van Dyck immersed himself in religious subjects with a sentimental transport and a dedication that could bloom only in a country as gloriously Catholic as Flanders in the middle of the seventeenth century. In *The Deposition*,

Peter Paul Rubens painted his sixteen-year-old bride, Hélène Fourment (above), in a dress of golden silk. She was the daughter of a cloth merchant, and the fabric for her gown was part of her dowry. Deeper, richer colors pervade the Rubens Deposition *opposite, which features Saint Simeon bracing himself on a ladder to receive Christ.*

painted at Antwerp in 1634, the red, purple, and turquoise colors in the figures of Mary and the angels, coupled with the rosy grey of Christ's form, constitute an extraordinary gesture of homage to Titian—and, at the same time, a personal participation in the sorrow and horror of the Crucifixion itself.

Even the origins of seventeenth-century Spanish painting can be traced back to Caravaggio. Jusepe de Ribera, who had worked in Naples, introduced full-bodied Caravaggian light to Spain, and Francisco de Zurbarán followed with incisive drawings that were colored with cold tints and strongly marked by light. His masterpiece, *The Exposition of Saint Bonaventure*, is the expression of a solitary soul closed in meditation and pledged to other-worldly hope. It was Diego Velázquez who was to emerge as the greatest Spanish painter of the seventeenth century, however. In contrast to the painters who had remained in the service of the Church, he became the favorite artist of the court. At the age of thirty Velázquez relinquished his court post and traveled to Italy, where he was deeply impressed by Venetian painting. The nobility and grandeur of Venetian forms in particular inspired his portraits, as evidenced by the works he executed upon his

When W. H. Auden wrote "About suffering they were never wrong, the old masters," he was speaking of older masters than Anthony Van Dyck. Yet in that artist's Deposition (below), every figure seems lost in sorrow. By contrast, little affects the poise of Infanta Margareta of Spain (opposite), who was eight years old when Diego Velázquez made his portrait of her. Velázquez sent his work to the infant's uncle, Emperor Leopold I, who married Margareta when she turned sixteen.

return home. In the equestrian portrait of the little prince Balthazar Carlos, for example, the deep, smooth Venetian tones make one think of late Titian. But Velázquez also revealed an extraordinary psychological penetration of character, expressed with a grandiloquence that is wholly and unmistakably Spanish.

Despite his numerous court duties as marshal of the palace, Velázquez made a second trip to Italy to acquire paintings by Tintoretto and Veronese. Although his artistic output decreased in his last decade, he nonetheless produced the most renowned masterpieces of his time.

Velázquez' vast—and vastly complex—masterpiece The Maids of Honor *(seen opposite) includes a self-portrait of the artist at his easel. The subjects of this painting-within-a-painting are the king and queen of Spain, who are visible in a mirror at rear. In the foreground, ladies in waiting and household servants attend the young infanta. In a later work (above), it is Venus that Velázquez mirrors. Curiously, the reflected features of the goddess of love belie the youthful beauty of her slender figure.*

The Rokeby Venus, which may have been painted in Italy between 1648 and 1651, contains echoes of classical statuary in the gorgeous figure of the nude young girl glimpsed from the back. The rosy body stretches with a soft suppleness upon a bed covered with a turquoise drape, while the red window curtain suggests a heated, sensual atmosphere. A little cupid holds the mirror within which Venus' face is reflected: it is a face that, in its overblown sensuality, seems unmatched to the firm, slim adolescent figure to which it belongs.

Velázquez's paintings often contain something hallucinatory or mysterious in their linearity of concept and color. The series of court dwarfs was painted with a hand at times cruel, at other times compassionate. Another late masterpiece, the portrait of *The Maids of Honor*, includes among its figures King Philip IV and his queen, their faces reflected in a mirror; the painter himself at the easel; the infanta with her ladies-in-waiting and the court dwarf, who tries to amuse her; a large silent dog; and a visitor, glimpsed through a door that opens in the background. A throbbing transparency defines the blacks, browns, and silver tones of the gowns and costumes, and thus the unexpected flashings of red, pink, and turquoise ribbons stand out like accent notes upon the powerful, deep chromatic register.

In 1657 Velázquez painted *The Spinners*, one of his last creations. The room where the women work is shown against the light, while in the background the figures of two ladies stand out before a tapestry that is touched by indefinite transparency. Shadows and lights alternate, presaging the possibilities that opened in the Impressionist era.

10

The Rococo Shell

THE CONVENTIONAL VIEW of the eighteenth century as an age of frivolity, eroticism, and *joie de vivre* is only partially accurate, for the eighteenth century was also marked by the triumph of the balance-of-power concept in international relations, by scientific and technological discoveries, by the rational philosophy of the Enlightenment, and by the French Revolution. Art naturally reflected these trends, and thus the beginning of the century saw the Baroque style transformed into the prettifying preciousness of Rococo. Realism gradually triumphed, however, and increasing numbers of paintings focused on scenes from daily life, landscape, caricature, and portraiture.

Painting was the major medium for artistic expression throughout the century, especially in such great artistic centers as Paris, Venice, and London. It was in France that a new eighteenth-century idiom emerged, following a long academic quarrel between supporters of Poussin's "classicism" and Rubens' "colorism." The argument itself was meaningless since it never involved first-rate artists, and it was soon put to rest by the transformation of Baroque taste into a passion for rocaille, or elegant, elaborate interior decoration with paneling cut or painted in festive, light garlands. The rocaille style, from which the more popular term Rococo is derived, took its name from the little rocks decorated with shells and mother-of-pearl that French gardeners were so fond of displaying among vines and flowering shrubs.

The initiator of the rocaille movement was Jean Antoine Watteau, who began his career as an interior decorator, painting panels in the Rococo style. His elegant designs included gay figures of dancers, animals, and jugglers, or ornaments of leaves and flowers in an intricate pattern that suggested a Chinese influence. Then, while admiring Rubens' Marie de Médicis series in the Luxembourg Palace, Watteau conceived of the notion of transforming that regal display into detailed little scenes of aristocratic life, amorous fêtes and meetings, music lessons, or episodes from the life of professional comedians. His thematic use of the *fêtes d'amour* in particular became popular with subsequent artists, who were deeply influenced by his work.

Watteau also discovered a new relationship between form and color, establishing a rapport that was to become one of the bases of painting in his century. Here outline became most minute, touched in by pen or brush point; the turn of line was accomplished by small

Long thought to show the embarkation of Venus from her birthplace near Cytherea in Crete but now believed to mark her return, John Antoine Watteau's painting of the goddess of love (detail opposite) heralded a new age of painting, one that stressed both form and color.

straight or curved strokes as elegant and sharp as the profile of a leaf; and chromatic scale broke up in a nervous vibration of changing surfaces, both thick and light at the same time, expressive but fanciful. One of Watteau's most famous works is *Return from Cytherea*, which depicts the festive close of celebrations in honor of Venus on her blessed isle. Typically, the mood is both light and sensuous, and the lyrical richness of the colors, especially of the golden atmosphere, blends into a symphonic song of joy.

Watteau's last great creation was *The Gersaint Shop*. In this work, both the setting and the figures are marvelously real: inside the shop, where the walls are completely covered by eighteenth-century paintings, some art lovers are examining a painting before purchasing it; other gentlemen are conversing amiably with the shop mistress, who is seated behind a counter. Yet there is a certain melancholy quality to the work—the color is low keyed, based on grey-silver or violet tones, and there is almost an elegiac air, perhaps arising from Watteau's presentiment of the illness that would soon cause his premature death.

The importance of Watteau in the history of French painting is immense because his works brought about a new pictorial orientation. Even the greater painter François Boucher found inspiration for his cold, sharp palette and for the great clarity and sensitivity of his design in Watteau's works. Boucher, who became the most famous French decorator of Louis XV's reign, had nothing else in common with his teacher, but *Venus' Toilet* or *Diana Coming from her Bath* or the delightful *Seasons* perfectly represented the spirit of the later artist's time, bound as they were to the salons of court favorites or intellectual ladies who offered a great deal of eroticism and a dash of philosophy. Boucher's art celebrated a personal style in which refined French drawing and brilliant color found unparalleled decorative synthesis.

Venetian painters, like the French, were also great decorators, and they too played an important role in the development of Rococo style.

With painted nudes viewing them from the walls, properly clothed gentlemen and ladies search for new acquisitions in Watteau's depiction of The Gersaint Shop *(above). The French master's decorative and sentimental style is reflected in the works of his student François Boucher. At right is a detail from Boucher's* Diana Coming from Her Bath, *which portrays the goddess as a mature woman with an adolescent face.*

In fact, by the beginning of the century both Sebastiano Ricci and Gian Antonio Pellegrini were already in possession of a style clearly differentiated from the prevalent late Baroque. As it appeared in paintings like Ricci's *Dream of Venus*, that style was clear, festive, and frothy, based on drawing that was full of verve. Because these Venetian artists could not easily find work at home, they pushed on into all of Europe —into England, where Pellegrini could be found in 1708 and Ricci in 1712; into Holland; and then into Germany, Paris, and Vienna. They were, in short, messengers who spread the style of the great Venetian school, taking for their model the decorative manner of Paolo Veronese. Certainly the work of Pellegrini offered the most characteristic model of Rococo style. One of his greatest undertakings, the series of canvases called *The Wedding of the Elector Wilhelm* in the castle of Schleissheim in Bavaria, is characterized by fluent mother-of-pearl hues combined with tints ranging from rose to green, from gold to blue.

The trend, already evident in Pellegrini, was to unravel color in an atmosphere as light as a spring breeze, and that trend was evident in the work of other artists who contributed to the glory of Rococo in Venice, among them Gian Antonio Guardi, the older brother of the famous landscape artist Francesco, and the portrait painter Rosalba Carriera, noted throughout Europe for her pastels and her understated touch. Carriera had a notable influence upon French painting, for it was her sojourn in Paris in the years 1720 and 1721 that inspired the great French pastel artists La Tour and Perroneau.

The heir to Ricci and Pellegrini's decorativism was Giovanni Battista Tiepolo, the greatest Venetian painter of the eighteenth century. In his innumerable frescoes and canvases, painted in churches and palaces across Europe, Tiepolo translated into figurative terms the century's festive vein. From the beginning his paintings were of large dimensions; his works included the decoration of entire rooms in great palaces like Ca Sandi or Ca Dolfin in Venice. The grandiose battle scenes in the latter mark a thematic return to the great sixteenth-century Venetian tradition, somewhere between Tintoretto and Veronese. As for his Rococo models, the youthful frescoes painted in the archbishopric of Udine around 1724 reflect the silvery, luminous painting of Ricci and Pellegrini. *Abraham and the Angels, Rebecca and Jacob,* and *The Announcement to Sarah* are alive with diaphanous and crystalline colors, the silvery sky enclosing a landscape that seems made of glass.

As Tiepolo matured, light became the element that enlivened his color, as is evident in countless palaces, villas, and churches in Bergamo, Vicenza, and Milan. In the Palazzo Labia in Venice, for example, Tiepolo adorned the ballroom with the story of Antony and Cleopatra. His masterpiece, however, was the series of paintings that he executed for the residence of the Bishop of Würzburg. These frescoes, relating

The angel at left is about to stay Abraham's hand and thereby prevent the sacrifice of Isaac. No such heavenly messenger intercedes on behalf of Lucius Junius Brutus, whose assassination (above) is the subject of another work by Giovanni Battista Tiepolo. The angel is from a ceiling fresco in Udine, and the canvas above is from a series commissioned in Venice. No sentimentalist, J. B. Siméon Chardin eschewed that trend in favor of serene works like Still Life with Pipe *at lower right.*

Overleaf: *England's Protestant middle class preferred morality tales to openly sensuous works from the Continent. They thus received a bit of unanticipated titillation from William Hogarth's* Orgy, *part of his 1735 series called* The Rake's Progress.

the histories of the bishop's ancestors and depicting allegorically the four corners of the world, revive for the modern viewer the splendid life of the Franconian court. The color is luminous, full of an intensity of tones and vibrant with changing lights and reflections.

Tiepolo did have his quieter moments. In the frescoes of the Villa Valmarana near Vicenza he depicted love stories involving ancient heroes taken from the poems of Virgil, Ariosto, and Tasso. These often melancholy themes offered Tiepolo the opportunity to express himself through delicately pensive images and in less resounding, more contained colors. The Valmarana episode was soon over, however, and Tiepolo began a new series of grandiose ceilings in his usual decorative vein, ending with a flourish at the royal palace in Madrid, where he completed a series of frescoes exalting the glory of Spain.

Tiepolo's sons were also painters. One of them, Giovanni Domenico, a sensitive painter of popular scenes, created a world full of bitter-

If Hogarth pleased the middle class, the portraitists of England gave pleasure to its aristocracy by preserving their faces for posterity. At left, Thomas Gainsborough's wedding portrait of William and Elizabeth Hallett, both aged twenty-one; above right, Sir Joshua Reynold's Little Girl with Cherries; and at right below, Thomas Lawrence's elegant Portrait of the Fluyder Children.

ness, one that seemed almost a grotesque contradiction of the sunny certitudes expressed by his father. In fact, the second half of the eighteenth century offered many such negations of the first. With the decline, after Tiepolo, of meritorious activity in the field of decoration, artists emerged whose style was much more intimate and realistic, and their works were more a part of the moral and social context of their times. These were the painters of the Enlightenment, the new philosophy that soon spread from France to the rest of Europe.

J. B. Siméon Chardin was a contemplative French painter whose earliest works recalled the style of the minor masters of the 1600's. Chardin's subjects were taken from real life, were drawn with boundless love of detail, and were colored with a faithful attention to true light. The Venetian Pietro Longhi also turned to reality, particularly as expressed in the costumes of his time. Common people and patricians, masked persons and mundane scenes were his favorite subjects. His style was in many ways similar to Chardin's, but his color had the exquisiteness of a miniature.

The English painter William Hogarth broke with the tradition of Watteau in a different way, for Hogarth was a satirist and a moralist whose depiction of the human comedy was at times humorous, at times terrifying, at times grotesque. As a result such works as *The Rake's Progress* and *Marriage á la Mode* left a deep mark upon the culture of the times. Hogarth's style in the field of portraiture was also extraordinary in its completely original psychological penetration and adherence to reality. Paintings such as *The Six Servants* and *The Shrimp Girl* were done in sober, shaded tones that suggest a realist's vision of life and an abiding moral concern.

Portraiture was a singularly rich field in eighteenth-century English painting, and Thomas Gainsborough was the most original and important painter in a notable group that included Reynolds, Raeburn, and Lawrence. Gainsborough took from the great Flemish portrait painters of the seventeenth century, Rubens and Van Dyck, the monumental measure of great figures; but he also knew how to imbue the faces and gestures of his subjects with delicacy and a touching melancholy. In addition to his portraits, his pre-Romantic feeling for landscape remains among the highest expressions of eighteenth-century painting.

Another characteristic aspect of the 1700's was the spread of "view painting." This trend was largely developed in Venice, where from the times of Carpaccio and Gentile Bellini a bent for topographical representation had been cultivated. In this singular city, with its wholly manmade landscape, it is not surprising that painters should be drawn to the sumptuous palaces lining the canals, to the sunny *campi*, or open squares, and to the theatrical setting of Piazza San Marco itself.

The first great view painter was Antonio Canaletto, son of a stage designer and active himself in Venetian and Roman theaters. A protégé of the English merchant Joseph Smith, who was later consul in Venice and who amassed the extraordinary collection of paintings and drawings that now adorn Windsor Castle, Canaletto was the favorite of English nobles, who commissioned dozens of views of Venice from him. It was for the Count of Carlisle that Canaletto painted one of his most beautiful views, *The Basin of St. Mark*. In the midday light, ships at anchor are mirrored in the tranquil lagoon, which is framed by Palladio's architecture on the island of San Giorgio and by the remarkable crenelations of the ducal palace.

Canaletto was always faithful to what was real, and before beginning a painting he patiently studied the Venice skyline with an "optical camera" that he used to determine the exact volume of monuments. While the light and the colorings of Venice retain all their poetic fascination in his paintings, Canaletto was bound to the same philosophical concept of faithful transposition from reality as the realist painters whom we have already noted.

In 1746 Canaletto went to England to seek his fortune, and he stayed almost ten years. Upon returning to Venice, he found himself faced with a rival view painter, Francesco Guardi, who worked in a style very different from Canaletto's. In contrast to Canaletto, Guardi was unschooled in perspective painting; in fact, his father and his older brother, Gian Antonio, worked in the style of the great decorators of the first Rococo period. At an early age Francesco had begun painting subjects from Roman history, mythology, and the Bible. However, Canaletto's absence from Venice, coupled with the disappearance of all the other major Venetian view painters, convinced Guardi to switch to view painting, which he did with immediate success.

Guardi's style always showed the effects of his "figurist" education. In fact, the figurines that enliven his paintings are true figures, well articulated and with autonomous color values. On the other hand, his topographical views themselves always keep a pictorial quality that is

The solidarity of cities and of society in the 1700's was reflected in a new art form: the view. Opposite below, Canaletto's The Basin of St. Mark, a panoramic view of Venice's boat-choked harbor. At left, above is Francesco Guardi's gouache of an arched portal in an old quarter of the lagoon city. Above, Francisco Goya's preliminary cartoon for a Bourbon Palace tapestry, a scene of bucolic serenity.

Overleaf: *A detail from Canaletto's 1763 view of London as seen from Somerset House terrace.*

different from the rather linear coldness of some of Canaletto's images. In his *Basin of St. Mark*, for example, the light takes on an imaginative transparency, and the atmosphere breaks up into a thousand changing vibrations, Guardi's being a world of fleeting impressions.

In his advanced age, Francesco Guardi was often called upon to portray public life in Venice. In 1782, for instance, Guardi painted *The Counts of the North* to commemorate their official visit to Venice. A work from this series, *Concert in the Philharmonic Hall*, is one of the most touching paintings of the late eighteenth century. Painted with a filtering of brown, dull green, red, turquoise, and silver lacquers, it conveys a profound melancholy—almost as if the decadence of the once-great city and the imminent fall of the thousand-year-old Venetian Republic had affected Guardi's brush strokes.

Eighteenth-century art came to an end with a last great painter from Catholic, reactionary Spain, Francisco de Goya y Lucientes. Goya's painting was a vivid, dramatic protest against the formulas and conventions of his time, whether social or aesthetic. Both the last flowering of the eighteenth century and the new neoclassical mode were swept away by the extremely forceful, direct insight of this revolutionary genius, who pointed ahead to the Romantic movement and marked the beginning of contemporary man's solitary explorations.

LIVES OF
THE PAINTERS

In 1550 Giorgio Vasari, an Italian painter, sculptor, and art critic, published Lives of the Eminent Painters, Sculptors, and Architects. *This book contained biographies of two hundred artists and was based on notes that Vasari had been collecting since boyhood. Although Vasari himself insisted his book represented only a minor facet of his work, we recognize it today as one of the most important documents in art history and an invaluable guide to understanding Renaissance Italy. Each of the following excerpts from Vasari—concerning the lives of Giotto, Leonardo da Vinci, Michelangelo, Titian, and Raphael—demonstrates the extraordinary nature of his achievement.*

Now in the year 1276, in the country of Florence, about fourteen miles from the city, in the village of Vespignano, there was born to a simple peasant named Bondone a son, to whom he gave the name of Giotto, and whom he brought up according to his station. And when he had reached the age of ten years, showing in all his ways though still child-ish an extraordinary vivacity and quickness of mind, which made him beloved not only by his father but by all who knew him, Bondone gave him the care of some sheep. And he leading them for pasture, now to one spot and now to another, was constantly driven by his natural inclination to draw on the stones or the ground some object in nature, or something that came into his mind. One day Cimabue, going on business from Florence to Vespignano, found Giotto, while his sheep were feeding, drawing a sheep from nature upon a smooth and solid rock with a pointed stone, having never learnt from any one but nature. Cimabue, marvelling at him, stopped and asked him if he would go and be with him. And the boy answered that if his father were con-tent he would gladly go. Then Cimabue asked Bondone for him, and he gave him up to him, and was content that he should take him to Flor-ence. There in a little time, by the aid of nature and the teaching of Cimabue, the boy not only equalled his master, but freed himself from the rude manner of the Greeks, and brought back to life the true art of painting, introducing the drawing from nature of living persons, which had not been practised for two hundred years; or at least if some had tried it, they had not succeeded very happily. Giotto painted among others, as may be seen to this day in the chapel of the Podestà's Palace at Florence, Dante Alighieri, his contemporary and great friend, and no less famous a poet than Giotto was a painter.

After this he was called to Assisi by Fra Giovanni di Muro, at that time general of the order of S. Francis, and painted in fresco in the upper church thirty-two stories from the life and deeds of S. Francis, which brought him great fame. It is no wonder therefore that Pope Benedict sent one of his courtiers into Tuscany to see what sort of a man he was and what his works were like, for the Pope was planning to have some paintings made in S. Peter's. This courtier, on his way to see Giotto and to find out what other masters of painting and mosaic there were in Florence, spoke with many masters in Sienna, and then, having

The Leonardo da Vinci sketch above, like those on the following pages, is part of the vast collection housed in the Royal Library of Windsor Castle.

received some drawings from them, he came to Florence. And one morning going into the workshop of Giotto, who was at his labours, he showed him the mind of the Pope, and at last asked him to give him a little drawing to send to His Holiness. Giotto, who was a man of courteous manners, immediately took a sheet of paper, and with a pen dipped in red, fixing his arm firmly against his side to make a compass of it, with a turn of his hand he made a circle so perfect that it was a marvel to see it. Having done it, he turned smiling to the courtier and said, "Here is the drawing." But he, thinking he was being laughed at, asked, "Am I to have no other drawing than this?" "This is enough and too much," replied Giotto, "send it with the others and see if it will be understood." The messenger, seeing that he could get nothing else, departed ill pleased, not doubting that he had been made a fool of. However, sending the other drawings to the Pope with the names of those who had made them, he sent also Giotto's, relating how he had made the circle without moving his arm and without compasses, which when the Pope and many of his courtiers understood, they saw that Giotto must surpass greatly all the other painters of his time. This thing being told, there arose from it a proverb which is still used about men of coarse clay, "You are rounder than the O of Giotto," which proverb is not only good because of the occasion from which it sprang, but also still more for its significance, which consists in its ambiguity, *tondo*, "round," meaning in Tuscany not only a perfect circle, but also slowness and heaviness of mind.

Leonardo da Vinci

. . . For the Dominican monks of Santa Maria delle Grazie at Milan, [Leonardo da Vinci] also painted a Last Supper, which is a most beautiful and admirable work; to the heads of the Apostles in this picture the master gave so much beauty and majesty that he was constrained to leave that of Christ unfinished, being convinced that he could not impart to it the divinity which should appertain to and distinguish an image of the Redeemer. But this work, remaining thus in its unfinished state, has been ever held in the highest estimation by the Milanese, and not by them only, but by foreigners also: Leonardo succeeded to perfection in expressing the doubts and anxiety experienced by the Apostles, and the desire by them to know by whom their Master is to be betrayed; in the faces of all appear love, terror, anger, or grief and bewilderment, unable as they are to fathom the meaning of their Lord. Nor is the spectator less struck with admiration by the force and truth with which, on the other hand, the master has exhibited the impious determination, hatred, and treachery of Judas. The whole work indeed is executed with inexpressible diligence even in its most minute part, among other things may be mentioned the table-cloth, the texture of which is copied with such exactitude, that the linen-cloth itself could scarcely look more real.

It is related that the Prior of the Monastery was excessively impor-

155

tunate in pressing Leonardo to complete the picture; he could in no way comprehend wherefore the artist should sometimes remain half a day together absorbed in thought before his work, without making any progress that he could see; this seemed to him a strange waste of time, and he would fain have had him work away as he could make the men do who were digging in his garden, never laying the pencil out of his hand. Not content with seeking to hasten Leonardo, the Prior even complained to the Duke, and tormented him to such a degree that the latter was at length compelled to send for Leonardo, whom he courteously entreated to let the work be finished, assuring him nevertheless that he did so because compelled by the importunities of the Prior. Leonardo, knowing the Prince to be intelligent and judicious, determined to explain himself fully on the subject with him, although he had never chosen to do so with the Prior. He therefore discoursed with him at some length respecting art, and made it perfectly manifest to his comprehension, that men of genius are sometimes producing most when they seem to be labouring least, their minds being occupied in the elucidation of their ideas, and in the completion of those conceptions to which they afterwards give form and expression with the hand. He further informed the Duke that there were still wanting to him two heads, one of which, that of the Saviour, he could not hope to find on earth, and had not yet attained the power of presenting it to himself in imagination, with all that perfection of beauty and celestial grace which appeared to him to be demanded for the due representation of the Divinity incarnate. The second head still wanting was that of Judas, which also caused him some anxiety, since he did not think it possible to imagine a form of feature that should properly render the countenance of a man who, after so many benefits received from his master, had possessed a heart so depraved as to be capable of betraying his Lord and the Creator of the world; with regard to that second, however, he would make search, and, after all—if he could find no better, he need never be at any great loss, for there would always be the head of that troublesome and impertinent Prior. This made the Duke laugh with all his heart, he declared Leonardo to be completely in the right, and the poor Prior, utterly confounded, went away to drive on the digging in his garden, and left Leonardo in peace; the head of Judas was then finished so successfully, that it is indeed the true image of treachery and wickedness; but that of the Redeemer remained, as we have said, incomplete.

Michelangelo

In the Casentino . . . in the year 1474, a son was born, under a fated and happy star, to the Signor Lodovico di Lionardo Buonarroti Simoni, who as it is said, was descended from the most noble and most ancient family of the Counts of Canossa; the mother being also a noble as well as excellent lady. Lodovico was that year Podestà, or Mayor of Chiusi-e-Caprese, near the Sasso della Vernia, where St. Francis received the

Stigmata, and which is in the diocese of Arezzo. The child was born on a Sunday, the 6th of March namely, at eight of the night, and the name he received was Michelangelo, because, without further consideration, and inspired by some influence from above, the father thought he perceived something celestial and divine in him beyond what is usual with mortals, as was indeed afterwards inferred from the constellations of his nativity, Mercury and Venus exhibiting a friendly aspect, and being in the second house of Jupiter, which proved that his works of art, whether as conceived in the spirit or performed by hand, would be admirable and stupendous. . . .

Lodovico had many children, and as he possessed but slender revenues, he placed his sons as they grew up with wool and silk weavers. When Michelangelo had attained the proper age he was sent to the school of learning kept by Messer Francesco of Urbino; but the genius of the boy disposing him to drawing, he employed his leisure secretly in that occupation, although reproached for it, and sometimes beaten by his father and other elders, they, perhaps, not perceiving his ability, and considering the pursuit he had adopted an inferior one and unworthy of their ancient family.

. . . Michelangelo formed a friendship with Francesco Granacci, who, although also but a boy, had placed himself with Domenico Ghirlandaio to learn the art of painting; and being fond of Michelangelo, Granacci supplied him daily with the designs of Ghirlandaio, who was then reputed one of the best masters, not in Florence only but through all Italy. The desire of Michelangelo for art thus increased from day to day, and Lodovio, finding it impossible to divert him from his drawings, determined to try if he could not derive benefit from this inclination, and being advised by certain friends, he decided on placing him with Domenico Ghirlandaio. . . .

The ability as well as the person of Michelangelo increased to such an extent, that Domenico was amazed thereat, since it appeared to him that Michelangelo not only surpassed his other disciples, of whom he had a large number, but even equalled himself, who was the master. One day for example, as one of Domenico's disciples had copied with the pen certain draped female figures by Ghirlandaio, Michelangelo took that sheet, and with a broader pen he passed over one of those women with new lines drawn in the manner which they ought to have been in order to produce a perfect form. A wonderful thing it was then to see the difference of the two, and to observe the ability and judgment of one who, though so young, had yet so much boldness as to correct the work of his master. This sheet I now keep as a relic, having obtained it from Granacci, to put it in my book of designs with other drawings by Michelangelo. And in the year 1550, being in Rome, I showed it to Michelangelo, who knew it at once and was rejoiced to see it again, but remarked out of his modesty, that he knew more when he was a boy than at that time when he had become old. . . .

During his abode in Rome [1496-1501], Michelangelo made so

much progress in art, that the elevation of thought he displayed, with the facility with which he executed works, in the most difficult manner, was considered extraordinary, by persons practised in the examination of the same, as well as by those unaccustomed to such marvels, all other works appearing as nothing in the comparison with those of Michelangelo. These things caused the Cardinal Saint Denis, a Frenchman, called Rovano, to form the desire of leaving in that renowned city some memorial of himself by the hand of so famous an artist. He therefore commissioned Michelangelo to execute a Pietà of marble in full relief; and this when finished, was placed in San Pietro, in the Chapel of Santa Maria della Febbre namely, at the Temple of Mars. To this work I think no sculptor, however distinguished an artist, could add a single grace, or improve it by whatever pains he might take, whether in elegance and delicacy, or force, and the careful perforation of the marble, nor could any surpass the art which Michelangelo has here exhibited.

Among other fine things may be remembered—to say nothing of the admirable draperies—that the body of the Dead Christ exhibits the very perfection of research in every muscle, vein, and nerve, nor could any corpse more completely resemble the dead than does this. There is besides a most exquisite expression in the countenance, and the limbs are affixed to the trunk in a manner that is truly perfect; the veins and pulses, moreover, are indicated with so much exactitude, that one cannot but marvel how the hand of the artist should in a short time have produced such a work, or how a stone which just before was without form or shape, should all at once display such perfection as Nature can but rarely produce in the flesh. The love and care which Michelangelo had given to this group were such that he there left his name—a thing he never did again for any work—on the cincture which girdles the robe of Our Lady; for it happened one day that Michelangelo, entering the place where it was erected, found a large assemblage of strangers from Lombardy there, who were praising it highly; one of these asking who had done it, was told "Our Hunchback of Milan"; hearing which, Michelangelo remained silent, although surprised that his work should be attributed to another. But one night he repaired to Saint Peter's with a light and his chisels, to engrave his name as we have said on the figure, which seems to breathe a spirit as perfect as her form and countenance. . . . From this work then Michelangelo acquired great fame; certain dullards do indeed affirm that he has made Our Lady too young, but that is because they fail to perceive the fact that unspotted maidens long preserve the youthfulness of their aspect, while persons afflicted as Christ was do the contrary; the youth of the Madonna, therefore, does but add to the credit of the master.

Michelangelo now received letters from friends in Florence advising him to return, since he might thus obtain that piece of marble which Pier Soderini, then Gonfaloniere of the city, had talked of giving to Leonardo da Vinci, but was now preparing to present to Andrea dal Monte Sansavino, an excellent sculptor who was making many efforts

to obtain it. It was difficult to get a statue out of it without the addition of several pieces, and no one, Michelangelo excepted, had the courage to attempt it; but he, who had long wished for the block, no sooner arrived in Florence than he made every effort to secure the same. This piece of marble was nine braccia high, and unluckily, a certain Maestro Simone da Fiesole had commenced a colossal figure thereon; but the work had been so grieviously injured that the Superintendents had suffered it to remain in the House of Works at Santa Maria del Fiore for many years, without thinking of having it finished, and there it seemed likely to continue.

Michelangelo measured the mass anew to ascertain what sort of figure he could draw from it, and accommodating himself to the attitude demanded by the injuries which Maestro Simone had inflicted on it, he begged it from the Superintendents and Soderini, by whom it was given to him as a useless thing, they thinking that whatever he might make of it must needs be preferable to the state in which it then lay, and wherein it was totally useless to the fabric. Michelangelo then made a model in wax, representing a young David, with the sling in his hand, as the ensigns of the Palace, and to intimate that, as he had defended his people and governed justly, so they who were then ruling that city should defend it with courage and govern it uprightly. He commenced his labours in the House of Work, at Santa Maria del Fiore, where he formed an enclosure of planks and masonry, which surrounded the marble; there he worked perpetually, permitting no one to see him until the figure was brought to perfection. The marble having been much injured by Simone, did not entirely suffice to the wishes of Michelangeo, who therefore permitted some of the traces of Simone's chisel to remain; these may be still perceived, and certainly it was all but a miracle that Michelangelo performed, when he thus resuscitated one who was dead. . . .

When Michelangelo returned to Rome [1508-12], therefore, he found Julius [Pope Julius II] no longer disposed to have the Tomb finished, but desiring that Michelangelo should paint the ceiling of the [Sistine] Chapel. This was a great and difficult labour, and our artist, aware of his own inexperience, did all he could to excuse himself from undertaking the work, proposing at the same time that it should be confided to Raphael. But the more he refused the more Pope Julius insisted, impetuous in all his desires, and stimulated by the competitors of Michelangelo, more especially by Bramante, he was on the point of making a quarrel with our artist, when the latter, finding His Holiness determined, resolved to accept the task. The Pope then ordered Bramante to prepare the scaffolding, which the latter suspended by ropes, perforating the ceiling for that purpose. Seeing this, Michelangelo inquired of the architect how the holes thus made were to be filled in when the painting should be completed; to which Bramante replied that they would think of that when the time came, and that it could not be done otherwise. But Michelangelo, perceiving that the architect was either incapable or unfriendly towards himself, went at once to the Pope, whom he assured that such a scaffolding was not the proper one, adding that Bramante did not know how to construct it; and Julius, in the presence of Bramante, replied, that Michelangelo might construct it himself after his own fashion. The latter then erected his scaffolding on props in such a manner that the walls were not injured, and this method has since been pursued by Bramante and others, who were hereby taught the best way in which preparations for the execution of pictures on ceilings, and other works of the kind could be made, the ropes used by Bramante and which Michelangelo's construction had rendered needless, the latter gave to the poor carpenter, by whom the scaffolding was rebuilt, and who sold them for a sum which enabled him to make up the dowry of his daughter.

Michelangelo now began to prepare the Cartoons [preliminary sketches] for the ceiling, His Holiness giving orders to the effect that all the paintings executed on the walls by older masters in the time of Pope Sixtus, should be destroyed, it was furthermore decided that Michelangelo should receive fifteen thousand ducats for the work, an estimation of its value which was made by Giuliano da San Gallo. But the extent of the work now compelled Michelangelo to seek assistance; he therefore sent for men to Florence, resolving to prove himself the conqueror of all who had preceded him, and to show modern artists how drawing and painting ought to be done. The circumstances of the case became a stimulus to his exertions, and impelled him forward, not for his own fame only, but for the welfare of Art also. He had finished the cartoons, but deferred commencing the frescoes until certain of the Florentine painters who were his friends should arrive in Rome, partly to decrease his labour by assisting in the execution of the work, but also in part to show him the processes of fresco-painting, wherein some of them were well-experienced. Among these artists were Granacci, Giuliano Bugiardini, Jacopo di Sandro, and the elder Indaco, with Agnolo da Donnino, and Aristotile da Sangallo.

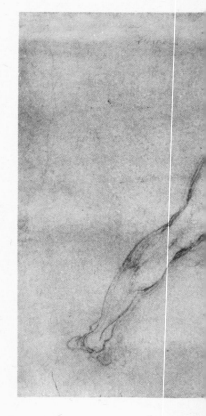

These masters having reached the city, the work was begun, and Michelangelo caused them to paint a portion by way of specimen, but what they had done was far from approaching his expectations or fulfilling his purpose, and one morning he determined to destroy the whole of it. He then shut himself up in the chapel, and not only would he never again permit the building to be opened to them, but he likewise refused to see any one of them at his house. Finally therefore, and when the jest appeared to them to be carried too far, they returned, ashamed and mortified, to Florence. Michelangelo then made arrangements for performing the whole work himself, sparing no care nor labour, in the hope of bringing the same to a satisfactory termination, nor would he ever permit himself to be seen, lest he should give occasion for a request to show the work; wherefore there daily arose, in the minds of all around him, a more and more earnest desire to behold it. Now Pope Julius, always greatly enjoyed watching the progress of the works he had undertaken, and more than ever desired to inspect anything that was purposely concealed from him: thus it happened that he one day went to see the chapel, as we have related, when the refusal of Michelangelo to admit him, occasioned that dispute which caused the master to leave Rome. . . .

Michelangelo afterwards told me the cause of this refusal, which was as follows: When he had completed about one-third of the painting, the prevalence of the north wind during the winter months had caused a sort of mould to appear on the pictures; and this happened from the fact that in Rome, the plaster, made of travertine and puzzolana, does not dry rapidly, and while in a soft state is somewhat dark and very fluent, not to say watery; when the wall is covered with this mixture, therefore, it throws out an efflorescence arising from the humid saltness which bursts forth; but this is in time evaporated and corrected by the air. Michelangelo was, indeed, in despair at the sight of these spots, and refused to continue the work, declaring to the Pope that he could not succeed therein, but His Holiness sent Giuliano da San Gallo to look at it, and he, telling our artist whence these spots arose, encouraged him to proceed, by teaching him how they might be removed.

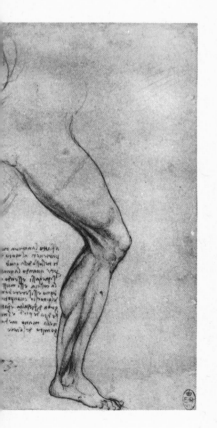

When the half was completed, Pope Julius, who had subsequently gone more than once to see the work (mounting ladders for that purpose with Michelangelo's aid), and whose temper was hasty and impatient, would insist on having the pictures opened to public view, without waiting until the last touches had been given thereto, and the chapel was no sooner thrown open than all Rome hastened thither, the Pope being the first; he had indeed, not patience to wait until the dust caused by removing the scaffold had subsided. Then it was that Raffaelo da Urbino, who was very prompt in imitation, having seen this work, instantly changed his manner, and to give proof of his ability, immediately executed the Prophets and Sibyls in the Church of the Pace. Bramante also then laboured to convince Pope Julius that he would do well to confide the second half of the Chapel to Raffaelo. Hearing of this Michelangelo complained to the Pope of Bramante, enumerating at the same time, without sparing him, many faults in the life, as well as errors in the works, of that architect; of the latter, indeed, he did himself become the corrector at a subsequent period. But Julius, who justly valued the ability of Michelangelo, commanded that he should continue the work, judging from what he saw of the first half, that our artist would be able to improve the second materially; and the master accordingly finished the whole, completing it to perfection in twenty months, without having even the help of a man to grind the colours. It is true that he sometimes complained of the manner in which the Pope hastened forward the work, seeing that he was thereby prevented from giving it the finish which he would have desired to bestow; His Holiness constantly inquiring when it would be completed. On one occasion, therefore, Michelangelo replied, "It will be finished when I shall have done all that I believe required to satisfy Art." "And we command," rejoined the Pontiff, "that you satisfy our wish to have it done quickly"; adding finally, that if it were not at once completed, he would have him, Michelangelo, thrown headlong from the scaffolding.

Hearing this, our artist, who feared the fury of the Pope, and with good cause, desisted instantly, without taking time to add what was wanting, and took down the remainder of the scaffolding, to the great satisfaction of the whole city, on All Saints' day, when Pope Julius went into that Chapel to sing mass; but Michelangelo had much desired to retouch some portions of the work *a secco*, as had been done by the older masters who had painted the stories on the walls; he would also gladly have added a little ultramarine to some of the draperies, and gilded other parts, to the end that the whole might have a richer and more striking effect. The Pope, too, hearing that these things were still wanting, and finding that all who beheld the Chapel praised it highly, would now fain have had the additions made, but as Michelangelo thought reconstructing the scaffold too long an affair, the pictures remained as they were, although the Pope, who often saw Michelangelo, would sometimes say, "Let the Chapel be enriched with bright colours and gold; it looks poor." When Michelangelo would reply familiarly, "Holy Father, the men of those days did not adorn themselves with gold; those who are painted here less than any, for they were none too rich; besides which, they were holy men, and must have despised riches and ornaments." . . .

When this work was completed, all the world hastened from every part to behold it, and having done so, they remained astonished and speechless. The Pope rewarded Michelangelo with rich gifts, and was encouraged by the success of this undertaking to project still greater works; wherefore, the artist would sometimes remark, in respect to the extraordinary favours conferred on him, that he saw well the Pope did esteem his abilities, and if he should now and then inflict some rudeness by a peculiar way of proving his amicable feeling towards him, yet he always cured the wound by gifts and distinguished favours.

Titian

Titian was born in the year 1480, at Cadore, a small place distant about five miles from the foot of the Alps; he belonged to the family of the Vecelli, which is among the most noble of those parts. Giving early proof of much intelligence, he was sent at the age of ten to an uncle in Venice, an honourable citizen, who seeing the boy to be much inclined to Painting, placed him with the excellent painter Gian Bellino, then very famous. . . . Under his care the youth soon proved himself to be endowed by nature with all the gifts of judgment and genius required for the art of painting. Now Gian Bellino, and the other masters of that country, not having the habit of studying antique, were accustomed to copy only what they saw before them, and that in a dry, hard,

laboured manner, which Titian also acquired; but about the year 1507, Giorgione da Castel Franco, not being satisfied with that mode of proceeding, began to give to his works an unwonted softness and relief, painting them in a very beautiful manner; yet he by no means neglected to draw from the life, or to copy nature with his colours as closely as he could, and in doing the latter he shaded with colder or warmer tints as the living object might demand, but without first making a drawing, since he held that, to paint with the colours only, without any drawing on paper, was the best mode of proceeding and most perfectly in accord with the true principles of design. . . .

Having seen the manner of Giorgione, Titian early resolved to abandon that of Gian Bellino, although well grounded therein. He now therefore devoted himself to this purpose, and in a short time so closely imitated Giorgione that his pictures were sometimes taken for those of that master. . . . Increasing in age, judgment, and facility of hand, our young artist executed numerous works in fresco which cannot here be named individually, having been dispersed in various places; let it suffice to say, that they were such as to cause experienced men to anticipate the excellence to which he afterwards attained. At the time when Titian began to adopt the manner of Giorgione, being then not more than eighteen, he took the portrait of a gentleman of the Barbarigo family who was his friend, and this was considered very beautiful, the co-labouring being true and natural, and the hair so distinctly painted that each one could be counted, as might also the stitches in a satin doublet, painted in the same work; at a word, it was so well and carefully done, that it would have been taken for a picture by Giorgione, if Titian had not written his name on the dark ground.

Giorgione meanwhile had executed the façade of the German Exchange, when, by the intervention of Barbarigo, Titian was appointed to paint certain stories in the same building, and over the Merceria. After which he executed a picture with figures the size of life, which is now in the Hall of Messer Andrea Loredano, who dwells near San Marcuola; this work represents Our Lady in her flight into Egypt, she is in the midst of a great wood, and the landscape of this picture is well done; Titian having practised that branch of art, and keeping certain Germans who were excellent masters therein for several months together in his own house: within the wood he depicted various animals, all painted from the life, and so natural as to seem almost alive. In the house of Messer Giovanni D'Anna, a Flemish gentleman and merchant, who was his gossip, he painted a portrait which appears to breathe, with an *Ecce Homo*, comprising numerous figures which, by Titain himself, as well as others, is considered to be a very good work. The same artist executed a picture of Our Lady, with other figures the size of life, men and children, being all taken from nature, and portraits of persons belonging to the D'Anna family.

In the year 1507, when the Emperor Maximilian was making war on the Venetians, Titian, as he relates himself, painted the Angel Raphael, with Tobit and a Dog, in the Church of San Marziliano. There is a distinct landscape in this picture, wherein San Giovanni Battista is seen at prayer in a wood; he is looking up to Heaven and his face is illumed by a light descending thence: some believe this picture to have been done before that on the Exchange of the Germans, mentioned above, was commenced. Now it chanced that certain gentlemen, not knowing that Giorgione no longer worked at this façade, and that Titian was doing it (nay, had already given that part over the Merceria to public view) met the former, and began as friends to rejoice with him, declaring that he was acquitting himself better on the side of the Merceria than he had done on that of the Grand Canal, which remark caused Giorgione so much vexation, that he would scarcely permit himself to be seen until the whole work was completed, and Titian had become generally known as the painter; nor did he thenceforward hold any intercourse with the latter and they were no longer friends. . . .

When Titian painted Filippo King of Spain, the son of Charles, he received another annuity of two hundred crowns; so that these four hundred added to the three hundred from the German Exchange, make him a fixed income of seven hundred crowns, which he possesses without the necessity of exerting himself in any manner. Titian presented the Portraits of Charles V and his son Filippo to the Duke Cosimo, who has them now in his Guardaroba. He also took the portrait of Ferdinand King of the Romans, who was afterwards Emperor, with those of his children, Maximilian that is to say, now Emperor, and his brother: he likewise painted the Queen Maria; and at the command of the Emperor Charles, he portrayed the Duke of Saxony, when the latter was in prison. But what a waste of time is this! when there has scarcely been a noble of high rank, scarcely a prince or lady of great name, whose portrait has not been taken by Titian, who in that branch of art is indeed an excellent painter. . . .

It is nevertheless true that his mode of proceeding in these last-mentioned works is very different from that pursued by him in those of his youth, the first being executed with a certain care and delicacy, which renders the work equally effective, whether seen at a distance or examined closely; while those of a later period, executed in bold strokes and with dashes, can scarcely be distinguished when the observer is near them, but if viewed from the proper distance they appear perfect. This mode of his, imitated by artists who have thought to show proof of facility, has given occasion to many wretched pictures, which probably comes from the fact that whereas many believe the works of Titian, done in the manner above described, to have been executed without labour, that is not the truth, and these persons have been deceived; it is indeed well known, that Titian went over them many times, nay, so frequently, that the labour expended on them, is most obvious. And this method of proceeding is a judicious, beautiful, and admirable one, since it causes the paintings so treated to appear living, they being executed with profound art, while that art is nevertheless concealed.

164

... Titian has been always healthy and happy; he has been favoured beyond the lot of most men, and has received from Heaven only favours and blessings. In his house he has been visited by whatever Princes, Literati, or men of distinction have gone to or dwelt in Venice; for, to say nothing of his excellence in art he has always distinguished himself by courtesy, goodness, and rectitude.

Titian has had some rivals in Venice, but not of any great ability, wherefore he has easily overcome them by the superiority of his art; while he has also rendered himself acceptable to the gentlemen of the city. He has gained a fair amount of wealth, his labours having always been well paid; and it would have been well if he had worked for his amusement alone during these latter years, that he might not have diminished the reputation gained in his best days by works of inferior merit, performed at a period of life when nature tends inevitably to decline, and consequent imperfection.

... when Vasari, the writer of the present History, was at Venice, he went to visit Titian, as one who was his friend, and found him, although then very old, still with the pencil in his hand and painting busily. Great pleasure had Vasari in beholding his works and in conversing with the master. ...

It may be affirmed then, that Titian, having adorned Venice, or rather all Italy, and other parts of the world, with excellent paintings, well merits to be loved and respected by artists, and in many things to be admired and imitated also, as one who has produced, and is producing, works of infinite merit; nay, such as must endure while the memory of illustrious men shall remain.

Raphael

Raphael ... painted a picture for the Cardinal and Vice-chancellor Giulio de' Medici, a Transfiguration namely, which was destined to be sent into France. This he executed with his own hand, and labouring at it continually, he brought it to the highest perfection, depicting the Saviour transfigured on Mount Tabor, with eleven of the disciples awaiting him at the foot of the Mount. To these is meanwhile brought a youth possessed of a spirit, who is also awaiting the descent of Christ, by whom he is to be liberated from the demon. The possessed youth is shown in a distorted attitude stretching forth his limbs, crying, rolling his eyes, and exhibiting in every movement the suffering he endures; the flesh, the veins, the pulses, are all seen to be contaminated by the malignity of the spirit, the terror and pain of the possessed being rendered further manifest by his pallid colour and writhing gestures. This figure is supported by an old man in whose widely open eyes the light is reflected, he is embracing and seeking to comfort the afflicted boy, his knitted brow and the expression of his face show at once the apprehension he feels, and the force with which he is labouring to combat his fears; he looks fixedly at the Apostles as if hoping to derive courage and consolation from their aspect. There is one woman among others in this picture who is the principal figure therein, and who, kneeling before the two just described, turns her head towards the apostles, and seems by the movement of her arms in the direction of the possessed youth, to be pointing out his misery to their attention. The Apostles also, some of whom are standing, some seated, and others kneeling, give evidence of the deep compassion they feel for that great misfortune.

In this work the master has of a truth, produced figures and heads of such extraordinary beauty, so new, so varied, and at all points so admirable, that among the many works executed by his hand, this, by the common consent of all artists, is declared to be the most worthily renowned, the most excellent, the most divine. Whoever shall desire to see in what manner Christ transformed into the Godhead should be represented, let him come and behold it in this picture. The Saviour is shown floating over the mount in the clear air; the figure, foreshortened, is between those of Moses and Elias, who, illumined by his radiance, awaken into life beneath the splendour of the light. Prostrate on the earth are Peter, James, and John, in attitudes of great and varied beauty, one has his head bent entirely to the ground, another defends himself with his hands from the brightness of that immense light, which proceeds from the splendour of Christ, who is clothed in vestments of snowy whiteness, his arms thrown open and the head raised towards heaven, while the essence and Godhead of all the three persons united in himself, are made apparent in their utmost perfection by the divine art of Raphael.

But as if that sublime genius had gathered all the force of his powers into one effort, whereby the glory and the majesty of art should be made manifest in the countenance of Christ; having completed that, as one who had finished the great work which he had to accomplish, he touched the pencils no more, being shortly afterwards overtaken by death.

GIORGIO VASARI
*Lives of the Eminent Painters, Sculptors,
and Architects*, 1550

Carel van Mander performed a service for Dutch and Flemish artists similar to that which Vasari did for the Italians by writing Dutch and Flemish Painters. *Contained in the volume are unique contemporary views and reminiscences of many great artists, among them the German portraitist Hans Holbein. As Van Mander relates, Holbein, who obtained the position of court painter to Henry VIII through the offices of Sir Thomas More, was favored not only with the king's patronage but his protection as well.*

At Basel [Holbein] became acquainted with the learned Erasmus of Rotterdam, who recognized the genius of the artist and tried to help him and to promote his interests. Erasmus esteemed the great artist; and

166

he had his portrait painted by Holbein, who was very proficient in portraiture. Holbein's study of Erasmus was so exquisitely painted that it could not have been surpassed by anyone; and no better resemblance could ever have been achieved.

Erasmus wrote for Holbein a polite letter of recommendation to his former fellow student, Thomas More, an Englishman in London, with the hope that Holbein might go into the service of King Henry VIII and gain the friendship of that monarch, who was very fond of art. Erasmus let Holbein take his portrait with him to England, and wanted him to give it to More. . . .

Holbein went to England and to Thomas More (who, owing to his great learning, was the High Chancellor to the King). He carried the letter and portrait with him as evidence of the excellence of his art.

Holbein was welcomed and well received by More, who was so delighted with the portrait of his friend, Erasmus, that he kept Holbein with him for about three years, and made him paint various things. And More, at first, neither informed the King about Holbein, nor let him see any of Holbein's paintings. . . . Holbein painted portraits of More and his family, relatives, and friends, and many other beautiful pictures, in the home of the Chancellor, until, finally, More was well satisfied. The King was then invited to a splendid banquet at More's house, to be shown all the pictures that Holbein had made there.

The King, who never had seen such excellent artistic work as Holbein's, was most amazed; for he seemed to see, before his eyes, various persons whom he knew, not in the form of the actual paintings but as if they were real and alive. More saw how greatly delighted the King was, and most politely offered the paintings to the King, as a present, saying, "They have been made for your Majesty." The King was very thankful and wanted to know if the master who had done this work could be engaged. More replied that the master was ready to render his services, and then introduced Holbein to the King. The King was very pleased. He told More to keep the paintings; and said, "Now that I have the master for myself, I shall obtain what I should like to have most certainly."

King Henry VIII appreciated Holbein, esteemed him highly, and was glad to have the great artist with him. Holbein, in the service of the King, made many beautiful portraits of the King and other persons. . . . The King's affection for Holbein increased, and he favored him more and more, as the artist served him so well according to his wishes. There is a story about Henry's regard for Holbein, which is a beautiful pearl in the crown of the artist.

It happened that an English Earl once came to visit Holbein. He wished to see the painter's pictures, and the work upon which he was engaged at that time. This did not please Holbein, who painted every one from life, and who just then needed to have privacy in doing his work. For this reason, the artist declined to receive the Earl, and he did so with the greatest politeness possible. He asked the Earl, again and again, to pardon him for his refusal, because something prevented the possibility of the visit; and he asked the Earl to please call at another time. No matter how politely and how humbly Holbein explained the matter, the Earl refused to give up, and tried to pass the artist on the stairway, showing forcefully that a person of his Grace's importance should be more feared, and treated with more deference, by a painter. Holbein warned the Earl not to carry out his impolite intention; but the Earl persisted, whereupon Holbein grappled with him and threw him down the stairs. As he fell, the Earl exclaimed, "O Lord, have mercy on me."

The noblemen in attendance on the Earl had their hands full in taking care of him. In the meantime, Holbein closed his door and secured it well, climbed out through a window leading to the roof, and hurried to the King to ask that he be pardoned, without telling what had happened. The King asked Holbein repeatedly what he had done, and was willing to pardon him, if he would confess his crime. Holbein did so, openly and completely. The King responded as if it was most difficult for him to pardon Holbein, and told him not to act so boldly again. His Majesty ordered the artist not to leave, and to remain in one of the royal chambers, until more could be learned about the Earl's condition.

Very soon the Earl arrived. Carried on a royal litter, he was brought before the King, wounded and in bandages. He complained, with a very weak voice, about the painter who had treated him so badly; but the truth was only partly told, and the charge was made worse by lies, just for spite, all to the detriment of Holbein—as the King well understood.

The Earl, after finishing his complaint, asked the King to punish the culprit adequately and justly, as such injury to his personage demanded. In his temper, the Earl noticed that the King was not greatly impressed and hardly eager to fulfill his wishes, had not asked much about the case, and had remained rather cool about the matter. It seemed to him that the King was not much inclined to punish Holbein sufficiently, so the Earl gave the King to understand that he wanted to take revenge himself.

The King became angry that the Earl should speak impertinently in his Majesty's presence, as if the Earl wanted to place himself in the position of the King. His Majesty said, "Now you have no more dealings with Holbein, but with my royal self." He raised his voice and began to threaten the Earl, and said: "Do you imagine that I care so little for that man? I tell you, Earl, that if it pleased me to make seven dukes of seven peasants, I could do so, but I could not make of seven earls one Hans Holbein, or any one as eminent as he."

The Earl, frightened by this answer, prayed for mercy and his life and wanted to do anything the King might order to regain his good grace. The King commanded that at no time should the Earl plan or commit any act of revenge on the person of Holbein, either by himself, or through others, for anything which had taken place; otherwise the King would punish the Earl as severely as if the offense were committed against the person of the King himself. This ended the quarrel.

CAREL VAN MANDER
Dutch and Flemish Painters, 1604

The German painter and engraver Albrecht Dürer achieved great fame and won widespread admiration during his lifetime. In the preface to a posthumous edition of Dürer's Four Books on Human Proportions, *Joachim Camerarius, a university professor and friend of the painter, described the impact upon both viewers and fellow artists of Dürer's celebrated technical skills.*

What shall I say of the steadiness and exactitude of his hand? You might swear that rule, square, or compasses had been employed to draw lines, which he, in fact, drew with the brush, or very often with pencil or pen, unaided by artificial means, to the great marvel of those who watched him. Why should I tell how his hand so closely followed the ideas of his mind that, in a moment, he often dashed upon paper, or, as painters say, composed, sketches of every kind of thing with pencil or pen? I see I shall not be believed by my readers when I relate, that sometimes he would draw separately, not only the·different parts of a composition, but even the different parts of bodies, which, when joined together, agreed with one another so well that nothing could have fitted better. In fact this consummate artist's mind, endowed with all knowledge and understanding of the truth and of the agreement of the parts one with another, governed and guided his hand and bade it trust to itself without any other aids. With like accuracy he held the brush, wherewith he drew the smallest things on canvas or wood without sketching them in beforehand, so that, far from giving ground for blame, they always won the highest praise. And this was a subject of greatest wonder to most distinguished painters, who from their own great experience, could understand the difficulty of the thing.

I cannot forbear to tell, in this place, the story of what happened between him and Giovanni Bellini. Bellini had the highest reputation as a painter at Venice and indeed throughout all Italy. When Albrecht was there he easily became intimate with him, and both artists naturally began to show one another specimens of their skill. Albrecht frankly admired and made much of all Bellini's works. Bellini also candidly expressed his admiration of various features of Albrecht's skill and particularly the fineness and delicacy with which he drew hairs. It chanced one day that they were talking about art, and when their conversation was done Bellini said: "Will you be so kind, Albrecht, as to gratify a friend in a small matter?" "You shall soon see," says Albrecht, "if you will ask of me anything I can do for you." Then says Bellini: "I want you to make me a present of one of the brushes with which you draw hairs." Dürer at once produced several, just like other brushes, and, in fact, of the kind Bellini himself used, and told him to choose those he liked best, or to take them all if he would. But Bellini, thinking he was misunderstood, said: "No, I don't mean these but the ones with which you draw several hairs with one stroke; they must be rather spread out and more divided, otherwise in a long sweep such regularity of curvature and distance could not be preserved." "I use no other than these" says Albrecht, "and to prove it, you may watch me." Then, taking up one of the same brushes, he drew some very long wavy tresses, such as women generally wear, in the most regular order and symmetry. Bellini looked on wondering, and afterwards, confessed to many that no human being could have convinced him by report of the truth of that which he had seen with his own eyes.

A similar tribute was given him, with conspicuous candour, by Andrea Mantegna, who became famous at Mantua by reducing painting to some severity of law—a fame which he was the first to merit, by digging up broken and scattered statues, and setting them up as examples of art. It is true all his work is hard and stiff, inasmuch as his hand was not trained to follow the perception and nimbleness of his mind; still it is held that there is nothing better or more perfect in art. While Andrea was lying ill at Mantua he heard that Albrecht was in Italy and had him summoned to his side at once, in order that he might fortify his (Albrecht's) facility and certainty of hand with scientific knowledge and principles. For Andrea often lamented in conversation with his friends that Albrecht's facility in drawing had not been granted to him nor his learning to Albrecht. On receiving the message Albrecht, leaving all other engagements, prepared for the journey without delay. But before he could reach Mantua Andrea was dead, and Dürer used to say that this was the saddest event in all his life; for high as Albrecht stood, his great and lofty mind was ever striving after something yet above him.

ALBRECHT DÜRER
Four Books on Human Proportions, 1528

The nineteenth-century Swiss art historian Jacob Burckhardt devoted much of his life to an intensive study of the Flemish painter Peter Paul Rubens. As a man as well as an artist Rubens cut a giant figure, and his genius and influence stretched across the entire European continent. In Recollections of Rubens, *Burckhardt drew upon his extensive knowledge of Rubens' life and work to produce an evocative and moving portrait of the artist.*

It is an exhilarating task to evoke the life and personality of Rubens; good fortune and kindliness abound in him as in hardly any other great master, and he is well enough known for us to feel sure of our judgment of him. In the consciousness of his own noble nature and great

powers he must have been one of the most privileged of mortals. No life is perfect, and trials came to him too, but the sum of his life so illuminates all its details that, looked at as a whole, it seems exemplary. It did not come to a premature end, like that of Masaccio, Giorgione or Raphael, while on the other hand he was spared the weakness of age, and it was in his last years that he created some of his grandest work. True, from a very early age he met with advancement on all hands, but not everyone could have taken advantage of it and made men and circumstances serve him as Rubens did, probably with the greatest composure. . . .

Rubens's return from Italy to Antwerp [in 1608] was followed by a time of great sorrow and a lengthy retirement. Having hurried back home on account of his mother's illness, he had arrived too late to see her alive. But good fortune at once joined forces with his own merits and he was appreciated at his true value. He did not rise by the passing whims of patronage, nor by the private tastes of the rich; powerful corporations entrusted him with their most important and solemn commissions, such as 'The Raising of the Cross' and the majestic altar-piece of 'St. Ildefonso,' while for the Council Hall of the City of Antwerp he painted an 'Adoration of the Magi' which is regarded as the most beautiful of his pictures on this subject. The Regents, who appointed him court painter and chamberlain, did not insist on his moving to Brussels, so that by far the most important centre of Flemish painting was permanently attached to Antwerp. Pupils at once crowded around him, he recognized the best of them and trained them to be the assistants his work absolutely required. . . .

It was the situation of a king, without land or subjects, maybe, but of great social brilliance. . . . From studio and art-collection a fascination spread to distant lands; ready-made pictures on all kinds of subjects, even pupils' copies, attracted connoisseurs; as early as 1616, Rubens was already painting for the distant city of Neuburg on the Danube, among other things, the 'Great Last Judgment,' and for Duke Maximilian the finest of his 'Lion Hunts.' And the tapestry weavers of the time made their greatest move by employing him for a whole series of huge compositions. For Genoese patricians he designed the six 'Histories of the Consul Decius' and by 1618 they were already on the Brussels looms. . . . In 1621 . . . Rubens appeared at the court of the Queen Dowager Marie de' Medici in Paris, and designed twenty-one huge paintings for a great gallery in the Palais du Luxembourg, containing an allegorized history of the Queen's life, which were finished in full size at Antwerp by 1625. The ambassador of the Archduke, de Vicq, had proposed Rubens for this enterprise, and the Florentine queen and the great Fleming had concluded their alliance over the heads of all French and other artists. From that time on the fame of this European studio knew no bounds, while for the master there existed only the inward bounds which he found good to set himself. . . .

The attempt has often been made to sum up the essential qualities of the master's greatness, yet no one has ever got far beyond mere asseverations. We all feel ourselves in the presence of a tremendous power; most of us feel it to be a lovable one, and catch a hint here and there of a personality whose dignity and nobility went hand in hand with that power. Nor is it necessary to make allowances for its gross and savage elements; we shall expect them from the outset, in order that the phenomenon may be complete. But the scope of the phenomenon is vast and touches the farthest bounds of painting. ... Animal painting as a genre first achieved true and splendid freedom with him. His wonderful intercourse with elemental nature speaks its own language in some fifty landscapes, and not even Titian can strike it dumb. In problems which had existed long before him, it is as if he were founding a genre, because for him there always exists an entirely fresh way of depicting everything, and where he has something of his own most personal feeling to give, he is really moved, and has passed far beyond mere calculation.

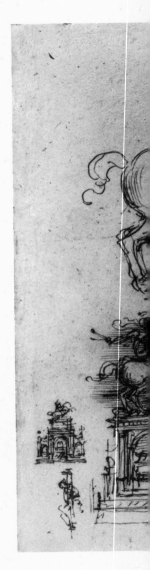

In the description of the static, of pure being, he has, so to speak, no more than his own place beside other great masters, and will enchant or repel us according to our temperament and mood; what he cannot do is to leave us indifferent. Sensitive minds find the full-bloodedness of these brilliantly healthy figures distasteful; but his ideal need not be anyone else's ideal, and there are more noble, delicate and blissful things in the heaven, on the Olympus and on the earth of other masters. But as soon as it comes to 'glorifying man in all his powers and instincts,' as soon as he embarks on his own great theme, movement, he goes his own way. Here, in countless pictures, 'the fire and truth of his physical and spiritual motion' provoke a perpetual amazement which no other artist has even approached. His enthusiasm and his enormous capacity for 'happenings,' whether in the subject as a whole or in single figures, make him launch out without misgivings where others would have reflected and considered. Was he too servile and yielding? Whatever tasks were set before him, whatever wishes he had to fulfil, particularly if they could find expression in movement, he saw at a glance what was paintable, and then it was worthy to be painted. Once given a subject, he had no need to wait long for the right 'mood,' for he lived in a permanent 'mood' for any problem, religious or secular, and no matter how great, which his time and civilization presented him with. 'Everyone according to his gift! My talent is of such a kind that no commission, however great in size or varied in subject matter, even daunted me,' he wrote in 1621, when just about to begin work on the paintings for the great gallery of the Palais du Luxembourg. Even in the apparently most intractable material, he senses its paintable aspect and answers: Give it me. He will and must do everything because he can. Yet the feeling in his painting, however stormy it may be, is nearly always pure and deep.

JACOB BURCKHARDT
Recollections of Rubens, 1898

Today Rembrandt's stature as one of the world's most eminent artists is unquestioned, but as his biographer Jakob Rosenberg points out, the contemporary response to Rembrandt's work fluctuated from acceptance to rejection—a condition that Rosenberg asserts brought out ever greater qualities in the artist.

Rembrandt's move to the Dutch capital was obviously induced by the greater advantages which this wealthy city offered to artists, particularly to gifted portraitists. The patronage in a small university town like Leyden was limited, and Rembrandt sought wider opportunities. Amsterdam was at this time one of the most flourishing trade centers of the world, and its colorful, cosmopolitan atmosphere must have attracted the young painter. A document of June 20, 1631, proves that Rembrandt had already formed a business connection with the Amsterdam art dealer and painter, Hendrik van Uylenburgh. It was shortly after this date that he moved to the capital and took up residence in van Uylenburgh's house in the Breestraat. Rembrandt's reputation as a portrait painter was very soon established by his first large-scale group portrait, the "Anatomy Lesson of Dr. Tulp". . . . In this work the twenty-six-year-old artist surpassed all the painters of Amsterdam in forceful illusionism and dramatic vividness of representation, the very qualities by which his teacher, Pieter Lastman, had previously captured the favor of the Amsterdam public. From 1632 on, Rembrandt's fame increased steadily, reaching its climax at the end of the decade. . . .

. . . Rembrandt's pictures were greatly in demand, and he was able to ask the highest prices from his patrons. His house was filled with pupils who had to pay dearly for the privilege of his instruction. Rembrandt was not the man to enjoy his new wealth soberly, and to build up a lasting fortune. He indulged all his extravagant tastes, and plunged impulsively into the collecting of objects of art and curiosities. Baldinucci describes Rembrandt's activity as a collector, and his extravagance as follows: "He often went to public sales by auction; and here he acquired clothes that were old-fashioned and disused as long as they struck him as bizarre and picturesque, and those, even though at times they were downright dirty, he hung on the walls of his studio among the beautiful curiosities which he also took pleasure in possessing, such as every kind of old and modern arms—arrows, halberds, daggers, sabers, knives and so on—innumerable quantities of drawings, engravings and medals and every other thing which he thought a painter might ever need." Baldinucci goes on to describe Rembrandt's rather provocative conduct at such public auctions, where he "bid so high at the outset that no one else came forward to bid; and he said that he did this in order to emphasize the prestige of his profession."

Rembrandt's possessions accumulated rapidly during these years, and in 1639 he purchased a large house in the Joden-Breestraat. This was an undertaking which strained his resources and contributed to his financial collapse. It may have been the mercantile atmosphere of

Amsterdam which exerted a strong effect upon Rembrandt, or the pompous and exuberant taste of the Baroque, with some influence coming from Rubens. At any rate, Rembrandt appears to have been more of an extrovert at this period, more ambitious and materially minded, than at any other phase of his career. He idolized his wife and represented her in a long series of portraits and allegories, not always in good taste. In the numerous Biblical and historical scenes of the thirties she appears as the ideal of womanhood as Rembrandt understood it. The conclusion has been drawn that Saskia's influence upon her husband was not a steadying one, that she encouraged this life of prodigality and ostentation, and that Rembrandt's lowly origin led him to overrate the qualities of finer breeding in her.

Too much emphasis should not be laid upon these external influences; Rembrandt's attitude may rather be explained by the strong contrasts in his own disposition. His human and artistic development cannot be fully understood without considering the exuberance of his first decade in Amsterdam. This period played an essential part in the dynamic unfolding of his nature, which swung to extremes before finding its ultimate balance. The power of his senses, the violence of his temperament, which burst forth so freely in this prosperous period, bore a clear relationship to the humility and spirituality of Rembrandt's maturity. Had the contrast been less, the inner crisis of his middle years would hardly have produced such profundity of feeling. Seen as a whole, the sensuous and the spiritual Rembrandt are two component parts of one vital personality. Each conditioned the other in strength and significance. Only a superficial judgment can separate the early from the late Rembrandt, or see a fundamental break in his development.

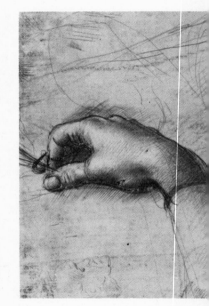

With the early 1640's began the series of tragic events which had some bearing upon the inner change in Rembrandt's human and artistic outlook. His mother died in 1640. In 1642 he lost his wife, Saskia, after a year of failing health following the birth of Titus, their only surviving child. Three other children had died in infancy. An etching of 1642, picturing Saskia as hopelessly weak, may be the last record Rembrandt was able to make of her features. The sad situation at home was not improved by the presence of Geertghe Dircx, a trumpeter's widow whom Rembrandt engaged as a nurse for Titus, after Saskia's death. The outcome of this unfortunate relationship was a breach-of-promise suit which dragged on until 1650, and ended only with Geertghe's confinement in a mental hospital.

In addition to all these blows, Rembrandt's financial situation, already strained by the purchase of the large house, grew steadily worse. His popularity as the foremost portrait painter of Amsterdam began to suffer. Rembrandt's increasing use of chiaroscuro, with less and less regard for merely naturalistic effects, caused dissatisfaction and contributed to the decline of his reputation. The brighter and more elegant style of Van Dyck was at this,time coming into fashion. Rembrandt's pupils, such as Ferdinand Bol, Govaert Flinck, and Jacob Backer, who yielded readily to the public taste, were soon more successful than their master and received the important commissions.

Such a piling up of misfortunes must have made these years bitter ones for Rembrandt. But disillusionment and suffering seem to have had only a purifying effect upon his human outlook. He began to regard man and nature with an even more penetrating eye, no longer distracted by outward splendor or theatrical display. A new contact with nature resulted in a large number of landscape drawings and etchings representing the environs of Amsterdam, and this contact must have helped to clarify, to widen, and to balance the artist's vision. It was not by chance that a change from Baroque theatricality to a more natural simplicity coincided with Rembrandt's new experiences in the open air. An altered sense of values is revealed in his art of this middle period. He was able to approach his immediate surroundings and his fellow men with a heightened sensitiveness to true human values and to interpret the Bible with a deeper sincerity. Rembrandt now began to study the Jewish population of Amsterdam, discovering there an inexhaustible source for Biblical types of an unprecedented verity. Such distinguished Jewish personalities as the Rabbi Manasseh Ben Israel and the physician Ephraim Bonus were among his acquaintances. His fond delight in his son Titus, as the boy began to grow up, Rembrandt expressed in many of the Biblical scenes of these years. We find Titus appearing again and again, as the young Christ, as Tobias, Daniel, or the young Joseph. It was also at this time that Rembrandt learned to appreciate the simple charm and warmheartedness of Hendrickje Stoffels, who entered his home about 1645 as a servant girl, to remain as his life companion. . . .

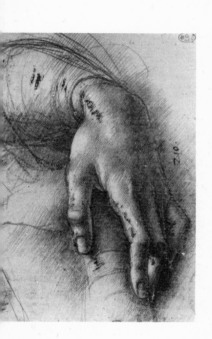

The outward events of Rembrandt's late years, in the fifties and sixties, took a final turn for the worse. Financial collapse came closer, and desperate efforts to avert it were unsuccessful. In July, 1656, Rembrandt asked the authorities to grant him a *cessio bonorum*, to avoid outright bankruptcy. This procedure was considered less degrading, and permission for it could be obtained on the basis of losses in trade or at sea. The *cessio* was granted, and the liquidation of Rembrandt's property was put into the hands of the Chamber of Insolvency. The results of the entire sale were disappointing, when compared to the purchase value of Rembrandt's estate, and the artist remained under a serious financial strain for the rest of his life. His son Titus and the faithful Hendrickje united to protect him from his creditors. The two formed a business partnership for dealing in paintings and objects of art, and in 1660 they made Rembrandt their employee. He was to deliver to them all he produced in return for his support, and by this subterfuge the old painter was able to save at least the earnings from his work. . . .

The loneliness of Rembrandt's late years has often been exaggerated by his biographers. Throughout his life Rembrandt was most closely attached to his family circle, and seldom felt the need of wider social contacts. One of his few patrician friends was Jan Six, afterward Burgomaster of Amsterdam. The painter's retirement from the public stage of Amsterdam, on which he had played a certain role during his prosperous period, was not wholly enforced upon him, but was partly his own decision. Most of the contemporary writers blamed Rembrandt for his slight regard for contacts with educated people and his constant association with common folk. Joachim von Sandrart remarks: "He did not know in the least how to keep his station, and always associated with the lower orders." Houbraken makes a similar observation, but with a more specific reference to the older Rembrandt: "In the autumn of his life Rembrandt kept company mostly with common people and such as practiced art." The extremely introspective character of Rembrandt's art required the utmost concentration on his part. Baldinucci has the following to say about his extraordinary intensity of application: "When Rembrandt worked he would not have granted an audience to the first monarch in the world, who would have had to return again and again until he found him no longer engaged." According to Houbraken, visitors to Rembrandt's studio who wished to examine his paintings too closely he frightened away by the words: "The smell of the colors will bother you." Baldinucci, who received his information on good authority, calls Rembrandt "a most temperamental man" who was inclined to "disparage everyone." As for the artist's appearance, he writes: "The ugly and plebeian face with which Rembrandt was ill-favored was accompanied by untidy and dirty clothes, since it was his custom, when working, to wipe his brushes on himself, and to do other things of a similar nature." Rembrandt in his late years clearly cared nothing for fine manners, nor had he any desire to be a gentleman-painter like Van Dyck or so many of his Dutch contemporaries. All the idiosyncrasies just mentioned fit convincingly into the picture of a man of overpowering directness, and with a complete disregard for social convention.

All the contemporary accounts of Rembrandt's life, even those which criticize him most severely, show a certain respect for the master's power and originality. And that Rembrandt in his old age was not an altogether forgotten figure we may confirm from a number of records. His international reputation had been established in the early 1640's. About that time some of his paintings came into the collection of Charles I of England. And as late as 1667, Cosimo de' Medici, afterward Grand Duke Cosimo III of Tuscany, visited the old painter in his studio. . . . Even though most of the public patronage went to his pupils who catered to the prevailing taste, Rembrandt still received a few large commissions during the fifties and early sixties. In 1654 he painted the "Anatomy Lesson of Dr. Deijman," of which only a fragment has survived, and in 1661-2 he created his greatest group portrait, the "Syndics [of the Drapers' Guild]." In 1661 he was asked to contribute to the decoration of Amsterdam's new Town Hall. His painting, a large historical subject representing the "Conspiracy of Julius Civilis," was delivered and hung, but apparently did not meet with favor. It was removed soon afterward and a work by Juriaen Ovens, one of Rembrandt's less gifted pupils, was put in its place. After this humiliating public rebuff, the canvas was cut down on all sides (probably by Rembrandt himself) in order to make the picture more salable. As for privately commissioned portraits, Rembrandt seems to have produced a fair number during the last ten years of his life.

There was, however, enough of failure and catastrophe in Rembrandt's late period—not to mention the burden of advancing age—to account for the somber undertone of his work. But the relationship between life and art is no longer so easily perceived. The old artist's innermost reactions found expression in a pictorial style that rose to symbolical heights. Without distorting visual reality, he expressed in this way a growing awareness of the transcendental background of human life. A deep feeling of humility penetrates the gloom of his late works and raises his art to a spiritual level in which individual experience takes on universal significance.

Rembrandt, in reaching this phase, went far beyond the bounds of ordinary Dutch realism. His contemporaries described the life and the world around them, but Rembrandt mirrored the world within himself.

JAKOB ROSENBERG
Rembrandt, 1948

William Hogarth has come to be regarded as the finest pictorial satirist in England's history. The artist's sharp and witty caricatures of upper-class and middle-class Englishmen obviously delighted future generations, including the novelist William Makepeace Thackeray, who was born 114 years after Hogarth and who composed the following humorous sketch of the artist's life.

What manner of man was he who executed these portraits [of English life]—so various, so faithful, and so admirable? In the National Collection of Pictures most of us have seen the best and most carefully finished series of his comic paintings, and the portrait of his own honest face, of which the bright blue eyes shine out from the canvas, and give you an idea of that keen and brave look with which William Hogarth regarded the world. No man was ever less of a hero; you see him before you and can fancy what he was,—a jovial, honest London citizen, stout and sturdy; a hearty, plain-spoken man, loving his laugh, his friend, his glass, his roast-beef of Old England, and having a proper *bourgeois* scorn for French frogs, for mounseers, and wooden shoes in general, for foreign fiddlers, foreign singers, and, above all, for foreign painters, whom he held in the most amusing contempt.

It must have been great fun to hear him rage against Correggio and the Caracci; to watch him thump the table, and snap his fingers, and say, "Historical painters be hanged! here's the man that will paint against any of them for a hundred pounds. Correggio's 'Sigismunda!' Look at Bill Hogarth's 'Sigismunda;' look at my altar-piece at St. Mary Redcliffe, Bristol; look at my 'Paul before Felix,' and see whether I'm not as good as the best of them."

Posterity has not quite confirmed honest Hogarth's opinion about his talents for the sublime. Although Swift could not see the difference between tweedle-dee and tweedle-dum, posterity has not shared the Dean's contempt for Handel; the world has discovered a difference between tweedle-dee and tweedle-dum, and given a hearty applause and admiration to Hogarth, too, but not exactly as a painter of scriptural subjects, or as a rival of Correggio. It does not take away from one's liking for the man, or from the moral of his story, or the humor of it—from one's admiration for the prodigious merit of his performances—to remember that he persisted to the last in believing that the world was in a conspiracy against him with respect to his talents as an historical painter, and that a set of miscreants, as he called them, were employed to run his genius down. . . . One of the most notorious of the "miscreants," Hogarth says, was Wilkes, who assailed him in "The North Briton;" the other was Churchill, who put "The North Briton" attack into heroic verse, and published his "Epistle to Hogarth." Hogarth replied by that caricature of Wilkes, in which the patriot still figures before us, with his Satanic grin and squint, and by a caricature of Churchill, in which he is represented as a bear with a staff, on which, lie the first, lie the second—lie the tenth, are engraved in unmistakable letters. There is very little mistake about honest Hogarth's satire: if he has to paint a man with his throat cut, he draws him with his head almost off; and he tried to do the same for his enemies in this little controversy. "Having an old plate by me," says he, "with some parts ready, such as the background, and a dog, I began to consider how I could turn so much work laid aside to some account, and so patched up a print of Master Churchill, in the character of a bear; the pleasure and pecuniary advantage which I derived from these two engravings, together with occasionally riding on horseback, restored me to as much health as I can expect at my time of life."

And so he concludes his queer little book of Anecdotes: "I have gone through the circumstances of a life which till lately passed pretty much to my own satisfaction, and I hope in no respect injurious to any other man. This I may safely assert, that I have done my best to make those about me tolerably happy, and my greatest enemy cannot say I ever did an intentional injury. What may follow, God knows."

A queer account still exists of a holiday jaunt taken by Hogarth and four friends of his, who set out, like the redoubted Mr. Pickwick and his companions, but just a hundred years before those heroes, and made an excursion to Gravesend, Rochester, Sheerness, and adjacent places. One of the gentlemen noted down the proceedings of the journey, for which Hogarth and a brother artist made drawings. The book is chiefly

curious at this moment from showing the citizen life of those days, and the rough jolly style of merriment, not of the five companions merely, but of thousands of jolly fellows of their time. Hogarth and his friends, quitting the "Bedford Arms," Covent Garden, with a song, took water to Billingsgate, exchanging compliments with the bargemen as they went down the river. At Billingsgate, Hogarth made "a caricatura" of a facetious porter, called the Duke of Puddledock, who agreeably entertained the party with the humors of the place. Hence they took a Gravesend boat for themselves; had a straw to lie upon, and a tilt over their heads, they say, and went down the river at night, sleeping, and singing jolly choruses.

They arrived at Gravesend at six, when they washed their faces and hands, and had their wigs powdered. Then they sallied forth for Rochester on foot, and drank by the way three pots of ale. At one o'clock they went to dinner with excellent port, and a quantity more beer, and afterwards Hogarth and Scott played at hopscotch in the town hall. It would appear that they slept, most of them, in one room, and the chronicler of the party describes them all as waking at seven o'clock, and telling each other their dreams. You have rough sketches by Hogarth of the incidents of this holiday excursion. The sturdy little painter is seen sprawling over a plank to a boat at Gravesend; the whole company are represented in one design, in a fisherman's room, where they had all passed the night. One gentleman in a nightcap is shaving himself; another is being shaved by the fisherman; a third, with a handkerchief over his bald pate, is taking his breakfast; and Hogarth is sketching the whole scene.

They describe at night how they returned to their quarters, drank to their friends, as usual, emptied several cans of good flip [a hot rum drink] all singing merrily.

It is a jolly party of tradesmen engaged at high jinks. These were the manners and pleasures of Hogarth, of his time very likely, of men not very refined, but honest and merry. It is a brave London citizen, with John Bull habits, prejudices, and pleasures.

WILLIAM MAKEPEACE THACKERAY
The Works of William Hogarth, 1876

A Chronology of Painting

Although painting has existed since prehistoric times, the Editors have begun this chronology in the thirteenth century because it is the earliest time that specific works can be reliably attributed to individual artists.

Nicola Pisano creates relief panel of scenes from the life of Christ for the baptistry at Pisa	1260	Gunpowder introduced to Europe from China
Anton Sanchez de Segovia creates frescoes for the Salamanca cathedral, Spain	1262	
	1271-95	Journey of Marco Polo to the Orient
	1273	Accession of Rudolph I establishes Habsburg rule in Austria
Florentine artist Cimabue paints the *Crucifix* at Santa Croce	1275	
Cimabue begins series of frescoes for basilica of St. Francis in Assisi; finished work includes the renowned *Madonna Enthroned with Angels and Saint Francis*	1280	
	1288	Ottoman dynasty founded by Osman I
Giotto takes up residence in Assisi	1290	
	1294	Election of Pope Boniface VIII, the last pope to claim universal political authority of the papacy
Master Honoré illuminates the breviary of Philip the Fair of France	1296	
Giotto goes to Rome to serve Pope Boniface VIII	1300	
Giotto commences work on frescoes for the Scrovegni Chapel in Padua	1303	
Frescoes in the Bardi Chapel of Santa Croce, in Florence, painted by Giotto	1320	
	1321	Dante completes *Divine Comedy*
Simone Martini paints *The Annunciation*, a lyrical study of the Virgin and angels	1333	
	1337	Outbreak of the Hundred Years' War
Ambrogio Lorenzetti prepares his frescoes *Good and Bad Government* in Siena's public palace	1340	
	1341	Petrarch crowned poet laureate of Rome
	1348	Beginning of Black Death, which spreads throughout Asia and Europe, claiming almost three-fourths of the population
The life of Christ is depicted in the *Cycle of Vissi Brod* by an unknown Bohemian painter	c. 1350	
	1353	Publication of Boccaccio's *Decameron*
	1368-1463	Ming dynasty rules China
	1382	John Wycliffe initiates translation of Vulgate Bible into English
	1387	Chaucer begins *Canterbury Tales*
	1391	Ottoman Turks launch campaign against Byzantine Empire
The Wylton Dyptich, painted by an anonymous Englishman, relates the story of Richard II	c. 1395	
Kano school is founded in Japan	1400	
	1415	English defeat French forces at Battle of Agincourt, a climactic event in the Hundred Years' War
The Limburg brothers complete *Les Très Riches Heures du duc de Berry*, a book of hours	1416	
	c. 1417	Donatello completes statue of *Saint George and the Dragon*

Masaccio paints his fresco *The Trinity* in the church of Santa Maria Novella, Florence	1425	
	1429	Joan of Arc leads French liberation of Orleans; she is captured by the English and executed two years later
Jan van Eyck completes *The Mystical Lamb* and *The Annunciation*, panels of his massive altarpiece in Ghent cathedral; a year later he paints *Man in a Red Turban*	1432	
	1434	Medici family establishes preeminence in cultural and economic affairs of Florence
Konrad Witz finishes the realistic *Saint Peter* panels; Rogier van der Weyden paints *The Deposition*	1435	
Leon Baptista Alberti writes his *Treatise on Painting*	1436	
Piero della Francesca paints *The Flagellation of Christ*	1444	
Jean Fouquet completes the *Portrait of Etiènne Chevalier* and his patron saint	c. 1450	
	1453	Fall of Constantinople to the Ottoman Turks
	c. 1454	Printing of the Mazarin Bible, first book printed from movable type, attributed to Gutenberg
	1461	François Villon writes *Grand Testament*
Dirk Bouts receives a commission to design an altarpiece showing the sacraments for the church of St. Peter, Louvain	1464	
	1469	Unification of Spain following the marriage of Ferdinand and Isabella
Leonardo da Vinci works as an apprentice in Verrocchio's studio in Florence	1470	
	1473	Pope Sixtus IV supervises building of the Sistine Chapel
Hugo van der Goes commissioned to paint the Portinari Altarpiece; Messina finishes the masterful San Cassiano Altarpiece	1476	
	1478	Ferdinand and Isabella order the Spanish Inquisition to commence
Completion of Botticelli's *The Birth of Venus*, commissioned by the Medici family	c. 1480	
Botticelli begins a series of frescoes in the Sistine Chapel	1481	
Hans Memling commissioned to paint *The Moreel Family*	1486	
	1489	Philippe Comines begins his *Mémoires*, a classic history of medieval times
Michelangelo is received in Florence at the court of Lorenzo the Magnificent	1490	
	1492	Christopher Columbus makes first of four voyages to the New World; fall of Granada marks the end of Moorish influence in Spain
Leonardo begins *The Last Supper* to decorate the refectory of Santa Maria delle Grazie, Milan; his masterwork is completed two years later	1495	
Albrecht Dürer designs a series of engravings entitled *Apocalypse*; twelve years later he matches this accomplishment with the series *Great Passion* and *Life of the Virgin*	1498	Portuguese explorer Vasco Da Gama reaches India following a route around Africa
Hieronymus Bosch paints the unique and puzzling triptych *The Garden of Earthly Delights*	c. 1500	
Leonardo's world-famous portrait *Mona Lisa* begun	1503	
Castelfranco Altarpiece attributed to Giorgione; Lucas Cranach paints *Rest on the Flight into Egypt.*	1504	
Giovanni Bellini renders the altarpiece *Madonna and Saints* in Saint Zaccaria, Venice	1505	
Raphael paints *The Madonna of the Goldfinch*	1506	
Michelangelo begins the frescoes in the Sistine Chapel; his task is completed four years later	1508	

Raphael paints *The School of Athens*, part of the decoration for papal apartments in the Vatican

1509
1511   Publication of Erasmus' *In Praise of Human Folly*

1513   Machiavelli writes his classic treatise on political power, *The Prince*; Balboa crosses the Isthmus of Panama and discovers the Pacific Ocean

Matthias Grünewald completes his finest work, the Isenheim Altarpiece; Titian paints *Sacred and Profane Love*

1515

Leonardo leaves Italy for France to work under the patronage of Francis I

1516

1517
1518   Martin Luther presents his "95 Theses"

Correggio, a disciple of Leonardo's, paints frescoes in the convent of St. Paul, Parma; Titian completes the altarpiece *Assumption of the Virgin*

1519   Magellan leads fleet of Spanish ships on first circumnavigation of the globe

Deposition from the Cross by Rosso Fiorentio, one of the first masterpieces in the Mannerist style

1521

Jacopo Pontormo begins *The Descent from the Cross*

1525

Titian paints *Madonna with Members of the Pesaro Family* in honor of a Venetian victory over the Turks

1526   Mogul Empire founded in India by Babar

Albrecht Altdorfer completes *The Battle of Issus*

1529

Correggio finishes *The Assumption of the Virgin*, a fresco decorating the dome of Parma cathedral; Cranach paints *The Judgment of Paris*

1530

1534   Act of Supremacy names Henry VIII head of the Church of England

Hans Holbein becomes court painter to Henry VIII; fours years later he paints his famous portrait of the monarch

1536

Titian commissioned by the Duke of Urbino to paint the Venus known as *The Venus of Urbino*

1538

Michelangelo completes his final masterpiece, *The Last Judgment*, for the Sistine Chapel

1541   John Calvin organizes first Protestant state in Geneva

1543   Copernicus publishes discoveries on the nature of the solar system

Giorgio Vasari publishes the first edition of *Lives of the Eminent Painters, Sculptors and Architects*

1550   *Book of Common Prayer*, a Protestant hymn book, compiled by John Marbeck

Veronese begins painting *The Story of Esther* in the church of St. Sebastian, Venice; the project takes twenty years to complete

1555

Tintoretto begins a series of sacred paintings for the Scuola di San Rocco depicting the life of Christ; Pieter Bruegel captures a country wedding celebration in *Peasant Wedding*

1565   Palestrina composes *Missa Papae Marcelli* in honor of Pope Marcellus II

1566   Outbreak of revolt by Netherlands against Spanish rule

Kyriakos Theotokopoulos, known as El Greco, settles in Toledo, Spain, and paints *Retablo de Santo Domingo el Antiguo*

1577

Tintoretto undertakes decoration of the Doges' Palace in Venice

1578

1582   Gregorian calendar introduced

El Greco receives a commission to paint *The Burial of Count Orgaz*

1586

1588   First performance of Christopher Marlowe's *Doctor Faustus*

1597   Francis Bacon begins publication of *Essays*, work is not completed for twenty-eight years

Caravaggio completes *The Calling of Saint Matthew*, presented to the Contralli Chapel, Rome

1598   Henry IV of France issues Edict of Nantes, granting Protestants equal political rights with Catholics

1601   First performance of Shakespeare's *Hamlet*

Portrait of Spanish poet and scholar Fray Felix Hortensio Paraviciano painted by El Greco

1605

182

Peter Paul Rubens marries Isabella Brant and paints *Self-portrait with His wife*	1609	*Avisa Relation oder Zeitun*, first newspaper published on European continent
	1611	King James version of the Bible compiled by scholars
Anthony Van Dyck opens his own studio at age sixteen	1615	Cervantes' epic novel *Don Quixote* is published
Beginning of collaboration between Rubens and Van Dyck	1618	
	1619	English architect Inigo Jones designs Banqueting House, Whitehall Palace
	1620	Pilgrims land at Plymouth Rock, Massachusetts
Marie de Médicis engages Rubens to decorate the Luxembourg Palace with scenes from her life; the work is completed in four years	1621	
Frans Hals, a master portraitist, completes *The Laughing Cavalier*	1624	
Georges de La Tour paints *Mary Magdalene with Oil Lamp*; Rembrandt opens a studio in Leyden	1625	
	1628	Experiments by William Harvey lead to discovery of blood circulation
Rembrandt moves from Leyden to Amsterdam and paints *The Anatomy Lesson of Doctor Tulp*	1632	Galileo publishes his work supporting Copernicus' theories on the solar system; the following year he is tried for heresy by the Inquisition
Van Dyck paints *Portrait of Charles I Hunting*	c. 1635	
	1637	Corneille's *Le Cid* performed in Paris
Georges de La Tour becomes court painter to Louis XIII	1639	
Poussin is directed to supervise decoration of the Grand Gallery in the Louvre	1640	
Louis Le Nain paints *La Charretté*	1641	
Rembrandt's so-called *Night Watch* both criticized and praised by commissioners	1642	
Diego Velázquez paints a portrait of his patron, *Philip IV of Spain on Horseback*	1644	Ch'ing dynasty comes to power in China
Academy of Painting founded in France; Poussin's *The Burial of Phocion*	1648	
Frans Hals completes the charming *Malle Bobbe*	c. 1650	
	1651	Publication of Hobbes' *Leviathan*
Rembrandt portrays his mistress Hendrijke in *Woman Bathing*	1654	
Velázquez completes *The Maids of Honor*, considered his finest work	1656	
Dutch artist Jan Vermeer paints *The Girl Reading a Letter*	1657	
	1666	Great London fire nearly engulfs the city
In the year of his death, Rembrandt paints the last of more than ninety self-portraits	1669	Royal Academy of Music founded in Paris
Jean Antoine Watteau settles in Paris	1701	Act of Settlement barring Catholics from the English monarchy passed by Parliament
	1707	Union of England and Scotland
Venetian artist Giovanni Battista Tiepolo paints *Isaac's Sacrifice*	1716	
Jean Antoine Watteau finishes *Return from Cytherea* as acceptance piece for admission to the Academy of Painting	1717	
	1721	Bach composes the six *Brandenburg Concertos*
Antonio Canal, known as Canaletto, paints a view of the Church della Carità	1726	Jonathan Swift's satire *Gulliver's Travels* published
Tiepolo paints frescoes in the Colleoni Chapel, Bergamo	1732	
François Boucher becomes a member of the Academy of Painting; illustrates an edition of Molière's works	1734	
William Hogarth publishes a series of engravings called *The Rake's Progress*	1735	
Jean Chardin, a master of views of French country life, paints *Grace at Table*	1740	War of the Austrian Succession embroils Europe in a major war

Canaletto works in London
Tiepolo decorates the salon of the Palazzo Labia with the *Tale of Antony and Cleopatra*

The Royal Academy of Arts is founded in England; Joshua Reynolds, famed portraitist, selected as first president

Francisco Jose Goya y Lucientes settles in Madrid

Francesco Guardi's *The Counts of the North* commemorates a state visit to Venice
English artist Thomas Gainsborough paints portraits of *Mrs. Siddons* and *Mrs. Richard Brinsley Sheridan*

Goya appointed court painter by King Charles IV of Spain; completes *The Nude Maja* and *The Clothed Maja*

1742	First performance of Handel's oratorio *Messiah*
1746-55	
1755	Earthquake devastates Lisbon
1758	Voltaire finishes *Candide*
1762	Rousseau publishes *The Social Contract*
1768	
1769	James Watt obtains patent for the steam engine
1773	
1776	American Declaration of Independence; publication of Adam Smith's *The Wealth of Nations*
1782	
1785	*The Times* of London founded by John Walter; publication of Boswell's *Life of Samuel Johnson*
1789	Parisians storm the Bastille; Declaration of the Rights of Man proclaimed
1799	Completion of Schiller's historical trilogy *Wallenstein*; a year later he writes *Maria Stuart*

Selected Bibliography

Akayama, Terukazu. *Japanese Painting*. Geneva: Skira, 1961.

Berenson, Bernard. *Italian Painters of the Renaissance*. London: Phaidon Publishers, 1968.

Byron, Robert and Talbot Rice, David. *The Birth of Western Painting*. New York: Hacker Art Books, 1968.

Cahill, James. *Chinese Painting*. Geneva: Skira, 1960.

Canaday, John. *The Lives of the Painters*. 4 vols. New York: W. W. Norton, 1969.

Clark, Kenneth and Pedretti, Carlo. *Leonardo da Vinci Drawings at Windsor Castle*. 2 vols. London: Phaidon Publishers, 1969.

Crowe, Joseph A. *Handbook of Painting: German, Flemish and Dutch Schools*. 2 vols. St. Clair Shores, Michigan: Scholarly Press, 1972.

Gardner, Helen. *Art Through the Ages*. New York: Harcourt Brace, 1959.

Godfrey, Frederick M. *History of Italian Painting*. New York: Taplinger Publishing Co., 1965.

Lassaigne, Jacques. *Spanish Painting*. 2 vols. Geneva: Skira, 1952.

Ruskin, Ariane: *Art of the High Renaissance*. New York: McGraw-Hill, 1968.

Rose, Barbara. *Golden Age of Dutch Painting*. New York: Praeger, 1969.

Swann, Peter C. *Chinese Painting*. New York: Universe Books, 1958.

Thuillier, Jacques. *French Painting*. 3 vols. Geneva: Skira, 1964.

Van Puyvelde, Leo. *Flemish Painting from Van Eyck to Metsys*. New York: McGraw-Hill, 1970.

——— *Flemish Painting: The Age of Rubens and Van Dyck*. New York: McGraw-Hill, 1971.

Welch, Stuart C. *The Art of Mughal India*. New York: Asia House Gallery, 1963.

Picture Credits

Index

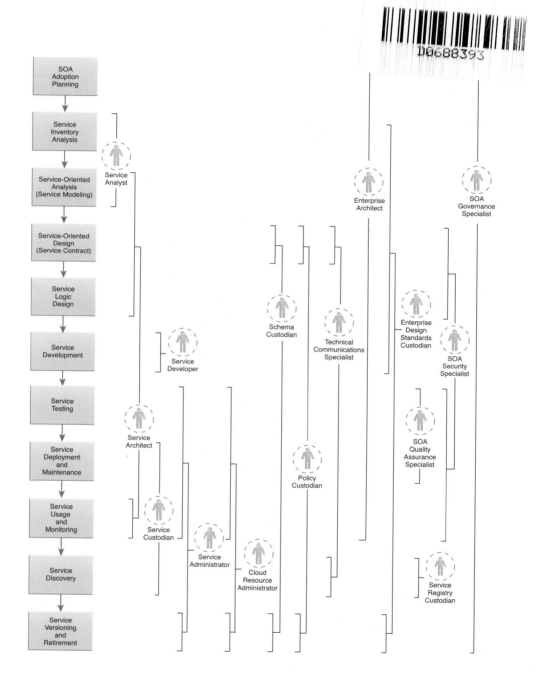

SOA
Adoption
Planning

Service
Inventory
Analysis

Service-Oriented
Analysis
(Service Modeling)

Service-Oriented
Design
(Service Contract)

Service
Logic
Design

Service
Development

Service
Testing

Service
Deployment
and
Maintenance

Service
Usage
and
Monitoring

Service
Discovery

Service
Versioning
and
Retirement

Service
Analyst

Service
Developer

Service
Architect

Service
Custodian

Service
Administrator

Cloud
Resource
Administrator

Schema
Custodian

Technical
Communications
Specialist

Policy
Custodian

Enterprise
Architect

Enterprise
Design
Standards
Custodian

SOA
Quality
Assurance
Specialist

Service
Registry
Custodian

SOA
Governance
Specialist

SOA
Security
Specialist

Praise for this Book

"With this book Thomas Erl [and his team] do a great job in outlining a framework to implement an SOA governance program. For each stage of the project lifecycle, necessary governance precepts and processes are described concretely by referring to the service-orientation principles and SOA patterns. This makes it an indispensable source of information for any SOA practitioner or any professional who plans to start an SOA initiative."

—Jean-Paul De Baets, Principal SOA Architect, Fedict (Belgian Federal Government Information and Communication Technology Service)

"Thomas Erl's *SOA Governance* fills in an important missing piece for any organization wanting to move to—and succeed with—an enterprise commitment to implement SOA and realize its overarching benefits. Of equal importance, however, is the fact that the basic concepts and frameworks that the book instantiates in the context of SOA can also be productively applied in other contexts that are not formally 'SOA-esque,' but where complexity is in need of formal governance. For example, we are using this book as our reference in both the SOA development and implementation work at the NCI CBIIT, as well as the enterprise architecture definition efforts within HL7, an international healthcare interoperability Standards Development Organization (SDO) whose purvey includes the development of specifications to support computable semantic interoperability using distributed computing paradigms of involving services, messages, and documents."

—Charles N. Mead, M.D., MSc., Senior Technical Advisor to the Director, National Cancer Institute Center for Bioinformatics and Information Technology (NCI CBIIT) Chair, Architecture Board, Health Level 7 (HL7)

"*SOA Governance* is a must-read that provides an in-depth look at the organizational, managerial, procedural, and technical aspects that any SOA project needs to consider. If you're investing in SOA, you'll benefit greatly by having this excellent resource available to you as you contend with the many challenges of creating your own SOA governance."

—David E. Michalowicz, Principal, Information Systems Engineer, The MITRE Corporation

"If you are not familiar with SOA governance, this book introduces you to all the relevant stuff needed in a very practical and easy-to-understand manner. Use the processes and precepts shown herein to enable your enterprise [to realize] SOA governance."

—Damian Kleer, SOA Architect, DB Systel

SOA Governance

The Prentice Hall Service-Oriented Computing Series
from Thomas Erl aims to provide the IT industry with
a consistent level of unbiased, practical, and
comprehensive guidance and instruction in the areas
of service-oriented architecture, service-orientation,
and the expanding landscape that is shaping
the real-world service-oriented computing platform.

For more information, visit www.soabooks.com.

SOA Governance

Governing Shared Services
On-Premise and in the Cloud

Co-authored and edited by Thomas Erl

Stephen G. Bennett, Clive Gee, Robert Laird, Anne Thomas Manes, Robert Schneider, Leo Shuster, Andre Tost, and Chris Venable

With contributions from Benjamin Carlyle, Robert Moores, and Filippos Santas

PRENTICE HALL

PRENTICE HALL

UPPER SADDLE RIVER, NJ • BOSTON • INDIANAPOLIS • SAN FRANCISCO

NEW YORK • TORONTO • MONTREAL • LONDON • MUNICH • PARIS • MADRID

CAPE TOWN • SYDNEY • TOKYO • SINGAPORE • MEXICO CITY

The publisher offers excellent discounts on this book when ordered in quantity for bulk purchases or special sales, which may include electronic versions and/or custom covers and content particular to your business, training goals, marketing focus, and branding interests. For more information, please contact:

U.S. Corporate and Government Sales
(800) 382-3419
corpsales@pearsontechgroup.com

For sales outside the United States please contact:

International Sales
international@pearson.com

Visit us on the Web: informit.com/ph

Library of Congress Cataloging-in-Publication Data

SOA governance : governing shared services on-premise and in the cloud / Thomas Erl ... [et al.].

p. cm.

Includes bibliographical references.

ISBN-13: 978-0-13-815675-6 (hardback : alk. paper)

ISBN-10: (invalid) 0-13-815672-1 (hardback : alk. paper) 1. Service-oriented architecture (Computer science) 2. Business enterprises--Computer networks--Management. I. Erl, Thomas. II. Title: Service-oriented architecture governance.

TK5105.5828.S59 2011

004.6'54--dc22

2011003181

ISBN-13: 978-0-13-815675-6
ISBN-10: 0-13-815675-1
Text printed in the United States on recycled paper.
First printing April 2011

Editor-in-Chief
Mark L. Taub

Development Editor
Infinet Creative Group

Managing Editor
Kristy Hart

Project Editor
Betsy Harris

Copy Editor
Infinet Creative Group

Senior Indexer
Cheryl Lenser

Proofreaders
Kam Chiu Mok
Shivapriya Nagaraj
Catherine Shaffer
Williams Woods
 Publishing
Pamela Janice Yau

Publishing Coordinator
Kim Boedigheimer

Cover Designer
Thomas Erl

Compositors
Bumpy Design
Nonie Ratcliff

Photos
Thomas Erl

Graphics
Infinet Creative Group

To my supportive wife, Marie, and my children, Sam and Sophia,
for allowing me to take some family time to work on this book.
—Stephen G. Bennett

To my family, my colleagues, and my Nespresso® machine,
all of whom supported the creation of this book.
—Thomas Erl

Many fine adventures for the past, present, and future for my wife, Amy,
and my sons, Thomas and Jack. You guys make it all worthwhile.
Thanks to all of the great people that I've worked with on SOA and governance.
I've learned a lot from you.
—Robert Laird

In memory of my father, Stanley Moores, who died at 45
and whose company and counsel I miss more each year.
—Robert Moores

To my family in appreciation of their continued support and encouragement.
—Robert D. Schneider

To all my friends and colleagues that helped me make this book a reality.
—Leo Shuster

Thanks and love to my wife, Silke, and my sons, Marc and Jonas.
—Andre Tost

To my wife, Kelly, and children, Ethan and Sarah, for their loving support;
and to my colleagues for putting up with my endless rants and pontification.
—Chris Venable

Contents at a Glance

Contents

PART I: FUNDAMENTALS

PART II: PROJECT GOVERNANCE

    8.1 Governing Service Inventory Analysis 192
        Precepts 193
            Service Inventory Scope Definition 193
        Processes 195
            Business Requirements Prioritization 195
        People (Roles) 197
            Service Analyst 197
            Enterprise Design Standards Custodian 198
            Enterprise Architect 199
            SOA Governance Specialist 200
        Case Study Example 201

    8.2 Governing Service-Oriented Analysis
    (Service Modeling) 206
        Precepts 206
            Service and Capability Candidate Naming Standards 206
            Service Normalization 207
            Service Candidate Versioning Standards 209
        Processes 210
            Service Candidate Review 210
        People (Roles) 212
            Service Analyst 212
            Service Architect 213
            Enterprise Design Standards Custodian 214
            Enterprise Architect 215
            SOA Governance Specialist 216
        Case Study Example 217

CHAPTER 9: Governing Service Design and
Development Stages 221

    9.1 Governing Service-Oriented Design (Service Contract) . . 223
        Precepts 223
            Schema Design Standards 223
            Service Contract Design Standards 225
            Service-Orientation Contract Design Standards 228
            SLA Template 229
        Processes 231
            Service Contract Design Review 231
            Service Contract Registration 234

Contents

xxvii

Foreword
by Massimo Pezzini

"What are the three key ingredients for successful SOA?" I was asked (in Sweden, if I remember well) by a pretty senior application architect several years ago. It was the time, circa 2004, when SOA was at the peak of what we at Gartner call "the hype cycle." Every vendor was busily trying to reposition as a SOA player, and users were struggling to understand what SOA was and why they should care about it.

When that application architect asked me the fatal question, I had luckily already investigated SOA, especially its key "dos" and "don'ts," for quite a while, starting in the late 1990s. I had by then spoken with quite a number of large organizations, in both North America and Europe, that had gone through the painful process of figuring out, through trial and error, how to manage a large-scale and business-critical set of SOA-based projects. Therefore, my answer was spontaneous and also came out with a rather unquestionable tone: "Discipline, discipline, and discipline!"

From my conversation with these leading-edge organizations, it was in fact pretty evident to me that what was later to be called SOA governance was a critical success factor for SOA initiatives. If you think about it for a second, this is obvious: The basic goals of SOA are

1. Reducing application development and maintenance costs, through run-time sharing of services across multiple applications

2. Increasing business agility, by effectively managing service and application life-cycle (discovery, definition, design, implementation, testing, deployment, management, maintenance, and retirement)

There is no way to achieve these goals without applying a proper set of rules and processes, which we now call SOA governance. SOA governance is in charge of making sure that services are designed and implemented to be truly reusable, that there are facilities in place (e.g., a *service repository* or *service inventory*, as it is called in this book) to enable a "reuse first" approach to application development, that ownership of (and accountability for) services is well defined and unambiguous, and that it is clear "who pays for what." (You would be surprised to know how many SOA initiatives I analyzed came to a stalemate because of cost allocation issues….) SOA pioneers also discovered it was not sufficient to define SOA governance rules and processes. Without an organizational entity (the *SOA Center of Excellence* or *SOA Governance Program Office*, as it is called in this book) in charge of not only defining but also enabling and enforcing these rules and processes, they simply don't happen.

You will find in this book a comprehensive and richly detailed interpretation of what these rules and processes are all about and how they can be concretely implemented. You may adopt and adapt these suggestions to your actual business and technical requirements, level of SOA maturity, organizational settings, and your company's business and IT culture. The variety of case studies discussed in the book will also give you a sense of how concretely SOA governance can be implemented to achieve real-life business goals.

Let me conclude with a final "lesson learned" from the SOA governance trenches: Your SOA initiative may be killed by lack of governance, but too much governance can be deadly, too. Figuring out what is the "just enough" amount of governance appropriate for your company is a difficult, but worthwhile task. This book will help you accomplish that goal.

—*Massimo Pezzini*
    VP and Research Fellow, Gartner, Inc.

Foreword
by Roberto Medrano

We have spent the better part of the last decade working on SOA governance programs at some of the world's largest and most complex IT organizations. We are very pleased, therefore, to see this important topic addressed in detail by Thomas Erl, one of this generation's truly great software architecture authors. Thomas' book is beyond timely, in our view, as it captures a serious truth that has crept up on even some of the most savvy CIOs. That is, SOA has gone from "nice to have," to "have to have," to today's reality that SOA is *just here*. Period. You have it. You don't have any choice but to have it. And now that you have, you have to govern it.

How did this happen? How did SOA emerge from the egghead shadows to become the de facto enterprise architecture across the globe? Many factors contributed to this situation, but perhaps most important has been the ascendancy of cloud computing. Though still in its infancy, cloud computing has been absolutely transformative in the role that SOA plays in day-to-day enterprise computing. The cloud is inherently service-oriented. Whether an organization is totally cloud-based, a hybrid of on-premise and cloud, or using a private cloud, its applications are now reaching out to consume and expose Web services in ways that would have been hard to imagine even a few years ago. Even organizations that shunned SOA now have one. It's called the cloud, and it's here to stay.

SOA governance and the cloud are vital companions, for better or worse. In a nutshell SOA governance is about making sure the enterprise builds the right things, build them right, and makes sure that what it has built is behaving right. With proper SOA governance, the cloud can be a strategic bonanza, smoothing the way for improving agility, reducing risks, reducing costs and economies that everyone should want. Companies realizing the most success are those that have built a Unified SOA Governance infrastructure that governs a wide range of assets and artifacts through their entire lifecycle. Without SOA governance, the cloud threatens operational disaster and exposure to multiple levels of risk. And now, we have a thorough and well thought out book on the subject. Thomas has done the industry a great service by delving deeply into this topic in a way that readers of many different backgrounds can understand.

This book works because it gives the reader a sense of SOA governance across the full IT lifecycle and spans the organizations that are charged with managing the SOA. Thomas offers valuable insights and pragmatic tips on how to implement governance that is sensible yet effective, touching on managerial and business issues as much as technology. He probes into the nature of rules and organizations, even human nature, as he lays out the groundwork for good governance. Thomas understands that all of these aspects of governance are relevant to the success of a program. Enjoy this book. If you are involved in IT management, you will find it an indispensible companion in your quest for success with SOA.

—Roberto Medrano
EVP, SOA Software

Acknowledgments

Special thanks to the following reviewers who generously volunteered their time and expertise (in alphabetical order):

Mohamad Afshar
Kristofer Ågren
Randy Atkins
Jean-Paul De Baets
Toufic Boubez
Benjamin Robert Carlyle
Pethuru Chelliah
Kevin P. Davis, Ph.D.
Mike Fields
Damian Kleer
Hanu Kommalapati
Nick Laqua
Charles N. Mead, MD, MSc
David E. Michalowicz
Thomas M. Michelbach
Kam Chiu Mok
Robert Moores
Eric Roch
David S. Rogers
Filippos Santas
Mark Sigsworth
Sanjay Kumar Singh
Herbjörn Wilhelmsen
Pamela Janice Yau
Dr. Jure Zakotnik
Dr. Matthias Ziegler

Chapter 1

Introduction

Imagine driving along a winding road. On the one side you have sheets of blasted rock that lead up into a mountain range, on the other side you have a steep cliff, with a freefall of several hundred feet, leading into a deep ocean. The faster you drive, the sooner you will reach your destination, but the more risky the drive. For example, you may need to swerve to avoid obstacles or adjust quickly to volatile weather conditions—risk factors that are elevated when moving at higher speeds. But, it's still tempting, because the sooner you reach that destination, the more successful your drive will be considered, by everyone.

When we design a roadmap for our SOA initiative, we lay out a direction that determines our route and a schedule that determines our rate of speed. We try to anticipate and plan for obstacles, but we know to expect the unexpected. With the necessary stakeholder support and financing in place (let's call it our "fuel in the tank"), we determine it's time to hit the road.

But before we do, let's go back to that decision point about choosing our route. A winding road with an open cliff constantly at our side represents the continuous risk of plunging over the edge, especially when maneuvering to avoid unanticipated obstacles. Such a road requires minimal work to put together and therefore a perceived opportunity to reach our goals in less time and with less expense. But, there's that risk factor we need to consider, especially of concern after we take a preliminary look over the edge to see the accumulated wreckage of the many vehicles that previously, unsuccessfully attempted this drive. We therefore reconsider.

The best analogy of IT governance I encountered was by Leo Shuster who, in his podcast interview for the International SOA + Cloud Symposium, stated that governance is like guardrails along a road. A governed roadmap is one that has, from beginning to end, controls that establish rules that we must comply with and parameters that we must function within, as we progress throughout SOA project stages.

In other words, we need to build a road with solid guardrails that keep our initiative from veering off its path. For many organizations, this realization was the result of losing significant investments to the heaps of wreckage already floating in the ocean below the cliffs of unregulated project plans. It has been a painful lesson that has, for some, shaken their very confidence in SOA. Fortunately, out of the numerous projects and efforts that have gone into establishing SOA governance as its own field of expertise, we now have a set of proven rules and parameters that provide a stable and healthy starting point for organizations to create successful SOA governance systems.

This book is the accumulated result of many years of practice and insight provided by SOA experts, IT governance experts, and technology innovation experts. It's about the nuts and bolts of guardrail construction, maintenance, and enforcement. It's also about helping us understand that establishing a sound system of governance requires an investment and an expected return on that investment. What we put into creating those guardrails will protect the greater investment we put into the overall SOA projects that will venture down that road.

Finally, this book is about highlighting the fact that once those guardrails are in place, that governed road we built can be used over and over again, each time allowing us to drive faster, without compromising our safety. Establishing a mature system of SOA governance within our IT enterprise gives us a form of regulated agility—a robust state whereby we can rapidly respond to on-going business change without assuming unnecessary risk.

—*Thomas Erl*

1.1 About this Book

This book has a very simple objective. Its focus is solely on IT governance as it applies to the adoption of SOA and service-orientation. To that effect, it makes a clear distinction between governance and management and methodology, and then proceeds to establish a generic governance system, comprised of a series of common precepts, processes, and associated organizational roles. It further addresses governance topics that pertain to specific forms of service technology innovation, including cloud computing.

The purpose of this book is to give SOA practitioners a concrete framework that can be further augmented and extended into custom SOA governance systems and programs.

Who this Book is For

There is much discussion about the role of the SOA Governance Specialist in the upcoming chapters. While this type of IT professional will need to become an expert at everything covered in this book, the actual intended audience is much broader.

Specifically, this book will be useful to:

- IT managers and project managers that need to understand how a governance system can and should be incorporated into an SOA initiative, its impacts, requirements, and benefits.

- Architects and analysts who will be in the midst of SOA governance activities, including contribution to governance precepts and standards, as well as participation in review and audit processes.

- Enterprise architects and those involved with the authoring and maintenance of custom design standards. These individuals will be part of governance activity in almost every SOA project stage.

- Business analysts that are part of analysis teams for service modeling and for the definition of enterprise business models, such as business dictionaries, ontologies, and business processes.

- Developers, administrators, quality assurance professionals, and security specialists, who all will find themselves participating in or being affected by various SOA governance controls.

- Cloud computing professionals interested in learning about IT governance considerations specific to SOA and service-oriented solutions that encompass one or more cloud-based services or resources.

What this Book Does Not Cover

This is Not a Book About SOA Management

SOA governance has historically often been mistaken or confused with SOA management. This is a book about SOA governance only, although related management requirements and project stages are occasionally referenced. See Chapter 6 for an explanation that helps clarify the difference between governance, management, and methodology.

This is Not a Book About Cloud Computing Governance

Wherever appropriate, this book references SOA governance considerations that can pertain to cloud computing. However, it is important to note that this is not a general book about cloud computing governance—only considerations specific to applying service-orientation within cloud-based environments are mentioned. General cloud computing governance is a much broader topic that delves beyond the service level, into the various mechanisms and IT resources that can comprise cloud environments.

1.2 **Recommended Reading**

To further ensure that you have a clear understanding of key terms used and referenced in the upcoming chapters, you can visit the online master glossary for this book series at www.soaglossary.com to look up definitions for terms that may not be fully described in this book.

Even if you are an experienced SOA practitioner, we suggest you take the time to have a look at this online resource. A great deal of ambiguity has surrounded SOA and service-oriented computing and these explanations and definitions will ensure that you fully understand key terms and concepts in relation to this book and the book series as a whole.

Here are some recommendations for additional books that elaborate on some of the topics covered by this title:

- *SOA Principles of Service Design* – A comprehensive documentation of the service-orientation design paradigm with full descriptions of all of the principles referenced in this book.

- *SOA Design Patterns* – This is the official SOA design patterns catalog containing descriptions and examples for most of the patterns referenced in this book. You can also look up concise descriptions for these patterns at www.soapatterns.org and in Appendix D.

- *Service-Oriented Architecture: Concepts, Technology, and Design* – The coverage of service-oriented analysis and design processes in this title supplements this book with more detailed methodology-related topics.

- The title *Web Service Contract Design & Versioning for SOA* provides a great deal of technical content that may not be relevant to governance topics, except for those that aim to establish technical design and development standards. However, this book does include four chapters dedicated to Web service contract versioning topics that will be useful when dealing with governance precepts associated with the Service Versioning and Retirement project stage (see Chapter 11 and Appendix F).

- *SOA with REST* – This book documents the convergence of REST and SOA by establishing how REST services can be realized in support of service-orientation. Salient topics are reinforced with comprehensive case studies using modern REST frameworks in combination with contemporary SOA models, patterns, practices, and concepts.

For the latest information regarding these and other titles in the *Prentice Hall Service-Oriented Computing Series from Thomas Erl*, visit www.soabooks.com.

1.3 How this Book is Organized

This book begins with Chapters 1 and 2 providing introductory content and case study background information respectively. All subsequent chapters are grouped into the following parts:

- Part I: Fundamentals
- Part II: Project Governance
- Part III: Strategic Governance
- Part IV: Appendices

Part I: Fundamentals

The first four chapters cover various introductory topics in preparation for the chapters in Parts II and III.

Chapter 3: Service-Oriented Computing Fundamentals

This chapter provides an overview of key terms and concepts associated with SOA, service-orientation, and cloud computing.

Chapter 4: SOA Planning Fundamentals

Foundational critical success factors (pillars), funding models, and basic maturity levels are described in this chapter. The "Pillars of Service-Orientation" are referenced in several subsequent chapters, especially in relation to maturity assessment and the SOA Adoption Planning project stage.

Chapter 5: SOA Project Fundamentals

This chapter provides introductory coverage of SOA project lifecycle stages, organizational roles, and the usage of service profiles. The project stages and organizational roles in particular are revisited through chapters in Parts II and III, as they relate to various SOA governance precepts and processes.

Chapter 6: Understanding SOA Governance

This must-read chapter establishes fundamental terminology and concepts pertaining to IT governance and SOA governance. Topics include an explanation of precepts and processes, the involvement of people and organizational roles, the SOA governance system, the SOA governance program, and the SOA Governance Program Office (SGPO).

Part II: Project Governance

This part of the book provides a series of chapters that step you through the SOA project lifecycle by exploring how and where various governance controls can be incorporated within different project stages. In many cases, governance controls provide entrance and exit criteria for the regulated transition from stage to stage.

Chapter 7: Governing SOA Projects

Part II begins with topics that explain how SOA project governance is approached, along with a series of overarching SOA governance precepts that apply to various project stages. This chapter concludes with a section dedicated to SOA Adoption Planning and establishes governance controls specific to this stage.

Precepts and processes covered in this chapter:

- Service Profile Standards
- SOA Governance Technology Standards
- Preferred Adoption Scope Definition
- Organizational Maturity Criteria Definition
- Standardized Funding Model
- Organizational Governance Maturity Assessment
- Adoption Impact Analysis
- Adoption Risk Assessment

Chapter 8: Governing Service Analysis Stages

A set of SOA governance controls, rules, and regulations are provided for the analysis and modeling of individual service candidates, as well as collections (or inventories) of services that need to be modeled in relation to each other.

Precepts and processes covered in this chapter:

- Service Inventory Scope Definition
- Service and Capability Candidate Naming Standards
- Service Normalization
- Service Candidate Versioning Standards
- Business Requirements Prioritization
- Service Candidate Review

Chapter 9: Governing Service Design and Development Stages

The physical design of service contracts and service architecture and logic are addressed in this chapter in relation to SOA governance precepts, processes, and organizational roles that are involved primarily to establish various standards, conventions, and compliance review processes.

Precepts and processes covered in this chapter:

- Schema Design Standards
- Service Contract Design Standards
- Service-Orientation Contract Design Standards
- SLA Template
- Service Logic Design Standards
- Service-Orientation Architecture Design Standards
- Service Logic Programming Standards
- Custom Development Technology Standards
- Service Contract Design Review
- Service Contract Registration
- Service Access Control
- Service Logic Design Review
- Legal Data Audit
- Service Logic Code Review

Chapter 10: Governing Service Testing and Deployment Stages

Quality assurance and testing activities are covered, along with steps required to deploy and maintain service implementations. For each of these topics, further governance controls and approaches are documented.

Precepts and processes covered in this chapter:

- Testing Tool Standards
- Testing Parameter Standards
- Service Testing Standards
- Cloud Integration Testing Standards
- Test Data Usage Guidelines
- Production Deployment and Maintenance Standards
- Service Test Results Review
- Service Certification Review
- Service Maintenance Review

Chapter 11: Governing Service Usage, Discovery, and Versioning Stages

We conclude this part with a look at governance topics and controls that regulate the runtime usage of services, as well as their post-implementation discovery and versioning. The Service Usage and Monitoring stage in particular is where a range of metrics are documented and further links to upcoming SOA governance vitality triggers and activities are established.

Precepts and processes covered in this chapter:

- Runtime Service Usage Thresholds
- Service Vitality Triggers
- Centralized Service Registry
- Service Versioning Strategy
- SLA Versioning Rules
- Service Retirement Notification
- Service Vitality Review

- Service Registry Access Control
- Service Registry Record Review
- Service Discovery
- Shared Service Usage Request
- Shared Service Modification Request
- Service Versioning
- Service Retirement

Part III: Strategic Governance

The next part of this book provides further governance topics that have broad or long-term applicability and are primarily relevant from a strategic perspective.

Chapter 12: Service Information and Service Policy Governance

Several additional SOA governance precepts and processes are documented in this chapter, primarily focused on the modeling, design, and standardization of business data and related models. Many of the artifacts advocated by these governance controls relate back to early SOA project stages.

Precepts and processes covered in this chapter:

- Enterprise Business Dictionary/Domain Business Dictionary
- Service Metadata Standards
- Enterprise Ontology/Domain Ontology
- Business Policy Standards
- Operational Policy Standards
- Policy Centralization
- Data Quality Review
- Communications Quality Review
- Information Alignment Audit
- Policy Conflict Audit

Chapter 13: SOA Governance Vitality

The concept of governance vitality is described in this chapter, along with explanations of common vitality triggers and vitality process activities. These are associated primarily with product service usage, but are also of strategic relevance for the on-going evolution of services and collections of services.

Chapter 14: SOA Governance Technology

This chapter begins by establishing primary categories of SOA governance technologies, and then proceeds to document common types of tools and products used to help automate various governance tasks throughout SOA project stages.

Part IV: Appendices

Appendix A: Case Study Conclusion

This appendix provides a brief conclusion of the case study storyline.

Appendix B: Master Reference Diagrams for Organizational Roles

Throughout the chapters in Parts II and III, SOA governance precepts and processes are mapped to each other and to organizational roles within a given project stage and beyond. However, the mapping of an organization's roles is limited to a given project stage because many of the same roles are associated with multiple project stages.

This appendix provides a global, cross-project stage mapping diagram for each organizational role.

Appendix C: Service-Orientation Principles Reference

This appendix provides the profile tables (originally from *SOA Principles of Service Design*) for the service-orientation design principles referenced in this book.

Appendix D: SOA Design Patterns Reference

This appendix provides the profile tables (originally from *SOA Design Patterns*) from the official SOA design patterns catalog.

Appendix E: The Annotated SOA Manifesto

This appendix provides the annotated version of the SOA Manifesto declaration, which is also published at www.soa-manifesto.com.

Appendix F: Versioning Fundamentals for Web Services and REST Services

As a supplement for Service Versioning topics and related governance precepts, a revised version of the Fundamental Service Versioning chapter from the *Web Service Contract Design & Versioning for SOA* book is provided here, updated with new content and examples for both Web services and REST services.

Appendix G: Mapping Service-Orientation to RUP

A newly published paper that provides concrete mapping of various aspects of service-orientation with the rational unified process (RUP).

Appendix H: Additional Resources

A list of relevant Web sites and supplementary resources.

1.4 Symbols, Figures, and Style Conventions

Symbol Legend

This book contains a series of diagrams that are referred to as *figures*. The primary symbols used throughout all figures are individually described in the symbol legend located on the inside of the front cover.

Mapping Diagrams

Chapters 7 through 12 provide concrete mapping of governance controls, as follows:

- SOA governance precepts are mapped to related processes and roles
- SOA governance processes are mapped to related precepts and roles
- relevant organizational roles are mapped to related SOA governance precepts and processes specific to the current chapter

This mapping is visually illustrated via a series of diagrams, such as the one shown in Figure 1.1.

As previously explained, Appendix B further provides a series of cross-project stage mapping diagrams for organization roles.

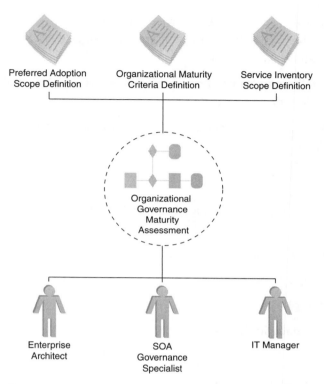

Figure 1.1

An example of a mapping diagram. The item in the center is an SOA
governance process that is being mapped to three precepts (top) and three
organizational roles (bottom).

SOA Principles & Patterns Sections

As a further supplement, this book occasionally references service-orientation principles and SOA patterns relevant to various governance topics. These references are
generally isolated to separate *SOA Principles & Patterns* sections and provided primarily
for those readers familiar with the principles and patterns covered in *SOA Principles of
Service Design* and *SOA Design Patterns* series titles. Prior knowledge of these principles
and patterns is not required and the corresponding references can be disregarded if
they are not of interest.

Principle and pattern names are always capitalized and followed by a page number
that points to their profile. Profile tables for principles are provided in Appendix C and

those for patterns are in Appendix D. In order to maintain a distinction between principles and patterns, the page number for each principle is placed in rounded parenthesis,
and for patterns, square brackets are used.

For example, the following statement first references a service-orientation design principle and then an SOA design pattern:

*"...the Service Loose Coupling (477) principle is supported via the application of the Decoupled
Contract [517] pattern..."*

Capitalization

The following are categories of topics for which terms are consistently capitalized
throughout this book:

- service-orientation pillars
- SOA project stage names
- organizational roles
- organizational maturity levels
- funding models
- SOA governance precept names
- SOA governance process names

This usage of capitalization is intended to help with the identification of key terms,
especially those for which mapping is provided.

1.5 Additional Information

These sections provide supplementary information and resources for the *Prentice Hall
Service-Oriented Computing Series from Thomas Erl*.

Updates, Errata, and Resources (www.soabooks.com)

Information about other series titles and various supporting resources can be found at
www.soabooks.com. You are encouraged to visit this site regularly to check for content
changes and corrections.

Master Glossary (www.soaglossary.com)

To avoid content overlap and to ensure constant content currency, the books in this series do not contain glossaries. Instead, a dedicated Web site at www.soaglossary.com provides a master glossary for all series titles. This site continues to grow and expand with new glossary definitions as new series titles are developed and released.

Referenced Specifications (www.soaspecs.com)

The www.soaspecs.com Web site provides a central portal to the original specification documents created and maintained by the primary standards organizations.

SOASchool.com® SOA Certified Professional (SOACP)

This text book is an official part of the SOA Certified Professional curriculum and is used in conjunction with courses and exams for the SOA Governance Specialist Certification program. The course materials that are part of this program provide additional content and lab exercises that further explore topics covered in this book.

For more information, visit www.soaschool.com.

CloudSchool.com™ Cloud Certified Professional (CCP)

Various SOA governance topics covered in this book address cloud computing considerations. Content pertaining to the governance of cloud-based services, as well as introductory content of general cloud computing topics and concepts, was provided by course material donated by the CloudSchool.com™ Cloud Certified Professional curriculum.

For more information, visit www.cloudschool.com.

The SOA Magazine (www.soamag.com)

The SOA Magazine is a regular publication provided by SOA Systems Inc. and Prentice Hall and is officially associated with the *Prentice Hall Service-Oriented Computing Series from Thomas Erl. The SOA Magazine* is dedicated to publishing specialized SOA articles, case studies, and papers by industry experts and professionals. The common criteria for contributions is that each explore a distinct aspect of service-oriented computing.

Notification Service

If you'd like to be automatically notified of new book releases in this series, new supplementary content for this title, or key changes to the previously listed Web sites, use the notification form at www.soabooks.com.

Chapter 2

Case Study Background

2.1 How Case Studies are Used

Part II of this book provides a series of case study examples that supplement the coverage of governance topics as they pertain to different lifecycle stages of SOA projects. These examples are based on the case study background content provided by this chapter. You can readily identify case study content by looking for sections with a light gray shading.

2.2 Raysmoore Corporation

Following the unexpected rise of precious metal values, the international mining industry has witnessed a dramatic increase in demand, production, and competition. Raysmoore is a five-year old mining corporation that has steadily established itself as a top producer of fine and coarse gold and silver. It has an internal supply chain that reaches directly into the retail sector where precious stones are sold as part of jewelry, watches, and other retail goods.

History

Two years ago, Raysmoore was comprised of a head office and three mining sites within North America. As a result of the strategic acquisition of Lovelt Inc. and Reeldrill Ltd. (two off-shore mining companies), Raysmoore has grown by almost 50%. Due to the specialized nature of the acquired companies, both Lovelt and Reeldrill remain as relatively independent subsidiaries within the overall Raysmoore corporate umbrella.

As a result of its increased size and multi-cultural market presence, Raysmoore has had to comply with a number of new regulations. Lovelt mining locations are based in South America and Reeldrill mining sites are scattered throughout Central America. Raysmoore management has noticed that governmental policies change more frequently and unexpectedly in these regions.

IT Environment

Raysmoore has a sizeable and diversified IT environment with a number of centralized systems, including a financials system, an enterprise resource planning (ERP) platform, and a separate human resources application. It further relies on its subsidiaries' proprietary systems to perform specialized business functions that require access to cross-domain business data. As a result, various forms of functional overlap exist throughout the Raysmoore ecosystem.

Raysmoore's technology stack includes a diverse set of legacy hardware and software. It has a sizeable AS/400 installation that houses legacy resources, some of which were purchased while others were custom-developed. As qualified AS/400 support began to erode, legacy applications were either migrated to distributed platforms, or maintained "as-is" with little or no changes. Raysmoore further has a large base of UNIX and Windows technologies that include its financials and HR systems.

Raysmoore has always been conservative in its technology evaluation and selection. Raysmoore's central IT group oversees its IT enterprise, as well as those from Lovelt and Reeldrill.

Business Goals and Obstacles

Raysmoore would like to keep growing. The CEO's growth strategy continues to be acquisition oriented, and the company's central functions (including IT) have therefore been mandated to become agile and flexible in order to minimize the impact of the integration of new assets.

In response to the agility mandate, the CIO that oversees the Raysmoore, Lovelt, and Reeldrill IT divisions recently kicked off a large-scale SOA initiative aimed at service-enabling their global IT enterprise. A primary objective of this effort is to integrate the respective divisions so as to span the supply chain across all business domains.

The project has been slow to get off the ground largely due to the company's size and political landscape. Raysmoore's subsidiaries have their own IT departments that operate in isolation, and have demanded to retain authority over their respective domains.

To make matters more challenging, Raysmoore IT has been asked to cut costs by 10% across the board. As a result, the CIO is considering reducing the planned amount of on-premise IT infrastructure technologies required for the SOA adoption project and instead investigate leasing options with third-party cloud providers.

With the pending complexities of a potentially expensive and pivotal SOA adoption project, the CIO decides that nothing will proceed until a solid governance system is in place.

2.3 Case Study Continuation

Additional case study content is provided throughout the following chapters:

- Chapter 7: *Governing SOA Projects*
- Chapter 8: *Governing Service Analysis Stages*
- Chapter 9: *Governing Service Design and Development Stages*
- Chapter 10: *Governing Service Testing and Deployment Stages*
- Chapter 11: *Governing Service Usage, Discovery, and Versioning Stages*

Sections in these chapters within Part II of this book are supplemented with sample case study scenarios and examples pertaining to the covered topic areas.

Part I

Fundamentals

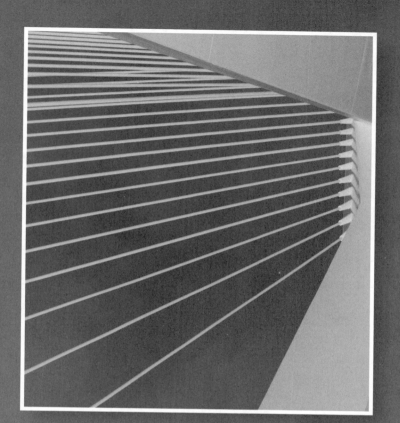

Chapter 3

Service-Oriented Computing Fundamentals

This chapter describes fundamental terms and concepts associated with service-oriented computing, including those related to service-oriented architecture, service-orientation, and cloud computing.

3.1 Basic Terminology

Upcoming sections provide definitions for the following terms:

- Service-Oriented Computing
- Service-Orientation
- Service-Oriented Architecture (SOA)
- Services
- SOA Manifesto
- Cloud Computing
- IT Resources
- Cloud
- On-Premise
- Cloud Deployment Models
- Cloud Consumers and Cloud Providers
- Cloud Delivery Models
- Service Models
- Service Composition
- Service Inventory
- Service Portfolio
- Service Candidate
- Service Contract

- Service-Related Granularity

- SOA Design Patterns

These terms are used throughout this book.

Service-Oriented Computing

Service-oriented computing is an umbrella term that represents a new generation distributed computing platform. As such, it encompasses many things, including its own design paradigm and design principles, design pattern catalogs, pattern languages, a distinct architectural model, and related concepts, technologies, and frameworks.

Service-orientation (explained shortly) emerged as a formal method in support of achieving the following goals and benefits associated with service-oriented computing:

- *Increased Intrinsic Interoperability* – Services within a given boundary are designed to be naturally compatible so that they can be effectively assembled and reconfigured in response to changing business requirements.

- *Increased Federation* – Services establish a uniform contract layer that hides underlying disparity, allowing them to be individually governed and evolved.

- *Increased Vendor Diversification Options* – A service-oriented environment is based on a vendor-neutral architectural model, allowing the organization to evolve the architecture in tandem with the business without being limited only to proprietary vendor platform characteristics.

- *Increased Business and Technology Domain Alignment* – Some services are designed with a business-centric functional context, allowing them to mirror and evolve with the business of the organization.

- *Increased ROI* – Most services are delivered and viewed as IT assets that are expected to provide repeated value that surpasses the cost of delivery and ownership.

- *Increased Organizational Agility* – New and changing business requirements can be fulfilled more rapidly by establishing an environment in which solutions can be assembled or augmented with reduced effort by leveraging the reusability and native interoperability of existing services.

- *Reduced IT Burden* – The enterprise as a whole is streamlined as a result of the previously described goals and benefits, allowing IT itself to better support the organization by providing more value with less cost and less overall burden.

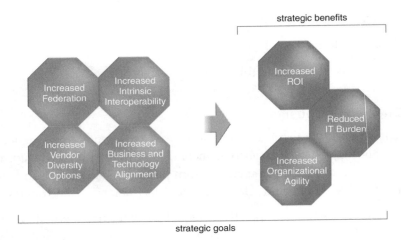

Figure 3.1
The latter three goals listed in the previous bulleted list represent target strategic benefits
that are achieved when attaining the first four goals.

Note that these strategic goals are also commonly associated with SOA, as explained in
the *SOA Manifesto* section.

Service-Orientation

Service-orientation is a design paradigm intended for the creation of solution logic units
that are individually shaped so that they can be collectively and repeatedly utilized in
support of the realization of the specific strategic goals and benefits associated with
service-oriented computing.

Solution logic designed in accordance with service-orientation can be qualified with
"service-oriented," and units of service-oriented solution logic are referred to as "services." As a design paradigm for distributed computing, service-orientation can be compared to object-orientation (or object-oriented design). Service-orientation, in fact, has
many roots in object-orientation (as first documented in Chapter 14 of *SOA Principles of
Service Design*) and has also been influenced by other industry developments.

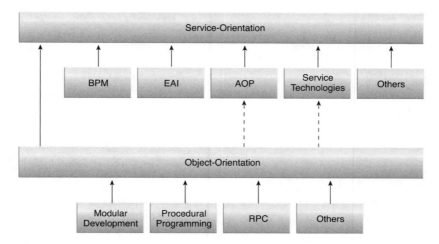

Figure 3.2
Service-orientation is very much an evolutionary design paradigm that owes much of its existence
to established design practices and technology platforms.

The service-orientation design paradigm is primarily comprised of eight specific design
principles:

- *Standardized Service Contract* – "Services within the same service inventory are in
  compliance with the same contract design standards."

- *Service Loose Coupling* – "Service contracts impose low consumer coupling requirements and are themselves decoupled from their surrounding environment."

- *Service Abstraction* – "Service contracts only contain essential information and
  information about services is limited to what is published in service contracts."

- *Service Reusability* – "Services contain and express agnostic logic and can be positioned as reusable enterprise resources."

- *Service Autonomy* – "Services exercise a high level of control over their underlying
  runtime execution environment."

- *Service Statelessness* – "Services minimize resource consumption by deferring the
  management of state information when necessary."

- *Service Discoverability* – "Services are supplemented with communicative metadata
  by which they can be effectively discovered and interpreted."

- *Service Composability* – "Services are effective composition participants, regardless
  of the size and complexity of the composition."

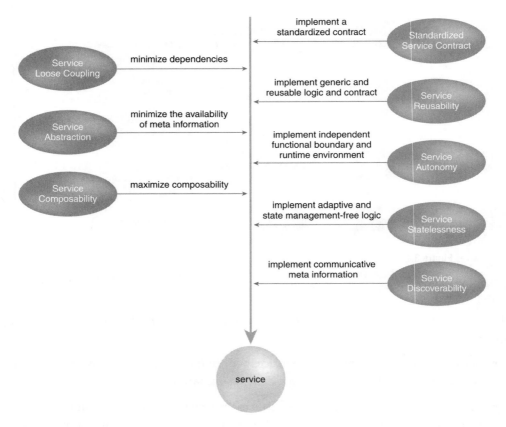

Figure 3.3
The principles on the left have a regulatory influence, whereas the application of the principles on the right primarily results in concrete characteristics being established within the service architecture.

Service-Oriented Architecture (SOA)

Service-oriented architecture is a technology architectural model for service-oriented solutions with distinct characteristics in support of realizing service-orientation and the strategic goals associated with service-oriented computing.

The four base characteristics we look to establish in any form of SOA are:

- *Business-Driven* – The technology architecture is aligned with the current business architecture. This context is then constantly maintained so that the technology architecture evolves in tandem with the business over time.

- *Vendor-Neutral* – The architectural model is not based solely on a proprietary vendor platform, allowing different vendor technologies to be combined or replaced over time in order to maximize business requirements fulfillment on an on-going basis.

- *Enterprise-Centric* – The scope of the architecture represents a meaningful segment of the enterprise, allowing for the reuse and composition of services and enabling service-oriented solutions to span traditional application silos.

- *Composition-Centric* – The architecture inherently supports the mechanics of repeated service aggregation, allowing it to accommodate constant change via the agile assembly of service compositions.

These characteristics collectively define the fundamental requirements a technology architecture must fulfill to be fully supportive of service-orientation.

As a form of technology architecture, an SOA implementation can consist of a combination of technologies, products, APIs, supporting infrastructure extensions, and various other parts. The actual complexion of a deployed service-oriented architecture is unique within each enterprise; however, it is typified by the introduction of new technologies and platforms that specifically support the creation, execution, and evolution of service-oriented solutions. As a result, building a technology architecture around the service-oriented architectural model establishes an environment suitable for solution logic that has been designed in compliance with service-orientation design principles.

Figure 3.4

The layered SOA model establishes the four common SOA types: service architecture, service composition architecture, service inventory architecture, and service-oriented enterprise architecture. (These different architectural types, along with the four SOA characteristics, are explained in detail in the book *SOA Design Patterns*.)

NOTE

Let's briefly recap the previous three terms to clearly establish how they relate to each other and specifically how they lead to a definition of SOA:

- There is a set of strategic goals associated with service-oriented computing.

- These goals represent a specific target state.

- Service-orientation is the paradigm that provides a proven method for achieving this target state.

- When we apply service-orientation to the design of software, we build units of logic called "services."

- Service-oriented solutions are comprised of one or more services.

- To build successful service-oriented solutions, we need a distributed technology architecture with specific characteristics.

- These characteristics distinguish the technology architecture as being service-oriented. This is SOA.

Services

A *service* is a unit of logic to which service-orientation has been applied to a meaningful extent. It is the application of service-orientation design principles that distinguishes a unit of logic as a service compared to units of logic that may exist solely as objects, components, Web services, REST services, and/or cloud-based services.

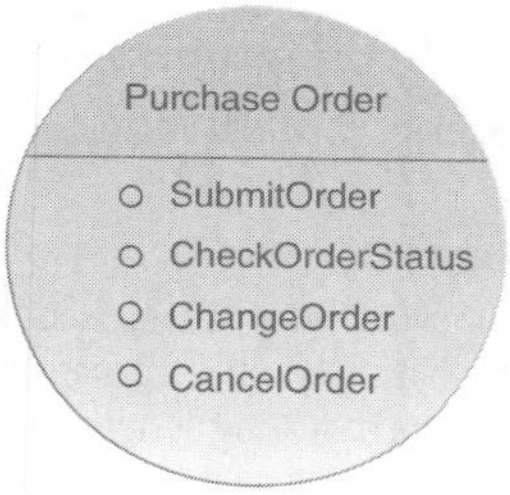

Subsequent to conceptual service modeling, design, and development stages implement a service as a physically independent software program with specific design characteristics that support the attainment of the strategic goals associated with service-oriented computing.

Purchase Order

○ SubmitOrder
○ CheckOrderStatus
○ ChangeOrder
○ CancelOrder

Figure 3.5

The chorded circle symbol is used to represent a service, primarily from a contract perspective.

Each service is assigned its own distinct functional context and is comprised of a set of capabilities related to this context. Therefore, a service can be considered a container of capabilities associated with a common purpose (or functional context).

It is important to view and position SOA and service-orientation as being neutral to any one technology platform. By doing so, you have the freedom to continually pursue the strategic goals associated with service-oriented computing by leveraging on-going service technology advancements.

Any implementation technology that can be used to create a distributed system may be suitable for the application of service-orientation. Three common service implementation mediums currently exist: components, Web services, and REST services. Any of these forms of service implementations can also exist as cloud-based services (as explained in the upcoming *Cloud* section).

Services as Components

A *component* is a software program designed to be part of a distributed system. It provides a technical interface comparable to a traditional application programming interface (API) through which it exposes public capabilities as *methods*, thereby allowing it to be explicitly invoked by other programs.

Components have typically relied on platform-specific development and runtime technologies. For example, components can be built using Java or .NET tools and are then deployed in a runtime environment capable of supporting the corresponding component communications technology requirements, as implemented by the chosen development platform.

Figure 3.6

The symbols used to represent a component. The symbol on the left is a generic component that may or may not have been designed as a service, whereas the symbol on the right is labeled to indicate that it has been designed as a service.

> **NOTE**
>
> Building service-oriented components is one of the topics covered in the books *SOA with .NET & Windows Azure* and *SOA with Java*, both titles in the *Prentice Hall Service-Oriented Computing Series from Thomas Erl.*

Services as Web Services

A *Web service* is a body of solution logic that provides a physically decoupled technical contract consisting of a WSDL definition, one or more XML Schema definitions and also possible WS-Policy expressions. The Web service contract exposes public capabilities as *operations*, establishing a technical interface but without any ties to a proprietary communications framework.

Service-orientation can be applied to the design of Web services. Web services provide an architectural model whereby the service contract is physically decoupled and vendor-neutral. This is conducive to several of the design goals associated with service-orientation.

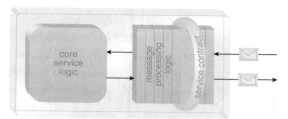

Web service acting as a service provider

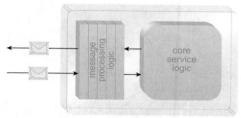

Portions of a Web service acting as a service consumer

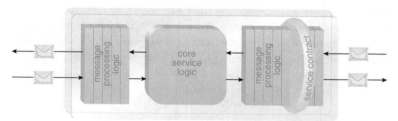

Web service transitioning through service consumer and provider roles

Figure 3.7

Three variations of a single Web service showing the different physical parts of its
architecture that come into play, depending on the role it assumes at runtime.

NOTE

Coverage of Web services in relation to SOA is provided by the series'
titles *Web Service Contract Design and Versioning for SOA* and *Service-
Oriented Architecture: Concepts, Technology, and Design*.

Services as REST Services

REST services (or RESTful services) are designed in compliance with the REST architectural style. A REST service architecture focuses on the resource as the key element of abstraction, with an emphasis on simplicity, scalability, and usability. REST services can be further shaped by the application of service-orientation principles.

Figure 3.8

A REST service, depicted similar to a Web service, except for the service contract symbol that indicates the service is accessed via a uniform contract.

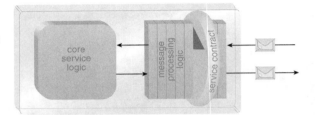

> **NOTE**
>
> How REST services can be designed in support of SOA and service-orientation is explored in the book *SOA with REST*, as part of the *Prentice Hall Service-Oriented Computing Series from Thomas Erl*. Note also that this book has been supplemented with new versioning content specific for REST services. This content can be found in Appendix F.

SOA Manifesto

Historically, the term "service-oriented architecture" (or "SOA") has been used so broadly by the media and within vendor marketing literature that it has almost become synonymous with service-oriented computing itself. *The SOA Manifesto* (published at www.soa-manifesto.org) is a formal declaration authored by a diverse working group comprised of industry thought leaders during the 2nd International SOA Symposium in Rotterdam in 2009. This document establishes, at a high level, a clear separation of service-oriented architecture and service-orientation in order to address the ambiguity that had been causing confusion in relation to the meaning of the term "SOA."

The Annotated SOA Manifesto is published at www.soa-manifesto.com and in Appendix E of this book. This version of the SOA Manifesto is recommended reading as it elaborates on statements made in the original SOA Manifesto.

Cloud Computing

Cloud computing is a specialized form of distributed computing that introduces utilization models for remotely provisioning scalable and measured IT resources. The primary benefits associated with cloud computing are:

- *Reduced Investment and Proportional Costs* – Cloud consumers that use cloud-based IT resources can generally lease them with a pay-for-use model, which allows them to pay a usage fee for only the amount of the IT resource actually used, resulting in directly proportional costs. This gives an organization access to IT resources without having to purchase its own, resulting in reduced investment requirements. By lowering required investments and incurring costs that are proportional to their needs, cloud consumers can scale their IT enterprise effectively and pro-actively.

- *Increased Scalability* – IT resources can be flexibly acquired from a cloud provider, almost instantaneously and at a wide variety of usage levels. By scaling with cloud-based IT resources, cloud consumers can leverage this flexibility to increase their responsiveness to planned and unforeseen changes.

- *Increased Availability and Reliability* – Cloud providers generally offer resilient IT resources for which they are able to guarantee high levels of availability. Cloud environments can be based on a modular architecture that provides extensive failover support to further increase reliability. Cloud consumers that lease access to cloud-based IT resources can therefore benefit from increased availability and reliability.

When appropriate, these benefits can help realize the strategic goals of service-oriented computing by extending and enhancing service-oriented architectures and increasing the potential of realizing certain service-orientation principles.

IT Resources

An *IT resource* is a broad term to refer to any physical or virtual IT-related artifact (software or hardware). For example, a physical server, a virtual server, a database, and a service implementation are all forms of IT resources.

Even though a service is considered an IT resource, it is important to acknowledge that a service architecture will commonly encapsulate and connect to other IT resources. This distinction is especially important in cloud-based environments, where a cloud service is classified as a remotely accessible IT resource that may encompass and depend on various additional cloud-based IT resources that are only accessible from within the cloud.

NOTE
The Cloud Resource Administrator role described in Chapter 5 can be involved with cloud service administration and the administration of internal cloud-based IT resources.

Cloud

A *cloud* is a distinct IT environment designed for the purpose of remotely provisioning scalable and measured IT resources. In order to remotely provision scalable and measured IT resources in an effective manner, an IT environment requires a specific set of characteristics. These characteristics need to exist to a meaningful extent for the IT environment to be considered an effective cloud.

- *On-Demand Usage* – This characteristic allows for the usage of self-provisioned IT resources to be automated so that no further human involvement by the provider or consumer of these resources is required.

- *Ubiquitous Access* – This is the ability for a cloud-based IT resource to be widely accessible.

- *Multitenancy* – Multitenancy is the characteristic of a software program that enables an instance of the program to serve different consumers (tenants), each of which is isolated from the other.

- *Elasticity* – This is the ability of a cloud to enable its consumers to scale cloud-based IT resources up or down, as required.

- *Measured Usage* – This represents the ability of a cloud platform to keep track of the usage of its IT resources by its consumers.

- *Resilient Computing* – This characteristic represents a form of failover that distributes redundant implementations of IT resources across physical locations.

Services that reside in cloud environments are referred to as *cloud services* or *cloud-based services*. Services are one form of IT resource hosted by clouds.

Figure 3.9
The symbol used to represent a
cloud environment.

On-Premise

The term *on-premise* is used as a qualifier to indicate that a service or IT resource (or some other artifact) resides within an internal IT enterprise environment, as opposed to a cloud-based environment. The use of "on-premise" within this book is primarily associated with discussions pertaining to cloud computing issues. By default, coverage of services, architectures, infrastructure, and other types of implementations are assumed to be on-premise, unless otherwise qualified.

Figure 3.10
A service shown on-premise, within an IT enterprise (left) and a cloud-based service, deployed within a cloud (right).

Cloud Deployment Models

A *cloud deployment model* represents a specific type of cloud environment, primarily distinguished by ownership and size.

There are four common deployment models:

- *Public Cloud* – A public cloud is a publically accessible cloud environment owned by a third-party cloud provider.

- *Community Cloud* – A community cloud is similar to a public cloud except that its access is limited to a specific community of cloud consumers.

- *Private Cloud* – A private cloud is owned by a single organization.

- *Hybrid Cloud* – A hybrid cloud is a cloud environment of two or more different cloud deployment models.

Variations of these models can also exist.

Cloud Consumers and Cloud Providers

The organization that uses cloud services is referred to as the *cloud consumer*, whereas the organization that owns and offers cloud IT resources and services is the *cloud provider*. With private clouds the cloud consumer and cloud provider can be the same organization, in which case these roles are assumed by departments or groups within the organization.

Cloud Delivery Models

A *cloud delivery model* represents a specific combination of IT resources offered by a cloud provider.

Three common delivery models are used:

- *Infrastructure-as-a-Service (IaaS)* – The IaaS delivery model provides a self-contained IT environment comprised of infrastructure-centric IT resources.

- *Platform-as-a-Service (PaaS)* – The PaaS delivery model provides a pre-defined cloud environment with already deployed and configured IT resources suitable for the development and deployment of applications.

- *Software-as-a-Service (SaaS)* – The SaaS delivery model generally represents a product that exists as a shared cloud service offered by a cloud provider to cloud consumers.

Variations of these models can also exist.

Service Models

A *service model* is a classification used to indicate that a service belongs to one of several predefined types based on the nature of the logic it encapsulates, the reuse potential of this logic, and how the service may relate to domains within its enterprise.

The following three service models are common to most enterprise environments and therefore common to most SOA projects:

- *Task Service* – A service with a non-agnostic functional context that generally corresponds to single-purpose, parent business process logic. A task service will usually encapsulate the composition logic required to compose several other services in order to complete its task.

- *Entity Service* – A reusable service with an agnostic functional context associated with one or more related business entities (such as invoice, customer, claim, etc.). For example, a Purchase Order service has a functional context associated with the processing of purchase order-related data and logic.

- *Utility Service* – Also a reusable service with an agnostic functional context, but this type of service is intentionally not derived from business analysis specifications and models. It encapsulates low-level technology-centric functions, such as notification, logging, and security processing.

NOTE

Due to their reuse potential, both entity and utility services are considered *shared services* (also referred to as *enterprise resources*). Most of the governance topics covered in this book pertain to the design-time and runtime regulation of shared services.

Service models play an important role during service-oriented analysis and service-oriented design phases. Although the just listed service models are well established, it is not uncommon for an organization to create its own service models. Often these new classifications tend to be derived from one of the aforementioned fundamental service models.

Agnostic Logic and Non-Agnostic Logic

The term "agnostic" originated from Greek and means "without knowledge." Therefore, logic that is sufficiently generic so that it is not specific to (has no knowledge of) a particular parent task is classified as *agnostic* logic. Because knowledge specific to single purpose tasks is intentionally omitted, agnostic logic is considered multi-purpose. On the flipside, logic that is specific to (contains knowledge of) a single-purpose task is labeled as *non-agnostic* logic.

Another way of thinking about agnostic and non-agnostic logic is to focus on the extent to which the logic can be repurposed. Because agnostic logic is expected to be multi-purpose, it has reuse potential and therefore forms the basis of shared service logic. Once reusable, this logic is truly multi-purpose in that it, as a single software program (or service), can be used to automate multiple business processes.

Non-agnostic logic does not have these types of expectations. It is deliberately designed as a single-purpose software program (or service) and therefore has different characteristics and requirements.

Service Composition

A *service composition* is an aggregate of services collectively composed to automate a particular task or business process. To qualify as a composition, at least two participating services plus one composition initiator need to be present. Otherwise, the service interaction only represents a point-to-point exchange.

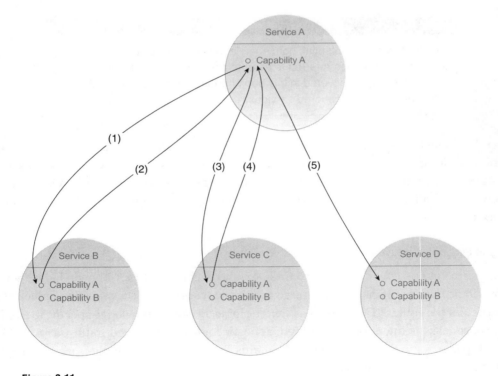

Figure 3.11

A service composition comprised of four services. The arrows indicate a sequence of modeled message exchanges. Note arrow #5 representing a one-way, asynchronous data delivery from Service A to Service D.

Service compositions can be classified into primitive and complex variations. In early service-oriented solutions, simple logic was generally implemented via point-to-point exchanges or primitive compositions. As the surrounding technology matured, complex compositions became more common.

Much of the service-orientation design paradigm revolves around preparing services for effective participation in numerous complex compositions—so much so that the Service Composability design principle exists, dedicated solely to ensuring that services are designed in support of repeatable composition.

Service Inventory

A *service inventory* is an independently standardized and governed collection of complementary services within a boundary that represents an enterprise or a meaningful segment of an enterprise. When an organization has multiple service inventories, this term is further qualified as *domain service inventory*.

Service inventories are typically created through top-down delivery processes that result in the definition of *service inventory blueprints*. The subsequent application of service-orientation design principles and custom design standards throughout a service inventory is of paramount importance so as to establish a high degree of native inter-service interoperability. This supports the repeated creation of effective service compositions in response to new and changing business requirements.

Service Portfolio

Service portfolio (also commonly referred to as a "service catalog") is a separate term used to represent a set of the services within a given IT enterprise. The distinction between service inventory and service portfolio is important as these and related terms are used within different contexts, as follows:

- Service inventory represents a collection of implemented services that are independently owned and governed.

- The Service Inventory Analysis is a modeling process by which service candidates are defined for a new or existing service inventory.

- A service inventory blueprint is a technical specification that represents the result of having performed a service inventory analysis. Subsequent iterations of the service inventory analysis process can expand or further refine a service inventory blueprint.

- The term "service portfolio" has a less specific definition than service inventory in that it can represent all or a subset of the services within an IT enterprise.

- A service portfolio often exists as a high-level documentation of services used for planning purposes.

- A service portfolio most commonly encompasses one or multiple service inventories.

Service portfolio management is the practice of planning the definition, delivery, and evolution of collections of services.

Service Candidate

When conceptualizing services during the service-oriented analysis and service modeling processes, services are defined on a preliminary basis and still subject to a great deal of change and refinement before they are handed over to the Service-Oriented Design project stage responsible for producing physical service contracts. The term *service candidate* is used to help distinguish a conceptualized service from an actual implemented service.

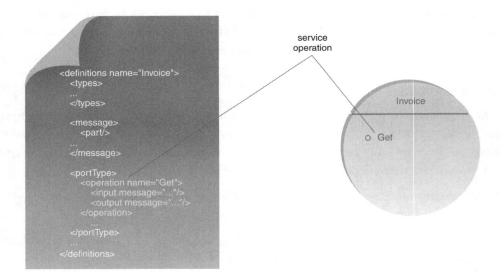

Figure 3.12
The Get operation (right) is first modeled and then forms the basis of the actual operation definition within a WSDL document (left).

Service Contract

A *service contract* is comprised of one or more published documents that express meta information about a service. The fundamental part of a service contract consists of the documents that express its technical interface. These form the technical service contract, which essentially establishes an API into the functionality offered by the service via its capabilities.

When services are implemented as Web services, the most common service description documents are the WSDL definition, XML Schema definition, and WS-Policy definition. A Web service generally has one WSDL definition, which can link to multiple XML Schema and policy definitions. When services are implemented as components, the technical service contract is comprised of a technology-specific API.

Services implemented as REST services are commonly accessed via a uniform contract, such as the one provided by HTTP. Service contracts are depicted differently depending on whether a uniform contract is involved.

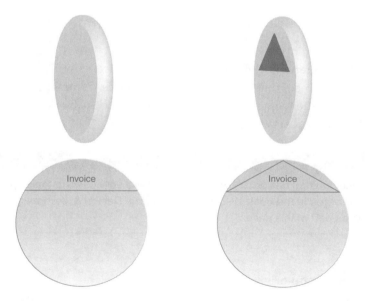

Figure 3.13

The standard symbol used to display a service contract (left) and one that is accessed via a uniform contract (right).

A service contract can be further comprised of human-readable documents, such as a Service Level Agreement (SLA) that describes additional quality-of-service features, behaviors, and limitations. Several SLA-related requirements can also be expressed in machine-readable format as policies.

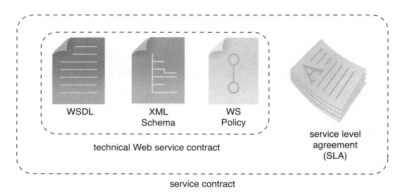

Figure 3.14
The common documents that comprise the technical Web service contract, plus a human-readable SLA.

Within service-orientation, the design of the service contract is of paramount importance—so much so, that the Standardized Service Contract (475) design principle and the aforementioned service-oriented design process are dedicated solely to the standardized creation of service contracts.

> **NOTE**
>
> Service contract design and versioning for Web services is a topic specifically covered in the book *Web Service Contract Design & Versioning for SOA*, as part of this series.

Service-Related Granularity

When designing services, there are different granularity levels that need to be taken into consideration, as follows:

- *Service Granularity* – This level of granularity represents the functional scope of a service. For example, fine-grained service granularity indicates that there is little logic associated with the service's overall functional context.

- *Capability Granularity* – The functional scope of individual service capabilities (operations) is represented by this granularity level. For example, a GetDetail capability will tend to have a finer measure of granularity than a GetDocument capability.

- *Constraint Granularity* – The level of validation logic detail is measured by constraint granularity. The more coarse constraint granularity is, the less constraints (or smaller the amount of validation logic) a given capability will have.

- *Data Granularity* – This granularity level represents the quantity of data processed. For example, from a Web service contract perspective, this corresponds to input, output, and fault messages. A fine level of data granularity is equivalent to a small amount of data.

Because the level of service granularity determines the functional scope of a service, it is usually determined during analysis and modeling stages that precede service contract design. Once a service's functional scope has been established, the other granularity types come into play and affect both the modeling and physical design of a service contract.

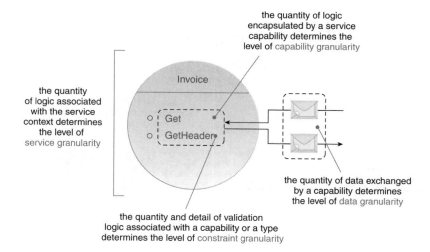

Figure 3.15

The four granularity levels that represent various characteristics of a service and its contract. Note that these granularity types are, for the most part, independent of each other.

SOA Design Patterns

A design pattern is a proven solution to a common design problem. The *SOA design pattern catalog* provides a collection of design patterns that provide practices and techniques for solving common problems in support of service-orientation.

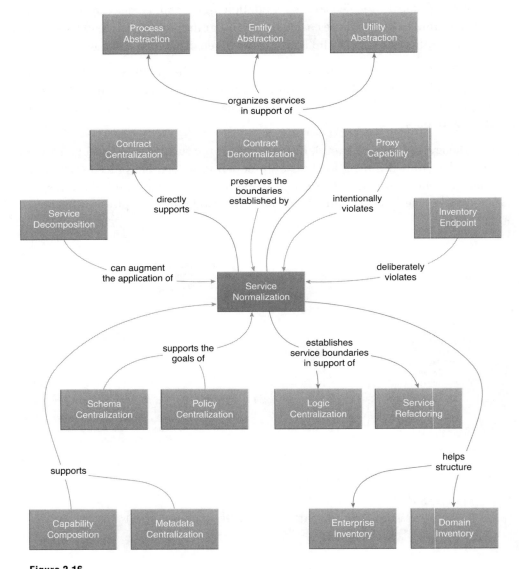

Figure 3.16

SOA design patterns form a design pattern language that allows patterns to be applied in different combinations and in different sequences in order to solve various complex design problems.

SOA design patterns do not only pertain to the actual design of services and related environments. Many patterns represent solutions that are realized by the application of standards and technologies highly relevant to SOA governance. Throughout this book you will notice references to patterns as a supplemental resource that further formalizes a given solution. In some cases, an SOA design pattern is even the primary basis of an SOA governance precept.

NOTE

Profiles of SOA design patterns are provided in Appendix D of this book and are also published online at www.soapatterns.org.

3.2 Further Reading

- Explanations of the service-oriented computing goals and benefits are available at www.whatissoa.com and in Chapter 3 of *SOA Principles of Service Design*.

- Explanations and definitions of concepts and terminology pertaining to cloud computing are available at www.whatiscloud.com.

- For information about SOA types and the distinct characteristics of the service-oriented technology architecture, see Chapter 4 of *SOA Design Patterns*.

- Design principles are referenced throughout this book but represent a separate subject matter that is covered in *SOA Principles of Service Design*. Introductory coverage of service-orientation as a whole is also available at www.soaprinciples.com and all eight principle profile tables are provided in Appendix C of this book.

- For a comparison of service-orientation and object-orientation concepts and principles, see Chapter 14 in *SOA Principles of Service Design*.

- Numerous design patterns are referenced in the upcoming chapters. These patterns are part of a greater SOA design patterns catalog that was published in the book *SOA Design Patterns*. Pattern profiles are available online at the SOAPatterns. org community site, and pattern profile tables for design patterns referenced in this book are further provided in Appendix D.

- Definitions for the terms introduced in this chapter can also be found at www.soaglossary.com.

- Read the Annotated SOA Manifesto in Appendix E (also published at www.soa-manifesto.com) for a formal, high level description of SOA and service-orientation.

See www.soabooks.com for additional reading resources, and visit www.soaschool.com and www.cloudschool.com for additional educational resources.

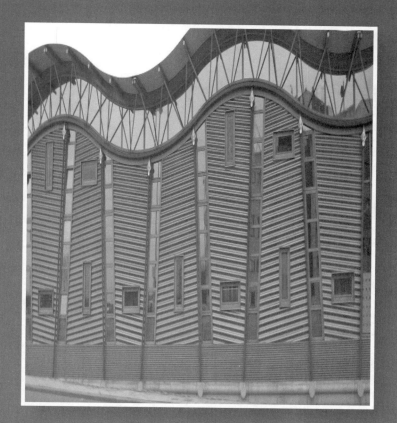

Chapter 4

SOA Planning Fundamentals

SOA PRINCIPLES & PATTERNS REFERENCED IN THIS CHAPTER

- Domain Inventory [520]
- Entity Abstraction [524]
- Process Abstraction [544]
- Service Layers [561]
- Utility Abstraction [573]

Governance, as with any other aspect of SOA adoption, begins with the planning stage. This chapter covers some general SOA planning considerations, all of which pertain to the definition of SOA governance strategies but are also themselves affected by the chosen governance approach. We begin with an overview of the foundations required for any SOA initiative, and then move on to describe common evolutionary stages and funding models.

4.1 The Four Pillars of Service-Orientation

As explained in Chapter 3, the attainment of the goals and benefits commonly associated with service-oriented computing and SOA require the application of the service-orientation paradigm. Service-orientation provides us with a well-defined method for shaping software programs into units of service-oriented logic that we can legitimately refer to as services. Each such service that we deliver, takes us a step closer to achieving the desired target state represented by these strategic goals and benefits.

Proven practices, patterns, principles, and technologies exist in support of service-orientation. However, because of the distinctly strategic nature of the target state that service-orientation aims to establish, there is a set of fundamental critical success factors that act as common pre-requisites for its successful adoption. These critical success factors are referred to as *pillars* because they collectively establish a sound and healthy foundation upon which to build, deploy, and govern services.

The four pillars of service-orientation are:

- *Teamwork* – Cross-project teams and cooperation are required.

- *Education* – Team members must communicate and cooperate based on common knowledge and understanding.

- *Discipline* – Team members must apply their common knowledge consistently.

- *Balanced Scope* – The extent to which the required levels of Teamwork, Education, and Discipline need to be realized is represented by a meaningful yet manageable scope.

The existence of these four pillars is considered essential to any SOA initiative. The absence of any one of these pillars to a significant extent introduces a major risk factor. If such an absence is identified in the early planning stages, it can warrant not proceeding with the project until it has been addressed—or the project's scope has been reduced.

Teamwork

Whereas traditional silo-based applications require cooperation among members of individual project teams, the delivery of services and service-oriented solutions requires cooperation across multiple project teams. The scope of the required teamwork is noticeably larger and can introduce new dynamics, new project roles, and the need to forge and maintain new relationships among  individuals and departments. Those on the overall SOA team need to trust and rely on each other; otherwise the team will fail.

Education

A key factor to realizing the reliability and trust required by SOA team members is to ensure that they use a common communications framework based on common vocabulary, definitions, concepts, methods, and a common understanding of the target state the team is collectively working to attain. To achieve a common understanding requires common education, not just in general topics pertaining to service-orientation, SOA, and service technologies, but also in specific  principles, patterns, and practices, as well as established standards, policies, and methodology specific to the organization.

Combining the pillars of teamwork and education establishes a foundation of knowledge and an understanding of how to use that knowledge among members of the SOA team. The resulting clarity eliminates many of the risks that have traditionally plagued SOA projects.

Discipline

A critical success factor for any SOA initiative is consistency in how knowledge and practices amongst a cooperative team are used and applied. To be successful as a whole, team members must therefore be disciplined in how they apply their knowledge and in how they carry out their respective roles. Required measures of discipline are commonly expressed in methodology, modeling, and design standards, as well as governance precepts. Even with the best intentions, an educated and cooperative team will fail without discipline.

Balanced Scope

So far we've established that we need:

- cooperative teams that have...

- a common understanding and education pertaining to industry and enterprise-specific knowledge areas and that...

- we need to consistently cooperate as a team, apply our understanding, and follow a common methodology and standards in a disciplined manner.

In some IT enterprises, especially those with a long history of building silo-based applications, achieving these qualities can be challenging. Cultural, political, and various other forms of organizational issues can arise to make it difficult to attain the necessary organizational changes required by these three pillars. How then can they be realistically achieved? It all comes down to defining a balanced scope of adoption.

The scope of adoption needs to be meaningfully cross-silo, while also realistically manageable. This requires the definition of a balanced scope of adoption of service-orientation.

NOTE

"The scope of SOA adoption can vary. Keep efforts manageable and within meaningful boundaries."

– SOA Manifesto

See Appendix E for the complete SOA Manifesto and the Annotated SOA Manifesto, which are also published at www.soa-manifesto.org and www.soa-manifesto.com, respectively.

Once a balanced scope of adoption has been defined, this scope determines the extent to which the other three pillars need to be established. Conversely, the extent to which you can realize the other three pillars will influence how you determine the scope (Figure 4.1).

Common factors involved in determining a balanced scope include:

- cultural obstacles

- authority structures

- geography

- business domain alignment

- available stakeholder support and funding

- available IT resources

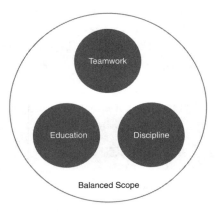

Figure 4.1

The Balanced Scope pillar encompasses and sets the scope at which the other three pillars are applied for a given adoption effort.

A single organization can choose one or more balanced adoption scopes (Figure 4.2). Having multiple scopes results in a domain-based approach to adoption. Each domain establishes a boundary for an inventory of services. Among domains, adoption of service-orientation and the delivery of services can occur independently. This does not result in application silos; it establishes meaningful service domains (also known as "continents of services") within the IT enterprise.

SOA PRINCIPLES & PATTERNS

The domain-based approach to the adoption of SOA and service-orientation originated with the Domain Inventory [520] pattern. However, it is important to acknowledge that logical domains within a domain service inventory can also be established by classifying services based on the nature of their respective functional contexts. This form of separation is relevant to service governance and is the basis of the Service Layers [561] pattern, as well as the related Utility Abstraction [573], Entity Abstraction [524], and Process Abstraction [544] patterns.

IT Enterprise

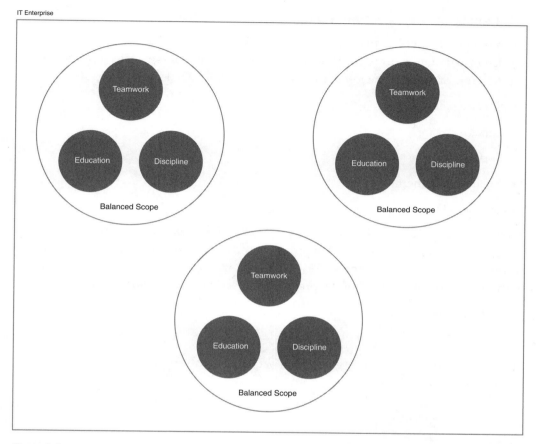

Figure 4.2

Multiple balanced scopes can exist within the same IT enterprise. Each represents a separate service inventory that is independently standardized, owned, and governed.

SUMMARY OF KEY POINTS

- Teamwork, education, and discipline represent foundational critical success factors for the successful adoption of service-orientation.

- Setting a meaningful and manageable scope of adoption establishes a boundary in which services are to be delivered and consequently determines the extent to which these three critical success factors need to be realized.

- Setting a balanced scope is a strategic planning decision and therefore itself a critical success factor.

4.2 Levels of Organizational Maturity

From the point at which an organization begins planning for the adoption of SOA and service-orientation up until the time it achieves its planned target state, it can transition through one or more of the following common evolutionary levels:

- Service Neutral
- Service Aware
- Service Capable
- Business Aligned
- Business Driven

Each of these levels represents a state of maturity of an organization on its way to carrying out a legitimate SOA adoption project based on the proper foundations. However, additional levels are worth noting for when organizations proceed with SOA initiatives in the absence of some or all of the previously described four pillars:

- Service Ineffectual
- Service Aggressive

Figure 4.3 displays how an organization will commonly transition through (positive and negative) maturity levels.

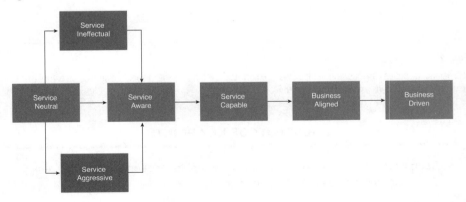

Figure 4.3
Common evolutionary levels of organizational maturity.

Service Neutral Level

This level indicates that there may be an awareness of SOA and service-orientation within the organization, but no meaningful extent of teamwork, education, or discipline has been established or yet identified. Every organization begins at the Service Neutral level, as it  represents the starting point in the evolutionary lifecycle. Whereas the Service Neutral level indicates an absence of maturity because the organization has not yet proceeded with an adoption effort, the Service Ineffectual and Service Aggressive levels represent an absence of maturity during the adoption effort. Figure 4.3 illustrates this by positioning this level at the beginning of the lifecycle. From this point, an organization can either move on to the Service Ineffectual or Service Aggressive levels, or it can proceed to the Service Aware level.

Service Aware Level

When reaching the Service Aware level, it has been confirmed that the four pillars have been established, that relevant business requirements and goals are defined, and that the overall necessary organizational foundation for the SOA initiative is in place. Within this context, the term "service aware" does not refer to an IT enterprise becoming aware of SOA and service-orientation; it refers to an early planning stage that validates that the necessary foundations (pillars) and business direction for a planned SOA initiative are identified and defined.

Service Capable Level

When the organization achieves the ability to deliver and govern services and service compositions in response to business automation requirements, it has reached the Service Capable level. An organization at this level will have avoided or overcome common adoption pitfalls and will therefore be positioned for a successful adoption. It will have a skilled, well trained team that has consistently delivered services within the required processes and regulations.

The principal risk at this level is that of stalling—remaining at a Service Capable level, without making further progress to move on to the Business Aligned level. This risk exists due to a potential sense of satisfaction with the current state of having services capable of composition.

Business Aligned Level

This level indicates that the organization has achieved meaningful alignment of (service-oriented) technology resources and current business automation requirements. In other words, the organization has successfully aligned services and service compositions with the current state of the business.

Attaining this state further implies that most or all of the services planned for a given service inventory have been delivered and are in operation. Therefore, the Business Aligned level represents a level of organizational maturity that has resulted from having established a relatively mature service inventory.

Business Driven Level

This evolutionary level represents a state where service-encapsulated technology resources are not just aligned with the current state of the business, but have proven themselves able to remain in alignment with how business requirements continue to change. This form of

evolutionary alignment is accomplished via the repeated or augmented composition of services. This level therefore represents the highest level of maturity for a service inventory as well as the highest level of success for the overall SOA adoption effort. The Business Driven level can last indefinitely as the organization continues to leverage the strategic benefits of its services.

> **NOTE**
>
> The attainment of this level is commonly associated with the successful utilization of an SOA governance vitality framework, as explained in Chapter 13.

Service Ineffectual Level

The Service Ineffectual level occurs when an organization descends into a technological backwater where the IT enterprise delivers services as silo-based or bottom-up automation solutions under the pretense that it is adopting SOA. Services delivered during this level are

generally not actual units of service-oriented logic. They are most likely single-purpose software programs labeled as services because they use one or more forms of service technology (such as technologies associated with Web services, REST service, and cloud platforms).

This level represents an IT initiative that, under the guise of "SOA," is tactically focused without much regard for service-orientation or the steps necessary to attain the strategic target state associated with SOA and service-oriented computing.

NOTE
So many IT projects have fallen victim to this pitfall that it has tarnished the perception of "SOA" in general, leading to the need for the SOA Manifesto to be declared in 2009.

Service Aggressive Level

When an organization is Service Aggressive, it is usually because IT's enthusiasm for SOA and service technology has led to a proliferation of services that the business doesn't want or need; in some cases, the business may not even be aware of their existence. The Service Aggressive level is different from the Service Ineffectual level in that there may be a sincere intention to adopt SOA and service-orientation in support of strategic goals. However, due to lack of teamwork or education or discipline or perhaps due to blatant incompetence, the SOA initiative fails to align its technology in support of the business. This misalignment therefore severely limits the usefulness and longevity of delivered services.

SUMMARY OF KEY POINTS

- There are common levels an organization can transition through when adopting SOA and service-orientation.

- The Service Neutral level is the typical starting point for an organization. From this level, it may transition to the Service Aware, Service Ineffectual, or Service Aggressive level.

- If an organization successfully transitions to the Service Aware level, it can move on to the Service Capable, Business Aligned, and Business Driven levels, each of which are supportive of achieving desired strategic goals.

- The Service Ineffectual and Service Aggressive levels are considered anti-patterns and inhibitors of successful SOA adoption.

4.3 SOA Funding Models

No IT project can succeed or proceed without funding. Traditional projects focused on the delivery of silo-based applications typically had straightforward funding models. Because of the single-purpose nature of the application logic, it was relatively simple to calculate the costs of delivery and the anticipated return on investment. In fact, this predictability factor is one of the strengths of silo-based delivery approaches.

With SOA projects, funding is more complex due to the strategic goals we aim to achieve and work toward with the delivery of each service. Funding becomes the concern of those delivering the services, those expecting to reuse the services, and those responsible for establishing an environment for multiple services. Furthermore, being able to show the returns on funding investments becomes another primary area of interest to those providing the funding and to those using the funds.

Therefore, establishing proper funding mechanisms and a means of proving consistent benefits and returns are critical to the success of any SOA governance program.

In this section, we explore two fundamental levels of SOA funding:

- *Platform Funding* – This level provides funds for the delivery of collections or inventories of services. Platform funding models are therefore generally focused on establishing the supporting infrastructure for a given service inventory.

- *Service Funding* – This level provides funds for the delivery of individual services. These services rely on an already-funded service inventory platform.

Furthermore, we will discuss how to capture and communicate the benefits and ROI of the platforms and services that have been funded. Once these models are in place and the necessary financial elements are identified, tangible and implied benefits can be calculated.

Platform (Service Inventory) Funding

This level of funding is focused on service inventory architecture and infrastructure. The intent is to establish an environment capable of hosting and enabling the runtime utilization of a collection of related services. One of the key factors here is that services need to be repeatedly leveraged as part of new and reconfigured service compositions.

Generally, the emphasis is on infrastructure components, such as service registries, ESBs, and various forms of service management frameworks. The important distinction is that this funding is not for the actual definition or creation of services.

There are three common platform funding models:

- *Project Funding Model* – This model identifies appropriate projects to acquire or to extend new or existing SOA platforms.

- *Central Funding Model* – With this model, the funding of the platform is provided centrally.

- *Usage Based Funding Model* – The initial platform is funded centrally but usage fees are charged for ongoing maintenance and support.

Let's look at each model individually:

Project Funding Model (Platform)

This model calls for attaching platform costs to individual service delivery projects (Figures 4.4 and 4.5). With this approach, projects are required to purchase and implement (or upgrade) any new infrastructure components necessary to automate their planned services. These implementations are limited to the pre-defined scope of the service inventory architecture. The project funding model enables a service inventory architecture to grow organically, based on individual project requirements.

Pros

- fits well with traditional, silo-based funding models

Cons

- high potential for conflicts with other projects that need to use platform resources or services funded by initial projects

- platform costs may inflate project budget

- project scope may not address service inventory-wide needs

- may result in unclear support and ownership requirements

- standardization issues may arise when different projects build upon a common platform (especially with cloud-based environments)

Although the simplicity of this model can be beneficial, it has several drawbacks. Despite this, there may be circumstances where a project funding model is the only option supported by stakeholders, primarily due to the familiarity of this model with traditional application development projects—or—simply due to a lack of sponsor support for the other funding models.

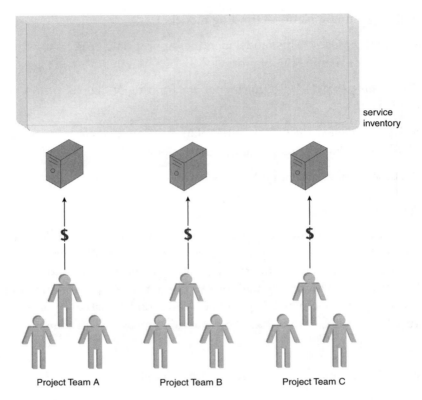

Figure 4.4

On-premise infrastructure resources for the service inventory is gradually (and often iteratively) assembled by individual service delivery projects. Shown are the physical servers being funded by individual project teams.

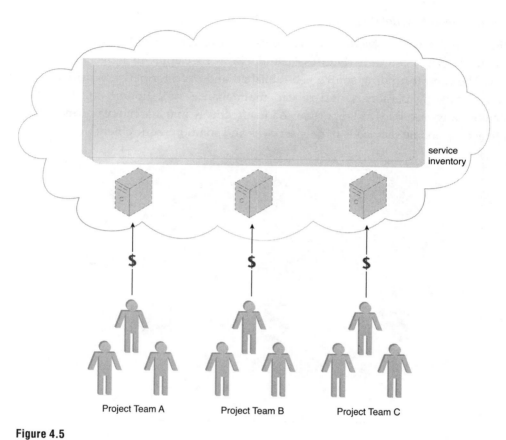

service inventory

Project Team A   Project Team B   Project Team C

Figure 4.5

Cloud-based infrastructure resources are leased, although up-front set-up costs and leasing terms can still require advance funding. Shown are virtual servers being leased by individual project teams.

Central Funding Model (Platform)

The Central Funding Model entails funding all of the SOA platform build-out and growth activities centrally (Figures 4.6 and 4.7), as they apply to a given service inventory. The central funding source is established and used for new acquisitions, expansion of existing platforms, and related maintenance and support efforts. This also includes any resources or labor required to effectively manage the platform and adjust it to accommodate the needs of new services and solution requirements.

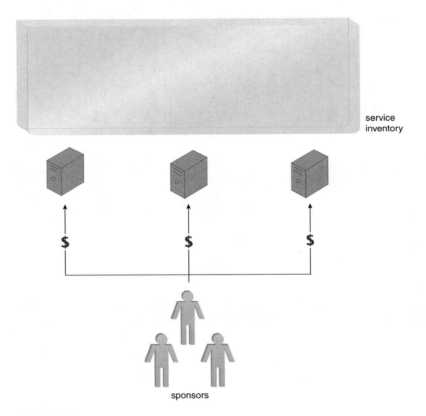

Figure 4.6

The SOA platform evolution is guided by the SOA roadmap under the Central Funding Model and the necessary on-site platform infrastructure is funded by one group of sponsors.

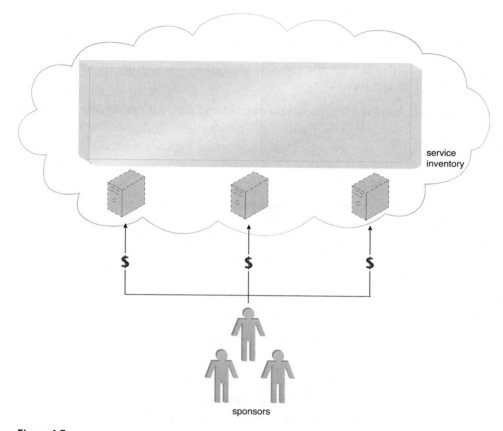

Figure 4.7
This model can also be applied to cloud-based infrastructure resources, whereby a central group of sponsors establishes a business relationship with a cloud provider and funds costs as they are incurred.

Central funding allows an organization to establish an independent roadmap for introducing and upgrading SOA platforms because cost, scaling, and availability issues are no longer relevant to individual projects.

Pros

- covers the platform needs of an entire service inventory with no additional funding sources required

- high visibility into platform expansion, scalability, and usage needs

- highly predictable support and ownership model

- funding occurs independent of individual project demands

Cons

- it can be difficult to secure consistent and ongoing enterprise level funding

- more accountability for spending and budgets may be required due to increased scope and responsibility

This model places increased emphasis on careful and diligent management in order to continually demonstrate how and where the funds went, while continuing to provide the necessary platform and infrastructure support for a growing service inventory.

Usage Based Funding Model (Platform)

This approach can be considered an extension of the Central Funding Model in that the platform builds out and expansion is still funded centrally; however, services and solutions that make use of platform resources are charged fees in order for investments to be recouped (Figures 4.8 and 4.9). The Usage Based Funding Model is especially commonplace when sharing resources via cloud environments. Depending on whether a public or private cloud is being used, usage fees may be charged by a central department within the organization or a third-party cloud provider.

Regardless of whether a cloud environment is being utilized, common types of fees can include the following:

- *Entry Fees* – These are standard one-time charges for new projects. These charges may be uniform across each service inventory platform or determined independently. Entry fees are typically calculated based on the general effort required to setup and support a new project on the platform, plus the prorated cost of the platform's portion being utilized.

- *Per Use Fees* – These charges are calculated using formulas based on unit costs and total fees for a predefined period of time. Total charges are based on the amount of units used within an invoiced period.

- *Supplemental Fees* – The more a service utilizes IT resources within the cloud, the more additional "supplemental" fees may be required to cover its build-out, maintenance, support, and growth.

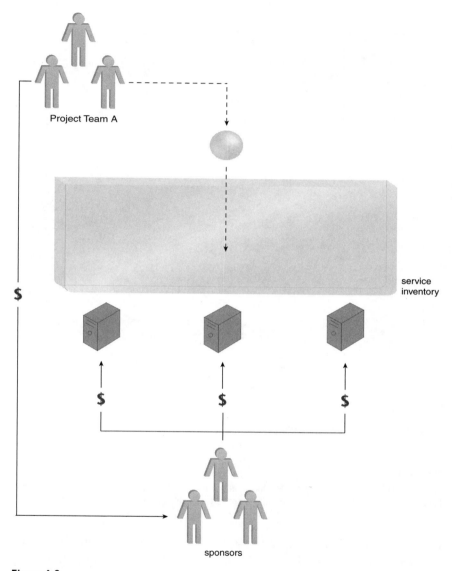

Figure 4.8
Under the Usage Based Funding Model, the SOA platform is still funded by a group of sponsors, but the on-site investment is recouped through usage fees.

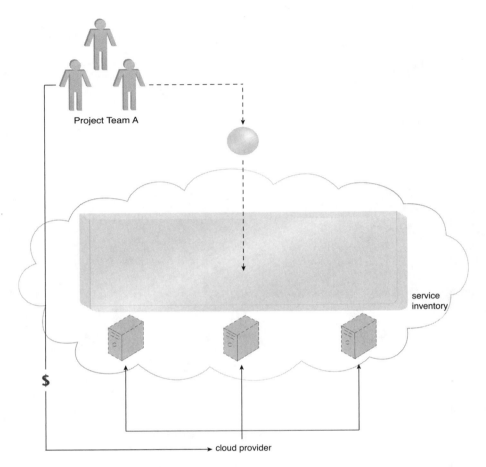

Figure 4.9
A variation of this model is comparable with the leasing arrangement of a public cloud provider, whereby the cloud provider simply charges the project team for infrastructure resources on a per-usage basis.

The following pros and cons apply to all forms of usage fees. Note that the pros and cons listed under the Central Funding Model generally also apply to the Usage Based Funding Model.

Pros

- can rapidly recoup the investment made in the platform

- charges are proportional to platform usage

- return on investment can be more easily demonstrated

Cons

- efficient and trusted chargeback mechanisms needed to monitor and bill for usage
- recovery of funds requires new billing processes
- improperly priced usage charges can deter projects from using platform resources

Service Funding

Agnostic services are created with the expectation that they will be reused and will provide repeated return on the investment originally required for their delivery. Because they are positioned as shared services, they are not dedicated to any one project. Instead, they are to be used to automate different business processes for which different projects build different solutions. Therefore, the funding of these reusable services requires special attention.

There are several different funding models that can be utilized:

- *Project Funding Model* – Individual projects build new or extend shared existing services.

- *Central Funding Model* – The funding of shared services is provided centrally.

- *Usage Based Funding Model* – The initial delivery of shared services is funded centrally but usage fees are subsequently charged.

- *Hybrid Funding Model* – A combination of project and central funding.

Let's look at each model individually:

Project Funding Model (Service)

With this model, a project responsible for delivering a solution for the automation of a specific business process is required to identify and build reusable services (Figure 4.10). Although it may seem a simple and familiar approach for organizations accustomed to silo-based application delivery, this model places the burden of creating (and possibly maintaining) services that may be used throughout the enterprise upon a single project. The project may be given additional funding, but it can be difficult for project team members, for whom the priority is the automation of a particular business process, to ensure that shared services are designed as truly reusable and re-composable enterprise resources.

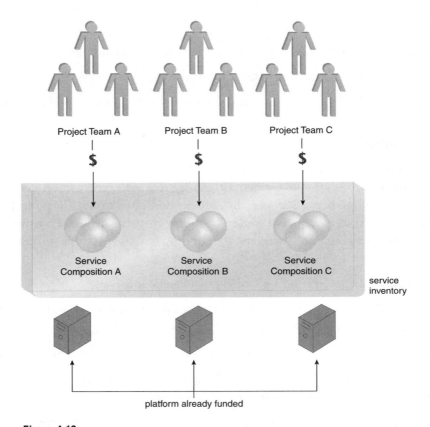

Figure 4.10
The service inventory grows based on project demand under the Project Funding Model.
(The same funding mechanism applies if services are deployed in a cloud.)

Pros

- more compatible with familiar silo-based delivery project models
- increased efficiency in the delivery of reusable services

Cons

- high risk of producing low-quality reusable services
- unclear support and ownership model
- can be difficult to measure the success of the project

Central Funding Model (Service)

Within the Central Funding Model the funding for building and maintaining shared and reusable services within the same service inventory comes from a sole pool of funds (Figure 4.11). As a result, individual project budgets are only impacted when:

- a new reusable service needs to be built (or an existing reusable service needs to be extended) and the project needs to wait for the central department to perform the development effort

- an existing reusable service needs to be used and there is cost and effort associated with incorporating it into the new solution

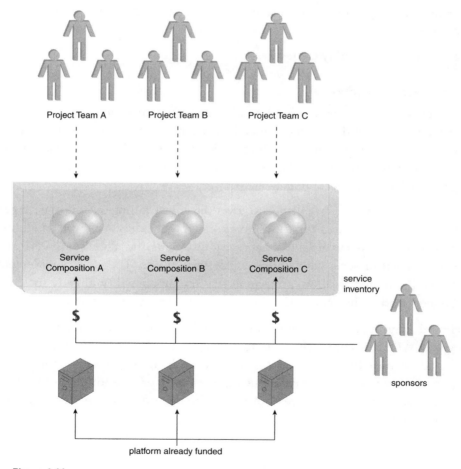

Figure 4.11

Under the Central Funding Model, the service inventory grows based on project demand but is funded by a central group of sponsors. (The same funding mechanism applies if services are deployed in a cloud.)

This model is common with organizations that have also chosen the Central Funding Model for platform funding purposes. In this case, the source of both forms of funding is likely the same.

Pros

- establishes a clear support and ownership model
- can help accelerate service reuse
- simplifies service governance

Cons

- can increase opportunity for wasteful spending or "gold-plating" of reusable services
- can introduce scalability challenges

Hybrid Funding Model (Service)

This model is based on a mixed funding framework where some funding comes from project budgets, while the rest is supplied by a central source. In other words, it's a hybrid of the Project and Central Funding Models (Figure 4.12). The intent is to increase the ability to deliver truly reusable services based on project demand without over-taxing the individual project budgets.

A central fund needs to be established to cover the efforts falling outside of each project scope. Since shared services typically incorporate other projects as well as additional enterprise requirements in order to meet reusability goals, the actual cost ends up being higher than what projects have budgeted for their needs. Therefore, supplementary funding is distributed to allow projects to pay for functionality already included in their budgets, and to then cover the additional costs through a central fund.

The Hybrid Funding Model attempts to balance between project demands and enterprise goals. With this approach, projects no longer have to be concerned about additional funds required to make services truly reusable, injecting additional enterprise requirements not relevant to their immediate solution, or accepting work from other teams. The central funds take care of these requirements and who performs the actual work also becomes largely irrelevant.

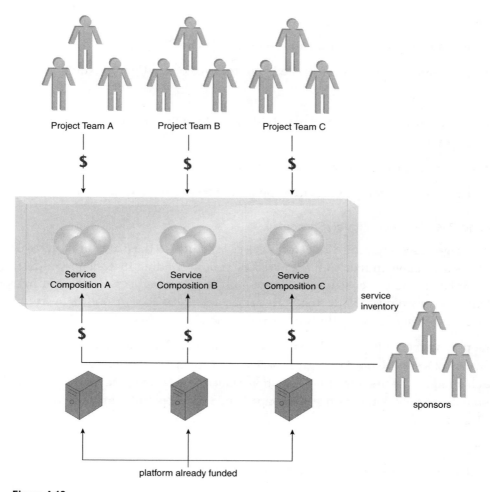

Figure 4.12

Under the Hybrid Funding Model, the service inventory grows based on project demand while the project funding is supplemented from the central SOA fund. (The same funding mechanism applies if services are deployed in a cloud.)

Pros

- can balance project (tactical) and enterprise (strategic) goals
- can eliminate problems associated with the Project and Central Funding models

Cons

- can be hard to establish and maintain throughout the growth of a service inventory
- creates opportunities for abuse by projects
- may introduce complex service support and ownership requirements

Usage Based Funding Model (Service)

The Usage Based Funding Model for services is similar to the platform funding model of the same name, in that both are based on central funding that then requires usage fees to be charged to consumers (Figure 4.13). Usage-based services hosted in cloud platforms are comparable to the Software-as-a-Service (SaaS) cloud delivery model, especially when offered by third-party public cloud providers (Figure 4.14).

The pricing model is generally based on a system of charging nominal fees for each instance of a service used by a given service consumer. Furthermore, an entry fee may be charged for the first time a new solution requests access to the service. Over time, the initial investment of the service is recouped and then, hopefully, far succeeded with the collected funds.

Pros

- defines a clear system for investment recovery
- eliminates the need for additional forms of non-project funding
- stream of funds help empower Service Custodians to evolve and improve reusable services

Cons

- depends on the usage of billing mechanisms
- can be difficult to set appropriate fee structures that accommodate and are fair to all potential service consumers

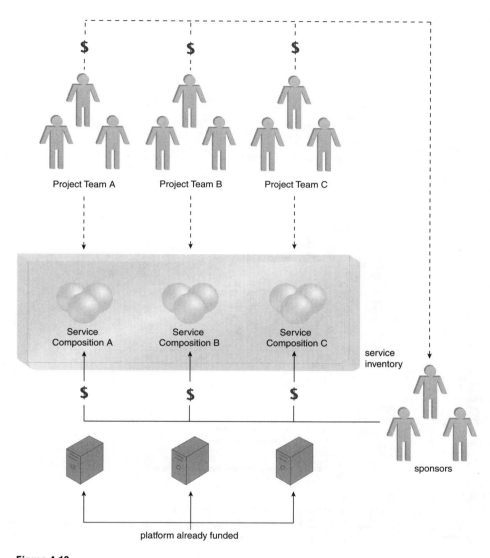

Figure 4.13

Under the Usage Based Funding Model, the sponsors that centrally fund the service delivery charge project teams for the usage of the services.

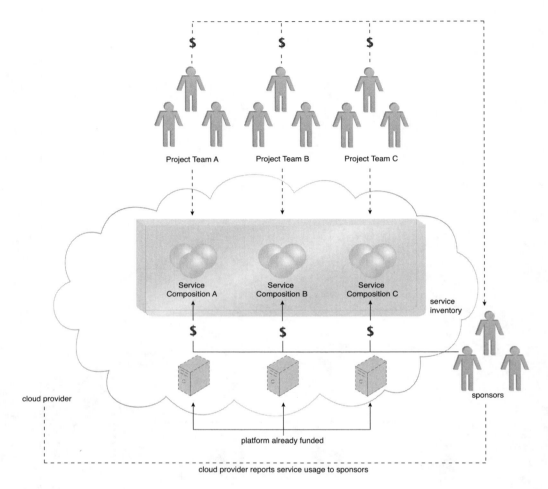

Figure 4.14

When the Central Funding Model is applied to a cloud-based service inventory, the sponsors can still fund the service delivery, but they can receive actual usage costs to bill the project teams via pay-for-use monitoring and reporting from the cloud provider.

SUMMARY OF KEY POINTS

- Funding is generally planned on two levels: platform (service inventory) and service.

- Project-specific funding models can be easier to implement but can result in problems that inhibit successful SOA adoption.

- Central funding models are more conducive to achieving SOA goals, but can be more challenging to establish (especially in organizations unaccustomed to shared funding and reusable resources).

- Other funding models can exist, some of which are comprised of a combination of common models.

Chapter 5

SOA Project Fundamentals

This book does not comprehensively define service project lifecycle stages or organizational roles associated with SOA projects. These areas, for the most part, have already been well-documented in previous titles in this book series. As an introductory resource, this chapter provides a set of sections comprised of summarized content from the following books and courses, along with new content introduced in support of upcoming chapters:

- *Service-Oriented Architecture: Concepts, Technology, and Design* – Contains content about SOA project delivery processes and roles.

- *SOA Principles of Service Design* – Contains additional content about SOA project roles, as well as the description of service profiles.

- *Web Service Contract Design and Versioning for SOA* – Contains detailed content about service contract versioning.

- *Module 4: SOA Project Delivery & Methodology* – Contains definitions for project stages and roles in relation to different methodologies (from the *SOA Certified Professional* curriculum).

- *Module 1: Cloud Computing Fundamentals* – Contains definitions for organizational roles and concepts specific to cloud computing (from the *Cloud Certified Professional* curriculum).

If you are new to service project lifecycle stages, organizational roles, and the use of service profiles, then it is recommended that you study the upcoming sections as these topics will be referenced throughout upcoming chapters.

NOTE
Several of the upcoming sections and sub-sections contain figures that do not have corresponding inline text references. This is intentional so as to improve the flow of content. The figures in question are displayed in close proximity to their sections, making the association evident.

5.1 Project and Lifecycle Stages

The following represent common and primary stages (or phases) related to SOA projects and the overall service lifecycle:

- SOA Adoption Planning

- Service Inventory Analysis

- Service-Oriented Analysis (Service Modeling)

- Service-Oriented Design (Service Contract)

- Service Logic Design

- Service Development

- Service Testing

- Service Deployment and Maintenance

- Service Usage and Monitoring

- Service Discovery

- Service Versioning and Retirement

Although Figure 5.1 displays stages sequentially, how and when each stage is carried out depends on the methodology being used. Different methodologies can be considered, depending on the nature and scope of the overall SOA project, the size and extent of standardization of the service inventory for which services are being delivered, and the

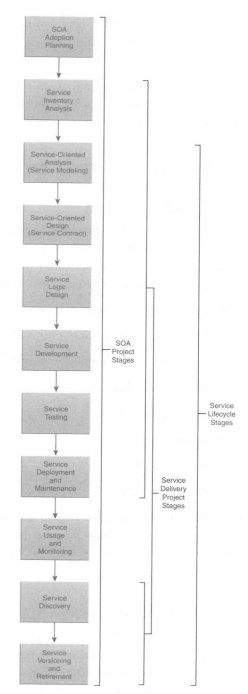

Figure 5.1

Common stages associated with SOA projects. Note the distinction between SOA project stages, service delivery project stages, and service lifecycle stages. These terms are used in subsequent chapters when referring to the overall adoption project, the delivery of individual services, and service-specific lifecycle issues, respectively.

manner in which tactical (short-term) requirements are being prioritized in relation to strategic (long-term) requirements.

A fundamental characteristic of SOA projects is that they tend to emphasize the need for some meaningful extent of strategic target state that the delivery of each service is intended to support. In order to realize this, some level of increased up-front analysis effort is generally necessary. Therefore, a primary way in which SOA project delivery methodologies differ is in how they position and prioritize analysis-related phases.

The upcoming sections briefly describe all stages:

SOA Adoption Planning

It is during this initial stage that foundational planning decisions are made. These decisions will shape the entire project, which is why this is considered a critical stage that may require separately allocated funding and time in order to carry out the studies required to assess and determine a range of factors, including:

- scope of planned service inventory and the ultimate target state
- milestones representing intermediate target states
- timeline for the completion of milestones and the overall adoption effort
- available funding and suitable funding model
- governance system
- management system
- methodology
- risk assessment

Additionally, prerequisite requirements need to be defined in order to establish criteria used to determine the overall viability of the SOA adoption. The basis of these requirements typically originates with the four pillars of service-orientation described earlier in Chapter 4.

Service Inventory Analysis

As explained in Chapter 3, a service inventory represents a collection of independently standardized, owned, and governed services. The scope of a service inventory is expected to be meaningfully "cross-silo," which generally implies that it encompasses multiple business processes or operational areas within an organization.

This stage is dedicated to conceptually defining the service inventory so that individual service candidates can be identified and assigned appropriate functional contexts in relation to each other. This ensures that services (within the service inventory boundary) are normalized in that they don't overlap. As a result, service reuse is maximized and the separation of concerns is cleanly carried out. A primary deliverable produced during this stage is the service inventory blueprint.

The scope of the initiative and the size of the target service inventory tend to determine the amount of up-front effort required to create a complete service inventory blueprint. More up-front analysis results in a better defined conceptual blueprint, which is intended to lead to the creation of a better quality inventory of services. Less up-front analysis leads to partial or less well-defined service inventory blueprints.

The Service Inventory Analysis stage is commonly carried out iteratively as part of the Service Inventory Analysis cycle (Figure 5.2). This is comprised of an iterative cycle during which the service inventory blueprint is incrementally defined as a result of repeated iterations of steps that include the Service-Oriented Analysis.

Figure 5.2

The Service Inventory Analysis cycle.

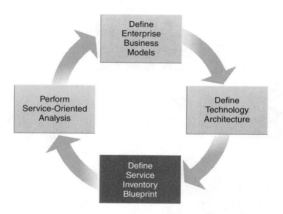

> ### NOTE
>
> The scope of the Service Inventory Analysis stage and the resulting service inventory blueprint directly relates to the Balanced Scope consideration explained in Chapter 4 as part of the section *The Four Pillars of Service-Orientation*.
>
> The enterprise business models referred to in the *Define Enterprise Business Models* step of the Service Inventory Analysis cycle relate to a number of the artifacts (and associated precepts and processes) covered in Chapter 12.

Service-Oriented Analysis (Service Modeling)

Service-Oriented Analysis represents one of the early stages in an SOA initiative and the first phase in the service delivery cycle. It is a process that begins with preparatory information gathering steps that are completed in support of a service modeling sub-process that results in the creation of conceptual service candidates, service capability candidates, and service composition candidates (Figures 5.3 and 5.4).

The Service-Oriented Analysis process is commonly carried out iteratively, once for each business process. Typically, the delivery of a service inventory determines a scope that represents a meaningful domain of the enterprise, or the enterprise as a whole. All iterations of a Service-Oriented Analysis then pertain to that scope, with each iteration contributing to the service inventory blueprint.

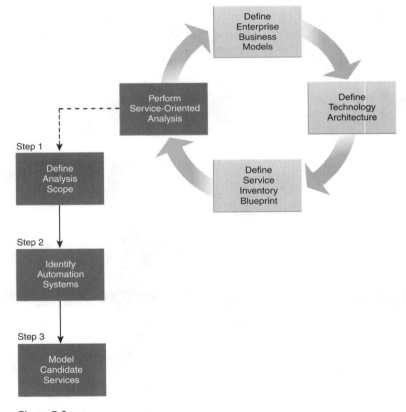

Figure 5.3
A generic Service-Oriented Analysis process that can be further customized. The first two steps essentially collect information in preparation for a detailed service modeling sub-process (Step 3).

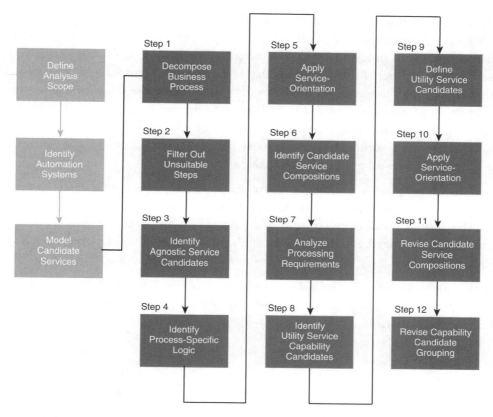

Figure 5.4

A generic service modeling process comprised of steps that raise key service definition considerations.

A key success factor of the Service-Oriented Analysis process is the hands-on collaboration of both Business Analysts and Technology Architects. The former group is especially involved in the definition of service candidates with a business-centric functional context because they best understand the business logic used as input for the analysis.

Service-Oriented Design (Service Contract)

The Service-Oriented Design phase represents a service delivery lifecycle stage dedicated to producing service contracts in support of the well-established "contract-first" approach to software development.

The typical starting point for the Service-Oriented Design process is a service candidate that was produced as a result of completing all required iterations of the Service-Oriented Analysis process (Figure 5.5). Service-Oriented Design subjects this service candidate to additional considerations that shape it into a technical service contract in alignment with other service contracts being produced for the same service inventory. Different approaches are used during this stage for the design of REST services, as these types of services share a common universal contract. For example, the design of media types, the determination of allowable HTTP method usage, and the definition of resource identifiers all require attention during this stage.

As a precursor to the Service Logic Design stage, Service-Oriented Design is comprised of a process that steps Service Architects through a series of considerations to ensure that the service contract being produced fulfills business requirements while representing a normalized functional context that further adheres to service-orientation principles.

Part of this process further includes the authoring of the SLA, which may be especially of significance for cloud-based services being offered to a broader consumer base via the SaaS cloud delivery model.

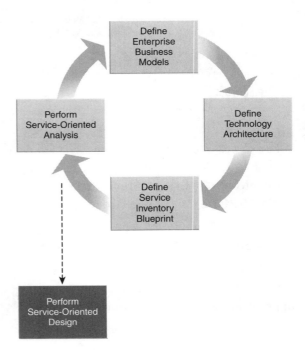

Figure 5.5

When a given service is deemed to have received sufficient analysis effort, it is subjected to the Service-Oriented Design process that produces a physical service contract.

Service Logic Design

By preceding the design of service logic with the Service-Oriented Design process, the service contract is established and finalized prior to the underlying service architecture and the logic that will be responsible for carrying out the functionality expressed in the service contract. This deliberate sequence of project stages is in support of the Standardized Service Contract (475) principle, which states that service contracts should be standardized in relation to each other within a given service inventory boundary.

The design of service logic and the service architecture is then further influenced by several service-orientation design principles and also whether or not the service will be deployed in a cloud environment (which can impact aspects of the service architecture design, especially when having to accommodate proprietary characteristics imposed by cloud providers).

Service Development

After all design specifications have been completed, the actual programming of the service can begin. Because the service architecture will already have been well-defined as a result of the previous stages and the involvement of custom design standards, service developers will generally have clear direction as to how to build the various parts of the service architecture.

For organizations employing the PaaS cloud delivery model, the service development platform itself may be offered by a ready-made environment hosted by virtual servers and geared toward the development and maintenance of cloud-based services and solutions.

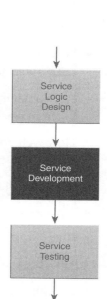

Service Testing

Services need to undergo the same types of testing and quality assurance cycles as traditional custom-developed applications. However, in addition, there are new requirements that introduce the need for additional testing methods and effort. For example, to support the realization of the Service Composability (486) principle, newly delivered services need to be tested individually and as part of service compositions. Agnostic services that provide reusable logic especially require rigorous testing to ensure that they are ready for repeated usage (both concurrently as part of the same service compositions and by different service compositions).

Below are examples of common Service Testing considerations:

- What types of service consumers could potentially access a service?

- Will the service need to be deployed in a cloud environment?

- What types of exception conditions and security threats could a service be potentially subjected to?

- Are there any security considerations specific to public clouds that need to be taken into account?

- How well do service contract documents communicate the functional scope and capabilities of a service?

- Are there SLA guarantees that need to be tested and verified?

- How easily can the service be composed and recomposed?

- Can the service be moved between on-premise and cloud environments?

- How easily can the service be discovered?

- Is compliance with any industry standards or profiles (such as WS-I profiles) required?

- If cloud-deployed, are there proprietary characteristics being imposed by the cloud provider that are not compatible with on-premise service characteristics?

- How effective are the validation rules within the service contract and within the service logic?

- Have all possible service activities and service compositions been mapped out?

- For service compositions that span on-premise and cloud environments, is the performance and behavior consistent and reliable?

Because services are positioned as IT assets with runtime usage requirements comparable to commercial software products, similar quality assurance processes are generally required.

Service Deployment and Maintenance

Service deployment represents the actual implementation of a service into the production environment. This stage can involve numerous inter-dependent parts of the underlying service architecture and supporting infrastructure, such as:

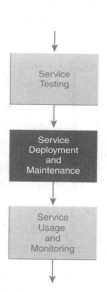

- distributed components

- service contract documents

- middleware (such as ESB and orchestration platforms)

- cloud service implementation considerations

- cloud-based IT resources encompassed by an on-premise or cloud-based service

- custom service agents and intermediaries

- system service agents and processors

- cloud-based service agents, such as automated scaling listeners and pay-for-use monitors

- on-demand and dynamic scaling and billing configurations

- proprietary runtime platform extensions

- administration and monitoring products

Service maintenance refers to upgrades or changes that need to be made to the deployment environment, either as part of the initial implementation or subsequently. It does not pertain to changes that need to be made to the service contract or the service logic, nor does it relate to any changes that need to be made as part of the environment that would constitute a new version of the service.

Service Usage and Monitoring

A service that has been deployed and is actively in use as part of one or more service compositions (or has been made available for usage by service consumers in general) is considered to be in the Service Usage and Monitoring stage. The on-going monitoring of the active service generates metrics that are necessary to measure service usage for evolutionary maintenance (such as scalability, reliability, etc.), as well as for business assessment reasons (such as when calculating cost of ownership and ROI).

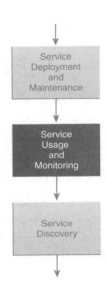

Special considerations regarding this stage apply to cloud-based services. For example:

- The cloud service may be hosted by virtualized IT resources that are further hosted by physical IT resources shared by multiple cloud consumer organizations.

- The cloud service usage may be monitored not only for performance, but also for billing purposes when its implementation is based on a per-usage fee license.

- The elasticity of the cloud service may be configured to allow for limited or unlimited scalability, thereby increasing the range of behavior (and changing its usage thresholds) when compared to an on-premise implementation.

This phase is often not documented separately, as it is not directly related to service delivery or projects responsible for delivering or altering services. It is noted in this book because while active and in use, a service can be subject to various governance considerations.

Service Discovery

In order to ensure the consistent reuse of agnostic services and service capabilities, project teams carry out a separate and explicitly defined Service Discovery process. The primary goal of this process is to identify one or more existing agnostic services (such as utility or entity services) within a given service inventory that can fulfill generic requirements for whatever business process the project team is tasked with automating.

The primary mechanism involved in performing Service Discovery is a service registry that contains relevant metadata about available and upcoming services, as well as pointers to the corresponding service contract documents, (which can include SLAs). The communications quality of the metadata and service contract documents play a significant role in how successful this process can be carried out. This is why one of the eight service-orientation principles (the Service Discoverability (484) principle) is dedicated solely to ensuring that information published about services is highly interpretable and discoverable.

Service Versioning and Retirement

After a service has been implemented and used in production environments, the need may arise to make changes to the existing service logic or to increase the functional scope of the service. In cases like this, a new version of the service logic and/or the service contract will likely need to be introduced. To ensure that the versioning of a service can be carried out with minimal impact and disruption to service consumers that have already formed dependencies on the service, a formal service versioning process needs to be in place.

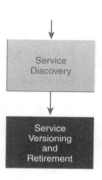

There are different versioning strategies, each of which introduces its own set of rules and priorities when it comes to managing the backwards and forwards compatibilities of services. Appendix F provides fundamental coverage of the three most common service versioning approaches (Loose, Flexible, Strict), along with examples for Web services and REST services.

The service versioning stage is associated with SOA governance because it can be a recurring and on-going part of the overall service lifecycle. As explained in Chapter 11, governance approaches that dictate how service versioning is to be carried out will have a significant influence on how a given service will evolve over time. Because this stage also encompasses the termination or retirement of a service, these influences can further factor into the service's overall lifespan.

SUMMARY OF KEY POINTS

- SOA delivery projects contain stages found in traditional IT projects, but also introduce new processes, such as Service Inventory Analysis and Service Discovery.

- One of the main considerations with SOA delivery projects is how much time is spent on the up-front analysis and modeling of services prior to their physical design and development.

5.2 Organizational Roles

To realize the distinct requirements that come with conceptualizing, designing, building, deploying, and evolving services and service-oriented solutions, a correspondingly distinct set of project roles and responsibilities exist.

Provided in this section are descriptions for the following set of roles:

- Service Analyst
- Service Architect
- Service Developer
- Service Custodian
- Cloud Service Owner
- Service Administrator
- Cloud Resource Administrator
- Schema Custodian
- Policy Custodian
- Service Registry Custodian
- Technical Communications Specialist
- Enterprise Architect
- Enterprise Design Standards Custodian (and Auditor)
- SOA Quality Assurance Specialist
- SOA Security Specialist
- SOA Governance Specialist

Note that this list represents *common* roles associated with SOA projects, as well as SOA-related roles within the overall IT enterprise. Variations of these project roles can exist, and additional roles can further be defined. It is also worth noting that a given role can be fulfilled by one or more individuals and that a single individual can be assigned one or more roles.

IMPORTANT

The organizational role/project stage associations displayed in Figure 5.6 are focused on overall project participation and therefore are <u>not</u> specific to governance activities. Governance-specific participation and involvement for each organizational role is described separately throughout Chapters 7 to 12 in this book.

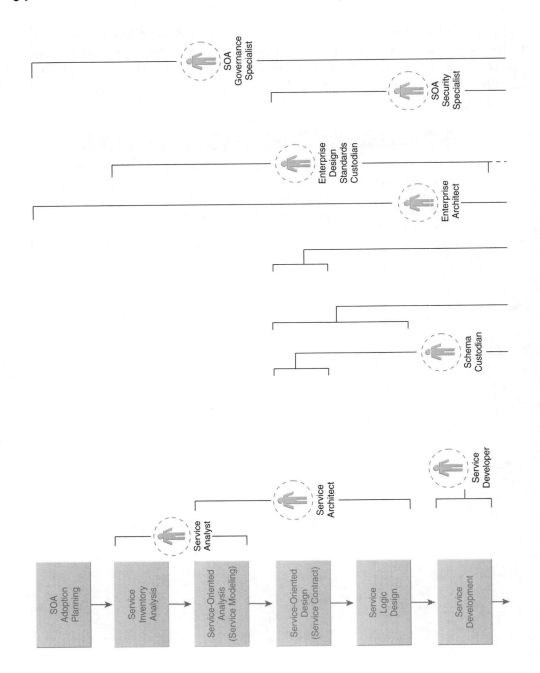

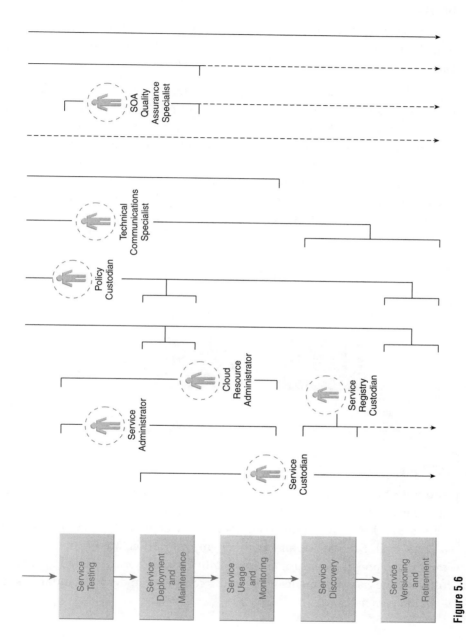

Figure 5.6

Shown here are common associations of organizational roles with different SOA project stages.

Service Analyst

The Service Analyst specializes in the areas of Service-Oriented Analysis and service modeling in order to provide expertise in the definition of service candidates, service capability candidates, and service composition candidates.

Service analysis (or SOA analysis) is a dedicated profession. However, the Service Analyst role can also be assumed by architects and Business Analysts that participate in a project's Service-Oriented Analysis phase. Alternatively, it can form the basis of a team leader role within this process; essentially a specialist in Service-Oriented Analysis that coordinates and leads Service Architects and Business Analysts throughout all process steps. The latter variation can be very effective in larger enterprise environments where every iteration through a business process can require the participation of different business and technology subject matter experts.

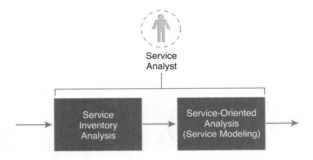

Figure 5.7
Service Analysts are focused primarily on analysis-related stages.

Service Architect

The Service Architect role is concentrated on the physical design of services. Therefore, this role is primarily associated with the Service-Oriented Design and Service Logic Design processes. Service Architects are commonly involved with the Service-Oriented Analysis stage as well. Service Architects therefore can participate in the definition of service candidates and then assume responsibility for authoring design specifications that fulfill business requirements while being compliant to design standards and service-orientation principles.

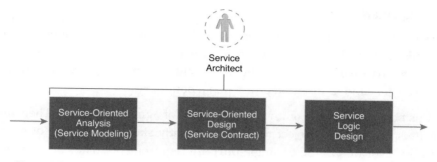

Figure 5.8

Service Architects will usually participate with the definition of service candidates during the Service-Oriented Analysis stage, in addition to their involvement with the actual physical design of service contracts and logic.

Service Developer

A Service Developer is a programmer proficient in the development tools, programming languages, industry markup languages and standards, and related technologies required to build service contracts, logic, and other parts of the service architecture. Service Developers are further versed in the custom design and development standards established by the Enterprise Design Standards Custodian (and others) and are accustomed to developing services in compliance with those standards.

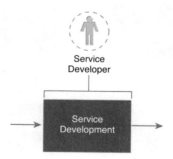

Figure 5.9

The Service Developer is primarily involved during the Service Development stage.

Service Custodian

A Service Custodian owns the management and governance responsibilities of one or more specific services. These duties do not just revolve around the extension and expansion and maintenance of service logic, but also include having to protect the integrity of the service context and its associated functional boundary.

Service Custodians are important to the evolution of agnostic services. Their involvement ensures that no one project team inadvertently skews the design of an agnostic service in favor of specific or single-purpose requirements. They are furthermore responsible for hiding non-essential information about service designs from the outside world (as per the access control levels established by the Service Abstraction (478) principle). As a result, Service Custodians often require a good amount of authority.

Note also that depending on how service details are documented, a Service Custodian may author, own, and maintain a service's corresponding service profile document (as explained in the upcoming *Service Profiles* section).

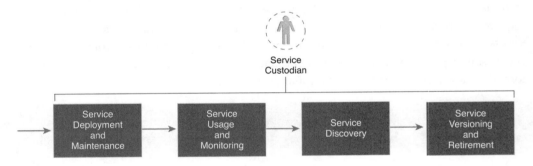

Figure 5.10

Even though a Service Custodian can take ownership of a service as early as when its context is first defined (and verified) during the Service-Oriented Analysis stage, they are typically assigned custodianship upon delivery of the implemented service by the development team.

Cloud Service Owner

A Cloud Service Owner is the person or organization that legally owns a service deployed in a cloud. The Cloud Service Owner can be either the cloud consumer or the cloud provider of the cloud within which the cloud service resides. This distinction is especially relevant when cloud services exist within public clouds owned by third-party cloud provider organizations.

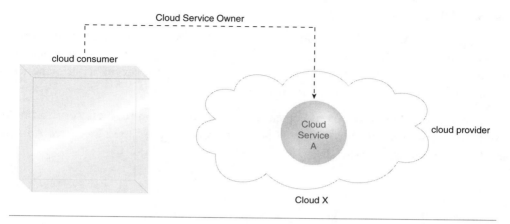

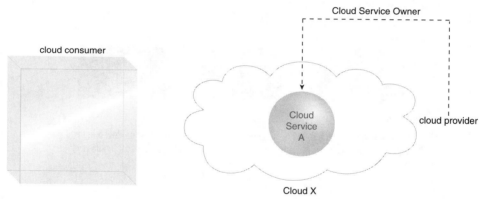

Figure 5.11

If Cloud X hosts Cloud Service A then either the organization acting as the cloud consumer of Cloud X can be the Cloud Service Owner (top) of Cloud Service A, or the cloud provider of Cloud X can be the Cloud Service Owner of Cloud Service A (bottom).

NOTE

Unlike other roles described in this chapter, the Cloud Service Owner is not directly mapped to SOA governance precepts and processes in Chapters 7 to 12. This is primarily because this role is used to identify the legal owner of the cloud service, and therefore does not necessarily represent a role actively involved with SOA project delivery stages. For project participation, the Cloud Service Owner will typically engage any number of individuals or groups that fulfill the other described roles, such as the Service Custodian or the Cloud Resource Administrator.

Service Administrator

A Service Administrator is responsible for administering a service implementation. This role is concerned with ensuring that the service and any resources it may share or depend on are properly configured and maintained so that the service's performance is consistent and in line with any guarantees published in its SLA.

The Service Administrator role is typically associated with on-premise service implementations. For services deployed in cloud environments, the Cloud Resource Administrator role is assumed instead.

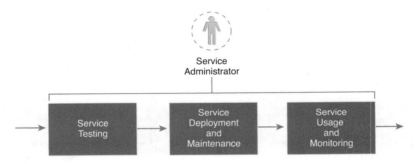

Figure 5.12

The Service Administrator generally gets involved when the service is first deployed in testing and then production environments, and subsequently maintains the service during its runtime existence.

Cloud Resource Administrator

A Cloud Resource Administrator is responsible for administering a cloud service and other types of cloud-based IT resources. This role is proficient with cloud computing technologies and mechanisms and will typically begin its involvement with the initial deployment of a service and then assume the responsibility of maintaining a cloud service implementation in relation to its surrounding cloud-based infrastructure and resources.

A primary concern of the Cloud Resource Administrator is the tuning of on-demand scalability and pay-per-usage mechanisms offered by the cloud environment. In third-party cloud platforms, there may be a variety of options for dynamic scaling and access to shared and virtualized IT resources. Some of these options may have billing implications, while others may introduce performance or behavioral factors.

Besides being dedicated to cloud-based administration requirements, this role is further distinguished from the Service Administrator role in relation to the role's affiliation. A Cloud Resource Administrator can be (or belong to) the organization acting as the consumer or client of a public cloud, or the organization that owns and provides the public cloud.

For example:

- A cloud consumer organization may deploy a service on a public cloud and then assign its own Cloud Resource Administrator to administer that service.

- A cloud provider organization may make a cloud service publically available on a pay-per-usage basis and will therefore have its own Cloud Resource Administrator administer that service. This type of cloud service (which would be categorized as a Software-as-a-Service offering) could then be used as part of a service composition developed by the cloud consumer organization.

Also worth noting is that Cloud Resource Administrators can be (or belong to) a third-party organization contracted to administer the cloud-based service or IT resource. For example, a Cloud Service Owner could outsource administration responsibilities to a Cloud Resource Administrator to administer its cloud service.

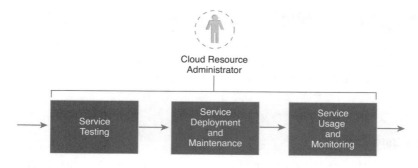

Figure 5.13

As with the Service Administrator, this role is generally involved from Service Testing through to Service Usage and Monitoring stages.

The reason this role is not named Cloud Service Administrator is because it may be responsible for administering cloud-based IT resources that don't exist as cloud services. For example, if the Cloud Resource Administrator belongs to (or is contracted by) the cloud provider organization, IT resources not made remotely accessible may be administered by this role (and these types of IT resources are not classified as cloud services). Figure 5.14 illustrates this in relation to the Cloud X and Service A scenario from Figure 5.11.

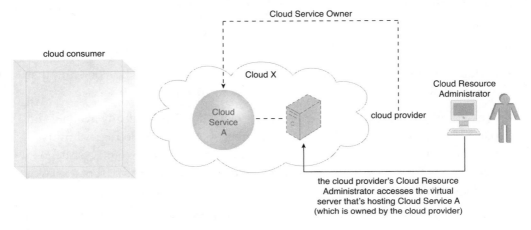

Figure 5.14

While Cloud Service A may be accessible to external cloud consumers, the cloud provider that acts as the Cloud Service Owner can have a Cloud Resource Administrator configure the underlying virtual server that hosts Cloud Service A.

NOTE

In the previous example, the virtual server is considered an IT resource. See Chapter 3 for a definition of the term "IT resource" and for further descriptions of fundamental cloud computing terms.

Schema Custodian

Schema Custodians are primarily responsible for ensuring that service contract schemas (and schemas used elsewhere as the basis of messaging data models), as well as custom media types for uniform contracts, are properly positioned as standardized and centralized parts of service inventories. Schema Custodians may even own design standards pertaining to service contracts and relevant data modeling.

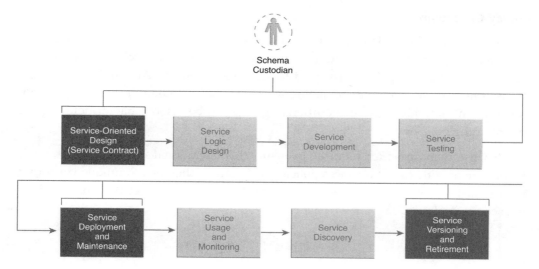

Figure 5.15

The Schema Custodian gets involved whenever the service contract's schema(s) are affected. It is part of its definition, implementation, and any subsequent versioning requirements. The Schema Custodian role was originally established in the book *Service-Oriented Architecture: A Field Guide to Integrating XML and Web Services*.

"XML Schema" vs. "XML schema"

The word "schema" is capitalized when referring to the XML Schema language or specification, and it is lower case when discussing schema documents.

For example, the following statement makes reference to the XML Schema language:

"One feature provided by XML Schema is the ability to…"

And this sentence explains the use of XML schema documents:

"When defining an XML schema it is important to…"

Note also that we often refer to XML schemas as just "schemas."

Policy Custodian

The Policy Custodian role is assigned the responsibility of defining and maintaining machine-language (technical) and natural-language (human-readable) policies used by service contracts and policies assigned to services in general. Although this role can be assumed by the same person acting as a Schema Custodian, it is not uncommon for different individuals (or even different groups) to be responsible for defining and maintaining policies.

Policy Custodians are often required to ensure that operational service policies remain in alignment with parent business policies. This can further lead to unique versioning requirements as business policies can be subject to various changes that end up affecting service contracts.

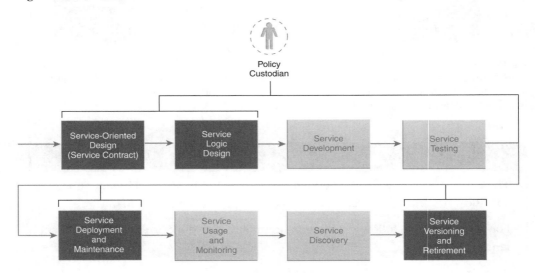

Figure 5.16
As with the Schema Custodian, this role is closely tied to the service contract. In this case, it is involved when service policies related to the service contract are affected.

Service Registry Custodian

The Service Registry Custodian is tasked with the overall administration of one or more service registries. This goes beyond the installation and maintenance of the registry product; it encompasses the constant responsibility of ensuring a high quality of registry record content, which ties directly into how discoverability-related meta information is defined and recorded for individual services.

A Service Registry Custodian needs to ensure that once a service registry is introduced into an IT enterprise, it is consistently maintained to avoid becoming stale or inaccurate. Although Service Registry Custodians will typically not author discoverability content themselves, they will often own standards or conventions that dictate the nature of metadata used to populate service registry profile records.

Figure 5.17

This role is focused almost exclusively in the Service Discovery stage. It is further affected when new versions of a service or service contract impact what is recorded in the service registry (which, in turn, eventually affects the Service Discovery stage again). Note that registry products are discussed in Chapter 14.

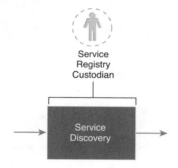

Technical Communications Specialist

A Technical Communications Specialist is usually someone with a background in technical writing who is enlisted to refine initial drafts of service profiles and associated service contracts and metadata.

The responsibility of this role is to express discoverability information, using standard vocabularies so that a range of project team members can effectively query and interpret service contracts and associated profiles. This makes information published about a service accessible to a broader range of project team members and reduces risk associated with misinterpretation and inadvertent non-discovery.

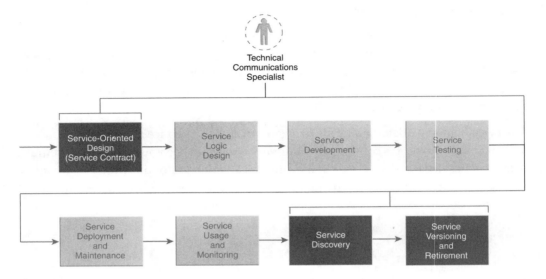

Figure 5.18

Stages pertaining to the authoring, definition, or expansion of content associated with what is published about a service are relevant to this role.

Enterprise Architect

Although this is not a new role by any means, it represents a position that is greatly empha-sized by the cross-application (cross-silo) scope of service inventory delivery projects.

Technology Architects with an enterprise perspective are expected to:

- assist with SOA Adoption Planning and strategy
- author or contribute to enterprise design standards
- become involved in service delivery projects to ensure that agnostic services are properly positioned
- assess service runtime usage and determine required infrastructure
- evaluate security concerns of individual service capabilities
- help define and perhaps even own service inventory blueprints

In larger organizations there may also be the need for Enterprise Domain Architects—a variation of this role that specializes in a particular segment of the overall enterprise. These architects would then be focused on the definition and governance of domain-specific service inventories.

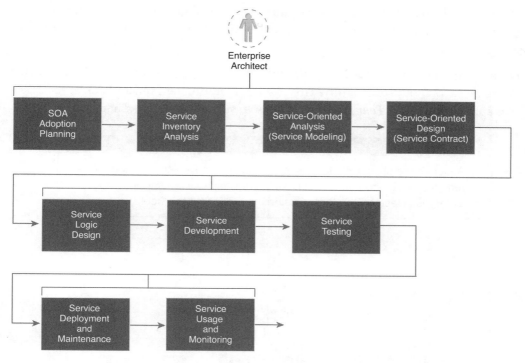

Figure 5.19

Enterprise Architects can be involved with just about every stage.

Enterprise Design Standards Custodian (and Auditor)

As enterprise architecture groups grow in response to the changes incurred by an SOA transition, design standards can be authored by multiple experts, each contributing conventions associated with a particular aspect of service design (security, performance, transactions, uniform contract usage, caching, etc.).

To ensure that design standards are kept in alignment and used wherever appropriate, it may very well be necessary to establish an official custodian for enterprise design specifications. This individual or group is responsible for the evolution of the design standards, as well as their enforcement. Therefore, this role often involves performing audits of proposed service or service-oriented solution designs.

The authority required to carry out auditing responsibilities can sometimes raise concerns within IT environments not accustomed to such formal use of design standards.

Therefore, this role can be more successfully established within the boundaries of a specific enterprise domain, where a given set of standards applies only to a specific domain service inventory, not the enterprise as a whole.

The authority needed to audit and *enforce* the use of standards is a requirement for this role to be carried out successfully. This essential requirement relates back to the *Discipline* sub-section of *The Four Pillars of Service-Orientation* section in Chapter 4.

NOTE

Although the official title for this role is Enterprise Design Standards Custodian (and Auditor), for the sake of brevity, this role is referred to as just Enterprise Design Standards Custodian throughout this book.

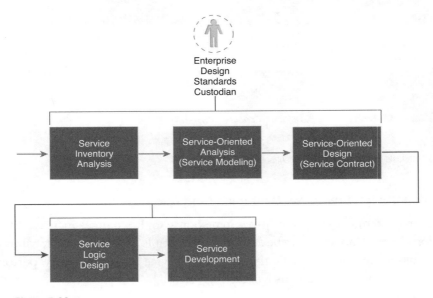

Figure 5.20
Although design standards can impact any part of a service's lifecycle, this role is primarily concerned with its initial delivery.

SOA Quality Assurance Specialist

This role is comparable to the traditional IT quality assurance profession, except that it requires further expertise in ensuring the quality of services—in particular, shared services that can be subjected to repeated reuse and composition.

SOA Quality Assurance Specialists are closely associated with the Service Testing stage, during which services can be subjected to various forms of tests either prior to their initial deployment or as part of the release of subsequent service versions.

> **NOTE**
>
> Several of the governance precepts and processes covered in this book are related to "ensuring the quality" of some aspect of SOA and the delivery of services. Although SOA Quality Assurance Specialists can be involved in these areas (as described in upcoming chapters), these types of quality assurance tasks are primarily associated with the SOA Governance Specialist role.

Figure 5.21

The SOA Quality Assurance Specialist usually gets involved during the Service Testing stage and can then further be required to ensure that required levels of quality are actually being met during subsequent stages.

SOA Security Specialist

Each service can have its own individual security requirements and security architecture. Further, with shared agnostic services, the requirements of the service compositions reusing the service to automate different types of business processes also need to be taken into account. In this case, the service may need to join a service composition architecture that introduces a parent security architecture that encompasses the service's individual security architecture.

Either way, the SOA Security Specialist role is dedicated to ensuring that services (individually and as part of service compositions) are properly secured and also that agnostic services are sufficiently flexible so that they can be incorporated into other security architectures when required.

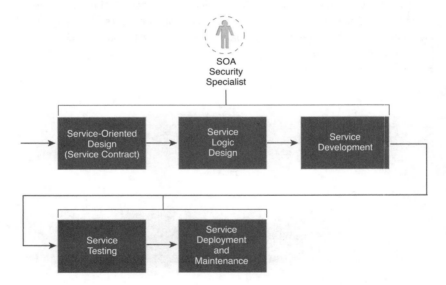

Figure 5.22
Security issues are of primary concern when physical design stages are entered, through to when the service is implemented. SOA Security Specialists will further be involved with subsequent stages, as new security requirements or threats surface.

SOA Governance Specialist

The SOA Governance Specialist is an expert in the definition and execution of governance precepts and processes, as well as the usage of related governance technology. All topics covered in this book pertain to this role.

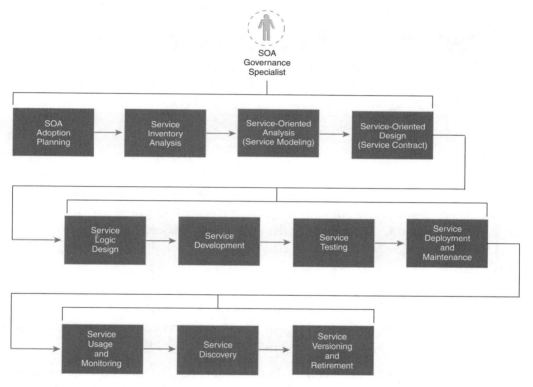

Figure 5.23

This role can be involved with all stages.

<table>
<tr><td>NOTE</td></tr>
<tr><td>Individuals assuming the SOA Governance Specialist, Enterprise Architect, and Enterprise Design Standards Custodian roles will generally end up joining the SOA Governance Program Office (explained in Chapter 6).</td></tr>
</table>

Other Roles

The following additional roles are also referred to in this book. These brief descriptions are by no means official definitions; they simply introduce the roles in relation to SOA project involvement. IT professionals focused on any of these areas can also assume one or more of the previously explained organizational roles.

NOTE
In the *People (Roles)* sections throughout Chapters 7 to 11, these roles are intentionally not always mapped to SOA governance precepts and processes.

Educator

A fundamental role that must be established and fulfilled on an on-going basis throughout SOA project stages is that of the Educator. Education (one of the four foundational pillars of service-orientation described in Chapter 4) is a critical success factor that impacts the successful fulfillment of *all* the other organizational roles described in this book, in terms of their involvement during SOA project activities, governance-related or otherwise.

Educators act as trainers (delivering instructor-led courses and workshops specific to the skill-set development requirements of a given SOA project) and as mentors (working with SOA project members individually to address knowledge gaps and other mismatches between their backgrounds and assigned responsibilities).

The role of the Educator is not mentioned in subsequent chapters because it is assumed to be ever-present. The Educator is there during the early stages to teach what project teams need to learn in preparation for a given SOA project. The Educator is then further there and available when the project commences to provide guidance, mentorship, and to deliver additional workshops, as required (such as when a new technology or tool is chosen to replace one originally selected during the planning stages).

In some cases, the SOA Governance Specialist may assume the role of a quasi-Educator when providing assistance to other project team members with the application and usage of SOA governance controls. However, to truly assume the role of Educator requires structured course development, dedicated tutorship, superior communication, and, typically, instructor-level accreditation. Therefore, an Educator specializing in SOA governance can exist separately from an SOA Governance Specialist.

Business Analyst

The job of a Business Analyst does not change drastically when defining business-centric services. While different organizations may have different business analysis practices and approaches, the primary objectives of this role as part of SOA projects are the creation of business use cases, business requirements, and the definition of business processes.

In relation to service modeling, Business Analysts are responsible for creating the business processes specifications that act as input for the Service-Oriented Analysis process. They are further expected to participate in the Service-Oriented Analysis process for the definition of business-centric service candidates.

Data Architect

Data Architects provide guidance for the identification of the data necessary for a service to comply with functional and non-functional requirements. They are usually also responsible for defining and maintaining the data models used to establish the structure of messages and the validation logic that can reside within service contracts and the underlying service implementations. As a result, it is fairly common for the Schema Custodian role to be assigned to a Data Architect.

> **NOTE**
>
> For the purpose of this book only, the term "Data Architect" encompasses information architects, data modelers, and data analysts.

Technology Architect

Although Service Architects will tend to already be Technology Architects, a distinction between these two roles is still necessary, especially when services need to access or encapsulate other IT resources. There may be Technology Architects (that are not qualified Service Architects) that need to be consulted or involved during SOA projects.

> **NOTE**
>
> For the purpose of this book only, the term "Technology Architect" encompasses application architects, systems architects, solution architects, and software architects.

Cloud Technology Professional

Any IT professional that is required to build, deploy, or work with cloud-based services and IT resources needs to be proficient with the core technologies, technical mechanisms, and fundamental security concerns that are relevant to contemporary cloud environments. The Cloud Technology Professional has obtained a proven understanding of the building blocks that comprise cloud solutions and enable key characteristics, such as elasticity and virtualization, and has further demonstrated ability to identify and address common security threats specific to cloud environments. This role is assumed by anyone working hands on with cloud-based IT resources, and is therefore typically combined with other roles, such as Service Developer and Service Administrator.

Cloud Architect

Cloud Architects specialize in cloud-based technology architecture, design patterns, mechanisms, and are proficient with contemporary analysis and design processes for authoring detailed architectural specifications of cloud-based solutions and platforms. The Cloud Architect's skill-set is not limited to cloud environments; this role is required to architect solutions and service compositions that span on-premise and cloud platforms and to further design dynamic and complex solutions using remote distribution techniques, such as cloud bursting and cross-cloud balancing. This role is most commonly coupled with the Service Architect role.

Cloud Security Specialist

These are IT professionals with expertise specific to security threats (and mechanisms used to counter those threats) pertaining to cloud-based services and supporting cloud-based IT resources. Cloud Security Specialists are distinct from SOA Security Specialists, in that they are focused solely on security issues related to cloud environments and IT resources, regardless of whether the underlying solutions are service-oriented or based on service-oriented technology architectures.

Cloud Governance Specialist

Public, private, and community clouds each have their own distinct characteristics and platforms, many of which are proprietary and vendor-specific. Amidst the diversity of these environments, there is a set of mechanisms and goals that are common to most initiatives that involve or are based on the use of cloud computing. Cloud Governance

Specialists are proficient in establishing IT governance precepts and processes in support of regulating general and proprietary mechanisms, technologies, solutions, and IT resources that reside and operate within cloud environments in order to ensure that the planned goals are attained.

This role is distinct from the SOA Governance Specialist role in that its focus is on regulating cloud environments and cloud-based IT resources, regardless of whether they are being used by or are associated with service-oriented solutions or service-oriented technology architectures.

IT Manager

IT management's primary focus is to manage IT resources and budgets, ensure proper staffing levels, and set the strategic direction for the department or group for which the IT Manager is responsible. Traditional IT Managers can be impacted by SOA initiatives and the need for new forms of IT Managers can further emerge.

SUMMARY OF KEY POINTS

- SOA projects introduce a number of unique project roles, several of which emerged from distinct SOA project and service lifecycle stages.
- One individual can assume one or more roles and a single role can be assumed by one or more individuals.
- The SOA Governance Specialist role is associated with all stages.

5.3 Service Profiles

When collecting discoverability-related meta information, it is helpful to use a standardized template or form that ensures the same type of data is documented for each service. This can be especially useful during the early analysis stages, when service candidates are just being conceptualized as part of the service modeling process. The document used to record details about a service is the *service profile* (Figure 5.24).

Figure 5.24

A service profile initially acts as a repository
of meta information when a service is first
conceptualized during early analysis stages, and
then later provides valuable details for design
and delivery-related documents used during
subsequent lifecycle phases.

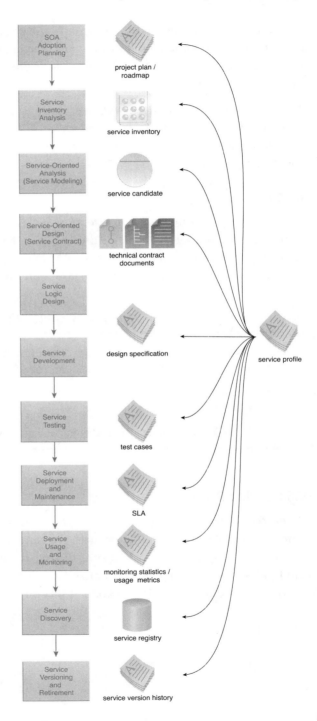

Service-Level Profile Structure

There is no one official industry format for service profiles. However, once in use, the service profile format must be standardized as part of the SOA initiative. With an understanding of how services typically transition and evolve throughout stages, the following baseline parts and fields are recommended:

- *Service Name*

- *Purpose Description (Short)* – A concise, one sentence description of the service context and purpose.

- *Purpose Description (Detailed)* – A full explanation of the service context and its functional boundary with as many details as necessary.

- *Service Model* – Entity, Utility, Task, Orchestrated Task, or a custom variation.

- *Capabilities* – The profile should document capabilities that exist and are in development, as well as those that are only planned and tentatively defined. Color coding is often useful to make these distinctions as is the use of the capability "status" field (described shortly).

- *Keywords* – This field can contain one or more keywords ideally taken from an official service inventory-level taxonomy or vocabulary. Service profile keywords should correspond to the keywords used by a service registry.

- *Version* – The version number of the service currently being documented is noted here. Depending on the version control system in use, version numbers may only be applicable to service capabilities.

- *Status* – The development status of the service (or service version) is expressed in this field using standard terms identifying a project lifecycle stage, such as "analysis," "contract design," "development," or "production." If the service is not in production, it can be helpful to include an estimated delivery date.

- *Custodian* – Details on how to reach the official Service Custodian or owner, as well as others that contributed to this documentation.

cribe these in plain English during the service modeling phase. The details

Capability Profile Structure

Because a service acts as a container for a collection of capabilities, additional "sub-profiles" need to be established to represent each individual capability separately, as follows:

- *Capability Name*

- *Purpose Description* – A concise explanation of the capability's overall purpose and functional context (similar to the short service description).

- *Logic Description* – A step-by-step description of the logic carried out by the capability. This can be supplemented with algorithms, workflow diagrams, or even entire business process definitions, depending on what stage the capability definition is at.

- *Input/Output* – These two fields provide definitions of a capability's allowable input and/or output value(s) and associated constraints. It can be helpful to describe these in plain English during the service modeling phase. The details established here can make reference to existing schema types.

- *Composition Role* – The execution of capability logic can place a service into various temporary runtime roles, depending on its position within service composition configurations. This field can filled out with a description of the capability's role or it can simply contain a term used to identify predefined runtime roles.

- *Composition Member Capabilities* – A list of services (and specifically their capabilities) composed by the capability logic. This provides a convenient cross-reference to other service capabilities the current capability has formed dependencies on. Ideally, identified composition member capabilities are mapped to the portions of the business process logic (documented in the *Logic Description* field) so that delegated logic is clearly indicated.

- *Keywords* – Often the same keywords that apply to the service can be carried over to the capability. But it is not uncommon for additional keywords to be added to individual capabilities so as to better classify their purpose. Keywords for services and capabilities should originate from the same parent vocabulary.

- *Version* – Depending on the versioning system in place, capabilities themselves may be versioned with a number or new capability versions may be added with the version number appended to the capability name.

- *Status* – The same lifecycle identifiers used for services can be applied to the status of individual capabilities. However, this field can also be used to earmark capabilities that were identified during the modeling stage, but for which no specific delivery date exists.

- *Custodian* – More often than not, the custodian of the service will be the custodian (or one of the custodians) of the related capabilities. However, when multiple business and technology experts collaborate on a given service, some are only there to assist with the definition of one service capability (or a subset of service capabilities). In this case separate custodians may need to be associated with individual capabilities.

Additional Considerations

Customizing Service Profiles

What we've established so far is fundamental profile documentation. Organizations are encouraged to customize and extend this to whatever extent required.

Service Profiles and Service Registries

Much of the information assembled into service profiles will form the basis for service registry records. Depending on whether a service registry exists within an organization at the time the profile is being defined, it is advisable to become familiar with the registry product's record format. This will allow you to better align the service profile template with how the profile information may need to be represented within the service registry.

Service Profiles and Service Catalogs

The structure of a service profile is ideally standardized so that different project teams consistently document the services they deliver. As more service profiles are created, they can be assembled into a *service catalog*. A service catalog is essentially a documentation of the services within a service inventory (much the same way a product catalog may describe the inventory of items a company may have in its warehouse). If an organization is creating multiple domain service inventories, each with its own design standards and governance processes, then service profile structures may vary. Therefore, a separate service catalog is generally created for each service inventory.

Service Profiles and Service Architecture

It's important to keep a clear separation between what is documented in a service profile document and the content of a service architecture specification. The latter form of document is authored by qualified Service Architects and contains the details of the service's design and implementation. As with the service profile, a service architecture specification can be a living document that evolves during the service lifecycle. However, few actual technical implementation details make their way into the corresponding service profile. It is up to the discretion of the Service Custodian (and the Service Architects and others involved with governing the service) to determine what extent of overlap is necessary. For example, it may be necessary to indicate that the service is located in a particular cloud environment and bound to pay-for-use leasing terms. This information is typically relevant to both service profile and service architecture documents. On the other hand, the fact that one of the service capabilities contains logic that accesses a legacy database may only belong in the service architecture specification.

> **NOTE**
>
> Service profiles were first introduced in the book *SOA Principles of Service Design*. See Chapter 15 of that book for a detailed example of a service profile.

SUMMARY OF KEY POINTS

- As services move from concept to candidate to physical design to production usage, it is important to consistently document them using standardized service profiles.

- The use of service profiles is most effective when combined with a standardized vocabulary or taxonomy.

- Multiple service profile documents can be compiled to create a service inventory-specific service catalog.

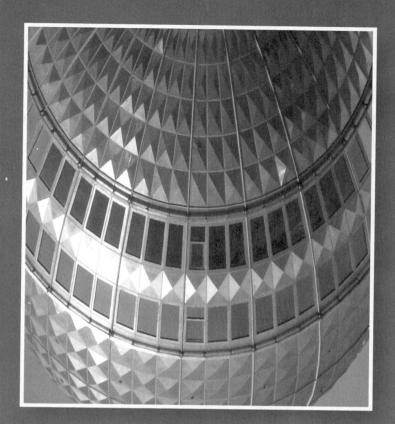

Chapter 6

Understanding SOA Governance

The expectation when adopting service-orientation is the realization of a number of specific strategic business benefits, as explained in Chapter 3. To accomplish this requires not only sound technology, mature practices, and sufficient stakeholder support, but also a firm grasp of the strategic target state being realized by the adoption and a firm system of ensuring its attainment and sustainment. Such a system cannot be purchased with technology products labeled as governance tools; it is a system that requires careful definition specific to overarching goals and requirements.

Structured governance is required to carry out and see through the commitments made when embarking on an SOA roadmap. It helps organizations succeed with SOA adoption efforts by mitigating risks through predefined constraints, rules, and the allocation of necessary authority. This chapter provides an introduction to general governance concepts and terms, as well as fundamental topics regarding governance systems for SOA projects.

6.1 Governance 101

Governance is the act of governing or administrating something. By far the most common form of governance is that of an organization. A system of governance is therefore generally a type of organizational system. For example, a society uses an organizational system to govern a public community. A company uses an organizational system to govern its own internal community.

A system for organizational governance exists as a meta-decision system. In other words, it is not just a means by which the organization makes decisions, it is the means by which the organization makes decisions *about* decision-making.

Within this context, a governance system:

- places constraints on decisions

- determines who has responsibility and authority to make decisions

- establishes constraints and parameters that control, guide, or influence decisions

- prescribes consequences for non-compliance

At the highest level in society, governance is established by a constitution. Within a company, it may be declared in the form of a business charter. Founding documents such as these establish a parent level of authority and constraints from which all other decision-making authorities and structures are derived. At deeper levels within the organization, a governance system can further influence the definition of policies, standards, and processes that guide and control day-to-day decision-making activities.

A good system of governance helps the members of an organization carry out responsibilities in a manner supportive of the organization's business goals and vision. It mitigates conflict by clearly defining responsibilities and assignments of authority, and further reduces ambiguity by articulating constraints and parameters in practical forms (such as rules and decision guidelines). It also helps balance tactical and strategic goals by expressing the intents and purposes of its rules.

The Scope of Governance

Within IT, a governance system is responsible for providing organization, direction, and guidance for the creation and evolution of IT assets and resources. To fully understand the scope of a governance system within a given IT department, we need to determine how a governance system relates to and is distinguished from methodology and management (Figure 6.1).

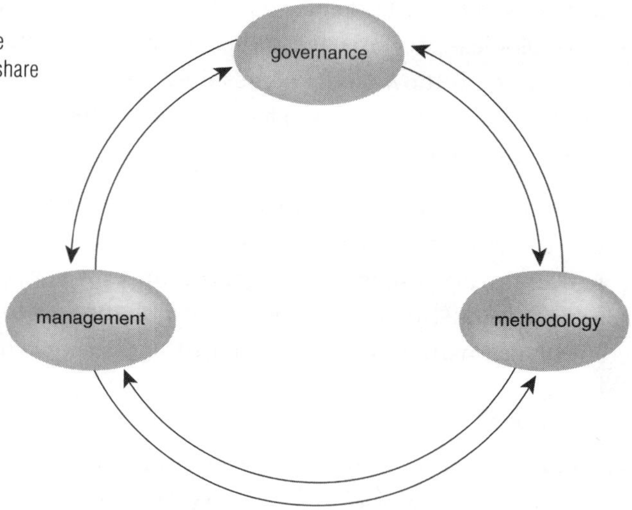

Figure 6.1

Governance, management, and methodology are distinct areas within an IT department that also share distinct relationships.

Governance and Methodology

Methodology represents a system of methods. Within IT, the form of methodology we are generally concerned with is that used to create software programs and business automation solutions. In this context, the methodology determines a system of methods used to conceptualize, design, program, test, and deploy a software program. These methods are generally formalized as a series of step-by-step processes that correspond to project delivery lifecycle stages.

> **NOTE**
>
> The Mainstream SOA Methodology (MSOAM) has established itself as a common, generic methodology for SOA project delivery. This methodology is explained in parts throughout the *Prentice Hall Service-Oriented Computing Series from Thomas Erl*, and is further summarized at www.soamethodology.com. Appendix G provides a supplementary paper that maps MSOAM to the Rational Unified Process (RUP).

Different software delivery methodologies exist. What commonly distinguishes one from the other is how they prioritize tactical and strategic requirements in relation to overarching business goals. These priorities will usually result in different processes (project lifecycle stages) being combined or organized in different ways. In some cases, one methodology may introduce a new process that does not exist in other methodologies—or it may exclude a process that commonly exists in other methodologies. Frequently, however, it comes down to how much time and effort a given process or project lifecycle stage receives, as determined by the tactical and strategic priorities of the methodology.

How a methodology is defined and carried out is heavily influenced by the governance system. Essentially, the methodology must be determined so that it follows the constraints established by the governance system and the corresponding methods (processes) must be carried out in compliance with these constraints, as well as any additional constraints that may be further introduced by the methodology itself.

Governance and Management

Whereas a governance system establishes rules and constraints, it is not responsible for enforcing them or overseeing related activities to ensure compliance. Management refers to the system and resources responsible for day-to-day operations.

Within an IT environment, this basically pertains to the execution of activities. In relation to governance, a management system provides the hands-on means by which the constraints and goals of the governance system are realized in the real world. Therefore, the management of a governance system represents a subset of the overall management responsibilities.

Management systems are assigned to and carried out by those with authority.

Methodology and Management

Management relates to methodology the same way it relates to governance. When building software programs according to a pre-defined methodology, a management system is used to ensure the proper execution of processes and project delivery lifecycle stages in compliance with the constraints of the methodology—and the constraints of the governance system.

Comparisons

The following list contains a series of sample distinctions to further help provide a clear separation between governance, methodology, and management:

- Governance establishes rules that control decision-making.

- Methodology establishes processes that comply to governance rules and may introduce additional rules.

- Management makes decisions according to governance rules.

- Governance does not dictate when or how to make a decision. It determines who should make the decision and establishes limits for that person or group.

- Methodology establishes processes that carry out specific types of decision logic that adhere to governance rules.

- Management is responsible for day-to-day operations and for ensuring that decisions made adhere to governance and methodology rules.

- Governance cannot replace management or methodology, nor can it compensate for poor management or poor (or inappropriate) methodology.

- Poorly defined and executed methodology can jeopardize the business goals associated with governance.

- Poor management can undermine a governance system and a methodology and will jeopardize associated business goals.

- Neither management nor methodology can replace governance, nor compensate for poor governance.

- A poor governance system inevitably inhibits the ability of a methodology to fulfill business automation requirement potential.

- A poor governance system inevitably inhibits the ability of management to make correct decisions.

As previously stated, while this book will make many references to management and methodology, it is primarily focused on governance.

STYLES OF GOVERNANCE

Governance must reflect and complement an organization's culture and structure. For example, when establishing suitable governance rules, considerations such as the following need to be raised:

- How much autonomy should each division, business unit, or department have?

- How much freedom should decision-makers have to delegate responsibilities to others?

- How much freedom should decision-makers have to use their own judgment when making decisions (as opposed to making decisions fully or partially based on pre-determined criteria)?

To determine what style of governance may be the best fit for a given organization, it can be helpful to refer to established forms of governance used historically in society. Figure 6.2 illustrates two dimensions that relate common governance styles.

Figure 6.2

The horizontal axis represents the degree of autonomy given to separate people or groups. The vertical axis represents the degree of control imposed on decision-makers.

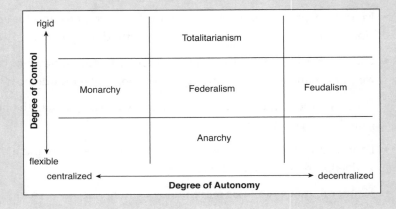

Looking at one end of the horizontal spectrum, all decision-making is centralized, which is comparable to a monarchy. At the other end, each group establishes its own policies and procedures, similar to a feudal society. Many IT departments opt for a federated model, which permits the separation of the department into individual business units or cost centers, each of which is given a degree of independence while still maintaining a level of consistency. This helps reduce contention between fiefdoms.

When we study the vertical spectrum, we have a totalitarian type of regime whereby rigid policies dictate required actions, and decision-makers have little freedom to apply their own judgment. Too much rigidity can generate resentment and inhibit creativity in an organization. On the other hand, allowing flexible policies that provide only suggestive guidance leaves decision-makers with so much freedom that there is little chance of achieving meaningful consistency.

Good governance empowers people to do what's right for the business. Poor governance unnecessarily constrains or inhibits decisions, or fails to provide enough decision-making guidance. All governance—whether good or bad—places limits on the decisions and behaviors of the people being governed. It also prescribes consequences for those choosing not to abide. There is no single governance style that is correct for all organizations. Each must strive to find a balance between centralization and decentralization, between rigidity and flexibility, and between its existing culture and its ability to adapt to new approaches.

The Building Blocks of a Governance System

So far we've established that governance provides a systematic way for organizations to make decisions. Let's take a closer look at the primary building blocks that comprise a governance system:

- *precepts* define the rules that govern decision-making
- *people* assume roles and make decisions based on precepts
- *processes* coordinate people and precept-related decision-making activities
- *metrics* measure compliance to precepts

Note that these building blocks can be collectively or individually referred to as *governance controls*.

Precepts

A *precept* is an authoritative rule of action. Precepts are the essence of governance because they determine who has authority to make decisions, they establish constraints for those decisions, and they prescribe consequences for non-compliance.

Precepts codify decision-making rules using:

- *objectives* – broadly define a precept and establish its overarching responsibility, authority, and goals

- *policies* – define specific aspects of a precept and establish decision-making constraints and consequences

- *standards* – specify the mandatory formats, technologies, processes, actions, and metrics that people are required to use and carry out in order to implement one or more policies

- *guidelines* – are non-mandatory recommendations and best practices

> **NOTE**
>
> Within some IT communities, the term "policy" is commonly used instead of "precept" in relation to governance systems. However, as just explained, a policy can be just one aspect of a precept.
>
> Also, even though a precept can contain standards, certain precepts themselves are considered standards. Therefore, it is important to not be confused when the precept name includes the word "standard" (such as Service Design Standard precept), and the precept itself further contains one or more standards that support corresponding precept policies.

People (Roles)

People (and groups of people) make decisions in accordance to and within the constraints stipulated by governance precepts. For a governance system to be successful, people must understand the intents and purposes of the precepts and they must understand and accept the responsibilities and authorities established by the precepts. Governance systems are therefore often closely associated with an organization's incentive system. This allows the organization to foster a culture that supports and rewards good behavior, while also deterring and punishing poor behavior.

When exploring the involvement of people in relation to governance systems, it is further necessary to identify the role or roles they assume. Organizational roles position people (and groups) in relation to governance models and further affect the relevance of precept compliance and enforcement.

There are two ways that people can relate to precepts and processes: they can help author the precepts and processes and they can be dictated by their application. In this book, we explore both types of relationships.

Processes

A process is an organized representation of a series of activities. It is important to make a distinction between governance processes and other types of processes related to IT. Governance processes provide a means by which to control decisions, enforce policies, and take corrective action in support of the governance system. Other processes, such as those employed to carry out project delivery stages, can be heavily influenced by governance precepts, but are not specifically processes that are directly related to carrying out the governance system. Technically, any process is considered a management activity, but a governance system is dependent on governance processes to ensure compliance with its precepts.

An organization is likely to use a variety of processes to support its precepts. Some may be automated, while others require human effort. Automated processes can help coordinate tasks (such as steps required to collect data for approvals), but can still rely on people to make important decisions (such as making the actual approvals based on the presented data).

Metrics

Metrics provide information that can be used to measure and verify compliance with precepts. The use of metrics increases visibility into the progress and effectiveness of the governance system. By analyzing metrics, we gain insight into the efficacy of governance rules and we can further discover whether particular precepts or processes are too onerous or unreasonable. Metrics also measure trends, such as the number of violations and requests for waivers. A large number of waiver requests may indicate that a given precept might not be appropriate or effective.

Governance and SOA

An organization establishes governance to mitigate risk and to help advance its strategy, goals, and priorities. When the organization invests in an SOA initiative, it expects to gain benefits worth more than the cost of the investment. This return on investment is measured in terms of business outcomes, and, presumably, those outcomes reflect the organization's strategy, goals, and priorities. Therefore, the primary business goal for SOA governance is to ensure that an SOA initiative achieves its targeted business outcome.

An SOA governance system is the meta-decision system that an organization puts in place to control and constrain decision-making responsibilities related to the adoption and application of service-orientation. There are many practices, considerations, models, and frameworks that can comprise a meta-decision system suitable for SOA governance, all of which are explored throughout this book. The foundation of an SOA governance system resides within an SOA Governance Program Office responsible for creating and administering an SOA governance program that encompasses and defines necessary SOA governance models and the tasks required to realize and sustain these models.

NOTE

The term "SOA Governance Program Office" is intentionally capitalized as it represents the official name of an IT department. The term "SOA governance program" is not capitalized, as it refers to a type of program that is commonly assigned its own unique name.

SUMMARY OF KEY POINTS

- There are clear distinctions between governance, methodology, and management.

- The building blocks of a governance system are precepts, people, processes, and metrics.

- The fundamental steps to laying the foundation for an SOA governance system are to create an SOA Governance Program Office that creates and administers an SOA governance program.

6.2 The SOA Governance Program Office (SGPO)

> **NOTE**
>
> For simplicity's sake this chapter frequently uses the acronym "SGPO" for the "SOA Governance Program Office." This is not an industry-standard acronym, nor is the book proposing it as such. It is an acronym used solely to simplify content by avoiding repeatedly spelling out this term.

The first step in any SOA governance effort is to establish a group (or department) that assumes the responsibility of defining and administering the various parts of an SOA governance system. This group forms the SOA Governance Program Office (SGPO), an organizational entity that is commonly comprised of trained SOA Governance Specialists, Enterprise Architects, and other types of IT decision-makers. The SGPO is given the authority to define and enforce the on-going activities and rules associated with SOA governance.

A primary responsibility of the SGPO is to author a series of formal precepts. In some cases, the SGPO may need to request amendments to existing IT governance precepts to accommodate the distinct needs of SOA projects, as the SGPO needs to avoid inadvertently defining conflicting precepts.

In general, SOA governance precepts are more balanced and more easily accepted when those who are governed have a voice. The SGPO may therefore need to solicit input from major stakeholders, including IT and business managers, senior IT staff, and even the legal department. Those contributing should have an opportunity to comment on pending precepts, propose amendments, and recommend new precepts. However, just because the SGPO solicits input does not imply that it is relinquishing its authority to establish the necessary SOA governance precepts.

Following are some basic guidelines for incorporating the SGPO into an IT environment:

- The SGPO must have the responsibility and authority to develop and manage the SOA governance system, and other teams must accept the SGPO's authority.

- The SGPO must ensure that the SOA governance system aligns with the organization's incentive and disciplinary systems.

- The SGPO must develop collaborative working relationships with other governance teams whose responsibilities intersect with those of the SGPO.

- The SGPO must ensure that its precepts align with other governance systems (Figure 6.3) within the company, or they must work with the other governance program offices to amend the conflicting precepts.

- The SGPO must have access to communication channels to disseminate information about the governance precepts and to provide training to people affected by them.

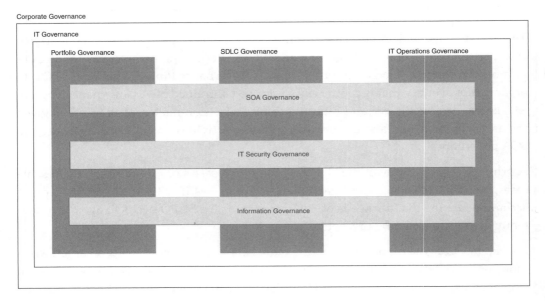

Figure 6.3
SOA governance must be defined through a program that can harmoniously co-exist alongside other IT governance programs.

What's of critical importance is that an appropriate scope be established for the SGPO. There are two primary factors that determine this scope: the reach of the SGPO within the overall IT enterprise and the areas of responsibility assumed by the SGPO within whatever domain it operates.

6.3 SGPO Jurisdiction Models

As explained in Chapter 3, a given IT enterprise can have one or more service inventories. Each service inventory represents a collection of independently standardized and governed services. When an IT enterprise has multiple service inventories, each is (ideally) associated with a well-defined domain, such as a line of business. In this case, service inventories are further qualified with the word "domain."

Depending on whether domain service inventories are being used and depending on how cooperative relations are between different service inventory owners, there may or may not be the opportunity to have one SGPO assume responsibility for multiple domain service inventories. As a result, different jurisdiction models exist, as follows:

Centralized Enterprise SGPO

If a single enterprise service inventory has been established, then it is generally expected that SOA governance responsibilities will be assigned to a single SGPO that oversees SOA governance on behalf of the entire IT enterprise.

Figure 6.4

A single SGPO responsible for the enterprise service inventory.

IT Enterprise

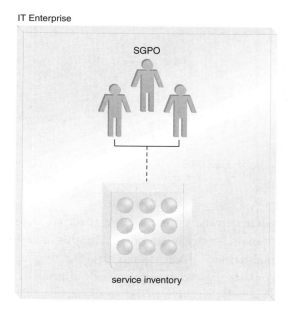

Centralized Domain SGPO

Even though individual domain service inventories can be independently standardized, managed, and owned, with enough cooperation between the owners, the IT department may be able to establish a single, enterprise-wide SGPO that subjects all service inventories to a common SOA governance system.

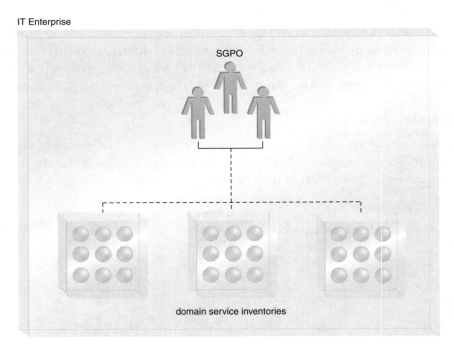

Figure 6.5
A single SGPO responsible for multiple domain service inventories.

Alternatively, different SOA governance programs can be created for each or select domain service inventories. With this model, separate programs can still be defined and maintained by the same central SGPO. The primary benefit of doing so is to maintain consistency and enterprise-wide alignment of how SOA governance programs are created and carried out, despite the fact that the respective SOA governance systems vary.

Federated Domain SGPOs

In this model, a central overarching SGPO exists in addition to individual SGPOs, each responsible for a separate domain service inventory. The domain SGPOs carry out individual SOA governance programs; however, these programs are required to comply to a set of conventions and standards defined by a single parent SGPO. The intent of this model is to strike a balance between domain-level independence and enterprise-wide consistency.

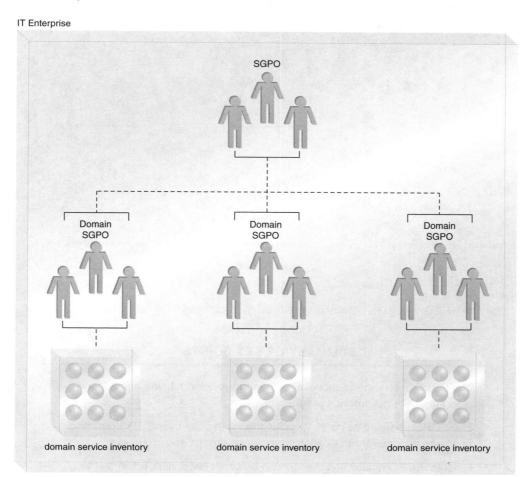

Figure 6.6
Multiple domain SGPOs are further "governed" by a central overarching SGPO.

Independent Domain SGPOs

Each domain service inventory has its own SGPO, which has full governance authority and jurisdiction over that domain. With the absence of a centralized SGPO presence, independent domain-level SGPOs have complete freedom to define and execute respective SOA governance programs.

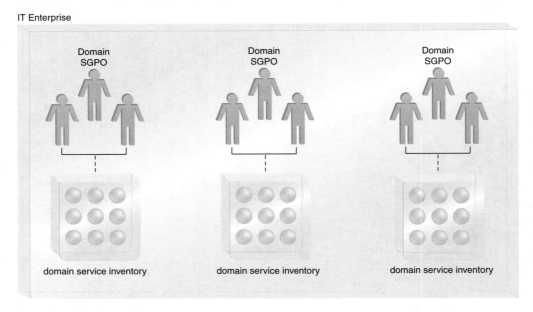

Figure 6.7
Multiple domain SGPOs independently govern multiple domain service inventories.

SUMMARY OF KEY POINTS

- The SGPO is an organizational entity responsible for defining and administering the SOA governance program.

- The SGPO needs to be carefully positioned within the overall IT department to ensure alignment with existing governance groups and programs.

- Different SGPO jurisdiction models can be considered, depending on the SOA adoption approach taken by an organization.

6.4 The SOA Governance Program

The SGPO exists to create and maintain an *SOA governance program*. This program encompasses the SOA governance system and all associated responsibilities for planning, implementing, and evolving this system. The best way to distinguish the program from the system is to view the SOA governance system as a set of formal precepts, roles, processes, metrics, and any associated models. The SOA governance program is dedicated to establishing and evolving the SOA governance system and therefore further provides real-world planning and implementation considerations, such as project plans, budgets, schedules, milestones, and further deliverables that map the SOA governance system to other parts of the existing IT enterprise (including already established IT governance systems).

The task of realizing an SOA governance program can be divided into three basic steps:

1. Assessing the Enterprise (or Domain)

2. Planning and Building the SOA Governance Program

3. Running the SOA Governance Program

Step 1: Assessing the Enterprise (or Domain)

Before creating appropriate precepts and formalizing the overall SOA governance system, the SGPO must first evaluate specific aspects of the current organizational state of the IT enterprise or whatever domain thereof for which that SOA adoption is being planned. This assessment may be limited to the domain in which the SGPO operates, but often also encompasses broader, organization-wide considerations that apply to most or all domains.

The assessment generally focuses on several specific areas:

- Current Governance Practices and Management Styles
- SOA Initiative Maturity
- Current Organizational Model
- Current and Planned Balance of On-Premise and Cloud-based IT Resources

Current Governance Practices and Management Styles

The organization's existing governance practices and management styles need to be studied to determine how best to introduce SOA governance-related processes and precepts. As previously described, no one governance model is suitable for every organization. A successful SOA governance program must take into account the organization's culture and management preferences.

Common issues that need to be addressed include:

- Are decisions tightly controlled by a central authority or widely delegated?

- Do the various groups within the organization collaborate or do they typically work autonomously?

- How do other governance program offices in the company work?

- How well does the organization articulate and disseminate governance precepts?

- How rigorously do people within the organization adhere to standard practices and processes?

- How much flexibility do managers and project leaders have in adapting to processes to meet the needs of a specific project?

- How much flexibility does management have to establish or modify incentive systems?

Concrete, well-researched answers to these questions can significantly influence an SOA governance program in that they can identify both strengths and weaknesses in relation to the types of governance and management practices required to see through a successful SOA initiative. This, in turn, helps determine the nature of precepts required and to what extent the existing IT culture will be impacted by the SOA governance system.

SOA Initiative Maturity

Ideally, an SOA governance program is established prior to the launch of an SOA initiative. However, in situations where existing SOA projects or activities are already underway, a further analysis of their progress and maturity is required to ensure that the introduction of the SOA governance program ends up supporting and aligning these efforts with overarching strategic goals. The SGPO may also need to spend time assessing existing SOA initiatives in relation to an IT department's readiness for SOA governance.

NOTE
Visit www.soaspecs.com for a list of industry maturity models relevant to the adoption of service-orientation and SOA.

Current Organizational Model

An organizational model defines roles and responsibilities within an organization. A given IT department will have a distinct organizational model that usually establishes a hierarchy with levels of authority. The SGPO must assess existing roles and responsibilities in order to identify how new roles and responsibilities specific to SOA governance will affect the organizational model.

Current and Planned Balance of On-Premise and Cloud-based IT Resources

In order to take an appropriate range of considerations into account when authoring SOA governance precepts and supporting processes, the SGPO needs to have a clear understanding of what cloud-based IT resources relevant to the SOA project currently exist, and to what extent the organization is planning to explore or proceed with cloud-based deployment of services and/or related IT resources. These considerations usually lead to additional standards, additional factors that apply to review processes, and additional organizational roles and skill-sets required for the definition of precepts and processes.

Step 2: Planning and Building the SOA Governance Program

After assessing the organization, the SGPO can get to work on actually planning and creating a concrete program for SOA governance. As previously established, the SOA governance program encompasses the SOA governance system and further provides supporting components to help establish and maintain this system.

To identify the primary components of an SOA governance program, we therefore begin by revisiting the precepts, people, and processes that are part of a governance system.

SOA Governance Precepts

The assessment completed in the previous stage is intended primarily to identify the aspects of a current or planned SOA initiative that pose the most risk and have the most urgent need for structured governance.

The following precepts are described individually in Chapters 7 to 12, where they are further associated with project lifecycle stages, processes, and organizational roles:

- Service Profile Standards (Chapter 7)

- SOA Governance Technology Standards (Chapter 7)

- Preferred Adoption Scope Definition (Chapter 7)

- Organizational Maturity Criteria Definition (Chapter 7)

- Standardized Funding Model (Chapter 7)

- Service Inventory Scope Definition (Chapter 8)

- Service and Capability Candidate Naming Standards (Chapter 8)

- Service Normalization (Chapter 8)

- Service Candidate Versioning Standards (Chapter 8)

- Schema Design Standards (Chapter 9)

- Service Contract Design Standards (Chapter 9)

- Service-Orientation Contract Design Standards (Chapter 9)

- SLA Template (Chapter 9)

- Service Logic Design Standards (Chapter 9)

- Service-Orientation Architecture Design Standards (Chapter 9)

- Service Logic Programming Standards (Chapter 9)

- Custom Development Technology Standards (Chapter 9)

- Testing Tool Standards (Chapter 10)

- Testing Parameter Standards (Chapter 10)

- Service Testing Standards (Chapter 10)

- Cloud Integration Testing Standards (Chapter 10)

- Test Data Usage Guidelines (Chapter 10)

- Production Deployment and Maintenance Standards (Chapter 10)

- Runtime Service Usage Thresholds (Chapter 11)

- Service Vitality Triggers (Chapter 11)

- Centralized Service Registry (Chapter 11)

- Service Versioning Strategy (Chapter 11)

- SLA Versioning Rules (Chapter 11)

- Service Retirement Notification (Chapter 11)

- Enterprise Business Dictionary/Domain Business Dictionary (Chapter 12)

- Service Metadata Standards (Chapter 12)

- Enterprise Ontology/Domain Ontology (Chapter 12)

- Business Policy Standards (Chapter 12)

- Operational Policy Standards (Chapter 12)

- Policy Centralization (Chapter 12)

It is important to document the reasoning behind each precept and define the circumstances in which it does or does not apply. Precepts need to be codified with clarifying policies and standards and consequences for non-compliance need to be further established. Also, supporting guidelines and compliance metrics are required. Where appropriate, conditions that might warrant a waiver need to be identified and a separate precept for allowing or denying waivers may further be required.

SOA Governance Processes

Depending on the size of the SGPO, internal processes may be required to coordinate activities within the group running the office. Governance process definition is another area of focus for the SOA governance program.

The following processes are covered in Chapters 7 to 12, where they are mapped to project lifecycle stages, precepts, and organizational roles:

- Organizational Governance Maturity Assessment (Chapter 7)

- Adoption Impact Analysis (Chapter 7)

- Adoption Risk Assessment (Chapter 7)

- Business Requirements Prioritization (Chapter 8)

- Service Candidate Review (Chapter 8)

- Service Contract Design Review (Chapter 9)

- Service Contract Registration (Chapter 9)

- Service Access Control (Chapter 9)

- Service Logic Design Review (Chapter 9)

- Legal Data Audit (Chapter 9)

- Service Logic Code Review (Chapter 9)

- Service Test Results Review (Chapter 10)

- Service Certification Review (Chapter 10)

- Service Maintenance Review (Chapter 10)

- Service Vitality Review (Chapter 11)

- Service Registry Access Control (Chapter 11)

- Service Registry Record Review (Chapter 11)

- Service Discovery (Chapter 11)

- Shared Service Usage Request (Chapter 11)

- Shared Service Modification Request (Chapter 11)

- Service Versioning (Chapter 11)

- Service Retirement (Chapter 11)

- Data Quality Review (Chapter 12)

- Communications Quality Review (Chapter 12)

- Information Alignment Audit (Chapter 12)

- Policy Conflict Audit (Chapter 12)

You may have noticed how several of these processes end with "review." Many SOA governance processes are designed specifically to support and enforce compliance to precepts, and therefore are carried out subsequent to other project delivery tasks as a formal review.

SOA Governance Roles

Organizational roles associated with SOA initiatives are of great interest to the SGPO because the various project stages for which governance precepts and processes can be defined will involve these roles in a governance capacity.

The following organizational roles were introduced in Chapter 5 and are further explored in Chapters 7 to 12, where they are associated with project lifecycle stages and SOA governance precepts and processes:

- Service Analyst
- Service Architect
- Service Developer
- Service Custodian
- Service Administrator
- Cloud Resource Administrator
- Schema Custodian
- Policy Custodian
- Service Registry Custodian
- Technical Communications Specialist
- Enterprise Architect
- Enterprise Design Standards Custodian (and Auditor)
- SOA Quality Assurance Specialist
- SOA Security Specialist
- SOA Governance Specialist

Figure 6.8 provides an overview of how these roles commonly map to SOA project lifecycle stages.

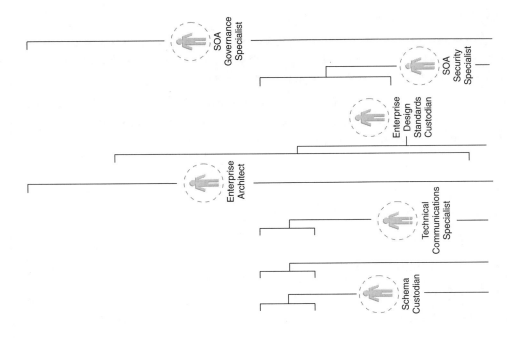

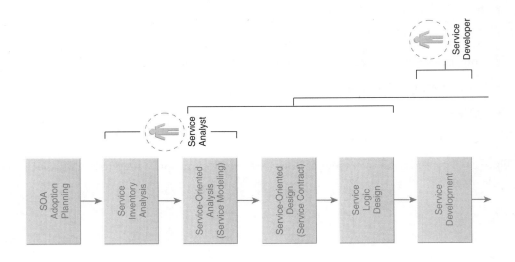

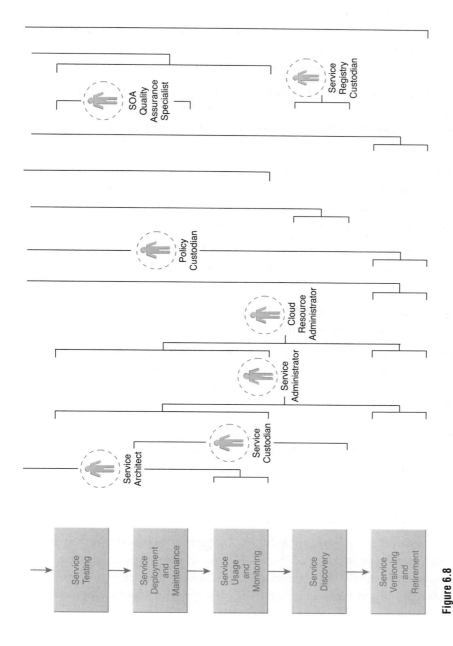

Figure 6.8

Each role can be involved in governance activities pertaining to multiple SOA project stages. Appendix B further provides master reference diagrams that illustrate the cross-project stage relationships of these roles with precepts and processes.

Additional Components

As previously stated, the scope of the SOA governance program goes beyond the definition of the SOA governance system. Some of the areas that the program will likely need
to further address in support of pre-defined precepts and processes include:

- *SOA Governance Tools* – Products and technologies that enable the automation of
  SOA governance processes or that can monitor and collect relevant statistical data
  need to be identified and chosen in order to establish a suitable SOA governance
  infrastructure.

- *SOA Governance Roadmap* – Also referred to as the SOA Governance Program
  Project Plan, this document establishes the timeline, resources, budget, and other
  real-world considerations required to actually realize the goals of the SGPO and,
  more specifically, a specific SOA governance program.

There can be many more parts and extensions to an SOA governance program specific
to the needs of a given IT department and its SOA project goals.

Step 3: Running the SOA Governance Program (Best Practices and Common Pitfalls)

The SOA governance program is a living entity that requires continuous maintenance.
Over time, and in response to real-world issues and challenges, the SOA governance
program will naturally evolve as precepts, roles, and processes are refined or added to
the overall SOA governance system.

This section contains a series of best practices that provide guidance for successfully
running an SOA governance program, as well as a set of common pitfalls that warn
against factors and circumstances that can inhibit the adoption and evolution of the
program.

Collect the Right Metrics and Have the Right People Use Them

Metrics, the fourth primary building block of a governance system, represent a vital
element in the on-going operation of the SOA governance program. Having the tools
and processes to consistently collect and disseminate key metrics is just as important
as having the right individuals and groups assigned the responsibility to interpret and
make decisions based on the reported metrics.

Provide Transparency and Foster Collaboration

Depending on its scope, an SOA governance program can affect a wide range of departments, groups, and individuals. Instead of creating the program in isolation, its development should be an open process, accessible for review and involvement to others within the IT department. Not only will this generate goodwill among those less enthusiastic about upcoming SOA adoption initiatives, but it will also allow people to voice concerns and provide suggestions. This type of feedback can help improve the SOA governance system, while also easing its eventual implementation.

Ensure Consistency and Reliability

SOA governance precepts need to be consistently enforced and SOA governance processes need to be consistently carried out. Providing a reliable means of managing and maintaining the SOA governance system is the foremost responsibility of the SGPO and depends heavily on the quality and detail with which the SOA governance program has been developed.

Besides human incompetence and poor SOA governance program definition, another reason this best practice may not be followed is an unexpected withdrawal of funding allocated to the SGPO. Should this occur, it is preferable to downsize the scope of the SOA governance program instead of trying to continue carrying out SOA governance activities without the necessary resources to ensure consistency and reliability.

Compliance and Incentives

An SOA governance system will introduce precepts that will sometimes restrict certain tasks that IT project team members have traditionally been free to complete by using their own judgment. At the same time, precepts also help make critical decisions for IT professionals that can ease their responsibilities while also guaranteeing consistency across services and service-oriented solutions. It is important that project teams embrace SOA governance precepts and processes and that they clearly understand how and why new types of compliance are required, while also fully acknowledging that their judgment and freedom in other areas are still required and relied upon.

Furthermore, offering formal incentives for regularly supporting precepts can go a long way to fostering consistent adherence. Because people will generally do that for which they are most rewarded, an absence of incentives can encourage them to violate or ignore SOA governance precepts. When this happens, something generally needs to change: the incentive, the precept, or the people.

Education and Communication

SOA governance systems can impose precepts more restrictive than traditional IT governance systems. Furthermore, some organizations can find it difficult to fully mandate the adoption of and compliance to SOA governance precepts. Even when compliance is required, in some IT cultures, groups or individuals can still choose to "rebel" by intentionally disregarding precepts because they are considered too burdensome.

Regardless of whether compliance to SOA governance precepts is voluntary or mandatory, it is critical that everyone affected fully understand why these precepts exist and how their compliance ultimately results in tangible benefits. Furthermore, it can be helpful to specifically address the common question: "What's in it for me?" Fostering a true understanding of how support for the SOA governance system can result in personal benefit will further help unify IT project teams and personnel.

For this purpose, the SGPO must put together an education and communications program. This program must begin by establishing SOA terminology, concepts, and practices using a common vocabulary that all project team members can understand. It must then introduce the SOA governance system and impress its virtues.

Common Pitfalls

From the many failed and successful SOA adoption initiatives has emerged a set of common pitfalls that pertain directly to establishing and running an SOA governance program:

- *Lack of Recognized Authority* – The SGPO must be endowed with the responsibility and authority to develop and execute the SOA governance program. For this to happen, other IT departments and project teams must accept that authority. When the SGPO's authority is ignored or not recognized, there needs to be recourse. If the lack of recognition persists, there need to be consequences for those who refuse to provide support.

- *Misalignment with IT Governance* – An SOA governance system must be consistent with and supportive of existing corporate and IT governance systems. If other IT governance precepts and processes are not taken into consideration, the SOA governance system can become inadvertently misaligned. This will result in conflicts and can further introduce risks to the IT department as a whole.

- *Overestimating or Underestimating Cloud Computing Factors* – There are various ways that cloud platforms and technologies can be made part of the planned SOA project. An organization may have or may plan to establish a private cloud comprised of standardized IT resources that require distinct administration processes, or it may be moving IT resources to a public cloud that imposes non-compliant requirements that may require even more distinct administration approaches. Either way, it is important for the SGPO to be open and flexible regarding these possibilities and—if cloud deployment is a possibility—to fully understand the consequences of having some or all services or IT resources of a given project deployed in cloud environments.

- *Impractical or Overly Formal Processes* – SOA governance processes are intended to help enforce and organize the application of precepts. Sometimes it can be tempting to create highly structured and detailed processes that cover all possible bases. Although such processes may be thorough, they can be too burdensome, onerous, or time consuming to carry out consistently in the real world. When designing SOA governance processes, consider the impact of the process on the project lifecycle and timeline and investigate any opportunity to streamline and automate parts of the process. Tools that integrate the governance process directly with development or administration platforms may further be helpful in allowing developers and administrators to efficiently identify and fix compliance issues.

- *Poor Documentation* – SOA governance precepts should be well-documented and disseminated. Many precepts require human interpretation, which means that people in the trenches will need to clearly understand how and when to apply them. Sometimes members of the SGPO take the formality of an SOA governance system too seriously. As a result, precepts and processes can be documented using overly academic or technical language. This can make the documents difficult to fully understand and, at times, inaccessible to some project team members.

- *Overspending on SOA Governance Tools* – SOA vendors have developed highly sophisticated administration and management tools (commonly labeled as "governance" products) with various design and runtime features. While powerful, these tools sometimes provide functionality that is not needed or not suitable for an organization's specific governance requirements. Further, these tools can be very expensive, especially in larger IT enterprises. Therefore, it is often worth waiting to invest in a full-blown SOA governance infrastructure until an SOA governance program has matured to the extent that the actual design and runtime automation requirements can be identified and well defined. Otherwise, over-spending or mis-spending on governance tools and technology can put a significant dent in an SOA initiative's overall ROI and further limit funds that may have been better allocated to supporting the SGPO in other areas.

SUMMARY OF KEY POINTS

- An SOA governance program encompasses the models that comprise an SOA governance system and further provides actionable artifacts that determine how the system will be established and maintained.

- A basic framework for an SOA governance program consists of three primary parts that address the assessment of the current organizational state, the planning and building of the program, as well as its evolutionary operation.

Part II

Project Governance

Chapter 7

Governing SOA Projects

SOA PRINCIPLES & PATTERNS REFERENCED IN THIS CHAPTER

- Brokered Authentication [496]
- Data Confidentiality [512]
- Data Origin Authentication [515]
- Direct Authentication [518]
- Entity Abstraction [524]
- Exception Shielding [526]
- Message Screening [534]
- Process Abstraction [544]
- Service Layers [561]
- Service Perimeter Guard [564]
- Trusted Subsystem [571]
- Utility Abstraction [573]

The foremost goal of an SOA governance program is to establish precepts for the effective, end-to-end governance of SOA project lifecycle stages. The chapters in this part of the book step through these stages (Figure 7.1) and highlight relevant governance considerations, including proposed precepts and supporting processes, roles, and metrics. It is best to consider the next six chapters as reference material, meaning that it is not necessary to read the chapters or the sections within chapters in sequence. You may want to focus on the project stages or organizational roles that are most relevant to you.

7.1 Overview

As explained in the previous chapter, the SOA Governance Program Office is not responsible for the definition of SOA project stages. Its concern is establishing entry and exit criteria for each stage. An effective approach to achieving this is to ensure that the quality and completeness of outputs from each individual lifecycle stage are reviewed and approved before proceeding to the next stage. For this reason, several review processes based on criteria established by related precepts are introduced over the next set of chapters. Adherence to these precepts is important. The longer it takes for an error or omission to be noticed, the greater its eventual impact and the cost of its correction.

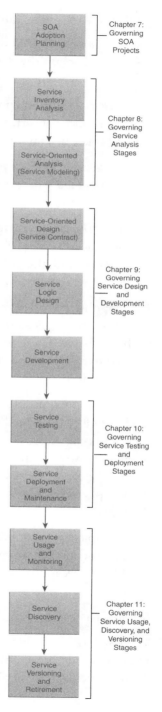

Figure 7.1

The SOA project lifecycle stages. Each of these stages was introduced in Chapter 5. The chapters in this part of the book focus solely on SOA governance controls that pertain to these stages.

Precepts, Processes, and People (Roles) Sections

The topic areas covered by Chapters 7 to 11 in Part II (as well as Chapter 12 in Part III) are further sub-divided into sections that correlate with the fundamental building blocks of a governance system:

- *Precepts* – Common precepts pertaining to an SOA project stage or an overarching governance concern are documented. A precept can be associated with processes and roles. In some special cases, a precept can be associated with another precept.

- *Processes* – Common processes used to apply and realize the goals of precepts are documented wherever appropriate. A process can be associated with precepts and roles.

- *People (Roles)* – Common organizational roles (as first described in Chapter 5) are identified and described, as they relate to covered precepts and/or processes. This section highlights roles involved in the creation of precepts and processes, as well as those regulated by them.

The mapping provided in this book between precepts, processes, and roles is based on proven associations as part of a generic SOA governance program structure common in the industry. These mappings are recommended, not required. Custom variations tailored to fulfill the specific needs of the SOA project and the organization as a whole are encouraged.

Note that some precepts can be associated with processes from different project stages (and therefore described in different chapters), and vice versa. In this case, the referenced precept or process is further qualified with its project stage name and chapter number. However, due to the fact that most organizational roles already span project stages, the roles described individually in the upcoming chapters make no reference to precepts or processes outside of the project stage section in which the role is being described.

For example, the Adoption Impact Analysis process introduced in the *Service Inventory Analysis* section later in this chapter includes a reference to the Service Inventory Scope Definition precept covered in Chapter 8. Therefore, the reference is further qualified, as follows:

Service Inventory Scope Definition (Service Inventory Analysis, Chapter 8)

The *People (Roles)* sections in the upcoming chapters are limited to the mapping of roles to precepts and processes for a given project stage. Appendix B provides a series of master reference diagrams that show cross-project stage relationships of roles to precepts and processes. Note also that mapping is provided only for the primary roles described in Chapter 5. Roles that are prefixed with "Other:" are provided for reference purposes but are not always mapped to precepts and processes.

HOW CASE STUDIES ARE USED IN PART II

Chapters 7, 8, 9, 10, and 11 are sub-divided into sections appended with associated case study examples. You may therefore want to revisit the case study background provided in Chapter 2 prior to reading these sections.

Many of the case study examples incorporate SOA governance precepts. Sometimes, precepts are further augmented to demonstrate how they can be customized and to highlight the fact that customization of the precepts and processes in this book is common and recommended.

7.2 General Governance Controls

Precepts

Before we look at precepts that are specific to individual SOA project stages, it is worth highlighting those that can apply to multiple stages or to the project as a whole.

Service Profile Standards

Services within a given service inventory need to be consistently documented, from when they are first conceived through all subsequent lifecycle stages, until they are eventually retired. Consistency in the type of information recorded about a service and in the format in which this information is organized is vital to effective service governance, especially considering how many different individuals and groups will make decisions based on this information.

The service profile described in Chapter 5 establishes a common format from which a custom standardized service profile can be derived for all services within a service inventory.

The generic service profile is organized into the following parts:

- Service-Level Profile Structure
- Capability Profile Structure

The various fields provided for each structure establish a flexible profile format in which different parts of the profile can be owned and maintained by different custodians and others involved with pre and post-deployment service lifecycle stages. However, governance regulations can limit this flexibility as required. For example, it may be necessary to restrict the maintenance of the service profile to a sole Service Custodian.

Service Information Precepts

Service information primarily represents business-centric data to which clear meaning and context has been assigned.

The following service information precepts are covered in Chapter 12:

- Business Dictionary
- Service Metadata Standards
- Ontology

Furthermore, the following supporting processes are described:

- Data Quality Review
- Communications Quality Review
- Information Alignment Audit

The use of service information has relevance to a number of stages, especially those that pertain to analysis (in that it assists with the identification of services and the definition of their functional boundaries).

Service Policy Precepts

As with service information precepts, regulations that govern the use of service policies are not stage-specific.

The following service policy precepts are also covered in Chapter 12:

- Business Policy Standards
- Operational Policy Standards
- Policy Centralization

These precepts tie into the Policy Conflict Audit process and they are further associated with service information precepts via the aforementioned Information Alignment Audit process.

Logical Domain Precepts

For many of the precepts that regulate the development, usage, and evolution of different services, there is the opportunity to further establish rules and guidelines (and perhaps even separate precepts) for services based on different types of service models.

Service models (explained in Chapter 3) form the basis of logical service layers within a given service inventory (Figure 7.2). Each service layer represents a type of service, classified by the nature of its functionality.

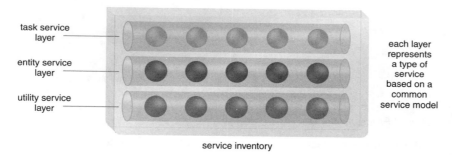

Figure 7.2

A service inventory with services organized into the three common types of service layers: utility, entity, and task, each based on a correspondingly named service model.

Different service layers can be governed in different ways when the governance precept in question pertains to differences in the functional context of the services (Figure 7.3). These service layer or service model-specific factors and considerations can apply to services when they are first conceptualized as part of early analysis stages, right through to when they are actively being used.

SOA PRINCIPLES & PATTERNS

The referenced service layers are based on the Service Layers [561] pattern, and the types of common service layers relate to the Utility Abstraction [573], Entity Abstraction [524], and Process Abstraction [544] patterns.

Figure 7.3
Each set of services is being governed by
different people or groups, based on the nature
of their functionality.

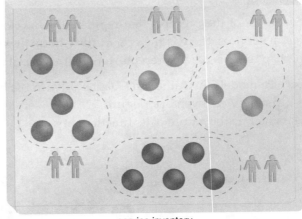

service inventory

Security Control Precepts

Throughout any of the project lifecycle stages covered in Chapters 7 to 11 there can be the need to create specific precepts to address unique security requirements and concerns. These precepts can vary significantly in that they can establish governance for a range of security controls for areas such as:

- Trust

- Claims

- Tokens

- Identification

- Authentication

- Authorization

- Confidentiality

- Integrity

- Non-Repudiation

Security control precepts can help standardize and position the usage of common SOA-related security technologies and mechanisms, including:

- Transport-Layer Security

- Message-Layer Security

- Security Policies

- Security Token Actions

- Trust Brokering

- Security Sessions

- Encryption

- Hashing

- Digital Signatures

- Identity and Access Management (IAM)

- Public Key Infrastructure (PKI)

- Digital Certificates

- Certificate Authority (CA)

- Single Sign-On

- Cloud-Based Security Groups (common to cloud-based architectures)

- Hardened Virtual Server Images (common to cloud-based architectures)

Similarly, security control precepts can further help identify approved industry security standards and further standardize their usage within the overall technology architecture.

Examples of common SOA-related security industry standards include:

- XML-Encryption

- XML-Signature

- Canonical XML

- Decryption Transform for XML Signature

- Web Services Security (WS-Security)

- Security Assertion Markup Language (SAML)

- WS-Trust

- WS-SecureConversation

- WS-SecurityPolicy

- WS-Policy

- WS-PolicyAttachment

As part of custom design standards (such as the standards that are established in the Service Contract Design Standards and Service Logic Design Standards precepts explained in Chapter 9), the use of SOA-related security design patterns can be regulated.

Examples of SOA design patterns that specifically address security concerns include:

- Data Confidentiality [512]

- Data Origin Authentication [515]

- Direct Authentication [518]

- Brokered Authentication [496]

- Exception Shielding [526]

- Message Screening [534]

- Trusted Subsystem [571]

- Service Perimeter Guard [564]

Finally, security control precepts can be authored to establish regulatory requirements to counter specific types of security threats. Such precepts are typically created for preventative reasons, in order to better equip services to deal with anticipated types of attacks—or reactively, after a service has been compromised as a result of an attack.

Common forms of SOA-related security attacks include:

- Buffer Overrun

- Information Leakage

- XPath Injection

- SQL Injection

- Exception Generation

- XML Parser Attack

- Malicious Intermediary (common to on-premise and cloud-based services)

- Denial of Service (common to on-premise and cloud-based services)

- Insufficient Authorization (common to on-premise and cloud-based services)

- Virtualization Attack (common to cloud-based services)

- Overlapping Trust Boundary (common to cloud-based services)

In the upcoming precept descriptions there are occasional references to security requirements and the potential involvement of the SOA Security Specialist role. However, security-specific precepts are not covered in this book due to the wide range of concerns and requirements they need to address, many of which are particular to an organization's individual needs.

SOA Governance Technology Standards

The application and enforcement of precepts documented in the upcoming chapters, as well as numerous steps within supporting processes, can be automated via SOA governance technology products. A fundamental precept governing the use of these products is that they are standardized for the regulation of services within a service inventory boundary. This means that different project teams or team members cannot use different products to perform the same governance task without prior approval.

The SOA governance technologies described in Chapter 14 are:

- Service Registries

- Repositories

- Service Agents

- Policy Systems

- Quality Assurance Tools

- SOA Management Suites

Other products mentioned include:

- Technical Editors and Graphic Tools

- Content Sharing and Publishing Tools

- Configuration Management Tools

The SOA Governance Technology Standards precept establishes general standards that are applied throughout SOA project stages to ensure consistency in the automation of governance tasks.

Metrics

A wide range of governance metrics can be collected throughout the SOA project lifecycle. This information provides important, real-world feedback for the SOA Governance Program Office and is almost always used to assess the success and effectiveness of the governance system.

Metrics of relevance to SOA governance are associated with common types of governance controls, as follows:

Cost Metrics

During initial SOA project lifecycle stages (ranging from planning to analysis), various types of cost metrics can be collected and analyzed to assess the asset value of planned investments, the cost impact of the planned adoption scope, the cost impact of encapsulating certain legacy resources with planned services, and so on.

As an example, this list contains common cost metrics used to compare the investment and operating costs of on-premise IT resources to cloud-based alternatives:

- *Up-front Costs* – The initial investment required to fund the IT resources.

- *On-going Costs* – The costs required to run and maintain the IT resources.

- *Cost of Capital* – The cost incurred as a result of raising the required funding for the IT resources.

- *Sunk Costs* – The prior investment that has been made in existing IT resources.

- *Integration Costs* – The costs required to carry out integration testing in an external (usually cloud-based) environment.

- *Locked-in Costs* – The costs associated with moving IT resources from one cloud to another.

These types of financial metrics not only help assess deployment and project scope factors, they also help stakeholders decide upon a suitable funding model for the SOA project (as covered in Chapter 4), and can even influence the choice of methodology for the overall delivery of the services.

Standards-related Precept Metrics

The most common types of metrics collected for standards-related precepts are those derived from the results of corresponding review processes.

Examples include:

- number of reviews resulting in approval

- number of reviews resulting in rejection or objection

- number of recorded standards violations

- number of requested waivers

- number of approved waivers

Collecting these statistics can help measure the effectiveness of a standards-based precept and can further help gauge whether the required standards are too strict or too flexible.

Threshold Metrics

Several of the regulations established by SOA governance precepts can put hard limitations on the design-time or runtime usage or management of a service. These types of thresholds create concrete parameters that those working with or managing services are required to respect.

Chapter 11 provides the following example thresholds associated with runtime service regulation:

- Service Composition Membership Threshold

- Service Instance Threshold

- Cloud Burst Threshold

- Service Billing Threshold

- Service Elasticity Threshold

- Service Exception Threshold

- Service Data Throughput Threshold

- Service Monitoring Footprint Threshold

Metrics derived from these types of parameters primarily relate to how well they are being adhered to.

For example:

- number of times a threshold was surpassed
- number of times the design-time usage of a service was rejected
- number of times the runtime usage of a service was rejected
- types of exceptions resulting from threshold-related service usage rejections
- number of times service usage neared a given threshold

The last type of metric in particular can be useful for planning purposes. Studying usage trends that indicate that thresholds are too close to actual required usage can help justify adjustments in the thresholds themselves (prior to services suffering from runtime performance fluctuations when thresholds are exceeded).

Vitality Metrics

Vitality metrics are collected to measure a service's on-going behavior. These metrics can, under pre-defined conditions, execute vitality triggers to help improve (or refresh) service implementations in response to new requirements.

The two types of vitality metrics discussed are:

- *Performance Metrics* – These are runtime metrics with defined thresholds that can execute various vitality triggers.
- *Compliance Metrics* – These can exist as manual or automated metrics. Manual compliance metrics are comparable to the aforementioned standards-related precept metrics. Automated compliance metrics are comparable to threshold metrics.

What distinguishes vitality metrics is that they are part of an overall vitality framework that can exist independently from other types of precepts. Vitality metrics are further explained in Chapter 13.

SUMMARY OF KEY POINTS

- There are several important precepts that are general in scope in that they can apply to multiple SOA project stages.
- As with stage-specific precepts, the application of most general precepts results in the need for standardization.

CASE STUDY EXAMPLE

Raysmoore wants to ensure that all upcoming SOA investments are justified and guaranteed to advance corporate objectives. A custom general governance precept (Table 7.1) is therefore created to establish regulations for project teams to follow when soliciting and evaluating vendor proposals. This precept is not considered specific to any one SOA project stage as IT asset investments can be made during any part of a project lifecycle.

SOA Investment Proposal Precept	
Objective: A financial investment in IT assets for the SOA adoption project will only be made if it is proven to advance Raysmoore's corporate strategy and business goals, as defined in the official Raysmoore Mission Statement.	
Policy: Each investment proposal must specify the anticipated costs incurred and benefits generated by the proposed IT assets. In addition to mapping each proposed investment to business goals, associated costs and risks must be accurately described. Failure to comply with this policy is cause for disciplinary action.	*Policy:* Each investment proposal must suggest at least one alternative solution that addresses the proposal requirements. The recommended solution must be justified in relation to Raysmoore's business goals and in comparison to alternatives.
Standard: An SOA Investment Committee needs to be established to authorize investments above $5,000. Investments over $50,000 further require the approval and sign-off of the CIO.	*Standard:* For purchases in excess of $50,000, the recommended solution and identified alternatives must be assessed by an outside consultant.
Standard: All presented investment proposals must be based on the standard Investment Proposal Template. The SOA Investment Committee is responsible for developing and maintaining this template.	*Guideline:* When comparing solutions, corporate-approved metrics can be used along with "soft," difficult-to-measure benefits that may be relevant to associating solution feature sets to corporate business goals.

Table 7.1

A custom governance precept that establishes intent and authority of a fundamental regulation.

In support of this precept, the Raysmoore SOA Governance Program Office defines a set of metrics for measuring precept efficiency:

- number of proposals submitted

- time required to make a proposal decision

- number of proposals rejected due to insufficient data

- number of proposals approved

- number of proposals approved without a CIO sign-off

- size of each approved investment

- length of time required to recoup the investment

- total return generated by an approved investment at 12, 18, and 24 months

- number of investments that did not break even within 12, 18, or 24 months

The statistical data collected by these metrics will help indicate how the precept can be improved or how it may need to be better communicated.

7.3 Governing SOA Adoption Planning

Some of the most critical and repercussive decisions are made during the planning stages of an SOA adoption effort. It is during this initial stage that an approach toward adoption is defined, leading to the authoring of baseline documents, such as the SOA Adoption Roadmap and a related SOA Adoption Project Plan.

The precepts introduced in the upcoming sections establish regulations and raise considerations pertaining to the SOA Adoption Planning stage to ensure that all bases are covered when it comes to factoring in common upfront concerns. Note that the precepts themselves do not dictate the creation of SOA Adoption Roadmap and Project Plan documents; it is assumed that these fundamental specifications are being actively authored during the SOA Adoption Planning stage. Instead, the application of the upcoming precepts results in new content and intelligence that acts as critical input for these documents.

Precepts

Preferred Adoption Scope Definition

In order to assess the viability of an SOA adoption, there must be an understanding as to the initial, preferred scope of adoption. For example, project managers and stakeholders must have a preliminary idea as to whether the adoption will be enterprise-wide or limited to a domain within the enterprise. This preferred scope will influence how other precepts are defined and the extent to which related processes are carried out.

> **NOTE**
>
> The Preferred Adoption Scope Definition precept remains subject to change until the Service Inventory Scope precept (Chapter 8) is applied during the Service Inventory Analysis stage, at which point the actual, real-world adoption scope is determined. Both Preferred Adoption Scope Definition and Service Inventory Scope precepts are based on the Balanced Scope pillar described in Chapter 4.

Related Processes

- Organizational Governance Maturity Assessment
- Adoption Impact Analysis
- Adoption Risk Assessment

Related Roles

- Enterprise Architect
- SOA Governance Specialist

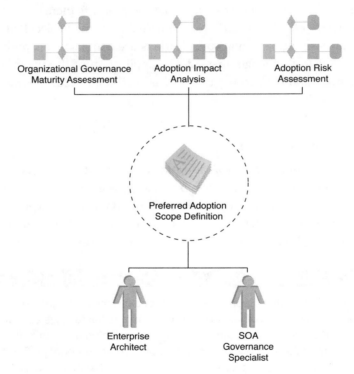

Figure 7.4
The Preferred Adoption Scope Definition
precept.

Organizational Maturity Criteria Definition

A basic starting point during the planning stage is to perform a study of the IT organization, as it exists today, in order to determine its level of maturity in relation to the specific and on-going requirements of the planned SOA adoption.

In order to carry out this type of study, specific criteria needs to be defined. This criteria is based on a combination of the distinct demands and impacts associated with SOA and service-orientation, along with the specific requirements and goals of the business.

Foundational criteria is based upon three of the pillars of service-orientation introduced earlier in Chapter 4:

- Teamwork

- Education

- Discipline

These and other considerations form criteria that can be organized into a series of checklists. This precept requires that this criteria be established as an initial step in the SOA Adoption Planning stage, applicable within the scope defined via the Preferred Adoption Scope precept.

Related Processes

- Organizational Governance Maturity Assessment

Related Roles

- Enterprise Architect

- SOA Governance Specialist

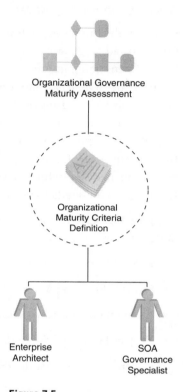

Figure 7.5
The Organizational Maturity Criteria Definition precept.

Standardized Funding Model

Based on the business goals associated with the planned SOA adoption, and with further information gathered as part of the creation of the SOA roadmap, there should be enough understanding of the gap between the current state of the IT enterprise and the target state expected from the SOA initiative. In support of this, a budget needs to be established for which a corresponding funding model needs to be chosen.

Chapter 4 described the following common SOA funding models:

- Project Funding Model (Platform)

- Central Funding Model (Platform)

- Usage Based Funding Model (Platform)

- Project Funding Model (Service)

- Central Funding Model (Service)

- Hybrid Funding Model (Service)

- Usage Based Funding Model (Service)

Adoption Impact Analysis   Adoption Risk Assessment

Standardized Funding Model

SOA Governance Specialist

Figure 7.6
The Standardized Funding Model precept.

The choice of funding model for establishing the platform (service inventory) and the delivery and evolution of individual services can have significant impacts in all areas of the initiative. Systems for methodology, management, and governance will all be influenced by that manner in which funds are allocated, the rate at which funds become available, and the source of the funds.

This precept dictates that these areas are clearly defined and established during the SOA Adoption Planning stage, because once a project is underway, unexpected changes in how funds are received and allocated can have numerous disruptive consequences.

NOTE
The chosen funding model can impact the preferred adoption scope and vice versa. Therefore, it is important to keep discussions pertaining to adoption scope inclusive of funding model definition.

Related Processes

- Adoption Impact Analysis
- Adoption Risk Assessment

Related Roles

- SOA Governance Specialist

Processes

Organizational Governance Maturity Assessment

This process incorporates all of the preceding precepts in addition to several other factors with the goal of assessing the maturity of an organization in relation to different areas affected by SOA governance. The purpose of the assessment is essentially to identify how ready and prepared an organization is to assume SOA governance responsibilities. The results of completing this assessment will not only help determine strengths and weaknesses within the organization, it will also help define the appropriate scope of the SOA adoption effort to ensure that it is both meaningful and manageable.

Another expected result of this assessment process is to increase the actual level of organizational maturity.

Chapter 4 introduced the following common organizational maturity levels:

- Service Neutral
- Service Aware
- Service Capable
- Business Aligned
- Business Driven
- Service Ineffectual (negative)
- Service Aggressive (negative)

The intelligence and insight gathered by the assessment can help educate key IT stakeholders, as well as the SOA Governance Program Office itself. This can effectively transition the IT enterprise from the Service Neutral to the Service Aware maturity level, thereby reducing the risk of an SOA initiative inadvertently moving to the negative Service Ineffectual or Service Aggressive levels.

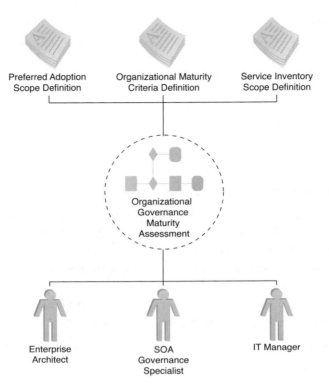

Figure 7.7

The Organizational Governance Maturity Assessment process.

NOTE

Although the Organizational Governance Maturity Assessment will be carried out by SOA Governance Specialists and others involved with the SOA Governance Program Office, the results of this assessment may end up impacting the structure of the SOA Governance Program Office itself. For example, additional resources may be added to address identified gaps or weaknesses. Or, perhaps the assessment results are lower than expected, thereby requiring a reduction in adoption scope and a corresponding reduction in the size of the SOA Governance Program Office.

To carry out an Organizational Governance Maturity Assessment process requires a framework that provides a quantitative means of measuring specific aspects of maturity in the organization. This framework may have its own structured methodology used to identify symptoms while at the same time diagnosing their root causes. Various industry and proprietary maturity assessments exist, some of which build on established IT maturity models and frameworks.

NOTE

Visit www.soaspecs.com for a list of maturity models and frameworks relevant to SOA and service-orientation. Note, however, that many of these models and frameworks are used to assess the overall maturity of an IT department or its maturity in relation to SOA adoption. Although this is helpful, it is not specific to assessing the *SOA governance* maturity of an IT department.

The Organizational Government Maturity Assessment can also be used to collect statistics about various domain-specific projects so that common pre-project maturity levels can be captured and so that common transitions between positive and negative maturity levels can be recorded. A valuable metric derived from collecting this information over time is how much easier and faster subsequent projects transition through or reach positive maturity levels compared to earlier initiatives. Measured improvements can be an indication of how early projects are raising awareness of requirements and critical success factors that can help other parts of the organization better prepare for future projects.

Related Precepts

- Preferred Adoption Scope Definition
- Organizational Maturity Criteria Definition
- Service Inventory Scope Definition (Service Inventory Analysis, Chapter 8)

Related Roles

- Enterprise Architect
- SOA Governance Specialist
- Other: IT Manager

Adoption Impact Analysis

With a solid understanding of an organization's current level of maturity in relation to the adoption of SOA and associated governance requirements, the scope of the adoption effort can be more accurately established. This will result in a clear definition of the target state that the organization expects to achieve as a result of a successful adoption.

With the current and target states well-defined, an analysis can be performed to document and assess both the technological and organizational impacts required to carry out the adoption of SOA and service-orientation.

The basic types of impacts addressed by this process are focused on:

- Cost

- Effort

- Disruption

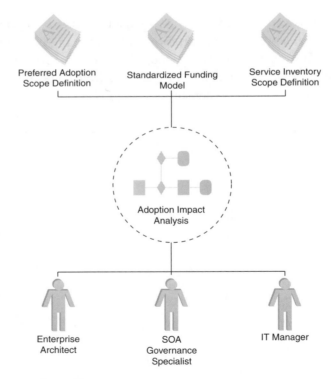

Figure 7.8
The Adoption Impact Analysis process.

The extent of this study will be directly related to the planned scope of the adoption, as well as the assessed maturity of the organization. The areas covered by an Adoption Impact Analysis process can vary dramatically, as they pertain specifically to the unique business and technology-related characteristics of a given organization's current and target state.

Provided here is a sampling of some common impact analysis areas:

- changes to traditional IT organizational and departmental structures

- introduction of new organizational roles and responsibilities

- changes to traditional IT management systems and methodologies (especially in relation to the governance, ownership, and evolution of shared services)

- impacts to legacy resources targeted for service encapsulation

- new technology products required for infrastructure and architecture upgrades

- planned shifts of on-premise IT resources to cloud environments (or vice-versa)

- new or augmented security requirements

- maturity issues related to planned service technologies

- performance and reliability impacts (especially in comparison to established silo-based applications)

The output of this process is typically a formal report detailing the cost, effort, and anticipated disruption of each identified area of impact. As with the completion of the Organizational Governance Maturity Assessment, the conclusions drawn from the completion of the Adoption Impact Analysis may lead to an adjustment in adoption scope.

NOTE

A more accurate analysis of impacts can be performed subsequent to the definition of the service inventory blueprint specification. Depending on the methodology being used for the SOA project, it may or may not be warranted to revisit and revise the results of the original Adoption Impact Analysis.

Related Precepts

- Preferred Adoption Scope Definition

- Standardized Funding Model

- Service Inventory Scope Definition (Service Inventory Analysis, Chapter 8)

Related Roles

- Enterprise Architect

- SOA Governance Specialist

- Other: IT Manager

Adoption Risk Assessment

There are several established assessment models and systems used by IT departments to help determine the risk of change. These models can be used to gauge risks associated with new technology adoption, the automation of new business processes or domains, the proposed expansion or reduction of IT staff and resources, the shifting of IT resources to external environments (such as third-party clouds), and/or the outsourcing of various IT functions.

With all of the intelligence gathered as a result of applying the preceding precepts and processes, a great amount of information will be available for stakeholders to perform a formal Adoption Risk Assessment of the planned SOA adoption project. This process may not result in any new concrete information pertaining to the project planning of the initiative; however, it may provide some fresh revelations and insights by focusing solely on risk factors.

Related Precepts

- Preferred Adoption Scope Definition

- Standardized Funding Model

- Service Inventory Scope Definition (Service Inventory Analysis, Chapter 8)

Related Roles

- Enterprise Architect

- SOA Governance Specialist

- Other: IT Manager

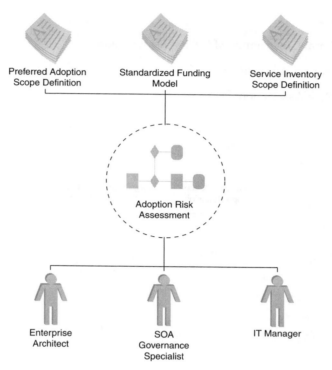

Figure 7.9
The Adoption Risk Assessment process.

People (Roles)

Enterprise Architect

Because of the broad knowledge Enterprise Architects have of the current and historical state of the IT enterprise, their involvement in most planning activities is required. Their insight into the intricacies of both organizational and technological aspects of the overall ecosystem can enable them to help define the appropriate adoption scope, assess organizational maturity, and identify impacts and risks. In many cases, they will also act as signing authorities for the SOA Roadmap and Project Planning documents.

Related Precepts

- Preferred Adoption Scope Definition
- Organizational Maturity Criteria Definition

Related Processes

- Organizational Governance Maturity Assessment
- Adoption Impact Analysis
- Adoption Risk Assessment

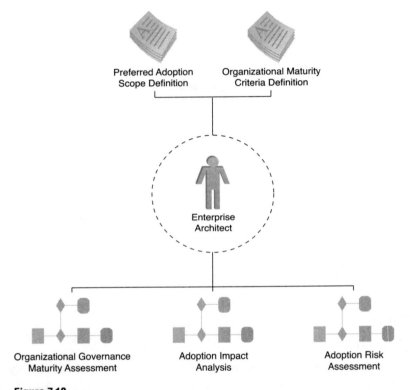

Figure 7.10
Service Adoption Planning governance precepts and processes associated with the
Enterprise Architect role.

SOA Governance Specialist

On behalf of the SOA Governance Program Office (which should already have been formed prior to the SOA Adoption Planning stage), one or more SOA Governance Specialists will be actively involved in establishing precepts and processes and to further provide guidance specifically in relation to maturity considerations, impacts, and risks that pertain to pre-deployment and on-going post-deployment SOA governance requirements.

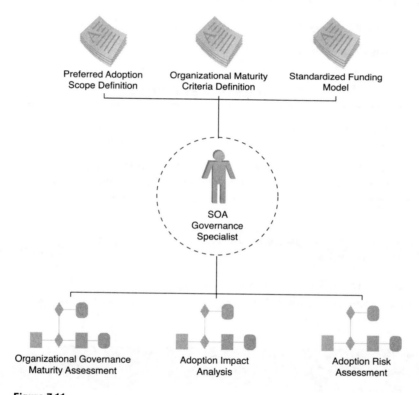

Figure 7.11

Service Adoption Planning governance precepts and processes associated with the SOA Governance Specialist role.

Related Precepts

- Preferred Adoption Scope Definition

- Organizational Maturity Criteria Definition

- Standardized Funding Model

Related Processes

- Organizational Governance Maturity Assessment

- Adoption Impact Analysis

- Adoption Risk Assessment

SUMMARY OF KEY POINTS

- Precepts applied during the SOA Adoption Planning stage are primarily focused on assessing the viability and suitable scope of the adoption project.

- Several of the governance processes can result in further input that can help shape original project plans, thereby introducing iterative planning cycles.

CASE STUDY EXAMPLE

The IT group leading the SOA adoption project at Raysmoore has embarked on an Organizational Governance Maturity Assessment using the following COBIT-inspired rating system (Table 7.2).

Governance Maturity Score	Description
0 - Non-Existent	There is a complete lack of support and the issue has not been recognized as an area to be addressed.
1 - Initial/Ad-hoc	There is evidence that the issue has been recognized as an area to be addressed. However, there are no standard-ized approaches, nor are there existing approaches applied consistently.

Governance Maturity Score	Description
2 - Repeatable but Intuitive	Approaches have been developed to the stage at which common procedures are being followed by different individuals or teams undertaking the same task. However, there is no formal training or communication of standardized procedures.
3 - Defined	Procedures have been standardized, documented, and communicated. It is mandated that these approaches be followed; however, it is unlikely that deviations will be detected and corrected.
4 - Managed and Measurable	Allocated authorities monitor and measure compliance with procedures and take action when approaches appear not to be working effectively. Approaches undergo regular revision. Automation and tools may also be used.
5 - Optimized	Approaches are refined to a level of mature practice and undergo continuous revision and refinement cycles.

Table 7.2
A COBIT-based rating system.

Using this rating system, the initial phase of the SOA governance maturity assessment focuses on the following areas:

- Cultural Readiness (Table 7.3)

- Centralization Factors (Table 7.4)

- Political Environment (Table 7.5)

- Technical Project Roles and Culture (Table 7.6)

The following series of tables further document the results of individual attributes of the assessed areas. Several of the comments were collected as a result of analysis and in-person interviews with relevant representatives and stakeholders.

Cultural Readiness		
Attribute	**Score**	**Scoring Comments**
Attitude Towards Governance	3 (defined)	Raysmoore has started the process of governance centralization by having established a parent SOA Governance Program Office in support of the adoption project. There are some additional governance activities that pertain specifically to developing traditional projects, but these are not consistently used and managed across Lovelt and Reeldrill.
Attitude Towards External Solutions	4 (managed)	Raysmoore has generally demonstrated a disciplined and managed approach to reusing services from outside sources. The enterprise architecture team performed a study of available Financial solutions and selected one that is now used throughout Raysmoore's environment. On the other hand, Lovelt had to be forced to use Reeldrill's ERP service-enabled system.
Power Balance in IT	3 (defined)	Raysmoore has a defined process for working across the Lovelt and Reeldrill business domains. In some areas, such as choosing a solution, they have experience in managing this process, but most areas have not had to deal with this level of potential conflict.
Attitude Towards Long-Term Strategy	1 (ad-hoc)	The Raysmoore enterprise architecture group has been strictly limited to an advisory role and has not had any real power to make decisions and shape the organization. Its attempts at formulating a long-term strategy have been ignored by both Lovelt and Reeldrill in the past, with no consequences
Attitude Towards Innovation	1 (ad-hoc)	After assessing past projects, it is determined that openness to innovation and risk taking has not been common at Raysmoore. The group pushing innovation is the enterprise architecture team and it has often been ignored.

Table 7.3
Assessment of cultural readiness factors.

Centralization Factors		
Attribute	**Score**	**Scoring Comments**
General Centralization	3 (defined)	Raysmoore is in the process of centralizing its practices, policies, and governance activities. However, those capabilities are not yet effectively managed across its existing silos.
Geography	3 (defined)	Raysmoore is geographically distributed across various regions. Remote staff make good use of conferencing technology to maintain consistent communication.
Shared Services	3 (defined)	Shared Services already exist within Raysmoore, including services from a previous SOA project held by Reeldrill prior to its acquisition. These shared services have so far received light management.

Table 7.4
Assessment of centralization factors.

Political Environment		
Attribute	**Score**	**Scoring Comments**
Leadership	1 (ad-hoc)	Raysmoore has weak IT leadership and Lovelt leadership is resistant to change. No one group is providing leadership to initiate enterprise-wide improvements.
Empire Building	1 (ad-hoc)	There has been rampant empire building at both Lovelt and Reeldrill.
Politics	1 (ad-hoc)	There is a high degree of political influence in decision making at Raysmoore. Lovelt and Reeldrill are constantly jockeying for authority with each other.
Relationship Between Business and IT	2 (repeatable)	Some good relationships exist between the business and IT, but both would like to see improvements.

Table 7.5
Assessment of political environment factors.

Technical Project Team		
Attribute	**Score**	**Scoring Comments**
Architect Roles	1 (ad-hoc)	Architect roles are dependent upon the personality of the architect and his/her relationship with the development staff.
Architecture Acceptance	1 (ad-hoc)	Acceptance of technology architecture and design is dependent on the relationship between the architect and the development team in a given project. In some projects, technology architecture is not planned for or even referenced.
Use of Standards by Development Teams	1 (ad-hoc)	The Lovelt and Reeldrill development teams are not used to working within a larger set of enterprise standards, and do so reluctantly.
Development Team Leadership	0 (non-existent)	Development teams at both Lovelt and Reeldrill have a "hero" leadership culture. The hero programmer fixes complex problems and rejects any attempts to govern the resulting code.
Developer and Architect Roles	0 (non-existent)	There are no clearly defined roles within project teams that separate development from technology architecture. When technology architecture is made part of a specification, it is generally documented by a senior developer (or, at times, by an outsourced developer).

Table 7.6
Assessment of technical project team factors.

This preliminary glimpse at the assessment results has already raised enough red flags to prompt the SOA project leaders to initiate meetings and even training sessions with key IT managers and staff. It has become clear that further education is required to ensure that those affected by the SOA adoption project will understand the necessity of certain changes and will further be supportive of the initiative overall. It is decided that these and other identified areas of weakness must be addressed before proceeding further with any analysis stages.

Chapter 8

Governing Service Analysis Stages

SOA PRINCIPLES & PATTERNS REFERENCED IN THIS CHAPTER

- Capability Composition [503]
- Canonical Expression [497]
- Contract Denormalization [510]
- Domain Inventory [520]
- Enterprise Inventory [522]
- Service Normalization [563]

Service analysis stages are a focal point when comparing SOA methodologies. Often, what distinguishes approaches to the delivery of services and collections of services is the extent to which analysis receives up-front attention, and how analysis is positioned in relation to other stages. From a governance perspective, the analysis of services is regulated to make the very most of the time and effort available to analysis-related project stages. The smaller the window allocated for analysis work, the greater the importance of firm governance.

In this chapter, we cover governance precepts for the two fundamental service analysis stages:

- Service Inventory Analysis
- Service-Oriented Analysis (Service Modeling)

As explained in Chapter 5, these stages are very much interrelated in that if a Service Inventory Analysis is carried out, it will establish a cycle in which the Service-Oriented Analysis stage will be performed iteratively (see Figure 8.2).

The maximum amount of iterations that can be executed is determined by the scope of the planned service inventory. The amount of *actual* iterations executed before post-analysis project stages take place is determined by the methodology. Therefore, it is important to understand the governance impact of allocating more or less time and effort to up-front analysis.

Specifically, the extent to which the Service Inventory Analysis cycle is iteratively (and competently) carried out has a direct bearing on the extent of pre-design and post-deployment governance burden services can impose.

Specifically, when more up-front time and effort is allocated:

- there is increased up-front burden, because the scope of governance responsibilities and required regulation for analysis tasks is broadened, but...
- there is a decrease in post-deployment governance burden, because the more advance effort invested in the definition of the service inventory blueprint, the better the quality of the resulting service candidates.

Better quality service candidates reduce the likelihood that subsequently delivered services will require refactoring, versioning, or will otherwise introduce avoidable governance-related impact to the IT enterprise in response to business change. In other words, increasing analysis effort helps increase the lifespan of service versions and can reduce the post-implementation governance burden of entire collections of services.

On the other hand, when going with a methodology that limits or minimizes the amount of time and effort allocated to service analysis stages:

- there is decreased up-front governance burden, because there is less analysis activity to regulate, but…

- there is an increase in post-deployment governance burden because of a greater likelihood that delivered services will require versioning and refactoring sooner than later.

Figure 8.1 contrasts these approaches. The large vertical arrows represent where, within the project lifecycle stages, this type of governance impact typically occurs.

Although it is often preferred to proceed with a Service Inventory Analysis prior to a business process-specific Service-Oriented Analysis, it is not always required or possible. There are cases where practical concerns or tactical business requirements take precedence over the strategic benefits of increased up-front analysis. As stated earlier, when less time within an SOA project is allocated to service analysis stages, it further amplifies the need for strong governance of the analysis effort.

Figure 8.1

Generally, the less time and effort
spent on the up-front service
analysis, the greater the on-going,
post-deployment governance
burden. The approach on the left is
comparable with bottom-up service
delivery and the approach on the right
is more akin to top-down delivery.
SOA methodologies that attempt to
combine elements of both approaches
also exist.

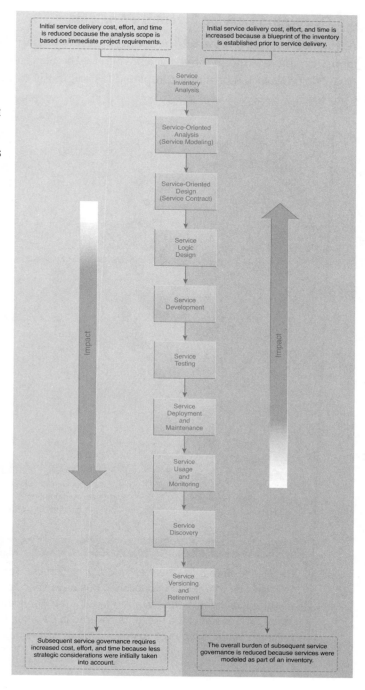

8.1 Governing Service Inventory Analysis

As further shown in Figure 8.2, the Service Inventory Analysis is commonly organized into iterative cycles whereby the Service-Oriented Analysis process is repeatedly completed (as originally explained in Chapter 5).

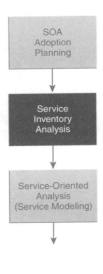

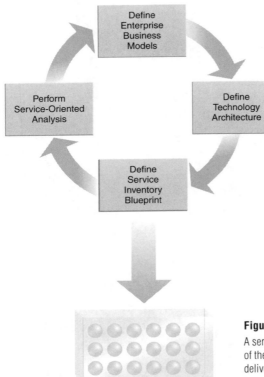

Figure 8.2

A service inventory blueprint (bottom) is the primary deliverable of the Service Inventory Analysis stage. Depending on the project delivery methodology used, several iterations of this cycle may occur to produce this deliverable.

NOTE

The *Define Enterprise Business Models* step in the Service Inventory Analysis lifecycle refers to published business specifications, documents, and artifacts that provide suitable input for the Service-Oriented Analysis stage. Several of the precepts covered in Chapter 12 pertain to the definition of these types of business models as the basis of governance precepts.

Precepts

Service Inventory Scope Definition

A key success factor in any Service Inventory Analysis effort is the correct scope definition for the service inventory blueprint. As stated in the SOA Manifesto (and the *Balanced Scope* section in Chapter 4), the scope of a service inventory needs to be "meaningful and manageable." The manageability of the planned service inventory is a foremost governance concern.

The application of this precept will need to involve the SOA Governance Program Office as this scope represents not only the magnitude of the SOA project delivery effort, but also the corresponding SOA governance effort. The definition of the service inventory scope is an overarching precept that establishes a concrete boundary within the IT enterprise for the delivery of a specific collection of services. As such, it further influences (but does not set) the scope of the Service Inventory Analysis stage.

Within the established boundary, services need to adhere to consistent governance, management, and methodology. Specifically, from a governance perspective, the service delivery lifecycle is required to adhere to the precepts established by the governance system applied to the service inventory.

Further, the service inventory blueprint scope represents a contract between IT and any related business operating units. This agreement establishes priorities that provide a means of carrying out a methodology for the identification, definition, development, and deployment of services within the service inventory in order to:

- match the value and urgency of relevant business needs

- most effectively support high-priority business goals (such as improving operational efficiency, profitability, organizational agility, etc.)

- cost-effectively leverage associated IT skills and resources

To achieve a governance system dedicated to Service Inventory Analysis with the aforementioned qualities depends on the successful usage and adherence of a number of additional stage-specific governance processes and precepts.

> **SOA PRINCIPLES & PATTERNS**
>
> This precept relates to the Enterprise Inventory [522] and Domain Inventory [520] patterns, each of which provides an alternative approach for the definition of a service inventory scope, in relation to the scope of the overall IT enterprise.

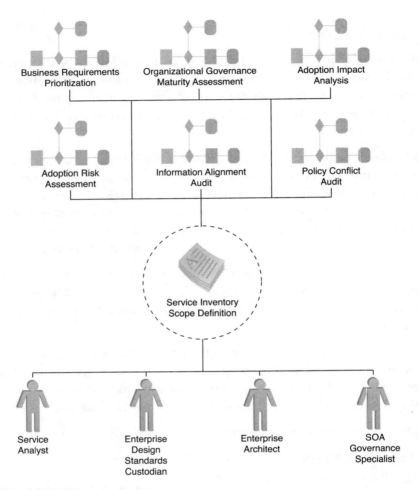

Figure 8.3

The Service Inventory Scope Definition precept.

Related Processes

- Business Requirements Prioritization

- Organizational Governance Maturity Assessment (Chapter 7)

- Adoption Impact Analysis (Chapter 7)

- Adoption Risk Assessment (Chapter 7)

- Information Alignment Audit (Chapter 12)
- Policy Conflict Audit (Chapter 12)

Related Roles

- Service Analyst
- Enterprise Design Standards Custodian
- Enterprise Architect
- SOA Governance Specialist

Processes

Business Requirements Prioritization

A primary consideration when carrying out the Service Inventory Analysis is how to prioritize business processes and requirements in order to determine the order in which they are subjected to the iterations of the Service-Oriented Analysis process. This relates directly to the *Define Enterprise Business Models* step that starts off each iteration of the Service Inventory Analysis cycle.

Business requirements prioritization involves a process whereby the business automation requirements within the domains or sub-domains of the Service Inventory Analysis scope are compared. This comparison can involve various criteria, including the urgency of requirements, cost of automation, impact on legacy systems, and so on.

A common deliverable used to organize the typical output of this process is the *business heat map*. This document contains tables consisting of columns that represent individual business units, each further containing a set of business activities (or responsibilities) specific to that unit. Heat maps are organized into business domains. For most large organizations, many of these domains will be split into sub-domains, each of which may be controlled by a separate IT Manager. In most cases, the top one or two domain levels suffice.

In order to fulfill its responsibilities, each domain has to be able to carry out certain business activities. Assigning a business activity to a specific domain implies assigning ownership of that activity to that domain. However, it does not imply that it is exclusively involved in the execution of that activity because many business activities can involve interaction between multiple business domains. Developing the heat map begins by creating a list of the business activities owned by each domain.

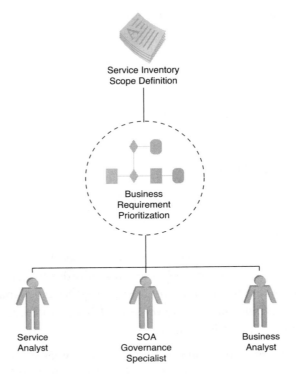

Figure 8.4
The Business Requirement Prioritization process.

The next step is to define which of those identified business activities needs to be improved or enhanced in some way to meet specific strategic business goals.

Examples include:

- business activities that are strategic but are being performed ineffectively
- business activities that reflect new business opportunities
- business activities that address new threats
- business functionality performance improvements
- areas of business activity that need to be downsized
- business activities that might be candidates for outsourcing or selling off

"Hot spot" areas, such as these, that require specific attention (based on the aforementioned criteria) are displayed in a different color. Separate explanatory text describes the type of attention of each focus area. (See the case study at the end of this section for an example of a business heat map.)

A business heat map can provide valuable governance input to help plan and carry out a Service Inventory Analysis. It represents a consensus view of business priorities and offers the additional benefit of providing a high-level view of the internal structure of one or more business domains.

Related Precepts

- Service Inventory Scope Definition

Related Roles

- Service Analyst
- SOA Governance Specialist
- Other: Business Analyst

People (Roles)

Service Analyst

The Service Inventory Analysis stage is essentially led by Service Analysts. Depending on how many are involved with the creation of a given service inventory blueprint, it may be necessary to designate a lead Service Analyst. This may especially be required when multiple teams of Service Analysts are working concurrently on producing service candidates for the same service inventory blueprint.

On the other hand, Service Analysts tend to take a secondary role when involved with the Business Requirements Prioritization process. Their contribution to this process primarily relates to ensuring a constant alignment between business processes and business domains used as input for the Service Inventory Analysis and Service-Oriented Analysis stages.

Service Inventory
Scope Definition

Service
Analyst

Business Requirements
Prioritization

Figure 8.5

Service Inventory Analysis governance precepts and processes associated with the Service Analyst role.

Related Precepts

- Service Inventory Scope Definition

Related Processes

- Business Requirements Prioritization

Enterprise Design Standards Custodian

Certain types of design standards can impose limitations or parameters that affect the definition of service inventory boundaries. For example, there may be product-specific platforms or proprietary technology or legacy resources that can impose hard perimeters that end up reducing or adjusting the planned scope of a service inventory. Enterprise Design Standards Custodians will be aware of these limitations (and may have themselves even defined them), making their involvement in this stage important. As a role that also commonly audits compliance to enterprise design standards, their participation may, in fact, be mandatory in that they may need to sign off on the proposed service inventory blueprint specification.

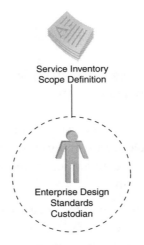

Figure 8.6

Service Inventory Analysis governance precepts and processes associated with the Enterprise Design Standards Custodian role.

Related Precepts

- Service Inventory Scope Definition

Related Processes

N/A

Enterprise Architect

Whereas the Enterprise Design Standards Custodian role is primarily concerned with the impact of and compliance to custom design standards, the Enterprise Architect will have a broader understanding of the overall IT ecosystem affected by the planned service inventory architecture. This insight will be helpful for providing guidance from a practical perspective, especially in relation to legacy resources that may need to be encapsulated by services within the planned service inventory scope.

Related Precepts

- Service Inventory Scope Definition

Related Processes

N/A

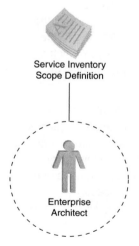

Figure 8.7
Service Inventory Analysis governance precepts and processes associated with the Enterprise Architect role.

SOA Governance Specialist

The primary responsibility of the SOA Governance Specialist during the Service Inventory Analysis stage is to provide input as to the governance requirements and impacts that the proposed service inventory scope (and associated business requirements scope) will introduce. Furthermore, this role will be assigned the task of ensuring that the Service Inventory Scope Definition precept and Business Requirements Prioritization process are carried out according to other predefined compliance criteria.

Related Precepts

• Service Inventory Scope Definition

Related Processes

• Business Requirements Prioritization

Service Inventory
Scope Definition

SOA
Governance
Specialist

Business Requirements
Prioritization

Figure 8.8
Service Inventory Analysis governance precepts and processes associated with the SOA Governance Specialist role.

SUMMARY OF KEY POINTS

• The definition of the service inventory scope correspondingly determines the scope of the Service Inventory Analysis effort and further establishes a concrete boundary in which a collection of services will subsequently be delivered.

• Business requirements prioritization helps determine the order and sequence of business processes and requirements that are processed through iterations of the Service Inventory Analysis cycle, which includes iterations of the Service-Oriented Analysis process.

CASE STUDY EXAMPLE

Subsequent to a series of executive board meetings, Raysmoore issues a new mission statement that identifies the following as the primary strategic business goals for the upcoming year:

- reduce business operating costs to increase overall profitability
- complete the creation of a seamless supply chain across all Raysmoore subsidiaries
- improve the ability of Raysmoore to monitor and control its supply chain
- improve the speed with which Raysmoore and its subsidiaries can respond to legislative changes
- improve Raysmoore's ability to respond to business opportunities through acquisitions, business partnerships, and outsourcing

The SOA governance program created by the SOA Governance Program Office for the first planned service inventory includes the Service Inventory Scope precept, as shown in Table 8.1.

Service Inventory Scope Precept	
Objective: Define a balanced service inventory scope.	
Policy: Ensure that the scope is meaningful.	*Policy:* Ensure that the scope is manageable.
Standard: Require the scope to be meaningfully cross-silo by encapsulating at least five well-defined business processes.	*Standard:* Require the scope to be realistically manageable by calculating cost, determining the length of required up-front analysis effort, and getting written approval from all affected IT Managers.
	Guideline: Use the Business Requirements Prioritization process to help define and refine the service inventory scope and to further assist with determining required up-front analysis effort.

Table 8.1

The Service Inventory Scope precept, as defined by Raysmoore's governance office.

Business Analysts within Raysmoore's strategic planning group intend to follow this precept by starting with the recommended Business Requirements Prioritization process. A team of Business Analysts and Service Analysts is assembled to carry out a prioritization of the corporation's business requirements across the Raysmoore, Lovelt and Reeldrill business domains.

The results of this effort are the heat maps displayed in Figures 8.9, 8.10, and 8.11. While there appears to be duplication across the heat maps, it is acknowledged that Raysmoore controls and coordinates the supply chain of its multiple subsidiaries, each of which is responsible for the scope of its own operations.

The initial plan was to establish one central enterprise service inventory that encompasses all of the business domains identified in each of the three business heat maps. However, when the group attempts to get sign-off from all of the affected IT Managers (as required by one of the precept standards), many objections arise. It becomes evident that for the scope of the service inventory to become manageable, it must be reduced.

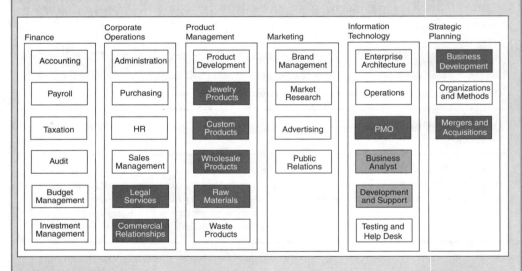

Figure 8.9
The Raysmoore business heat map.

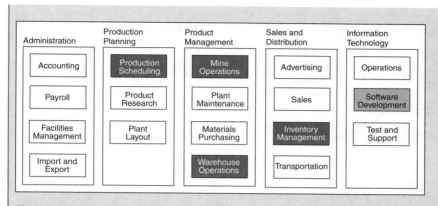

Figure 8.10
The Lovelt business heat map.

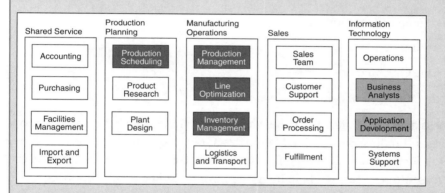

Figure 8.11
The Reeldrill business heat map.

The group is determined to establish a level of federation across the Raysmoore IT enterprise and those of its two subsidiaries (Lovelt and Reeldrill). After further analysis based on the hot spots identified in the heat maps, the service inventory scope is limited to productions and operations areas, which encompass the following business units:

• Raysmoore Product Management

• Lovelt Production Management

• Reeldrill Manufacturing Operations

The result is the definition of the Productions and Operations domain service inventory.

After sign-off from IT Managers and other required stakeholders, the group turns its attention back to the business heat maps where the following business activities are identified as the immediate priority for the Service Inventory Analysis:

- Raysmoore Jewelry Products (retail)
- Raysmoore Custom Products (retail)
- Raysmoore Wholesale Products
- Raysmoore Raw Materials
- Lovelt Mine Operations
- Lovelt Warehouse Operations
- Reeldrill Production Management
- Reeldrill Line Optimization
- Reeldrill Inventory Management

These business activities reflect the perceived need to streamline development support activities and reduce duplication of effort as a means of achieving the first strategic goal of reducing operating costs. The Raysmoore team feels that the creation of federated, cross-silo services will help integrate Lovelt and Reeldrill's supply chains. To meet all of the strategic business goals is likely going to require enhancements to both the processes and tools involved in the business activities.

Specifically, in order to meet the third strategic business goal, the Raysmoore product management groups are required to improve their ability to monitor all aspects of the product supply chains across subsidiaries. This activity needs to be closely aligned with the enhancements to the subsidiaries' production management supply chain processes.

Because of the risk of heavy fines for non-compliance with increasingly complex government legislation, the Raysmoore Business Development and Legal Services teams are given the task to create an improved compliance process.

Finally, Raysmoore Business Development, Mergers and Acquisitions, Commercial Relationships and PMO groups are given the mission of creating a more structured and reliable process for integrating future acquisitions, outsourcing, and enhanced commercial relationships.

The board recognizes that these are ambitious goals and that there are several dependencies between them. Because the constraints on investment are tight, the strategic planning team has been given the authority to approve or reject all new proposed development projects with budgets exceeding $100,000 on the basis of the degree to which they support these business priorities. The first of these projects to receive approval is for the optimized automation of the cross-subsidiary supply chain.

8.2 Governing Service-Oriented Analysis (Service Modeling)

The following precepts and processes pertain specifically to the Service-Oriented Analysis project stage, regardless of whether Service-Oriented Analysis is carried out as part of the Service Inventory Analysis cycle.

Precepts

Service and Capability Candidate Naming Standards

Of the various service modeling conventions that may exist, having a system for the consistent labeling of service candidates and service capability candidates is important for governance purposes.

The naming established when individual service candidates are defined will need to be compatible with service candidates defined by other project teams during separate iterations of the Service-Oriented Analysis process. Further, service and capability names will carry over to the Service-Oriented Design process where these names then become solidified as part of the service's physical design.

Related Processes

- Service Candidate Review

Related Roles

- Service Analyst

- Enterprise Design Standards Custodian

- SOA Governance Specialist

Service Inventory Analysis

Service-Oriented Analysis (Service Modeling)

Service-Oriented Design (Service Contract)

SOA PRINCIPLES & PATTERNS

This precept relates to Canonical Expression [497], a pattern commonly applied to establish service naming standards.

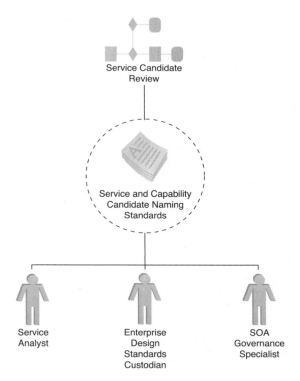

Figure 8.12

The Service and Capability Candidate Naming Standards precept.

Service Normalization

The Service Normalization precept dictates that service candidates within a given service inventory cannot have overlapping boundaries. This guarantees that no two services will introduce redundant logic, which maximizes reuse opportunities for shared services and forces services to compose other services when functionality outside of their boundaries is required.

Although the need for this precept typically emerges during the Service-Oriented Analysis stage when individual business process

SOA PRINCIPLES & PATTERNS

This precept relates to the Service Normalization [563] and Capability Composition [503] patterns, both of which are concerned with establishing independent functional contexts for services and preserving these functional boundaries within the scope of a service inventory.

definitions are being decomposed, it is a precept that actually affects and applies to the service inventory blueprint as a whole. Therefore, this precept can also be associated with the Service Inventory Analysis stage.

Related Processes

- Service Candidate Review

Related Roles

- Service Analyst
- Service Architect

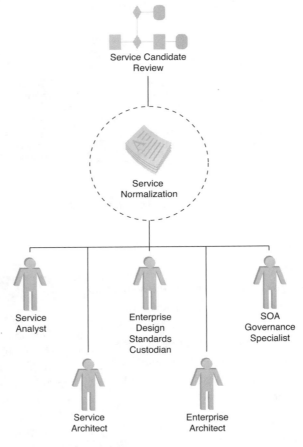

Figure 8.13

The Service Normalization precept.

- Enterprise Design Standards Custodian
- Enterprise Architect
- SOA Governance Specialist

Service Candidate Versioning Standards

Though services are only conceptualized during the Service-Oriented Analysis stage, the need for versioning can still arise when service candidates and even entire service inventory blueprints are required to be re-aligned with how deployed services have been changed or versioned. There may even be a service candidate versioning system that facilitates the versioning of service candidates during the Service Inventory Analysis cycles. In this case, agnostic service candidates undergo repeated refinement as a result of being reviewed as part of multiple service composition candidate definitions.

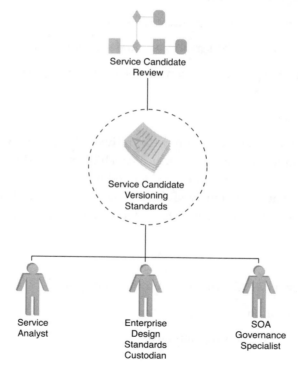

Figure 8.14
The Service Candidate Versioning Standards precept.

Related Processes

• Service Candidate Review

Related Roles

• Service Analyst

• Enterprise Design Standards Custodian

• SOA Governance Specialist

Processes

Service Candidate Review

A formal review is recommended when a service candidate is first defined and whenever it undergoes significant changes.

Possible outcomes of the service candidate review are:

• changes or extensions to the service candidate are approved

• approval of the changes or extensions is deferred pending additional remedial service modeling activity

• changes to the service are rejected

In some cases, reviews may be required for individual service capability candidates. This requirement may surface when service capabilities have different custodians or when an already implemented service is extended by the addition of one or more new service capabilities that are first modeled prior to actual design and development. In the latter case, the review may also check for compliance to service candidate versioning standards.

Related Precepts

• Service and Capability Candidate Naming Standards

• Service Normalization

• Service Candidate Versioning Standards

Related Roles

- Service Analyst
- Service Architect
- Enterprise Design Standards Custodian
- Enterprise Architect
- SOA Governance Specialist

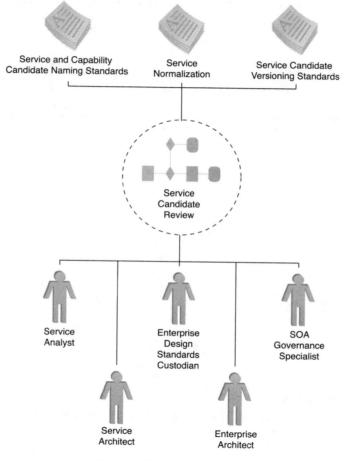

Figure 8.15

The Service Candidate Review process.

People (Roles)

Service Analyst

Service Analysts are typically involved with both the application and definition of precepts and processes that pertain to the Service-Oriented Analysis stage. Because of their hands-on participation in service modeling processes, they have the highest level of expertise required to help establish modeling standards in cooperation with SOA Governance Specialists and Enterprise Design Standards Custodians. Although it will generally be a Service Analyst that proposes one or more modeled services for the Service Candidate Review, it is common for a peer Service Analyst to participate as a reviewer as well.

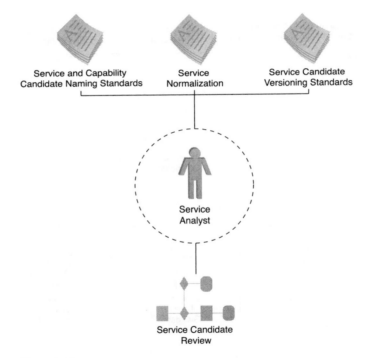

Figure 8.16
Service-Oriented Analysis governance precepts and processes associated with the Service Analyst role.

Related Precepts

- Service and Capability Candidate Naming Standards
- Service Normalization
- Service Candidate Versioning Standards

Related Processes

- Service Candidate Review

Service Architect

The involvement of Service Architects with the Service Normalization precept is typically more peripheral than Service Analysts. Service Architects can assist with the definition and application of these precepts by providing input regarding the practical considerations of establishing functional service boundaries. This can influence the extent to which some service candidates can be normalized as well as the granularity of their functional boundaries. The same practical issues can require a Service Architect to act as one of the reviewers during the Service Candidate Review process.

Related Precepts

- Service Normalization

Related Processes

- Service Candidate Review

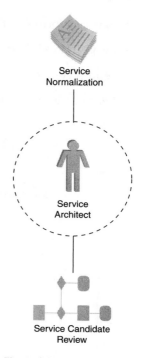

Service Normalization

Service Architect

Service Candidate Review

Figure 8.17
Service-Oriented Analysis governance precepts and processes associated with the Service Architect role.

Enterprise Design Standards Custodian

The definition of any standards pertaining to service modeling and Service-Oriented Analysis in general will require the involvement or, at minimum, the approval of the Enterprise Design Standards Custodian. To verify compliance to these standards during the Service Candidate Review may further require attendance by the person assuming this role; however, it is not uncommon for the Enterprise Design Standards Custodian to delegate this responsibility to a senior Service Analyst.

Related Precepts

- Service and Capability Candidate Naming Standards

- Service Normalization

- Service Candidate Versioning Standards

Related Processes

- Service Candidate Review

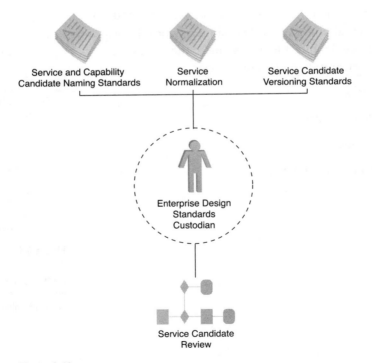

Figure 8.18
Service-Oriented Analysis governance precepts and processes associated with the Enterprise Design Standards Custodian role.

Enterprise Architect

Whereas Service Architects can provide input regarding service-specific encapsulation considerations, Enterprise Architects can comment on broader platform and resource issues that can further affect the application and definition of the Service Normalization precept. For the same reasons, an Enterprise Architect may need to serve on the review team for the Service Candidate Review process.

Related Precepts

- Service Normalization

Related Processes

- Service Candidate Review

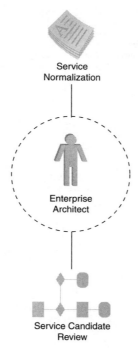

Figure 8.19

Service-Oriented Analysis governance precepts and processes associated with the Enterprise Architect role.

SOA Governance Specialist

Bringing together the precepts and a supporting process for the Service-Oriented Analysis stage falls upon the SOA Governance Specialist. A primary task in accomplishing this is coordinating the involvement of Service Analysts, Service Architects, and possibly also an Enterprise Architect and Enterprise Design Standards Custodian.

Especially challenging can be the incorporation of the precepts with a methodology that only allows limited or partial service analysis, prior to proceeding with post-analysis project stages. In this case, judgment is required to ensure that the most important standards are adhered to and that some form of meaningful review can occur before service candidates are transposed to concrete service contract designs.

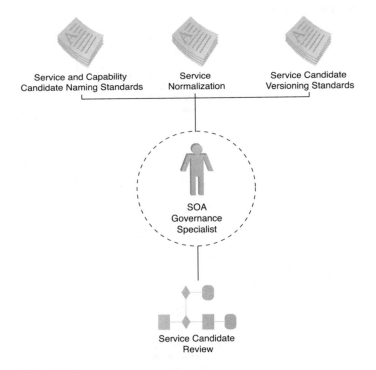

Figure 8.20
Service-Oriented Analysis governance precepts and processes associated with the SOA Governance Specialist role.

Related Precepts

- Service and Capability Candidate Naming Standards
- Service Normalization
- Service Candidate Versioning Standards

Related Processes

- Service Candidate Review

SUMMARY OF KEY POINTS

- The Service-Oriented Analysis stage is responsible for producing the very first incarnations of services and service capabilities, and therefore presents an opportunity to establish precepts that can support eventual governance tasks.

- The primary governance responsibilities relate to the consistent definition and versioning of service candidates, and to ensuring their review before moving on to the Service-Oriented Design stage.

CASE STUDY EXAMPLE

The first iteration of the Service-Oriented Analysis process focuses on the decomposition of the business process that encompasses supply chain management across Raysmoore, Lovelt, and Reeldrill. Several service candidates and service capability candidates are derived from the subsequent service modeling effort. The Product service is an agnostic service candidate that in particular appears to have high reuse potential throughout the planned service inventory.

Initially, Business Analysts encountered confusion caused by different subsidiary legacy environments using different terms to refer to the same types of functionality and, worse, the same terms referring to different types of functionality.

Fortunately, the SOA governance program includes the Service and Capability Naming precept (Table 8.2) that addresses this problem. The SOA Governance Program Office, in cooperation with Service Analysts, supplement this precept by authoring a lexicon that encompasses a vocabulary of naming conventions for service candidates and service capability candidates.

Service and Capability Naming Precept	
Objective: Service candidates and service capability candidates within the same service inventory must adhere to the same naming conventions.	
Policy: Ensure that a common vocabulary is used.	*Policy:* Ensure that a common name format is used.
Standard: Require that all service candidates and service capability candidates are assigned names based on a pre-defined lexicon and/or pre-defined naming conventions.	*Standard:* Require that pre-defined formats are applied to all service and service capability candidate names so that the name structure and sequence of combined words is consistent.
Standard: Require that all service and service capability names are reviewed for compliance in accordance with the vocabulary and format standards as part of the Service Candidate Review process.	

Table 8.2
The Raysmoore Service and Capability Naming precept.

The required usage of this precept further ensures that service modeling tasks carried out by different project teams remain in alignment. Newly defined service candidates will be able to encapsulate and abstract disparate legacy applications (and the disparity among the terms and vocabulary used by these legacy environments), and still provide a conceptual set of services that establish standardized endpoints.

This level of consistency among service candidates allows Raysmoore to consolidate similarities across supply chain business requirements from its subsidiaries and essentially enables the definition of service candidates that represent parts of supply chain processes as logical wholes. However, as service modeling efforts proceed, Business Analysts begin to uncover some significant differences between the requirements of Raysmoore and Lovelt in relation to supply chain business rules used for authorization and access to product inventory data. Specifically, Lovelt has traditionally allowed customers to view its product inventory levels, whereas Raysmoore has always had a policy that regarded overall corporate stock levels as a trade secret available only to internal staff.

This conflict affects the definition of the Product service that is being modeled. Initially, the project team proposes to create two variations of the service, one specific to Raysmoore and the other specific to Lovelt (Figure 8.21). This would allow each service to incorporate different business rules that could be further independently evolved.

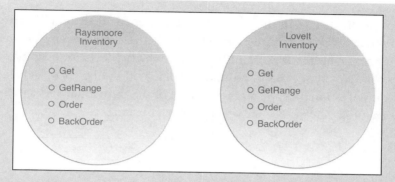

Figure 8.21
Two service candidates with overlapping functional boundaries.

SOA Governance Specialists, however, push back on this approach and state that ultimately this service inventory is intended to establish a unified view of business automation that spans the Raysmoore and Lovelt IT enterprises. Further, they point to the Service Normalization precept (Table 8.3), which states that the creation of separate service candidates with comparable functional boundaries is not allowed.

Service Normalization Precept	
Objective: Service candidates within the same service inventory cannot have overlapping functional boundaries.	
Policy: Ensure that no two services within the same service inventory contain redundant logic.	*Policy:* Ensure that no two services within the same service inventory have overlapping functional contexts (regardless of their actual implemented logic).
Standard: Require that the logic of all service candidates is explicitly documented in service profiles.	*Guideline:* Register service candidates in the service registry with a status of "analysis."
Standard: Require that the functional context of each service candidate is reviewed in relation to other services in the service inventory blueprint, as part of the Service Candidate Review process.	

Table 8.3
The Raysmoore Service Normalization precept.

Subsequent to further analysis and discussion, it is decided to only proceed with a single Product service (Figure 8.22). The conflict is addressed by the application of the Contract Denormalization [510] pattern, which allows for a single service to contain capabilities that express redundant logic without being in violation of the Service Normalization precept. Access control of the individual service capabilities is further ensured via appropriate security mechanisms.

Figure 8.22

A single Product service candidate containing service capability candidates that provide an extent of redundant functionality. The capabilities further qualified with "Full" allow for the retrieval of product inventory stock values for Lovelt customers only.

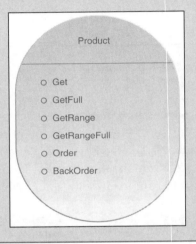

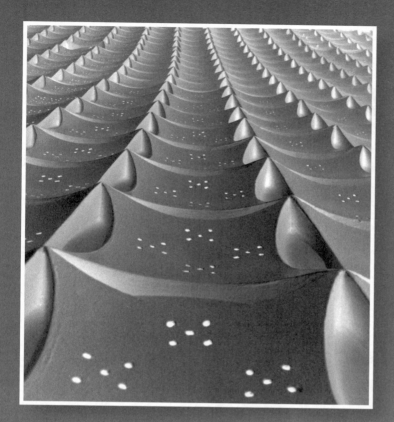

Chapter 9

Governing Service Design and Development Stages

SOA PRINCIPLES & PATTERNS REFERENCED IN THIS CHAPTER

- Canonical Expression [497]

- Canonical Protocol [498]

- Canonical Schema [500]

- Concurrent Contracts [508]

- Contract Centralization [509]

- Decoupled Contract [517]

- Dual Protocols [521]

- Legacy Wrapper [532]

- Metadata Centralization [536]

- Schema Centralization [551]

- Service Abstraction (478)

- Service Autonomy (481)

- Service Composability (486)

- Service Discoverability (484)

- Service Façade [558]

- Service Loose Coupling (477)

- Service Reusability (479)

- Service Statelessness (482)

- Standardized Service Contract (475)

- Validation Abstraction [574]

All of the project stages so far lead up to the actual concrete design and creation of the service architecture and service logic. The stages in this chapter result in the realization of services as IT assets, which makes their regulation a critical success factor.

Governance considerations addressed by the upcoming precepts focus primarily on establishing and validating compliance to standards. While various organizational roles are involved with specifics pertaining to precepts and processes in particular stages, governance professionals participate in all aspects of service design and development regulation to ensure continuity and consistency from prior analysis stages through to subsequent deployment and usage stages.

9.1 Governing Service-Oriented Design (Service Contract)

Service contracts within a given service inventory boundary are intended to establish a federated service endpoint layer within which services can intrinsically interoperate (as per the Increased Federation and Increased Intrinsic Interoperability goals described in Chapter 3). Therefore, having governance controls to help keep service contracts consistent and in alignment with each other is crucial to the success of an SOA initiative.

Precepts

Schema Design Standards

This precept is dedicated to standardizing the use of common schemas by services and applications, inter-schema sharing and linking, as well as constructs and elements used within schemas.

Standards that relate to the design of common schemas and data models used by service contracts can be part of the overall Service Contract Design Standards precept. A separate Schema Design Standards precept is required when shared schemas are part of an independent data architecture that may be used by other parts of the IT enterprise, outside of service boundaries.

For example, a common design standard is that schemas defining data models for common business documents be canonical across a pre-defined scope or domain. An Invoice schema used by an Invoice service may also be used by a middleware broker managing the exchange of invoice data between disparate legacy accounting applications.

Note that this precept may also address the design of single-purpose or service-specific schemas. In this case, specific standards are created to govern the use of schema syntax, functions, validation logic, and structure. Additionally, these standards may further indicate when service-specific schemas must still make use of common schemas—and—for REST service design, Schema Design Standards may also address uniform contract aspects, such as the custom standardization of media types (see the upcoming *Schema Custodian* section for examples).

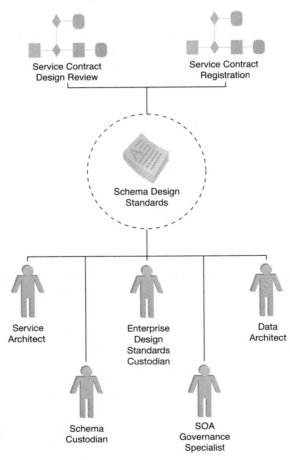

Figure 9.1
The Schema Design Standards precept.

Related Processes

- Service Contract Design Review
- Service Contract Registration

Related Roles

- Service Architect
- Schema Custodian
- Enterprise Design Standards Custodian
- SOA Governance Specialist
- Other: Data Architect

NOTE

Corresponding precepts that govern policy design further establish common standards. Precepts and processes that pertain to both business and operational policy design are covered in Chapter 12.

Service Contract Design Standards

Custom design standards need to be in place to ensure that the technical contracts for services within a given service inventory adhere to established and required conventions.

Common examples of custom service contract design standards include those that:

- identify allowed service contract-related industry standards and languages (such as WSDL, WADL, SOAP, etc.)
- identify what parts of allowed industry standards and languages can and cannot be used
- require compliance to custom or industry determined use of industry standards and languages (such as WS-I profiles)

SOA PRINCIPLES & PATTERNS

This precept can relate to any patterns that shape or standardize service contract characteristics. Common examples include the Decoupled Contract [517], Contract Centralization [509], Concurrent Contracts [508], Canonical Protocol [498], Dual Protocols [521], Canonical Expression [497], and Validation Abstraction [574] patterns.

Furthermore, concerns addressed by custom Service Contract Design Standards are often closely tied to the application of the Standardized Service Contract (475), Service Loose Coupling (477), Service Abstraction (478), and Service Discoverability (484) design principles, as explained in the upcoming *Service-Orientation Architecture Design Standards* section.

- position and/or limit the use of canonical data models and schemas within service contracts
- position and/or limit the use or quantity of service-specific schemas
- position and/or limit the use of shared or service-specific policies
- establish naming and syntax conventions
- address communications quality requirements in support of service interpretability and discoverability
- custom design standards that address the method usage and resource identifier syntax for uniform contracts used by REST services
- custom design standards that address the usage of media types for REST services

This precept may optionally introduce architectural standards that relate to how the service contract (as a physical artifact) is positioned within the overall service technology architecture. These types of standards do not define the underlying technology architecture; they only establish certain requirements that may impact how the service contract is designed independently.

> **NOTE**
>
> Depending on how precepts are applied and associated with corresponding review processes, it may be more practical to broaden the scope of the Service Contract Design Standards precept to encompass any of the following related precepts:
>
> - Schema Design Standards
> - Service Metadata Standards (Chapter 12)
> - Business Policy Standards (Chapter 12)
> - Operational Policy Standards (Chapter 12)
> - Service-Orientation Contract Design Standards
> - SLA Template

Related Processes

- Service Contract Design Review
- Service Contract Registration
- Policy Conflict Audit (Chapter 12)

Related Roles

- Service Architect
- Schema Custodian
- Policy Custodian
- Enterprise Design Standards Custodian
- SOA Security Specialist
- SOA Governance Specialist

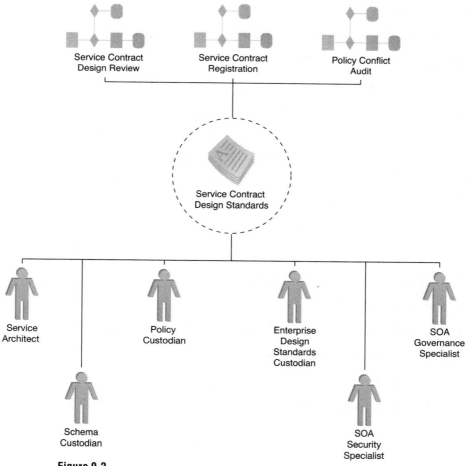

Figure 9.2
The Service Contract Design Standards precept.

Service-Orientation Contract Design Standards

The service-orientation paradigm establishes eight design principles that, when applied, shape software programs into units of service-oriented logic so that they are equipped with specific characteristics that help realize the strategic goals of service-oriented computing (see the *Service-Orientation* and *Service-Oriented Computing* sections in Chapter 3). A subset of these design principles specifically affects the design and positioning of the service contract, and are therefore highly relevant to the governance of the Service-Oriented Design project stage.

In addition to the aforementioned custom design standards, a meaningful level of compliance needs to be ensured with the following contract-related service-orientation design principles:

- Standardized Service Contract (475)
- Service Loose Coupling (477)
- Service Abstraction (478)

As mentioned shortly, when associated with the *Service Contract Registration* process, compliance to the Service Discoverability (484) principle is also measured during this stage.

Related Processes

- Service Contract Design Review
- Service Contract Registration

Related Roles

- Service Architect
- Schema Custodian
- Technical Communications Specialist
- Enterprise Design Standards Custodian
- SOA Security Specialist
- SOA Governance Specialist

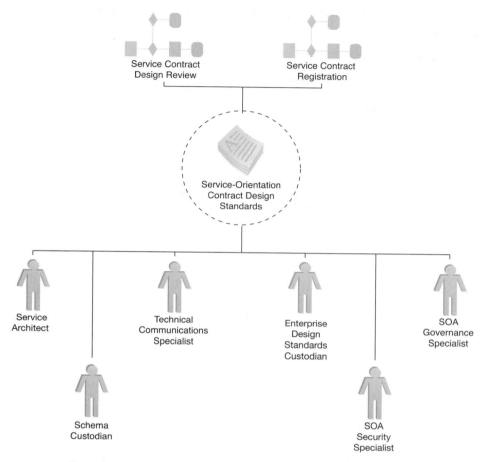

Figure 9.3

The Service-Orientation Contract Design Standards precept.

SLA Template

The SOA Governance Program Office needs to mandate the use of a standard template for human-readable service-level agreements (SLAs). The template can include required and optional parts, the former of which is commonly dedicated to expressing availability and reliability guarantees.

A different SLA template may be needed for cloud-deployed services in order to conform to proprietary conventions of the third-party cloud provider, or to address service-level guarantees that are distinct to the cloud environment. Every effort should be made to add unique parts to the SLA template as extensions to the same base template used for all services.

Related Processes

- Service Contract Design Review
- Service Contract Registration

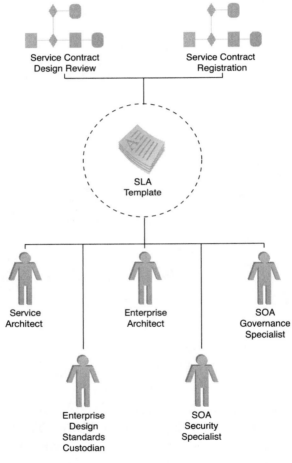

Figure 9.4
The SLA Template precept.

Related Roles

- Service Architect

- Enterprise Design Standards Custodian

- Enterprise Architect

- SOA Security Specialist

- SOA Governance Specialist

Processes

Service Contract Design Review

A service contract design review is the principal process for governing the quality and completeness of the service contract, as well as its required compliance to design standards. The SOA Governance Program Office can establish a checklist to be used during this review to ensure consistency so that the service logic (that will be subsequently constructed during the Service Development stage) will conform to the specified contract when it is delivered.

The purpose of the review is to confirm that the service contract meets design standards, and truly reflects the functional scope originally defined during analysis stages. Each aspect of the service contract must be approved by technically qualified reviewers before it is deemed ready for release. Since expensive resources may be committed to developing both the service itself and other software programs that will consume the service, based solely on the service contract, it is worthwhile to give this review significant attention.

Probable outcomes of this review are:

- The service contract is accepted and then handed over to the Service Logic Design stage, where the underlying logic and architecture of the service implementation will be specified in support of realizing the functionality expressed in the service contract.

- The service contract fails one or more of the technical or content reviews and is returned for rework.

It can be helpful to conduct an informal requirements review immediately before the Service Contract Design Review to ensure that both the functional and non-functional requirements are stable before the service contract is published. There may also be follow-up issues that need to be addressed before the service contract is actually finalized, which may result in the need for additional "mini-reviews."

NOTE
It can be beneficial to have regular "review days" that handle all or most outstanding reviews, rather than attempting to schedule a larger number of small reviews. This approach is especially helpful with Service Contract Design Reviews, as it provides the opportunity to review several service contracts in relation to each other.

Related Precepts

- Schema Design Standards
- Service Contract Design Standards
- Service-Orientation Contract Design Standards
- SLA Template
- Service Metadata Standards (Chapter 12)
- Business Policy Standards (Chapter 12)
- Operational Policy Standards (Chapter 12)

Related Roles

- Service Architect
- Schema Custodian
- Technical Communications Specialist
- Enterprise Design Standards Custodian
- SOA Security Specialist
- Enterprise Architect
- SOA Governance Specialist

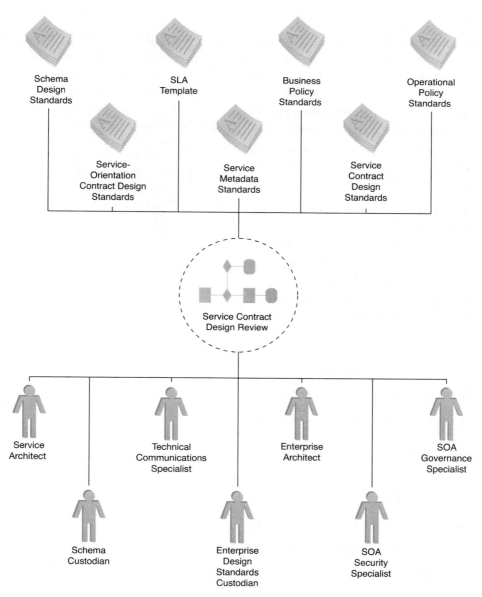

Figure 9.5

The Service Contract Design Review process.

Service Contract Registration

If the review of the service design was successful, it may be desirable, at that point, to initiate
a separate process for the formal registration
of service metadata in the service registry (or
repository). This will give other project teams
concrete information about a service that is near-
ing development and deployment stages. The
registry information can further include a status
value and a target availability date.

If a service contract is available, any of its technical or human-readable parts can be recorded in
the service registry, thereby allowing for the preliminary design of potential service consumer
programs. Note that the Service Contract Registration process may include steps dedicated to
the review of the proposed metadata.

> **SOA PRINCIPLES & PATTERNS**
>
> Considerations pertaining to this
> process are closely related to the
> application of the Service Discov-
> erability (484) principle, which
> ensures that published service
> metadata is both discoverable
> and interpretable by a range of
> project team members in support
> of service reuse by new service
> consumers. Also, the pattern that
> represents the centralization of
> service metadata is Metadata
> Centralization [536].

Related Precepts

- Schema Design Standards

- Service Contract Design Standards

- Service-Orientation Contract Design Standards

- SLA Template

Related Roles

- Service Architect

- Technical Communications Specialist

- Enterprise Design Standards Custodian

- Enterprise Architect

- SOA Governance Specialist

> **NOTE**
>
> Although the Service Registry Custodian is involved in the actual imple-mentation and governance of the service registry, this role is generally not required for governance-related tasks pertaining to the Service Contract Registration process that occurs during this stage.

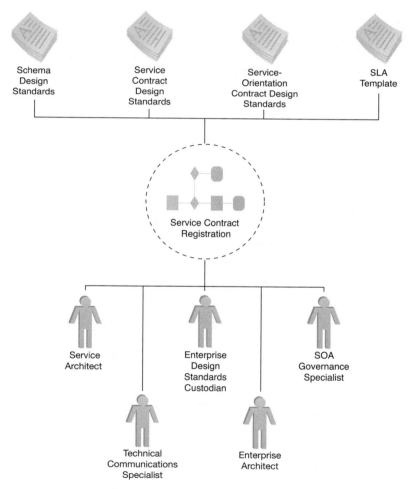

Figure 9.6

The Service Contract Registration process.

People (Roles)

Service Architect

Service-Oriented Design is of primary concern to the Service Architect, and this role's expertise supports all precepts and processes pertaining to this stage. Service Architects, together with Enterprise Design Standards Custodians, will lead the creation of design standards, as well as the subsequent compliance reviews.

Related Precepts

- Schema Design Standards

- Service Contract Design Standards

- Service-Orientation Contract Design Standards

- SLA Template

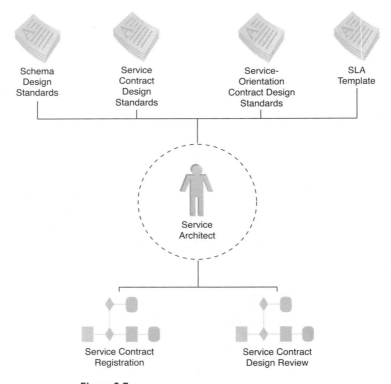

Figure 9.7

Service-Oriented Design governance precepts and processes associated with the Service Architect role.

Related Processes

- Service Contract Registration
- Service Contract Design Review

Schema Custodian

The Schema Custodian's governance responsibilities can extend to contributing to the definition of design standards pertaining to schemas and data models used by service contracts, as well as taking part in the corresponding compliance review.

> **SOA PRINCIPLES & PATTERNS**
>
> This role's association with the Service-Orientation Design Standards precept is specifically related to the application of the Standardized Service Contract (475) principle.

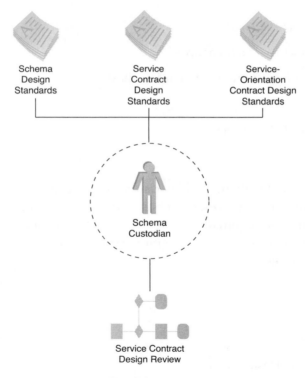

Figure 9.8

Service-Oriented Design governance precepts and processes associated with the Schema Custodian role.

When working with REST services, the Schema Custodian may further be tasked with identifying and defining the usage of service-specific and service inventory-wide media types. Specifically, the Schema Custodian may be responsible for:

- Ensuring that the most widely used and standardized media type applicable is used in the service contracts.

- Ensuring that new media types are as reusable as possible across service contracts.

- Ensuring that when new media types are defined for a given service, they are further promoted to foster discovery and reuse in support of other services within the same service inventory.

These tasks are in addition to the use of custom XML Schema definitions that may be required for data passed between REST services.

Related Precepts

- Schema Design Standards
- Service Contract Design Standards
- Service-Orientation Contract Design Standards

Related Processes

- Service Contract Design Review

Policy Custodian

As explained in Chapter 12, this role is central to precepts and processes associated with the standards and centralization of business and operational policies. Policy Custodians may further be required to share expertise for the definition of design standards for service contracts (especially with regards to the development and usage of service-specific policies).

Related Precepts

- Service Contract Design Standards

Related Processes

- Service Contract Design Review

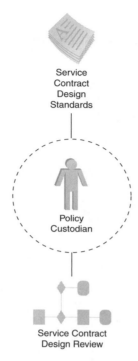

Figure 9.9
Service-Oriented Design
governance precepts and
processes associated with the
Policy Custodian role.

Technical Communications Specialist

The Technical Communications Specialist is not expected to be able to contribute governance expertise for precepts associated with the Service-Oriented Design stage. However, it may be helpful to include these specialists during review processes to ensure that service contract content (including SLA content) and associated discovery metadata being submitted is adequately clear and understandable to a range of IT professionals.

SOA PRINCIPLES & PATTERNS

During the Service Contract Design Review process, there is usually no one better qualified to check for compliance to the Service Discoverability (484) principle than the Technical Communications Specialist. Proofing the interpretability and discoverability of information published about a service also carries over into the Service Contract Registration process.

Related Precepts

- Service-Orientation Contract Design Standards

Related Processes

- Service Contract Registration

- Service Contract Design Review

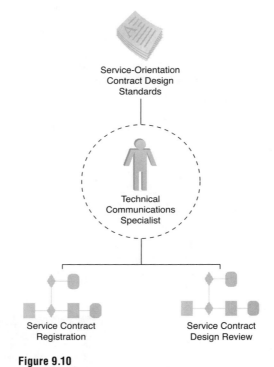

Figure 9.10
Service-Oriented Design governance precepts and processes associated with the Technical Communications Specialist role.

Enterprise Design Standards Custodian

Several of the design standards that affect and shape service contracts will be contributed by roles focused on specific subsets of the contract content or specific aspects of the contract design. For example, Schema Custodians are concerned with the schema(s) used by a service contract, whereas Policy Custodians are focused on the contract's polices. The Enterprise Design Standards Custodian collaboratively participates with these and other individuals to create the necessary design standards, but further provides a more global perspective to ensure that individual standards do not conflict with each other or with design standards that apply to other parts of the service architecture, and the service inventory architecture as a whole. This same enterprise perspective can be helpful during subsequent review processes.

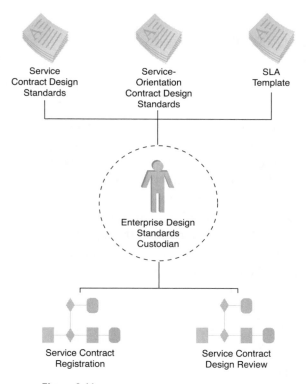

Figure 9.11

Service-Oriented Design governance precepts and processes associated with the Enterprise Design Standards Custodian role.

Additionally, the Enterprise Design Standards Custodian may be responsible for defining service contract design standards not addressed by other SOA governance-specific roles. For example, when standardizing the use of the uniform contract for REST services, the Enterprise Design Standards Custodian may need to complement media type standards provided by the Schema Custodian with further custom design standards that govern HTTP method usage and resource identifier syntax conventions.

Related Precepts

- Service Contract Design Standards
- Service-Orientation Contract Design Standards
- SLA Template

Related Processes

- Service Contract Registration
- Service Contract Design Review

Enterprise Architect

While Enterprise Architects can become involved in any area of Service-Oriented Design governance, their primary point of interest is not as much the design of the service contract, but how the service will be positioned to perform amidst other services and the enterprise platform overall. This consideration brings Enterprise Architects into the definition of the SLA Template precept, as well as the review for compliance to requirements expressed in service SLAs. This role is especially important when SLA standards need to be established for foreign or third-party cloud environments, as service quality guarantees may be tied to these cloud platforms and therefore may lie outside of the Enterprise Architects direct control.

Related Precepts

- SLA Template

Related Processes

- Service Contract Design Review
- Service Contract Registration

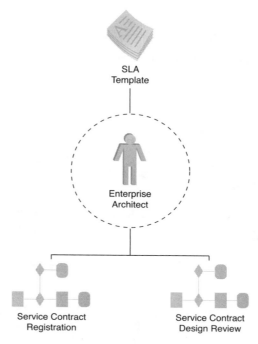

Figure 9.12

Service-Oriented Design governance precepts and
processes associated with the Enterprise Architect role.

SOA Security Specialist

SOA Security Specialists can join governance groups responsible for standards definition and review when service security requirements need to be expressed within the
technical interface of a service contract or as part of the service's published SLA. In this
circumstance, the expertise provided by this role can assist in determining appropriate
security technologies and constraints, primarily with the intention of protecting message data and transmissions.

Shared services being created with high reusability expectations will be of particular
concern to SOA Security Specialists. At the service contract level there may be certain
controls that need to be established to ensure that some types of potentially harmful
message content cannot make it through to the service logic. Further, service contracts
published for cloud-based services will likely require extra rigor in their security assessment, especially with SaaS offerings that are being made available to larger communities of service consumers.

Related Precepts

- Service Contract Design Standards
- Service-Orientation Contract Design Standards
- SLA Template

Related Processes

- Service Contract Design Review

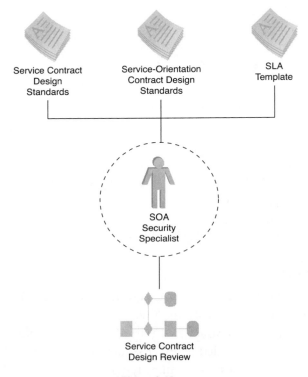

Figure 9.13
Service-Oriented Design governance precepts and processes associated with the SOA Security Specialist role.

SOA Governance Specialist

Service-Oriented Design represents the first stage within the SOA project lifecycle wherein physical service artifacts are defined and created. In addition to their regular involvement with establishing required standards, SOA Governance Specialists therefore need to assist with the coordination of other roles as well as the coordination of affected artifacts, as they transition through review processes over to the Service Logic Design stage.

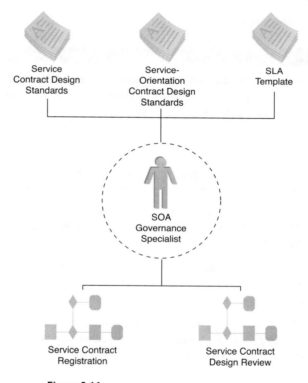

Figure 9.14
Service-Oriented Design governance precepts and processes associated with the SOA Governance Specialist role.

Related Precepts

- Service Contract Design Standards

- Service-Orientation Contract Design Standards

- SLA Template

Related Processes

- Service Contract Registration

- Service Contract Design Review

NOTE
Service Developers can be involved in the creation and delivery of technical service contract definitions during this stage; however, they do not commonly contribute to governance tasks.

SUMMARY OF KEY POINTS

- One of the main reasons a separate project stage dedicated to the definition and creation of service contracts exists is to provide an opportunity for service contracts across a service inventory to be standardized and aligned.

- Governance precepts that relate to the Service-Oriented Design project stage help ensure endpoint federation and intrinsic interoperability among services within a service inventory.

- The Service Contract Design Review process further helps ensure standards compliance prior to proceeding to the Service Logic Design stage.

CASE STUDY EXAMPLE

One of several Service Contract Design Standard precepts within Raysmoore's SOA governance program is a custom Canonical Messaging Schema precept, which supports the Standardized Service Contract (475) principle by requiring that service contracts share the same schemas for primary business documents. The precept is explained in Table 9.1.

Canonical Messaging Schema Precept	
Objective: All services within the same service inventory must share data based on canonical data models wherever possible.	
Policy: Ensure that canonical schemas are defined for shared business documents and records.	*Policy*: Ensure that canonical schemas are sufficiently flexible to accommodate reusability by agnostic services.
Standard: All canonical schemas must be defined and implemented using the XML Schema Definition Language.	*Guideline*: Have canonical schema validation logic (in particular required fields) reviewed by Data Architects to ensure the schema validation granularity is properly balanced for reuse within the service inventory.
Standard: Require that all service contracts are reviewed for compliance in accordance with the canonical schemas as part of the Service Contract Design Review process.	

Table 9.1
The Canonical Messaging Schema precept.

Raysmoore's Service Architects and Data Architects collaborate to establish a canonical schema to be used by messages containing product data.

The data model is comprised of the following fields:

- location code (a unique code for each physical location within the Raysmoore corporation)

- location description

- universal SKU

- local stock number

- item short description

- QoH (Quantity on Hand)

- date (when the requested QoH is needed or is available)

- UoM (Unit of Measure)

- price (before any applicable discounts)

- discount percentage (when applied)

- inter-company billing price

- item description

All the fields in the product record are optional, and the actual amount of information depends on the details of the service being invoked.

For example:

- The Local Stock service might generate a message that includes an inventory record with only the location code and universal SKU fields completed. This service may then return one or more complete records with the inventory level of the specified item, as well as other items that are possible substitutes.

- The Report service can issue messages wherein the date field is used to determine inventory levels for a specified date range.

- The Product service uses the same basic structure but generally leaves the location code blank.

- The Stock Locations service, on the other hand, might include an inventory record containing just a universal SKU value in order to return a more complete inventory record for each warehouse location with non-zero stock of that item.

Fields containing confidential information (such as an inter-company billing price value) are normally blank, except when the service is invoked by accredited service consumers authorized to receive such information. This data structure can be extended in the future by adding new fields in compliance with the existing versioning strategy.

After a few minor corrections, the SOA Governance Program Office approves the service contract design standards and requests that the project team publish the service contracts (using this schema) to the service registry.

9.2 Governing Service Logic Design

The completion of the Service-Oriented Design stage results in the physical definition of a service's technical interface and associated definitions related to the overall service contract. Creating the corresponding design of the internal service logic requires further regulation to ensure that the underlying service architecture and associated programming and encapsulated resources can collectively fulfill the functionality promised by the service contract, while continuing to maintain required levels of cross-service consistency.

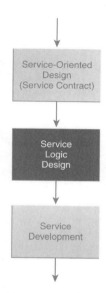

Therefore, governance efforts continue to be focused on standardization. Unlike Service-Oriented Design activities, which commonly produce actual markup code for the technical service contract, this stage is about the authoring of a design specification that will be handed over to developers for implementation. This can make the quality of the content being reviewed and assessed for compliance to governance precepts more challenging. Not only do those participating in these governance activities need to verify that a given service design specification is compliant with precepts, they must also ensure that stated compliance is realistic with regards to available resources and tools.

Precepts

Service Logic Design Standards

Service architectures and programming are subject to a range of custom design standards.

Areas that commonly require formal standardization include:

- legacy resource encapsulation

- shared or replicated resource encapsulation

- involvement of cloud computing mechanisms and other cloud-based IT resources

- composition member involvement or limitations

SOA PRINCIPLES & PATTERNS

Numerous SOA design patterns can relate to this precept. Some common examples include the Service Façade [558] and Legacy Wrapper [532] patterns.

As further explained in the upcoming *Service-Orientation Architecture Design Standards* section, several design principles also directly impact the Service Logic Design and can themselves form the basis of various design standards.

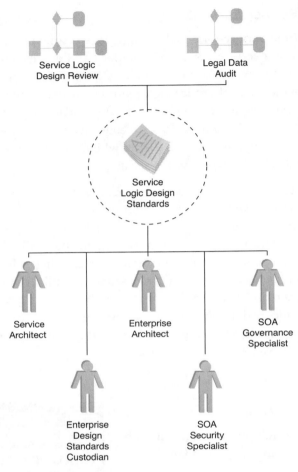

Figure 9.15

The Service Logic Design Standards precept.

- invocation of third-party or cloud-based services

- multi-tenancy requirements

- security controls and the involvement of security mechanisms

- performance and response times

- reliability, failover, and resiliency

- scalability thresholds

- data volume throughput

- REST service capabilities to defer session state back to service consumers at the end of each request

- supply of runtime metadata for REST services, such as introspection capabilities and cache directives

- the required behavior of service consumers (for example, including a virtual server to execute logic on behalf of services invoked by service consumer logic as part of the code on-demand REST constraint)

This precept is important as it demands the existence of custom design standards and avoids a common pitfall with this stage where compliance only to service-orientation design principles is considered.

Related Processes

- Service Logic Design Review

- Legal Data Audit

Related Roles

- Service Architect

- Enterprise Design Standards Custodian

- Enterprise Architect

- SOA Security Specialist

- SOA Governance Specialist

Service-Orientation Architecture Design Standards

The design of service-oriented logic requires that compliance be checked for all eight service-orientation principles. When focusing on the logic that underlies the service contract, the following principles are primarily relevant:

- Service Reusability (479)

- Service Autonomy (481)

- Service Statelessness (482)

- Service Composability (486)

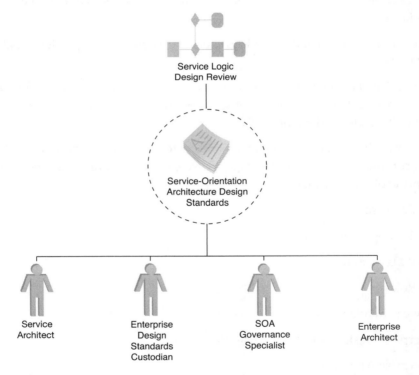

Figure 9.16
The Service-Orientation Architecture Design Standards precept.

The service contract-related principles referred to in the preceding Service-Orientation Contract Design Standards precept are revisited, especially in relation to coupling concerns. The Service Loose Coupling (477) principle in particular can play a significant role in Service Logic Design, as several negative coupling types can result from how the service logic and implementation relate to the service contract.

Related Processes

- Service Logic Design Review

Related Roles

- Service Architect

- Enterprise Design Standards Custodian

- Enterprise Architect

- SOA Governance Specialist

Processes

Service Access Control

Services are preferably delivered as "black boxes" where the only information that is published about each service is the service contract and its associated SLA, as well as service registry metadata. Details about the service architecture and its underlying implementation are hidden from project teams wanting to potentially build service consumers. This access limitation is put in place to protect those project teams from building consumer programs that inadvertently (or indirectly) form dependencies upon aspects of the underlying service implementation that may be subject to change.

As a result, a process needs to be established to control access to private service design specifications. Figure 9.17 depicts different levels of access service consumer designers can be granted. Although shown, the open access option is not usually a viable option as it does not introduce any level of access control.

Related Precepts

N/A

Related Roles

- Service Architect

- SOA Governance Specialist

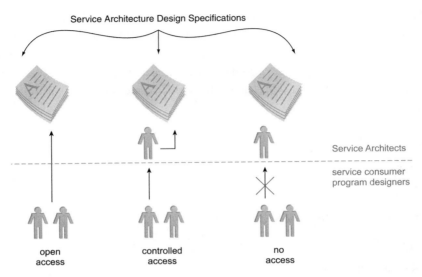

Figure 9.17

Higher levels of access control allow for abstraction levels to be consistently preserved during the lifetime of a service. (This figure is borrowed from Chapter 8 of the *SOA Principles of Service Design* book.)

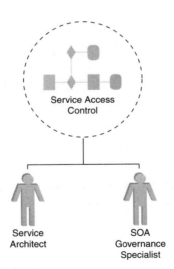

Figure 9.18

The Service Access Control process.

Service Logic Design Review

This process establishes a series of steps during which qualified team members assess the Service Logic Design specification to validate compliance with both the custom design standards and service-orientation design principles. Additionally, this process revisits the service contract information in relation to the Service Logic Design to ensure alignment and to confirm that all documented parts of the design completely and accurately provision the functionality expressed in the service contract.

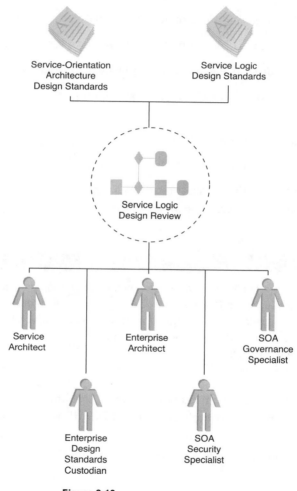

Figure 9.19
The Service Logic Design Review process.

Because a large part of governing compliance to Service Logic Design Standards involves verification that preceding analysis and design steps have been performed successfully, use of checklists is recommended.

For example, checklists can be created to verify that a service:

- conforms to the interface and SLA terms specified in the published service contract

- supports known functional requirements

- supports non-functional requirements and security requirements

- has been subject to the application of all relevant and required design patterns

- is addressing required levels of runtime quality and behavioral consistency

- can or must be deployed in a cloud environment (or, alternatively, cannot be cloud-based)

- is using optimal and authorized technologies

- is correctly implementing identified business rules

The main value of a checklist is that it requires a physical or electronic signature of an approver or set of approvers, creating an audit trail of responsibility in the event of later inquiries.

NOTE

Although related to the Service Testing stage, a common deliverable required as part of the Service Logic Design stage exit criteria is a test plan containing functional and non-functional areas for which the service should be tested, as derived from the Service Logic Design specification and the review results.

For any services where the design is taking an excessive amount of effort, or where one or more checklists cannot be completed satisfactorily, those involved with the Service Logic Design Review can take extra steps to identify the root cause of the problem to provide guidance in support of any necessary remedial action.

Related Precepts

- Service Logic Design Standards
- Service-Orientation Architecture Design Standards

Related Roles

- Service Architect
- Enterprise Design Standards Custodian
- Enterprise Architect
- SOA Security Specialist
- SOA Governance Specialist

Legal Data Audit

There may be occasions where certain types of data processed by the service logic have legal requirements.

Examples include:

- The data has privacy requirements that must be fulfilled by appropriate security controls and logic.
- The data has geographical requirements that may limit options for the service and/or the data repository from being deployed in certain types of cloud environments and remote data centers.
- The data may be subject to legal policies prone to change, which may limit or altogether eliminate the possibility of deploying the service and/or the data in a cloud environment that can impose mobility restrictions.

The Legal Data Audit precept establishes a process whereby data accessed, stored, or processed in relation to the service logic is checked against any known or identified legal requirements. This can be a potentially involved process when cloud services (in particular cloud storage services) are being reviewed—or—when cloud services or cloud storage repositories are being invoked or accessed by the service being reviewed. In the latter case, a previously existing service may never have had a legal compliance issue until made part of a new service composition.

Related Precepts

- Service Logic Design Standards

Related Roles

- Service Architect
- Enterprise Design Standards Custodian
- Enterprise Architect
- SOA Security Specialist
- SOA Governance Specialist
- Other: Data Architect

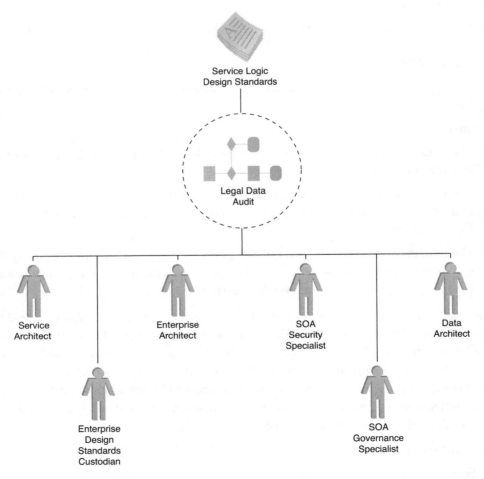

Figure 9.20
The Legal Data Audit process.

People (Roles)

Service Architect

Service Logic Design is all about defining the service architecture, from the service contract all the way down to the processing layers that interact with platform resources, such as databases, legacy applications, and other services. This makes governance tasks pertaining to this stage a focal point for Service Architects. This role tends to participate in all covered areas of Service Logic Design governance.

Related Precepts

- Service Logic Design Standards
- Service-Orientation Architecture Design Standards

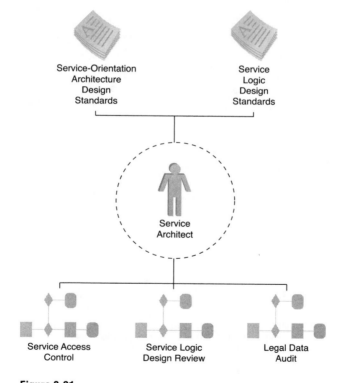

Figure 9.21

Service Logic Design governance precepts and processes associated with the Service Architect role.

Related Processes

- Service Access Control

- Service Logic Design Review

- Legal Data Audit

Enterprise Design Standards Custodian

Service Architects will typically team up with the Enterprise Design Standards Custodian to finalize proposed service logic and architecture design standards, some of which can be influenced by legal requirements. This role will further participate in the subsequent review.

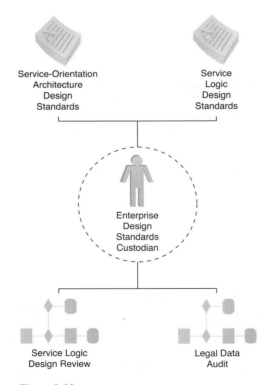

Figure 9.22
Service Logic Design governance precepts and processes associated with the Enterprise Design Standards Custodian role.

Related Precepts

- Service Logic Design Standards
- Service-Orientation Architecture Design Standards

Related Processes

- Service Logic Design Review
- Legal Data Audit

Enterprise Architect

How the Enterprise Architect takes part in Service Logic Design governance activities can vary greatly, mostly dependent on the nature of a given service architecture. For example, autonomous on-premise service architectures may require less governance attention from enterprise architectures than those that are cloud-based or require access to a great deal of shared enterprise resources, such as central databases. Either way, it

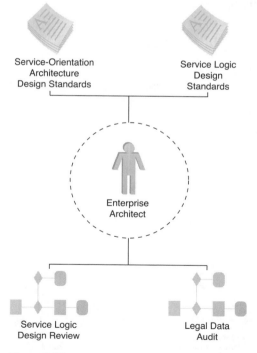

Figure 9.23
Service Logic Design governance precepts and processes associated with the Enterprise Architect role.

is common for the Enterprise Architect to be part of the actual Service Logic Design Review process and for this person's sign-off to be required as part of the exit criteria.

Related Precepts

- Service Logic Design Standards
- Service-Orientation Architecture Design Standards

Related Processes

- Service Logic Design Review
- Legal Data Audit

SOA Security Specialist

A given service architecture specification can include preventative and reactive security processing logic and the use of external security mechanisms. The definition of security-related design standards and their approval will generally require the involvement of an SOA Security Specialist.

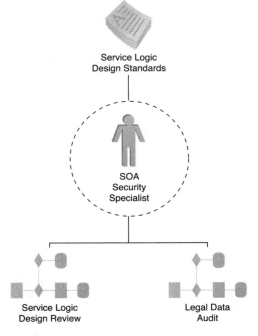

Figure 9.24

Service Logic Design governance precepts and processes associated with the SOA Security Specialist role.

As explained in Chapter 7, depending on the extent of security requirements and the level of importance assigned to fulfilling these requirements, a separate Security Audit process may be needed (especially when there are security requirements with legal implications). Such a process would be led by the individual or group taking on this role.

Related Precepts

- Service Logic Design Standards

Related Processes

- Service Logic Design Review
- Legal Data Audit

SOA Governance Specialist

The exit criteria for the Service Logic Design is especially important to the SOA Governance Specialist, because it represents the final step before the service moves on to Service Development, where it will be actually created. Further, the SOA Governance Specialist will be responsible for overseeing (and possibly carrying forward) Service Logic Design precepts in relation to precepts from previous stages, in particular the Service-Oriented Design stage.

For example, issues may arise during the Service Logic Design Review that end up impacting the design of the service contract. This may require that previously applied precepts be revisited or that a waiver may be issued or that the Service Contract Design Review process be carried out again. The SOA Governance Specialist can provide guidance to help ensure that these and other necessary governance responsibilities are carried out in preparation for Service Development.

Finally, the SOA Governance Specialist can assist the Service Architect with establishing the Service Access Control process, as this type of regulatory procedure may have various organizational governance implications.

Related Precepts

- Service Logic Design Standards
- Service-Orientation Architecture Design Standards

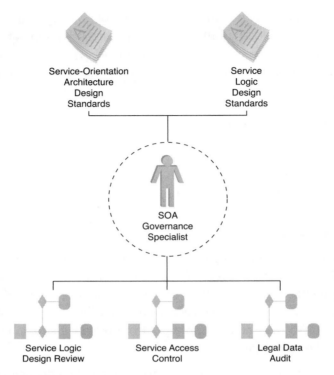

Figure 9.25
Service Logic Design governance precepts and processes associated with the SOA Governance Specialist role.

Related Processes

- Service Access Control

- Service Logic Design Review

- Legal Data Audit

NOTE
Policy Custodians are not typically involved in governance tasks during this stage, unless specific policy processing requirements (internal to the service architecture) exist that warrant governance attention.

SUMMARY OF KEY POINTS

- The Service Logic Design Review is the fundamental means by which the Service Logic Design stage is governed.

- In addition to adhering to custom design standards, service designs need to be compliant to service-orientation design principles. This ensures foundational, baseline consistency across all services in support of the strategic goals of service-oriented computing.

CASE STUDY EXAMPLE

The SOA Governance Program Office creates the following set of checklists in support of the Service Logic Design Standards and Compliance with Service-Orientation Architecture Design Principles precepts:

- A *service functionality checklist* to validate that each service design fully meets its business requirements.

- A *service non-functional requirements checklist* to validate that each service design fully supports its performance and behavioral requirements.

- A *service security checklist* to validate that the service design fully meets the security requirements.

- A *service architecture checklist* to validate that the service design meets all architectural standards in compliance with the overall service inventory architecture.

Using their service registry, the SOA Governance Program Office further automates the distribution of these checklists to authorized reviewers and approvers in order to implement a policy that prevents the Service Development stage from beginning until all checklists have been formally approved and signed off.

When the Service Custodian responsible for the Product service submits this service to the Service Logic Design Review, she raises a concern regarding one of the non-functional requirements on the SOA Governance Program Office checklists. The requirement corresponds to a design standard produced by the Enterprise Design Standards Custodian that demands that all service capabilities respond within a maximum period of 2 seconds. Depending on the criteria submitted, the GetRange capability of the Product service may need to query multiple product inventory locations, some of which are geographically distributed. Although these types of queries are expected to be rare, the fact that they are possible means that the upcoming Service Testing stage will likely reveal this as an area of non-compliance.

The SOA Governance Program Office joins the Service Custodian and a group of Service Architects to discuss the issue. During the meeting they identify four possible options:

1. Use a database replication approach to maintain a centralized "super table" that contains a copy of all product inventory data across Raysmoore and its subsidiaries. The Product service would then only need to query this one table, resulting in improved performance.

2. Create additional logic that detects when geographically separated product inventory repositories need to be queried, and then respond with a message to the service consumer warning that the query will take extra time (and asking for further confirmation).

3. Do nothing until performance test results can be obtained to determine actual service response times.

4. Issue a waiver for the Product service's GetRange capability so that the service can proceed with an approved extent of non-compliance.

It is decided that the cost of Option #1 will be too high considering the infrequency with which this performance lag will occur. Option #2 is also not chosen, as it would have too much of an impact on service consumer requirements. Although some voted for Option #3, it was Option #4 that was finally selected with one condition: the service logic will need to be further enhanced so that a query will timeout after 5 seconds, in which case the service capability will return an error back to the service consumer.

The design of the service is updated to reflect this change, and all other checklist items are signed off, allowing the Product service to be released to development.

9.3 Governing Service Development

The development of service logic can be challenging to formally govern, especially when IT enterprises are accustomed to outsourcing development projects or to giving internal development teams a great deal of autonomy. Even within standardized SOA delivery projects, there is sometimes a tendency to grant developers creative freedom as to how a given service should be programmed, as long as the logic created conforms to approved design specifications.

Governance precepts for this stage are not intended to constrict or negatively inhibit this creativity; their purpose is to regulate development activities and approaches in support of consistency, standardization, and quality maintenance.

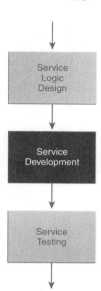

Precepts

Service Logic Programming Standards

Various programming language conventions can be established to ensure consistency across services.

Some common considerations include:

- naming standards

- consistent documentation and comments

- in-line maintenance logs identifying the developers that performed work on a given part of the service logic code

- reusable routines, variable names, use of global and shared variables, etc.

These types of conventions are well-established as programming best practices. However, their importance within SOA projects is amplified due to the potential need for shared services to be reused, recomposed, and perhaps maintained and expanded by different project teams at different points in time.

Furthermore, the positioning and use of industry standards will be dictated in order to ensure that proprietary programming languages are not employed when industry standardization is required. In this regard, there will tend to be overlap with the aforementioned service logic and service contract design standards. Regardless of how or where the programming standards are documented, it is important that they be made available specifically to Service Developers.

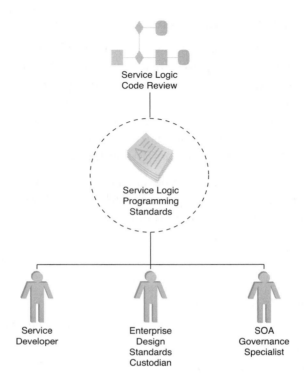

Figure 9.26
The Service Logic Programming Standards precept.

Related Processes

- Service Logic Code Review

Related Roles

- Service Developer
- Enterprise Design Standards Custodian
- SOA Governance Specialist

Custom Development Technology Standards

Existing enterprise and design standards will commonly dictate which programming languages are allowed. This will often be based on the current development platform (Java, .NET, etc.) already established within the IT enterprise, but can also be influenced by new and unique business requirements.

Also, the use of industry standards (such as XML-based markup languages) will be identified in the design specifications and further regulated (and elaborated) by custom programming standards. For example, whereas a design specification may indicate the WS-Security standard is to be used, the Custom Development Technology Standards document will identify exactly which features and elements of the standard are actually allowed and under what circumstances they may not be allowed.

Tool standards are also common to ensure that the building and subsequent maintenance processes are not bound to disparate tools and skill-sets. Having a common set of tools used throughout development-related project phases makes it easier for different developers to work with each other's code. The choice of tools will depend on the development platform and industry standards dictated by the Service Logic Programming Standards.

NOTE

One of the strategic goals of service-oriented computing explained in Chapter 3 was Increased Vendor Diversity Options. It may seem contrary to this goal to support the standardization of development tools and technologies. This precept can be augmented if the need to diversify emerges and is sufficiently justified. This is why the goal emphasizes having the "option" of diversifying (when it makes sense to do so), but it does not advocate unwarranted diversification.

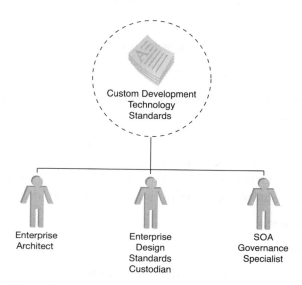

Figure 9.27

The Custom Development Technology Standards precept.

Related Processes

N/A

Related Roles

- Enterprise Design Standards Custodian
- Enterprise Architect
- SOA Governance Specialist

Processes

Service Logic Code Review

The primary purpose of the Service Logic Code Review is to verify that the programming code created and used by the service is in compliance with the Service Logic Programming Standards. The extent to which this review needs to delve into the specifics of the code is directly related to the level of detail of the programming standards. For example, some standards may dictate how certain types of routines need to be programmed, whereas others may require that existing generic routines be reused for specific types of programming requirements.

When carrying out this process, it is very common to incorporate additional types of reviews that go beyond the Service Logic Programming Standards. Examples of typical areas to further proof include:

- the service is programmed according to its design specification
- the quality of the programming code
- the level of documentation is adequate to enable future maintenance by different Service Developers

A Service Logic Code Review typically consists of structured code walkthroughs, where a group of peer developers inspects and constructively criticizes the code in sessions moderated by an SOA Governance Specialist. These walkthroughs can also help mentor junior programmers new to the use of the custom standards.

Possible outcomes of the review include:

- The code is approved as it stands.
- Potential improvement areas are identified and the Service Developer is tasked to incorporate them.

- The code is so non-compliant to the Service Logic Programming Standards that it is rejected and assigned to new Service Developers.

When the final approval is received, the service state in the registry should be updated to indicate its promotion to the next stage. Changes to the service metadata made during coding can also be reflected in the repository.

Related Precepts

- Service Logic Programming Standards

Related Roles

- Service Developer

- Enterprise Design Standards Custodian

- SOA Governance Specialist

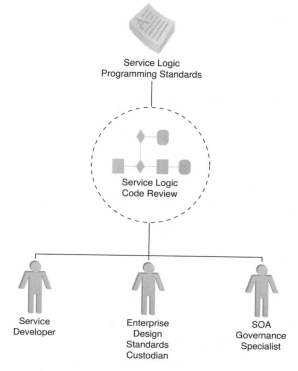

Figure 9.28

The Service Logic Code Review process.

People (Roles)

Service Developer

Although Service Developers will be the ones carrying out the programming activities during the Service Development stage, their expertise is useful and often necessary to help establish suitable Service Logic Programming Standards, especially in relation to the distinct requirements introduced by the application of service-orientation design principles (as will have likely been documented in the design specifications from the Service Logic Design stage). Service Logic Code Reviews will also require participation by peer Service Developers to verify compliance to the corresponding Service Logic Programming Standards.

Related Precepts

- Service Logic Programming Standards

Related Processes

- Service Logic Code Review

Service Logic
Programming Standards

Service
Developer

Service Logic
Code Review

Figure 9.29

Service Development governance precepts and processes
associated with the Service Developer role.

Enterprise Design Standards Custodian

This role will generally act in a peripheral capacity with regards to the definition of Service Logic Programming Standards. Similarly, involvement in the Service Logic Code Review may also be secondary to the Service Developers actually performing the detailed code audits.

The Enterprise Design Standards Custodian may communicate, in advance, specific regulations or requirements of importance to the Service Developers authoring the standards and performing the reviews. The Enterprise Design Standards Custodian may then need to rely on confirmation from the Service Developers that those requirements have been met. Upon receiving confirmation (perhaps in the form of a signature), the Enterprise Design Standards Custodian can sign off on the standards or review.

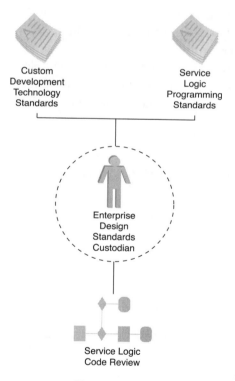

Figure 9.30

Service Development governance precepts and processes associated with the Enterprise Design Standards Custodian role.

This role is further involved with the definition of Custom Development Technology Standards, for which collaboration with the Enterprise Architect and other technology experts may be required.

Related Precepts

- Service Logic Programming Standards
- Custom Development Technology Standards

Related Processes

- Service Logic Code Review

Enterprise Architect

Enterprise Architects will usually have a regulatory interest in the technologies and tools being used to build software programs for deployment within the enterprise. They will therefore commonly lead the creation of Custom Development Technology Standards in cooperation with the Enterprise Design Standards Custodian and an SOA Governance Specialist.

Custom Development
Technology Standards

Enterprise
Architect

Related Precepts

- Custom Development Technology Standards

Related Processes

N/A

Figure 9.31
Service Development governance precepts and processes associated with the Enterprise Architect role.

SOA Governance Specialist

During the Service Development stage, SOA Governance Specialists provide any necessary guidance for the definition and application of precepts and processes on behalf of the SOA Governance Program Office.

Together with the Enterprise Design Standards Custodian, they may further assist with the mapping of development standards to design standards to ensure consistency.

Related Precepts

- Service Logic Programming Standards
- Custom Development Technology Standards

Related Processes

- Service Logic Code Review

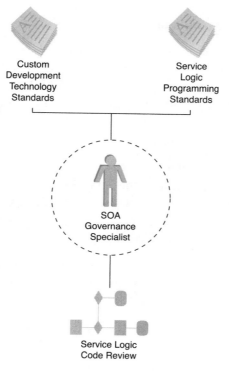

Figure 9.32

Service Development governance precepts and processes associated with the SOA Governance Specialist role.

SUMMARY OF KEY POINTS

- The focal point of the Service Development stage, from a governance perspective, is the use of development standards and the involvement of a review for checking on the compliance of those standards.

- Service Development can be a challenging stage to effectively govern because developers may not be accustomed to the form of regulation required by SOA governance precepts.

CASE STUDY EXAMPLE

The SOA Governance Program Office mandates code walkthroughs for every newly developed or updated service. During these sessions Service Developers join Service Architects to compare the programming logic with the functionality defined in the corresponding design specifications.

During the code walkthrough for the Product service a Service Architect notices that it contains several complex routines that seem to include superfluous code not relevant to the nature of the service logic. The Service Architect asks the newly hired Service Developer responsible for these routines about their origin and, when pressed on that point, the developer admits that some code routines from a project he worked on for a previous employer had been reused.

The SOA Governance Program Office representative joins the Service Architect and they have a counseling session with the Service Developer to explain that not only have these actions caused the Product service to fail its code review, but that the inclusion of code routines from another company may have violated that company's copyright and perhaps even introduced a security breach.

The Product service logic is handed back to the development team where it will undergo rework to replace the foreign routines.

Chapter 10

Governing Service Testing and Deployment Stages

The methodology and management system used by an IT enterprise for the analysis, design, and development of services can vary based on strategic and tactical priorities and business goals. However, approaches and procedures that oversee the testing and deployment of software programs are often well established, regardless of how the programs were created. Although service delivery does introduce unique testing and deployment requirements, the same tendency to follow consistent procedures holds true. From a governance perspective, we are concerned with maintaining this consistency, especially across project teams that may be delivering different services at different times into the same service inventory.

10.1 Governing Service Testing

Service testing efforts aim to ensure compliance with functional and non-functional requirements, as well as related policies, SLAs, and other pre-defined and measurable features and behaviors.

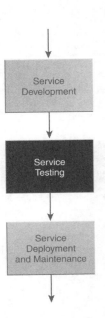

Common types of tests and test cycles include:

- *Unit Tests* (service is tested to ensure that it performs as expected)

- *Standards Compliance Tests* (service is tested to ensure it complies with required standards)

- *Functional Tests* (service is tested to ensure it adheres to functional requirements)

- *Security Tests* (service is tested to ensure it adheres to security requirements)

- *Policy Tests* (service is tested for compliance to service-specific and cross-service policies)

- *Regression Tests* (service is tested to ensure that changes do not negatively impact existing service consumers)

- *Performance Tests* (service is tested to ensure that it adheres to non-functional requirements, including performance, SLAs, and scalability)

- *Integration Tests* (service is tested within a new or foreign environment to identify any compatibility issues and to ensure it behaves and performs as expected)

The last item on this list is discussed specifically in relation to cloud environments in this chapter.

Precepts

Testing Tool Standards

Several of the previously listed tests can be automated and executed continuously throughout the service development lifecycle. In order to maintain consistency across services and service and solution delivery projects, a common set of testing tools should be used.

Establishing Testing Tool Standards helps avoid different services within the same service inventory from being subjected to the same tests with variance in test method, test quality, and the metrics used to measure test results. The last consideration is especially important in support of the Test Parameters Standards precept (explained next).

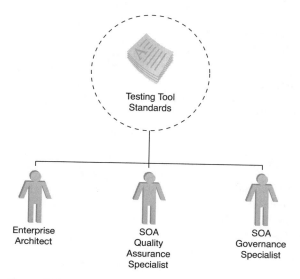

Figure 10.1

The Testing Tools Standards precept.

Related Processes

N/A

Related Roles

- Enterprise Architect
- SOA Quality Assurance Specialist
- SOA Governance Specialist

Testing Parameter Standards

Many IT departments define standards that specify which tests need to be performed along with common sets of testing parameters that services (especially shared services) must be required to meet in order to be approved for deployment. This type of service inventory-wide standardization is important to ensure behavioral predictability among services.

When certain parameters cannot be met (perhaps due to limitations imposed by legacy resources encapsulated by the service), exceptions may be allowed. In this case, there is typically a requirement to document these limitations in the service's SLA.

Related Processes

- Service Test Results Review

Related Roles

- Service Administrator
- Cloud Resource Administrator
- SOA Security Specialist
- SOA Quality Assurance Specialist
- SOA Governance Specialist

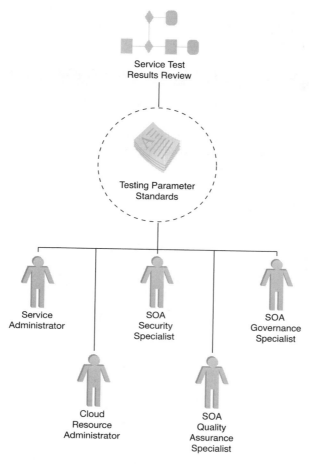

Figure 10.2

The Testing Parameter Standards precept.

Service Testing Standards

Each service architecture is unique and testing processes are commonly based on the specific set of functions and processing requirements of a given service. However, there are baseline standards that can be established to ensure a minimum guarantee of runtime performance and behavior. These base Service Testing Standards often correlate to the Runtime Service Usage Thresholds precept (and associated metrics) documented in the *Governing Service Usage and Monitoring* section in Chapter 11.

Further, this precept can encompass additional testing standards specific to different service models (task, entity, utility, etc.), as each will tend to have specific types of processing responsibilities and performance expectations.

NOTE

Due to the variance in functionality across different services and service models, some parts of this precept may be better suited as guidelines. It is therefore useful to make a clear distinction between voluntary testing guidelines and mandatory, baseline testing standards.

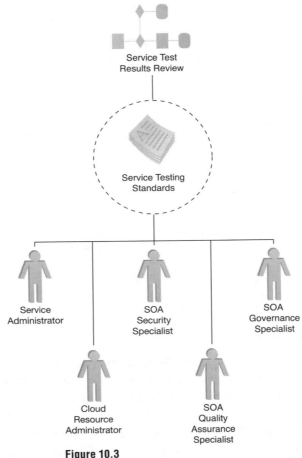

Figure 10.3
The Service Testing Standards precept.

Related Processes

- Service Test Results Review

Related Roles

- Service Administrator

- Cloud Resource Administrator

- SOA Security Specialist

- SOA Quality Assurance Specialist

- SOA Governance Specialist

Cloud Integration Testing Standards

For services identified for deployment within third-party cloud platforms, further baseline testing standards can be defined to guarantee that services behave and perform to a level of acceptable consistency with on-premise services. This is especially important when service compositions can span cloud and on-premise deployed services.

Cloud Integration Testing Standards include criteria and checklists that confirm compatibility with specific implementation characteristics required to maintain cross-service standardization. The identification of non-compliant (and non-flexible) platform requirements can lead to the rejection of the cloud as a deployment option during the subsequent Service Test Results Review.

Conversely, a primary motivation for targeting the deployment of a service within a cloud platform may be the availability of IT resources (especially in relation to dynamic scaling and pay-per-use billing) that do not exist within the IT enterprise's on-premise environment. In this case, cloud integration tests may be further extended to validate that the cloud-specific features do, in fact, address the service requirements and expectations.

Related Processes

- Service Test Results Review

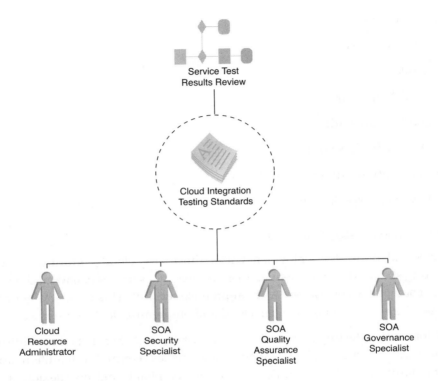

Figure 10.4
The Cloud Integration Testing Standards precept.

Related Roles

- Cloud Resource Administrator
- SOA Security Specialist
- SOA Quality Assurance Specialist
- SOA Governance Specialist
- Other: Cloud Architect
- Other: Cloud Security Specialist
- Other: Cloud Governance Specialist

Test Data Usage Guidelines

Because the testing phase results in the creation of data specific to services and service compositions (such as performance statistics, measured exceptions, etc.), it is important to have guidelines (or, in some cases, even standards) in place to govern the usage of that data.

Some common considerations include:

- Where will test data be stored?
- Who is responsible for the analysis of test data?
- How are testing-related metrics communicated?
- How are testing-related metrics mapped to business requirements?
- How are testing-related metrics mapped to design specifications?
- Who is responsible for the management of test scripts and the configuration of testing tools?

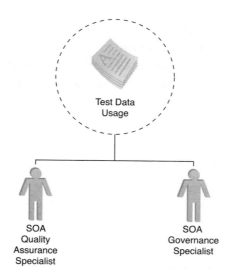

Figure 10.5
The Test Data Usage Guidelines precept.

These and other issues should be addressed by a guidelines document that depicts the flow of test data from its initial raw, collected state to its presentation in metrics reports.

Related Processes

N/A

Related Roles

- SOA Quality Assurance Specialist
- SOA Governance Specialist

Processes

Service Test Results Review

One or more review processes can be established to approve or reject a given service based on the statistics and results made available from whatever tests the service underwent. As part of this review, it should also be confirmed that a given service was, in fact, subjected to all of the appropriate tests.

It is important to note that if failures are encountered in any of the testing steps, the service logic may need to be revised which, in turn, will necessitate cycles of re-testing. Further, test results data can be stored in the service profile as well as a central location (preferably a repository) along with all other service metadata.

Related Precepts

- Testing Parameter Standards
- Service Testing Standards
- Cloud Integration Standards

Related Roles

- SOA Security Specialist
- SOA Quality Assurance Specialist
- SOA Governance Specialist

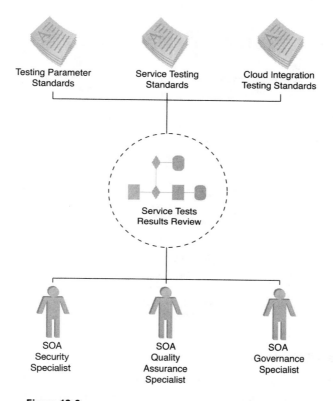

Figure 10.6

The Service Test Results Review process.

People (Roles)

Service Administrator

Service Administrators are usually peripherally involved with establishing governance controls for the Service Testing stage in that they can provide guidance and advice regarding the recommended testing parameters and standards, and the synchronization of testing environments with target production environments.

Related Precepts

- Testing Parameter Standards
- Service Testing Standards

Related Processes

N/A

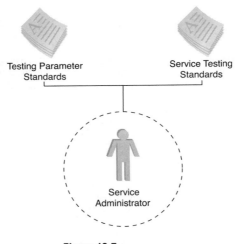

Figure 10.7
Service Testing governance
precepts and processes
associated with the Service
Administrator role.

Cloud Resource Administrator

Similar to the role of the Service Administrator, Cloud Resource Administrators provide their expertise and understanding of the target cloud environment for a service to ensure that testing standards are authored correctly and that all cloud-specific considerations are accounted for. When working with PaaS platforms that provide a ready-made environment within which services can be built, tested, and then deployed to production, the Cloud Resource Administer may need to collaborate with the SOA Quality Assurance Specialist to properly govern the Service Testing stage.

Related Precepts

• Testing Parameter Standards

• Service Testing Standards

• Cloud Integration Testing Standards

Related Processes

N/A

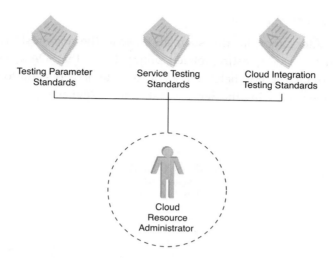

Figure 10.8

Service Testing governance precepts and processes associated with the Cloud Resource Administrator role.

Enterprise Architect

In relation to SOA governance, the primary area of interest for the Enterprise Architect during the Service Testing stage is the toolset used by SOA Quality Assurance Specialists. When different project teams are delivering services for the same service inventory, the standardization of testing tools helps maintain consistency when carrying out any of the precepts associated with this stage.

Related Precepts

- Testing Tool Standards

Related Processes

N/A

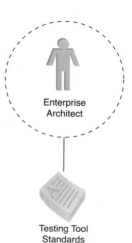

Figure 10.9

Service Testing governance precepts and processes associated with the Enterprise Architect role.

SOA Quality Assurance Specialist

As the subject matter expert for this stage and also as the role most involved with the actual execution of Service Testing-related project tasks, the SOA Quality Assurance Specialist can provide input to help define appropriate precepts and to further participate as a peer reviewer during the Service Test Results Review process.

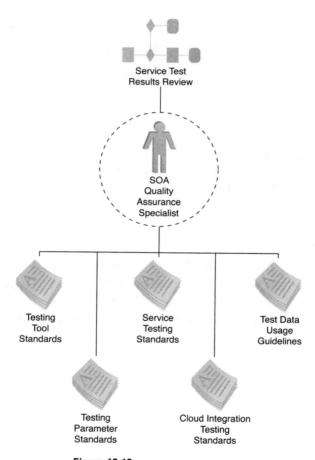

Figure 10.10

Service Testing governance precepts and processes associated with the SOA Quality Assurance Specialist role.

Related Precepts

- Testing Tool Standards

- Testing Parameter Standards

- Service Testing Standards

- Cloud Integration Testing Standards

- Test Data Usage Guidelines

Related Processes

- Service Test Results Review

SOA Security Specialist

As with other project stages, the involvement of the SOA Security Specialist is required when certain security concerns are being addressed within the service architecture. This role will possess the expertise to not only identify types of security-related tests, but will further be able to set the individual thresholds and tolerances pertaining to service security requirements.

For example, the SOA Security Specialist may devise a series of tests to simulate a malicious attack in order to expose encrypted data transmitted in messages sent by a service. The attack may succeed at some point, indicating a certain level of encryption weakness or strength. This level may or may not be deemed acceptable, depending on the standards set by the SOA Security Specialist.

Further, SOA Security Specialists will be particularly involved with testing security controls with cloud-based services, as some of the security mechanisms in use may be supplied by the cloud provider. As briefly explained in Chapter 7, cloud environments can introduce new security concerns, especially in third-party clouds where resources used by the service are shared by other cloud consumer organizations (leading to the need to share corresponding trust boundaries).

Related Precepts

- Testing Parameter Standards

- Service Testing Standards

- Cloud Integration Testing Standards

Related Processes

- Service Test Results Review

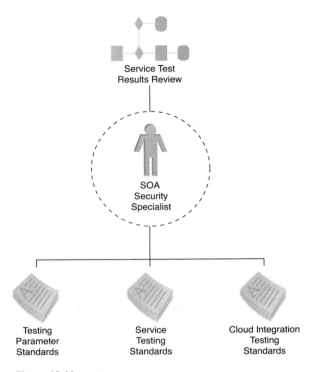

Figure 10.11
Service Testing governance precepts and processes associated with the SOA Security Specialist role.

SOA Governance Specialist

The SOA Governance Specialist participates in an advisory role throughout the definition and application of Service Testing precepts. However, this role can further aid this governing stage by identifying and involving other technology or subject matter experts that may be required to assist with the identification and creation of testing standards, as well as participation during the Service Test Results Review.

Related Precepts

- Testing Tool Standards
- Testing Parameter Standards
- Service Testing Standards

- Cloud Integration Testing Standards
- Test Data Usage Guidelines

Related Processes

- Service Test Results Review

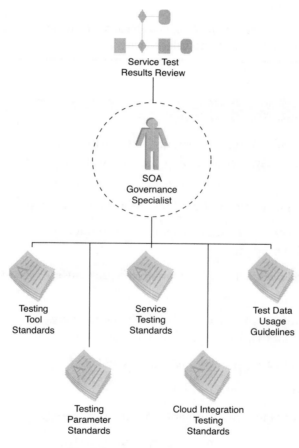

Figure 10.12
Service Testing governance precepts
and processes associated with the SOA
Governance Specialist role.

SUMMARY OF KEY POINTS

- Service Testing governance precepts intend to ensure that services fulfill testing requirements within required parameters and in compliance with pre-defined standards.

- Test data is a primary governance concern to ensure its on-going use and value in the form of metrics.

- Cloud-based services introduce special testing requirements, some of which are related to distinct security concerns.

CASE STUDY EXAMPLE

Following the guidance and requirements set forth by the SOA Governance Program Office precepts, the Raysmoore quality assurance department establishes an SOA testing program.

Some distinguishing characteristics of the program include the following:

- a standardized set of performance metrics created for evaluating service performance and SLA compliance

- business-centric parameters documented to verify business requirements compliance

Multiple test environments are made available in order to accurately mirror the production environment in all aspects (except for capacity).

Specifically, the following environments are established:

- development environments for unit testing

- systems functional test environments for systems testing

- performance test environments for performance testing

- pre-production environments for certification testing

Each test environment holds smaller-scale copies of production databases to allow for functional and performance testing with real data. The performance test and pre-production environments have network connectivity to all subsidiaries' test environments in order to test for service inter-system connectivity and network performance under realistic conditions.

Performance and regression testing is automated using a commercial software product that can generate combinations of random input data. This data can be valid and realistic (for functional or performance testing) or deliberately invalid (for testing that systems generate the correct responses during exception conditions). The testing tool can also run scripts to generate pre-determined volumes of requests to assist performance testing.

For larger service compositions, the SOA Governance Program Office specifies a six week "soak" period in the pre-production environment under a simulated traffic load to determine if there are any further bugs, memory leaks, or other types of flaws.

All initial service testing and certification is performed using Raysmoore's test and staging environments, except for services that wrap legacy systems unique to one or more subsidiaries. Any services that are later deployed to the subsidiary's operations environment are required to be re-certified for that environment.

The SOA Governance Program Office further mandates that the service repository be used to store test results and capture test history. This allows for the identification of recurring issues and helps keep track of which services are certified for which subsidiary's production environment.

Following one of the Test Data Management Guidelines published by the SOA Governance Program Office, the quality assurance team creates a standardized testing profile, as shown in Table 10.1.

Test Type	Entry Criteria	Exit Criteria	Next Steps
unit test	• code being tested is complete (if test-driven development practices are used, tests are written before any code is produced)	• all unit tests pass • code coverage criteria is met	• store results in service repository along with other service metadata • proceed to compliance testing

continues

Test Type	Entry Criteria	Exit Criteria	Next Steps
compliance test	• code being tested is complete • compliance rules have been documented	• all compliance tests pass	• store results in service repository along with other service metadata • proceed to security testing • deploy code into system test environment
security test	• code being tested is complete • security policies have been documented and implemented	• all security tests pass	• store results in service repository along with other service metadata • proceed to functional testing
functional test	• code being tested is complete and unit tested • test cases are defined • optional: functional tests are automated	• all functional tests pass	• store results in service repository along with other service metadata • proceed to regression testing
regression test	• code being tested is complete and unit and functionally tested • regression test cases have been documented • optional: regression tests are automated	• all regression tests pass	• store results in service repository along with other service metadata • add functional tests to the regression testing suite • proceed to performance testing • deploy code into performance test environment

Test Type	Entry Criteria	Exit Criteria	Next Steps
performance test	• code being tested is complete and unit, functionally, and regression tested • performance test cases are defined for the new consumer • performance test cases are defined for the existing consumers	• all non-functional criteria is met for the new consumer • combined non-functional criteria set is met for all service consumers • all SLA requirements are met	• store results in service repository along with other service metadata • add new performance tests to the performance testing suite • deploy code to production

Table 10.1
A testing profile that organizes service testing and related governance steps.

10.2 Governing Service Deployment and Maintenance

Production environments in most IT enterprises are supported by governance controls. With service-oriented solutions these controls can become more stringent. For example, because a single service deployment can establish a point of failure for multiple future service compositions, the amount of checkpoints and rigor that deployments for a reusable service must undergo can be significant.

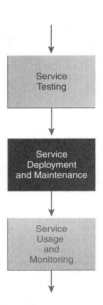

The primary goal of governing the deployment of services within a production environment is to ensure the stability of the services and to further guarantee that all maintenance changes face the appropriate scrutiny to preserve the service's (stable) production status.

> **NOTE**
>
> It is important, for the purpose of this chapter, to distinguish service maintenance from service versioning. This governance stage is concerned with maintenance issues that usually relate to an initial service deployment. Technology upgrades and bug fixes are the two most common types of maintenance deployments that fall under this category.
>
> The upcoming *Governing Service Versioning and Retirement* section in Chapter 11 is dedicated solely to service versioning issues. Depending on the configuration system and versioning strategy being employed, any maintenance deployment may actually constitute a new service version (in which case you should consider the maintenance-related content in this chapter part of the Service Versioning and Retirement stage).

Precepts

Production Deployment and Maintenance Standards

A typical IT enterprise will have already established governance requirements for any software programs to be deployed or upgraded in the production environment.

These requirements can include:

- production entrance criteria

- specific steps to be followed for production deployments and upgrades

- forms and approvals needed to apply for and carry out a deployment or an upgrade

- guidelines for dealing with common production deployments issues

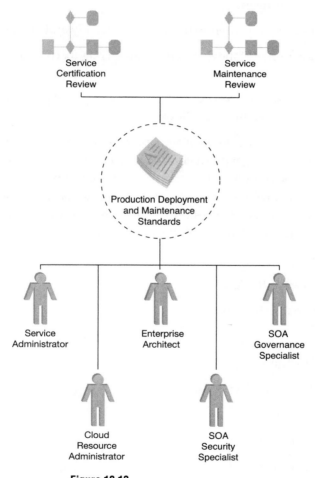

Figure 10.13

The Production Deployment and
Maintenance Standards precept.

The deployment and maintenance of services can introduce additional considerations, especially in relation to surrounding services that share the same service inventory environment. For example, it may be necessary to analyze the impact of a newly deployed, reusable service on pooled infrastructure resources that are already being shared by other services.

Upgrades and bug fixes can be challenging because they carry a potential impact to the stability of the existing service and its consumers.

Example considerations include:

- Is enough data being captured to resolve bugs quickly and efficiently?
- Is the resolution process followed to introduce a bug fix consistent with issue severity?
- For a cloud-based service deployment, are there required procedures specified by the cloud provider that must be followed?

This precept represents the deployment and maintenance requirements, standards, and guidelines specific to the target production environment for a given service. As noted in the last bullet from the preceding list, services deployed in public cloud environments may be subject to deployment and maintenance limitations imposed by third-party cloud providers. In this case, the resulting standards and guidelines may need to be based on or defined in compliance with these limitations.

Related Processes

- Service Certification Review
- Service Maintenance Review

Related Roles

- Service Administrator
- Cloud Resource Administrator
- Enterprise Architect
- SOA Security Specialist
- SOA Governance Specialist

Processes

Service Certification Review

Before any new service is deployed into a production environment, it must receive formal approval. Typically, this is achieved as a result of the completion of the Service Certification Review process, which is necessary to ensure that:

- the correct service is being deployed to the correct location

- the deployment location is consistent with the preceding testing and staging environments (a consideration especially relevant when deploying services to third-party cloud platforms)

- all advertised quality characteristics (as documented in the SLA and service profile) have been fulfilled

- any required service monitoring and management tools and processes are in place

- all applicable billing rates (for services deployed on leased IT resources) have been verified

Many individuals can participate in this process, each potentially involved in a different aspect of the review. If, subsequently, the review is successful, the service is considered "certified" and ready to enter the production environment. Prior to this point, production support teams should have been notified so that they are prepared for the new service deployment and its requirements. (This type of notification can contain a pointer to the corresponding service registry record.)

Related Precepts

- Production Deployment and Maintenance Standards

Related Roles

- Service Administrator

- Cloud Resource Administrator

- Enterprise Architect

- Service Custodian

- SOA Quality Assurance Specialist

- SOA Security Specialist

- SOA Governance Specialist
- Other: Cloud Architect
- Other: Cloud Security Specialist
- Other: Cloud Governance Specialist

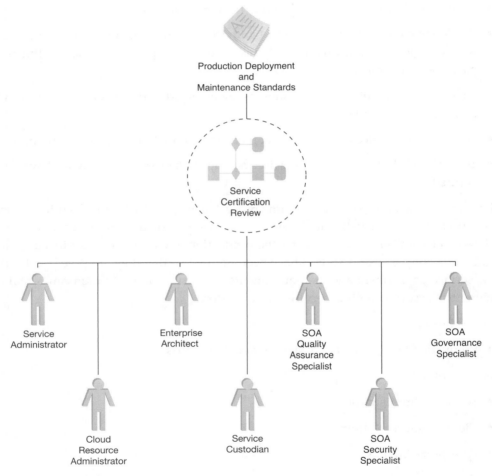

Figure 10.14
The Service Certification Review precept.

Service Maintenance Review

Maintenance changes that affect the service code, such as bug fixes, must be stored in the source code repository alongside the original service code. These changes need to be introduced in such a way that they do not interfere with any new work being performed against the same code base. In most typical development platforms this is achieved by introducing a new branch in the source control tool. Although several roles can be involved in this process, the Service Custodian in particular needs to approve any such changes prior to deployment. Maintenance changes can be further logged in the service's registry record.

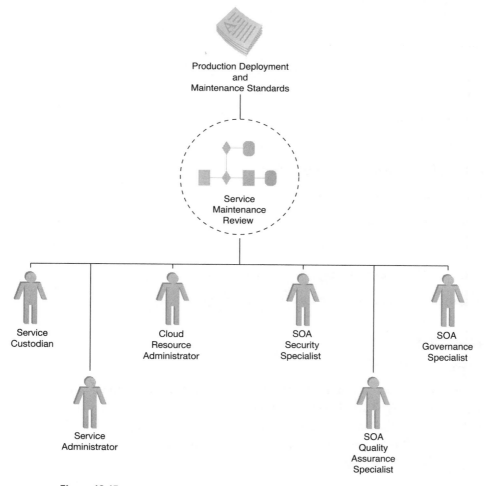

Figure 10.15
The Service Maintenance Review precept.

If maintenance changes are classified as fixes or upgrades that do not constitute a new major service version, then, depending on the change management system and methodology in use by the IT department, it may or may not be necessary to subject the revised service to another complete Service Certification Review.

> **NOTE**
>
> In some cases, the Production Deployment and Maintenance Requirements precept will dictate that if a maintenance change warrants a re-certification of the service, it must result in a new service version and therefore become subject to further service versioning precepts.

Related Precepts

- Production Deployment and Maintenance Standards

Related Roles

- Service Custodian
- Service Administrator
- Cloud Resource Administrator
- SOA Quality Assurance Specialist
- SOA Security Specialist
- SOA Governance Specialist
- Other: Cloud Computing Security Specialist
- Other: Cloud Computing Governance Specialist

People (Roles)

Service Administrator

For on-premise service implementations, the Service Deployment and Maintenance stage is primarily associated with this role. The Service Administrator, together with the Service Custodian and SOA Governance Specialist, typically lead the efforts to establish the Production Deployment and Maintenance Standard precept and associated processes.

Related Precepts

- Production Deployment and Maintenance Standards

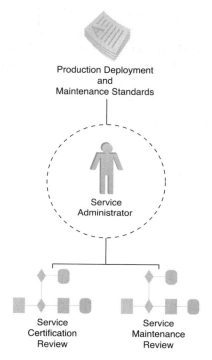

Figure 10.16
Service Deployment governance precepts
and processes associated with the Service
Administrator role.

Related Processes

- Service Certification Review

- Service Maintenance Review

Cloud Resource Administrator

For services destined for deployment within a cloud environment, this role will lead
necessary governance activities together with the Service Custodian and SOA Governance Specialist. The Cloud Resource Administrator's involvement may not be limited
to the service implementation, as further cloud-based IT resources may need to be set
up and maintained to ensure consistent performance behavior, especially in cloud environments shared by multiple cloud consumer organizations.

A primary task during this stage is the configuration of on-demand and dynamic scaling settings. Mechanisms, such as the automated scaling listener and the pay-for-use monitor, may need to be positioned and tuned via cloud-based desktop tools so that the cloud service can leverage cloud provided IT resources within pre-defined parameters.

Related Precepts

- Production Deployment and Maintenance Standards

Related Processes

- Service Certification Review
- Service Maintenance Review

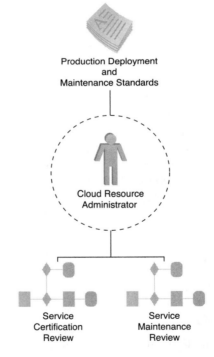

Figure 10.17
Service Deployment governance precepts and processes associated with the Cloud Resource Administrator role.

Service Custodian

Although the owner or custodian of a service may have been involved in previous service lifecycle stages, it is often as part of Service Deployment where ownership is officially assigned to a designated Service Custodian. As a result, this role will be involved with the Service Certification Review, during which it will act as a primary point of contact for any issues or objections that may arise. The Service Custodian is also a standard participant of Service Maintenance Reviews, as this individual may be required to approve any planned upgrades or fixes that affect the service architecture.

Related Precepts

N/A

Related Processes

- Service Certification Review
- Service Maintenance Review

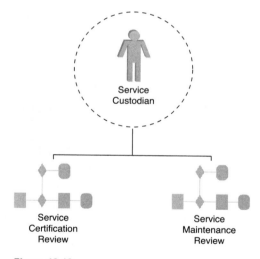

Figure 10.18

Service Deployment governance precepts and processes associated with the Service Custodian role.

Enterprise Architect

Many of the standards and requirements defined in the Production Deployment and Maintenance Standards specifications will be influenced by or even derived from underlying platform technology architecture and infrastructure. Enterprise Architects therefore can become a primary contributor to these standards and their sign-off may further be required for the deployment of any service implementation that introduces new or previously non-standardized technologies or resources.

Related Precepts

- Production Deployment and Maintenance Standards

Related Processes

- Service Certification Review

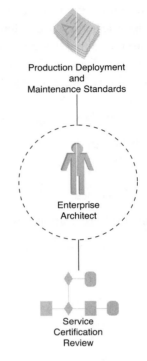

Production Deployment
and
Maintenance Standards

Enterprise
Architect

Service
Certification
Review

Figure 10.19

Service Deployment governance precepts and processes associated with the Enterprise Architect role.

SOA Quality Assurance Specialist

Quality assurance concerns can extend to the Service Deployment stage in order to validate that a service is functioning and performing in the production environment as it was previously when in testing and staging environments. In this capacity, the SOA Quality Assurance Specialist can take part in the Service Certification Review and Service Maintenance Review processes.

Related Precepts

N/A

Related Processes

- Service Certification Review
- Service Maintenance Review

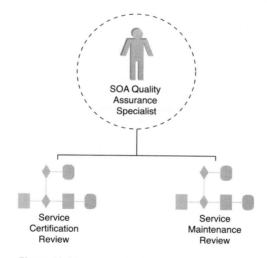

Figure 10.20

Service Deployment governance precepts and processes associated with the SOA Quality Assurance Specialist role.

SOA Security Specialist

The SOA Security Specialist will be asked to join the Service Certification Review and/ or the Service Maintenance Review process when it's necessary to perform a security audit on the service's production implementation. This may involve assessing the service as it relates to and interacts with other services.

The Production Deployment and Maintenance Standards may also benefit from having the SOA Security Specialist contribute to ensure that existing standards don't inhibit the use of required security mechanisms or inadvertently introduce security vulnerabilities.

Related Precepts

- Production Deployment and Maintenance Standards

Related Processes

- Service Certification Review
- Service Maintenance Review

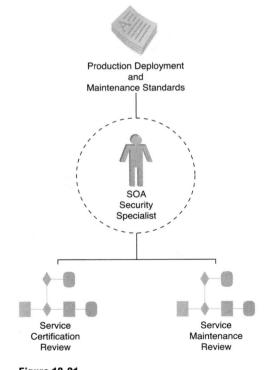

Figure 10.21
Service Deployment governance precepts and processes associated with the SOA Security Specialist role.

SOA Governance Specialist

In addition to providing guidance and coordination for the transition of the developed and tested service to its production deployment, the SOA Governance Specialist can further help ensure that Service Deployment exit criteria is in alignment with Service Usage precepts that will already be in place.

Related Precepts

- Production Deployment and Maintenance Standards

Related Processes

- Service Certification Review
- Service Maintenance Review

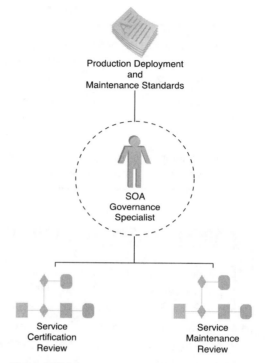

Figure 10.22
Service Deployment governance precepts and processes associated with the SOA Governance Specialist role.

NOTE

The Schema Custodian and Policy Custodian may be asked to participate in the Service Deployment stage to ensure that implementation of schemas and policies (especially when shared by multiple services) is carried out correctly. Often their involvement is required to resolve conflicts that may occur with runtime schema and policy processing and validation. However, these roles are not usually required to contribute to governance tasks.

Of course, other IT professionals, such as System Administrators (and various production support personnel), are also commonly involved in the actual management and execution of deployment and maintenance processes.

SUMMARY OF KEY POINTS

- Changes to the production environment needs to be introduced in a very deliberate and pragmatic fashion, especially when dealing with shared services.

- Before any new service code is deployed into the production environment, it must receive formal approval, typically through a Service Certification Review.

- Maintenance deployments and upgrades can constitute a new major service version and therefore can be subject to additional governance controls.

CASE STUDY EXAMPLE

The SOA Governance Program Office recognized early on that Raysmoore required a rapid and effective resolution of maintenance issues (such as minor software bugs and unforeseen SLA violations) pertaining to newly deployed services. Rapid problem resolution and consistently meeting promised service SLAs was a critical success factor clearly defined in the original SOA roadmap and one that is becoming increasingly important as the new Raysmoore service inventory grows steadily more reliant on agnostic services to support core business operations.

To this end, the SOA Governance Program Office arranges for the help desk to handle technical problems and SLA violations with services, according to pre-defined severity codes:

- *Severity 1 (service unavailable)* – Respond to consumers within one hour during normal business hours, or within three hours during evenings and weekends. Target 95% resolution of Severity 1 problems in the same business day.

- *Severity 2 (significant impairment of service function or violation of SLA by 20% or more)* – Respond to consumer within two hours during normal business hours or next business day. Target of 95% resolution of Severity 2 problems within two working days.

- *Severity 3 (minor functional issues or SLA violations)* – Respond to consumer within two working days. Target 95% of Severity 3 problems to be resolved within five working days.

When a problem occurs, the fix is made available to all service consumers as soon as the service has completed any necessary regression testing and re-certification. In order to meet the deadlines for Severity 1 and 2 issues, emergency certification reviews can be called at any time.

The SOA Governance Program Office helps establish a process that ensures that all the changes to the code made as a result of bug fixes are checked into a central code repository. (This helps avoid a previous problem where support personnel inadvertently re-introduced previously identified bugs into new service deployments.)

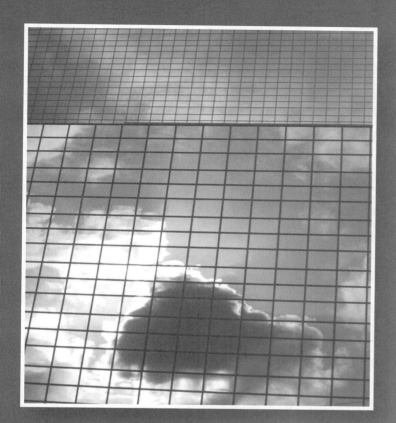

Chapter 11

Governing Service Usage, Discovery, and Versioning Stages

The SOA governance precepts covered in this chapter are dedicated to post-deployment stages during which services are active and available for use by service consumers, and further subject to evolutionary changes.

11.1 Governing Service Usage and Monitoring

The runtime governance of deployed services is a critical regulatory focal point because it represents the stage during a service's lifecycle during which we have the opportunity to actively receive value and benefit in return for the investment we made to create the service.

Precepts for service usage governance are, for the most part, dedicated to establishing parameters that limit how services can be used. These precepts are geared to protecting the service from excess or inappropriate usage so as to ensure stability, reliability, and consistent behavior. This, in return, protects all service consumers that rely on the service. Furthermore, these parameters help ensure that the service does not compromise resources shared by other services within the same service inventory or shared by other parts of the IT enterprise.

The Service Usage and Monitoring stage is also the part of the service lifecycle during which the majority of runtime metrics are collected both for use by precepts in processes related to this stage, but also for use by other (pre- and post-deployment) precepts and processes, to help assess their effectiveness.

Precepts

Runtime Service Usage Thresholds

This precept establishes a set of thresholds, some applied generally to most or all services within a service inventory, others are applied or adjusted specifically for individual services.

Common types of usage thresholds include:

- *Service Composition Membership Threshold* – The amount of service compositions an agnostic service can participate in. This value is usually based on scalability limitations or limitations imposed by shared and legacy resources encapsulated by the service.

- *Service Instance Threshold* – This value represents the amount of instances of a service that can exist concurrently. This scalability limitation is usually based on available infrastructure and memory resources.

- *Cloud Burst Threshold* – This threshold represents the point at which a given service will scale into a cloud. Often, the Cloud Burst Threshold is the same as the Service Instance Threshold in that the latter value represents the on-premise limit which, when reached, prompts further service instances to be invoked in a correlated cloud-hosted environment.

- *Service Billing Threshold* – When pay-per-usage mechanisms are used to monitor service usage, this value can represent a limit imposed by the usage budget (or credit) associated with the service configuration. This type of threshold is common in cloud-based environments where services are deployed on leased infrastructure resources that support dynamic and on-demand scaling.

- *Service Elasticity Threshold* – Service elasticity is a general measure of a service's dynamic scalability. This type of threshold is broader than other scalability-related thresholds and may therefore be used as a baseline or as a parent limitation for other thresholds (such as those pertaining to service billing or service instances).

- *Service Exception Threshold* – Services runtime exceptions can be the result of problems originating from inside the service architecture or from its surrounding infrastructure or even from other services participating in the same runtime activity. When a service encounters an abnormally large amount of exceptions, it can be an indication that the service (or a part of its surroundings) is being attacked or that there are critical issues with its implementation. Either way, when this threshold is reached, it is often necessary to shut the service down and, if available, invoke a failover system to defer processing to a backup service implementation.

- *Service Data Throughput Threshold* – Various factors can be taken into account to set the data throughput limit of a given service. For example, the data may be subject to complex calculations that consume memory and therefore require the quantity of data to be limited. Or, there may be bandwidth or connectivity limitations, especially when transmitting data to remote or geographically disbursed cloud-based services via third-party internet connections.

- *Service Monitoring Footprint Threshold* – There are several governance products and platforms that introduce sophisticated monitoring features, usually implemented via intelligent, processing-rich service agents. These types of event-driven programs can track individual services and service instances, collecting data for metrics and invoking notification and logging routines, as required. In larger environments with greater quantities of services and service compositions residing alongside each other, the amount of runtime processing and memory consumed by monitoring-related programs can take its toll on the overall resources shared by services. Therefore, governance thresholds that limit service monitoring may be required.

An important consideration when applying this precept is that some thresholds may need to be set at the service capability level instead of at the service level. For example, different service capabilities within the same service may be assigned different Service Billing Thresholds depending on the nature and importance of their processing logic.

There are many more thresholds that can be established by this precept. Some may be specific to the monitoring product or technology being used, while others may be specific to business requirements or general project constraints.

Related Processes

- Service Vitality Review

Related Roles

- Service Administrator

- Cloud Resource Administrator

- Enterprise Architect

- Service Architect

- Service Custodian

- SOA Security Specialist

- SOA Governance Specialist

- Other: Cloud Architect

- Other: Cloud Security Specialist

- Other: Cloud Governance Specialist

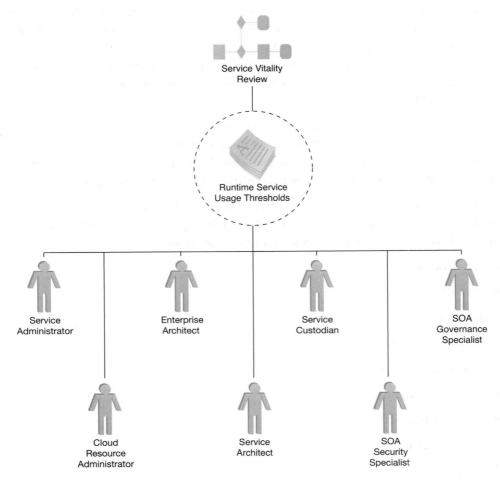

Figure 11.1

The Runtime Service Usage Thresholds precept.

Service Vitality Triggers

Over time, after a service is in production and actively being used by service consumers, various events can impact the service logic, its implementation, or resources it may depend upon. In order to maintain maximum value as an IT asset, it is generally necessary to review and check on the service's "vitality" to either confirm that it is still in an optimum state or to confirm that it requires attention.

Service vitality triggers represent anticipated events that execute vitality activities as part of a Vitality Review process. These activities step those involved with the service's governance through a series of considerations to determine whether or not the service should be subjected to a "refresh" in order to update or adjust any part of its implementation.

Common vitality triggers include:

- Strategic Business Adjustment

- Strategic IT Adjustment

- Business Shift

- Technology Shift

- Performance Metrics

- Compliance Metrics

- Scheduled Milestone

- Scheduled Time Period

Note that the Performance Metrics and Compliance Metrics vitality triggers generally encompass metrics collected in relation to the thresholds established by the Runtime Service Usage Thresholds precept. For example, if an allowable threshold is exceeded, it may warrant a violation logged as a compliance metric. If service responsiveness fluctuates, it may be measured in relation to corresponding usage thresholds.

The listed vitality triggers are described individually in Chapter 13.

Related Processes

- Service Vitality Review

Related Roles

- Service Administrator

- Cloud Resource Administrator

- Enterprise Architect

- Service Architect

- Service Custodian

- SOA Security Specialist

- SOA Governance Specialist

- Other: Cloud Architect

- Other: Cloud Security Specialist

- Other: Cloud Governance Specialist

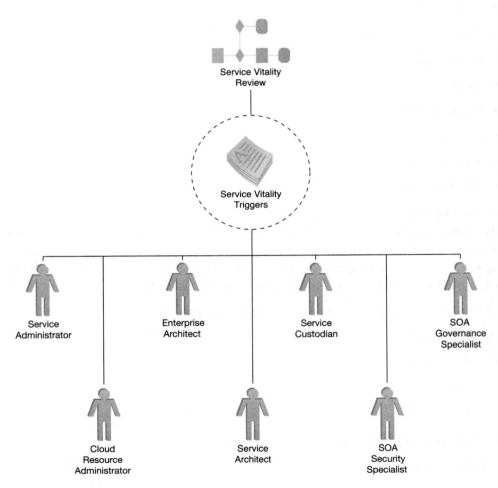

Figure 11.2
The Service Vitality Triggers precept.

Processes

Service Vitality Review

When a vitality trigger is executed, it initiates a review of the service status and implementation. Each such review aims to assess the service vitality in order to determine whether there is a need (and justification) to make improvements and the extent of improvements required.

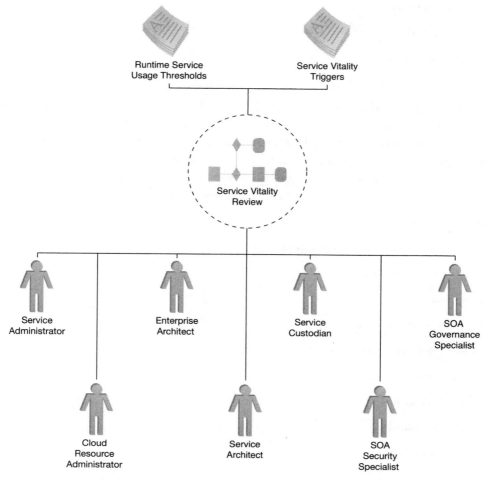

Figure 11.3
The Service Vitality Review process.

For example, the outcome of a service vitality review could result in a recommendation that the service be re-factored, discontinued, superseded by a new version, or that no changes are needed at all.

The base vitality process that is executed to perform this assessment and, if necessary, act upon it, contains the following common steps:

- Identify Activity
- Assess Activity
- Refresh Activity
- Approve Activity
- Communicate Activity

These steps are explained separately in Chapter 13. Custom vitality review processes are generally required based on the organization's preferences, the nature of the vitality trigger responsible for initiating the review, and the nature of metrics collected relevant to the trigger and review. Some metrics will likely correspond to the parameters established by the Runtime Service Usage Thresholds precept, in which case the review can further act as a means of assessing the effectiveness of service usage thresholds.

Related Precepts

- Runtime Service Usage Thresholds
- Service Vitality Triggers

Related Roles

- Service Administrator
- Cloud Resource Administrator
- Enterprise Architect
- Service Architect
- Service Custodian
- SOA Security Specialist
- SOA Governance Specialist
- Other: Cloud Architect
- Other: Cloud Security Specialist
- Other: Cloud Governance Specialist

People (Roles)

Enterprise Architect

Because the service, during the Service Usage and Monitoring stage, resides and actively participates in the production environment of an IT enterprise, the Enterprise Architect will generally be involved in any related precepts or processes. The extent of required participation will often depend on the extent to which a service implementation relies upon or accesses shared resources and legacy systems. For example, service implementations with high levels of autonomy (or those deployed in isolated or cloud-based environments) may require the Enterprise Architect to be only peripherally involved.

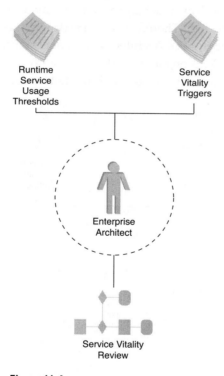

Figure 11.4

Service Usage and Monitoring governance precepts and processes associated with the Enterprise Architect role.

Related Precepts

- Runtime Service Usage Thresholds
- Service Vitality Triggers

Related Processes

- Service Vitality Review

Service Architect

The Service Architect has intimate knowledge of the service implementation and any related resources or mechanisms (such as those that may have been introduced by service composition architectures). Therefore, when setting usage thresholds or exploring vitality improvements, the Service Architect will generally become a primary point of contact and will often end up negotiating (together with the Service Custodian) proposed improvements and refresh updates with the Enterprise Architect.

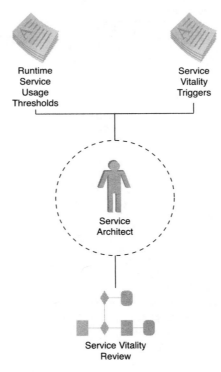

Figure 11.5

Service Usage and Monitoring governance precepts and processes associated with the Service Architect role.

Related Precepts

- Runtime Service Usage Thresholds
- Service Vitality Triggers

Related Processes

- Service Vitality Review

Service Administrator

Throughout a service's runtime existence, the Service Administrator will be a central part of its on-going usage monitoring and performance maintenance. As a result, this role is a primary participant in establishing the necessary usage threshold and vitality trigger governance precepts, as well as associated Service Vitality Reviews.

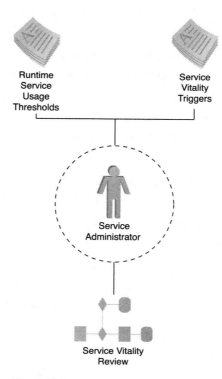

Figure 11.6

Service Usage and Monitoring governance precepts and processes associated with the Service Administrator role.

Related Precepts

- Runtime Service Usage Thresholds
- Service Vitality Triggers

Related Processes

- Service Vitality Review

Cloud Resource Administrator

For cloud-based services, the Cloud Resource Administrator will perform tasks similar to the Service Administrator, but, depending on the nature of the cloud environment, may be further required to take additional considerations into account.

For example, the following are common issues addressed by Cloud Resource Administrators acting on behalf of cloud consumer organizations that have deployed a service in a public cloud:

- runtime usage and performance fluctuations resulting from reliance on IT resources being shared by multiple cloud services from different cloud consumer organizations
- proprietary runtime service agents and monitoring tools provided by the cloud environment and perhaps not compatible with corresponding on-premise products
- automated or manual configuration of scaling characteristics of a service or of one or more of its underlying IT resources (in relation to scaling thresholds)
- billing limitations or options as they may apply, depending on the licensing or leasing model used by the cloud consumer organization

Furthermore, there may be unique security concerns that arise from making the service available via a cloud. These would be investigated by the Cloud Resource Administrator in collaboration with an SOA Security Specialist and/or a Cloud Security Specialist.

Related Precepts

- Runtime Service Usage Thresholds
- Service Vitality Triggers

Related Processes

- Service Vitality Review

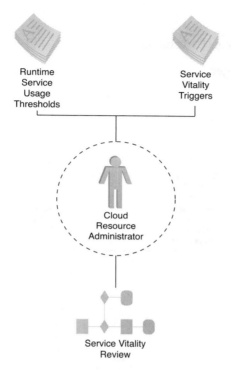

Figure 11.7

Service Usage and Monitoring governance precepts and processes associated with the Cloud Resource Administrator role.

Service Custodian

The Service Usage and Monitoring stage represents an on-going period of time during which the Service Custodian remains actively involved with any issues pertaining to the service's runtime behavior and performance, as well as its overall functional scope and integrity (in relation to how the purpose and functional context of the service was initially defined during the Service-Oriented Analysis stage). As with the Service Architect, this role takes part in all precepts and processes associated with this stage.

For cloud-based services, the Service Custodian, together with the Cloud Resource Administrator, will stay on top of any vitality-related issues that may arise (as a result of vitality triggers having executed). If significant changes are required to a service implementation, they will usually need to report the estimated impacts to the Cloud Service Owner for approval.

Related Precepts

- Runtime Service Usage Thresholds
- Service Vitality Triggers

Related Processes

- Service Vitality Review

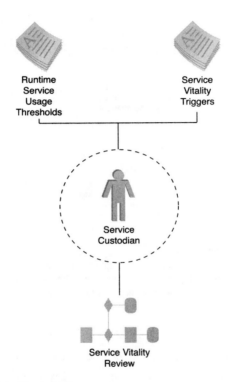

Figure 11.8
Service Usage and Monitoring governance
precepts and processes associated with the
Service Custodian role.

SOA Security Specialist

This role is pulled into precept definition and process reviews whenever security issues arise or when preventative measures need to be considered. For example, if a service's exception threshold is constantly exceeded, a vitality trigger may be executed resulting in a vitality review that could involve the SOA Security Specialist to help determine whether the increased number of recorded exceptions were the result of malicious service consumers carrying out periodic attacks on the service.

Related Precepts

- Runtime Service Usage Thresholds
- Service Vitality Triggers

Related Processes

- Service Vitality Review

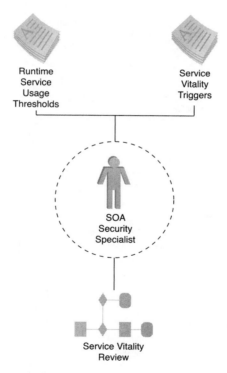

Figure 11.9

Service Usage and Monitoring governance precepts and processes associated with the SOA Security Specialist role.

SOA Governance Specialist

The SOA Governance Specialist will aid in defining and establishing the precepts associated with the Service Usage and Monitoring stage, and will further assist with carrying out vitality reviews. As explained in Chapter 13, SOA governance vitality can exist as a sub-framework to the overall SOA governance system. The definition and positioning of this framework (which encompasses vitality triggers, activities, and processes) are the responsibility of the SOA Governance Specialist.

Related Precepts

- Runtime Service Usage Thresholds
- Service Vitality Triggers

Related Processes

- Service Vitality Review

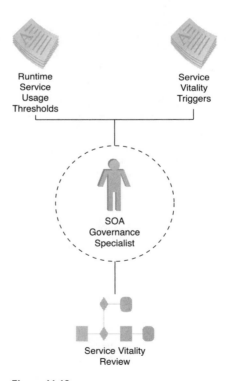

Figure 11.10

Service Usage and Monitoring governance precepts and processes associated with the SOA Governance Specialist role.

SUMMARY OF KEY POINTS

- Runtime thresholds can be set to help control and measure the usage of a service.

- Vitality triggers can be assigned to a given service in order to automate notification of the service status based on pre-defined criteria.

- Vitality reviews are carried out as a result of executed vitality triggers.

CASE STUDY EXAMPLE

The Raysmoore Product service has finally made its way into the Raysmoore production environment. As first explained in the *Case Study Example* section at the end of Chapter 8, this service was modeled to contain four variations of the Get service capability in order to accommodate business requirements specific to Raysmoore and Lovelt, while complying to the Service Normalization precept (Figure 11.11).

Figure 11.11
The Raysmoore Product service contract.

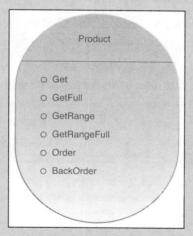

Specifically, the GetFull and GetRangeFull service capabilities allow for the retrieval of product inventory information for customers of Lovelt. The information provided includes current stock levels, which is something the corresponding Get and GetRange service capabilities do not provide, as per Raysmoore policy.

While deciding on threshold values for the application of the Runtime Service Usage Thresholds precept, the Service Architect, together with the SOA Governance Specialist, further examine these and related processing requirements of the four Get service capabilities. In addition to the general thresholds being applied to new services, they determine that the GetRangeFull service capability allows service consumers to issue queries that can return an unusually large amount of Product data (including historical and statistical data).

The Service Architect is concerned that some of the more complex queries could take a long time to execute and that the volume of returned data could put a strain on shared bandwidth, especially if the service is being accessed concurrently by multiple service consumers. As a result, they determine that the GetRangeFull service capability needs to be more strictly regulated than the Product service's other service capabilities, as follows:

- Whereas other Product service capabilities are assigned a Service Instance Threshold of 22, the GetRangeFull service capability is limited to spawning 10 service instances, when concurrently invoked.

- Similarly, the Service Data Throughput Threshold for the GetRangeFull service capability is set to half of what is allowed by the Product service's other service capabilities.

The Service Custodian makes note of these limitations in the Product service profile document and further warns that if usage demands exceed what the imposed thresholds allow, then a new version of this service capability may need to be developed, supporting a reduced query range in order to maintain higher thresholds.

11.2 Governing Service Discovery

The dynamic of discovering reusable services for inclusion in new service-oriented solutions is fundamental to service-orientation and the realization of shared services, and perhaps one of the primary reasons that this stage has historically been most associated with SOA governance in general.

The following sections explore precepts and processes that help regulate the Service Discovery stage and, in particular, the use of the service registry.

NOTE
The service registry is an SOA governance technology explained in Chapter 14.

Service
Usage
and
Monitoring

Service
Discovery

Service
Versioning
and
Retirement

Precepts

Centralized Service Registry

IT enterprises can have multiple collections of services that exist as service inventories. For each well-defined collection, there should be a service registry, which is centralized so that it establishes itself as the sole source for official service discovery information.

When multiple domain service inventories exist, the following centralization rules usually apply:

- For every domain service inventory there should be only one central domain service registry.

- When a subset of services is shared across multiple domain service inventories, a central service registry can represent multiple service inventories or separate service registries can share a common set of data (most likely via replication).

SOA PRINCIPLES & PATTERNS

It is important to acknowledge that it is the application of the Service Discoverability (484) principle during the early design stages that helps make information published about a service both interpretable and discoverable. The Service Discovery stage then relies on these qualities to enable project teams to locate and understand upcoming and existing services when designing and assembling their new service-oriented solutions in compliance with governance regulations.

- When the shared subset of services corresponds cleanly to a service model (or some form of clearly distinguished service category), a separate service registry can be positioned as a central, cross-domain repository of service metadata specifically for that type of service.

This precept is applied to establish a centralized service registry and to mandate its use in support of the Service Discovery stage. Project teams delivering new services need to be required to have them recorded in the service registry in order to keep service registry data current and accurate.

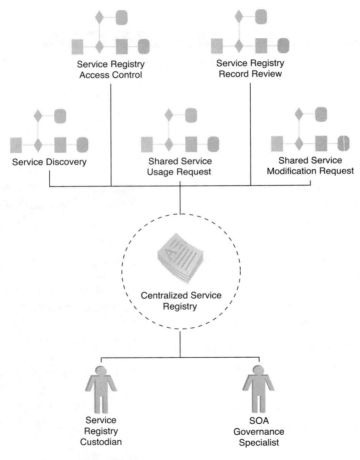

Figure 11.12
The Centralized Service Registry precept.

Related Processes

- Service Registry Access Control
- Service Registry Record Review
- Service Discovery
- Shared Service Usage Request
- Shared Service Modification Request

Related Roles

- Service Registry Custodian
- SOA Governance Specialist

> **SOA PRINCIPLES & PATTERNS**
>
> The Centralized Service Registry precept is based on the consistent application of the Metadata Centralization [536] pattern. The Cross-Domain Utility Layer [511] pattern defines an approach whereby reusable utility services can be shared across multiple domain service inventories.

Processes

Service Registry Access Control

A primary issue when governing Service Discovery is establishing the appropriate level of access to service registry records. An access control process enforcing specific rules and policies may need to be put in place to ensure that only authorized parties are able to locate and access some or all of the services or service capabilities within certain service registries.

> **SOA PRINCIPLES & PATTERNS**
>
> The Service Registry Access Control process relates to intentional limitations imposed by the application of the Service Abstraction (478) principle.

The following are sample access control considerations and rules:

- Some services can be selectively marked as "discoverable," thereby making them undiscoverable to some users and groups. The need for this may be related to security requirements, but it can also be the result of service versioning in that a retired service may need to remain active to support existing service consumers (but its retired version should no longer be discoverable to new service consumers).

- If necessary, only a portion of service capabilities can be made discoverable or accessible. This may be required if a subset of service capabilities is intended only for certain types of service consumers.

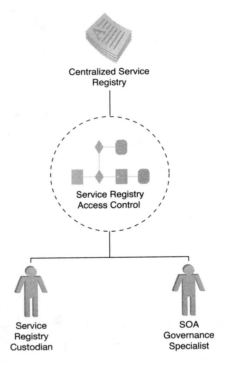

Figure 11.13
The Service Registry Access Control process.

Note that security controls used to limit access to a service's registry record are separate from any security mechanisms and requirements with which the service itself may have been designed. A service may be discoverable but still off-limits to those service consumers that do not possess the appropriate security credentials.

Related Precepts

- Centralized Service Registry

Related Roles

- Service Registry Custodian
- SOA Governance Specialist

> **NOTE**
>
> Although this precept raises security requirements, it does not directly relate to the involvement of the SOA Security Specialist role. The nature of the access control system that may need to be set up for a service registry is usually an internal administration matter and does not affect the security requirements of services or service-oriented solutions. However, if the service registry is made accessible outside of the organization boundary, then the SOA Security Specialist may need to participate with the application of this precept.

Service Registry Record Review

When adding to or updating a centralized service registry, a review process may be required to verify that new service registry records comply to all required authoring and technology standards (including access control rules). This review process is almost always carried out by the Service Registry Custodian together with the Technical Communications Specialist, but can also involve other roles, such as the SOA Governance Specialist and the Service Custodian.

Related Precepts

- Centralized Service Registry
- Service Metadata Standards (Chapter 12)

Related Roles

- Service Registry Custodian
- Service Custodian
- Technical Communications Specialist
- SOA Governance Specialist

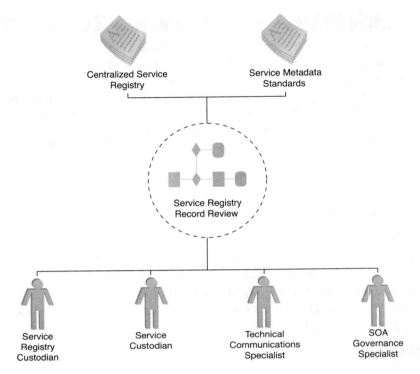

Figure 11.14
The Service Registry Record Review process.

Service Discovery

A formal discovery process needs to be in place, providing clear, step-by-step instructions for all project teams planning or actively delivering services and service-oriented solutions for a given service inventory.

The following is a sample discovery process that also includes steps pertaining to access control:

1. A project team member accesses a service registry and performs a search based on provided criteria.

2. Services marked discoverable for this user (or the group to which the user belongs) are searched and those with metadata matching the search criteria are returned.

3. The user chooses an agnostic service based on the provided service metadata and the request is routed to the corresponding Service Custodian.

4. The Service Custodian approves or rejects the request.

5. If access can be granted, a process to provision access to the actual service is invoked (and those involved with the service management are notified of the new service consumer).

6. If the request is rejected, the user is notified. Human contact with the Service Custodian may be required to address or clarify the reasons for the rejection.

> **SOA PRINCIPLES & PATTERNS**
>
> The Service Discovery process relates directly to the application of the Service Discoverability (484) principle, which encompasses metadata that is defined during the Service-Oriented Analysis and Service-Oriented Design stages, as well as any additional metadata authored for service registry records. In many ways, the success by which the Service Discovery stage is carried out by project teams can be traced back to the extent to which the Service Discoverability (484) principle was correctly applied during early analysis and design stages.

Ensuring that service metadata within service registry records is authored consistently and in adherence to a common vocabulary and pre-defined standards is vital to the successful use of a service registry and the successful execution of the Service Discovery project stage.

The standards that govern service registry records are primarily concerned with guaranteeing that the metadata for a given service provides all of the keywords and other search criteria required for effective discovery queries and that, once discovered, the service metadata is easily understood and interpreted by those performing the searches.

Related Precepts

- Centralized Service Registry
- Service Metadata Standards (Chapter 12)

Related Roles

- Service Registry Custodian
- Service Custodian
- SOA Governance Specialist

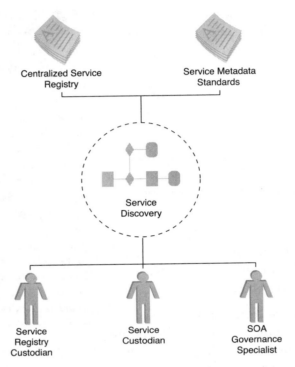

Figure 11.15
The Service Discovery process.

Shared Service Usage Request

When agnostic services with reusable logic are discovered by project teams wanting to share them within new service compositions, a formal process can be established to issue a request for reuse, along with information about how the service will be used within the new solution.

This type of process enables those overseeing the governance of a service to ensure that a given service implementation will not be stretched too thin or that a service will not be used in an inappropriate manner. Further, it allows for different service consumers to be prioritized based on the importance or urgency of each request.

For example, the request to reuse an agnostic service for a mission critical business automation requirement may receive a higher priority than other usage requests. In this case, a higher Service Instance Usage Threshold value may be assigned to the higher ranking service consumer.

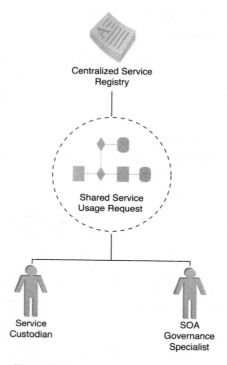

Figure 11.16

The Shared Service Usage Request process.

Related Precepts

- Service Registry

Related Roles

- Service Custodian

- SOA Governance Specialist

Shared Service Modification Request

There will commonly be situations when the project team requesting the use of a shared service will further request modifications to the service. This requires a separate process to address the following important considerations:

- The shared service contains reusable logic that will have typically been carefully designed based on a previously defined agnostic functional context. The integrity of this context must be retained in order for the service to continue being an effective, shared enterprise resource.

- If a change or enhancement can be made to the service without compromising its agnostic functional context, then there will need to be an understanding of who will carry out this change and/or how the additional development effort will be funded.

- Functional changes to services (especially services already being actively shared) will almost always introduce a new major version. This will require that the modified service undergo the full delivery lifecycle plus be subject to existing version management precepts and processes.

When the custodian of a service (together with involvement from the SOA Governance Program Office) rejects a change request, it may alleviate the project team from having to use the discovered service. However, it may not provide them with the freedom to build the requested logic on their own.

Note that this type of request process may not necessarily be considered part of the Service Discovery stage. As it raises analysis and design concerns, it may be positioned as a pre-deployment process or as part of the Service Versioning and Retirement stage.

> **SOA PRINCIPLES & PATTERNS**
>
> Service Normalization [563] is a prime concern within any service inventory, and it requires that if the newly identified service logic is also deemed as reusable, that it either be placed in another shared service with the appropriate functional context or that it form the basis of a new agnostic functional context (requiring the delivery of a new reusable service).

Related Precepts

- Centralized Service Registry

Related Roles

- Service Custodian

- SOA Governance Specialist

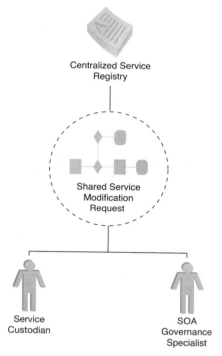

Figure 11.17

The Shared Service Modification Request process.

People (Roles)

Service Custodian

At the center of activity during the Service Discovery stage is the Service Custodian, who is a primary contact point for project teams attempting to locate, identify, and understand service metadata published for discoverability purposes. Further, the Service Custodian will often have the authority to determine whether new requests for different types of service usage are acceptable.

The Service Custodian is typically involved in all of the processes associated with this project stage, with the exception of the Service Registry Access Control process (unless access control rules specific to the custodian's service need to be defined).

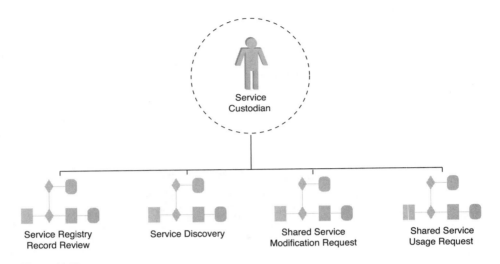

Figure 11.18
Service Discovery governance precepts and processes associated with the Service Custodian role.

Related Precepts

N/A

Related Processes

- Service Registry Record Review

- Service Discovery

- Shared Service Modification Request

- Shared Service Usage Request

Service Registry Custodian

All governance tasks that involve the service registry during the Service Discovery project stage will also involve the registry's custodian. This role will lead the effort to establish centralized service registries and further acts as a principal participant in the Service Registry Access Control and Service Registry Record Review processes. In support of the Service Discovery process, the Service Registry Custodian assumes more of an advisory role.

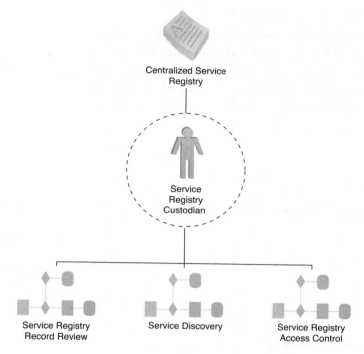

Figure 11.19

Service Discovery governance precepts and processes associated with the Service
Registry Custodian role.

Related Precepts

- Centralized Service Registry

Related Processes

- Service Registry Access Control
- Service Registry Record Review
- Service Discovery

Technical Communications Specialist

With the responsibility of ensuring the communications quality of service metadata authored and published in support of the Service Discovery stage and the Service Discovery process, the Technical Communications Specialist is an expected participant in the Service Registry Record Review process.

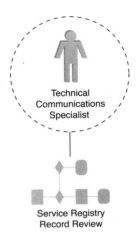

Technical Communications Specialist

Service Registry Record Review

Figure 11.20
Service Discovery governance precepts and processes associated with the Technical Communications Specialist role.

Related Precepts

N/A

Related Processes

- Service Registry Record Review

SOA Governance Specialist

The SOA Governance Specialist works closely with the Service Registry Custodian to help establish the Centralized Service Registry precept and related processes, and will further aid the Service Custodian (and other roles) with governance processes and activities pertaining to the discovery of agnostic services.

Related Precepts

- Centralized Service Registry

Related Processes

- Service Registry Access Control
- Service Registry Record Review
- Service Discovery
- Shared Service Modification Request
- Shared Service Usage Request

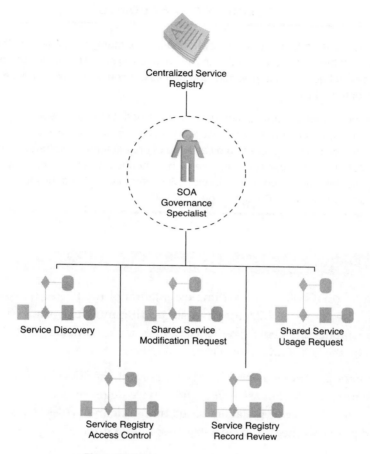

Figure 11.21

Service Discovery governance precepts and processes associated with the SOA Governance Specialist role.

SUMMARY OF KEY POINTS

- The success of the Service Discovery stage is primarily dependent on the quality of the metadata recorded in the service registry. This is why there are several governance precepts and processes concerned with service metadata definition.

- The importance of service metadata pertains both to the discoverability of the service during the Service Discovery stage, as well as the interpretability of the discovered metadata by a range of project team members. These characteristics are instilled within service contracts and service registry data via the application of the Service Discoverability (484) principle during the Service-Oriented Design stage.

CASE STUDY EXAMPLE

During the original definition and implementation of the Productions and Operations service inventory architecture and supporting infrastructure, the Raysmoore project team applies the Centralized Service Registry precept (Table 11.1) previously established by the SOA Governance Program Office.

In support of the Centralized Service Registry precept, the SOA Governance Program Office introduces a custom variation of the Service Registry Access Control process that limits access to service metadata based on pre-defined rules. These access control rules require that the service registry be split into three principal sections:

- the *public* section that is open to external business partners

- the *internal* section that is restricted to Raysmoore and its subsidiaries

- the *restricted* section that is limited to individuals on project teams building service consumer programs authorized for a given service

The SOA Governance Program Office also helps create a formal certification process for "on-boarding" new consumers of each service (which leads to an additional precept and process).

Centralized Service Registry Precept	
Objective: Each service inventory must have one central service registry used to record metadata for all services within the service inventory.	
Policy: Ensure that a common metadata vocabulary is used.	*Policy:* Ensure that standardized access control rules are used.
Standard: The metadata vocabulary must incorporate and be in alignment with existing service candidate and service naming conventions. Therefore, this precept must be applied together with the Service Metadata Standards precept (described separately in Chapter 12).	*Standard:* Pre-defined security groups or categories must be used for all service registry records. Custom variations of pre-defined access control rules must be subject to a review and application for a waiver.
	Guideline: When carrying out Service Discovery, this precept can be enforced by a manual or automated Service Registry Access Control process, depending on the preference of the project team members requesting access to protected service registry records. A manual process may be required when project teams need to request information about registered services that are hidden from discovery searches. In this case, the Service Registry Custodian will need to manually administer the request and, if approved, manually provide the requested service metadata.
Standard: Require that the service registry is configured to limit access control to pre-defined groups and to further establish parameters that support the standardization of metadata, as per the conventions defined in the Service Metadata Standards precept.	

Table 11.1
The Centralized Service Registry precept.

11.3 Governing Service Versioning and Retirement

Service versioning represents the most evolutionary stage in a service's lifecycle. When the need for a new version of a service emerges, clear rules and regulations are required to ensure that whatever changes are introduced by the new service version do not negatively impact or disrupt other services and service consumers within the service inventory—especially those that already have dependencies on the updated service.

Similarly, the actual termination or deactivation of a service or service version is another natural part of a service's overall lifecycle, and an occurrence for which governance attention needs to be planned to further ensure no inadvertent disruption. The precepts in this section help establish fundamental regulatory controls to establish a structured system for service versioning and retirement in support of an IT enterprise's configuration management preferences.

Precepts

Service Versioning Strategy

The most important aspect of performing service versioning is that a set of rules is in place to ensure that each service within a given service inventory is versioned consistently. Versioning rules are primarily concerned with how services can be versioned in response to compatible or incompatible changes, as they relate to backwards and forwards compatibility.

These rules form the basis of a versioning strategy, of which three common types exist:

- *Strict* – Any compatible or incompatible changes result in a new version of the service contract. This approach does not support backwards or forwards compatibility.

- *Flexible* – Any incompatible change results in a new version of the service contract and the contract is designed to support backwards compatibility but not forwards compatibility.

- *Loose* – Any incompatible change results in a new version of the service contract and the contract is designed to support backwards compatibility and forwards compatibility.

NOTE

Appendix F explores each of these strategies in more detail, and further explains the differences between compatible and incompatible changes, as well as backwards and forwards compatibility.

Each service versioning strategy approaches the governance of the Service Versioning stage in a distinct manner. Therefore, each service versioning strategy will tend to further establish a set of distinct precepts that address more granular service versioning issues, such as:

- service version identification and labeling within service contracts and service registry records

- moderating the number of service versions that are allowed to exist concurrently in the production environment

- establishing when service consumers are required to switch to a new service version, even when this change impacts the service consumer design

SOA PRINCIPLES & PATTERNS

Depending on the nature of the precepts, various patterns can be involved, including:

- Compatible Change [505]
- Version Identification [575]
- Service Refactoring [565]
- Service Decomposition [556]
- Proxy Capability [547]

Note that some of these patterns relate to service contract versioning, while others are focused on versioning requirements resulting from service logic changes.

Further precepts pertaining to the versioning of service logic changes and changes to the underlying service implementation and resources can also be defined as part of the overall versioning strategy.

Related Processes

- Service Versioning

Related Roles

- Enterprise Design Standards Custodian

- Schema Custodian

- Policy Custodian

- SOA Governance Specialist

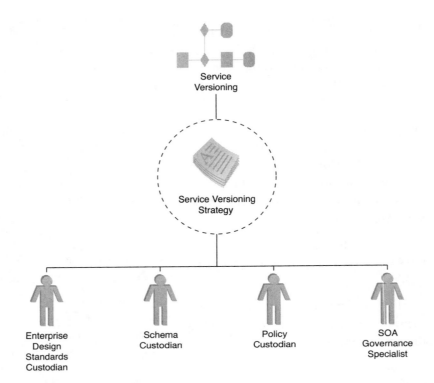

Figure 11.22

The Service Versioning Strategy precept.

SLA Versioning Rules

In addition to the rules defined in the chosen service versioning strategy, additional versioning rules and preferences can be added for individual services. Most commonly, these rules are expressed in human-readable language as part of a service's SLA.

Examples of such rules include:

- The maximum number of versions of a service that can be supported at any one time.

- How the consumers of a service are notified when the service version is changed and/or about to become unsupported.

- The predefined period of time that service consumers of a retiring service version have to migrate to the new version.

- When and how access to unsupported or retired service versions will be revoked.

- How to access a test environment, together with realistic simulated data, that will be made available to allow service consumers to test new service versions before they migrate their production systems to use them. This applies even when the new versions are expected to be backwards compatible.

These and other types of rules can also be part of the overarching service versioning strategy.

> **NOTE**
>
> Various forms of individual service versioning rules can be expressed in technical policy definitions instead of SLAs. One such example is the use of ignorable or optional WS-Policy assertions. Policy-related governance topics are covered in Chapter 12. Policy assertions are explained in the book *Web Service Contract Design & Versioning for SOA*.

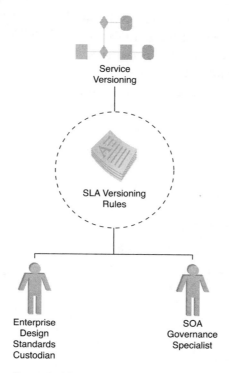

Figure 11.23

The SLA Versioning Rules precept.

Related Processes

*   Service Versioning

Related Roles

*   Enterprise Design Standards Custodian
*   SOA Governance Specialist

Service Retirement Notification

A standardized mechanism or system needs to be in place in order to communicate the pending and completed retirement of a service. This mechanism must issue notifications to raise awareness of the service termination, beyond the mere change of the service status within the central service registry.

> **SOA PRINCIPLES & PATTERNS**
>
> An SOA design pattern developed specifically in support of the Service Retirement Notification precept is Termination Notification [569], which can be applied by adding an ignorable WS-Policy assertion in a service contract to indicate the scheduled retirement date of the service.

These notification requirements, along with the mechanisms used to carry out the notification, are standardized by this precept so that communication of pending and past service terminations remains consistent throughout a service inventory.

Related Processes

*   Service Retirement

Related Roles

*   Service Administrator
*   Cloud Resource Administrator
*   Enterprise Design Standards Custodian
*   SOA Governance Specialist

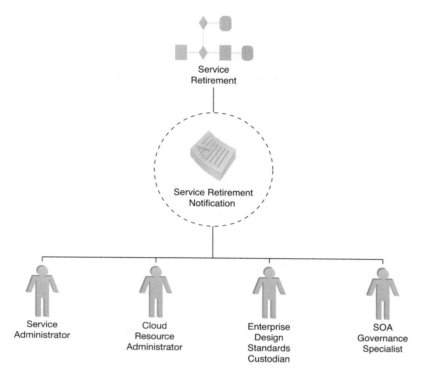

Figure 11.24
The Service Retirement Notification precept.

Processes

Service Versioning

With the chosen service versioning strategy comes one or more formal service versioning processes that establish step-by-step procedures for phasing new versions of services into a service inventory. These processes may trigger other project stages (or parts of project stages), such as testing and deployment. Generally, these stages are further customized to accommodate various factors.

For example, the new service version may need to:

- be deployed alongside one or more older service versions

- immediately support a number of service consumers that have so far been using the older version of the service

- introduce new logic and capabilities that require additional testing effort as well as new forms of tests

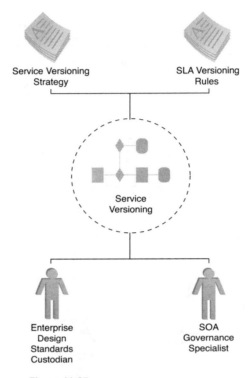

Figure 11.25
The Service Versioning process.

Service versioning processes will further include review steps to ensure that the service has complied with all requirements prior to being deployed into the production environment.

Related Precepts

- Service Versioning Strategy
- SLA Versioning Rules

Related Roles

- Enterprise Design Standards Custodian
- SOA Governance Specialist

Service Retirement

The retirement of a service that has been actively in use for an extended period of time is an important and formal process that needs to be defined and administered to ensure that the planned termination occurs without disruption. Often this is possible with proper advance planning because the actual termination date of the service can usually be pre-determined.

The Service Retirement process includes steps that carry out the Service Retirement Notification precept, but the primary purpose of this process is to investigate all possible (past and current) dependencies upon the to-be-terminated service.

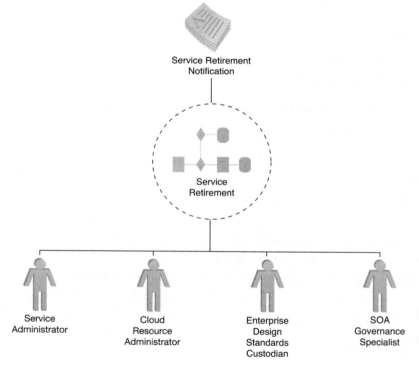

Figure 11.26
The Service Retirement process.

For example:

- service consumers that currently or periodically access and use the service

- service composition architectures that encompass the service architecture

- shared resources and legacy systems that are being accessed by the service (and may therefore be behaviorally impacted by the service's absence)

Furthermore, project teams that may be planning or actively designing new consumer programs for the service may need to be located and notified.

Related Precepts

- Service Retirement Notification

Related Roles

- Service Administrator

- Cloud Resource Administrator

- Enterprise Design Standards Custodian

- SOA Governance Specialist

People (Roles)

Enterprise Design Standards Custodian

Process and precepts that pertain to the Service Versioning and Retirement stage are primarily based on standards and conventions that need to be established to ensure consistency in how the logic and contracts of services within a given service inventory are evolved and then terminated. This requires the involvement of the Enterprise Design Standards Custodian to help define these standards and strategies and to further ensure they are created in alignment with and in support of other design standards.

Related Precepts

- Service Versioning Strategy

- SLA Versioning Rules

- Service Retirement Notification

Related Processes

- Service Versioning

- Service Retirement

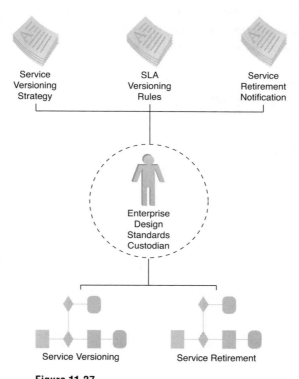

Figure 11.27

Service Versioning and Retirement governance precepts and processes associated with the Enterprise Design Standards Custodian role.

Service Administrator

The Service Retirement Notification precept and the Service Retirement process collectively regulate the termination of an active service. The Service Administrator can be a primary contributor to establishing these governance controls to ensure that they are defined in compliance with production runtime environments and affected IT resources.

Related Precepts

- Service Retirement Notification

Related Processes

- Service Retirement

Figure 11.28

Service Versioning and Retirement governance precepts and processes associated with the Service Administrator role.

Cloud Resource Administrator

There will likely be special considerations that need to be addressed by the Service Retirement Notification precept and the Service Retirement process for cloud-based services. For example, there may be licensing and billing arrangements that require termination or deferral to different cloud services. The cloud provider organization may require advance notice of a pending cloud service retirement and if the cloud service has been accessible to multiple external cloud consumer organizations (as it would be as part of an SaaS offering), a more elaborate notification system may be required. These and other issues are the responsibility of the Cloud Resource Administrator.

Related Precepts

• Service Retirement Notification

Related Processes

• Service Retirement

Service Retirement
Notification

Cloud Resource
Administrator

Service
Retirement

Figure 11.29
Service Versioning and Retirement governance precepts and processes associated with the Cloud Resource Administrator role.

Schema Custodian

Part of the Service Versioning Strategy precept includes strategies and standards that govern the versioning of XML schemas and data models. For this subset of the precept, the Schema Custodian can provide input and recommendations.

Related Precepts

• Service Versioning Strategy

Related Processes

N/A

Figure 11.30
Service Versioning and Retirement governance precepts and processes associated with the Schema Custodian role.

Policy Custodian

As with the involvement of the Schema Custodian, the Policy Custodian can provide guidance for the versioning of technical business and operational policies, especially in relation to considerations raised by the Policy Centralization precept (as described in Chapter 12).

Related Precepts

• Service Versioning Strategy

Related Processes

N/A

Figure 11.31
Service Versioning and Retirement governance precepts and processes associated with the Policy Custodian role.

SOA Governance Specialist

The effort required to establish the precepts and processes that govern the versioning and termination of services may fall squarely on the shoulders of the SOA Governance Specialist. Assistance from the Enterprise Design Standards Custodian will be required, but this role may also involve other specialists as needed.

Related Precepts

- Service Versioning Strategy
- SLA Versioning Rules
- Service Retirement Notification

Related Processes

- Service Versioning
- Service Retirement

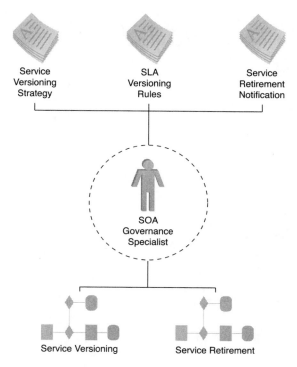

Figure 11.32
Service Versioning and Retirement governance
precepts and processes associated with the SOA
Governance Specialist role.

SUMMARY OF KEY POINTS

- The Service Versioning Strategy precept requires that a service inventory-wide service versioning system be established. Additional, more detailed precepts are then defined, specific to the overarching strategy.

- In addition to a Service Versioning process, there is the need for a Service Retirement process that is further supported by a formal Service Retirement Notification precept.

NOTE
Examples pertaining to the Service Versioning Strategy precept are provided in Appendix F. Note that these are technical examples that display code for Web services and REST services.

Part III

Strategic Governance

Chapter 12

Service Information and Service Policy Governance

SOA PRINCIPLES & PATTERNS REFERENCED IN THIS CHAPTER

- Messaging Metadata [535]

- Policy Centralization [543]

- Service Abstraction (478)

- Validation Abstraction [574]

The adoption of service-orientation breaks down silos within the organization by establishing a layer of normalized functional boundaries, each represented by a separate service. So far in this book we've been focusing a great deal on the governance issues that pertain to this service layer as they relate to individual stages of the SOA project lifecycle.

In this chapter we focus on the governance requirements of data exchanged by services, its origin, its definition, and its usage to further add definition to the data and its relationships with services.

NOTE

This chapter is primarily focused on business data related to business-centric services, such as entity and task services. For a description of how business services differ from non-business services (such as utility services), see the *Service Models* section in Chapter 3.

Also, unlike Chapters 7 to 11 where precepts, processes, and roles were organized according to project stages, in this chapter they are grouped into dedicated sections, as each may apply to one or more stages.

12.1 Overview

This chapter is about the governance of service information and service policies. Service information governance is the practice of identifying and evolving governance controls that ensure the provision of timely and accurate information. Service policy governance is focused on the regulation of operational and business policies that can be machine- or human-readable.

Let's begin by clarifying the key terminology used in the upcoming sections, namely the terms *data*, *information*, and *policy*.

Service Data vs. Service Information

The first step to understanding the scope and purpose of service information governance is to make a clear distinction between data and information. In the science of knowledge management, there is an established concept referred to as the *knowledge hierarchy* and also known as the *DIKW hierarchy*.

The acronym DIKW represents the following:

- *Data* – raw facts and symbols without context and meaning
- *Information* – data given meaning by placing it within a context
- *Knowledge* – information that is understood, making it useful and actionable
- *Wisdom* – experience applied to knowledge, providing the ability to make appropriate decisions

How these parts of the hierarchy relate to each other is illustrated in Figure 12.1.

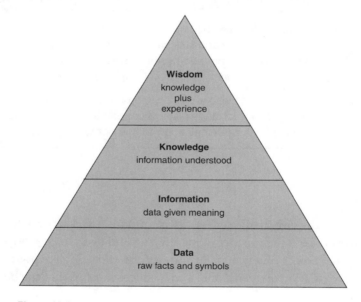

Figure 12.1
The DIKW pyramid shows how raw facts and figures (data) are the foundation for ultimately understanding and being able to (wisely) act upon information.

Within this chapter only, we will use the terminology established by the DIKW hierarchy to make a distinction between *data* (raw facts and symbols) and *information* (data given meaning). When defining and using business-centric services (as opposed to utility services), we are more concerned with information rather than just data. This is because each business service's functional boundary is derived from a source of business intelligence (such as a business entity or a business process) that gives the data meaning (hence our use of the term "information").

Business services provide service consumers information in the form of messages associated with business intelligence. This is how business services place data in context, giving it meaning. Because of this ontological commitment made by business services, an SOA governance system must address the governance of both the data and its meaning. This is because SOA governance precepts can help ensure that services provide this information accurately and that service consumers can trust this information without requiring knowledge of its origins.

Policies 101

Just about any organization works with policies that provide parameters and guidance for how tasks and responsibilities need to be carried out. Some of these requirements are mandated by external organizations (such as government agencies or industry standards bodies), while others may be imposed by internal organizational entities (such as accounting, human resources, or legal departments).

In general, policies are stated as real-world requirements or rules. For example:

- An order cannot be shipped until payment has been received.

- An employee cannot work more than 40 hours per week without approval.

- Each aircraft engine needs to be inspected after every 50 hours of flying.

Policies have traditionally been published as human-readable (or natural language) documents. Such policies therefore rely on manual processes, carried out by humans, to ensure enforcement. Failing to enforce policies can lead to serious consequences, with potential legal, financial, and operational ramifications. Because manual enforcement by humans can be prone to human error and inconsistency, it can introduce risk.

As a result, organizations have sought ways to automate policy enforcement via the use of machine-readable (or technical) policies. Technologies, such as WS-Policy (Figure 12.2) and policy management products (explained in Chapter 14) have emerged to provide various features for technical policy definition and runtime enforcement.

Although the substance and content quality of individual policies can vary, technical policies tend to be more focused on processing data and human-readable policies are generally authored with more information (data with meaning). Depending on the nature of the policy content and its purpose and intended consumers, different types of policies can be authored. The precepts described in this chapter focus on business and operational policies, each of which can exist in human-readable or machine-readable format.

Figure 12.2

A WS-Policy definition as part of a Web service contract.

WSDL   XML Schema   WS Policy   Service Level Agreement (SLA)

technical Web service contract

service contract

Regardless of their type, technical policies can be associated with services as an extension to the service contract or as part of the underlying service logic. Using a technical language (such as WS-Policy), machine-readable policies can express service contract level constraints and qualities that relate to and express service behavior and requirements.

Although it is possible and sometimes required, it is less common to embed policy processing logic as part of the service logic. Embedded policy logic can be difficult to maintain, especially when one policy applies to multiple services. Furthermore, having technical policies defined as part of the service contract makes the policy requirements clear in advance to service consumer designers.

SOA PRINCIPLES & PATTERNS

An SOA design pattern that advocates placing less validation logic in the service contract is Validation Abstraction [574]. This pattern is applied primarily in support of the Service Abstraction (478) principle that aims to minimize what is published about a service in order to foster positive coupling between services and service consumers. The usage of the Validation Abstraction [574] pattern may lead to justification for locating some forms of policy processing within the service logic.

NOTE

The policies discussed in this chapter are focused exclusively on service contract-related policy definitions. However, the associated technologies used to create policy definitions are beyond the scope of this book.

Chapters 10, 16, and 17 in the book *Web Service Contract Design & Versioning for SOA* are dedicated to fundamental and advanced topics pertaining to the use of WS-Policy related syntax and technologies.

12.2 Governance Controls

A core objective of service-oriented computing is to achieve a state of intrinsic interoperability among software programs delivered as services. A baseline requirement for doing so is ensuring that the data exchanged is understood by services and their consumers. To help foster an understanding of the meaning of service data, governance precepts are required to position and regulate service information and policy content.

Precepts

Enterprise Business Dictionary/Domain Business Dictionary

When integrating disparate and silo-based applications, the incompatibility of data meaning has historically caused problems. For example, when different systems colloquially refer to a "claim" without further qualification, we can end up with different meanings being associated to this term. One system may deal with property insurance claims, while the other processes employee health insurance claims. These types of issues have historically been resolved with traditional integration architectures, whereby point-to-point integration channels were created between each system. Each channel contained custom programming comprised of data mapping and transformation logic that was executed at runtime, each time data exchange needed to occur.

As previously explained, one of the primary goals of service-orientation is to avoid having to resort to integration architectures. However, suppose, within a services environment, two disparate service consumers become aware of and decide to use a Claim Submission service. With no additional information about the service (or its information) available, neither service consumer may have a reason to believe that "claim" means anything other than what it understands it to be. This precept aims to avoid this scenario by requiring that a business dictionary be established.

There are two variations of this precept:

- Enterprise Business Dictionary
- Domain Business Dictionary

The difference is a matter of scope. An Enterprise Business Dictionary applies to the IT enterprise as a whole. It mandates the creation of a central dictionary to be used by all services within all service inventories. The Domain Business Dictionary precept requires that business dictionaries focus on specific subsets of the IT enterprise. The most common application of this precept is to establish a business dictionary with a scope equal to a particular domain service inventory.

The reason separate precepts exist is because they can be used together. For example, an Enterprise Business Dictionary may be developed to regulate a common set of business terms (such as those that perhaps represent common business documents), but it may not include definitions for all possible business terms. Additional Domain Business Dictionaries can be authored to standardize domain-specific terminology, even if it results in some terms having different definitions.

Either way, each business dictionary provides an official and centralized resource for the definition of information. Each term within the dictionary is given an individual meaning, and qualifiers (such as "medical" claim) are used to give terms more specific (yet still individual) meanings.

Although the creation of a business dictionary (or the updating of an existing business dictionary) is a common initial step during SOA adoption projects, its usage is by no means limited to service information or to the SOA adoption scope.

> **NOTE**
>
> A business dictionary is different from a data dictionary. Whereas the latter is focused on the definition of data residing within database tables, the former aims to establish a "single source of truth" for *information* so as to foster a common business understanding.

Related Processes

- Data Quality Review
- Communications Quality Review
- Information Alignment Audit

Related Roles

- Business Analyst
- Service Registry Custodian
- Technical Communications Specialist
- SOA Governance Specialist

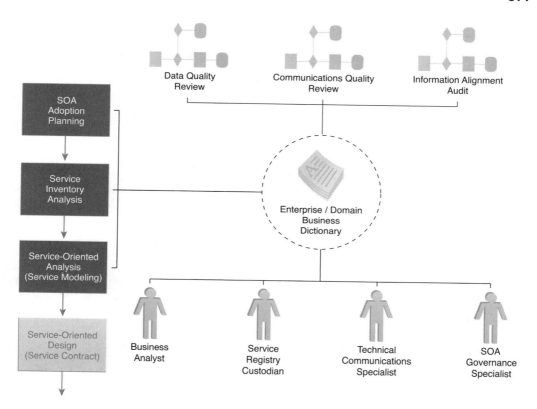

Figure 12.3

This precept can be applied as early as the SOA Adoption Planning stage, but also throughout the Service Inventory Analysis and Service-Oriented Analysis stages.

Service Metadata Standards

Metadata is typically defined as "data about data." But given the terminology we established earlier in this chapter, it can more accurately be defined as "information about data." Essentially, metadata is information about data of importance to an organization. Those responsible for designing and administering databases have long cataloged technical metadata that describes databases, tables, columns, and other aspects of physical data management systems. However, functional metadata—descriptions of business meaning and relevancy of data—is less commonly captured and documented.

Metadata, as it pertains to services and information exchanged by services, is very much focused on establishing functional meaning and context.

Established forms of service metadata include:

- *Technology Information* – Metadata that describes the technical implementation of the underlying service logic.

- *Functional Information* – Metadata that describes what the service is capable of.

- *Programmatic Logic Information* – Metadata that describes how the service carries out its capabilities.

- *Quality of Service Information* – Metadata that describes service behavior, limitations, and interaction requirements.

Depending on the implementation medium used to build services, service metadata standards can be encompassed within the Service Contract Design Standards precept (explained in the *Governing Service-Oriented Design* section of Chapter 9). However, if the scope of an organization's overall information governance initiative is beyond that of any one SOA adoption project, metadata standards can exist independently and then referenced by Service Contract Design Standards or other forms of standards pertaining to the definition of service information or the structure of data exchanged by services.

Common examples of service metadata include:

- keywords used within message headers, service contract documents, service registries, and SLAs

- elements and attribute names used by different XML schemas (including canonical XML schemas)

As with establishing a centralized business dictionary, creating an official collection of service metadata will often be limited in scope to a particular service inventory. Further, service metadata items commonly can (and should) be mapped to terms defined in the overarching business dictionary.

SOA PRINCIPLES & PATTERNS

The Messaging Metadata [535] pattern represents a form of service metadata, as commonly separated into the header portion of a message. The four metadata types (Functional, Technology, Programming Logic, Quality of Service) listed earlier pertain to the Service Abstraction (478) principle, as it is applied to determine what forms of service metadata to publish and hide.

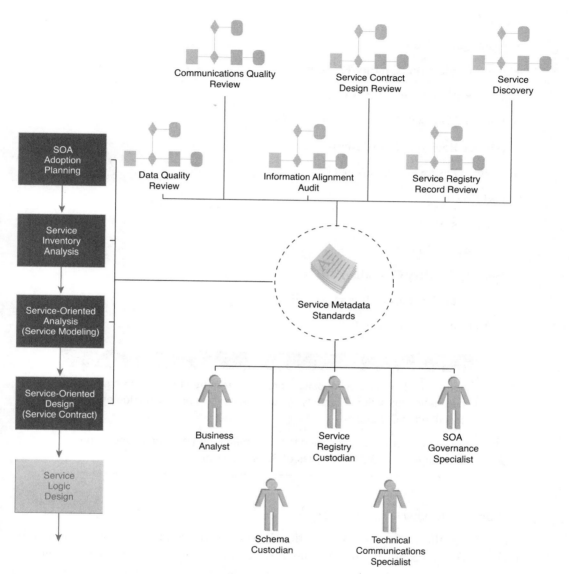

Figure 12.4

Service metadata governance can begin with the SOA Adoption Planning stage and can continue throughout the Service Inventory Analysis and Service-Oriented Analysis stages. However, it is within the Service-Oriented Design stage where the actual metadata is commonly incorporated and when this precept needs to be fully applied to ensure standardization across services.

Related Processes

- Data Quality Review
- Communications Quality Review
- Information Alignment Audit
- Service Contract Design Review (Chapter 9)
- Service Registry Record Review (Chapter 11)
- Service Discovery (Chapter 11)

Related Roles

- Business Analyst
- Schema Custodian
- Service Registry Custodian
- Technical Communications Specialist
- SOA Governance Specialist

NOTE

Service registry and/or repository products are often used to store service metadata information. These types of SOA governance technologies are described in Chapter 14.

For more information regarding the aforementioned metadata types, see Chapter 8 in the *SOA Principles of Service Design* book.

Enterprise Ontology/Domain Ontology

An ontology allows the semantic relationship between two pieces of information to be inferred. This precept requires that the information that forms the basis of an ontology originates from or relates to information in the business dictionary, as well as service metadata. The level of insight established by the relationships defined within an ontology can help provide increased depth and clarity of the data's meaning.

As with the business dictionary, enterprise and domain versions of the precept for establishing an ontology exist. The same considerations explained in relation to business dictionary scope apply even more so to the definition of an ontology. For larger IT enterprises, the creation of a proper Enterprise Ontology can be an exhaustive analysis exercise because of the multitude of relationships that need to be mapped and considered. The Domain Ontology precept is therefore more commonly applied, even when the Enterprise Business Dictionary has been established.

In cases where an ontology already exists within the IT enterprise, this precept is concerned with ensuring that the ontology is current and in alignment with business dictionary and service metadata content.

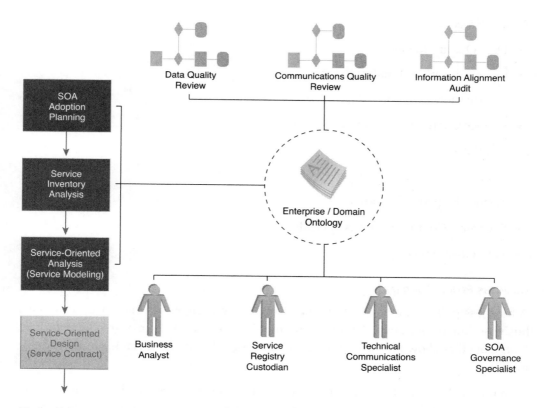

Figure 12.5

When an ontology is available, this precept is applied to the same stages as the Enterprise Business Dictionary/Domain Business Dictionary precept, namely SOA Adoption Planning, Service Inventory Analysis, and Service-Oriented Analysis.

> **NOTE**
>
> An ontology can be created using industry standards, such as the Web Ontology Language (OWL) and Resource Description Framework (RDF). Both of these standards allow for the definition of machine-readable concepts and relationships. Further, the Open Group developed the SOA Ontology standard to help bridge the gap between common business and IT concepts and terminology.

Related Processes

- Data Quality Review

- Communications Quality Review

- Information Alignment Audit

- Service Contract Design Review (Chapter 9)

Related Roles

- Business Analyst

- Service Registry Custodian

- Technical Communications Specialist

- SOA Governance Specialist

Business Policy Standards

A business policy describes a certain aspect of how business is conducted. It can be a business rule or objective. Although commonly expressed in human-readable format, tools exist that allow for the definition of business policy content via machine-readable formats.

A common challenge to establishing technical business policies is the requirement to create and standardize a technical business policy vocabulary, proprietary to the organization. Although such a vocabulary can be derived from an existing business dictionary, making it machine-readable requires that its usage is standardized as part of precepts associated with the Service-Oriented Design project stage (and perhaps also the Service Logic Design stage for when embedded policy logic exists).

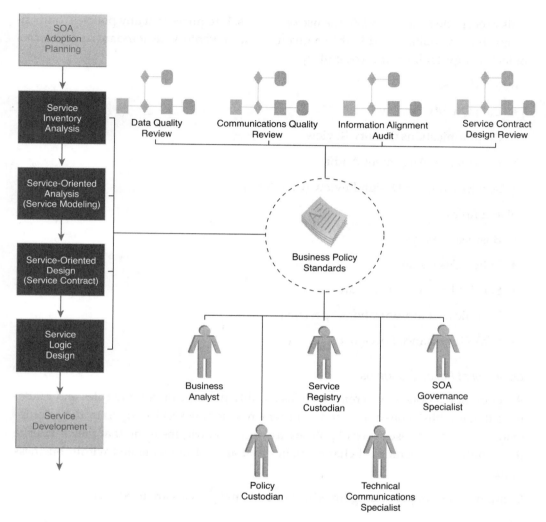

Figure 12.6

The standardization of business policies can become a concern during initial analysis stages, but then becomes an important requirement when technical policies are physically defined during the Service-Oriented Design stage or, if necessary, during the actual Service Logic Design stage.

This precept does not mandate the use of policies. It requires that any policies (human- or machine-readable) used within a given service inventory be standardized in terms of technology, tooling, and vocabulary.

Related Processes

- Data Quality Review
- Communications Quality Review
- Information Alignment Audit
- Service Contract Design Review (Chapter 9)

Related Roles

- Business Analyst
- Policy Custodian
- Service Registry Custodian
- Technical Communications Specialist
- SOA Governance Specialist

Operational Policy Standards

An operational policy (also referred to as a utility policy) can provide rules and guidelines that establish constraints and requirements for how services operate and interoperate at runtime. These types of policies are utility-centric, meaning that they influence the handling of operational characteristics that are not implemented within business policies.

Common types of processing for which operational policies are used include:

- security
- logging
- messaging protocol
- versioning

While any of these policies can be expressed in human-readable format, operational policies are almost always represented in machine-readable form. As with technical business policies, operational policies can be defined via custom vocabularies. However, the WS-Policy standard, together with various associated industry standards, provide a range of pre-defined sets of XML vocabularies for common functional areas.

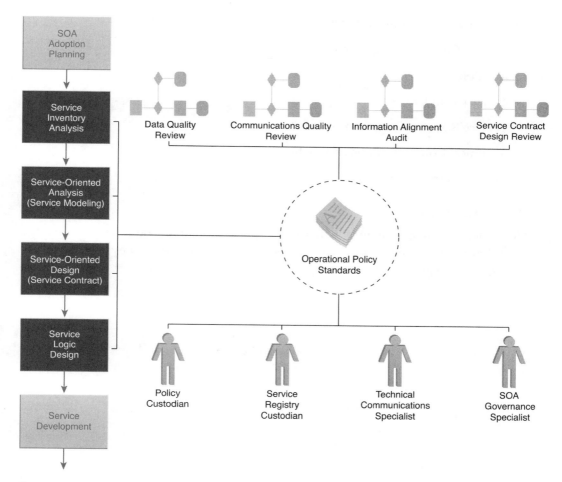

Figure 12.7

Because operational policies can be human-readable and machine-readable (as with business policies), the same project stage associations apply, namely Service Inventory Analysis, Service-Oriented Analysis, Service-Oriented Design, and Service Logic Design.

As with the Business Policy Standards precept, this precept does not mandate the usage of operational policies. It only dictates that policies that are in use are standardized within the service inventory boundary.

Related Processes

- Data Quality Review
- Communications Quality Review

- Information Alignment Audit
- Service Contract Design Review (Chapter 9)

Related Roles

- Policy Custodian
- Service Registry Custodian
- Technical Communications Specialist
- SOA Governance Specialist

Policy Centralization

More often than not, a technical policy will apply to more than one service. In this case, the policy definition needs to be centralized so that it can be shared by all affected service contracts (Figure 12.8).

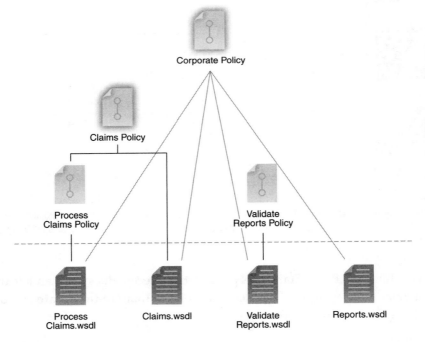

Figure 12.8

The highlighted policy documents in this diagram are being shared by multiple Web service contracts. (This figure is taken from the Policy Centralization [543] pattern description in the *SOA Design Patterns* book.)

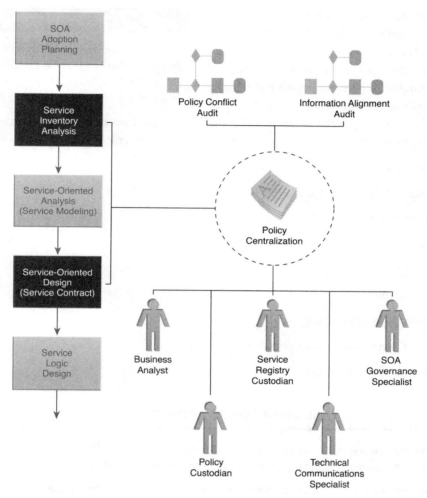

Figure 12.9

This precept is concerned with centralizing policy content for use by multiple services and therefore becomes applicable during the Service Inventory Analysis stage and then the actual Service-Oriented Design stage.

By applying the Policy Centralization precept, we effectively establish logical policy domains (or layers). For business policies these policy domains are commonly aligned with line of business domains, whereas operational policies often establish independent domains that may

> **SOA PRINCIPLES & PATTERNS**
>
> The Policy Centralization precept is directly based upon the Policy Centralization [543] pattern.

reside within or overlap business policy domains. Some policies are considered global in that they simply apply to all services within the service inventory.

Related Processes

- Information Alignment Audit
- Policy Conflict Audit

Related Roles

- Business Analyst
- Policy Custodian
- Service Registry Custodian
- Technical Communications Specialist
- SOA Governance Specialist

SUMMARY OF KEY POINTS

- Governance precepts that pertain to service information focus on the definition of a business dictionary, ontology, and business-centric metadata.

- Governance precepts that pertain to service policies focus on the standardization of business and operational policies, as well as the centralization of policies within a service inventory.

Processes

The following governance processes support the application of the preceding precepts and further provide controls for maintaining the quality and alignment of service information and policies.

Data Quality Review

As previously established, information represents data with meaning. However, for us to assign the correct meaning to data, the data itself must be correct. The purpose of the Data Quality Review process is to ensure data correctness.

To address quality concerns we must first understand the characteristics and dimensions of data quality most important to the organization. Common areas of data quality that can be incorporated into this review include:

- completeness
- accuracy
- consistency
- timeliness
- relevance

When assessing data quality and undertaking quality improvement programs it is necessary to identify and prioritize these characteristics according to business requirements. SOA Quality Assurance Specialists can then establish metrics used to track quality improvement over time.

Once key data quality characteristics and associated metrics have been identified, data profiling can be conducted against existing data sources to assess current-state quality. Subsequently, data cleansing and "de-duplication" efforts can be carried out to further improve the quality of existing data. Several vendors provide supporting tools for these tasks.

Related Precepts

- Enterprise Business Dictionary / Domain Business Dictionary
- Service Metadata Standards
- Enterprise Ontology / Domain Ontology
- Business Policy Standards
- Operational Policy Standards

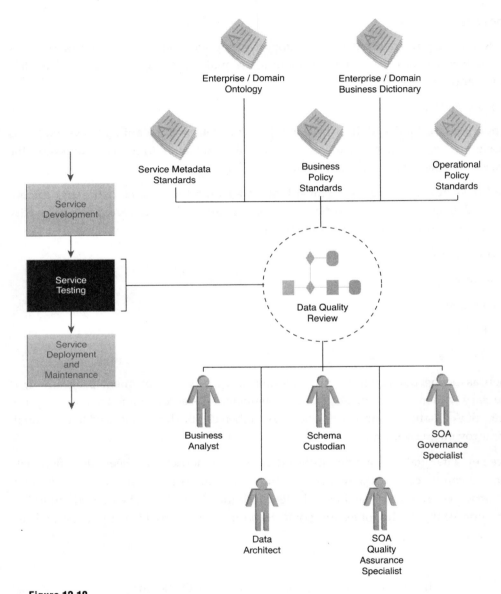

Figure 12.10
The Data Quality Review is generally considered a quality assurance process and is therefore commonly carried out as part of the Service Testing stage.

Related Roles

- Business Analyst

- Data Architect

- Schema Custodian

- SOA Quality Assurance Specialist

- SOA Governance Specialist

Communications Quality Review

While the Data Quality Review is focused on the correctness quality of data, it does not typically address the communications quality of data. Communications quality is the primary concern of the Technical Communications Specialist role and is focused on making published data (and information) interpretable and discoverable.

> **SOA PRINCIPLES & PATTERNS**
>
> Depending on the nature of the data, this precept can relate to the application of the Service Discoverability (484) principle, which requires that service metadata be authored for discoverability and interpretability by a wide range of project team members.

This review can be carried out for any body of content published as a result of the aforementioned precepts, regardless of whether the deliverable artifacts are human-readable or machine-readable.

Related Precepts

- Enterprise Business Dictionary / Domain Business Dictionary

- Service Metadata Standards

- Enterprise Ontology / Domain Ontology

- Business Policy Standards

- Operational Policy Standards

Related Roles

- Business Analyst

- Technical Communications Specialist

- SOA Quality Assurance Specialist

- SOA Governance Specialist

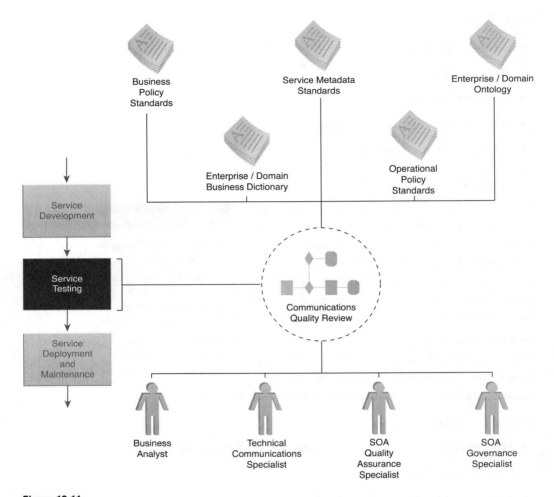

Figure 12.11
Also classified as a quality assurance process, the Communications Quality Review is commonly performed during the Service Testing stage.

Information Alignment Audit

When establishing bodies of content that define information (give data specific meaning) or bodies of content that then use or build upon previously defined information, we need to ensure that the meaning is kept consistent throughout the scope in which all bodies of content are utilized.

This process essentially validates the alignment of information across different bodies of content, such as the previously described business dictionary, metadata, policies, and ontology. It involves steps that trace one piece of data or information back to its origin where meaning was first assigned.

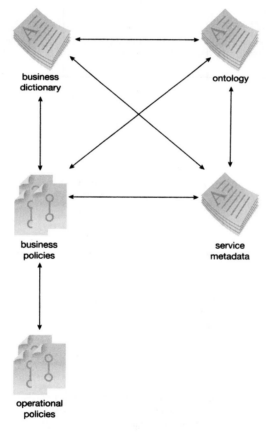

Figure 12.12

An example of how different bodies of business intelligence can relate to and depend upon each other. The Information Alignment Audit needs to trace and validate all of these relationships and dependencies.

Typically, an Information Alignment Audit is carried out iteratively, for each newly delivered or expanded service or service-oriented solution that introduces relevant business data or information.

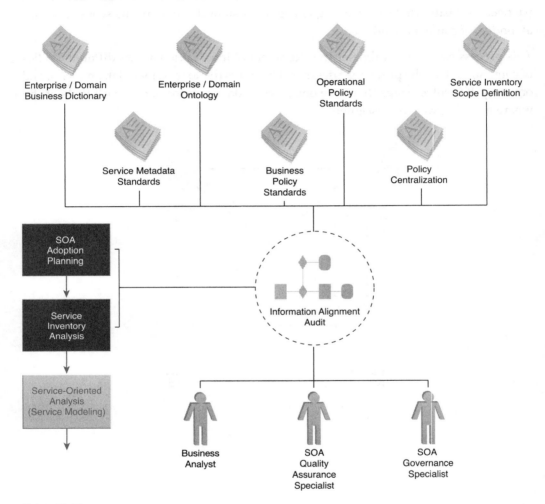

Figure 12.13

Tracing the alignment between different bodies of business information needs to be performed as early in the project lifecycle as possible, before services are built to actually incorporate and use the data. As a result, this process is commonly carried out during the initial SOA Project Planning and Service Inventory Analysis stages. Although the governance of several precepts further extend into Service-Oriented Analysis, cross-artifact alignment concerns should have been resolved prior to that stage.

Related Precepts

- Enterprise Business Dictionary / Domain Business Dictionary
- Service Metadata Standards
- Enterprise Ontology / Domain Ontology
- Business Policy Standards
- Operational Policy Standards
- Policy Centralization
- Service Inventory Scope Definition (Chapter 7)

Related Roles

- Business Analyst
- SOA Quality Assurance Specialist
- SOA Governance Specialist

Policy Conflict Audit

When centralizing policies (as per the Policy Centralization precept and pattern), each policy establishes its own scope of application (or domain). Because one service can be associated with multiple policies, it is natural for policy domains to overlap. When defining a centralized policy, it is therefore important to take into account the nature of the constraints and rules the policy is imposing upon affected services. If a constraint or rule in a newly shared policy conflicts with a constraint or rule in an existing policy (shared by the same service), then various unpredictable runtime exceptions and behaviors can occur. The greater the domain or applicability of a policy, the greater the risk of conflicts with existing policies.

The Policy Conflict Audit process requires that, prior to introducing a new policy within a service inventory, the constraints and rules in the proposed policy are cross-checked against any affected policies (as well as other relevant service contract content that defines constraints and rules).

Related Precepts

- Policy Centralization
- Service Inventory Scope Definition (Chapter 7)
- Service Contract Design Standards (Chapter 9)

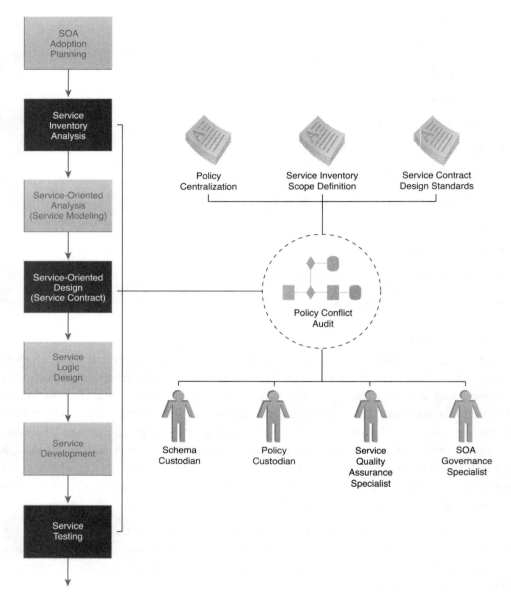

Figure 12.14

Policy conflicts are ideally resolved before policy definitions are even introduced to the service contract and service architecture. This process can therefore be part of the Service Inventory Analysis, Service-Oriented Design, or Service Testing stages.

Related Roles

- Schema Custodian
- Policy Custodian
- SOA Quality Assurance Specialist
- SOA Governance Specialist

SUMMARY OF KEY POINTS

- Service information governance processes are primarily concerned with the quality assurance of business information relevant to services.
- Policy conflict resolution is a key factor for successfully using shared policies within service inventories.
- All of the artifacts resulting from the application of service information and policy precepts need to be kept in alignment in order to maintain their value.

People (Roles)

The availability of service information and policy deliverables and artifacts can end up affecting just about any organizational role within an SOA project. Service Analysts in particular are required to work with business-centric and human-readable deliverables when identifying and defining service candidates during early analysis stages. However, our focus is on roles associated with the *governance* of service information and policies. This brings us back to the previously described precepts and processes and the people commonly involved in their definition and execution.

Business Analyst

Business Analysts and other types of business subject experts are generally the most qualified people to contribute to the authoring of a business dictionary and related ontology. Their insight into how lines of business and related business processes have and continue to operate gives them a clear understanding of how different business entities exist, how they relate, and how they should be represented by terms and definitions. This same business-centric expertise can also be valuable for the identification and definition of business-centric metadata and policies, as well as participation in processes that involve the review of business information.

- Related Precepts

  - Enterprise Business Dictionary/Domain Business Dictionary

  - Service Metadata Standards

  - Enterprise Ontology/Domain Ontology

  - Business Policy Standards

  - Policy Centralization

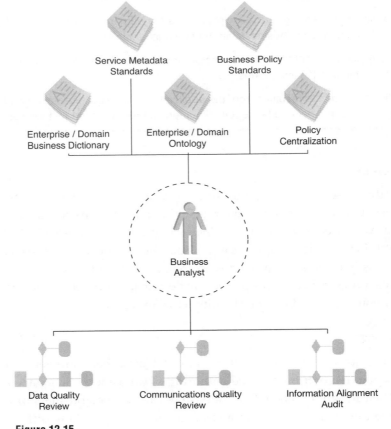

Figure 12.15
Service Information and Service Policy governance precepts and processes associated with the Business Analyst role.

Related Processes

- Data Quality Review
- Communications Quality Review
- Information Alignment Audit

Data Architect

Because of their intimate knowledge of data sources and how data and data relationships, at a physical storage level, have been modeled, Data Architects are generally the primary participants of the Data Quality Review process.

Related Precepts

N/A

Related Processes

- Data Quality Review

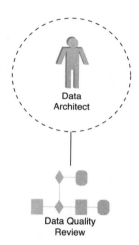

Figure 12.16
Service information and service policy governance precepts and processes associated with the Data Architect role.

Schema Custodian

XML schemas, and other forms of data models that may be used or referenced by service contracts and message structures, are often derived from (or required to encapsulate) underlying data sources and architectures. Schema Custodians have expertise in the definition of schemas (and often also the definition of schema design standards). This expertise can be helpful or even required for the identification and definition of suitable service metadata. Further, Schema Custodians can assist with Data Quality Reviews and may be asked to help resolve issues raised during Policy Conflict Audits.

Related Precepts

- Service Metadata Standards

Related Processes

- Data Quality Review
- Policy Conflict Audit

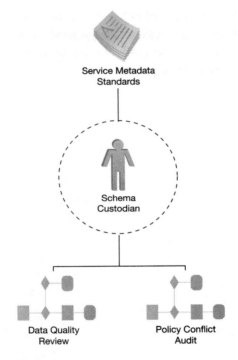

Figure 12.17
Service information and service policy governance
precepts and processes associated with the
Schema Custodian role.

Policy Custodian

The Policy Custodian role is most commonly associated with the definition and maintenance of machine-readable policies. However, part of this responsibility often requires the interpretation (and, in some cases, the initial definition) of parent human-readable policies. Either way, this role is directly involved with all policy-related precepts and processes.

Related Precepts

- Business Policy Standards

- Operational Policy Standards

- Policy Centralization

Related Processes

- Policy Conflict Audit

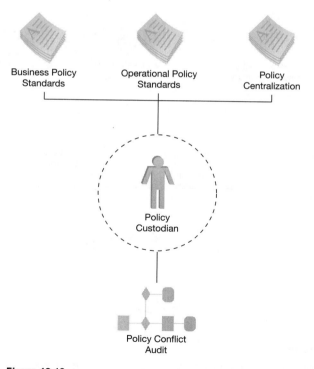

Figure 12.18
Service information and service policy governance precepts and processes associated with the Policy Custodian role.

Service Registry Custodian

Any of the bodies of content resulting from service information and policy-related precepts can be stored or represented within a central service registry. In this case, the Service Registry Custodian can contribute to the governance tasks pertaining to the application of the precepts and the delivery of the resulting information and policy artifacts. For example, the chosen service registry product may have certain features or constraints that end up shaping the format of business data or the manner in which meaning is associated with the data.

Related Precepts

- Enterprise Business Dictionary / Domain Business Dictionary

- Service Metadata Standards

- Enterprise Ontology / Domain Ontology

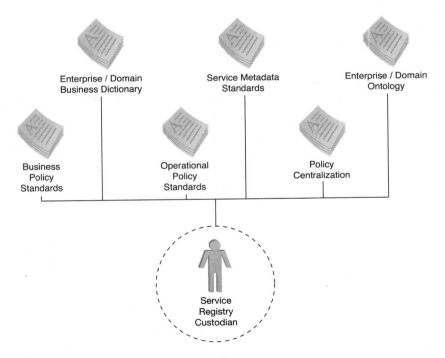

Figure 12.19
Service information and service policy governance precepts and processes associated with the Service Registry Custodian role.

- Business Policy Standards

- Operational Policy Standards

- Policy Centralization

Related Processes

N/A

Technical Communications Specialist

Precepts that govern the delivery of bodies of content that are published in human-readable and machine-readable format will usually make the quality of such content a priority. The Technical Communications Specialist's responsibility is to incorporate governance controls that help regulate published content in support of ensuring interpretability and discoverability for a range of project team members.

To improve the quality of interpretation, the Technical Communications Specialist will often need to establish review and revision cycles that enable content to undergo required wording and vocabulary changes. To increase discoverability, the expression of content will sometimes need to be simplified. Although the Technical Communications Specialist will be involved in the development of the content, this role may also be part of the actual review of the content's communications quality.

Related Precepts

- Enterprise Business Dictionary / Domain Business Dictionary

- Service Metadata Standards

- Enterprise Ontology / Domain Ontology

- Business Policy Standards

- Operational Policy Standards

Related Processes

- Communications Quality Review

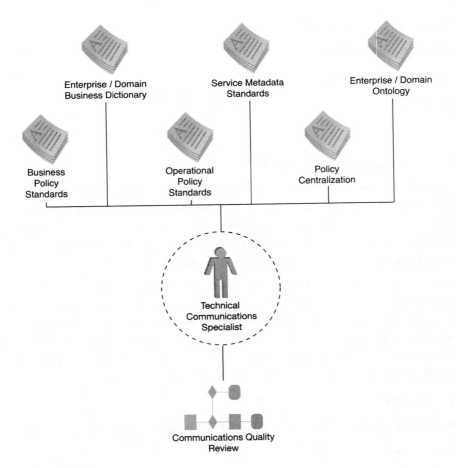

Figure 12.20

Service information and service policy governance precepts and processes associated with the Technical Communications Specialist role.

SOA Quality Assurance Specialist

The participation of this role is vital for the Data Quality Review and Policy Conflict Audit processes, as well as the Communications Quality Review process. It also makes sense to have an SOA Quality Assurance Specialist act in an advisory capacity for the governance of any of the service information and policy processes.

Specifically, these professionals can be involved in the following areas:

- ensuring that relevant quality assurance practices and metrics are applied

- incorporating processes within (and relating the processes to) quality assurance methodologies and processes already being used

Basically, whenever any of the service information and service policy precepts can be associated with the Service Testing stage, an SOA Quality Assurance Specialist should participate to ensure proper positioning of the precepts within the overall testing methodology.

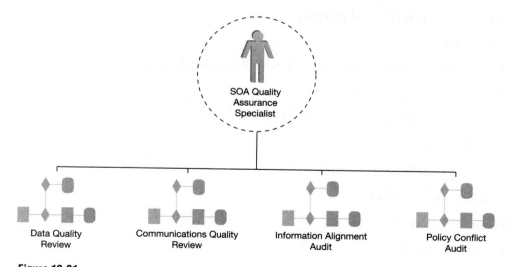

Figure 12.21

Service information and service policy governance precepts and processes associated with the SOA Quality Assurance Specialist role.

Related Precepts

N/A

Related Processes

- Data Quality Review
- Communications Quality Review
- Information Alignment Audit
- Policy Conflict Audit

SOA Governance Specialist

The SOA Governance Specialist is required to be involved in the identification, definition, and governance of all service information and policy precepts and processes. As members and representatives of the SOA Governance Program Office, individuals fulfilling this role will be required to supervise and, in some cases, lead efforts required to establish these precepts and processes.

Related Precepts

- Enterprise Business Dictionary/Domain Business Dictionary
- Service Metadata Standards
- Enterprise Ontology/Domain Ontology
- Business Policy Standards
- Operational Policy Standards
- Policy Centralization

Related Processes

- Data Quality Review
- Communications Quality Review
- Information Alignment Audit
- Policy Conflict Audit

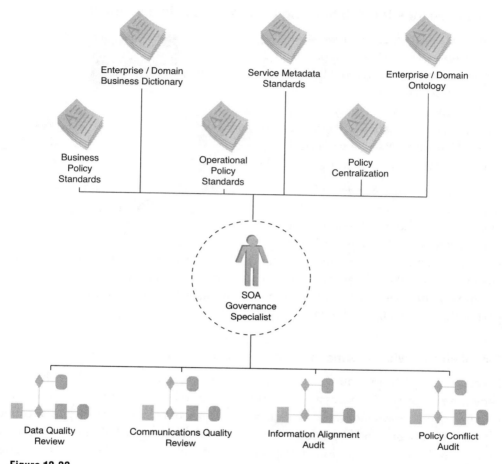

Figure 12.22

Service information and service policy governance precepts and processes associated with the SOA Governance Specialist role.

SUMMARY OF KEY POINTS

- Multiple organizational roles can be involved with any one service information or policy precept or process.

- Especially for business information governance, it can be necessary to draw upon the expertise of several business subject matter experts.

12.3 Guidelines for Establishing Enterprise Business Models

Several of the artifacts referenced in the preceding *Precepts* section of this chapter represent foundational business intelligence used as input for the Service Inventory Analysis and Service-Oriented Analysis project stages. These are collectively referred to as *enterprise business models*.

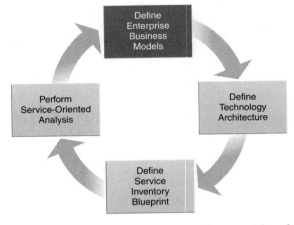

The *Define Enterprise Business Models* step in the Service Inventory Analysis lifecycle is dedicated to ensuring that the necessary business artifacts are in place and sufficiently up-to-date. All of this business content can be considered business information (business data with meaning). The following guidelines provide recommendations for establishing and maintaining enterprise business models in support of the overall SOA initiative.

Establish a Service Information Governance Council

Because business information spans organizational boundaries, it can be helpful (and sometimes necessary) to form a council (or steering committee) comprised of members or department representatives from all affected lines of business. This type of council would typically be joined by senior members of management with high-level decision-making authority. It is positioned as a sub-office or sub-group of the SOA Governance Program Office and receives its mandate from that office, as well as executive sponsors. If a general Business Information Council or governing body also exists, then it would need to be aligned (or also become a parent entity to) the Service Information Governance Council.

Assign Business Information Custodians

A role not defined in this book is the Business Information Custodian. Although it is not specific to SOA projects, it can be a valuable role to establish in support of creating and keeping current a business dictionary and ontology. This form of custodianship responsibility can be assigned to multiple individuals, each with specific business subject matter expertise. They would typically receive authority and direction from the Service Information Governance Council.

When available, Business Information Custodians can be effective contributors to the Information Alignment Audit process.

Assign Value to Business Information

Some forms of business information are core and critical to an organization's primary business tasks, while others may be peripheral or supplementary in nature. When documenting business information in the form of a business dictionary, it can be helpful to assign individual terms and business entities a value ranking indicating its relative importance to the organization. These ranks can help Business Analysts, Service Analysts, and SOA Governance Specialists prioritize the definition, maintenance, and incorporation of business information within SOA project lifecycle stages. This consideration is especially relevant when a project delivery methodology is being employed whereby only limited time and effort is being assigned to up-front analysis stages.

Relate Service Information Governance to Master Data Management

Master data management (MDM) is an accepted practice for governing reference data that is deemed core to an organization's business. It has become a data governance-related discipline with its own well-defined roles, responsibilities, processes, and technology products. As a result, if MDM is in use within an IT enterprise that is adopting SOA, it should be related to and incorporated with service information and policy governance precepts and processes.

For example, MDM data domains are usually classified according to fundamental business entities common to an entire organization (such as customer, product, location, supplier, etc.). Given that this same data and information can form the basis of business entity services that are commonly modeled as part of Service-Oriented Analysis processes, advance planning will help ensure that MDM and SOA governance systems are complementary.

SUMMARY OF KEY POINTS

- Business enterprise models encompass several of the service information artifacts relevant to SOA governance and SOA projects in general.

- The usage of business enterprise models, such as the business dictionary and ontology, can go well beyond the scope of an SOA project. Therefore additional practices can apply.

Chapter 13

SOA Governance Vitality

Investments made into SOA initiatives need to be viewed as living assets. Once deployed and in use, services, service-oriented solutions, and the technology architectures and infrastructure resources that support and realize their runtime enablement need to continue to fulfill the expectations and requirements of the business. The SOA governance program must therefore provide a means by which these assets are routinely reviewed, kept current and accurate and, most importantly, relevant to (often changing) business needs.

To address this evolutionary aspect, the SOA governance program needs to make the notion of *vitality* part of the SOA governance system being employed. *SOA governance vitality* is a proactive approach for maintaining the validity and applicability of an SOA governance system and the many artifacts, assets, and people it oversees.

SOA governance vitality typically exists as a sub-framework that is part of the overall SOA governance system. This chapter introduces common parts of this framework that pertain to on-premise and cloud-based assets.

13.1 Vitality Fundamentals

Many IT enterprises have traditionally applied governance reactively when confronted with change. The essence of service-orientation is to create an IT environment inherently capable of accommodating change. Therefore, an SOA governance program must establish a system of governance that is fully prepared for business change and that will react to this change with unwavering support for the strategic goals of the business.

An SOA governance vitality framework utilizes *vitality triggers* as a mechanism of notification and reaction. An executed trigger can result in one or more predefined activities to address the needs of whatever change "pulled the trigger." Common forms of triggers and resulting *vitality activities* are described in the upcoming sections.

> **NOTE**
>
> SOA governance vitality is sometimes classified as a subset of an overall approach to SOA vitality. SOA vitality, as a topic area, can be broader. It can deal with the vitality of the overall initiative, starting with early delivery stages to post-implementation stages. As previously explained, our coverage of SOA *governance* vitality is focused on maintaining the relevancy and accuracy of the existing SOA governance system, its precepts and processes. As such, it is a framework that, when successfully applied, is commonly associated with maintaining the Business Driven level of organizational maturity (as first explained in Chapter 4).

Figure 13.1 provides an overview of how an SOA governance vitality framework can connect with other parts of the SOA governance program and areas of the IT enterprise in general. Several of these relationships are explored in this chapter.

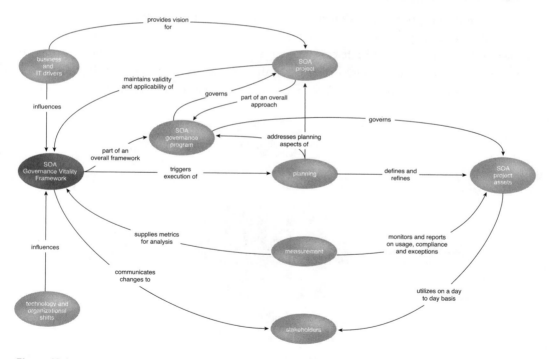

Figure 13.1

Common relationships of an SOA governance vitality framework.

SUMMARY OF KEY POINTS

- Vitality, within the context of SOA, is a quality measured by an SOA initiative's ability to maintain a desired direction and attain desired goals in the face of on-going change.

- SOA governance vitality is a subset of SOA governance that is focused on extending SOA governance practices to the governance of an SOA initiative's vitality.

- An SOA governance vitality framework commonly exists as a part of the overall SOA governance system. This framework is typically comprised of one or more processes comprised of pre-defined vitality activities executed by pre-defined vitality triggers.

13.2 Vitality Triggers

Vitality triggers represent pre-determined events and conditions that execute pre-determined activities as part of a vitality process. It is important to enable a wide range of project team members to initiate certain triggers so that a broad variety of concerns can be encompassed by the SOA governance vitality framework. Figure 13.2 shows the five main categories of vitality triggers, each of which is described in the upcoming sections.

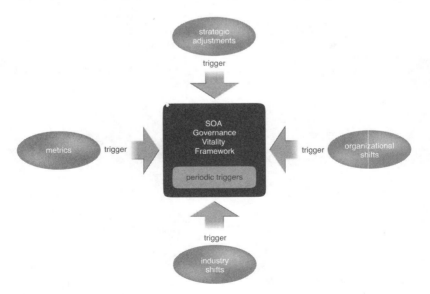

Figure 13.2

Common types of vitality triggers that can execute an SOA governance vitality process.

Vitality triggers need to be balanced in terms of importance and impact. Imbalanced vitality triggers can impose an ineffectual framework or one that unnecessarily introduces governance burden. Therefore, asset update and refresh requirements must be weighed against the importance of the trigger. The responsibility of choosing and balancing collections of vitality triggers lies with SOA Governance Specialists.

In most cases, a trigger will execute activities that result in some form of asset update or refresh. The cost and effort associated with this type of activity must be carefully considered to ensure it is justified and worthwhile. On the other hand, choosing to not trigger some activities can result in undesirable consequences to the overall SOA initiative (which can lead to new costs, effort, and other negative impacts down the road).

Business vs. Technology Changes

Vitality activities are triggered by change. Change can originate from the IT and business divisions or communities within an organization. Figure 13.3 illustrates the never-ending cycle that most organizations find themselves iterating through over time. When adopting service-orientation, the focus is mainly on business-centric requirements, which is usually the primary source of change affecting SOA initiatives. However, it is important to acknowledge and be prepared for changes that originate within the IT community, as these types of changes can, in turn, impact the business.

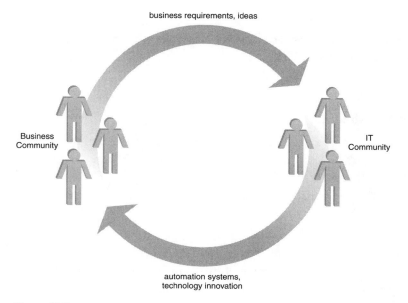

Figure 13.3

The on-going cycle of change that service-orientation is geared to inherently accommodate.

Types of Vitality Triggers

There are five common types of vitality triggers:

- Strategic Adjustments

- Industry Shifts

- Metrics

- Organizational Shifts

- Periodic

Most of these categories have further, more specific types of related triggers. The upcoming sections explain each of these triggers in more detail.

NOTE

The cycle displayed in Figure 13.3 relates specifically to the following vitality triggers:
 	
  • Strategic Business Adjustment
 	
  • Strategic IT Adjustment
 	
  • Business Shift
 	
  • Technology Shift
 	
Other types of triggers can also fall within this cycle, depending on their nature and origin.

Strategic Adjustments

Sometimes changes are unexpected; other times they are the result of an intentional decision to change or *adjust* strategic direction. Strategic adjustments are usually significant and will almost always act as vitality triggers. Following are descriptions of business and IT strategic adjustments.

Strategic Business Adjustment

A strategic business adjustment trigger is driven by changes to the organization's business direction or vision. An example of this type of change is a corporation altering its overall business strategy as a result of a recent merger.

When business drivers are augmented to such an extent, it can reprioritize various aspects of an SOA initiative. The resulting ripple effects can be far-reaching, ranging from delivery processes to technology to the governance system itself. Therefore, this type of trigger is usually considered the most significant and potentially impactful.

Strategic IT Adjustment

IT departments can initiate changes pertaining to technology and resources (human and automated). Sometimes these changes are in support of fostering greater business requirements fulfillment (such as when new technology innovation is made available to the business) or they can be limiting and prohibitive (such as when automation requirements requested by the business cannot be fulfilled due to infrastructure, skill-sets, security, or other forms of IT limitations).

For example, an IT department traditionally limited by its budget and on-premise resources may discover that it can now begin to offer greater scalability of its automated systems to business stakeholders by leveraging cloud-based environments.

These types of adjustments to IT strategy can alter the entire complexion of a service architecture or even the service inventory architecture itself. Therefore, in some cases, regular vitality refresh activities may be insufficient.

Industry Shifts

Whereas strategic adjustment triggers generally represent situations when change is the result of deliberate decision-making by management or stakeholders, changes imposed by industry developments are generally considered triggers out of the control of the affected organization.

Business Shift

Within most public and private sectors, an organization can find itself impacted by changes in business law, governmental policy, or even economic or political factors. When external developments affect how a business can and should carry out its operations, it generally warrants the use of this vitality trigger. For example, an accounting firm may find several of its business processes heavily influenced by the release of a new tax law or subsidy.

Technology Shift

This trigger represents industry technology shifts that occur within proprietary vendor platforms and product lines, as well as industry technology standards communities.

Examples include:

- A new version of an infrastructure product becomes available and the version currently being used by the organization will no longer be supported after a period of time.

- The Service Custodian decides that a service is to be moved from an on-premise environment to a cloud-based environment (or vice versa).

- A product vendor announces that it will discontinue a product used in the IT enterprise.

- A new version of a currently utilized technology or application is now service-enabled.

- A new security industry standard is released, superseding the standard to which an enterprise's solutions currently comply.

- A cloud provider offers new leasing models for IT resources with greater amounts of scalability, or perhaps at lower rates.

These types of changes can impact various parts of technology architecture and infrastructure, as well as the skill-sets and resources required to implement and support the required technology changes.

Metrics

The most common form of vitality trigger is based on the use of metrics. An SOA governance framework can utilize quantitative and qualitative metrics to identify inadequacies, exceptions, violations, and other problem areas. Not only do metrics provide visibility into the effectiveness of an SOA governance system, they can also indicate if parts of the system are too strict, arduous, or otherwise unsuccessful.

It is important that a manageable set of metrics is created and that each metric has a clearly defined rationale. Too many metrics can be overwhelming, too few ineffectual. Initial metrics are likely to be subject to further refinement as the SOA governance vitality framework matures.

A variety of metrics can be defined in support of vitality requirements. Provided here are descriptions for two common types.

Performance Metrics

Metrics with defined thresholds can raise triggers to assist in measuring the performance of various parts of an SOA ecosystem.

Example areas of focus include:

- the operational efficiency of services or specific service capabilities
- the operational burden of a service-oriented solution in relation to its ROI
- the utilization of a given on-premise physical server compared to its purchase and administration cost
- the usage costs of a cloud-based service that is incurring per-usage fees
- the administration costs associated with resolving recurring security problems of cloud-based services being periodically attacked

It should be noted that not all metrics are equally important and resulting decisions should normally not be based on a single metric but on a set of related metrics. Further, performance-related metrics need to be assessed in relation to usage parameters set by the Runtime Service Usage Thresholds precept (explained in Chapter 11).

Compliance Metrics

This type of metric can be collected manually or automatically. Manual compliance metrics are generally derived from the results of governance review processes (such as those described in Chapters 7–11). These results help determine the amount of compliance failures (or violations) that occur, which can then trigger corresponding vitality activities.

Automated compliance metrics are usually focused on runtime exceptions or logged events that occur when messages or data exchanged by services fail validation rules within technical policies, schemas, or other operational definitions. Alternatively, compliance metrics can apply when the usage of a service violates the parameters or limits set by the Runtime Service Usage Thresholds precept (see Chapter 11).

Organizational Shifts

This type of trigger occurs when internal changes are made to an organizational structure, or when other forms of internal events affect the IT enterprise, deliberately or inadvertently.

Examples of organizational shifts include:

- two departments are combined due to budgetary constraints
- a line of business is temporarily suspended due to a strike or labor protest
- there is a change in IT management, resulting in the reallocation of resources
- adjustments are made to the existing funding model

The Organizational Shifts trigger is differentiated from Strategic Adjustment triggers in that the organizational shift may not be the result of a change in strategic direction or policy. However, some strategic adjustments can lead to organizational shifts, in which case separately defined triggers may not be necessary.

Periodic

Periodic triggers are pre-scheduled, preventative reviews utilized primarily for quality assurance purposes. They are employed as a means of measuring and validating that an SOA ecosystem is performing as expected and in support of the overarching strategic direction. The following sections describe two common types of periodic triggers.

Milestone

A milestone trigger is associated with pre-defined vitality activities that are carried out at scheduled intervals. As an example, a series of reviews of a service inventory technology architecture may be scheduled to correspond with service quantity milestones. The first review is carried out upon the delivery of 10 services, the second review when the quantity reaches 20, and so on.

Time

Time triggers force a review of an asset using a pre-defined timescale. This facilitates the flexibility to define different classes of SOA assets with different time trigger durations. For example, every shared service deployed in a public cloud may be subjected to a statistics report on a monthly basis to collect usage and billing data. This information can then be used to compile ROI reports as the basis of a business metric.

SUMMARY OF KEY POINTS

- SOA governance vitality triggers represent common events and changes that force the execution of an SOA governance vitality process.

- Some vitality triggers are associated with business change, while others originate with technology change.

- Metrics are the most common form of vitality trigger.

13.3 SOA Governance Vitality Process

An SOA governance vitality process is comprised of a series of activities that are carried out in response to certain vitality concerns or requirements. Each of the previously described vitality triggers can result in different vitality activities (or different combinations of activities) being performed.

Figure 13.4 displays a generic sample process with five common types of vitality activities. The upcoming sections describe these activities in more detail. Note that vitality processes and activities need to be customized to ensure they address the specific needs of the organization.

Figure 13.4

Five common activities as part of a generic SOA governance vitality process. This process is usually carried out manually by SOA Governance Specialists and other members of the SOA Governance Program Office.

Identify Activity

This base activity centers on capturing relevant information surrounding the trigger and the circumstances of its execution. The collected data can help determine which subsequent activities should be carried out and whether minor or more substantial vitality measures are required. Therefore, it is important that the identification criteria used by this activity is accurate and balanced.

Assess Activity

To enable the SOA Governance Program Office to make informed vitality decisions, it will need to assess the validity, impact, and value of each proposed refresh of an IT asset. The Assess activity encompasses tasks that focus on determining the effect of carrying out a refresh, prior to moving on to the actual Refresh activity.

Example assessment criteria includes:

- the motivation for the refresh
- concrete benefits of the proposed refresh
- degree of impact on existing and future projects
- the effect on other SOA assets
- the effect on consumers of the asset to be refreshed
- implications if the refresh is rejected
- legitimate alternatives to the refresh
- refresh limitations imposed by current deployment environments (such as when the environment is controlled by a third-party cloud provider)

Armed with this type of assessment information, those carrying out the SOA governance vitality process can make informed recommendations or decisions for approving, delaying, or rejecting proposed refresh requests.

Refresh Activity

The Refresh activity governs the actual actions performed in response to the previously identified vitality concern. As a task that is part of a governance process, this activity provides direction and regulation with regards to the necessary changes that need to be applied to the affected asset (or to the affected part of the SOA ecosystem).

Here are some examples:

- An SOA Governance Specialist carrying out the vitality process may develop a custom refresh plan that identifies the team, schedule, and budget required to perform necessary infrastructure upgrades to counter an identified scalability threshold.

- The Enterprise Architect involved with a vitality process identifies a flaw in an existing design standard and creates a plan to regulate the revision of the corresponding design standards specification.

- As a result of usage demands that exceed on-premise infrastructure capacity, the Service Custodian consults a Cloud Governance Specialist and they collectively decide to move the service implementation into a public cloud.

- Alternatively, a cloud-based service may have been the victim of repeated attacks that have compromised its performance. After receiving a report from the Cloud Resource Administrator that there is no immediate solution in sight, the Service Custodian decides to bring the service back to an on-premise environment.

Regardless of the nature of the required refresh tasks, the primary deliverable of this activity is generally a plan with proposed details for carrying out the actual refresh.

Approve Activity

The plan produced by the Refresh activity is subjected to an authority within the SOA Governance Program Office for formal approval. This activity is basically a review that can result in the acceptance or rejection of the refresh plan. Often, a rejection may simply be a request for more details or refinements.

In addition to cost and effort, a primary factor that weighs into this review process is the impact of the refresh on the existing SOA ecosystem. Because assets commonly affected by vitality activities are currently in production usage, impacts upon resources and consumers relying on the targeted assets can be significant. So much so, that there may be cases where legitimate refresh plans are rejected because they are not considered worth the disruption they would end up causing.

Communicate Activity

Once approved, the planned refresh needs to be communicated to the affected stakeholders, project teams, and others involved with the targeted asset (such as the Service Custodians).

Documents and reports need to be provided to ensure that all affected understand the objectives and consequences of the upcoming refresh. Note that this is communication that occurs *after* the Approve activity. The intent is to notify others of the refresh activities that will occur.

SUMMARY OF KEY POINTS

- An SOA governance vitality process is initiated as a result of the execution of a vitality trigger.

- Each vitality process can be customized in relation to the nature of the trigger and the organization's requirements.

- Common vitality process steps include Identify, Assess, Refresh, Approve, and Communicate.

Chapter 14

SOA Governance Technology

It's no secret that SOA underwent an identity crisis during its earlier stages. As the acronym became an increasingly common part of IT media vocabulary, there were many associations and definitions. Most were wrong. One of the primary contributing factors to the resulting confusion was that some vendors wanting to capitalize on the hype began branding products with "SOA." Many trusting practitioners who invested in these products eventually failed in their attempts to realize project goals. Either the products were not legitimately supportive of SOA, or practitioners were led to believe that the purchase of the products alone would lead to the creation of a service-oriented enterprise, or both.

In the later stages of the SOA hype cycle, governance was being highlighted as the most common critical success factor overlooked by early adopters. This oversight was blamed as the reason for past failed projects and as the justification for organizations to "try to do it right" this time around. Unfortunately, the subsequent emergence of SOA governance technologies resulted in a related, yet separate stage of "mis-branding." This led to a new, yet familiar round of ambiguity and confusion.

In this chapter we establish what is and is not SOA governance technology. We describe common products used to support SOA governance systems for both design-time and runtime stages with reference to on-premise and cloud-based services. The chapter concludes with guidelines for choosing SOA governance products and vendors.

> **NOTE**
>
> While the upcoming products are discussed in relation to SOA governance, they are not necessarily exclusive to that purpose. For example, many of these products are used for hands-on management activities.

14.1 Understanding SOA Governance Technology

To fully understand what constitutes an SOA governance product and to further comprehend its meaning and purpose, we need to go back to the foundational definition of a governance system introduced in Chapter 6. A governance system is a meta-decision system used by an organization to make decisions about decision-making. A governance system therefore places constraints on decisions, determines who has responsibility and authority to make decisions, establishes constraints and parameters that control, guide, or influence decisions, and prescribes consequences for non-compliance.

The purpose of the many governance precepts, processes, and roles throughout this book is to help you establish and maintain a governance system specific to SOA and service-orientation. It is this context we must remain aware of when exploring and assessing suitable technologies.

NOTE

In addition to the term "technology," the terms "products" and "tools" are used throughout this chapter. Neither term is formally defined. A tool is most commonly a type of product with a front-end user interface. For the purpose of this chapter, both products and tools are considered forms of technologies.

SOA Governance Task Types

Let's first begin with some common terms used to label types of SOA governance tasks. These categories will help us classify technologies based on their function and purpose.

Manual Governance

These are primarily decision-based tasks that need to be performed by people or as part of processes that are not fully automated. An example of a manual governance task is the review of a service architecture specification by an SOA architect.

Automated Governance

Automated governance tasks can include the collection of metrics used to support decision-making or tasks performed automatically to support or enforce governance precepts and processes. An example of an automated governance task is the use of a security mechanism to prevent access to a service architecture specification by an outside project team.

Design-time Governance

The "design-time" part of this term refers to manual or automated tasks performed prior to runtime service usage. An example of a design-time governance task is the review of modeled service candidates to ensure compliance to naming conventions. (SOA Adoption Planning and Service-Oriented Analysis stages are, for the purpose of this chapter, still considered design-time governance tasks.)

Runtime Governance

Runtime governance begins where design-time governance ends. This type of task therefore becomes primarily relevant after the service has been implemented for active usage. An example of a runtime governance task is the monitoring of a service's runtime behavior to ensure compliance to published SLA guarantees.

> **NOTE**
>
> Runtime governance is often associated with the Service Usage and Monitoring stage. However, during the Service Deployment and Maintenance stage a service implementation moves from its pre-production to its production environment, making this stage relevant to both design-time and runtime governance controls.

On-Premise Governance

When the focus of governance activity is limited to controlled, on-premise environments, then it qualifies as on-premise governance tasks. An example of an on-premise governance task is the impact analysis performed by an SOA planning tool in order to determine the effect a new service version may have on existing service consumers and related artifacts within the on-premise service inventory.

Cloud Governance

Cloud governance tasks are those specific to governing services and related IT resources that are deployed in cloud environments. An example of a cloud governance task is the monitoring of per usage fees incurred by a SaaS deployment within a public cloud.

Passive Governance

This classification is used to label tasks that do not directly impact or interfere with the current state of a service or service-oriented solution. An example of a passive governance task is the collection and reporting of runtime or design-time metrics.

Active Governance

When governance tasks do have an immediate effect on the current state of a service or service-oriented solution, they are classified as "active." An example of an active governance task is a review process, such as the compliance checking of a proposed XML schema. Upon failing compliance, the schema is rejected.

NOTE

A given governance task will belong to one of each of the previously described type pairs. For example, a task can be categorized as automated or manual, design-time or runtime, on-premise or cloud-based, and passive or active.

SOA Governance Technology Types

Let's now establish some common categories that help group governance products based on their overall purpose.

Administrative

This category mostly represents tools used for manual governance purposes at design-time and runtime. An administrative tool is typically utilized to document and share published content pertaining to precepts and processes, or details about the governance system and the SOA Governance Program Office in general. Some forms of automated governance products may incorporate the usage of administrative functionality or may include a front-end tool allowing for administrative tasks.

Monitoring

A key means of measuring the effectiveness and success of an SOA governance system is to keep track of the performance of the people and solutions being governed. Monitoring products can range from front-end tools used to manually trace a service through its lifecycle stages to automated runtime technologies that observe services and service-oriented solution behavior. Monitoring products can carry out passive or active tasks, depending on how they are designed to respond to certain events or conditions encountered while monitoring.

Reporting

For governance professionals to assess and stay in touch with the design-time state of service delivery projects and the runtime performance of individual services, it is crucial to have reporting mechanisms in place that collect and communicate various metrics and statistics. This information is commonly used by the SOA Governance Program Office as vitality input for evolving the governance system.

Enforcement

Those participating in manual processes are often assigned the responsibility of checking for compliance to SOA governance precepts. Depending on the nature of the compliance-checking being performed, this type of active governance task can be supported by front-end tools and back-end technologies that help validate or automatically determine compliance or non-compliance.

> **NOTE**
>
> There can be a natural overlap between products that provide monitoring and reporting features. Depending on the nature of the information being gathered, reporting functionality often needs to encompass an extent of monitoring.

> **NOTE**
>
> The Service Discovery stage can also be considered a design-time stage when an existing agnostic service (that has likely already been active in runtime) is discovered during the design-time stages of a new project.

SUMMARY OF KEY POINTS

- There are eight task types that can be used to classify SOA governance products based on how and when they are typically applied in support of governance activities.

- There are five technology types that can be used to categorize SOA governance products based on the nature of their functionality.

14.2 Common SOA Governance Technology Products

The upcoming section contains descriptions for a set of primary products, each of which further includes sub-sections that map a product to related task types and technology types, as well as commonly associated SOA project stages. How and where technologies can be involved can vary greatly, depending on the nature of the governance system and the scope and reach of the SOA Governance Program Office.

Specifically, the following SOA governance technologies and products are covered:

- Service Registries
- Repositories
- Service Agents
- Policy Systems
- Quality Assurance Tools
- SOA Management Suites

It's important to acknowledge that other types of governance-branded products exist. The listed products were chosen because they are established and have proven themselves valuable specifically in support of SOA governance systems.

NOTE

For many examples of current vendor products for each of the upcoming categories, visit www.soabooks.com/governance/. The screenshots and information published at this part of the book series Web site is intended to help readers associate the described SOA governance technology product categories with real world products. Vendors have an open invitation to freely contribute content to this part of the Web site; however, none of the products displayed are endorsed by the *Prentice Hall Service-Oriented Computing Series from Thomas Erl*.

Service Registries

A service registry is used to store metadata about services, including descriptions of their functional contexts and capabilities, as well as pointers to the locations of their service contracts.

Private and public service registries can exist, depending on the scope of intended consumers. A private service registry is typically intended for access by consumers within the IT enterprise and is often specific to a particular service inventory.

To locate services, people typically search service registries using specialized query tools. A number of different technologies have been employed to provide service registry functionality, from relational databases to flat files registry to products compliant with the Universal Description, Discovery, and Integration (UDDI) industry standard.

The usage of a service registry is mandated by SOA governance precepts and related processes, most commonly in relation to discovery requirements (as explained in Chapter 10). The metadata within the service registry can further support the SOA Governance Program Office by providing a central data source used to report on the status of upcoming and existing services, as well as the overall status of an entire service inventory.

Task Types

The service registry can be used for all forms of SOA governance tasks. Members of the SOA Governance Program Office can contribute to or maintain registered service metadata the same way project teams delivering the service can. Metadata can be added or updated at design-time and further updated and accessed at runtime. The data can be used for passive reporting purposes, or it may lead to the need for responsive, active governance action. Although service registries can exist in cloud platforms, it is more common for them to be positioned in on-premise environments, with pointers to cloud-based services.

Manual	x
Automated	x
Design-time	x
Runtime	x
On-Premise	x
Cloud	x
Passive	x
Active	x

Technology Types

The recording and maintenance of service metadata within the service registry can be classified as an administrative task. Some service registries are equipped with built-in reporting features (comparable to search results), and the structure of the service records within the registry can force compliance to service registry standards and conventions. Furthermore, the usage of the service registry itself can be (and often is) the focal point of a primary compliance requirement for project teams.

Administrative	x
Monitoring	
Reporting	x
Enforcement	x

SOA Project Stages

Because service metadata can be added and updated throughout the project and service life-cycles, the service registry can be associated with all lifecycle stages. However, it is most commonly known for its association with the Service Discovery stage.

Besides acting as a central administrative resource for users to keep track of the status of services, a primary function it fulfills is to provide access to service metadata for project teams that need to locate (discover) agnostic services for reuse purposes.

SOA Adoption Planning	x
Service Inventory Analysis	x
Service-Oriented Analysis	x
Service-Oriented Design	x
Service Logic Design	x
Service Development	x
Service Testing	x
Service Deployment & Maintenance	x
Service Usage & Monitoring	x
Service Discovery	x
Service Versioning & Retirement	x

Repositories

An SOA repository is a specialized database used as a storage mechanism for a range of design-time artifacts that can pertain to individual services or entire service-oriented solutions. Examples of artifacts commonly stored in repositories include:

- service profiles and design specifications
- programming code, including executable business process logic (such as WS-BPEL)
- data models (such as those defined using the XML Schema Definition language)
- technical service contract documents (such as WSDL and policy definitions)
- human-readable service contract documents (such as SLAs)
- business analysis documents (such as process models)

In addition to serving as a general storage container, repository products are also often capable of automatically parsing artifacts to determine relationships, as well as enabling additional input. Users interact with repositories the same way they do with service registries—by using query tools and user-interfaces provided by the repository vendor.

Although most of the artifacts stored in a repository are technical in nature and administered by Service Architects and Service Developers, Service Custodians and SOA Governance Specialists also can contribute to and maintain certain types of artifacts, most notably service profiles and SLAs.

Task Types

The typical artifacts stored in a repository are most relevant to both manual and automated governance tasks that occur at design-time. This is because the repository simply provides central storage for related documents and technical artifacts that are most used during and relevant to the lifecycle stages that lead up to service implementation and runtime usage. Although it is technically possible for repositories to be used to store these types of artifacts in cloud-based environments, they are more commonly kept on-premise where they can be centrally administered. (An exception may be the use of a private cloud to make a repository accessible to other internal cloud consumers. In this case, a Cloud Storage Specialist may become involved to determine the best repository implementation and access methods.)

Manual	x
Automated	x
Design-time	x
Runtime	
On-Premise	x
Cloud	
Passive	x
Active	

Technology Types

The storage and maintenance of documents and artifacts within the repository are considered administrative governance tasks, especially as they serve the purpose of making the repository contents centrally shareable by a range of project team members. Some repository products are capable of reporting various types of information about stored artifacts in relation to services and service composition, and more recent repositories can even parse and validate some forms of artifacts (such as

Administrative	x
Monitoring	
Reporting	x
Enforcement	x

service contract definitions). Furthermore, the repository can be subject to access control limitations to help SOA Governance Specialists prevent unauthorized project teams from gaining access to confidential service implementation information.

SOA Project Stages

Just about any form of documentation and technical component can be stored in a repository. Therefore, this type of SOA governance technology can be potentially associated with all service lifecycle stages.

The Service Discovery stage is also included as it is common for project teams, subsequent to identifying agnostic services they would like to reuse as part of a new solution, to request further access to technical and human-readable artifacts. For example, after choosing a service listed in a service registry, an SOA architect on a project team may then want to retrieve the service's actual service contract definitions.

SOA Adoption Planning	x
Service Inventory Analysis	x
Service-Oriented Analysis	x
Service-Oriented Design	x
Service Logic Design	x
Service Development	x
Service Testing	x
Service Deployment & Maintenance	x
Service Usage & Monitoring	x
Service Discovery	x
Service Versioning & Retirement	x

> **NOTE**
>
> Several vendors provide products that combine service registry and repository features.

Service Agents

A service agent is an event-driven software program capable of passively tracking runtime activity and actively responding when encountering pre-defined conditions. Service agents are a common part of SOA governance products that contain back-end technology and processing logic.

Typical functions carried out by service agents include:

- validation
- enforcement
- monitoring
- notification
- logging

- exception handling

- billing and payment data collection

- dynamic scaling

A service agent is different from a service in that it does not provide a published contract and is therefore not explicitly invoked. Further, the type of logic encapsulated by service agents is generally utility-centric.

Service agents can be custom-developed to support various types of runtime governance requirements. A popular example is a service agent that issues a notification each time it detects a violation of a runtime governance precept. These notifications can be logged, forming the basis of a regular report published for the SOA Governance Program Office.

NOTE
For an introductory description of service agents, see the definition in Chapter 3.

Task Types

Service agents are specifically used for automated governance tasks that occur at runtime. Service agent logic can be designed to carry out both passive and active governance tasks, depending on how the service agent is utilized and also on whether the service agent is part of a larger product environment or was custom-developed for specific governance automation requirements. Note that some service agents can perform a range of processing, whereby only a subset of this functionality may actually be directly related to supporting SOA governance activities.

Manual	
Automated	x
Design-time	
Runtime	x
On-Premise	x
Cloud	x
Passive	x
Active	x

Cloud environments, in particular, rely heavily on the use of service agents that are native parts of cloud platforms. For example, cloud-based service agents are commonly used to support administrative cloud services that expose APIs or provide user interfaces for the configuration and reporting of monitoring and diagnostic functions. Some of these agents can dynamically seek and collect instrumentation information about active cloud services or entire cloud-based service compositions.

Technology Types

As previously discussed, common types of utility-centric processing provided by service agents include monitoring, reporting, and enforcement. Cloud-based service agents further focus on billing and on-demand scaling capabilities. These forms of runtime functions can be used to assist with a wide range of SOA governance tasks.

Administrative	
Monitoring	x
Reporting	x
Enforcement	x

SOA Project Stages

Although development tools and various design-time platforms may employ service agents in support of common SOA governance tasks, they are primarily utilized for runtime processing and are therefore used to passively observe and/or actively respond to runtime conditions.

For example, service agents may keep track of requests or inquiries issued against a service registry in order to collect discovery-related metrics. Similarly, service agents may be used to monitor the usage of a particular service version, especially when a new version of the service co-exists with the old version.

SOA Adoption Planning	
Service Inventory Analysis	
Service-Oriented Analysis	
Service-Oriented Design	
Service Logic Design	
Service Development	
Service Testing	
Service Deployment & Maintenance	
Service Usage & Monitoring	x
Service Discovery	x
Service Versioning & Retirement	x

Policy Systems

A typical policy system provides three types of functions: policy definition, policy enforcement, and policy monitoring. This type of governance product generally provides front-end UIs that enable you to create policy logic that is then exported in the form of technical policy definitions. The back-end of the system then makes use of service agents to monitor policy processing activity and, when necessary, enforce the policy conditions.

When policy violations occur, the service agents can be configured to actively or passively respond by either preventing the activity from completing or merely issuing a notification that the violation happened. Policy systems allow for the central maintenance of collections of policies, often for an entire service inventory. Some systems even tie in to service registries and repositories.

> **NOTE**
>
> For introductory coverage of operational and business policies, see the *Policies 101* section in Chapter 12.

Task Types

As technical artifacts that exist as part of back-end architectures, policies can be considered a runtime technology comparable in scope to service agents. Because a policy system will typically employ the use of specialized service agents, policies (and the service agent logic used to validate and enforce them) can result in passive or active responses to various runtime conditions.

Manual	
Automated	x
Design-time	
Runtime	x
On-Premise	x
Cloud	x
Passive	x
Active	x

Technology Types

As runtime artifacts, the usage of policies primarily pertains to runtime processing, which can encompass monitoring and enforcement. Further, various policy metrics (especially compliance-related) form the basis for reporting input.

Administrative	
Monitoring	x
Reporting	x
Enforcement	x

SOA Project Stages

A policy system is comprised of policy definitions that can be business or utility-centric in the type of logic they contain. The logic behind policies can be collected as early as the analysis stages when service candidates are derived from various forms of business intelligence. Although policy definitions will typically be positioned as extensions of service contracts, the results of compliance checks can impact how the underlying service processing logic needs to respond.

SOA Adoption Planning	
Service Inventory Analysis	x
Service-Oriented Analysis	x
Service-Oriented Design	x
Service Logic Design	x
Service Development	x
Service Testing	x
Service Deployment & Maintenance	x
Service Usage & Monitoring	x
Service Discovery	x
Service Versioning & Retirement	x

Quality Assurance Tools

When services pass through the SOA project stages they can be subjected to multiple governance review processes, each of which is responsible for ensuring compliance to certain precepts. Many of these compliance checks are related to verifying a baseline measure of quality as it pertains to the service's compatibility with its platform and surrounding services, as well as the service itself.

Prior to being implemented in the production environment, the service must undergo testing and other forms of quality assurance controls as part of the Service Testing lifecycle stage. Tools are typically used by SOA Quality Assurance Specialists to perform various tests and to collect information for subsequent test reports.

Of the sample precepts associated with the Service Testing stage (listed in Chapter 10), the Testing Parameters Standards and Service Model Testing Standards represent a set of regulations that can be incorporated within customizable quality assurance tools. This can make steps of the Service Test Review process automated or, even if still manual, more seamlessly part of processes carried out by SOA Quality Assurance Specialists.

It can be further valuable to the SOA Governance Program Office for metrics to be collected at this stage to report on how well services responded to various types of tests. For example, if a high level of failure for a certain type of test is encountered, SOA Governance Specialists can consider whether new precepts should be introduced to help alleviate these types of recurring problems.

Task Types

Quality assurance tools are generally used at design-time during which, for governance purposes, both manual and automated tasks can be carried out. The focus of the processing performed by these tools is on compliance checking and therefore, the results of failed or successful checks can be configured. Some forms of checking will demand an active response that results in the service (or part of the service architecture) being rejected. Passive responses are also possible, especially when compliance is optional. Cloud-based quality assurance tools are commonly limited to reporting functions with primary governance tasks being carried out on-premise (especially when the cloud environment itself is the focal point of quality assurance concerns).

Manual	x
Automated	x
Design-time	x
Runtime	
On-Premise	x
Cloud	x
Passive	x
Active	x

Technology Types

Depending on how a quality assurance tool is customized to support SOA governance precepts and processes, it may assume various types of reporting functions to provide metrics and other forms of reports of particular interest to the SOA Program Governance Office. Enforcement is the natural task performed by these tools; however, not all forms of service testing enforcement are necessarily pertinent to SOA governance precepts.

Administrative	
Monitoring	
Reporting	x
Enforcement	x

SOA Project Stages

Due to the nature of the processing performed by quality assurance tools, their involvement is generally limited to the Service Testing stage.

SOA Adoption Planning	
Service Inventory Analysis	
Service-Oriented Analysis	
Service-Oriented Design	
Service Logic Design	
Service Development	
Service Testing	x
Service Deployment & Maintenance	
Service Usage & Monitoring	
Service Discovery	
Service Versioning & Retirement	

SOA Management Suites

Several SOA product vendors have made large-scale SOA management systems available, some of which can handle environments containing thousands of services, comprising hundreds of compositions that exchange vast amounts of messages per second.

Such systems can provide broad feature sets, including:

- governance impact planning
- service administration
- service monitoring
- service mediation
- auditing and logging
- service management
- error diagnosis and remediation

An SOA management system is often comprised of a set of products and therefore also referred to as a management suite. The products in the suite tend to be more about the hands-on management of services and their respective runtime environments, meaning that if we revisit the distinction we made back in Chapter 6 between management and governance, these systems are primarily relevant to the former. However, because of the all-encompassing nature of these solutions, they often contain features suitable for SOA governance purposes.

> **NOTE**
>
> Because SOA management suites can vary significantly in terms of feature-sets and relevancy to SOA governance support, the *Task Types*, *Technology Types*, and *SOA Project Stages* sections are not provided. If they were shown, all items in all three tables would be checked off.

Other Tools and Products

There are no limitations as to the types of technologies that can be used for SOA governance purposes. As long as their usage legitimately supports SOA governance precepts and processes, they can be considered SOA governance technologies.

Provided here are further common examples.

Technical Editors and Graphic Tools

Several of the review processes and compliance-related precepts introduced by an SOA governance program can require validation of technical data. In order for SOA Governance Specialists to perform this validation, there may be the need to use tools capable of displaying the data in a structured or graphical manner. Some technical editors have the ability to render programming code into a graphical representation, which can make a manual audit easier to perform.

Content Sharing and Publishing Tools

Communication of SOA governance regulations and related information is extremely important to the success of an SOA Governance Program Office. Within the office, new or updated precepts and processes need to be centrally maintained and published for access to all that work within or in relation to the SOA Governance Program Office. Furthermore, having an open, two-way communications channel between the SOA

Governance Program Office and other departments and project teams within the organization is vital for SOA Governance Specialists to measure and assess the effectiveness of the SOA governance system.

Traditional Web-based content sharing mediums, such as intranets, content management systems, or document sharing and versioning systems, can be used to ensure consistent and accurate dissemination of governance information. Ideally, IT professionals outside of the SOA Governance Program Office are given the ability to subscribe to the SOA governance program so that they are automatically notified of changes or additions to the SOA governance system.

Configuration Management Tools

The same way that quality assurance tools can be used to support SOA governance precepts and processes specific to the Service Testing lifecycle stage, configuration management and versioning tools can be utilized in relation to precepts and processes established to help regulate the Service Versioning stage. Note that these tools can provide metrics for versioning issues pertaining to technical service contracts as well as SLAs. One of the metrics of most interest to the SOA Governance Program Office is the frequency of service or service contract versions, as this can shed light on flaws or problems that are inhibiting the longevity of services.

Custom SOA Governance Solutions

When vendor or open-source products are insufficient or, for other reasons, not the correct choice for adding SOA governance technology to your environment, there always exists the option of building your own. Sometimes this approach is justified, especially when your organization's governance requirements are so distinct that commercially available technologies are simply not sufficient.

When the choice between existing products and custom solutions does exist, it is important to weigh the consequences of each before deciding on a direction. Although SOA governance products are by no means inexpensive, it is generally significantly more costly to develop and then maintain your own solutions, especially when having to scale those solutions in tandem with a growing inventory of services.

Furthermore, factors such as security, reliability, and expected ROI need to be addressed. In many cases, it makes more sense to find a packaged product that can be customized to an extent that most technical SOA governance requirements are fulfilled. But, if your organization is accustomed to building robust software programs (especially if your line of business is already the delivery of packaged software), then you may be able to leverage existing resources and expertise to create and evolve the best possible governance technologies and tools for your requirements.

SUMMARY OF KEY POINTS

- Any technology can be considered an SOA governance technology if it can be used to effectively support the precepts and/or processes defined for a given SOA governance system.
- Common SOA governance technologies include service registries, repositories, service agents, policy systems, quality assurance tools, and SOA management suites.

14.3 Guidelines for Acquiring SOA Governance Technology

Provided in this final section are some general strategies and best practices for choosing SOA governance products.

Acquisition Strategies

How you go about choosing your SOA technology vendor will have long-term consequences, not just in relation to how you will (and will not) be able to govern your service inventory, but also as to how cost-effective and effort-intensive that governance responsibility will be.

There are four common approaches that you can take: single vendor, multiple vendors, open source, and leasing from a cloud vendor. Let's take a closer look at each.

Single Vendor

Purchasing all (or the majority) of your SOA governance technology from a sole vendor can simplify the acquisition process, but can also impose some long-term limitations. The following lists explore the pros and cons.

Pros

- *Standardization* – By sticking to a single vendor, it will be easier to standardize SOA governance processes as well as the usage of the governance products themselves.

All SOA Governance Specialists working for the SOA Governance Program Office can be required to use the same line of products.

- *Skill-Set* – With a single source for SOA governance products, it will be easier to train and develop proficiency among the governance team, as well as others that may want to use the products for non-governance activities.

- *Seamless Integration* – If your technical SOA governance platform is comprised of various moving parts, having them all belong to the same product line will make any required integration significantly easier than if they came from different vendors.

Cons

- *Vendor Lock-In* – Vendor products are often designed to encourage customers to form dependencies upon the vendor. Entrusting just one vendor with all of your SOA governance software needs will likely lock you into the direction they choose for their product line. This may end up inhibiting your ability to evolve your SOA governance precepts and goals.

- *Vendor Credibility* – Some vendor organizations are acquisition targets for other, larger product vendors. If you have invested only in one vendor product line and the vendor company is acquired, it could have serious impacts on future support and product line direction.

- *Integration Issues* – As previously stated, a typical advantage to this approach is improved integration. However, that is not always the case. Some vendors provide SOA governance platforms that appear (from a packaging perspective) to be uniform, but are in fact assembled from a hodgepodge of disparate products, some of which may have been the result of corporate acquisitions.

Multiple Vendors

This is the best-of-breed approach, whereby you pick and choose the most suitable SOA governance products from different vendors. The result is that you intentionally create a heterogeneous SOA governance platform.

Pros

- *Leverage Innovation* – By deciding to assemble your SOA governance environment from the best possible solutions, you're much more likely to end up with highly sophisticated feature-sets capable of maximizing your requirements potential.

- *Independence* – By not committing to any single vendor vision and product road-map, you greatly increase your freedom to evolve your SOA governance platform in response to future needs.

- *Cost-Effectiveness* – This approach may more easily enable you to generate competition among vendors in order to drive down costs.

Cons

- *Integration Challenges* – The disparity within a diverse SOA governance platform will most likely increase the cost and effort required to make different governance tools and products connect. This further increases the likelihood that custom development may be required. These types of integration challenges can be further compounded when different vendors choose to take new directions with their products over time.

- *Skill-Set* – Supporting a range of products from different vendors can be burdensome when having to train staff to use and maintain multiple products.

Open Source

Some SOA governance technologies (and products providing governance-related functionality) exist as open source offerings. An approach can be used whereby the SOA governance platform is assembled entirely or partially from open source technology.

Pros

- *Usually it's Free* – The common basis of the open source model is that the software is made available to the community at no charge. This, of course, makes an open source SOA governance product more desirable from a budgetary perspective.

- *Access to Source Code* – Another common basis of the open source model is that the entire source code of the software is also made available to the community. The advantage here is that you are able to extend and fully customize the product as long as you have sufficient development resources.

Cons

- *Extra Support Agreements* – Another common revenue stream for open source organizations is support contracts. Because you will likely be relying on your SOA governance software to oversee vital daily operations, it's quite possible that you'll decide to pay for a support plan.

- *Lack of Features* – As we'll describe in a moment, open source solutions may offer noticeably less functionality than their proprietary brethren. In some cases, not having access to these important capabilities may outweigh the cost savings of an open source package.

- *Reliability Problems* – Because open source products may not be subjected to the same quality assurance rigor as commercial software products, they can be less stable. This can lead to serious consequences (or a significant maintenance burden) when relying on these products for SOA governance purposes.

Leased from Cloud Vendor

Various cloud providers offer virtualized desktop tools that can assist with cloud governance tasks. These are used for the remote governance and overall administration of cloud-hosted services and supporting IT resources.

Pros

- *You Don't Need to Buy* – Instead of having the up-front cost of purchasing governance technology, you can lease it as part of a licensing package with the cloud provider.

- *Optimized to Environment* – Generally, a cloud provider will offer tools that are very compatible to the nature of the cloud environment hosting the services and IT resources you would want to perform the governance tasks on.

Cons

- *Limited Options* – By working with the governance tool(s) a cloud provider makes available, you may be limited as to the functionality and extent of the governance activities you can actually perform.

- *Shared Hosting* – The governance tools you may be remotely accessing will commonly be virtualized and hosted by shared servers that can impact performance and reliability.

Of course, depending on the location of services within a given service inventory and the extent of additional on-premise governance tasks required, it may be necessary to combine leased cloud-based governance tools with on-premise governance tools.

Best Practices

The following best practices can form the basis of a checklist for assessing SOA governance vendors and products.

Establish Criteria Based on Your Specific Requirements

SOA governance technology is best evaluated after you have documented a comprehensive draft of your planned SOA governance system, along with the various parts of the supporting SOA governance program and even the organizational structure of the SOA Governance Program Office. With all of this in place, you will be able to define very specific criteria for technologies that can help realize the goals of the SOA governance program. It is with this criteria in hand that you will be in the best position to judge the applicability and usefulness of the various features offered by different SOA governance systems, products, and platforms.

Investigate Customizability

Some vendor products are extremely sophisticated, but allow for little opportunity to further change how they function or what boundaries they can function within. Regardless of whether you initially need to perform any major customization work on an SOA governance product, be sure to fully understand the extent to which the product can, in fact, be tailored. The more flexible the product is with regards to accommodating a range of requirements or parameters or even governance styles, the greater the chances that the investment you are making in the product today will last.

Investigate APIs

SOA governance product integration is often a key success factor to the long-term usage of an SOA governance platform. If products can be easily connected to share data and functionality, the platform can more responsively be evolved to accommodate new and changing governance requirements. If identified integration points result in actual integration and development projects, the SOA governance platform itself may be in need of its own system of governance.

Understand Both Initial and Long-Term Costs

The immediate costs required to establish SOA governance products, along with the long-term implications of licensing costs, need to be fully understood and compared before deciding on a given product. It is very helpful to have a service inventory blueprint at hand to fully assess the potential scope at which governance technology may need to be deployed and utilized. Estimates pertaining to scalability of products (in terms of concurrent users and runtime capacity) together with supplementary expenses (such as training and integration) can form the basis of cost projections that help reveal required budgets.

Understand Actual Governance Support

As discussed earlier in this chapter, what constitutes a product that provides true SOA governance-related features can vary, depending on how vendors choose to brand and market their offerings. The best approach is, with your requirements criteria already defined, to disregard brands and labels and focus on the actual features and functions provided. Sometimes a subset of SOA governance product features will be relevant to your requirements and in other cases products not labeled with "SOA governance" at all will contain useful features.

Take the Time to Create a Quality RFP

Whether you are following the single vendor or multiple vendor strategy described earlier, it is worthwhile to put together a comprehensive RFP before approaching any vendor with your requirements. The most effective RFPs are created with the involvement of numerous IT professionals, not just the SOA Governance Specialists who may be leading the acquisition effort. It's further important that the RFP be the culmination of an honest, unbiased assessment of your SOA governance requirements and expectations.

SUMMARY OF KEY POINTS

- When choosing SOA governance technologies, a single vendor, multiple vendor and/or open source acquisition approach can be considered—or—you may be required to lease governance tools from a cloud provider.

- Key best practices for deciding on the most suitable SOA governance products focus on ensuring compatibility with your specific governance requirements and fully understanding the extent to which a product can be customized and integrated with other products.

- A fundamental criterion for assessing SOA governance offerings is to have a clear understanding of what actually constitutes SOA governance activity within your organization.

Part IV

Appendices

Appendix A

Case Study Conclusion

When Raysmoore was still in the planning stages of their SOA adoption project, they performed an Organizational Governance Maturity Assessment (see the case study example at the end of Chapter 7) whereby the following areas were evaluated:

- Cultural Readiness

- Centralization Factors

- Political Environment

- Technical Project Roles

The results of the initial assessment were not sufficient to proceed with the project at that time. Subsequent efforts to improve communication and education among affected departments and personnel led to a follow-up assessment with scores high enough to proceed.

While SOA Governance Specialists were in the midst of coordinating and documenting necessary vitality precepts (Chapter 11), they reflected on how the initial two maturity assessments differed after a concentrated effort to address identified shortcomings. If pre-project improvements in communications and skill-set development among project teams could increase organizational maturity, then what about the actual hands-on experience of carrying out the project with governance controls and the experience of the on-going governance of deployed services? This type of real-world exposure should, in theory, further help affect and help evolve the organization's maturity.

It is therefore decided to add a new scheduled vitality trigger. The same Organizational Governance Maturity Assessment will be carried out annually to determine the following:

- areas where organizational maturity has continued to grow

- areas where organizational maturity has begun to regress

Scores collected will help identify upward and downward trends in any of the measured areas. This, in turn, will help assess the effectiveness of precepts and processes that address or impact those areas.

Finally, this yearly assessment will highlight how the repeated application of SOA governance precepts and processes themselves will influence and shape different aspects of the organization, its culture, its technology, and its success in leveraging governed services in support of realizing business goals.

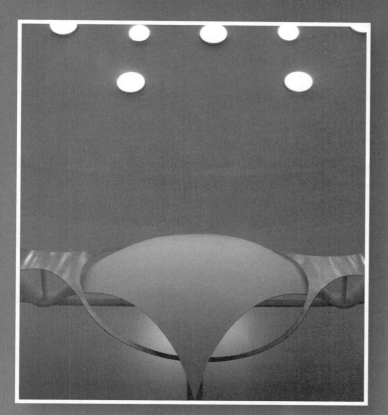

Appendix B

Master Reference Diagrams
for Organizational Roles

This appendix contains a series of reference diagrams that illustrate the mapping between organizational roles and SOA governance precepts and processes. Each identified precept and process is further labeled with its chapter of origin.

Service Analyst

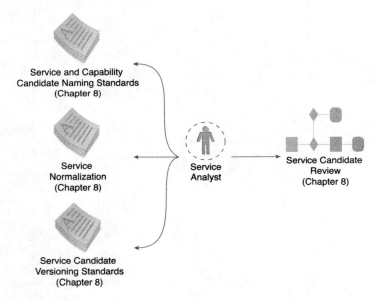

Figure B.1

SOA governance precepts and processes associated with the Service Analyst role.

Service Architect

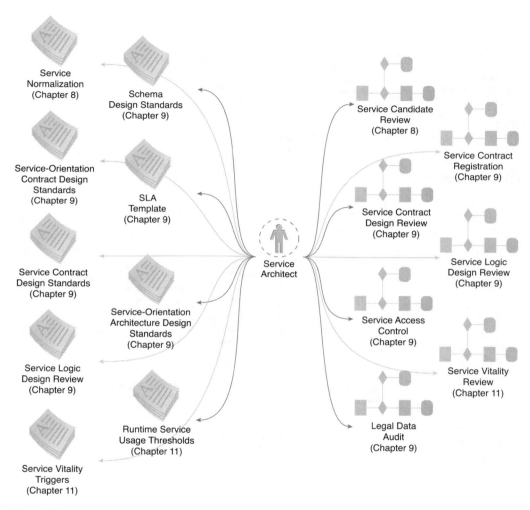

Figure B.2

SOA governance precepts and processes associated with the Service Architect role.

Service Developer

Figure B.3
SOA governance precepts and processes associated with the Service Developer role.

Service Custodian

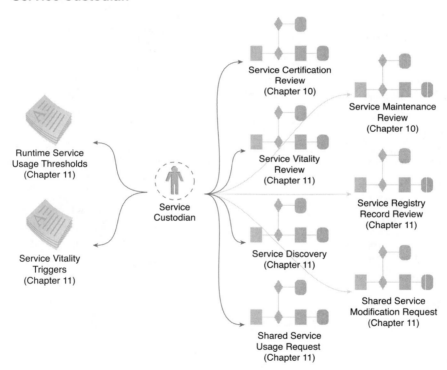

Figure B.4
SOA governance precepts and processes associated with the Service Custodian role.

Service Administrator

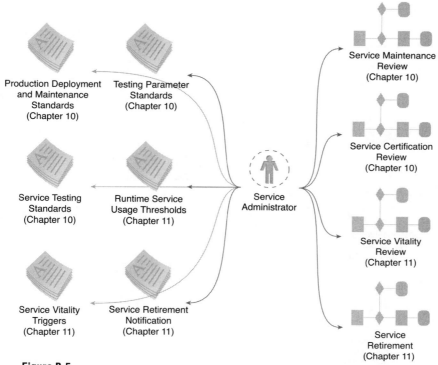

Figure B.5
SOA governance precepts and processes associated with the Service Administrator role.

Cloud Resource Administrator

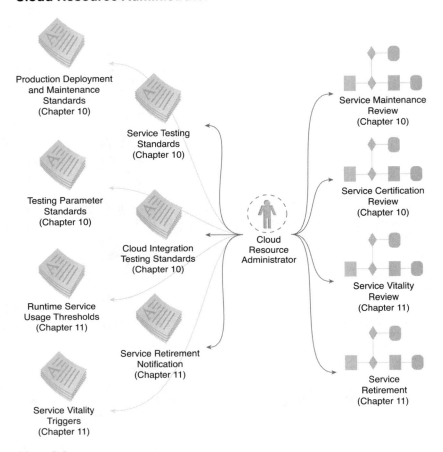

Production Deployment
and Maintenance
Standards
(Chapter 10)

Service Testing
Standards
(Chapter 10)

Testing Parameter
Standards
(Chapter 10)

Cloud Integration
Testing Standards
(Chapter 10)

Runtime Service
Usage Thresholds
(Chapter 11)

Service Retirement
Notification
(Chapter 11)

Service Vitality
Triggers
(Chapter 11)

Cloud
Resource
Administrator

Service Maintenance
Review
(Chapter 10)

Service Certification
Review
(Chapter 10)

Service Vitality
Review
(Chapter 11)

Service
Retirement
(Chapter 11)

Figure B.6

SOA governance precepts and processes associated with the Cloud Resource
Administrator role.

Schema Custodian

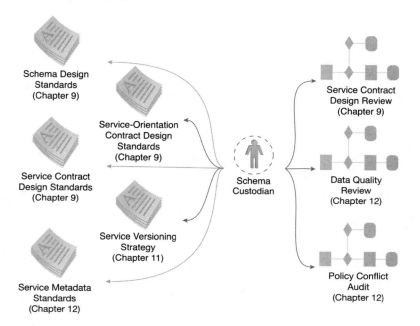

Figure B.7

SOA governance precepts and processes associated with the Schema Custodian role.

Policy Custodian

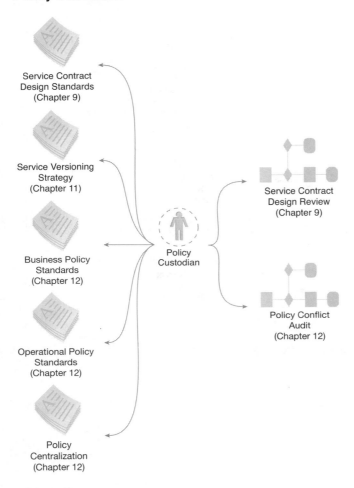

Figure B.8
SOA governance precepts and processes associated with the Policy Custodian role.

Service Registry Custodian

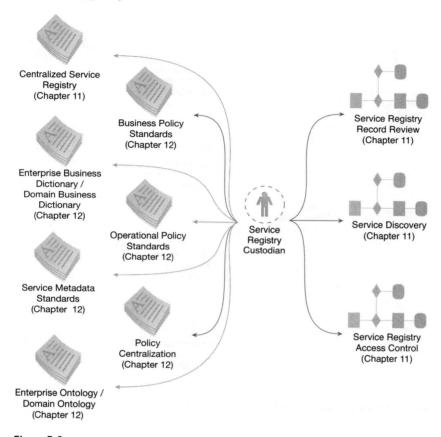

Figure B.9

SOA governance precepts and processes associated with the Service Registry Custodian role.

Technical Communications Specialist

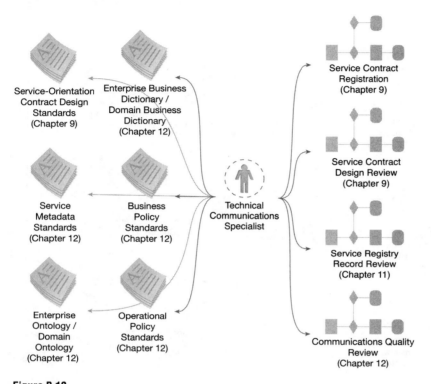

Figure B.10

SOA governance precepts and processes associated with the Technical Communications
Specialist role.

Enterprise Architect

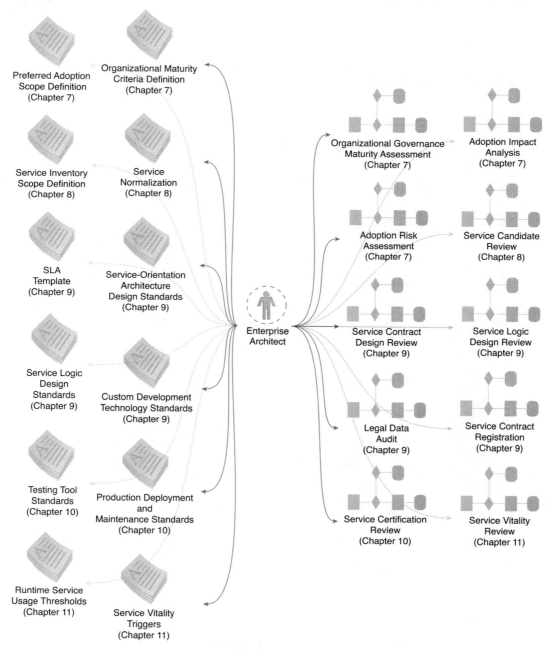

Figure B.11

SOA governance precepts and processes associated with the Enterprise Architect role.

Enterprise Design Standards Custodian (and Auditor)

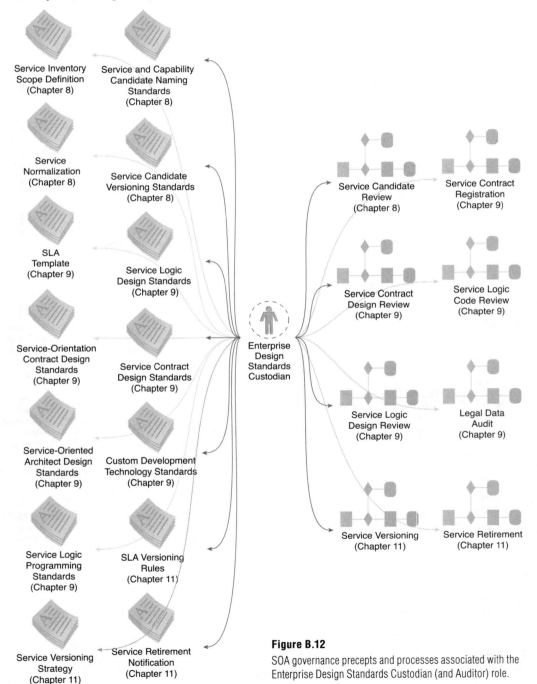

Figure B.12

SOA governance precepts and processes associated with the Enterprise Design Standards Custodian (and Auditor) role.

SOA Quality Assurance Specialist

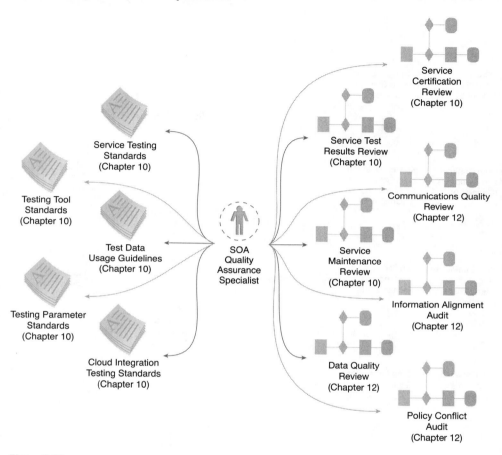

Figure B.13

SOA governance precepts and processes associated with the SOA Quality Assurance Specialist role.

SOA Security Specialist

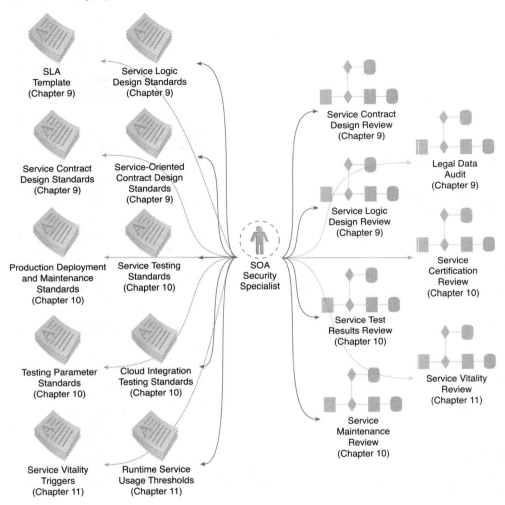

Figure B.14
SOA governance precepts and processes associated with the SOA Security Specialist role.

SOA Governance Specialist (precepts)

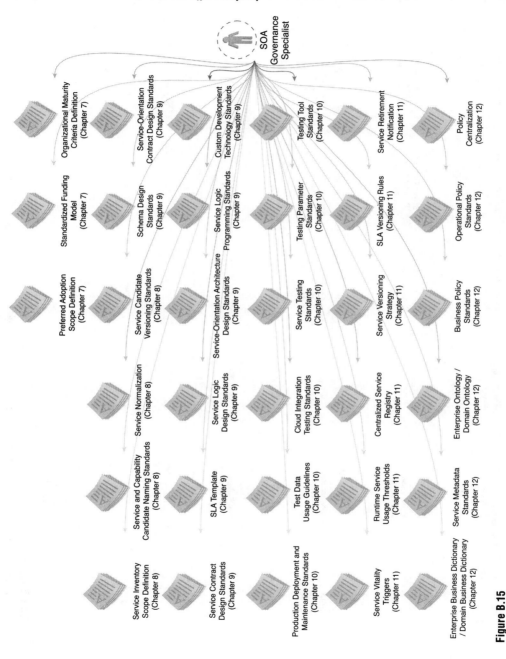

Figure B.15

SOA governance precepts associated with the SOA Governance Specialist role.

SOA Governance Specialist (processes)

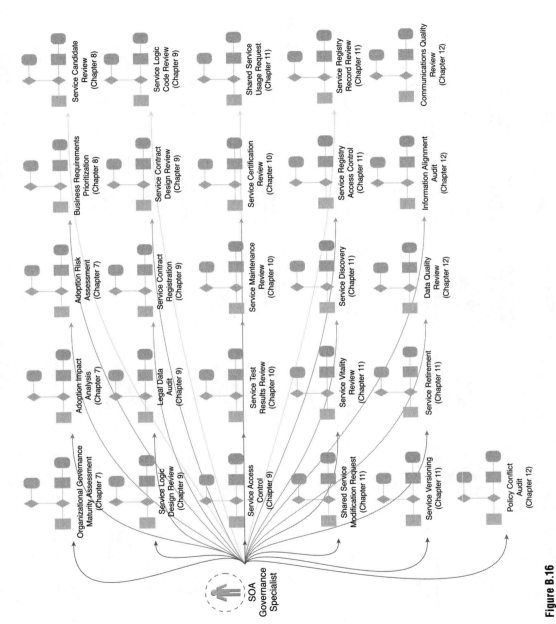

Figure B.16

SOA governance processes associated with the SOA Governance Specialist role.

Appendix C

Service-Orientation Principles Reference

This appendix provides profile tables for the eight design principles that are documented in *SOA Principles of Service Design*, a title that is part of this book series. Each principle that is referenced in this book is suffixed with the page number of its corresponding profile table in this appendix.

Every profile table contains the following sections:

- *Short Definition* – A concise, single-statement definition that establishes the fundamental purpose of the principle.

- *Long Definition* – A longer description of the principle that provides more detail as to what it is intended to accomplish.

- *Goals* – A list of specific design goals that are expected from the application of the principle. Essentially, this list provides the ultimate results of the principle's realization.

- *Design Characteristics* – A list of specific design characteristics that can be realized via the application of the principle. This provides some insight as to how the principle ends up shaping the service.

- *Implementation Requirements* – A list of common prerequisites for effectively applying the design principle. These can range from technology to organizational requirements.

Note that these tables provide only summarized content from the original publication. Information about service-orientation principles is also published online at www.soaprinciples.com.

Standardized Service Contract	
Short Definition	*"Services share standardized contracts."*
Long Definition	*"Services within the same service inventory are in compliance with the same contract design standards."*
Goals	• To enable services with a meaningful level of natural interoperability within the boundary of a service inventory. This reduces the need for data transformation because consistent data models are used for information exchange. • To allow the purpose and capabilities of services to be more easily and intuitively understood. The consistency with which service functionality is expressed through service contracts increases interpretability and the overall predictability of service endpoints throughout a service inventory. Note that these goals are further supported by other service-orientation principles as well.
Design Characteristics	• A service contract (comprised of a technical interface or one or more service description documents) is provided with the service. • The service contract is standardized through the application of design standards.
Implementation Requirements	The fact that contracts need to be standardized can introduce significant implementation requirements to organizations that do not have a history of using standards. For example: • Design standards and conventions need to ideally be in place prior to the delivery of any service in order to ensure adequately scoped standardization. (For those organizations that have already produced ad-hoc Web services, retro-fitting strategies may need to be employed.) • Formal processes need to be introduced to ensure that services are modeled and designed consistently, incorporating accepted design principles, conventions, and standards.

- Because achieving standardized Web service contracts generally requires a "contract first" approach to service-oriented design, the full application of this principle will often demand the use of development tools capable of importing a customized service contract without imposing changes.

- Appropriate skill-sets are required to carry out the modeling and design processes with the chosen tools. When working with Web services, the need for a high level of proficiency with XML schema and WSDL languages is practically unavoidable. WS-Policy expertise may also be required.

These and other requirements can add up to a noticeable transition effort that goes well beyond technology adoption.

Table C.1
A profile for the Standardized Service Contract principle.

Service Loose Coupling	
Short Definition	*"Services are loosely coupled."*
Long Definition	*"Service contracts impose low consumer coupling requirements and are themselves decoupled from their surrounding environment."*
Goals	By consistently fostering reduced coupling within and between services we are working toward a state where service contracts increase independence from their implementations and services are increasingly independent from each other. This promotes an environment in which services and their consumers can be adaptively evolved over time with minimal impact on each other.
Design Characteristics	• The existence of a service contract that is ideally decoupled from technology and implementation details. • A functional service context that is not dependent on outside logic. • Minimal consumer coupling requirements.
Implementation Requirements	• Loosely coupled services are typically required to perform more runtime processing than if they were more tightly coupled. As a result, data exchange in general can consume more runtime resources, especially during concurrent access and high usage scenarios. • To achieve the right balance of coupling, while also supporting the other service-orientation principles that affect contract design, requires increased service contract design proficiency.

Table C.2
A profile for the Service Loose Coupling principle.

Service Abstraction	
Short Definition	*"Non-essential service information is abstracted."*
Long Definition	*"Service contracts only contain essential information and information about services is limited to what is published in service contracts."*
Goals	Many of the other principles emphasize the need to publish *more* information in the service contract. The primary role of this principle is to keep the quantity and detail of contract content concise and balanced and prevent unnecessary access to additional service details.
Design Characteristics	• Services consistently abstract specific information about technology, logic, and function away from the outside world (the world outside of the service boundary). • Services have contracts that concisely define interaction requirements and constraints and other required service meta details. • Outside of what is documented in the service contract, information about a service is controlled or altogether hidden within a particular environment.
Implementation Requirements	The primary prerequisite to achieving the appropriate level of abstraction for each service is the level of service contract design skill applied.
Web Service Region of Influence	The *Region of Influence* part of this profile has been moved to the *Types of Meta Abstraction* section (in the book *SOA Principles of Service Design*) where a separate Web service figure is provided for each form of abstraction.

Table C.3

A profile for the Service Abstraction principle.

Service Reusability	
Short Definition	*"Services are reusable."*
Long Definition	*"Services contain and express agnostic logic and can be positioned as reusable enterprise resources."*
Goals	The goals behind Service Reusability are tied directly to some of the most strategic objectives of service-oriented computing: • To allow for service logic to be repeatedly leveraged over time so as to achieve an increasingly high return on the initial investment of delivering the service. • To increase business agility on an organizational level by enabling the rapid fulfillment of future business automation requirements through wide-scale service composition. • To enable the realization of agnostic service models. • To enable the creation of service inventories with a high percentage of agnostic services.
Design Characteristics	• *The service is defined by an agnostic functional context*—The logic encapsulated by the service is associated with a context that is sufficiently agnostic to any one usage scenario so as to be considered reusable. • *The service logic is highly generic*—The logic encapsulated by the service is sufficiently generic, allowing it to facilitate numerous usage scenarios by different types of service consumers. • *The service has a generic and extensible contract*—The service contract is flexible enough to process a range of input and output messages. • *The service logic can be accessed concurrently*—Services are designed to facilitate simultaneous access by multiple consumer programs.

Implementation Requirements	From an implementation perspective, Service Reusability can be the most demanding of the principles we've covered so far. Below are common requirements for creating reusable services and supporting their long-term existence: • A scalable runtime hosting environment capable of high-to-extreme concurrent service usage. Once a service inventory is relatively mature, reusable services will find themselves in an increasingly large number of compositions. • A solid version control system to properly evolve contracts representing reusable services. • Service analysts and designers with a high degree of subject matter expertise who can ensure that the service boundary and contract accurately represent the service's reusable functional context. • A high level of service development and commercial software development expertise so as to structure the underlying logic into generic and potentially decomposable components and routines. These and other requirements place an emphasis on the appropriate staffing of the service delivery team, as well as the importance of a powerful and scalable hosting environment and supporting infrastructure.

Table C.4

A profile for the Service Reusability principle.

Service Autonomy	
Short Definition	*"Services are autonomous."*
Long Definition	*"Services exercise a high level of control over their underlying runtime execution environment."*
Goals	• To increase a service's runtime reliability, performance, and predictability, especially when being reused and composed. • To increase the amount of control a service has over its runtime environment. By pursuing autonomous design and runtime environments, we are essentially aiming to increase post-implementation control over the service and the service's control over its own execution environment.
Design Characteristics	• Services have a contract that expresses a well-defined functional boundary that should not overlap with other services. • Services are deployed in an environment over which they exercise a great deal (and preferably an exclusive level) of control. • Service instances are hosted by an environment that accommodates high concurrency for scalability purposes.
Implementation Requirements	• A high level of control over how service logic is designed and developed. Depending on the level of autonomy being sought, this may also involve control over the supporting data models. • A distributable deployment environment, so as to allow the service to be moved, isolated, or composed as required. • An infrastructure capable of supporting desired autonomy levels.

Table C.5

A profile for the Service Autonomy principle.

Service Statelessness	
Short Definition	*"Services minimize statefulness."*
Long Definition	*"Services minimize resource consumption by deferring the management of state information when necessary."*
Goals	• To increase service scalability. • To support the design of agnostic service logic and improve the potential for service reuse.
Design Characteristics	What makes this somewhat of a unique principle is the fact that it is promoting a condition of the service that is temporary in nature. Depending on the service model and state deferral approach used, different types of design characteristics can be implemented. Some examples include: • Highly business process-agnostic logic so that the service is not designed to retain state information for any specific parent business process. • Less constrained service contracts so as to allow for the receipt and transmission of a wider range of state data at runtime. • Increased amounts of interpretative programming routines capable of parsing a range of state information delivered by messages and responding to a range of corresponding action requests.
Implementation Requirements	Although state deferral can reduce the overall consumption of memory and system resources, services designed with statelessness considerations can also introduce some performance demands associated with the runtime retrieval and interpretation of deferred state data. Here is a short checklist of common requirements that can be used to assess the support of stateless service designs by vendor technologies and target deployment locations: • The runtime environment should allow for a service to transition from an idle state to an active processing state in a highly efficient manner.

- Enterprise-level or high-performance XML parsers and hardware accelerators (and SOAP processors) should be provided to allow services implemented as Web services to more efficiently parse larger message payloads with less performance constraints.

- The use of attachments may need to be supported by Web services to allow for messages to include bodies of payload data that do not undergo interface-level validation or translation to local formats.

The nature of the implementation support required by the average stateless service in an environment will depend on the state deferral approach used within the service-oriented architecture.

Table C.6
A profile for the Service Statelessness principle.

Service Discoverability	
Short Definition	*"Services are discoverable."*
Long Definition	*"Services are supplemented with communicative meta data by which they can be effectively discovered and interpreted."*
Goals	• Services are positioned as highly discoverable resources within the enterprise. • The purpose and capabilities of each service are clearly expressed so that they can be interpreted by humans and software programs. Achieving these goals requires foresight and a solid understanding of the nature of the service itself. Depending on the type of service model being designed, realizing this principle may require both business and technical expertise.
Design Characteristics	• Service contracts are equipped with appropriate meta data that will be correctly referenced when discovery queries are issued. • Service contracts are further outfitted with additional meta information that clearly communicates their purpose and capabilities to humans. • If a service registry exists, registry records are populated with the same attention to meta information as just described. • If a service registry does not exist, service profile documents are authored to supplement the service contract and to form the basis for future registry records. (See Chapter 15 in *SOA Principles of Service Design* for more details about service profiles.)

Implementation Requirements	<ul><li>The existence of design standards that govern the meta information used to make service contracts discoverable and interpretable, as well as guidelines for how and when service contracts should be further supplemented with annotations.</li><li>The existence of design standards that establish a consistent means of recording service meta information outside of the contract. This information is either collected in a supplemental document in preparation for a service registry, or it is placed in the registry itself.</li></ul> You may have noticed the absence of a service registry on the list of implementation requirements. As previously established, the goal of this principle is to implement design characteristics within the service, not within the architecture.

Table C.7
A profile for the Service Discoverability principle.

Service Composability	
Short Definition	*"Services are composable."*
Long Definition	*"Services are effective composition participants, regardless of the size and complexity of the composition."*
Goals	When discussing the goals of Service Composability, pretty much all of the goals of Service Reusability (479) apply. This is because service composition often turns out to be a form of service reuse. In fact, you may recall that one of the objectives we listed for the Service Reusability (479) principle was to enable wide-scale service composition.
	However, above and beyond simply attaining reuse, service composition provides the medium through which we can achieve what is often classified as the ultimate goal of service-oriented computing. By establishing an enterprise comprised of solution logic represented by an inventory of highly reusable services, we provide the means for a large extent of future business automation requirements to be fulfilled through... you guessed it: service composition.
Design Characteristics for Composition Member Capabilities	Ideally, every service capability (especially those providing reusable logic) is considered a potential composition member. This essentially means that the design characteristics already established by the Service Reusability (479) principle are equally relevant to building effective composition members.
	Additionally, there are two further characteristics emphasized by this principle:
	• The service needs to possess a highly efficient execution environment. More so than being able to manage concurrency, the efficiency with which composition members perform their individual processing should be highly tuned.
	• The service contract needs to be flexible so that it can facilitate different types of data exchange requirements for similar functions. This typically relates to the ability of the contract to exchange the same type of data at different levels of granularity.

	The manner in which these qualities go beyond mere reuse has to do primarily with the service being capable of optimizing its runtime processing responsibilities in support of multiple, simultaneous compositions.
Design Characteristics for Composition Controller Capabilities	Composition members will often also need to act as controllers or sub-controllers within different composition configurations. However, services designed as designated controllers are generally alleviated from many of the high-performance demands placed on composition members.
	These types of services therefore have their own set of design characteristics:
	• The logic encapsulated by a designated controller will almost always be limited to a single business task. Typically, the task service model is used, resulting in the common characteristics of that model being applied to this type of service.
	• While designated controllers may be reusable, service reuse is not usually a primary design consideration. Therefore, the design characteristics fostered by Service Reusability (479) are considered and applied where appropriate, but with less of the usual rigor applied to agnostic services.
	• Statelessness is not always as strictly emphasized on designated controllers as with composition members. Depending on the state deferral options available by the surrounding architecture, designated controllers may sometimes need to be designed to remain fully stateful while the underlying composition members carry out their respective parts of the overall task.
	Of course, any capability acting as a controller can become a member of a larger composition, which brings the previously listed composition member design characteristics into account as well.

Table C.8

A profile for the Service Composability principle.

Appendix D

SOA Design Patterns Reference

This appendix provides profile tables for all 85 patterns that are documented in *SOA Design Patterns*, a title that is part of this book series. Each pattern that is referenced in this book is suffixed with the page number of its corresponding profile table in this appendix.

Every profile table contains the following sections:

- *Requirement* – A requirement is a concise, single-sentence statement that presents the fundamental requirement addressed by the pattern in the form of a question. Every pattern description begins with this statement.

- *Icon* – Each pattern description is accompanied by an icon image that acts as a visual identifier. The icons are displayed together with the requirement statements in each pattern profile as well as on the inside book cover.

- *Problem* – The issue causing a problem and the effects of the problem. It is this problem for which the pattern is expected to provide a solution.

- *Solution* – This represents the design solution proposed by the pattern to solve the problem and fulfill the requirement.

- *Application* – This part is dedicated to describing how the pattern can be applied. It can include guidelines, implementation details, and sometimes even a suggested process.

- *Impacts* – This section highlights common consequences, costs, and requirements associated with the application of a pattern and may also provide alternatives that can be considered.

- *Principles* – References to related service-orientation principles.

- *Architecture* – References to related SOA architecture types (as described in Chapter 3).

Note that these tables provide only summarized content from the original publication. All pattern profile tables in this book are also published online at SOAPatterns.org.

Agnostic Capability

How can multi-purpose service logic be made effectively consumable and composable?

Problem	Service capabilities derived from specific concerns may not be useful to multiple service consumers, thereby reducing the reusability potential of the agnostic service.
Solution	Agnostic service logic is partitioned into a set of well-defined capabilities that address common concerns not specific to any one problem. Through subsequent analysis, the agnostic context of capabilities is further refined.
Application	Service capabilities are defined and iteratively refined through proven analysis and modeling processes.
Impacts	The definition of each service capability requires extra up-front analysis and design effort.
Principles	Standardized Service Contract (475), Service Reusability (479), Service Composability (486)
Architecture	Service

Agnostic Context

How can multi-purpose service logic be positioned as an effective enterprise resource?

Problem	Multi-purpose logic grouped together with single purpose logic results in programs with little or no reuse potential that introduce waste and redundancy into an enterprise.
Solution	Isolate logic that is not specific to one purpose into separate services with distinct agnostic contexts.
Application	Agnostic service contexts are defined by carrying out service-oriented analysis and service modeling processes.
Impacts	This pattern positions reusable solution logic at an enterprise level, potentially bringing with it increased design complexity and enterprise governance issues.
Principles	Service Reusability (479)
Architecture	Service

Agnostic Sub-Controller

How can agnostic, cross-entity composition logic be separated, reused, and governed independently?

Problem	Service compositions are generally configured specific to a parent task, inhibiting reuse potential that may exist within a subset of the composition logic.
Solution	Reusable, cross-entity composition logic is abstracted or made accessible via an agnostic sub-controller capability, allowing that subset of the parent composition logic to be recomposed independently.
Application	A new agnostic service is created or a task service is appended with an agnostic sub-controller capability.
Impacts	The addition of a cross-entity, agnostic service can increase the size and complexity of compositions and the abstraction of agnostic cross-entity logic can violate modeling and design standards established by Service Layers [561].
Principles	Service Reusability (479), Service Composability (486)
Architecture	Composition, Service

Asynchronous Queuing
By Mark Little, Thomas Rischbeck, Arnaud Simon

How can a service and its consumers accommodate isolated failures and avoid unnecessarily locking resources?

Problem	When a service capability requires that consumers interact with it synchronously, it can inhibit performance and compromise reliability.
Solution	A service can exchange messages with its consumers via an intermediary buffer, allowing service and consumers to process messages independently by remaining temporally decoupled.
Application	Queuing technology needs to be incorporated into the surrounding architecture, and back-up stores may also be required.
Impacts	There may be no acknowledgement of successful message delivery, and atomic transactions may not be possible.
Principles	Standardized Service Contract (475), Service Loose Coupling (477), Service Statelessness (482)
Architecture	Inventory, Composition

Atomic Service Transaction

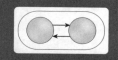

How can a transaction with rollback capability be propagated across messaging-based services?

Problem	When runtime activities that span multiple services fail, the parent business task is incomplete and actions performed and changes made up to that point may compromise the integrity of the underlying solution and architecture.
Solution	Runtime service activities can be wrapped in a transaction with rollback feature that resets all actions and changes if the parent business task cannot be successfully completed.
Application	A transaction management system is made part of the inventory architecture and then used by those service compositions that require rollback features.
Impacts	Transacted service activities can consume more memory because of the requirement for each service to preserve its original state until it is notified to rollback or commit its changes.
Principles	Service Statelessness (482)
Architecture	Inventory, Composition

Brokered Authentication

By Jason Hogg, Don Smith, Fred Chong, Tom Hollander, Wojtek Kozaczynski, Larry Brader, Nelly Delgado, Dwayne Taylor, Lonnie Wall, Paul Slater, Sajjad Nasir Imran, Pablo Cibraro, Ward Cunningham

How can a service efficiently verify consumer credentials if the consumer and service do not trust each other or if the consumer requires access to multiple services?

Problem	Requiring the use of Direct Authentication [518] can be impractical or even impossible when consumers and services do not trust each other or when consumers are required to access multiple services as part of the same runtime activity.
Solution	An authentication broker with a centralized identity store assumes the responsibility for authenticating the consumer and issuing a token that the consumer can use to access the service.
Application	An authentication broker product introduced into the inventory architecture carries out the intermediary authentication and issuance of temporary credentials using technologies such as X.509 certificates or Kerberos, SAML, or SecPAL tokens.
Impacts	This pattern can establish a potential single point of failure and a central breach point that, if compromised, could jeopardize an entire service inventory.
Principles	Service Composability (486)
Architecture	Inventory, Composition, Service

Canonical Expression

How can service contracts be consistently understood and interpreted?

Problem	Service contracts may express similar capabilities in different ways, leading to inconsistency and risking misinterpretation.
Solution	Service contracts are standardized using naming conventions.
Application	Naming conventions are applied to service contracts as part of formal analysis and design processes.
Impacts	The use of global naming conventions introduces enterprise-wide standards that need to be consistently used and enforced.
Principles	Standardized Service Contract (475), Service Discoverability (484)
Architecture	Enterprise, Inventory, Service

Canonical Protocol

How can services be designed to avoid protocol bridging?

Problem	Services that support different communication technologies compromise interoperability, limit the quantity of potential consumers, and introduce the need for undesirable protocol bridging measures.
Solution	The architecture establishes a single communications technology as the sole or primary medium by which services can interact.
Application	The communication protocols (including protocol versions) used within a service inventory boundary are standardized for all services.
Impacts	An inventory architecture in which communication protocols are standardized is subject to any limitations imposed by the communications technology.
Principles	Standardized Service Contract (475)
Architecture	Inventory, Service

Canonical Resources

How can unnecessary infrastructure resource disparity be avoided?

Problem	Service implementations can unnecessarily introduce disparate infrastructure resources, thereby bloating the enterprise and resulting in increased governance burden.
Solution	The supporting infrastructure and architecture can be equipped with common resources and extensions that can be repeatedly utilized by different services.
Application	Enterprise design standards are defined to formalize the required use of standardized architectural resources.
Impacts	If this pattern leads to too much dependency on shared infrastructure resources, it can decrease the autonomy and mobility of services.
Principles	Service Autonomy (481)
Architecture	Enterprise, Inventory

Canonical Schema

How can services be designed to avoid data model transformation?

Problem	Services with disparate models for similar data impose transformation requirements that increase development effort, design complexity, and runtime performance overhead.
Solution	Data models for common information sets are standardized across service contracts within an inventory boundary.
Application	Design standards are applied to schemas used by service contracts as part of a formal design process.
Impacts	Maintaining the standardization of contract schemas can introduce significant governance effort and cultural challenges.
Principles	Standardized Service Contract (475)
Architecture	Inventory, Service

Canonical Schema Bus

By Clemens Utschig-Utschig, Berthold Maier, Bernd Trops, Hajo Normann, Torsten Winterberg, Thomas Erl

While Enterprise Service Bus [523] provides a range of messaging-centric functions that help establish connectivity between different services and between services and resources they are required to encapsulate, it does not inherently enforce or advocate standardization.

Building upon the platform established by Enterprise Service Bus [523], this pattern positions entry points into the logic, data, and functions offered via the service bus environment as independently standardized service contracts.

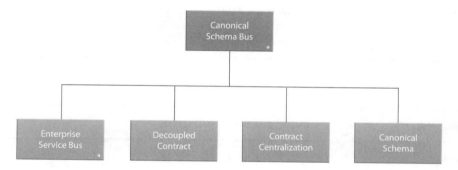

Canonical Schema Bus is comprised of the co-existent application of Enterprise Service Bus [523], Decoupled Contract [517], Contract Centralization [509], and Canonical Schema [500].

Canonical Versioning

How can service contracts within the same service inventory be versioned with minimal impact?

$$v1 = v2$$

Problem	Service contracts within the same service inventory that are versioned differently will cause numerous interoperability and governance problems.
Solution	Service contract versioning rules and the expression of version information are standardized within a service inventory boundary.
Application	Governance and design standards are required to ensure consistent versioning of service contracts within the inventory boundary.
Impacts	The creation and enforcement of the required versioning standards introduce new governance demands.
Principles	Standardized Service Contract (475)
Architecture	Service, Inventory

Capability Composition

How can a service capability solve a problem that requires logic outside of the service boundary?

Problem	A capability may not be able to fulfill its processing requirements without adding logic that resides outside of its service's functional context, thereby compromising the integrity of the service context and risking service denormalization.
Solution	When requiring access to logic that falls outside of a service's boundary, capability logic within the service is designed to compose one or more capabilities in other services.
Application	The functionality encapsulated by a capability includes logic that can invoke other capabilities from other services.
Impacts	Carrying out composition logic requires external invocation, which adds performance overhead and decreases service autonomy.
Principles	All
Architecture	Inventory, Composition, Service

Capability Recomposition

How can the same capability be used to help solve multiple problems?

Problem	Using agnostic service logic to only solve a single problem is wasteful and does not leverage the logic's reuse potential.
Solution	Agnostic service capabilities can be designed to be repeatedly invoked in support of multiple compositions that solve multiple problems.
Application	Effective recomposition requires the coordinated, successful, and repeated application of several additional patterns.
Impacts	Repeated service composition demands existing and persistent standardization and governance.
Principles	All
Architecture	Inventory, Composition, Service

Compatible Change
By David Orchard, Chris Riley

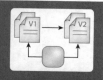

How can a service contract be modified without impacting consumers?

Problem	Changing an already-published service contract can impact and invalidate existing consumer programs.
Solution	Some changes to the service contract can be backwards-compatible, thereby avoiding negative consumer impacts.
Application	Service contract changes can be accommodated via extension or by the loosening of existing constraints or by applying Concurrent Contracts [508].
Impacts	Compatible changes still introduce versioning governance effort, and the technique of loosening constraints can lead to vague contract designs.
Principles	Standardized Service Contract (475), Service Loose Coupling (477)
Architecture	Service

Compensating Service Transaction

By Clemens Utschig-Utschig, Berthold Maier, Bernd Trops, Hajo Normann, Torsten Winterberg, Brian Loesgen, Mark Little

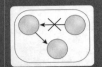

How can composition runtime exceptions be consistently accommodated without requiring services to lock resources?

Problem	Whereas uncontrolled runtime exceptions can jeopardize a service composition, wrapping the composition in an atomic transaction can tie up too many resources, thereby negatively affecting performance and scalability.
Solution	Compensating routines are introduced, allowing runtime exceptions to be resolved with the opportunity for reduced resource locking and memory consumption.
Application	Compensation logic is pre-defined and implemented as part of the parent composition controller logic or via individual "undo" service capabilities.
Impacts	Unlike atomic transactions that are governed by specific rules, the use of compensation logic is open-ended and can vary in its actual effectiveness.
Principles	Service Loose Coupling (477)
Architecture	Inventory, Composition

Composition Autonomy

How can compositions be implemented to minimize loss of autonomy?

Problem	Composition controller services naturally lose autonomy when delegating processing tasks to composed services, some of which may be shared across multiple compositions.
Solution	All composition participants can be isolated to maximize the autonomy of the composition as a whole.
Application	The agnostic member services of a composition are redundantly implemented in an isolated environment together with the task service.
Impacts	Increasing autonomy on a composition level results in increased infrastructure costs and government responsibilities.
Principles	Service Autonomy (481), Service Reusability (479), Service Composability (486)
Architecture	Composition

Concurrent Contracts

How can a service facilitate multi-consumer coupling requirements and abstraction concerns at the same time?

Problem	A service's contract may not be suitable for or applicable to all potential service consumers.
Solution	Multiple contracts can be created for a single service, each targeted at a specific type of consumer.
Application	This pattern is ideally applied together with Service Façade [558] to support new contracts as required.
Impacts	Each new contract can effectively add a new service endpoint to an inventory, thereby increasing corresponding governance effort.
Principles	Standardized Service Contract (475), Service Loose Coupling (477), Service Reusability (479)
Architecture	Service

Contract Centralization

How can direct consumer-to-implementation coupling be avoided?

Problem	Consumer programs can be designed to access underlying service resources using different entry points, resulting in different forms of implementation dependencies that inhibit the service from evolving in response to change.
Solution	Access to service logic is limited to the service contract, forcing consumers to avoid implementation coupling.
Application	This pattern is realized through formal enterprise design standards and the targeted application of the Service Abstraction (478) design principle.
Impacts	Forcing consumer programs to access service capabilities and resources via a central contract can impose performance overhead and requires on-going standardization effort.
Principles	Standardized Service Contract (475), Service Loose Coupling (477), Service Abstraction (478)
Architecture	Composition, Service

Contract Denormalization

How can a service contract facilitate consumer programs with differing data exchange requirements?

Problem	Services with strictly normalized contracts can impose unnecessary functional and performance demands on some consumer programs.
Solution	Service contracts can include a measured extent of denormalization, allowing multiple capabilities to redundantly express core functions in different ways for different types of consumer programs.
Application	The service contract is carefully extended with additional capabilities that provide functional variations of a primary capability.
Impacts	Overuse of this pattern on the same contract can dramatically increase its size, making it difficult to interpret and unwieldy to govern.
Principles	Standardized Service Contract (475), Service Loose Coupling (477)
Architecture	Service

Cross-Domain Utility Layer

How can redundant utility logic be avoided across domain service inventories?

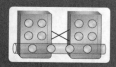

Problem	While domain service inventories may be required for independent business governance, they can impose unnecessary redundancy within utility service layers.
Solution	A common utility service layer can be established, spanning two or more domain service inventories.
Application	A common set of utility services needs to be defined and standardized in coordination with service inventory owners.
Impacts	Increased effort is required to coordinate and govern a cross-inventory utility service layer.
Principles	Service Reusability (479), Service Composability (486)
Architecture	Enterprise, Inventory

Data Confidentiality

By Jason Hogg, Don Smith, Fred Chong, Tom Hollander, Wojtek Kozaczynski,
Larry Brader, Nelly Delgado, Dwayne Taylor, Lonnie Wall, Paul Slater,
Sajjad Nasir Imran, Pablo Cibraro, Ward Cunningham

How can data within a message be protected so that it is not disclosed to unintended recipients while in transit?

Problem	Within service compositions, data is often required to pass through one or more intermediaries. Point-to-point security protocols, such as those frequently used at the transport-layer, may allow messages containing sensitive information to be intercepted and viewed by such intermediaries.
Solution	The message contents are encrypted independently from the transport, ensuring that only intended recipients can access the protected data.
Application	A symmetric or asymmetric encryption and decryption algorithm, such as those specified in the XML-Encryption standard, is applied at the message level.
Impacts	This pattern may add runtime performance overhead associated with the required encryption and decryption of message data. The management of keys can further add to governance burden.
Principles	Service Composability (486)
Architecture	Inventory, Composition, Service

Data Format Transformation
By Mark Little, Thomas Rischbeck, Arnaud Simon

How can services interact with programs that communicate with different data formats?

Problem	A service may be incompatible with resources it needs to access due to data format disparity. Furthermore, a service consumer that communicates using a data format different from a target service will be incompatible and therefore unable to invoke the service.
Solution	Intermediary data format transformation logic needs to be introduced in order to dynamically translate one data format into another.
Application	This necessary transformation logic is incorporated by adding internal service logic, service agents, or a dedicated transformation service.
Impacts	The use of data format transformation logic inevitably adds development effort, design complexity, and performance overhead.
Principles	Standardized Service Contract (475), Service Loose Coupling (477)
Architecture	Inventory, Composition, Service

Data Model Transformation

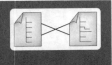

How can services interoperate when using different data models for the same type of data?

Problem	Services may use incompatible schemas to represent the same data, hindering service interaction and composition.
Solution	A data transformation technology can be incorporated to convert data between disparate schema structures.
Application	Mapping logic needs to be developed and deployed so that data compliant to one data model can be dynamically converted to comply to a different data model.
Impacts	Data model transformation introduces development effort, design complexity, and runtime performance overhead, and overuse of this pattern can seriously inhibit service recomposition potential.
Principles	Standardized Service Contract (475), Service Reusability (479), Service Composability (486)
Architecture	Inventory, Composition

Data Origin Authentication

By Jason Hogg, Don Smith, Fred Chong, Tom Hollander, Wojtek
Kozaczynski, Larry Brader, Nelly Delgado, Dwayne Taylor, Lonnie Wall,
Paul Slater, Sajjad Nasir Imran, Pablo Cibraro, Ward Cunningham

*How can a service verify that a message originates from a known
sender and that the message has not been tampered with in transit?*

Problem	The intermediary processing layers generally required by service compositions can expose sensitive data when security is limited to point-to-point protocols, such as those used with transport-layer security.
Solution	A message can be digitally signed so that the recipient services can verify that it originated from the expected consumer and that it has not been tampered with during transit.
Application	A digital signature algorithm is applied to the message to provide "proof of origin," allowing sensitive message contents to be protected from tampering. This technology must be supported by both consumer and service.
Impacts	Use of cryptographic techniques can add to performance requirements and the choice of digital signing algorithm can affect the level of security actually achieved.
Principles	Service Composability (486)
Architecture	Composition

Decomposed Capability

How can a service be designed to minimize the chances of capability logic deconstruction?

Problem	The decomposition of a service subsequent to its implementation can require the deconstruction of logic within capabilities, which can be disruptive and make the preservation of a service contract problematic.
Solution	Services prone to future decomposition can be equipped with a series of granular capabilities that more easily facilitate decomposition.
Application	Additional service modeling is carried out to define granular, more easily distributed capabilities.
Impacts	Until the service is eventually decomposed, it may be represented by a bloated contract that stays with it as long as proxy capabilities are supported.
Principles	Standardized Service Contract (475), Service Abstraction (478)
Architecture	Service

Decoupled Contract

How can a service express its capabilities independently of its implementation?

Problem	For a service to be positioned as an effective enterprise resource, it must be equipped with a technical contract that exists independently from its implementation yet still in alignment with other services.
Solution	The service contract is physically decoupled from its implementation.
Application	A service's technical interface is physically separated and subject to relevant service-orientation design principles.
Impacts	Service functionality is limited to the feature-set of the decoupled contract medium.
Principles	Standardized Service Contract (475), Service Loose Coupling (477)
Architecture	Service

Direct Authentication

By Jason Hogg, Don Smith, Fred Chong, Tom Hollander, Wojtek Kozaczynski,
Larry Brader, Nelly Delgado, Dwayne Taylor, Lonnie Wall, Paul Slater,
Sajjad Nasir Imran, Pablo Cibraro, Ward Cunningham

How can a service verify the credentials provided by a consumer?

Problem	Some of the capabilities offered by a service may be intended for specific groups of consumers or may involve the transmission of sensitive data. Attackers that access this data could use it to compromise the service or the IT enterprise itself.
Solution	Service capabilities require that consumers provide credentials that can be authenticated against an identity store.
Application	The service implementation is provided access to an identity store, allowing it to authenticate the consumer directly.
Impacts	Consumers must provide credentials compatible with the service's authentication logic. This pattern may lead to multiple identity stores, resulting in extra governance burden.
Principles	Service Composability (486)
Architecture	Composition, Service

Distributed Capability

How can a service preserve its functional context while also fulfilling special capability processing requirements?

Problem	A capability that belongs within a service may have unique processing requirements that cannot be accommodated by the default service implementation, but separating capability logic from the service will compromise the integrity of the service context.
Solution	The underlying service logic is distributed, thereby allowing the implementation logic for a capability with unique processing requirements to be physically separated, while continuing to be represented by the same service contract.
Application	The logic is moved and intermediary processing is added to act as a liaison between the moved logic and the main service logic.
Impacts	The distribution of a capability's logic leads to performance overhead associated with remote communication and the need for new intermediate processing.
Principles	Standardized Service Contract (475), Service Autonomy (481)
Architecture	Service

Domain Inventory

How can services be delivered to maximize recomposition when enterprise-wide standardization is not possible?

Problem	Establishing an single enterprise service inventory may be unmanageable for some enterprises, and attempts to do so may jeopardize the success of an SOA adoption as a whole.
Solution	Services can be grouped into manageable, domain-specific service inventories, each of which can be independently standardized, governed, and owned.
Application	Inventory domain boundaries need to be carefully established.
Impacts	Standardization disparity between domain service inventories imposes transformation requirements and reduces the overall benefit potential of the SOA adoption.
Principles	Standardized Service Contract (475), Service Abstraction (478), Service Composability (486)
Architecture	Enterprise, Inventory

Dual Protocols

How can a service inventory overcome the limitations of its canonical protocol while still remaining standardized?

Problem	Canonical Protocol [498] requires that all services conform to the use of the same communications technology; however, a single protocol may not be able to accommodate all service requirements, thereby introducing limitations.
Solution	The service inventory architecture is designed to support services based on primary and secondary protocols.
Application	Primary and secondary service levels are created and collectively represent the service endpoint layer. All services are subject to standard service-orientation design considerations and specific guidelines are followed to minimize the impact of not following Canonical Protocol [498].
Impacts	This pattern can lead to a convoluted inventory architecture, increased governance effort and expense, and (when poorly applied) an unhealthy dependence on Protocol Bridging [546]. Because the endpoint layer is semi-federated, the quantity of potential consumers and reuse opportunities is decreased.
Principles	Standardized Service Contract (475), Service Loose Coupling (477), Service Abstraction (478), Service Autonomy (481), Service Composability (486)
Architecture	Inventory, Service

Enterprise Inventory

How can services be delivered to maximize recomposition?

Problem	Delivering services independently via different project teams across an enterprise establishes a constant risk of producing inconsistent service and architecture implementations, compromising recomposition opportunities.
Solution	Services for multiple solutions can be designed for delivery within a standardized, enterprise-wide inventory architecture wherein they can be freely and repeatedly recomposed.
Application	The enterprise service inventory is ideally modeled in advance, and enterprise-wide standards are applied to services delivered by different project teams.
Impacts	Significant upfront analysis is required to define an enterprise inventory blueprint and numerous organizational impacts result from the subsequent governance requirements.
Principles	Standardized Service Contract (475), Service Abstraction (478), Service Composability (486)
Architecture	Enterprise, Inventory

Enterprise Service Bus
By Thomas Erl, Mark Little, Thomas Rischbeck, Arnaud Simon

An enterprise service bus represents an environment designed to foster sophisticated interconnectivity between services. It establishes an intermediate layer of processing that can help overcome common problems associated with reliability, scalability, and communications disparity.

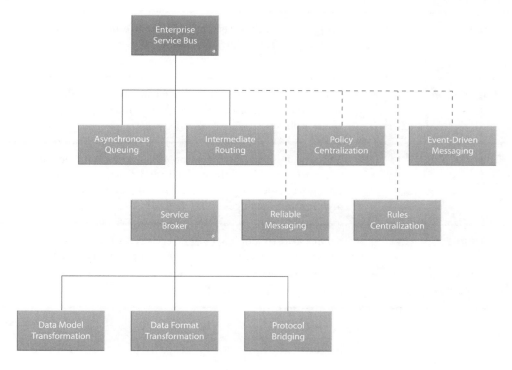

Enterprise Service Bus is fundamentally comprised of the co-existent application of Asynchronous Queuing [494], Intermediate Routing [530], and Service Broker [553], and can be further extended via Reliable Messaging [549], Policy Centralization [543], Rules Centralization [550], and Event-Driven Messaging [525].

Entity Abstraction

How can agnostic business logic be separated, reused, and governed independently?

Problem	Bundling both process-agnostic and process-specific business logic into the same service eventually results in the creation of redundant agnostic business logic across multiple services.
Solution	An agnostic business service layer can be established, dedicated to services that base their functional context on existing business entities.
Application	Entity service contexts are derived from business entity models and then establish a logical layer that is modeled during the analysis phase.
Impacts	The core, business-centric nature of the services introduced by this pattern require extra modeling and design attention and their governance requirements can impose dramatic organizational changes.
Principles	Service Loose Coupling (477), Service Abstraction (478), Service Reusability (479), Service Composability (486)
Architecture	Inventory, Composition, Service

Event-Driven Messaging

By Mark Little, Thomas Rischbeck, Arnaud Simon

How can service consumers be automatically notified of runtime service events?

Problem	Events that occur within the functional boundary encapsulated by a service may be of relevance to service consumers, but without resorting to inefficient polling-based interaction, the consumer has no way of learning about these events.
Solution	The consumer establishes itself as a subscriber of the service. The service, in turn, automatically issues notifications of relevant events to this and any of its subscribers.
Application	A messaging framework is implemented capable of supporting the publish-and-subscribe MEP and associated complex event processing and tracking.
Impacts	Event-driven message exchanges cannot easily be incorporated as part of Atomic Service Transaction [495], and publisher/subscriber availability issues can arise.
Principles	Standardized Service Contract (475), Service Loose Coupling (477), Service Autonomy (481)
Architecture	Inventory, Composition

Exception Shielding

By Jason Hogg, Don Smith, Fred Chong, Tom Hollander, Wojtek
Kozaczynski, Larry Brader, Nelly Delgado, Dwayne Taylor, Lonnie Wall,
Paul Slater, Sajjad Nasir Imran, Pablo Cibraro, Ward Cunningham

*How can a service prevent the disclosure of information about its internal
implementation when an exception occurs?*

Problem	Unfiltered exception data output by a service may contain internal implementation details that can compromise the security of the service and its surrounding environment.
Solution	Potentially unsafe exception data is "sanitized" by replacing it with exception data that is safe by design before it is made available to consumers.
Application	This pattern can be applied at design time by reviewing and altering source code or at runtime by adding dynamic sanitization routines.
Impacts	Sanitized exception information can make the tracking of errors more difficult due to the lack of detail provided to consumers.
Principles	Service Abstraction (478)
Architecture	Service

Federated Endpoint Layer

Federation is an important concept in service-oriented computing. It represents the desired state of the external, consumer-facing perspective of a service inventory, as expressed by the collective contracts of all the inventory's services.

The more federated and unified this collection of contracts (endpoints) is, the more easily and effectively the services can be repeatedly consumed and leveraged.

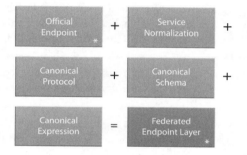

The joint application of Official Endpoint [539], Service Normalization [563], Canonical Protocol [498], Canonical Schema [500], and Canonical Expression [497] results in Federated Endpoint Layer.

File Gateway
By Satadru Roy

How can service logic interact with legacy systems that can only share information by exchanging files?

Problem	Data records contained in flat files produced by a legacy system need to be processed individually by service logic, but legacy systems are not capable of directly invoking services. Conversely, service logic may need to produce information for the legacy system, but building file creation and transfer functionality into the service can result in an inflexible design.
Solution	Intermediary two-way file processing logic is positioned between the legacy system and the service.
Application	For inbound data the file gateway processing logic can detect file drops and leverage available broker features to perform Data Model Transformation [514] and Data Format Transformation [513]. On the outbound side, this logic intercepts information produced by services and packages them (with possible transformation) into new or existing files for consumption by the legacy system.
Impacts	The type of logic provided by this pattern is unsuitable when immediate replies are required by either service or legacy system. Deployment and governance of two-way file processing logic can further add to operational complexity and may require specialized administration skills.
Principles	Service Loose Coupling (477)
Architecture	Service

Functional Decomposition

How can a large business problem be solved without having to build a standalone body of solution logic?

Problem	To solve a large, complex business problem a corresponding amount of solution logic needs to be created, resulting in a self-contained application with traditional governance and reusability constraints.
Solution	The large business problem can be broken down into a set of smaller, related problems, allowing the required solution logic to also be decomposed into a corresponding set of smaller, related solution logic units.
Application	Depending on the nature of the large problem, a service-oriented analysis process can be created to cleanly deconstruct it into smaller problems.
Impacts	The ownership of multiple smaller programs can result in increased design complexity and governance challenges.
Principles	n/a
Architecture	Service

Intermediate Routing

By Mark Little, Thomas Rischbeck, Arnaud Simon

How can dynamic runtime factors affect the path of a message?

Problem	The larger and more complex a service composition is, the more difficult it is to anticipate and design for all possible runtime scenarios in advance, especially with asynchronous, messaging-based communication.
Solution	Message paths can be dynamically determined through the use of intermediary routing logic.
Application	Various types of intermediary routing logic can be incorporated to create message paths based on message content or runtime factors.
Impacts	Dynamically determining a message path adds layers of processing logic and correspondingly can increase performance overhead. Also the use of multiple routing logic can result in overly complex service activities.
Principles	Service Loose Coupling (477), Service Reusability (479), Service Composability (486)
Architecture	Composition

Inventory Endpoint

How can a service inventory be shielded from external access while still offering service capabilities to external consumers?

Problem	A group of services delivered for a specific inventory may provide capabilities that are useful to services outside of that inventory. However, for security and governance reasons, it may not be desirable to expose all services or all service capabilities to external consumers.
Solution	Abstract the relevant capabilities into an endpoint service that acts as a the official inventory entry point dedicated to a specific set of external consumers.
Application	The endpoint service can expose a contract with the same capabilities as its underlying services, but augmented with policies or other characteristics to accommodate external consumer interaction requirements.
Impacts	Endpoint services can increase the governance freedom of underlying services but can also increase governance effort by introducing redundant service logic and contracts into an inventory.
Principles	Standardized Service Contract (475), Service Loose Coupling (477), Service Abstraction (478)
Architecture	Inventory

Legacy Wrapper
By Thomas Erl, Satadru Roy

How can wrapper services with non-standard contracts be prevented from spreading indirect consumer-to-implementation coupling?

Problem	Wrapper services required to encapsulate legacy logic are often forced to introduce a non-standard service contract with high technology coupling requirements, resulting in a proliferation of implementation coupling throughout all service consumer programs.
Solution	The non-standard wrapper service can be replaced by or further wrapped with a standardized service contract that extracts, encapsulates, and possibly eliminates legacy technical details from the contract.
Application	A custom service contract and required service logic need to be developed to represent the proprietary legacy interface.
Impacts	The introduction of an additional service adds a layer of processing and associated performance overhead.
Principles	Standardized Service Contract (475), Service Loose Coupling (477), Service Abstraction (478)
Architecture	Service

533 の Logic Centralization

Logic Centralization

How can the misuse of redundant service logic be avoided?

Problem	If agnostic services are not consistently reused, redundant functionality can be delivered in other services, resulting in problems associated with inventory denormalization and service ownership and governance.
Solution	Access to reusable functionality is limited to official agnostic services.
Application	Agnostic services need to be properly designed and governed, and their use must be enforced via enterprise standards.
Impacts	Organizational issues reminiscent of past reuse projects can raise obstacles to applying this pattern.
Principles	Service Reusability (479), Service Composability (486)
Architecture	Inventory, Composition, Service

Message Screening

By Jason Hogg, Don Smith, Fred Chong, Tom Hollander, Wojtek
Kozaczynski, Larry Brader, Nelly Delgado, Dwayne Taylor, Lonnie Wall,
Paul Slater, Sajjad Nasir Imran, Pablo Cibraro, Ward Cunningham

How can a service be protected from malformed or malicious input?

Problem	An attacker can transmit messages with malicious or malformed content to a service, resulting in undesirable behavior.
Solution	The service is equipped or supplemented with special screening routines that assume that all input data is harmful until proven otherwise.
Application	When a service receives a message, it makes a number of checks to screen message content for harmful data.
Impacts	Extra runtime processing is required with each message exchange, and the screening logic requires additional, specialized routines to process binary message content, such as attachments. It may also not be possible to check for all possible forms of harmful content.
Principles	Standardized Service Contract (475)
Architecture	Service

Messaging Metadata

How can services be designed to process activity-specific data at runtime?

Problem	Because messaging does not rely on a persistent connection between service and consumer, it is challenging for a service to gain access to the state data associated with an overall runtime activity.
Solution	Message contents can be supplemented with activity-specific metadata that can be interpreted and processed separately at runtime.
Application	This pattern requires a messaging framework that supports message headers or properties.
Impacts	The interpretation and processing of messaging metadata adds to runtime performance overhead and increases service activity design complexity.
Principles	Service Loose Coupling (477), Service Statelessness (482)
Architecture	Composition

Metadata Centralization

How can service metadata be centrally published and governed?

Problem	Project teams, especially in larger enterprises, run the constant risk of building functionality that already exists or is already in development, resulting in wasted effort, service logic redundancy, and service inventory denormalization.
Solution	Service metadata can be centrally published in a service registry so as to provide a formal means of service registration and discovery.
Application	A private service registry needs to be positioned as a central part of an inventory architecture supported by formal processes for registration and discovery.
Impacts	The service registry product needs to be adequately mature and reliable, and its required use and maintenance needs to be incorporated into all service delivery and governance processes and methodologies.
Principles	Service Discoverability (484)
Architecture	Enterprise, Inventory

Multi-Channel Endpoint

By Satadru Roy

How can legacy logic fragmented and duplicated for different delivery channels be centrally consolidated?

Problem	Legacy systems custom-built for specific delivery channels (mobile phone, desktop, kiosk, etc.) result in redundancy and application silos when multiple channels need to be supported, thereby making these systems burdensome to govern and difficult to federate.
Solution	An intermediary service is designed to encapsulate channel-specific legacy systems and expose a single standardized contract for multiple channel-specific consumers.
Application	The service established by this pattern will require significant processing and workflow logic to support multiple channels while also coordinating interaction with multiple backend legacy systems.
Impacts	The endpoint processing logic established by this pattern often introduces the need for infrastructure upgrades and orchestration-capable middleware and may turn into a performance bottleneck.
Principles	Service Loose Coupling (477), Service Reusability (479)
Architecture	Service

Non-Agnostic Context

How can single-purpose service logic be positioned as an effective enterprise resource?

Problem	Non-agnostic logic that is not service-oriented can inhibit the effectiveness of service compositions that utilize agnostic services.
Solution	Non-agnostic solution logic suitable for service encapsulation can be located within services that reside as official members of a service inventory.
Application	A single-purpose functional service context is defined.
Impacts	Although they are not expected to provide reuse potential, non-agnostic services are still subject to the rigor of service-orientation.
Principles	Standardized Service Contract (475), Service Composability (486)
Architecture	Service

Official Endpoint

As important as it is to clearly differentiate Logic Centralization [533] from Contract Centralization [509], it is equally important to understand how these two fundamental patterns can and should be used together.

Applying these two patterns to the same service realizes the Official Endpoint [539] compound pattern. The repeated application of Official Endpoint [539] supports the goal of establishing a federated layer of service endpoints, which is why this compound pattern is also a part of Federated Endpoint Layer [527].

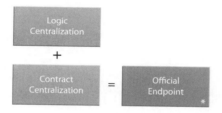

The joint application of Logic Centralization [533] and Contract Centralization [509] results in Official Endpoint.

Orchestration
By Thomas Erl, Brian Loesgen

An orchestration platform is dedicated to the effective maintenance and execution of parent business process logic. Modern-day orchestration environments are especially expected to support sophisticated and complex service composition logic that can result in long-running runtime activities.

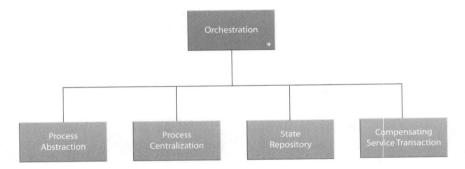

Orchestration is fundamentally comprised of the co-existent application of Process Abstraction [544], State Repository [567], Process Centralization [545], and Compensating Service Transaction [506], and can be further extended via Atomic Service Transaction [495], Rules Centralization [550], and Data Model Transformation [514].

Partial State Deferral

How can services be designed to optimize resource consumption while still remaining stateful?

Problem	Service capabilities may be required to store and manage large amounts of state data, resulting in increased memory consumption and reduced scalability.
Solution	Even when services are required to remain stateful, a subset of their state data can be temporarily deferred.
Application	Various state management deferral options exist, depending on the surrounding architecture.
Impacts	Partial state management deferral can add to design complexity and bind a service to the architecture.
Principles	Service Statelessness (482)
Architecture	Inventory, Service

Partial Validation

By David Orchard, Chris Riley

How can unnecessary data validation be avoided?

Problem	The generic capabilities provided by agnostic services sometimes result in service contracts that impose unnecessary data and validation upon consumer programs.
Solution	A consumer program can be designed to only validate the relevant subset of the data and ignore the remainder.
Application	The application of this pattern is specific to the technology used for the consumer implementation. For example, with Web services, XPath can be used to filter out unnecessary data prior to validation.
Impacts	Extra design-time effort is required and the additional runtime data filtering-related logic can reduce the processing gains of avoiding unnecessary validation.
Principles	Standardized Service Contract (475), Service Loose Coupling (477)
Architecture	Composition

Policy Centralization

How can policies be normalized and consistently enforced across multiple services?

Problem	Policies that apply to multiple services can introduce redundancy and inconsistency within service logic and contracts.
Solution	Global or domain-specific policies can be isolated and applied to multiple services.
Application	Up-front analysis effort specific to defining and establishing reusable policies is recommended, and an appropriate policy enforcement framework is required.
Impacts	Policy frameworks can introduce performance overhead and may impose dependencies on proprietary technologies. There is also the risk of conflict between centralized and service-specific policies.
Principles	Standardized Service Contracts (475), Service Loose Coupling (477), Service Abstraction (478)
Architecture	Inventory, Service

Process Abstraction

How can non-agnostic process logic be separated and governed independently?

Problem	Grouping task-centric logic together with task-agnostic logic hinders the governance of the task-specific logic and the reuse of the agnostic logic.
Solution	A dedicated parent business process service layer is established to support governance independence and the positioning of task services as potential enterprise resources.
Application	Business process logic is typically filtered out after utility and entity services have been defined, allowing for the definition of task services that comprise this layer.
Impacts	In addition to the modeling and design considerations associated with creating task services, abstracting parent business process logic establishes an inherent dependency on carrying out that logic via the composition of other services.
Principles	Service Loose Coupling (477), Service Abstraction (478), Service Composability (486)
Architecture	Inventory, Composition, Service

Process Centralization

How can abstracted business process logic be centrally governed?

Problem	When business process logic is distributed across independent service implementations, it can be problematic to extend and evolve.
Solution	Logic representing numerous business processes can be deployed and governed from a central location.
Application	Middleware platforms generally provide the necessary orchestration technologies to apply this pattern.
Impacts	Significant infrastructure and architectural changes are imposed when the required middleware is introduced.
Principles	Service Autonomy (481), Service Statelessness (482), Service Composability (486)
Architecture	Inventory, Composition

Protocol Bridging
By Mark Little, Thomas Rischbeck, Arnaud Simon

How can a service exchange data with consumers that use different communication protocols?

Problem	Services using different communication protocols or different versions of the same protocol cannot exchange data.
Solution	Bridging logic is introduced to enable communication between different communication protocols by dynamically converting one protocol to another at runtime.
Application	Instead of connecting directly to each other, consumer programs and services connect to a broker, which provides bridging logic that carries out the protocol conversion.
Impacts	Significant performance overhead can be imposed by bridging technologies, and their use can limit or eliminate the ability to incorporate reliability and transaction features.
Principles	Standardized Service Contract (475), Service Composability (486)
Architecture	Inventory, Composition

Proxy Capability

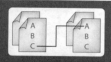

How can a service subject to decomposition continue to support consumers affected by the decomposition?

Problem	If an established service needs to be decomposed into multiple services, its contract and its existing consumers can be impacted.
Solution	The original service contract is preserved, even if underlying capability logic is separated, by turning the established capability definition into a proxy.
Application	Façade logic needs to be introduced to relay requests and responses between the proxy and newly located capabilities.
Impacts	The practical solution provided by this pattern results in a measure of service denormalization.
Principles	Service Loose Coupling (477)
Architecture	Service

Redundant Implementation

How can the reliability and availability of a service be increased?

Problem	A service that is being actively reused introduces a potential single point of failure that may jeopardize the reliability of all compositions in which it participates if an unexpected error condition occurs.
Solution	Reusable services can be deployed via redundant implementations or with failover support.
Application	The same service implementation is redundantly deployed or supported by infrastructure with redundancy features.
Impacts	Extra governance effort is required to keep all redundant implementations in synch.
Principles	Service Autonomy (481)
Architecture	Service

Reliable Messaging

By Mark Little, Thomas Rischbeck, Arnaud Simon

How can services communicate reliably when implemented in an unreliable environment?

Problem	Service communication cannot be guaranteed when using unreliable messaging protocols or when dependent on an otherwise unreliable environment.
Solution	An intermediate reliability mechanism is introduced into the inventory architecture, ensuring that message delivery is guaranteed.
Application	Middleware, service agents, and data stores are deployed to track message deliveries, manage the issuance of acknowledgements, and persist messages during failure conditions.
Impacts	Using a reliability framework adds processing overhead that can affect service activity performance. It also increases composition design complexity and may not be compatible with Atomic Service Transaction [495].
Principles	Service Composability (486)
Architecture	Inventory, Composition

Rules Centralization

How can business rules be abstracted and centrally governed?

Problem	The same business rules may apply across different business services, leading to redundancy and governance challenges.
Solution	The storage and management of business rules are positioned within a dedicated architectural extension from where they can be centrally accessed and maintained.
Application	The use of a business rules management system or engine is employed and accessed via system agents or a dedicated service.
Impacts	Services are subjected to increased performance overhead, risk, and architectural dependency.
Principles	Service Reusability (479)
Architecture	Inventory

Schema Centralization

How can service contracts be designed to avoid redundant data representation?

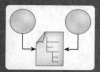

Problem	Different service contracts often need to express capabilities that process similar business documents or data sets, resulting in redundant schema content that is difficult to govern.
Solution	Select schemas that exist as physically separate parts of the service contract are shared across multiple contracts.
Application	Up-front analysis effort is required to establish a schema layer independent of and in support of the service layer.
Impacts	Governance of shared schemas becomes increasingly important as multiple services can form dependencies on the same schema definitions.
Principles	Standardized Service Contract (475), Service Loose Coupling (477)
Architecture	Inventory, Service

Service Agent

How can event-driven logic be separated and governed independently?

Problem	Service compositions can become large and inefficient, especially when required to invoke granular capabilities across multiple services.
Solution	Event-driven logic can be deferred to event-driven programs that don't require explicit invocation, thereby reducing the size and performance strain of service compositions.
Application	Service agents can be designed to automatically respond to predefined conditions without invocation via a published contract.
Impacts	The complexity of composition logic increases when it is distributed across services, and event-driven agents and reliance on service agents can further tie an inventory architecture to proprietary vendor technology.
Principles	Service Loose Coupling (477), Service Reusability (479)
Architecture	Inventory, Composition

Service Broker
By Mark Little, Thomas Rischbeck, Arnaud Simon

Although all of the Service Broker patterns are used only out of necessity, establishing an environment capable of handling the three most common transformation requirements can add a great deal of flexibility to a service-oriented architecture implementation, and also has the added bonus of being able to perform more than one transformation function at the same time.

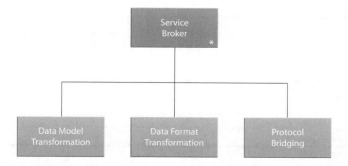

Service Broker is comprised of the co-existent application of Data Model Transformation [514], Data Format Transformation [513], and Protocol Bridging [546].

Related Patterns in Other Catalogs

Broker (Buschmann, Henney, Schmidt, Meunier, Rohnert, Sommerland, Stal)

Related Service-Oriented Computing Goals

Increased Intrinsic Interoperability, Increased Vendor Diversification Options, Reduced IT Burden

Service Callback
By Anish Karmarkar

How can a service communicate asynchronously with its consumers?

Problem	When a service needs to respond to a consumer request through the issuance of multiple messages or when service message processing requires a large amount of time, it is often not possible to communicate synchronously.
Solution	A service can require that consumers communicate with it asynchronously and provide a callback address to which the service can send response messages.
Application	A callback address generation and message correlation mechanism needs to be incorporated into the messaging framework and the overall inventory architecture.
Impacts	Asynchronous communication can introduce reliability concerns and can further require that surrounding infrastructure be upgraded to fully support the necessary callback correlation.
Principles	Standardized Service Contract (475), Service Loose Coupling (477), Service Composability (486)
Architecture	Inventory, Service, Composition

Service Data Replication

How can service autonomy be preserved when services require access to shared data sources?

Problem	Service logic can be deployed in isolation to increase service autonomy, but services continue to lose autonomy when requiring access to shared data sources.
Solution	Services can have their own dedicated databases with replication to shared data sources.
Application	An additional database needs to be provided for the service and one or more replication channels need to be enabled between it and the shared data sources.
Impacts	This pattern results in additional infrastructure cost and demands, and an excess of replication channels can be difficult to manage.
Principles	Service Autonomy (481)
Architecture	Inventory, Service

Service Decomposition

How can the granularity of a service be increased subsequent to its implementation?

Problem	Overly coarse-grained services can inhibit optimal composition design.
Solution	An already implemented coarse-grained service can be decomposed into two or more fine-grained services.
Application	The underlying service logic is restructured, and new service contracts are established. This pattern will likely require Proxy Capability [547] to preserve the integrity of the original coarse-grained service contract.
Impacts	An increase in fine-grained services naturally leads to larger, more complex service composition designs.
Principles	Service Loose Coupling (477), Service Composability (486)
Architecture	Service

Service Encapsulation

How can solution logic be made available as a resource of the enterprise?

Problem	Solution logic designed for a single application environment is typically limited in its potential to interoperate with or be leveraged by other parts of an enterprise.
Solution	Solution logic can be encapsulated by a service so that it is positioned as an enterprise resource capable of functioning beyond the boundary for which it is initially delivered.
Application	Solution logic suitable for service encapsulation needs to be identified.
Impacts	Service-encapsulated solution logic is subject to additional design and governance considerations.
Principles	n/a
Architecture	Service

Service Façade

How can a service accommodate changes to its contract or implementation while allowing the core service logic to evolve independently?

Problem	The coupling of the core service logic to contracts and implementation resources can inhibit its evolution and negatively impact service consumers.
Solution	A service façade component is used to abstract a part of the service architecture with negative coupling potential.
Application	A separate façade component is incorporated into the service design.
Impacts	The addition of the façade component introduces design effort and performance overhead.
Principles	Standardized Service Contract (475), Service Loose Coupling (477)
Architecture	Service

Service Grid
By David Chappell

How can deferred service state data be scaled and kept fault-tolerant?

Problem	State data deferred via State Repository or Stateful Services can be subject to performance bottlenecks and failure, especially when exposed to high-usage volumes.
Solution	State data is deferred to a collection of stateful system services that form a grid that provides high scalability and fault tolerance through memory replication and redundancy and supporting infrastructure.
Application	Grid technology is introduced into the enterprise or inventory architecture.
Impacts	This pattern can require a significant infrastructure upgrade and can correspondingly increase governance burden.
Principles	Service Statelessness (482)
Architecture	Enterprise, Inventory, Service

Service Instance Routing
By Anish Karmarkar

How can consumers contact and interact with service instances without the need for proprietary processing logic?

Problem	When required to repeatedly access a specific stateful service instance, consumers must rely on custom logic that more tightly couples them to the service.
Solution	The service provides an instance identifier along with its destination information in a standardized format that shields the consumer from having to resort to custom logic.
Application	The service is still required to provide custom logic to generate and manage instance identifiers, and both service and consumer require a common messaging infrastructure.
Impacts	This pattern can introduce the need for significant infrastructure upgrades and when misused can further lead to overly stateful messaging activities that can violate the Service Statelessness (482) principle.
Principles	Service Loose Coupling (477), Service Statelessness (482), Service Composability (486)
Architecture	Inventory, Composition, Service

Service Layers

How can the services in an inventory be organized based on functional commonality?

Problem	Arbitrarily defining services delivered and governed by different project teams can lead to design inconsistency and inadvertent functional redundancy across a service inventory.
Solution	The inventory is structured into two or more logical service layers, each of which is responsible for abstracting logic based on a common functional type.
Application	Service models are chosen and then form the basis for service layers that establish modeling and design standards.
Impacts	The common costs and impacts associated with design standards and up-front analysis need to be accepted.
Principles	Service Reusability (479), Service Composability (486)
Architecture	Inventory, Service

Service Messaging

How can services interoperate without forming persistent, tightly coupled connections?

Problem	Services that depend on traditional remote communication protocols impose the need for persistent connections and tightly coupled data exchanges, increasing consumer dependencies and limiting service reuse potential.
Solution	Services can be designed to interact via a messaging-based technology, which removes the need for persistent connections and reduces coupling requirements.
Application	A messaging framework needs to be established, and services need to be designed to use it.
Impacts	Messaging technology brings with it QoS concerns such as reliable delivery, security, performance, and transactions.
Principles	Standardized Service Contract (475), Service Loose Coupling (477)
Architecture	Inventory, Composition, Service

Service Normalization

How can a service inventory avoid redundant service logic?

Problem	When delivering services as part of a service inventory, there is a constant risk that services will be created with overlapping functional boundaries, making it difficult to enable wide-spread reuse.
Solution	The service inventory needs to be designed with an emphasis on service boundary alignment.
Application	Functional service boundaries are modeled as part of a formal analysis process and persist throughout inventory design and governance.
Impacts	Ensuring that service boundaries are and remain well-aligned introduces extra up-front analysis and on-going governance effort.
Principles	Service Autonomy (481)
Architecture	Inventory, Service

Service Perimeter Guard

By Jason Hogg, Don Smith, Fred Chong, Tom Hollander, Wojtek Kozaczynski,
Larry Brader, Nelly Delgado, Dwayne Taylor, Lonnie Wall, Paul Slater,
Sajjad Nasir Imran, Pablo Cibraro, Ward Cunningham

*How can services that run in a private network be made available to
external consumers without exposing internal resources?*

Problem	External consumers that require access to one or more services in a private network can attack the service or use it to gain access to internal resources.
Solution	An intermediate service is established at the perimeter of the private network as a secure contact point for any external consumers that need to interact with internal services.
Application	The service is deployed in a perimeter network and is designed to work with existing firewall technologies so as to establish a secure bridging mechanism between external and internal networks.
Impacts	A perimeter service adds complexity and performance overhead as it establishes an intermediary processing layer for all external-to-internal communication.
Principles	Service Loose Coupling (477), Service Abstraction (478)
Architecture	Service

Service Refactoring

How can a service be evolved without impacting existing consumers?

Problem	The logic or implementation technology of a service may become outdated or inadequate over time, but the service has become too entrenched to be replaced.
Solution	The service contract is preserved to maintain existing consumer dependencies, but the underlying service logic and/or implementation are refactored.
Application	Service logic and implementation technology are gradually improved or upgraded but must undergo additional testing.
Impacts	This pattern introduces governance effort as well as risk associated with potentially negative side-effects introduced by new logic or technology.
Principles	Standardized Service Contract (475), Service Loose Coupling (477), Service Abstraction (478)
Architecture	Service

State Messaging
By Anish Karmarkar

How can a service remain stateless while participating in stateful interactions?

Problem	When services are required to maintain state information in memory between message exchanges with consumers, their scalability can be comprised, and they can become a performance burden on the surrounding infrastructure.
Solution	Instead of retaining the state data in memory, its storage is temporarily delegated to messages.
Application	Depending on how this pattern is applied, both services and consumers may need to be designed to process message-based state data.
Impacts	This pattern may not be suitable for all forms of state data, and should messages be lost, any state information they carried may be lost as well.
Principles	Standardized Service Contract (475), Service Statelessness (482), Service Composability (486)
Architecture	Composition, Service

State Repository

How can service state data be persisted for extended periods without consuming service runtime resources?

Problem	Large amounts of state data cached to support the activity within a running service composition can consume too much memory, especially for long-running activities, thereby decreasing scalability.
Solution	State data can be temporarily written to and then later retrieved from a dedicated state repository.
Application	A shared or dedicated repository is made available as part of the inventory or service architecture.
Impacts	The addition of required write and read functionality increases the service design complexity and can negatively affect performance.
Principles	Service Statelessness (482)
Architecture	Inventory, Service

Stateful Services

How can service state data be persisted and managed without consuming service runtime resources?

Problem	State data associated with a particular service activity can impose a great deal of runtime state management responsibility upon service compositions, thereby reducing their scalability.
Solution	State data is managed and stored by intentionally stateful utility services.
Application	Stateful utility services provide in-memory state data storage and/or can maintain service activity context data.
Impacts	If not properly implemented, stateful utility services can become a performance bottleneck.
Principles	Service Statelessness (482)
Architecture	Inventory, Service

Termination Notification
By David Orchard, Chris Riley

How can the scheduled expiry of a service contract be communicated to consumer programs?

Problem	Consumer programs may be unaware of when a service or a service contract version is scheduled for retirement, thereby risking runtime failure.
Solution	Service contracts can be designed to express termination information for programmatic and human consumption.
Application	Service contracts can be extended with ignorable policy assertions or supplemented with human-readable annotations.
Impacts	The syntax and conventions used to express termination information must be understood by service consumers in order for this information to be effectively used.
Principles	Standardized Service Contract (475)
Architecture	Composition, Service

Three-Layer Inventory

This compound pattern is simply comprised of the combined application of the three service layer patterns. Three-Layer Inventory exists because the combined application of these three patterns results in common layers of abstraction that have been proven to complement and support each other by establishing services with flexible variations of agnostic and non-agnostic functional contexts.

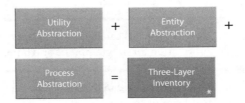

The joint application of Utility Abstraction [573], Entity Abstraction [524], and Process Abstraction [544] results in Three-Layer Inventory.

Trusted Subsystem

By Jason Hogg, Don Smith, Fred Chong, Tom Hollander, Wojtek
Kozaczynski, Larry Brader, Nelly Delgado, Dwayne Taylor, Lonnie Wall,
Paul Slater, Sajjad Nasir Imran, Pablo Cibraro, Ward Cunningham

*How can a consumer be prevented from circumventing a service
and directly accessing its resources?*

Problem	A consumer that accesses backend resources of a service directly can compromise the integrity of the resources and can further lead to undesirable forms of implementation coupling.
Solution	The service is designed to use its own credentials for authentication and authorization with backend resources on behalf of consumers.
Application	Depending on the nature of the underlying resources, various design options and security technologies can be applied.
Impacts	If this type of service is compromised by attackers or unauthorized consumers, it can be exploited to gain access to a wide range of downstream resources.
Principles	Service Loose Coupling (477)
Architecture	Service

UI Mediator

By Clemens Utschig-Utschig, Berthold Maier,
Bernd Trops, Hajo Normann, Torsten Winterberg

*How can a service-oriented solution provide a consistent,
interactive user experience?*

Problem	Because the behavior of individual services can vary depending on their design, runtime usage, and the workload required to carry out a given capability, the consistency with which a service-oriented solution can respond to requests originating from a user-interface can fluctuate, leading to a poor user experience.
Solution	Establish mediator logic solely responsible for ensuring timely interaction and feedback with user-interfaces and presentation logic.
Application	A utility mediator service or service agent is positioned as the initial recipient of messages originating from the user-interface. This mediation logic responds in a timely and consistent manner regardless of the behavior of the underling solution.
Impacts	The mediator logic establishes an additional layer of processing that can add to the required runtime processing.
Principles	Service Loose Coupling (477)
Architecture	Composition

Utility Abstraction

How can common non-business centric logic be separated, reused, and independently governed?

Problem	When non-business centric processing logic is packaged together with business-specific logic, it results in the redundant implementation of common utility functions across different services.
Solution	A service layer dedicated to utility processing is established, providing reusable utility services for use by other services in the inventory.
Application	The utility service model is incorporated into analysis and design processes in support of utility logic abstraction, and further steps are taken to define balanced service contexts.
Impacts	When utility logic is distributed across multiple services it can increase the size, complexity, and performance demands of compositions.
Principles	Service Loose Coupling (477), Service Abstraction (478), Service Reusability (479), Service Composability (486)
Architecture	Inventory, Composition, Service

Validation Abstraction

How can service contracts be designed to more easily adapt to validation logic changes?

Problem	Service contracts that contain detailed validation constraints become more easily invalidated when the rules behind those constraints change.
Solution	Granular validation logic and rules can be abstracted away from the service contract, thereby decreasing constraint granularity and increasing the contract's potential longevity.
Application	Abstracted validation logic and rules need to be moved to the underlying service logic, a different service, a service agent, or elsewhere.
Impacts	This pattern can somewhat decentralize validation logic and can also complicate schema standardization.
Principles	Standardized Service Contract (475), Service Loose Coupling (477), Service Abstraction (478)
Architecture	Service

Version Identification

By David Orchard, Chris Riley

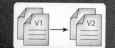

How can consumers be made aware of service contract version information?

Problem	When an already-published service contract is changed, unaware consumers will miss the opportunity to leverage the change or may be negatively impacted by the change.
Solution	Versioning information pertaining to compatible and incompatible changes can be expressed as part of the service contract, both for communication and enforcement purposes.
Application	With Web service contracts, version numbers can be incorporated into namespace values and as annotations.
Impacts	This pattern may require that version information be expressed with a proprietary vocabulary that needs to be understood by consumer designers in advance.
Principles	Standardized Service Contract (475)
Architecture	Service

Appendix E

The Annotated SOA Manifesto

The SOA Manifesto was authored and announced during the 2nd Annual International SOA Symposium in Rotterdam by a working group comprised of 17 experts and thought leaders from different organizations. Two of the SOA Manifesto Working Group members (Anne Thomas Manes and Thomas Erl) are co-authors of this book.

The original SOA Manifesto is published at www.soa-manifesto.org. You are encouraged to visit this site and enter your name on the *Become a Signatory* form to show your support for the values and principles declared in the manifesto.

Subsequent to the announcement of the SOA Manifesto, Thomas Erl authored an annotated version that supplements individual statements from the original manifesto with additional commentary and insights. The Annotated SOA Manifesto is published at www.soa-manifesto.com and has been further provided as a supplementary resource in this appendix.

The Annotated SOA Manifesto

Commentary and Insights about the SOA Manifesto from Thomas Erl

Service-orientation is a paradigm that frames what you do. Service-oriented architecture (SOA) is a type of architecture that results from applying service-orientation.

From the beginning it was understood that this was to be a manifesto about two distinct yet closely related topics: the service-oriented architectural model and service-orientation, the paradigm through which the architecture is defined. The format of this manifesto was modeled after the Agile Manifesto, which limits content to concise statements that express ambitions, values, and guiding principles for realizing those ambitions and values. Such a manifesto is not a specification, a reference model or even a white paper, and without an option to provide actual definitions, we decided to add this preamble in order to clarify how and why these terms are referenced in other parts of the manifesto document.

We have been applying service-orientation...

The service-orientation paradigm is best viewed as a method or an approach for realizing a specific target state that is further defined by a set of strategic goals and benefits. When we apply service-orientation, we shape software programs and technology architecture in support of realizing this target state. This is what qualifies technology architecture as being service-oriented.

...to help organizations consistently deliver sustainable business value, with increased agility and cost effectiveness...

This continuation of the preamble highlights some of the most prominent and commonly expected strategic benefits of service-oriented computing. Understanding these benefits helps shed some light on the aforementioned target state we intend to realize as a result of applying service-orientation.

Agility at a business level is comparable to an organization's responsiveness. The more easily and effectively an organization can respond to business change, the more efficient and successful it will be to adapting to the impacts of the change (and further leverage whatever benefits the change may bring about).

Service-orientation positions services as IT assets that are expected to provide repeated value over time that far exceeds the initial investment required for their delivery. Cost-effectiveness relates primarily to this expected return on investment. In many ways, an increase in cost-effectiveness goes hand-in-hand with an increase in agility; if there is more opportunity to reuse existing services, then there is generally less expense required to build new solutions.

"Sustainable" business value refers to the long-term goals of service-orientation to establish software programs as services with the inherent flexibility to be continually composed into new solution configurations and evolved to accommodate ever-changing business requirements.

...in line with changing business needs.

These last six words of the preamble are key to understanding the underlying philosophy of service-oriented computing. The need to accommodate business change on an on-going basis is foundational to service-orientation and considered a fundamental over-arching strategic goal.

Through our work we have come to prioritize:

The upcoming statements establish a core set of values, each of which is expressed as a prioritization over something that is also considered of value. The intent of this value system is to address the hard choices that need to be made on a regular basis in order for the strategic goals and benefits of service-oriented computing to be consistently realized.

Business value over technical strategy

As stated previously, the need to accommodate business change is an overarching strategic goal. Therefore, the foundational quality of service-oriented architecture and of any software programs, solutions, and eco-systems that result from the adoption of service-orientation is that they are business-driven. It is not about technology determining the direction of the business, it is about the business vision dictating the utilization of technology.

This priority can have a profound ripple effect within the regions of an IT enterprise. It introduces changes to just about all parts of IT delivery lifecycles, from how we plan for and fund automation solutions, to how we build and govern them. All other values and principles in the manifesto, in one way or another, support the realization of this value.

Strategic goals over project-specific benefits

Historically, many IT projects focused solely on building applications designed specifically to automate business process requirements that were current at that time. This fulfilled immediate (tactical) needs, but as more of these single-purpose applications were delivered, it resulted in an IT enterprise filled with islands of logic and data referred to as application "silos." As new business requirements would emerge, either new silos were created or integration channels between silos were established. As yet more business change arose, integration channels had to be augmented, even more silos had to be created, and soon the IT enterprise landscape became convoluted and increasingly burdensome, expensive, and slow to evolve.

In many ways, service-orientation emerged in response to these problems. It is a paradigm that provides an alternative to project-specific, silo-based, and integrated application development by adamantly prioritizing the attainment of long-term, strategic business goals. The target state advocated by service-orientation does not have traditional application silos. And even when legacy resources and application silos exist in environments where service-orientation is adopted, the target state is one where they are harmonized to whatever extent feasible.

Intrinsic interoperability over custom integration

For software programs to share data they need to be interoperable. If software programs are not designed to be compatible, they will likely not be interoperable. To enable interoperability between incompatible software programs requires that they be integrated. Integration is therefore the effort required to achieve interoperability between disparate software programs.

Although often necessary, customized integration can be expensive and time consuming and can lead to fragile architectures that are burdensome to evolve. One of the goals of service-orientation is to minimize the need for customized integration by shaping software programs (within a given domain) so that they are natively compatible. This is a quality referred to as intrinsic interoperability. The service-orientation paradigm encompasses a set of specific design principles that are geared toward establishing intrinsic interoperability on several levels.

Intrinsic interoperability, as a characteristic of software programs that reside within a given domain, is key to realizing strategic benefits, such as increased cost-effectiveness and agility.

Shared services over specific-purpose implementations

As just explained, service-orientation establishes a design approach comprised of a set of design principles. When applied to a meaningful extent, these principles shape a software program into a unit of service-oriented logic that can be legitimately referred to as a service.

Services are equipped with concrete characteristics (such as those that enable intrinsic interoperability) that directly support the previously described target state. One of these characteristics is the encapsulation of multi-purpose logic that can be shared and reused in support of the automation of different business processes.

A shared service establishes itself as an IT asset that can provide repeated business value while decreasing the expense and effort to deliver new automation solutions. While there is value in traditional, single-purpose applications that solve tactical business requirements, the use of shared services provides greater value in realizing strategic goals of service-oriented computing (which again include an increase in cost-effectiveness and agility).

Flexibility over optimization

This is perhaps the broadest of the value prioritization statements and is best viewed as a guiding philosophy for how to better prioritize various considerations when delivering and evolving individual services and inventories of services.

Optimization primarily refers to the fulfillment of tactical gains by tuning a given application design or expediting its delivery to meet immediate needs. There is nothing undesirable about this, except that it can lead to the aforementioned silo-based environments when not properly prioritized in relation to fostering flexibility.

For example, the characteristic of flexibility goes beyond the ability for services to effectively (and intrinsically) share data. To be truly responsive to ever-changing business requirements, services must also be flexible in how they can be combined and aggregated into composite solutions. Unlike traditional distributed applications that often were relatively static despite the fact that they were componentized, service compositions need to be designed with a level of inherent flexibility that allows for constant augmentation. This means that when an existing business process changes or when a new business process is introduced, we need to be able to add, remove, and extend services within the composition architecture with minimal (integration) effort. This is why service composability is one of the key service-orientation design principles.

Evolutionary refinement over pursuit of initial perfection

There is a common point of confusion when it comes to the term "agility" in relation to service-orientation. Some design approaches advocate the rapid delivery of software programs for immediate gains. This can be considered "tactical agility," as the focus is on tactical, short-term benefit. Service-orientation advocates the attainment of agility on an organizational or business level with the intention of empowering the organization, as a whole, to be responsive to change. This form of organizational agility can also be referred to as "strategic agility" because the emphasis is on longevity in that, with every software program we deliver, we want to work toward a target state that fosters agility with long-term strategic value.

For an IT enterprise to enable organizational agility, it must evolve in tandem with the business. We generally cannot predict how a business will need to evolve over time and therefore we cannot initially build the perfect services. At the same time, there is usually a wealth of knowledge that already exists within an organization's existing business intelligence that can be harvested during the analysis and modeling stages of SOA projects.

This information, together with service-orientation principles and proven methodologies, can help us identify and define a set of services that capture how the business exists and operates today while being sufficiently flexible to adapt to how the business changes over time.

That is, while we value the items on the right, we value the items on the left more.

By studying how these values are prioritized, we gain insight into what distinguishes service-orientation from other paradigms. This type of insight can benefit IT practitioners in several ways. For example, it can help establish fundamental criteria that we can use to determine how compatible service-orientation is for a given organization or IT enterprise. It can further help determine the extent to which service-orientation can or should be adopted.

An appreciation of the core values can also help us understand how challenging it may be to successfully carry out SOA projects within certain environments. For example, several of these prioritizations may clash head-on with established beliefs and preferences. In such a case, the benefits of service-orientation need to be weighed against the effort and impact their adoption may have (not just on technology, but also on the organization and IT culture).

The upcoming guiding principles were provided to help address many of these types of challenges.

We follow these principles:

So far, the manifesto has established an overall vision as well as a set of core values associated with the vision. The remainder of the declaration is comprised of a set of principles that are provided as guidance for adhering to the values and realizing the vision.

It's important to keep in mind that these are guiding principles specific to this manifesto. There is a separate set of established design principles that comprise the service-orientation design paradigm and there are many more documented practices and patterns specific to service-orientation and service-oriented architecture.

Respect the social and power structure of the organization.

One of the most common SOA pitfalls is approaching adoption as a technology-centric initiative. Doing so almost always leads to failure because we are simply not prepared for the inevitable organizational impacts.

The adoption of service-orientation is about transforming the way we automate business. However, regardless of what plans we may have for making this transformation effort happen, we must always begin with an understanding and an appreciation of the organization, its structure, its goals, and its culture.

The adoption of service-orientation is very much a human experience. It requires support from those in authority and then asks that an IT culture adopt a strategic, community-centric mindset. We must fully acknowledge and plan for this level of organizational change in order to receive the necessary long-term commitments required to achieve the target state of service-orientation.

These types of considerations not only help us determine how to best proceed with an SOA initiative, they further assist us in defining the most appropriate scope and approach for adoption.

Recognize that SOA ultimately demands change on many levels.

There's a saying that goes: "Success is being prepared for opportunity." Perhaps the number one lesson learned from SOA projects carried out so far is that we must fully comprehend and then plan and prepare for the volume and range of change that is brought about as a result of adopting service-orientation. Here are some examples.

Service-orientation changes how we build automation solutions by positioning software programs as IT assets with long-term, repeatable business value. An upfront investment is required to create an environment comprised of such assets and an on-going commitment is required to maintain and leverage their value. So, right out of the gate, changes are required to how we fund, measure, and maintain systems within the IT enterprise.

Furthermore, because service-orientation introduces services that are positioned as resources of the enterprise, there will be changes in how we own different parts of systems and regulate their design and usage, not to mention changes to the infrastructure required to guarantee continuous scalability and reliability.

The scope of SOA adoption can vary. Keep efforts manageable and within meaningful boundaries.

A common myth has been that in order to realize the strategic goals of service-oriented computing, service-orientation must be adopted on an enterprise-wide basis. This means establishing and enforcing design and industry standards across the IT enterprise so as to create an enterprise-wide inventory of intrinsically interoperable services. While there is nothing wrong with this ideal, it is not a realistic goal for many organizations, especially those with larger IT enterprises.

The most appropriate scope for any given SOA adoption effort needs to be determined as a result of planning and analysis in conjunction with pragmatic considerations, such as the aforementioned impacts on organizational structures, areas of authority, and cultural changes that are brought about.

These types of factors help us determine a scope of adoption that is manageable. But for any adoption effort to result in an environment that progresses the IT enterprise toward the desired strategic target state, the scope must also be meaningful. In other words, it must be meaningfully cross-silo so that collections of services can be delivered in relation to each other within a pre-defined boundary. In other words, we want to create "continents of services," not the dreaded "islands of services."

This concept of building independently owned and governed service inventories within domains of the same IT enterprise reduces many of the risks that are commonly attributed to "big-bang" SOA projects and furthermore mitigates the impact of both organizational and technological changes (because the impact is limited to a segmented and managed scope). It is also an approach that allows for phased adoption where one domain service inventory can be established at a time.

Products and standards alone will neither give you SOA nor apply the service-orientation paradigm for you.

This principle addresses two separate but very much related myths. The first is that you can buy your way into SOA with modern technology products, and the second is the assumption that the adoption of industry standards (such as XML, WSDL, SCA, etc.) will naturally result in service-oriented technology architecture.

The vendor and industry standards communities have been credited with building modern service technology innovation upon non-proprietary frameworks and platforms. Everything from service virtualization to cloud computing and grid computing has helped advance the potential for building sophisticated and complex service-oriented solutions. However, none of these technologies are exclusive to SOA. You can just as easily build silo-based systems in the cloud as you can on your own private servers.

There is no such thing as "SOA in a box" because in order to achieve service-oriented technology architecture, service-orientation needs to be successfully applied; this, in turn, requires that everything we design and build be driven by the unique direction, vision, and requirements of the business.

SOA can be realized through a variety of technologies and standards.

Service-orientation is a technology-neutral and vendor-neutral paradigm. Service-oriented architecture is a technology-neutral and vendor neutral architectural model. Service-oriented computing can be viewed as a specialized form of distributed computing. Service-oriented solutions can therefore be built using just about any technologies and industry standards suitable for distributed computing.

While some technologies (especially those based on industry standards) can increase the potential of applying some service-orientation design principles, it is really the potential to fulfill business requirements that ultimately determines the most suitable choice of technologies and industry standards.

Establish a uniform set of enterprise standards and policies based on industry, de facto, and community standards.

Industry standards represent non-proprietary technology specifications that help establish, among other things, consistent baseline characteristics (such as transport, interface, message format, etc.) of technology architecture. However, the use of industry standards alone does not guarantee that services will be intrinsically interoperable.

For two software programs to be fully compatible, additional conventions (such as data models and policies) need to be adhered to. This is why IT enterprises must establish and enforce design standards. Failure to properly standardize and regulate the standardization of services within a given domain will begin to tear at the fabric of interoperability upon which the realization of many strategic benefits relies.

This principle not only advocates the use of enterprise design standards, it also reminds us that, whenever possible and feasible, custom design standards should be based upon and incorporate standards already in use by the industry and the community in general.

Pursue uniformity on the outside while allowing diversity on the inside.

Federation can be defined as the unification of a set of disparate entities. While allowing each entity to be independently governed on the inside, all agree to adhere to a common, unified front.

A fundamental part of service-oriented architecture is the introduction of a federated endpoint layer that abstracts service implementation details while publishing a set of endpoints that represent individual services within a given domain in a unified manner. Accomplishing this generally involves achieving unity based on a combination of industry and design standards. The consistency of this unity across services is key to realizing intrinsic interoperability.

A federated endpoint layer further helps increase opportunities to explore vendor-diversity options. For example, one service may need to be built upon a completely different platform than another. As long as these services maintain compatible endpoints, the governance of their respective implementations can remain independent. This not only highlights that services can be built using different implementation mediums (such as EJB, .NET, SOAP, REST, etc.), it also emphasizes that different intermediary platforms and technologies can be utilized together, as required.

Note that this type of diversity comes with a price. This principle does not advocate diversification itself—it simply recommends that we allow diversification when justified, so that "best-of-breed" technologies and platforms can be leveraged to maximize business requirements fulfillment.

Identify services through collaboration with business and technology stakeholders.

In order for technology solutions to be business-driven, the technology must be in synch with the business. Therefore, another goal of service-oriented computing is to align technology and business. The stage at which this alignment is initially accomplished is during the analysis and modeling processes that usually precede actual service development and delivery.

The critical ingredient to carrying out service-oriented analysis is to have both business and technology experts working hand-in-hand to identify and define candidate services. For example, business experts can help accurately define functional contexts pertaining to business-centric services, while technology experts can provide pragmatic input to ensure that the granularity and definition of conceptual services remains realistic in relation to their eventual implementation environments.

Maximize service usage by considering the current and future scope of utilization.

The extent of a given SOA project may be enterprise-wide or it may be limited to a domain of the enterprise. Whatever the scope, a pre-defined boundary is established to encompass an inventory of services that need to be conceptually modeled before they can be developed. By modeling multiple services in relation to each other we essentially establish a blueprint of the services we will eventually be building. This modeling exercise is critical when attempting to identify and define services that can be shared by different solutions.

There are various methodologies and approaches that can be used to carry out service-oriented analysis stages. However, a common thread among all of them is that the functional boundaries of services be normalized to avoid redundancy. Even then, normalized services do not necessarily make for highly reusable services. Other factors come into play, such as service granularity, autonomy, state management, scalability, composability, and the extent to which service logic is sufficiently generic so that it can be effectively reused.

These types of considerations guided by business and technology expertise provide the opportunity to define services that capture current utilization requirements while having the flexibility to adapt to future change.

Verify that services satisfy business requirements and goals.

As with anything, services can be misused. When growing and managing a portfolio of services, their usage and effectiveness at fulfilling business requirements need to be verified and measured. Modern tools provide various means of monitoring service usage, but there are intangibles that also need to be taken into consideration to ensure that services are not just used because they are available, but to verify that they are truly fulfilling business needs and meeting expectations.

This is especially true with shared services that shoulder multiple dependencies. Not only do shared services require adequate infrastructure to guarantee scalability and reliability for all of the solutions that reuse them, they also need to be designed and extended with great care to ensure their functional contexts are never skewed.

Evolve services and their organization in response to real use.

This guiding principle ties directly back to the "Evolutionary refinement over pursuit of initial perfection" value statement, as well as the overall goal of maintaining an alignment of business and technology.

We can never expect to rely on guesswork when it comes to determining service granularity, the range of functions that services need to perform, or how services will need to be organized into compositions. Based on whatever extent of analysis we are able to initially perform, a given service will be assigned a defined functional context and will contain one or more functional capabilities that likely involve it in one or more service compositions.

As real world business requirements and circumstances change, the service may need to be augmented, extended, refactored, or perhaps even replaced. Service-orientation design principles build native flexibility into service architectures so that, as software programs, services are resilient and adaptive to change and to being changed in response to real world usage.

Separate the different aspects of a system that change at different rates.

What makes monolithic and silo-based systems inflexible is that change can have a significant impact on their existing usage. This is why it is often easier to create new silo-based applications rather then augment or extend existing ones.

The rationale behind the separation of concerns (a commonly known software engineering theory) is that a larger problem can be more effectively solved when decomposed into a set of smaller problems or concerns. When applying service-orientation to the separation of concerns, we build corresponding units of solution logic that solve individual concerns, thereby allowing us to aggregate the units to solve the larger problem in addition to giving us the opportunity to aggregate them into different configurations in order to solve other problems.

Besides fostering service reusability, this approach introduces numerous layers of abstraction that help shield service-comprised systems from the impacts of change. This form of abstraction can exist at different levels. For example, if legacy resources encapsulated by one service need to be replaced, the impact of that change can be mitigated as long as the service is able to retain its original endpoint and functional behavior.

Another example is the separation of agnostic from non-agnostic logic. The former type of logic has high reuse potential if it is multi-purpose and less likely to change. Non-agnostic logic, on the other hand, typically represents the single-purpose parts of parent business process logic, which are often more volatile. Separating these respective logic types into different service layers further introduces abstraction that enables service reusability while shielding services, and any solutions that utilize them, from the impacts of change.

Reduce implicit dependencies and publish all external dependencies to increase robustness and reduce the impact of change.

One of the most well-known service-orientation design principles is that of service loose coupling. How a service architecture is internally structured and how services relate to programs that consume them (which can include other services) all comes down to dependencies that are formed on individually moving parts that are part of the service architecture.

Layers of abstraction help ease evolutionary change by localizing the impacts of the change to controlled regions. For example, within service architectures, service facades can be used to abstract parts of the implementation in order to minimize the reach of implementation dependencies.

On the other hand, published technical service contracts need to disclose the dependencies that service consumers must form in order to interact with services. By reducing internal dependencies that can affect these technical contracts when change does occur, we avoid proliferating the impact of those changes upon dependent service consumers.

At every level of abstraction, organize each service around a cohesive and manageable unit of functionality.

Each service requires a well-defined functional context that determines what logic does and does not belong within the service's functional boundary. Determining the scope and granularity of these functional service boundaries is one of the most critical responsibilities during the service delivery lifecycle.

Services with coarse functional granularity may be too inflexible to be effective, especially if they are expected to be reusable. On the other hand, overly fine grained services may tax an infrastructure in that service compositions will need to consist of increased quantities of composition members.

Determining the right balance of functional scope and granularity requires a combination of business and technology expertise, and further requires an understanding of how services within a given boundary relate to each other.

Many of the guiding principles described in this manifesto will help in making this determination in support of positioning each service as an IT asset capable of furthering an IT enterprise toward that target state whereby the strategic benefits of service-oriented computing are realized.

Ultimately, though, it will always be the attainment of real world business value that dictates, from conception to delivery to repeated usage, the evolutionary path of any unit of service-oriented functionality.

—Thomas Erl (November 22, 2009)
www.soa-manifesto.com

Appendix F

Versioning Fundamentals for Web Services and REST Services

After a service contract is deployed, consumer programs will naturally begin forming dependencies on it. When we are subsequently forced to make changes to the contract, we need to figure out:

- whether the changes will negatively impact existing (and potentially future) service consumers

- how changes that will and will not impact consumers should be implemented and communicated

These issues result in the need for versioning. Any time you introduce the concept of versioning into an SOA project, a number of questions will likely be raised, for example:

- What exactly constitutes a new version of a service contract? What's the difference between a major and minor version?

- What do the parts of a version number indicate?

- Will the new version of the contract still work with existing consumers that were designed for the old contract version?

- Will the current version of the contract work with new consumers that may have different data exchange requirements?

- What is the best way to add changes to existing contracts while minimizing the impact on consumers?

- Will we need to host old and new contracts at the same time? If yes, for how long?

We will address these questions and provide a set of options for solving common versioning problems. The upcoming sections begin by covering some basic concepts, terminology, and strategies specific to service contract versioning.

F.1 Versioning Basics

So when we say that we're creating a new version of a service contract, what exactly are we referring to? The following sections explain some fundamental terms and concepts and further distinguish between Web service contracts and REST service contracts.

Versioning Web Services

As we've established many times over in this book, a Web service contract can be comprised of several individual documents and definitions that are linked and assembled together to form a complete technical interface.

For example, a given Web service contract can consist of:

- one (sometimes more) WSDL definitions

- one (usually more) XML Schema definitions

- some (sometimes no) WS-Policy definitions

Furthermore, each of these definition documents can be shared by other Web service contracts.

For example:

- a centralized XML Schema definition will commonly be used by multiple WSDL definitions

- a centralized WS-Policy definition will commonly be applied to multiple WSDL definitions

- an abstract WSDL description can be imported by multiple concrete WSDL descriptions or vice versa

Of all the different parts of a Web service contract, the part that establishes the fundamental technical interface is the abstract description of the WSDL definition. This represents the core of a Web service contract and is then further extended and detailed through schema definitions, policy definitions, and one or more concrete WSDL descriptions.

When we need to create a new version of a Web service contract, we can therefore assume that there has been a change in the abstract WSDL description or one of the contract documents that relates to the abstract WSDL description. How the different constructs of a WSDL can be versioned is covered in Chapter 21 (*Web Service Contract Design and Versioning for SOA*).

The Web service contract content commonly subject to change is the XML schema content that provides the types for the abstract description's message definitions. Chapter 22 (*Web Service Contract Design and Versioning for SOA*) explores the manner in which the underlying schema definitions for messages can be changed and evolved.

Finally, the one other contract-related technology that can still impose versioning requirements but is less likely to do so simply because it is a less common part of Web service contracts is WS-Policy. How policies in general relate to contract versioning is explained as part of the advanced topics in Chapter 23 (*Web Service Contract Design and Versioning for SOA*).

Versioning REST Services

If we follow the REST model of using a uniform contract to express service capabilities, the sharing of definition documents between service contract is even clearer.

For example:

- all HTTP methods used in contracts are standard across the architecture

- XML Schema definitions are standard, as they are wrapped up in general media types

- the identifier syntax for lightweight service endpoints (known as resources) are standard across the architecture

Changes to the uniform contract facets that underlie each service contract can impact any REST service in the service inventory.

Fine and Coarse-Grained Constraints

Regardless of whether XML schemas are used with Web services or REST services, versioning changes are often tied to the increase or reduction of the quantity or granularity of constraints expressed in the schema definition. Therefore, let's briefly recap the meaning of the term constraint granularity in relation to a type definition.

Note the bolded and italicized parts in the following example:

```
<xsd:element name="LineItem" type="LineItemType"/>
<xsd:complexType name="LineItemType">
  <xsd:sequence>
    <xsd:element name="productID" type="xsd:string"/>
    <xsd:element name="productName" type="xsd:string"/>
    <xsd:any minOccurs="0" maxOccurs="unbounded"
      namespace="##any" processContents="lax"/>
  </xsd:sequence>
  <xsd:anyAttribute namespace="##any"/>
</xsd:complexType>
```

Example F.1

A `complexType` construct containing fine and coarse-grained constraints.

As indicated by the bolded text, there are elements with specific names and data types that represent parts of the message definition with a *fine* level of constraint granularity. All of the message instances (the actual XML documents that will be created based on this structure) must conform to the these constraints in order to be considered valid (which is why these are considered the absolute "minimum" constraints).

The italicized text shows the element and attribute wildcards also contained by this complex type. These represent parts of the message definition with an extremely *coarse* level of constraint granularity in that messages do not need to comply to these parts of the message definition at all.

The use of the terms "fine-grained" and "coarse-grained" is highly subjective. What may be a fine-grained constraint in one contract may not be in another. The point is to understand how these terms can be applied when comparing parts of a message definition or when comparing different message definitions with each other.

F.2 Versioning and Compatibility

The number one concern when developing and deploying a new version of a service contract is the impact it will have on other parts of the enterprise that have formed or will form dependencies on it. This measure of impact is directly related to how compatible the new contract version is with the old version and its surroundings in general.

This section establishes the fundamental types of compatibility that relate to the content and design of new contract versions and also tie into the goals and limitations of different versioning strategies introduced at the end of this appendix.

Backwards Compatibility

A new version of a service contract that continues to support consumer programs designed to work with the old version is considered *backwards-compatible*. From a design perspective, this means that the new contract has not changed in such a way that it can impact existing consumer programs that are already using the contract.

Backwards Compatibility in Web Services

A simple example of a backwards-compatible change is the addition of a new operation to an existing WSDL definition:

```
<definitions name="Purchase Order" targetNamespace=
  "http://actioncon.com/contract/po"
  xmlns="http://schemas.xmlsoap.org/wsdl/"
  xmlns:tns="http://actioncon.com/contract/po"
  xmlns:po="http://actioncon.com/schema/po">
  ...
  <portType name="ptPurchaseOrder">
    <operation name="opSubmitOrder">
      <input message="tns:msgSubmitOrderRequest"/>
      <output message="tns:msgSubmitOrderResponse"/>
    </operation>
    <operation name="opCheckOrderStatus">
      <input message="tns:msgCheckOrderRequest"/>
      <output message="tns:msgCheckOrderResponse"/>
    </operation>
    <operation name="opChangeOrder">
      <input message="tns:msgChangeOrderRequest"/>
      <output message="tns:msgChangeOrderResponse"/>
    </operation>
    <operation name="opCancelOrder">
      <input message="tns:msgCancelOrderRequest"/>
      <output message="tns:msgCancelOrderResponse"/>
```

```
   </operation>
   <operation name="opGetOrder">
     <input message="tns:msgGetOrderRequest"/>
     <output message="tns:msgGetOrderResponse"/>
   </operation>
  </portType>
</definitions>
```

Example F.2

The addition of a new operation represents a common backwards-compatible change.

NOTE

In this example we're borrowing the abstract description of the Purchase Order service that was initially built at the end of Chapter 7 (*Web Service Contract Design and Versioning for SOA*).

By adding a brand new operation, we are creating a new version of the contract, but this change is backwards-compatible and will not impact any existing consumers. The new service implementation will continue to work with old service consumers because all of the operations that an existing service consumer might invoke are still present and continue to meet the requirements of the previous service contract version.

Backwards Compatibility in REST Services

A backwards-compatible change to a REST-compliant service contract might involve adding some new resources or adding new capabilities to existing resources. In each of these cases the existing service consumers will only invoke the old methods on the old resources, which continue to work as they previously did.

```
Service: po.actioncon.com
Capabilities:
POST /orders
      In = application/vnd.com.actioncon.po+xml
GET /orders/{order-id}/status
      Out = text/plain
PUT /orders/{order-id}
      In = application/vnd.com/actioncon.po+xml
DELETE /orders/{order-id}
GET /orders/{order-id}
      Out = application/vnd.com.actioncon.po+xml
```

Example F.3

The addition of a new resource or new supported method on a resource is a backwards-compatible change for a REST service.

As demonstrated in Example F.3, supporting a new method that existing service consumers don't use results in a backwards-compatible change. However, in a service inventory with multiple REST services, we can take steps to ensure that new service consumers will continue to work with old versions of services.

As shown in Example F.4, it may be important for service consumers to have a reasonable way of proceeding with their interaction if the service reports that the new method is not implemented.

```
Legal methods for actioncon.com service inventory:
* GET
* PUT
* DELETE
* POST
* SUBSCRIBE (consumers must fall back to periodic GET if service
reports "not implemented")
```

Example F.4

New methods added to a service inventory's uniform contract need to provide a way for service consumers to "fall back" on a previously used method if they are to truly be backwards-compatible.

Changes to schemas and media types approach backwards compatibility in a different manner, in that they describe how information can be encoded for transport, and will often be used in both request and response messages. The focus for backwards compatibility is on whether a new message recipient can make sense of information sent by a legacy source. In other words, the new processor must continue to understand information produced by a legacy message *generator*.

An example of a change made to a schema for a message definition that is backwards-compatible is the addition of an optional element (as shown in bolded markup code in Example F.5).

```
Media type = application/vnd.com.actioncon.po+xml
<xsd:schema xmlns:xsd="http://www.w3.org/2001/XMLSchema"
  targetNamespace="http://actioncon.com/schema/po"
  xmlns="http://actioncon.com/schema/po">
  <xsd:element name="LineItem" type="LineItemType"/>
  <xsd:complexType name="LineItemType">
    <xsd:sequence>
      <xsd:element name="productID" type="xsd:string"/>
      <xsd:element name="productName" type="xsd:string"/>
      <xsd:element name="available" type="xsd:boolean"
        minOccurs="0"/>
```

```
     </xsd:sequence>
   </xsd:complexType>
</xsd:schema>
```

Example F.5

In an XML Schema definition, the addition of an optional element is also considered backwards-compatible.

Here we are using a simplified version of the XML Schema definition for the Purchase Order service. The optional `available` element is added to the `LineItemType` complex type. This has no impact on existing generators because they are not required to provide this element in their messages. New processors must be designed to cope without the new information if they are to remain backwards-compatible.

Changing any of the existing elements in the previous example from required to optional (by adding the `minOccurs="0"` setting) would also be considered a backwards-compatible change. When we have control over how we choose to design the next version of a Web service contract, backwards compatibility is generally attainable. However, mandatory changes (such as those imposed by laws or regulations) can often force us to break backwards compatibility.

NOTE

Both the Flexible and Loose versioning strategies explained at the end of this appendix support backwards compatibility.

Forwards Compatibility

When a service contract is designed in such a manner so that it can support a range of future consumer programs, it is considered to have an extent of *forwards compatibility*. This means that the contract can essentially accommodate how consumer programs will evolve over time.

Supporting forwards compatibility for Web service operations or uniform contract methods requires exception types to be present in the contract to allow service consumers to recover if they attempt to invoke a new and unsupported operation or method. For example, a "method not implemented" response enables the service consumer to detect that it is dealing with an incompatible service, thereby allowing it to handle this exception gracefully.

Redirection exception codes help REST services that implement a uniform contract change the resource identifiers in the contract when required. This is another way in which service contracts can allow legacy service consumers to continue using the service after contract changes have taken place.

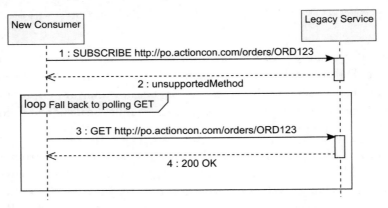

Example F.6

A REST service ensures forwards compatibility by raising an exception whenever it does not understand a reusable contract or uniform contract method.

Forwards compatibility of schemas in REST services requires extension points to be present where new information can be added so that it will be safely ignored by legacy processors.

For example:

- any validation that the processor does must not reject a document formatted according to the new schema

- all existing information that the processor might need must remain present in future versions of the schema

- any new information added to the schema must be safe for legacy processors to ignore (if processors must understand the new information then the change cannot be forwards compatible)

- the processor must ignore any information that it does not understand

A common way to ensure validation does not reject future versions of the schema is to use wildcards in the earlier version. These provide extension points where new information can be added in future schema versions:

```
<xsd:schema xmlns:xsd="http://www.w3.org/2001/XMLSchema"
  targetNamespace="http://actioncon.com/schema/po"
  xmlns="http://actioncon.com/schema/po">
  <xsd:element name="LineItem" type="LineItemType"/>
  <xsd:complexType name="LineItemType">
    <xsd:sequence>
      <xsd:element name="productID" type="xsd:string"/>
      <xsd:element name="productName" type="xsd:string"/>
      <xsd:any namespace="##any" processContents="lax"
        minOccurs="0" maxOccurs="unbounded"/>
    </xsd:sequence>
    <xsd:anyAttribute namespace="##any"/>
  </xsd:complexType>
</xsd:schema>
```

Example F.7

To support forwards compatibility within a message definition generally requires the use of XML Schema wildcards.

In this example, the `xsd:any` and `xsd:anyAttribute` elements are added to allow for a range of unknown elements and data to be accepted by the service contract. In other words, the schema is being designed in advance to accommodate unforeseen changes in the future.

> **NOTE**
>
> How wildcards can be used in support of forwards compatibility with Web services and the limited options that exist in support of forwards compatibility when it comes to WSDL definitions are discussed in Chapters 22 and 21 (*Web Service Contract Design and Versioning for SOA*), respectively.

It is important to understand that building extension points into service contracts for forwards compatibility by no means eliminates the need to consider compatibility issues when making contract changes. New information can only be added to schemas in a forwards compatible manner if it is genuinely safe for processors to ignore. New operations are only able to be made forwards compatible if a service consumer has an existing operation to fall back on when it finds the one it initially attempted to invoke is unsupported.

A service with a forwards compatible contract will often not be able to process all message content. Its contract is simply designed to accept a broader range of data unknown at the time of its design.

> **NOTE**
>
> Forwards compatibility forms the basis of the Loose versioning strategy that is explained shortly.

Compatible Changes

When we make a change to a service contract that does not negatively affect existing consumers, then the change itself is considered a *compatible change*.

> **NOTE**
>
> In this book, the term "compatible change" refers to backwards compatibility by default. When used in reference to forwards compatibility it is further qualified as a *forwards compatible change*.

A simple example of a compatible change is when we set the `minOccurs` attribute of an element from "1" to "0", effectively turning a required element into an optional one, as shown here.

```
<xsd:schema xmlns:xsd="http://www.w3.org/2001/XMLSchema"
  targetNamespace="http://actioncon.com/schema/po"
  xmlns="http://actioncon.com/schema/po">
  <xsd:element name="LineItem" type="LineItemType"/>
  <xsd:complexType name="LineItemType"    <xsd:sequence>
      <xsd:element name="productID" type="xsd:string"/>
      <xsd:element name="productName" type="xsd:string"
        minOccurs="0"/>
      <xsd:element name="available" type="xsd:boolean"
        minOccurs="0"/>
    </xsd:sequence>
  </xsd:complexType>
</xsd:schema>
```

Example F.8

The default value of the `minOccurs` attribute is "1". Therefore because this attribute was previously absent from the `productName` element declaration, it was considered a required element. Adding the `minOccurs="0"` setting turns it into an optional element, resulting in a compatible change. (Note that making this change to a message output from the service would be an incompatible change.)

This type of change will not impact existing consumer programs that are used to sending the element value to the Web service, nor will it affect future consumers that can be designed to optionally send that element.

Another example of a compatible change was provided earlier in Example F.5, when we first added the optional `available` element declaration. Even though we extended the type with a whole new element, because it is optional it is considered a compatible change.

Here is a list of common compatible changes:

- adding a new WSDL operation definition and associated message definitions

- adding a new standard method to an existing REST resource

- adding a set of new REST resources

- changing the identifiers for a set of REST resources (including splitting and merging of services) using redirection response codes to facilitate migration of REST service consumers to the new identifiers

- adding a new WSDL port type definition and associated operation definitions

- adding new WSDL binding and service definitions

- extending an existing uniform contract method in a way that can be safely ignored by REST services that can fall back on old service logic (for example, adding "If-None-Match" as a feature of the HTTP GET operation so that if the service ignores it, the consumer will still get the current and correct representation for the resource)

- adding a new uniform contract method when an exception response exists for services that do not understand the method to use (and consumers can recover from this exception)

- adding a new optional XML Schema element or attribute declaration to a message definition

- reducing the constraint granularity of an XML Schema element or attribute of a message definition type used for input messages

- adding a new XML Schema wildcard to a message definition type

- adding a new optional WS-Policy assertion

- adding a new WS-Policy alternative

Other chapters in the *Web Service Contract Design and Versioning for SOA* book provide examples for several of these types of changes and further explore techniques whereby changes that are not normally compatible can still be implemented as compatible changes.

Incompatible Changes

If after a change a contract is no longer compatible with consumers, then it is considered to have received an *incompatible change*. These are the types of changes that can break an existing contract and therefore impose the most challenges when it comes to versioning.

NOTE

As with the term "compatible change," this term also indicates backwards compatibility by default. When referring to incompatible changes that affect forwards compatibility, this term will be qualified as *forwards-incompatible change*.

Going back to our example, if we set an element's `minOccurs` attribute from "0" to any number above zero, then we are introducing an incompatible change for input messages, as follows:

```
<xsd:schema xmlns:xsd="http://www.w3.org/2001/XMLSchema"
  targetNamespace="http://actioncon.com/schema/po"
  xmlns="http://actioncon.com/schema/po">
  <xsd:element name="LineItem" type="LineItemType"/>
  <xsd:complexType name="LineItemType">
    <xsd:sequence>
      <xsd:element name="productID" type="xsd:string"/>
      <xsd:element name="productName" type="xsd:string"
        minOccurs="3"/>
      <xsd:element name="available" type="xsd:boolean"
        minOccurs="3"/>
    </xsd:sequence>
  </xsd:complexType>
</xsd:schema>
```

Example F.9

Incrementing the `minOccurs` attribute value of any established element declaration is automatically an incompatible change.

What was formerly an optional element is now required. This will certainly affect existing consumers that are not designed to comply with this new constraint, because adding a new required element introduces a mandatory constraint upon the contract.

Common incompatible changes include:

- renaming an existing WSDL operation definition
- removing an existing WSDL operation definition
- changing the MEP of an existing WSDL operation definition
- adding a fault message to an existing WSDL operation definition
- adding a new required XML Schema element or attribute declaration to a message definition
- increasing the constraint granularity of an XML Schema element or attribute declaration of a message definition
- renaming an optional or required XML Schema element or attribute in a message definition
- removing an optional or required XML Schema element or attribute or wildcard from a message definition
- adding a new required WS-Policy assertion or expression
- adding a new ignorable WS-Policy expression (most of the time)

Incompatible changes cause most of the challenges with service contract versioning. These and other types of incompatible changes are demonstrated in upcoming chapters (*Web Service Contract Design and Versioning for SOA*).

F.3 REST Service Compatibility Considerations

REST services within a given service inventory typically share a uniform contract for every resource, including uniform methods and media types. The same media types are used in both requests and responses, and new uniform contract facets are reused much more often than they are added to. This emphasis on service contract reuse within REST-compliant service inventories results in the need to highlight some special considerations, because changes to the uniform contract will automatically impact a range of service consumers because:

- the uniform contract methods are shared by all services
- the uniform contract media types are shared by both services and service consumers

As a result, both backwards compatibility and forwards compatibility considerations are almost equally important.

NOTE

Service contracts that make use of the Schema Centralization pattern without necessarily being REST-compliant will often need to impose a similarly rigid view of forward-compatibility and backwards compatibility.

Uniform contract methods codify the kinds of interactions that can occur between services and their consumers. For example, GET codifies "fetch some data," while PUT codifies "store some data."

Because the kinds of interactions that occur between REST services within the same service inventory tend to be relatively limited and stable, methods will usually change at a low rate compared to media types or resources. Compatibility issues usually pertain to a set of allowable methods that are only changed after careful case-by-case consideration.

An example of a compatible change to HTTP is the addition of `If-None-Match` headers to GET requests. If a service consumer knows the last version (or `etag`) of the resource that it fetched, it can make its GET request conditional. The `If-None-Match` header allows the consumer to state that the GET request should be shortcut and not executed if the version of the resource is still the same as it was for the consumer's last fetch. If the service does not understand this new header, it will not shortcut its processing. Instead, it will return the normal GET response, although it will do so in a non-optimal mode.

An example of an incompatible change to HTTP is the addition of a `Host` header used to support multi-homing of Web servers. HTTP/1.0 did not require the name of the service to be included in request messages, but HTTP/1.1 does require this. If the special `Host` header is missing, HTTP/1.1 services must reject the request as being badly formed. However, HTTP/1.1 services are also required to be backwards-compatible, so if a HTTP/1.0 request comes into the REST service it will still be handled according to HTTP/1.0 rules.

Uniform contract media types further codify the kinds of information that can be exchanged between REST services and consumers. As previously stated, media types tend to change at a faster rate than HTTP methods in the uniform contract; however media types still change more slowly than resources. Compatible change is more of a live concern for the media types, and we can draw some more general rules about how to deal with them.

For example, if the generator of a message indicates to a processor of the message that it conforms to a particular media type, the processor generally does not need to know which version of the schema was used, nor does the processor need to have been built against the same version of the schema. The processor expects that all versions of the schema for a particular media type will be both forwards compatible and backwards-compatible with the type it was developed to support. Likewise, the generator expects that when it produces a message conformant with a particular schema version, that all processors of the message will understand it.

When incompatible changes are made to a schema, a new media type identifier is generally required to ensure that:

- the processor can decide how to parse a document based on the media type identifier

- services and consumers are able to *negotiate* for a specific media type that will be understood by the processor when the message has been produced

Content negotiation is the ultimate fall-back to ensure compatibility in REST-compliant service inventories. For a fetch interaction this often involves the consumer indicating to the service what media types it is able to support, and the service returning the most appropriate type that it supports. This mechanism allows for incompatible changes to be made to media types, as required.

NOTE

One way to better understand versioning issues that pertain to media types is to look at how they are used in HTML. An example of a compatible change to HTML that did not result in the need for a new media type was the addition of the `abbr` element to version 4.0 of the HTML language. This element allows new processors of HTML documents to support a mouse-over to expand abbreviations on a web page and to better support accessibility of the page. Legacy processors safely ignore the expansion, but will continue correctly showing the abbreviation itself.

> An example of an incompatible change to HTML that did require a new
> media type was the conversion of HTML 4.0 to XML (resulting in version
> 1.0 of XHTML). The media type for the traditional SGML version remained
> `text/html`, while the XML version became `application/xhtml+xml`.
> This allowed content negotiation to occur between the two types, and for
> processors to choose the correct parser and validation strategy based on
> which type was specified by the service.
>
> Some incompatible changes have also been made to HTML without
> changing the media type. HTML 4.0 deprecated APPLET, BASEFONT,
> CENTER, DIR, FONT, ISINDEX, MENU, S, STRIKE, and U elements in
> favor of newer elements. These elements must continue to be understood
> but their use in HTML documents is being phased out. HTML 4.0 made
> LISTING, PLAINTEXT, and XMP obsolete. These elements should not be
> used in HTML 4.0 documents and no longer need to be understood.
>
> Deprecating elements over a long period of time and eventually identify-
> ing them as obsolete once they are no longer used by existing services
> or consumers is a technique that can be used for REST media types to
> incrementally update a schema without having to change the media type.

F.4 Version Identifiers

One of the most fundamental design patterns related to Web service contract design is
the Version Identification pattern. It essentially advocates that version numbers should
be clearly expressed, not just at the contract level, but right down to the versions of the
schemas that underlie the message definitions.

The first step to establishing an effective versioning strategy is to decide on a common
means by which versions themselves are identified and represented within Web service
contracts.

Versions are almost always communicated with version numbers. The most common
format is a decimal, followed by a period and then another decimal, as shown here:

```
version="2.0"
```

Sometimes, you will see additional period + decimal pairs that lead to more detailed
version numbers like this:

```
version="2.0.1.1"
```

The typical meaning associated with these numbers is the measure or significance of the change. Incrementing the first decimal generally indicates a major version change (or upgrade) in the software, whereas decimals after the first period usually represent various levels of minor version changes.

From a compatibility perspective, we can associate additional meaning to these numbers. Specifically, the following convention has emerged in the industry:

- A minor version is expected to be backwards-compatible with other minor versions associated with a major version. For example, version 5.2 of a program should be fully backwards-compatible with versions 5.0 and 5.1.

- A major version is generally expected to break backwards compatibility with programs that belong to other major versions. This means that program version 5.0 is not expected to be backwards-compatible with version 4.0.

> **NOTE**
>
> A third "patch" version number is also sometimes used to express changes that are both forwards-compatible and backwards-compatible. Typically these versions are intended to clarify the schema only, or to fix problems with the schema that were discovered once it was deployed. For example, version 5.2.1 is expected to be fully compatible with version 5.2.0, but may be added for clarification purposes.

This convention of indicating compatibility through major and minor version numbers is referred to as the *compatibility guarantee*. Another approach, known as "amount of work," uses version numbers to communicate the effort that has gone into the change. A minor version increase indicates a modest effort, and a major version increase predictably represents a lot of work.

These two conventions can be combined and often are. The result is often that version numbers continue to communicate compatibility as explained earlier, but they sometimes increment by several digits, depending on the amount of effort that went into each version.

There are various syntax options available to express version numbers. For example, you may have noticed that the declaration statement that begins an XML document can contain a number that expresses the version of the XML specification being used:

```
<?xml version="1.0"?>
```

That same `version` attribute can be used with the root `xsd:schema` element, as follows:

```
<xsd:schema version="2.0" ...>
```

You can further create a custom variation of this attribute by assigning it to any element you define (in which case you are not required to name the attribute "version").

```
<LineItem version="2.0">
```

An alternative custom approach is to embed the major version number into a namespace or media type identifier, as shown here:

```
<LineItem xmlns="http://actioncon.com/schema/po/v2">
```

or

```
application/vnd.com.actioncon.po.v2+xml
```

Note that it has become a common convention to use date values in namespaces when versioning XML schemas, as follows:

```
<LineItem xmlns="http://actioncon.com/schema/po/2010/09">
```

In this case, it is the date of the change that acts as the major version identifier. In order to keep the expression of XML Schema definition versions in alignment with WSDL definition versions, we use version numbers instead of date values in upcoming examples. However, when working in an environment where XML Schema definitions are separately owned as part of an independent data architecture, it is not uncommon for schema versioning identifiers to be different from those used by WSDL definitions.

Regardless of which option you choose, it is important to consider the Canonical Versioning pattern that dictates that the expression of version information must be standardized across all service contracts within the boundary of a service inventory. In larger environments, this will often require a central authority that can guarantee the linearity, consistency, and description quality of version information. These types of conventions carry over into how service termination information is expressed, as further explored in Chapter 23 (*Web Service Contract Design and Versioning for SOA*).

> **NOTE**
>
> Of course you may also be required to work with third-party schemas and WSDL definitions that may already have implemented their own versioning conventions. In this case, the extent to which the Canonical Versioning pattern can be applied will be limited.

F.5 Versioning Strategies

There is no one versioning approach that is right for everyone. Because versioning represents a governance-related phase in the overall lifecycle of a service, it is a practice that is subject to the conventions, preferences, and requirements that are distinct to any enterprise.

Even though there is no de facto versioning technique for the WSDL, XML Schema, and WS-Policy content that comprises Web service contracts, a number of common and advocated versioning approaches have emerged, each with its own benefits and tradeoffs.

Here we are going to single out the following three common strategies:

- *Strict* – Any compatible or incompatible changes result in a new version of the service contract. This approach does not support backwards or forwards compatibility.

- *Flexible* – Any incompatible change results in a new version of the service contract and the contract is designed to support backwards compatibility but not forwards compatibility.

- *Loose* – Any incompatible change results in a new version of the service contract and the contract is designed to support backwards compatibility and forwards compatibility.

These strategies are explained individually in the upcoming sections.

The Strict Strategy (New Change, New Contract)

The simplest approach to Web service contract versioning is to require that a new version of a contract be issued whenever any kind of change is made to any part of the contract.

This is commonly implemented by changing the target namespace value of a WSDL definition (and possibly the XML Schema definition) every time a compatible or incompatible change is made to the WSDL, XML Schema, or WS-Policy content related to the contract. Namespaces are used for version identification instead of a version attribute because changing the namespace value automatically forces a change in all consumer programs that need to access the new version of the schema that defines the message types.

This "super-strict" approach is not really that practical, but it is the safest and sometimes warranted when there are legal implications to Web service contract modifications, such as when contracts are published for certain inter-organization data exchanges. Because both compatible and incompatible changes will result in a new contract version, this approach supports neither backwards or forwards compatibility.

Pros and Cons

The benefit of this strategy is that you have full control over the evolution of the service contract, and because backwards and forwards compatibility are intentionally disregarded, you do not need to concern yourself with the impact of any change in particular (because all changes effectively break the contract).

On the downside, by forcing a new namespace upon the contract with each change, you are guaranteeing that all existing service consumers will no longer be compatible with any new version of the contract. Consumers will only be able to continue communicating with the Web service while the old contract remains available alongside the new version or until the consumers themselves are updated to conform to the new contract.

Therefore, this approach will increase the governance burden of individual services and will require careful transitioning strategies. Having two or more versions of the same service co-exist at the same time can become a common requirement for which the supporting service inventory infrastructure needs to be prepared.

The Flexible Strategy (Backwards Compatibility)

A common approach used to balance practical considerations with an attempt at minimizing the impact of changes to Web service contracts is to allow compatible changes to occur without forcing a new contract version, while not attempting to support forwards compatibility at all.

This means that any backwards-compatible change is considered safe in that it ends up extending or augmenting an established contract without affecting any of the service's existing consumers. A common example of this is adding a new operation to a WSDL definition or adding an optional element declaration to a message's schema definition.

As with the Strict strategy, any change that breaks the existing contract does result in a new contract version, usually implemented by changing the target namespace value of the WSDL definition and potentially also the XML Schema definition.

Pros and Cons

The primary advantage to this approach is that it can be used to accommodate a variety of changes while consistently retaining the contract's backwards compatibility. However, when compatible changes are made, these changes become permanent and cannot be reversed without introducing an incompatible change. Therefore, a governance process is required during which each proposed change is evaluated so that contracts do not become overly bloated or convoluted. This is an especially important consideration for agnostic services that are heavily reused.

The Loose Strategy (Backwards and Forwards Compatibility)

As with the previous two approaches, this strategy requires that incompatible changes result in a new service contract version. The difference here is in how service contracts are initially designed.

Instead of accommodating known data exchange requirements, special features from the WSDL, XML Schema, and WS-Policy languages are used to make parts of the contract intrinsically extensible so that they remain able to support a broad range of future, unknown data exchange requirements.

For example:

- The `anyType` attribute value provided by the WSDL 2.0 language allows a message to consist of any valid XML document.

- XML Schema wildcards can be used to allow a range of unknown data to be passed in message definitions.

- Ignorable policy assertions can be defined to communicate service characteristics that can optionally be acknowledged by future consumers.

These and other features related to forwards compatibility are discussed in upcoming chapters (*Web Service Contract Design and Versioning for SOA*).

Pros and Cons

The fact that wildcards allow undefined content to be passed through Web service contracts provides a constant opportunity to further expand the range of acceptable message element and data content. On the other hand, the use of wildcards will naturally result in vague and overly coarse service contracts that place the burden of validation on the underlying service logic.

Summary Table

Provided here is a table that broadly summarizes how the three strategies compare based on three fundamental characteristics.

	Strategy		
	Strict	**Flexible**	**Loose**
Strictness	high	medium	low
Governance Impact	high	medium	high
Complexity	low	medium	high

Table F.1
A general comparison of the three versioning strategies.

The three characteristics used in this table to form the basis of this comparison are as follows:

- *Strictness* – The rigidity of the contract versioning options. The Strict approach clearly is the most rigid in its versioning rules, while the Loose strategy provides the broadest range of versioning options due to its reliance on wildcards.

- *Governance Impact* – The amount of governance burden imposed by a strategy. Both Strict and Loose approaches increase governance impact but for different reasons. The Strict strategy requires the issuance of more new contract versions, which impacts surrounding consumers and infrastructure, while the Loose approach introduces the concept of unknown message sets that need to be separately accommodated through custom programming.

- *Complexity* – The overall complexity of the versioning process. Due to the use of wildcards and unknown message data, the Loose strategy has the highest complexity potential, while the straight-forward rules that form the basis of the Strict approach make it the simplest option.

Throughout this comparison, the Flexible strategy provides an approach that represents a consistently average level of strictness, governance effort, and overall complexity.

F.6 REST Service Versioning Considerations

REST services that share the same uniform contract maintain separate versioned specifications for the following:

- the version number or specification of the resource identifier syntax (as per the "Request for Comments 6986 - Uniform Resource Identifier (URI): Generic Syntax" specification)

- the specification of the collection of legal methods, status codes, and other interaction protocol details (as per the "Request for Comments 2616 - Hypertext Transfer Protocol - HTTP/1.1" specification)

- individual specifications for legal media types (for example. HTML 4.01 and the "Request for Comments 4287 - The Atom Syndication Format" specification)

- individual specifications for service contracts that use the legal resource identifier syntax, methods, and media types

Each part of the uniform contract is specified and versioned independently of the others. Changing any one specification does not generally require another specification to be updated or versioned. Likewise, changing any of the uniform contract facet specifications does not require changes to individual service contracts, or changes to their version numbers.

This last point is in contradiction to some conventional versioning strategies. One might expect that if a schema used in a service contract changed, then the service contract would need to be modified. However, with REST services there is a tendency to maintain both forwards compatibility and backwards compatibility. If a REST service consumer sends a message that conforms to a newer schema, the service can process it as if it conformed to the older schema. If compatibility between these schemas has been maintained then the service will function correctly. Likewise, if the service returns a message to the consumer that conforms to an old schema the newer service consumer can still process the message correctly.

REST service contracts only need to directly consider the versioning of the uniform contract when media types used become deprecated, or when the schema advances so far that elements and attributes the service depends on are on their way to becoming obsolete. When this occurs, the service contract needs to be updated, and with it, the underlying service logic that processes the media types.

Appendix G

Mapping Service-Orientation to RUP

The Rational Unified Process (RUP) is commonly used for projects with identified areas of complexity and risk, and that can involve numerous potential stakeholders. RUP has been successfully applied in many organizations; today, a large number of RUP practitioners use a growing library of best practices to guide software development projects.

This appendix is intended for IT professionals with a RUP background who want to better understand how RUP can apply or relate to SOA projects, as well as those with an SOA background required to work with RUP. The upcoming sections will present an overview of how RUP can relate to service-orientation, SOA and MSOAM, the Mainstream SOA Methodology [REF-3]. We will explore how key RUP principles align with the goals, benefits, and pillars introduced in Chapters 3 and 4 of this book. We then further provide a high level mapping of service-orientation to RUP phases, milestones, disciplines, roles, activities and artifacts.

The purpose of this mapping is to determine:

- gaps between RUP and service-orientation
- how RUP emphasizes particular elements of SOA and service-orientation
- how service-orientation emphasizes particular aspects of RUP
- how RUP can be extended with service-orientation elements
- how the application of service-orientation can benefit from RUP practices

Compatibility of RUP and SOA

The findings from "Suitability of Extreme Programming and RUP Software Development Methodologies for SOA Applications" [REF-1] provides an abstract mapping between RUP and SOA methodologies. Five criteria were used to demonstrate how RUP can support service delivery projects (Table G.1).

Characteristic	SOA (requires)	RUP (supports)
Size of Development Team	multidisciplinary teams	multidisciplinary teams
Level of Documentation	very high	high
Development Time	long when first designing the architecture, short when the architecture is in place	long, but steady development
Scope of Software	enterprise, domain	any scope
Type of Orientation	service	object

Table G.1
Five process characteristics required by SOA and supported by RUP.

RUP supports four of the listed characteristics, but does not support the fifth (type of orientation). The suggestion is that RUP needs can support service-oriented architecture development by incorporating SOA methodology to add a layer on top of the object-oriented design features.

This paper and other previous work on mapping or combining RUP with SOA concentrated mainly on introducing activities specific to SOA into RUP, or partially distributing basic SOA project stages into RUP phases.

When mapping aspects of service-orientation to RUP, further alternatives come to light. The main building blocks, principles, and best practices of RUP and MSOAM can be combined to elaborate on the relationships and gaps between the two methodologies. That is, we can establish a mapping among all areas of MSOAM related to service delivery and all the engineering disciplines of RUP with the associated processes, roles, artifacts, activities, and guidelines. When gaps are identified, we can decide to extend one process by introducing elements of the other. When mapping is established, the processes can leverage features, patterns, and best practices from each other.

Overview of RUP (and MSOAM)

The main building blocks of RUP, or content elements, are the following:

- Roles (who) – A Role defines a set of related skills, competencies and responsibilities.

- Artifacts/Work Products (what) – A work product represents something resulting from a task, including all the documents and models (artifacts) produced while working through the process.

- Activities/Tasks (how) – A task describes a unit of work assigned to a Role that provides a meaningful result.

The above are organized into phases, iterations, disciplines, and workflow details (when). Within each iteration, the tasks are categorized into nine disciplines:

- six engineering disciplines: business modeling, requirements, analysis and design, implementation, test, deployment

- three supporting disciplines: configuration and change management, project management, environment

RUP is architecture-centric and risk-driven in that values are produced by the engineering disciplines. MSOAM is business-driven and enterprise-centric and constantly targets the delivery of value to the business, regardless of how the business changes.

The upcoming sections focus on the engineering disciplines of RUP and associated roles, along with the project delivery stages of MSOAM and corresponding roles.

The Pillars of Service-Orientation and the RUP Principles

The four pillars of service-orientation (introduced in Chapter 4) are summarized in Table G.2.

Pillar	Description
Teamwork	Cross-project and cross-functional teams and cooperation are required.
Education	Team members must communicate and cooperate based on common knowledge (common vocabulary, definitions, concepts, methods) and understanding of the target state the team is collectively working to attain.
Discipline	Consistent application of common knowledge by all members of the teams.
Balanced Scope	Establish teamwork, education, and discipline within a meaningful and manageable scope.

Table G.2
The four SOA Pillars.

One of the key RUP principles (known as "ABCDEF") is entirely devoted to Teamwork and collaboration. Furthermore, RUP supports education and common understanding in the following ways:

- by providing training and mentoring as activities [REF-8]

- by using multiple levels of abstraction with well defined concepts and methods

- by using UML as a graphical language

The pillar of discipline is supported by RUP's six best practices, while the key principles contribute toward the attainment of a balanced scope. Table G.3 elaborates on this comparison.

Pillar	RUP Support
Teamwork	Key principle - Collaborate across teams: • Motivate people to perform at their best. • Collaborate cross-functionally across analysts, developers, testers. • Manage evolving artifacts and tasks to enhance collaboration and progress/quality insight with integrated environments. • Ensure that business, development, and operations teams work effectively as an integrated whole.
Education	Key principle - Elevate the level of abstraction: • Reuse existing assets • Reduce the amount of human-generated stuff through higher-level tools and languages. • Architect for resilience, quality, understandability, and complexity control. Use UML as standard language in analysis and design. Training and mentoring are further supported activities throughout practices that introduce RUP into organizations.

continues

Pillar	RUP Support
Discipline	Systematic, methodical way to analyze, design, develop, and validate with the six best practices:
	1. Develop software iteratively.
	2. Manage requirements.
	3. Use component-based architectures.
	4. Visually model software.
	5. Verify software quality.
	6. Control changes to software.
Balanced Scope	Key principle – Adapt the process.
	Key principle – Demonstrate value iteratively.

Table G.3
How RUP supports the four pillars of service-orientation.

It should be noted here that although the service-orientation pillars correspond to RUP principles, activities, and roles, RUP still needs to be extended in the following areas:

- The collaboration across teams requires additional attention due to the potential complexity of incorporating additional enterprise and governance roles within the project.

- Educational materials need to be extended with the eight service-orientation principles, patterns that address service analysis and service design, and precepts and processes specific to shared service governance.

Note that the business vocabulary is optional in RUP but mandatory in SOA.

There are two further RUP key principles that have not been mapped:

- Balance competing stakeholder priorities.

- Focus continuously on quality.

These can contribute to the successful execution of several service delivery stages in MSOAM.

Breadth and Depth Roles and Role Mapping

RUP role definitions are consistent with the notion of separating *breadth and depth* [REF-7]. As the name implies, depth roles perform tasks that add details and precision to the artifacts produced by the breadth roles. Breadth roles are related to leadership, impact and integrity, definition of standards, and guidelines. The breadth and depth are not related to the discipline. Each of RUP's nine disciplines has one role that focuses on breadth, and a different role that focuses on depth for that discipline.

Furthermore, roles can be grouped in role sets. There are four role sets: Analysts, Developers, Testers and Managers. Once this basic principle is understood, it is easy to classify the roles in meaningful groups and map them to MSOAM roles (Table G.4).

MSOAM Project Stage	MSOAM Role	RUP Role Set	RUP Discipline	RUP Breadth Role	RUP Depth Role
Service Inventory Analysis	Business Analyst	Analyst	Business Modeling	Business Process Analyst	Business Designer
Service-Oriented Analysis	Service Analyst	Analyst	Requirements	Systems Analyst	Requirements Specifier
Service-Oriented Design Service Logic Design	Service Architect	Developer	Analysis and Design	Software Architect	Designer
Service Development	Service Developer	Developer	Implementation	Integrator	Implementer
Service Testing	SOA Quality Assurance Specialist	Manager/ Analyst/ Developer/ Tester	Test	Test Manager Test Analyst Test Designer	Test Designer Tester

continues

MSOAM Project Stage	MSOAM Role	RUP Role Set	RUP Discipline	RUP Breadth Role	RUP Depth Role
Service Deployment and Maintenance	Service Administrator	Manager	Deployment	Deployment Manager	Tech Writer, Course Developer, Graphic Artist
All	IT Manager	Manager	Project Management	Project Manager	Project Manager

Table G.4
MSOAM roles and project stages mapped to RUP breadth/depth roles, disciplines, and role sets.

It is important to note that there is no distinction between breadth and depth for the above MSOAM roles. However, in larger programs it will become necessary to make this distinction, especially in relation to Service Analysts where the concept of *Lead Analyst* emerges.

One further key observation is the gravity that testing has in RUP. The Test Discipline includes roles from all the role sets: Managers, Analysts, Developers, and Testers. This fully supports the importance placed upon the Testing stage within SOA delivery projects (where services need to be tested rigorously as if they were commercial products).

Enterprise and Governance Roles

Parallel to the traditional roles, MSOAM introduces:

- Four enterprise or domain level custodian roles: Schema Custodian, Policy Custodian, Service Registry Custodian, Enterprise Design Standards Custodian (and Auditor). These roles are active mainly during the Service-Oriented Design, Service Logic Design, Service Deployment and Maintenance, and Service Versioning and Retirement stages.

- One generic enterprise architecture role: Enterprise Architect. This role is present in just about all stages of an SOA delivery project, but the only project-specific artifact directly produced is the inventory blueprint.

- Two service management roles: Service Custodian, Service Administrator

- One general governance role: SOA Governance Specialist

All of these roles are responsible in defining some form of standards and participate in reviews. Additionally, MSOAM introduces the concept of the SOA Governance Program Office, which has a scope well beyond that of the Change Control Board established during the Inception phase in RUP.

Mapping Service Delivery Project Stages to Disciplines

MSOAM defines eleven project lifecycle stages, nine of which are service delivery stages. Only the service delivery stages are relevant for mapping to RUP (Table G.5), because RUP does not support generic product lifecycle stages.

Service Delivery Project Stages	RUP Disciplines
Service Inventory Analysis Service-Oriented Analysis Service-Oriented Design Service Logic Design	Business Modeling Requirement Analysis and Design
Service Development	Implementation
Service Testing	Test
Service Deployment and Maintenance	Deployment
—	Project Management
—	Environment
Service Discovery	—
Service Versioning and Retirement	Configuration and Change Management

Table G.5
Mapping of MSOAM service delivery stages with RUP disciplines.

The service delivery stages are further divided into sub-processes or activities. This subdivision allows us to make the mapping between the Service Inventory Analysis, Service-Oriented Analysis, and Service-Oriented Design stages more granular with the corresponding RUP disciplines.

As mentioned previously, we need to be careful when applying this level of mapping; even if we assume that the roles, activities, and artifacts correspond entirely, we still must consider the gaps associated by the followed principles, patterns, and methods. (These gaps are briefly discussed in the upcoming *Service-Orientation and RUP: Gaps* section.)

Mapping MSOAM Analysis and Design Stages to RUP Disciplines

In the top-down project approach, the Service Inventory Analysis lifecycle consists of four processes that are applied iteratively (Figure G.1). These processes can be mapped to three different RUP disciplines (Table G.6).

Figure G.1

The four primary steps that comprise the Service Inventory Analysis stage.

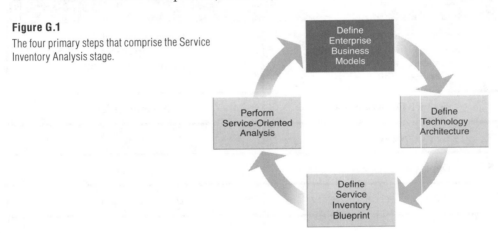

The Define Enterprise Business Models process corresponds to RUP Business Modeling. It is the process in which all business concepts, terms, and architecture are defined and modeled. It is probably the only mapping between MSOAM and RUP which is completely free of gaps. That is, one can safely apply the Business Modeling of RUP to the Service Inventory Analysis lifecycle.

The mapping of the Define Technology Architecture process to the RUP Analysis and Design discipline is also straightforward. What may appear odd at first is that the Analysis and Design seems to be applied together with Business Modeling without any mention of the Requirements discipline. However, this is not an issue because in RUP there is no sequence of disciplines; only sequences of iterations and phases. All principles can be combined together in the same iteration. (That is, the three disciplines that appear in Table G.6 can be applied simultaneously in each iteration in the inception and elaboration phase.)

Service Inventory Analysis Process	MSOAM Role	RUP Discipline	RUP Breadth Role	Primary RUP Artifacts
Define Enterprise Business Models	Business Analyst	Business Modeling	Business Process Analyst	Business Vision Business Architecture Business Glossary Suppl. Business Specification Business UCM Business Object Model
Define Technology Architecture	Service Architect	Analysis and Design	Software Architect	Software Architecture Document (Inception)
Define Service Inventory Blueprint	Service Analyst	Requirement (Workflow: Define the System)	System Analyst	Vision Glossary UCM Supplemental Specification
Perform Service-Oriented Analysis	Service Analyst	Requirement	System Analyst	Vision Glossary UCM Supplemental Specification

Table G.6
Mapping Service Inventory Analysis processes and roles to RUP disciplines, roles, and artifacts.

The mapping of the Definition of the Service Inventory Blueprint process to the Requirement RUP discipline deserves some further elaboration: The primary role assigned to the Definition of the Service Inventory Blueprint process is the Service Analyst. This role corresponds to the System Analyst in RUP, and is the breadth role for the Requirement discipline. Furthermore, the service inventory blueprint represents a collection of conceptual service candidates, and is therefore not restricted to the service inventory architecture. This aligns very well with the Define System Workflow process in RUP, which is part of the workflow of the Requirement discipline. The artifacts processed by this Workflow include the Use Case Model, the Vision, and the Object Model, which, when combined, correspond to the modeling of service candidates.

Service-Orientation and RUP: Gaps

As a result of the mapping performed, some notable gaps were identified. For example, the four characteristics of service-oriented technology architecture (vendor-neutral, business-driven, enterprise-centric, composition-centric) are not present in RUP. Furthermore, core service-orientation concepts, like services and service compositions, replace the RUP concepts of objects and object-oriented applications. Other observations include the fact that service-oriented solutions place a greater emphasis on security, standardization, centralization, and cross-project collaboration.

The proper application of the pillars of service-orientation will help organizations overcome these gaps.

Related Reading

It is worth acknowledging other work that has been done in the area of mapping SOA with RUP. For example:

- A RUP for SOA plug-in was made available in 2005 to help extend the RUP analysis and design approach with workflows and artifacts required for service-oriented analysis and design.

- A mapping of high level service design stages to RUP phases was published in "Mapping of SOA and RUP" [REF-5], but this work did not cover service-oriented analysis.

- A combination of RUP and the MSOAM appeared in the March 2008 issue of the *SOA Magazine* [REF-4]. This article uses RUP to elaborate service inventories and it focuses on processes related to top-down Service-Oriented Analysis stages in relation to the RUP activities related to Business Modeling.

- The "Enterprise Unified Process" [REF-6] delves into extending RUP with activities related to SOA or enterprise architecture in general. The limitations of RUP for operation and support of software after its deployment are treated by the Enterprise Unified Process (EUP), an extension of RUP.

Bibliography

[REF-1] Suitability of Extreme Programming and RUP Software Development Methodologies for SOA Applications, Guillermo A. Callahan, 2006 (www.soberit.hut.fi/T-86/T-86.5165/2007/final_callahan.pdf).

[REF-2] *The Rational Unified Process: an Introduction*, P. Kruchten, Addison Wesley, 2000.

[REF-3] "MSOAM, The Mainstream SOA Methodology," Thomas Erl (www.soamethodology.com).

[REF-4] "Working with SOA and RUP," Solmaz Boroumand, *SOA Magazine*, Issue XVI, March 2008.

[REF-5] "Mapping of SOA and RUP: DOA as Case Study," Shahid Hussain, Bashir Ahmad, Shakeel Ahmad, Sheikh Muhammad Saqib, *Journal of Computing*, January 2010.

[REF-6] *Enterprise Unified Process: Extending the Rational Unified Process*, Scott W. Ambler, John Nalbone, and Michael Vizdos, Prentice Hall (www.enterpriseunifiedprocess.com).

[REF-7] *Understanding RUP Roles*, Anthony Crain, IBM (www.ibm.com/developerworks/rational/library/apr05/crain/index.html).

[REF-8] "Introducing the RUP into an organization," DJ de Villiers, 2003 (www.ibm.com/developerworks/rational/library/916.html)

[REF-9] "Rational Unified Process: Best Practices for Software Development Teams," Rational Software White Paper (www.ibm.com/developerworks/rational/library/content/03July/1000/1251/1251_bestpractices_TP026B.pdf).

Appendix H

Additional Resources

Following is a list of resource Web sites that provide supplementary content for books in this series. If you'd like to be automatically notified of new book releases, new supplementary content for this title, or key changes to these Web sites, send a blank e-mail to notify@soabooks.com.

www.soabooks.com

The official site of the *Prentice Hall Service-Oriented Computing Series from Thomas Erl*. Numerous resources are provided, including sample chapters from available books and updates and corrections.

www.soaschool.com, www.cloudschool.com

These two educational sites describe the vast curricula dedicated to SOA and Cloud Computing. Books from the *Prentice Hall Service-Oriented Computing Series from Thomas Erl* are official parts of these programs. In particular, SOASchool.com offers a series of courses for the Certified SOA Governance track for which this book is a primary resource.

www.soamag.com

This site is the home of The SOA Magazine, a monthly publication officially associated with this book series. This magazine is dedicated to publishing specialized articles, case studies, and papers that explore various aspects of service-oriented computing.

www.soaglossary.com

A master glossary for all books in the *Prentice Hall Service-Oriented Computing Series by Thomas Erl* is hosted by this site. This site is constantly growing as new titles are developed and released.

www.soaspecs.com

This Web site establishes a convenient central portal to industry standards and specifications covered or referenced by titles in this book series.

www.soapatterns.org

The official site of the master catalog of SOA design patterns. This site allows for the online submission and community review of candidate patterns proposed for inclusion in the master patterns catalog.

www.serviceorientation.com, www.whatissoa.com, www.whatiscloud.com

These sites provide papers, book excerpts, and various content dedicated to describing and defining the service-orientation paradigm, cloud computing concepts, associated principles, and the service-oriented technology architectural model.

www.soasymposium.com, www.cloudsymposium.com

Two sites dedicated to the conference series featuring the world's largest SOA and Cloud Computing events. These co-located conferences are held throughout the world and frequently feature authors from the *Prentice Hall Service-Oriented Computing Series from Thomas Erl*.

About the Authors

Stephen G. Bennett

Stephen G. Bennett currently holds the role of Senior Enterprise Architect at Oracle, prior to which he worked with BEA where he was the Americas SOA Practice Lead within BEA's consulting division. Stephen is a 25-year experienced manager and technologist, with a wide range of leadership, architecture, and implementation experience around SOA and Cloud Computing gained in high profile environments. Before becoming a consultant, Stephen spent 12 years in the investment banking industry delivering global trading systems.

Alongside many white papers and magazine articles, Stephen's previous literary efforts include the book *Silver Clouds, Dark Linings: A Concise Guide to Cloud Computing* (Prentice Hall 2010). Stephen is a regular speaker at executive events and conferences on topics such as SOA adoption, service engineering, SOA Governance, service-oriented architecture, and cloud computing. Stephen has been involved in multiple standards efforts around SOA and Enterprise Architecture. Stephen has co-chaired a number of working groups within the Open Group organization around SOA Governance and TOGAF/SOA.

Thomas Erl

Thomas Erl is the founder of SOASchool.com® and CloudSchool.com™, as part of Arcitura Education Inc. Thomas has been the world's top-selling SOA author for more than five years and is the series editor of the *Prentice Hall Service-Oriented Computing Series from Thomas Erl*, as well as the editor of the *SOA Magazine*. With more than 140,000 copies in print world-wide, his seven published books have become international bestsellers and have been formally endorsed by senior members of major IT organizations, such as IBM, Microsoft, Oracle, Intel, Accenture, IEEE, MITRE, SAP, CISCO, and HP.

In cooperation with SOASchool.com® and CloudSchool.com™, Thomas has helped develop curricula for the internationally recognized SOA Certified Professional (SOACP) and Cloud Certified Professional (CCP) accreditation programs, which have established a series of formal, vendor-neutral industry certifications.

Thomas is the founding member of the SOA Manifesto Working Group (www.soa-manifesto.org), founder of the APQC Service-Orientation Maturity Model (SOMM) initiative, co-chair of the SOA Education Committee, and he further oversees the SOAPatterns.org initiative, a community site dedicated to the on-going development of a master patterns catalog for service-oriented computing.

Thomas has toured more than 20 countries as a speaker and instructor for public and private events, and regularly participates in SOA Symposium (www.soasymposium. com) and Gartner conferences. More than 100 articles and interviews by Thomas have been published in numerous publications, including the *Wall Street Journal* and *CIO Magazine*.

Clive Gee, Ph.D.

After developing an interest in computers while studying for a Ph.D. in Theoretical Physics from the University of Stirling, Scotland, Clive joined IBM United Kingdom in 1976 to pursue a career in the emerging IT industry. He worked initially in telecommunications and office automation, and then moved to the field of application development in the 1980s where he spent the remainder of his career.

An early proponent of Object Orientation, he was one of the founders of IBM's European Object Technology Practice, where he worked on major client application development projects and internal CASE tool development. In 1997 Clive moved to the United States, joining IBM's North American Object Technology Practice as a consultant architect, working on major client projects in the Banking, Retail, Telecommunication, and Transportation Industries. During his tenure with IBM he worked on developing solutions that ranged from wireless telecommunications network infrastructure to mobile applications for the airline industry.

As well as being closely involved in the technical architecture and design of complex IT solutions, Clive developed an interest in the field of software engineering, improving the IT application design and development process by adopting production management techniques such as those used by the engineering and manufacturing industries. One of the very first IBM architects to work on SOA, Clive was involved with most of IBM's flagship SOA engagements, initially as a Solution or Lead Architect, then increasingly as a specialist in SOA governance, where he is considered to be one of IBM's pre-eminent worldwide practitioners. Clive worked on numerous major client projects in the USA, Canada, Latin America, Europe, Japan, and Australia. Semi-retired in 2008, Clive has since returned to live in the UK's Northern Isles. He is a co-author of the book *SOA Governance: Achieving and Sustaining Business and IT Agility* (IBM Press 2008).

Robert Laird

Robert is the lead architect of the IBM Software Group in areas of SOA governance and SOA policy; he currently leads the automation of the SOA Policy Lifecycle. Prior to that, Robert co-authored the *SOA Governance and Management Method (SGMM)* for usage of SOA governance capabilities and maturity assessment. Robert has several years of international consulting experience and was responsible for supporting and leading service-oriented architecture (SOA) governance and SOA architecture engagements for worldwide IBM customers.

With more than 20 years experience in the telecom industry at MCI and Verizon, Robert has been the MCI chief architect, leading the enterprise architecture group and has worked across the entire order-to-cash suite of applications. He led the development of the SOA based single stack strategy to simplify the multiple network and applications silos; he has driven the strategy, planning, and execution of MCI's product development in the area of contact centers, IP/VPN, VOIP, IMS, and managed services; and, for OSS, he has led successful implementations to automate network provisioning, network restoration, and network management.

Prior to joining MCI, Robert worked as a consultant for American Management Systems (AMS) and Ideation, Inc. He has an MS and a BS degree in Computer Science from Purdue University and has been granted two patents in the area of telephony, with three patents pending in the area of computing. As well as speaking at various industry forums, Robert has written for *The SOA Magazine*, been quoted in *CIO Insight*, *Telecommunications*, *Infoworld*, and *Computerworld*, and has co-authored two books including *SOA Governance* (IBM Press 2008) and *Executing SOA* (IBM Press 2008).

Anne Thomas Manes

Anne Thomas Manes is the Vice President and Research Director for Burton Group Application Platform Strategies. Her expertise includes SOA, web services, XML, governance, Java, application servers, super platforms, and application security.

Prior to joining Burton Group, Anne was the Chief Technology Officer at Systinet, an SOA governance vendor (now part of HP) and Director of Market Innovation in Sun Microsystems's software group. With 28 years of experience, Anne was named one of the 50 most powerful people in networking 2002 by Network World and among the "Power 100 IT Leaders," by Enterprise Systems Journal.

Anne has authored *Web Services: A Manager's Guide* (Addison-Wesley, 2003) and contributed the foreword for the new book *Next Generation SOA* (Prentice Hall, 2011). Anne has also participated in Web services standards development efforts at the W3C, OASIS, WS-I, and JCP.

Robert Schneider

Robert Schneider is a Partner at WiseClouds, LLC. WiseClouds offers vendor-neutral, unbiased consulting and training services that help customers understand and manage cloud computing business concerns, select the right mixture of enabling technologies, and identify and deploy the ideal configuration required.

Robert has provided database optimization, distributed computing, and other technical expertise to a wide variety of enterprises in the financial, technology, and public sectors. Clients have included Amazon, JP Morgan Chase & Co, VISA, HP, S.W.I.F.T., and numerous governments such as the United States, Brazil, Malaysia, Mexico, Australia, and the United Kingdom.

Robert has written six books and numerous articles on database technology and other complex topics such as cloud computing, and SOA. Robert is a frequent organizer and presenter at technology industry events, worldwide.

Leo Shuster

Leo Shuster is a seasoned IT professional. He has directed Enterprise Architecture and SOA strategy and execution for a number of organizations including Nationwide Insurance, National City Corporation, Ohio Savings Bank, and Progressive Insurance.

Leo holds an MS in Computer Science and Engineering from Case Western Reserve University and an MBA from Cleveland State University. Thus far, in his 15 year IT career, Leo has held a variety of roles including Director, Manager, Team Lead, Project Manager, Architect, and Developer. Leo has presented on Enterprise Architecture, SOA, and related topics for groups of all sizes at a variety of industry events and conferences. He is passionate about technology and regularly blogs about advanced software architecture issues at leoshuster.blogspot.com.

Andre Tost

Andre Tost works as a Senior Technical Staff Member in the IBM Software Group where he assists IBM's customers in establishing service-oriented architectures. His special focus is on Web services, Enterprise Service Bus technology, and SOA governance.

Before his current assignment, Andre spent ten years in various partner enablement, development, and architectural roles in IBM software development. Andre has spoken at industry conferences worldwide on topics related to SOA and is a frequent publisher of articles and papers. He is also a co-author of several books on Web services and related technologies including *Web Service Contract Design and Versioning for SOA* (Prentice Hall 2008). Originally from Germany, he now lives and works in Rochester, Minnesota.

Chris Venable

Chris Venable is an architect and member of the SOA Center of Competency at Wal-Mart Stores, Inc. He has 16 years of experience in the IT industry with the past nine focused on SOA, data integration, and other modern software engineering practices. Current areas of interest include business architecture, event processing, variation analysis, and conceptual modeling.

About the Contributors

Benjamin Carlyle

Benjamin is a long-time Australian employee of Invensys Rail Group and has been involved in projects worldwide as a founding developer of the "SystematICS" product line, as a software architect and systems engineer. Benjamin has been working with REST and related technologies since 2004 through his blog (soundadvice.id.au/blog), his day job, and various other forums.

Benjamin's work has been referenced in books on RESTful Web services and on microformats. He has presented at the SOA Symposium, was a member of the program committee for the first and second international workshop on RESTful Design, and is co-author of *SOA with REST* (Prentice Hall, 2011). He is credited with helping inspire the RESTlet framework for Java and coined the term "REST Triangle" to describe the structure of a REST uniform contract. He has a deep understanding of both the theory and practice of REST and related styles, as well as broader software and systems architecture topics.

Robert Moores

Robert Moores lives and works in Leeds, England, where he is currently Head of Information & Media Services at Leeds Metropolitan University. Robert has worked in IT for more than 25 years, starting his career as a COBOL programmer. Robert's career has encompassed higher education, government, health, and insurance sectors and he has worked in the UK, Australia, and the USA as a Developer, Business Analyst, Project Manager and most recently as an Operational Manager. You can read more writings from Robert at robmoores.wordpress.com.

Filippos Santas

Filippos is an IT Architect for Credit Suisse Private Banking in Switzerland and an SOASchool.com Certified SOA Trainer, Analyst, Architect, Consultant, and Security Specialist; additionally, he is certified by IBM on the Rational Unified Process V7.0. In the last 10 years, Filippos has been the lead for the analysis and architecture of a number of successful SOA projects and for transforming legacy architectures to service-oriented architectures, primarily in the financial sector. His achievements include the conceptual and physical design of the international insurance claims service network that connects insurance policies, customer companies, and state authorities in 44 countries across the globe, combining legislation, business processes, business rules, business objects, knowledge bases, and different platforms.

Filippos's recent work with Credit Suisse has been as an SOA Architect, combining the profitable and established functionality of legacy systems with centralized business process services, decentralized business rule services, domain specific BOMs and entity services, end-to-end traceability, and service composability at every level.

About the Foreword Contributors

Massimo Pezzini

Massimo Pezzini is a vice president and distinguished analyst in Gartner Research. His research focus is currently on application platforms, ultra high-end transaction processing technology, composite applications, service-oriented and event-driven architecture infrastructure and best practices, and application integration including integration appliances and mobile middleware. Pezzini has decades of experience in distributed computing, middleware technology, and software architectures. Throughout his career, he has had responsibilities in software development, project management, pre-sales support, consulting, and product marketing. Prior to joining Gartner, Mr. Pezzini was managing director of the Internet Business Unit of Infostrada, an Italian telecom provider. Before that, he held various positions in the Olivetti group.

Roberto Medrano

A recognized executive in the information technology fields of SOA, Internet security, governance, and compliance, Medrano has extensive experience with both start-ups and large companies, having been involved at the beginning of four IT industries: EDA, Open Systems, Computer Security, and now SOA.

Medrano holds an MBA from UCLA, a MSEE from MIT, BSEE from USC and prior to joining SOA Software, he was CEO of PoliVec, a leader in security policy. Before joining PoliVec, he was one of the top 100 Sr. Executives at Hewlett-Packard. At Hewlett-Packard (HP) he served as the General Manager of the E-Services and Internet Security Divisions. Medrano has held executive positions at Finjan, Avnet Inc, and Sun Microsystems. Medrano participated in President Clinton's White House Security Summit and has been an active member on National Cyber Security Summits and the White House National Strategy to Secure Cyberspace. Medrano has been selected as one of "The 100 most influential Hispanics in US," "The 100 most influential Latinos in Silicon Valley" "Top 100 most influential Hispanics in Information Technology" and is co-founder and CEO for Hispanic-Net, a non-profit organization.

Index

THE PRENTICE HALL SERVICE-ORIENTED COMPUTING SERIES FROM THOMAS ERL

SOA with .NET and Windows Azure: Realizing Service-Orientation with the Microsoft Platform
ISBN 9780131582316

Top Microsoft technology experts team up with Thomas Erl to explore service-oriented computing with Microsoft's latest .NET service technologies and Windows Azure innovations.

Service-Oriented Architecture: Concepts, Technology, and Design
ISBN 9780131858589

Widely regarded as the definitive "how-to" guide for SOA, this best-selling book presents a comprehensive end-to-end tutorial that provides step-by-step instructions for modeling and designing service-oriented solutions from the ground up.

SOA: Principles of Service Design
ISBN 9780132344821

Published with over 240 color illustrations, this hands-on guide contains practical, comprehensive, and in-depth coverage of service engineering techniques and the service-orientation design paradigm. Proven design principles are documented to help maximize the strategic benefit potential of SOA.

SOA: Design Patterns
ISBN 9780136135166

Software design patterns have emerged as a powerful means of avoiding and overcoming common design problems and challenges. This new book presents a formal catalog of design patterns specifically for SOA and service-orientation. All patterns are documented using full-color illustrations and further supplemented with case study examples.

Several additional series titles are currently in development and will be released soon. For more information about any of the books in this series, visit www.soabooks.com.

PRENTICE HALL

SOA & Cloud Computing Training & Certification

◎ SOASchool.com

Content from this book and other series titles has been incorporated into the SOA Certified Professional (SOACP) program, an industry-recognized, vendor-neutral SOA certification curriculum developed by author Thomas Erl in cooperation with industry experts and academic communities and provided by SOASchool.com and licensed training partners.

The SOA Certified Professional curriculum is comprised of a collection of 23 courses and labs that can be taken with or without formal testing and certification. Training can be delivered anywhere in the world by certified instructors. A comprehensive self-study program is available for remote, self-paced study, and exams can be taken world-wide via Prometric testing centers.

Certifications include:
- Certified SOA Professional
- Certified SOA Architect
- Certified SOA Analyst
- Certified SOA Consultant
- Certified SOA Java Developer
- Certified SOA .NET Developer
- Certified SOA Governance Specialist
- Certified SOA Security Specialist
- Certified SOA Quality Assurance Specialist

All courses are reviewed and revised on a regular basis to stay in alignment with industry developments

For more information, visit: **www.soaschool.com**

◎ CloudSchool.com

The Cloud Certified Professional (CCP) program, provided by CloudSchool.com, establishes a series of vendor-neutral industry certifications dedicated to areas of specialization in the field of cloud computing. Also founded by author Thomas Erl, this program exists independently from the SOASchool.com courses, while preserving consistency in terminology, conventions, and notation. This allows IT professionals to study cloud computing topics separately or in combination with SOA topics, as required.

The Cloud Certified Professional curriculum is comprised of 15 courses and labs, each of which has a corresponding Prometric exam. Private and public training workshops can be provided throughout the world by certified instructors. Self-study kits are further available for remote, self-paced study and in support of instructor-led workshops.

Certifications include:
- Certified Cloud Professional
- Certified Cloud Technology Professional
- Certified Cloud Architect
- Certified Cloud Governance Specialist
- Certified Cloud Security Specialist
- Certified Cloud Storage Specialist

All courses are reviewed and revised on a regular basis to stay in alignment with industry developments

For more information, visit: **www.cloudschool.com**

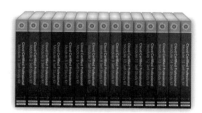

SOASchool.com® SOA CERTIFIED *Professional*
SOASchool.com® SOA CERTIFIED *Consultant*
SOASchool.com® SOA CERTIFIED *Analyst*
SOASchool.com® SOA CERTIFIED *Architect*
SOASchool.com® SOA CERTIFIED *Java Developer*
SOASchool.com® SOA CERTIFIED *.NET Developer*
SOASchool.com® SOA CERTIFIED *Governance Specialist*
SOASchool.com® SOA CERTIFIED *Quality Assurance Specialist*
SOASchool.com® SOA CERTIFIED *Security Specialist*

CloudSchool.com™ CLOUD CERTIFIED *Professional*
CloudSchool.com™ CLOUD CERTIFIED *Technology Professional*
CloudSchool.com™ CLOUD CERTIFIED *Architect*
CloudSchool.com™ CLOUD CERTIFIED *Security Specialist*
CloudSchool.com™ CLOUD CERTIFIED *Governance Specialist*
CloudSchool.com™ CLOUD CERTIFIED *Storage Specialist*

SOASchool.com and CloudSchool.com exams offered world-wide through Prometric testing centers (www.prometric.com).

Self-Study Kits available for remote, self-paced study and exam preparation.

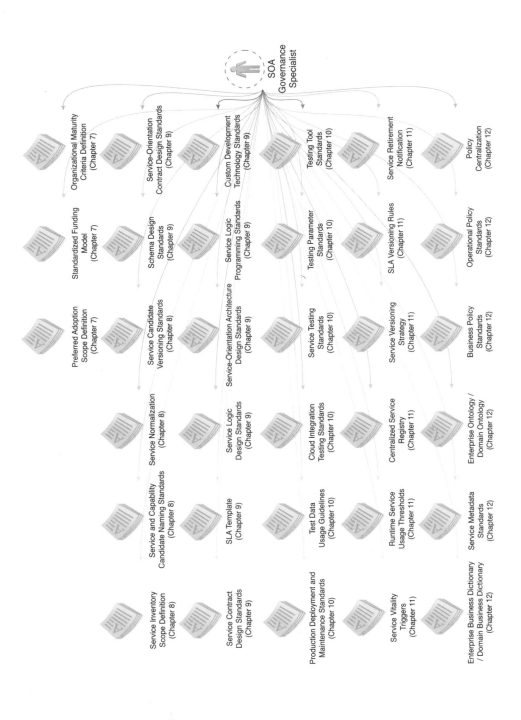

SOA Governance Specialist

Organizational Maturity Criteria Definition (Chapter 7)

Service-Orientation Contract Design Standards (Chapter 9)

Custom Development Technology Standards (Chapter 9)

Testing Tool Standards (Chapter 10)

Service Retirement Notification (Chapter 11)

Policy Centralization (Chapter 12)

Standardized Funding Model (Chapter 7)

Schema Design Standards (Chapter 9)

Service Logic Programming Standards (Chapter 9)

Testing Parameter Standards (Chapter 10)

SLA Versioning Rules (Chapter 11)

Operational Policy Standards (Chapter 12)

Preferred Adoption Scope Definition (Chapter 7)

Service Candidate Versioning Standards (Chapter 8)

Service-Orientation Architecture Design Standards (Chapter 9)

Service Testing Standards (Chapter 10)

Service Versioning Strategy (Chapter 11)

Business Policy Standards (Chapter 12)

Service Normalization (Chapter 8)

Service Logic Design Standards (Chapter 9)

Cloud Integration Testing Standards (Chapter 10)

Centralized Service Registry (Chapter 11)

Enterprise Ontology / Domain Ontology (Chapter 12)

Service and Capability Candidate Naming Standards (Chapter 8)

SLA Template (Chapter 9)

Test Data Usage Guidelines (Chapter 10)

Runtime Service Usage Thresholds (Chapter 11)

Service Metadata Standards (Chapter 12)

Service Inventory Scope Definition (Chapter 8)

Service Contract Design Standards (Chapter 9)

Production Deployment and Maintenance Standards (Chapter 10)

Service Vitality Triggers (Chapter 11)

Enterprise Business Dictionary / Domain Business Dictionary (Chapter 12)